The Three Worlds

The Three Worlds

CULTURE AND WORLD DEVELOPMENT

Peter Worsley

THE UNIVERSITY OF CHICAGO PRESS

The University of Chicago Press, Chicago 60637
George Weidenfeld & Nicolson Ltd., London SW4
© 1984 by Peter Worsley
All rights reserved. Published 1984

Printed in the United States of America

The extract from Regis Debray, *A Critique of Arms*,
vol. 1 (1974), on pp. 322–3 is printed by permission of Penguin Books Limited.

93 92 91 90   54

Library of Congress Cataloging in Publication Data

Worsley, Peter.
  The three worlds.

  Bibliography: p.
  Includes index.
  1. Developing countries. 2. Rural development.
3. Social history——modern, 1500–   . I. Title.
HC59.7.W685   1984   306'.09172'4   84–2609
ISBN 0–226–90754–6
ISBN 0–226–90755–4 (pbk).

In memory of Ruth First, a White communist
who spent her life fighting for a
multi-racial South Africa and who died working
for a Black revolutionary country.

Murdered in Maputo,
17 August 1982.

First Priest: Great Sarastro, dost thou
think that Tamino will withstand the stern trials that
await him? Consider well: he is a prince.
Sarastro: More than that! He is a man!

Emanuel Schikaneder, *The Magic Flute*, Act II

And at last he realized that man never knows who it is he suffers for and
who it is he waits and toils for. He suffers and waits and toils for people
he will never know, who in their turn will suffer and wait and toil for
others who will not find happiness either, because man always yearns for
more happiness than the little granted him. But the greatness of man
consists precisely in wanting to improve on what exists. In setting himself
Tasks. In the Kingdom of Heaven there is no greatness to be conquered,
for there all is fixed and hierarchical; nothing is unknown, all is revealed;
since there is no limit to existence, sacrifice, rest and pleasure are
impossibilities. So, weighed down by suffering and by Tasks, splendid in
the midst of his misery, capable of love in the midst of affliction, man can
only reach greatness, his highest stature, in the Kingdom of this World.

Alejo Carpentier, *The Kingdom of this World*

Contents

Tables

Preface

I first entered the Third World at Port Said in 1944, though I didn't know it at the time. To us, Egypt was part of 'the Empire'. Thirty yards down the road from the troopship, I saw a man sitting against a wall amongst the rubbish and the ordure, with his nightshirt raised above his knees. Between them was a football, over which he was engaged in pouring water from a bowl. A closer look showed me that the football was his scrotum, monstrously swollen with elephantiasis.

Nearly forty years later, I arrived in La Paz, Bolivia. A peasant in a poncho stopped me in the street, begging for money. He didn't use words, because he couldn't. He simply pointed into his mouth, from which strangled sounds issued. The inside was filled with a swollen, yellow thing. It was his tongue. In horror, I recoiled, shoving a note into his hand, and fled. Then I turned back, racked with guilt, and stuffed more money into his hands, for antibiotics, than he could have earned in a month.

He may have come from the Cochabamba Valley. There, Frank Cajka has written:

> in a man's lifetime, he will buy one suit, one white shirt, perhaps a hat and one pair of rubber boots. The only things which have to be purchased in the market are a small radio-record player, the batteries to run it, plaster religious figures, a bicycle, a picture of a popular ex-President, and some cutlery.[1]

The Third World seemed to have changed little. Yet I had just experienced arriving at work every day with a headache and smarting eyes due to the industrial pall and the motor fumes that afflict cities like Mexico City and – yes – even the old centre of Rio (though not the residential zones where the rich live or the beaches where they disport themselves). Nor had I had to live in the far worse zones where the poor live and work: in Cantagem in Belo Horizonte or in North Rio. Plainly, the Third World had changed.

This book is an effort to reconcile that contradiction. It has taken me a lifetime, which began with the speeded-up changes and the sharpened contradictions of the time of Stalingrad and El Alamein. I was myself one of those contradictions: a communist officer in the colonial forces, who, like so many, later came to reject Stalinism, though not socialism (the biggest party in Britain, it has been said, is the ex-Communist Party). In 1964, I wrote a book about the Third World, which I have frequently been asked to update. I did so once, in 1967. But the Third World has changed massively since then. So has social science; and so have I. It is not updating – a few new statistics – that is needed, but a radical reappraisal of one's whole framework and its constituent categories. Thus, this book is not about the Third World alone, though my main preoccupation is with the majority of humankind who live there, for the directions that world has taken have been shaped (not determined – because they react against First and Second World models as well as being influenced by them) by the two major historic models of development.

Nor is it a history. I have drawn freely, as one must, on the work of historians. I have, however, assumed that people know what happened in Vietnam or in the American Civil War, though I do discuss less widely appreciated aspects of such major events. I use references for two purposes: to draw attention to works which I regard as worth reading, and to back up statements that some might challenge. Though today we have nothing equivalent to the histories of the world written by Jawaharlal Nehru or H. G. Wells, we do now possess a magisterial account of the growth of the Third World in L. S. Stavrianos' *Global Rift* (1981), which has made it unnecessary for me to go over the same ground (with less scholarship). Eric Wolf's path-breaking *Europe and the People without History* (1983) appeared too late to take into account as much as I would have liked to; Benedict Anderson's *Imagined Communities* (1983) even later. By publishing my *Marx and Marxism* in 1981, I have avoided yet another general discussion about the strengths and weaknesses of Marx's work. Ian Roxborough's *Theories of Underdevelopment* (1979) also made it unnecessary to repeat his perspicacious criticisms. Finally, the *Guía del Tercer Mundo 1981* is as exhaustive a handbook as one could hope for as a guide to the contemporary Third World, while Kidron and Segal's *State of the World Atlas* (1981) is a useful visual accompaniment. The *Third World Atlas* that forms part of the series of course materials put out for Open University students on the Third World Studies course (U 204) is outstanding.

My framework is not one of events, then, but one of meta-theory: of theory set against and lodged in history, focused on the theories and categories that have been used by others, both by actors in the world of everyday life and by specialists in theorizing, to make sense of what is happening to them. I am unimpressed by disciplinary boundaries except for the most part negatively, and make no apology therefore for ranging from T. S. Eliot to Pol Pot. Though I will surely be accused of the sin of 'culturalism', I think there is more than enough political economy in this book, while two of the three inner chapters are about classes. Most of that discussion is not very original, though I hope it is useful as synthesis. My main hope is that I may have thrown some theoretical light on ethnicity and nationalism and their relationship to class, because of the inadequacy of theorizing about these important forms of social life, particularly in Marxist materialism, which has had such dire consequences.

Finding out about the Third World is a labour of Sisyphus, or, in more modern terms, like painting Sydney Harbour Bridge. By the time you have covered one end, you need to start again at the other. Where there was a great deal about Africa in my 1964 book this one has much less, and a great deal more about Latin America. There is a further reason for this: that the research literature now coming from Mexico and Brazil (though no longer from Chile and Argentina, the former main centres for the social sciences) is very large, and usually higher both in quality and quantity than most of the work on Africa. This reflects the poverty of the latter continent, whereas Mexico and Brazil are industrializing countries which therefore have large tertiary education sectors in which a considerable amount of social research is carried out. There is a danger, then, of generalizing about the Third World as a whole on the basis of material which relates to a few countries of exceptionally rapid industrial growth.

There is certainly not enough in this book on India. I was so horrified at life in that huge subcontinent when I was there in the army that I have never been back. But it seems to me likely that which way India goes may well determine the future of the world. There is also virtually nothing on Japan, the great Asian capitalist 'late-comer'.

I did not do 'research' in the usual, field-work sense of that word, nor would it have been possible to have studied the world in that way. What I did do was to visit as much of it as possible, keeping my eyes and ears open, talking to people, and reading the specialized studies others had spent years producing. One depends heavily on such work. I would nevertheless disclaim responsibility when – as sometimes happens – one's sources lead one astray. But I now wish to publish this life-work before it becomes the death of me, and even if it is a case of 'publish and be damned'.

The two years I spent writing it would have been five had it not been for a grant from the UK Social Sciences Research Council which enabled me to exchange the hurly-burly of Manchester for the pastoral calm of Greenwich Village. That wonderful institution, the sabbatical year (which *everyone* should have), enabled me to fill in the major blank on my intellectual map of the world, South America. Without access to the great John Rylands Library of the University of Manchester and to the Elmer Holmes Bobst Library of New York University I would have lacked the means of modern intellectual production.

I communed almost exclusively with myself while writing – a lonely business which also made me cut down on activities important to me and on associations with people I value. My daughter, Deborah, did, however, help me to come to some conclusions. Without her optimism and drive, too, I would never have hunted for the accumulated notes of ten years which were stolen from my car a few hours before I was due to fly to the USA, and which we found scattered in the garden of an abandoned house – with not a sheet missing! I owe my wife, Sheila, special thanks and apologies: for responding to the love she has given me by dragging her to so many places – some terrible, some marvellous, some both – that she never wanted to go to in the first place (though she enjoyed most of them in the end); for her healthy disbelief that academia and intellectuals are the centre of the universe (which includes never reading anything I write); and for keeping me living a normal life when I would otherwise probably have worked until I made myself ill. I thank, too, Linda Ollerenshaw, Jeanne Ashton, Florene Daniel, Hilary Thornber and Julie Gorton, as well as the unknown typist at Typing Etc., New York, who sent me encouraging comments, for deciphering the jigsaw-puzzles of successive drafts. All the translations are by me.

Sydel Silverman and Eric Wolf did, however, give me one major opportunity to expose my ideas to criticism in the shape of the members of 'U 819', whom I thank deeply, both as critics and friends: John Antici, Jeffrey Aron, Beatrice Duret, Christine Grabowski, Wendy Hoefler, Susan Ikenberry, Karen Judd, Donna Kerner, David Leonard, Sonja Nelson, Alessandro Scassellati, and Robyn Wishengrad, and last, but not least, Jim Ryan; as well as for the chance to sit in on seminars with other graduate students and faculty. Stanley Diamond made me equally welcome at seminars in the New School for Social Research, and outside it. Finally, Glennon and Summerlyne Harrison read early drafts for me; Rod Watson read Chapters 1 and 4; Teodor Shanin picked up errors on Russia; Paul Kelemen vetted Chapter 1; and Alan Middleton and Ian Roxborough commented on Chapter 3. And I owe special thanks to Sally Mapstone's precise and critical editing, which brought light into innumerable dark places, and decimated my ironic quotation-marks. The perspicacious, gentle and devastating comments of Phil Leeson, that fount of knowledge about the Third World (though he rarely writes about it) and to which he is so dedicated (though he rarely visits it), forced me to rewrite the whole last chapter at the last minute. I suppose I should thank him: with the deepest respect and affection. The usual disclaimers that these friends do not necessarily agree with what I have written is no mere form of words.

Peter Worsley
Stockport

I Prolegomena

The Creation of the Third World

Poverty on a world scale is commonly thought of as a fact of Nature. Thus a recent popular overview of the condition of the majority of humankind – the peoples of the Third World – by a writer passionately committed to the eradication of their poverty, begins by discussing the 'cruel sun', 'droughts and downpours' and the 'disastrous environment' – though he does go on to observe that 'colonial powers laid the foundation of the present division of the world into industrial nations on the one hand and hewers of wood and drawers of water on the other' and concludes that 'the international economic order adds injustice to natural handicap'.[1] The notion that 'the tropics' lie under some kind of primordial curse makes it difficult to explain, however, why the great civilizations of the ancient world – Egypt, Mesopotamia, the Indus Valley – or the later Mayan and Chinese Empires, all flourished in mainly tropical regions which are now the most under-developed parts of the globe. 'Geography', as Christopher Hill has remarked, 'provides conditions "without which"': it does not offer a causal explanation of why'.[2]

Though 'development' is a post-Second World War concept, the whole of human history is the history of development. But during those long millennia during which the life of one generation was very like that not only of their parents, but even of their remote ancestors, change was commonly conceived of either as repetition or as very slow cumulation. Knowledge consisted of learning what was already known, even if the world was never as static or as coherent as ideology represented it to be: technical change might be gradual to the point of invisibility, but new religious cults could sweep whole societies and across societal boundaries.

The Great Transformation, as Karl Polanyi has called the rise of modern capitalism, involved a total re-making of the entire institutional order of society: not only the Industrial Revolution of applying science to industry and replacing manufacture by machinofacture, but the concomitant trans-formation of social and political institutions, a tidal wave that soon spread outside its original centres and within a century had engulfed the globe.

The overthrow not only of ancient structures of Church and State and their replacement by new ones involved a transformation not just of institutions, but of modes of thought, culminating in the discovery that the very order of Nature was itself not immutable, but had evolved and would continue to evolve in the future. Change, it seemed, was the only constant. Yet change must always be change of something: in the social sphere, of social structures and cultural values. It now became important, therefore, to work out a theory of society which would also be a theory of social change.

The dynamic of industrial capitalism in Europe had been intellectually codified in the shape of the 'laws' of *laissez-faire* economics and positivist sociology, which, it was assumed, were of universal validity, true irrespective of time and place. Knowledge of those laws gave mankind, for the first time in history, the 'positive' capacity to overcome scarcity and therefore to do away with conflict, even to change Nature: the possibility of a rationally ordered world summed up in the phrase *savoir pour prévoir, prévoir pour pouvoir*. To conservatives, we had already entered this new realm of freedom. For radicals, that freedom was contradicted because it was confined to a few; for the majority, it was only potential. In the richest countries on earth, millions lived in hunger and sickness.

The spread of Western capitalism wrought a parallel transformation of social life across the globe at the cost of the immiserization of far more millions. By the 1880s, the world had been divided up among a few Western industrial Powers. But within only a generation, capitalism was overthrown in one of the largest countries on earth. The USSR was thenceforward to be the model for those who wanted to overthrow capitalism in their countries also. For all its size, however, the Soviet Union did not become the leader of a Second World of other socialist states until after the Second World War. And there were far more who wanted to overthrow not capitalism, but *foreign* capitalism; nationalists who were neither social revolutionaries nor desirous of restoring the past, to whom the West was a far more acceptable and more impressive model of modernization. All that was needed, it seemed, was control of one's own political institutions. The support of the masses for that project was won by telling them that independence was the precondition for economic expansion which would benefit everyone.

The rapid growth of even the capitalist 'late-comers', in Europe, Germany, and Italy; in Asia, Japan, was so impressive that it blinded many people to the failure of the countries of Latin America, politically independent since the early nineteenth century, either to industrialize themselves or to emancipate themselves from the economic domination of the West. It was these countries, inevitably, though unconcerned with the 'nation-building' that preoccupied those recent ex-colonies that came together as the Third World after the Second World War, that were the first to develop the modern theories of dependency and underdevelopment which were rapidly taken up by the newly-independent countries.

'Underdevelopment', of course, is a relative concept. It does not mean *un*developed, for all societies are the end-products of thousands of years of development. They are *under*developed in relation to the 'advanced', industrialized countries. But when Europeans first arrived in Africa and the Americas, they often found themselves dealing with societies whose levels of economic development and cultural sophistication were superior or equal to anything Europe could show. Their underdevelopment, today, is not a natural condition, but an unnatural one, a social state which is the product of history; not a passive condition, but the consequence of conscious action; not something that just happened, governed by the logic of an impersonal system, but something that was done to people by other people. Underdevelopment did not mean ossification – the absence of change. Nor was it just an economic process. It meant the transformation of every dimension of life for the majority of the people of the world who lived in those countries that underwent underdevelopment. That is why a Caribbean historian entitled his study of African history, 'How Europe *Underdeveloped* Africa' (my italics).[3]

The continent most resistant to European conquest was Asia, not just because of its size, or the distances involved, but because until the eighteenth century, Europe possessed neither the military superiority nor the capacity to offer in trade anything much that Asia needed. Rather, the Asian commodities of spices, silks and fine textiles were eagerly sought after. They were paid for, not in the products of Europe, but with the wealth: gold and silver bullion plundered from America.

The conquest and settlement of the New World – 'by far the most important thing in the history of the Old'[4] – was the first phase in a process that was to end in the creation, for the first time in human history, of a world system of society.[5] But it was a system with two major components, divided by a 'global rift'[6] between the imperialist countries and their victims: politically, in the domination of new constructs called colonies by the metropolitan countries; economically, in the conversion of the colonies into producers of raw materials supplied to consumers and manufacturers in the West; and culturally, in the reduction of the extraordinary variety of institutions and ways of thought developed in innumerable societies to a simple dichotomy: in Sartre's words, a world divided into 'five hundred million men and one thousand five hundred million natives'.[7]

The societies the Europeans encountered were as diverse in their political structures – acephalous bands and chiefdoms; loose federal states in which the kingship rotated round a number of royal houses; highly centralized despotisms, and 'bureaucratic' empires – as in the bewildering variety of their exotic cultures. The logic of conquest was to stamp all of the new colonies with certain common features: political control from Europe; unbridled economic exploitation; and the construction of a racist social order. But the colonial relationship was a relationship between societies, each of which had its own distinctive social institutions and its own internal social differences, its own culture and subcultures. Despite the political power of the conqueror, each colony was the product of a dialectic, a synthesis, not just a simple imposition, in which the social institutions and cultural values of the conquered was one of the terms of the dialectic. Histories of colonialism written by imperialists ignore one of these terms: history is the story of what the White man did. Nationalist historiography has developed a contrary myth: a legend of 'national' resistance which omits the uncomfortable fact of collaboration.

How it was possible for Cortés to set out to defeat the might of the Aztecs with a force of only 600 Spaniards, and succeed, or for Pizarro to conquer Peru with only 180, has to be explained. In later centuries, the British in India and in Africa similarly defeated armies many times larger than their own. In the nineteenth century, technological – especially military – superiority seemed an adequate enough explanation: we had the Gatling gun and they did not. The horses and muskets of the Spaniards, and the ships of the Portuguese had also been superior to the equipment of their opponents. But by no means decisively so. Brutality is a second explanation, from the Spanish massacres at Cholula and Cajamarca to Leopold's Congo, where 10 million were killed in thirteen years and those who failed to bring in their ivory or rubber quota had their hands chopped off. It was enough to demoralize even the bravest. When his chief minister and old friend, Ras Engada, was blown to pieces before his eyes by a British shell in 1868, Theodorus, the Emperor of Abyssinia, 'showed no outward sign of emotion'. All he said was, ' "How can one fight with people who use such terrible missiles?" ' But he refused to surrender, saying, ' "Let us not fall into men's hands; they have no pity. Let us fall into God's". Soon afterwards, he . . . put his pistol into his mouth and pulled the trigger.'[8]

But the Abyssinians did continue to resist European invasion, and in 1896 defeated the Italian army at Adowa. Smaller societies would usually give in without a fight once they had seen the fate of those who did resist.

Yet Aztec wars for sacrificial victims, or African kingdoms which raided their neighbours for slaves to sell to the White man, had been just as brutal. And other highly-organized societies besides the Abyssinians were able to defeat European forces even in the nineteenth century: the Afghans, the Zulus and the Ashanti all defeated British armies.

The victories of earlier conquerors, less well-equipped, had depended, more than anything else, on their understanding of the social systems and cultures of their opponents. Cortés' victory was only possible because he was able to exploit the enmity between Tenochtitlán and Texcoco and Tlaxcala, which provided him with tens of thousands of men. Pizarro's arrival was welcomed by the Cañari and other peoples and factions who had paid the penalty for choosing the wrong side in the succession war between Atahualpa, ruler of the northern part of the Empire based on Quito, and Huascar, ruler of Cuzco, that had only just finished. Plassey, which won India for Britain, was 'hardly a battle at all'. Clive, with a motley force of only 950 European infantry and 150 gunners, half of them 'topasses' and French turncoats, and 2,000 sepoys, against Nawab Suraj-ud-Daulah's 50,000 foot and 18,000 horsemen plus superior artillery, triumphed, in the end, because one of the Nawab's generals, Mir Jafar, defected with his troops.[9] Cortés and Pizarro also exploited the cultural vulnerability of peoples to whom their kings were gods. Following a tactic they had learned among simpler peoples in the Caribbean, Moctezuma and Atahualpa were seized as hostages and killed. Cortés, a bearded White man, had been addressed by Moctezuma as 'Quetzalcóatl', the god who had returned and whom he welcomed back to his throne. He had appeared at the end of one of the fifty-two-year cycles, when, it was believed, the continuity, not just of society, but of the whole cosmic order was uncertain. Without elaborate rituals, the sun itself, the source of life, might never rise again.

The Spaniards, for their part, had been massively ignorant about what they would find: searching for the Indies, they found America. The Governor of Havana had particularly charged Cortés to keep an eye out for those 'strange beings with big flat ears and others with dogs' faces who live in the lands of the Aztecs'. What they actually found, in present-day Mexico and in the Andes, were two gigantic empires.

Their initial hopes had been dashed. In the islands of the Caribbean there had been little gold, and barbarous tribes. They themselves came from a country in which capitalism was little developed. Spain, a 'dry, barren, impoverished land',[10] a country of only eight million people, had acquired an empire more populous than any country in Europe.

After Conquest, there were only handfuls of men available to administer the tens of millions of their new subjects. 'Indirect rule' – the co-option of indigenous rulers, chiefs, nobles, and the use of existing structures of administration, especially at lower levels – was no nineteenth-century invention of Lord Lugard. It was an unavoidable necessity from the beginnings of colonization, and one which had the merit of providing a patina of legitimacy. In the Spanish and Portuguese colonies, in the absence of European women, the conquerors took native wives and concubines, a physical miscegenation that was to eventuate in social miscegenation: in American, *mestizo* cultures instead of Spanish, metropolitan culture. By the time the last colonies were established in the late nineteenth century, such cultural miscegenation was no longer possible, not just because the colonial period was too short to permit ancient religions to be wiped out, or because the colonized were numbered in hundreds of millions – the Spaniards had faced similar odds – nor because the British were Protestants and the extirpation of heresy and conversion to Catholicism a primary rationale of conquest for Spain, but because in the four hundred years in between, human relations between the West and the colonial world had been poisoned by the central fact of the slave trade. Economic and political domination was now buttressed by racist barriers to social intercourse of every kind. The British in India married only their own women back home or those who came out on the annual 'fishing fleet', looking for husbands.

The force that had driven the Spaniards to undertake the lunatic project of defeating empires of many millions with powerful armies was not religion. Cortés tells us what it was: 'We Spaniards', he wrote, 'suffer from an affliction of the heart which can only be cured by gold . . . I came in search of gold and not to work the land like a labourer.' He was to end up a marquis; his followers, mainly men of humble origins from the poorer regions of Spain,[11] a new settler class endowed with estates and the Indians to work them. Yet there could have been no conquest without fanatical faith and bottomless arrogance. The faith of the Spaniards was no other-worldly philosophy: it was an historical product, part and parcel of a fierce nationalism born of eight centuries of rule by Muslim conquerors whose yoke had finally been thrown off only seven months before Columbus sailed. Under Indian attack in Central America, half a century later, Coronado, the captain-general, invoked that tradition: 'You are Spaniards, sons of noble parentage. Now is the time to show your qualities. Be not afraid, for it is natural that the Spanish nation should accomplish feats that outshine in their greatness all others.'[12]

An elaborate apparatus of political control was now brought into being to keep these bold spirits firmly under metropolitan control. The Indies, in true Absolutist style, were annexed, not to Spain, but to the Crown of Castile. All trade with America was the monopoly of the port of Seville. And under Philip II, Spain 'passed out of the age of the *conquistador* into the age of the civil servant'.[13] Though all colonies are 'administrative societies', no states, Elliott has written, 'were more governed in the sixteenth century than those of the King of Spain'.[14]

At the apex of the overall bureaucratic machine stood the Council of the Indies. Within the colonies, political, administrative, and judicial power was carefully distributed between the Viceroys and the *audiencias*. Lest they become too powerful or develop local attachments, officials were regularly rotated, and their actions subjected to continuous monitoring and periodic inspections.[15]

The contradictions inherent in this system were not simply technical – that, for instance, it took eight months to get letters back and forth. They were also social. But they were only to mature with the emergence of a propertied class whose prosperity was frustrated by the prohibition on trade with other colonies, and who were the descendants of generations of *criollos*

born in America; with the defection of similarly local-born civil servants who
resented superiors, usually Spaniards, appointed from Spain; and with
political leadership from specialists in ideology in close contact with the
ordinary people: the lower-level clergy of a Church unique even in Europe
for its degree of subjection to royal control and subject to even more
stringent and detailed interference in the New World, which included a ban
on direct contacts with Rome.

The Spanish economy was dominated by a wool industry strongly
controlled by the Crown; its agriculture was 'distinctly unhealthy'. Manorial
tenants had only been released from servile tenure and allowed to sell their
own property and to move in 1480, twelve years before Columbus' voyage.[16]
Colonial 'adventurers' were especially uninterested in agriculture or any
other form of manual toil. Their voyages, like those of their counterparts in
other countries, were financed by wealthy backers, including the Crown,
who hoped for profits which could amount to fifty times the original
investment. What they were engaged in, however, was not production in the
sense of industry: the transformation of raw materials through the application of human labour. Even less was it founded upon capitalist relations of
production: the relationship of wage-labour to capital. It was not even trade
very·often, but what Weber termed 'booty capitalism' and ordinary people
called piracy or pillage: the use of force either to seize goods produced by
others in quite non-capitalist ways or to compel them to collect what nature
provided, not so much mercantile activity as a kind of indirect hunting-
and-collecting under duress. Based on the use of means of violence and
often backed by the power of the State, these were supremely *political* forms
of economic activity, a phase Marx called 'primitive' accumulation, which
other areas were only to experience in the nineteenth century, with the
ransacking of the islands of Melanesia for sandalwood, of New Guinea for
bird-of-Paradise feathers, and of the Amazon for wild rubber.

Production proper began with the introduction of farming on a limited
scale by White settlers who produced a variety of crops, mainly for local
consumption. But they were soon driven out by a revolutionary form of
agriculture first developed by the Portuguese in the islands off the west coast
of Africa, especially Madeira: sugar plantations worked by slave labour,
which at first included Whites, but of which Africa soon became the main
supplier. Columbus' idea of compensating for the limited supply of gold and
other natural resources in the Indies by exporting its human resources was
now reversed as Africa became the main arena for the hunting and gathering
of human beings.

The new, centralized organization of the plantation, which involved a new
work-discipline as well as a new division of labour, was to provide a model or
prototype for the later organization, in Europe and in the colonial *obrajes*,
of new kinds of non-agricultural productive enterprises: the manufacturing

units, named 'factories', like the trading-posts of early colonial times, which employed wage-labourers under conditions of such intensive labour and such loss of control over their work that the workers called it 'wage-slavery', analogous to the true slavery of the West Indies.

Sugar was so immensely profitable a crop – a 'licence to print money', as we now say of television – that in some colonies the cultivation of anything else was actually forbidden. But even these figurative gold-mines in the tropical lowlands were to remain of secondary importance for over a century and a half once the Spaniards had discovered what they had really come for: real gold and silver, not in handfuls of alluvial dust as in Hispaniola, but in huge quantities in the mines of Mexico and Peru. To a priest who complained that the Indians were being exploited, not converted, Pizarro retorted: 'I have not come for any such reason. I have come to take away from them their gold.'[17] The payment of tribute in kind had been heavy enough:

> The Indians of Parinacocha have to carry their tribute over two hundred miles to Cuzco: wheat, maize, cloth, bars of silver, etc. Indian men are loaded with it, and so are the women, the pregnant ones with their heads on their swollen bellies and those who have given birth with their babies on top of the loads. [They] climb with their loads up slopes that a horse could not climb.[18]

By the middle of the sixteenth century, it was their labour they were supplying to the mines of Potosí, from one province alone

> . . . with their wives and children . . . more than seven thousand souls. Every Indian . . . takes with him eight or ten sheep and a few alpacas to eat . . ., Indian corn and potato flour, their covers for sleeping, mats to guard against the cold, which is sharp, for they sleep in the open. All this cattle generally exceeds thirty thousand head . . . [The journey] takes two months, since the cattle cannot travel quicker, nor their children of five and six years whom they take with them . . . No more than two thousand souls ever return . . . at the end of six months, four in the mines, working twelve hours a day, going down at times seven hundred feet, down to where night is perpetual . . ., taking quite four to five hours, step by step, and if they make the slightest false step, they may fall . . . and when they arrive . . . a mineowner scolds them because they did not come quickly enough or because they did not bring enough load, and for the slightest reason makes them go down again.[19]

To the churchmen who sailed with the expeditions, however, conquest was merely a divine instrument, a means to the higher end of saving the souls of the unbaptized from perdition. For most of them, the barbarities of conquest and the harshness of colonial rule could therefore be justified. But there were others, some inspired by the millenarian beliefs of Joachim of Fiores newly published in the year Cortés landed, others by the new humanism, who reminded laymen that the Church was not a mere arm of the State, but superior to it: the City of God on earth. Ancient beliefs and garbled versions of the new marvels discovered by explorers were jumbled together in fantastic amalgam: wondrous animals and plants; bestial men with only one eye; hermaphrodites; people who lived on the perfume of fruits like the tropical birds which lived off flowers; women who removed one breast the better to fire their arrows – images projected onto the peoples and places they found and today preserved in the name of the world's largest river. Others sought not only the gold of El Dorado, but the land of Eternal Youth, where sickness was unknown. Inspired by reports that Christians converted by Saint Thomas centuries ago had been found in India, they shifted the myth to the new Indies. The Garden of Eden, they believed, had not been in the Middle East, but in America; the fruit which gave knowledge of Good and Evil had not been the apple, but the *maracujá*, the passion-fruit.[20] By the time these myths were being abandoned by Europeans, they were being taken up with fervour by those they had christianized. The worship of the black Virgin of Guadalupe, who had miraculously appeared to an Indian, became the main expression of the counter-culture of the oppressed Indians of colonial Mexico. By the time of Independence, it had become the symbol of *Mexican* nationhood.[21] By the 1930s, the most serious resistance to the new secularism of the revolutionary state was that offered by the fanatical Cristeros.[22] The hopes poured into these religious movements fuelled millenarian outbreaks in Yucatán among the Maya every few decades, and often far more frequently, from the Conquest right through to the nineteenth century, many of which had to be put down by force.[23]

The economic exploitation of the Indian thus bore no resemblance to the theoretical categories developed in *laissez-faire* economic theory to describe a later phase of capitalism. The bonds between *encomendero* and Indian were not those of the cash-nexus or of a market in labour: they were extra-economic, political ties of bondage. They also involved the construction not merely of an economic system, but of a whole new social order based on racial categories. The mass of the people, we shall see, were assigned to the hitherto unknown category of 'Indian'.

These new Indians turned in their suffering to those whose authority derived from their specialized role as interpreters of the Christian religion: the friars who lived close to them and who supplied cultural images of the world and interpretations of the meaning of life in this vale of tears. Religion was not just, as functionalist accounts would have it, solely an arm of the State. It was also the 'heart of a heartless world'. The Word of the God of the conquerors was susceptible of different interpretations by different priests – and by the Indians themselves. Indian Christianity was no more solely a religion of protest than was resistance the only political response to conquest. More often, it expressed identification with the bleeding Christ. Just as political opportunists and economic entrepreneurs seized the new openings available to them, often exploiting their fellows in the process, so many jumped at the chance to learn new skills and acquire Spanish education through the Church.

Nor was the Church the only source of images and explanations, or the only vehicle for expressing ideas and feelings. In village versions of Spanish folk-plays celebrating the victory of the Christians over the Moors, the Indians identified with the Moors.[24] Brilliant intellectuals like the *mestizo* Garcilaso de la Vega, and the Indian Guzmán Poma, tried, in the aftermath of the Conquest, to make sense of it all, producing sophisticated cosmological histories which drew upon both indigenous and European worldviews. Garcilaso's evolutionist historiography, which idealized the Inca past and denigrated Spanish dominion, embraced everything from the differences in the fauna and flora of the Old and the New Worlds to the existence of monotheism in traditional religion. Guzmán, despite his professed Christianity, developed an even more elaborate cosmology, in over one thousand pages, in which, however, it was Indian categories which supplied the framework of time and space: Adam and Eve and Christ, David and Abraham, the mummies of the Emperors and the Day of the Dead, were fitted together within a new, proto-nationalist synthesis. The world had passed through five ages (which were given precise dates) before the Spaniards arrived, the Inca Empire being the fifth of these. Today, he wrote, the kingdom of Castile was paramount in a world divided between the kingdom of the Indies in the West; the kingdom of Rome in the East; the kingdom of Guinea in the North; and the kingdom of Turkey in the South. But clearly Cuzco was destined to be the future 'new Rome', owing to its location at the centre of the world, the intersection of these four divisions, which clearly correspond to the four Inca divisions: Chinchasuyo (the West), Antisuyo (the North), Collasuyo (the East) and Cuntisuyo (the South). Guzmán actually proposed the establishment of a world council presided over by the king of Spain, who had clearly taken over the role of the Inca emperor as monarch of the Universe.

But the Indies were the *top* of the world, the zone of light, under heaven; Castile lay in the *lower* half, above the infernal region. Socially, what the schema meant was that the rights of the traditional Inca aristocracy had been pre-empted by jumped-up Spaniards; the future would see the displacement of Spain and the ushering-in of a messianic epoch of 'good Christianity'.[25]

We have paid particular attention to Spanish colonialism because Spain succeeded first in establishing a world empire. That colonial relationship was fateful both for the colonized and the colonizer. For the colonies, it meant ruthless exploitation, the loss of political autonomy, and savage cultural colonization. For Spain, it meant the distortion of her economy, ultimately economic paralysis; imperial delusions of grandeur and social and cultural stagnation.

But Spanish colonialism was not the prototype of colonialism generally. Each colony, and each empire, was to develop its own special character. All of them were stamped with the branding-iron of colonialism which marked them as property. But it also marked them as the private property of particular masters. Each colony was the product of a particular colonial equation in which the two sets of terms were never identical with those in any other colonial equation: differences not only of economic and political structure, but also social and cultural. The outcomes were necessarily vastly dissimilar: the encounter between a newly-forged Spanish Absolutist state atop a feudal society and powerful indigenous states was to result in a doubly Absolutist colonial system; that between Britain, undergoing political revolution against the monarchy and recalcitrant Nonconformist settlers in New England, produced a new kind of democracy in America. By the time of the East India Company's conquest of India, Britain was a changed country: the outcome was a vastly different society, India. Before long, Christianity began to be displaced as the dominant mode of thought of the rulers. The colonized now fastened upon new ideologies, of positivistic science, of liberalism, nationalism, and, eventually, of socialism, in order to express their own aspirations.

These changes were not simply points along a linear continuum of the development of capitalism. They were *discontinuities*. By the time of the conquest of India, capitalism had entered a new phase, one of radical disjuncture from the mercantile capitalism of the past, as capitalism became the dominant mode of *production* at home and, eventually, abroad. It also involved the construction of a new international division of labour, in which a subordinate role was allocated to the colonies.

The crucial commodity supplied to Europe by the colonies during the first phase of colonialism was not raw materials for European industry, or even consumer goods, but capital. Nationalist historiography in the Third World often attributes the development of Europe to colonial primitive accumulation: Africans ascribe it to the slave trade, Latin Americans to the silver and gold of the Americas, Indians to the introduction of capitalism in agriculture and the destruction of Indian industry, Caribbean writers to the triangular trade in sugar and rum, Chinese to the profits from opium and tea. Those contributions, however, should not be exaggerated, and they could become significant to Europe only because modernization was already the order of the day. Even in Spain, less than a quarter of the king's revenues came from American silver.[26] And while the capital accumulated by the nabobs of the East India Company gave Britain an invaluable edge over other competitors and imperial rivals, most of the capital that went to modernize agriculture and industry in those countries which were to emerge in the nineteenth century as the first industrial countries and eventually as the major imperialist Powers came mainly from profits generated at home. Once invested, in any case, the origins of the different capitals became a matter of historical interest only. But the colonies became an increasingly important market for British goods. By 1700, 'colonial trade amounted to 15 per cent of [British] commerce [and] by 1775 to as much as a fifth'.[27] By the middle of the nineteenth century, 'between £200 million and £300 million of British capital investment – a quarter in the USA, almost a fifth in Latin America – brought back dividends and orders from all parts of the world.[28] '[The British] industrial economy grew out of commerce and especially commerce with the underdeveloped world.'[29] Even then, European production was to remain inferior to Asian, both in quantity and quality, and was only able to eventually outstrip the latter, not through its ability to compete on the free market, but through the use of political force to destroy the Indian textile and shipping industries.

The new industrializing countries, notably Britain, were able to displace Spain because that country, instead of using the wealth of the Indies to modernize its metropolitan economy, dissipated it in consumption and imperial adventure in Europe. The decline of the supply of gold and silver in the eighteenth century, then, was not the cause of the decline of Spain; rather that decline had begun precisely because those commodities had been superabundant for two centuries. From the first decades of the arrival of the treasure-ships, bankruptcy became a chronic condition for Spain: in 1557, 1575, 1596, 1607, 1627, 1647, 1653 and 1680, by which year 'two-thirds of the silver in the treasure-fleet went straight to foreigners without even entering Spain',[30] to pay for goods and services provided by more advanced countries. There was no need for pirates like Drake. By 1703 Portugal had become a client state of Britain, where a half to three-quarters of the gold of Brazil ended up.

Stavrianos has divided the history of the Third World into three stages. In the first, between 1400 and 1770, commercial capitalism became the dominant framework within which, firstly Eastern Europe, then Latin America, was underdeveloped, transformed into appendages of the economies of Western Europe. The second phase, from 1770 to 1870, marked the transition to the epoch of industrial capitalism and its spread across the globe. The third, from 1870 to 1914, its consolidation, with the rise of monopoly capitalism and a world system of imperialism. No sooner was it established than backwards-looking primary resistance was to give way to movements for national independence, many of which, after the Russian Revolution of 1917, had strong socialist and communist components.

Underdevelopment thus began, not in the Americas, in Africa or in Asia, but in Europe, with the transformation of Eastern Europe into a region supplying wheat and other primary materials to the more dynamic economies of Western Europe. The contemporary division into East and West thus long antedates the rise of communism.

These economic developments could not have occurred without concomitant wholesale political transformations: in Eastern Europe, the 'second serfdom'; outside Europe, the establishment of colonies and trading-posts and their eventual consolidation into empires. In the Americas, initial piratical primitive accumulation and mercantilist trade gave way to the setting-up of productive enterprises – plantations and mines – worked by unfree, including slave, labour, relations which were totally different from the capitalist organization of production based on wage- labour. The arrival of capitalism in Asia at first involved no such disjunctural invention of new kinds of production-unit, simply the subordination of the major traditional unit of production, the household, to the new controls of the market and to new capitalist work-disciplines.

In the first, mercantilist phase, the colonial economy had been based on the ownership of land and other resources conferred or confirmed as private property, or converted into it, by the State. Much of the crop would end up in the hands of the State, which could market that part of this tribute that it did not use directly. Landowners, as the legal owners of the product of other people's labour on their land, also marketed grain, as did land*lords*, who acquired it as rent, and as those peasants able to market the product of their own labour surplus to subsistence needs. By the second, industrial phase, capitalist companies were becoming directly involved in the productive process itself, especially in manufacture. By the turn of the nineteenth century, the output of the Indian weaver was controlled by one of the East India Company's servants, a 'man with a cane who would watch over the weaver and beat him to "quicken his deliveries" '.[31]

A great deal of what arrived on the market, however, both agricultural commodities as well as manufactures, was not produced by wage-labour at all, but by unfree producers of all kinds – slaves, serfs, and into this century, those in debt-peonage. Capitalist market relations, then, have been perfectly compatible with non-capitalist ways of producing, all of which are commonly lumped together, sloppily, as the 'capitalist mode of production'. In the Third World today, production by landless proletarians, working land and machines owned by others and paid wages for the hours they put in – the pure form of the capitalist labour process – though fast becoming the dominant mode of production, still co-exists with agricultural and even manufacturing still based on the use of family labour.

The linking together of all these forms of economic activity across the globe into a single, interconnected economic system was necessarily a protracted and uneven process. By the nineteenth century, whole societies had already been converted into zones of monocultural agriculture, 'factories without chimneys', as Furnivall called Burma. Some, like Egypt, were to become vast cotton plantations; others banana plantations; yet others dependent, literally, on peanuts, or in extreme cases, on such specialized commodities as cloves. Scientific imperialism was an integral part of the process. The tropics were ransacked for the seeds of rubber, quinine, tea, coffee, and other plants, which were brought back to Kew, subjected to careful selection, and then disseminated to Imperial Botanic Gardens in Ceylon, Malaya, the West Indies and elsewhere.[32] By the twentieth century, whole regions were specializing in the production of cocaine and heroin for the US market.

Europe's irruption into the Asian scene had begun in 1498, when Vasco da Gama, led by the Arab pilot, Ahmad ibn-Madjid, discovered the Cape route to the East. From then on, the historic trade-routes between Asia and the West, centred upon the Middle East, were to be bypassed, and cities like Cairo were to sink into decay. Only a century after Columbus, Asian spices were reaching the Middle East from North-west Europe, via the new route round the Cape. The Portuguese, first in the field, tried to keep the new wealth of the East under their control by making maps of the sea-route top secret. Their initial success provoked even more boundless ambition: the Spaniards, inspired by their conquests in America, dreamed of displacing the Portuguese in Asia. Some believed that 5,000 Spaniards could take China as easily as they had conquered the Aztecs and the Incas, or that they might break Muslim resistance by diverting the Nile to the Red Sea or raiding Mecca and seizing the Prophet's body.

Portuguese naval artillery and gunnery, and the manoeuvrability of their ships, proved superior enough to that of their opponents to give them the edge in the somewhat inconclusive battle of Diú, against the Egyptian fleet, in 1509. After that engagement, there was little to stop them at sea. Albuquerque, the Portuguese admiral and governor, could soon boast that 'at the rumour of our coming, the native ships all vanished, and even the birds ceased to skim over the water'.[33] By 1513, they were in Canton.

This maritime superiority, however, was by no means so effective when it came to tackling the empires of the Asian land-mass. The inferiority of the Europeans – cultural as well as economic – seemed self-evident to Asian potentates when they first encountered them. The Ottoman Empire had 50 million subjects when England had 5 million. In 1666, the Grand Vizier of the Ottoman Empire addressed the French ambassador as a '*Giaour*' [unbeliever], 'a hogge, a dogge, a turde cater'. A century later, news of the alliance between France and Austria was treated as of no more consequence than 'the union of one hog with another'. When John Russell, Cromwell's grandson, arrived in Mogul India in 1712, he had to make obeisance to the Emperor, requesting 'the smallest particle of sand . . . with his forehead at command rub'd on the Ground, and reverence due from a Slave'.[34]

But Europe was fast outstripping the East. Only thirty-two years after that last insult, the French ambassador could describe the Ottoman Empire as 'one of the richest colonies of France'.[35]

Spanish and Portuguese expansion in the East fizzled out, leaving behind a few decaying forts in stagnant coastal enclaves. In much of East Africa, they were expelled by superior Arab forces. But even at their height, the Portuguese in Asia had 'functioned merely as carriers and middlemen in a purely intra-Asian trade'.[36] Before the nineteenth century, Asian handicrafts had 'never left any important place for European goods, and European factory products found no admittance in Asia before the advent of . . . mass production of consumer goods in Western Europe'.[37] 'For two and a half centuries after da Gama, Europeans were effectively excluded from the Indian subcontinent'.[38]

The same initial conceit and hauteur were displayed by Ch'ien Lung, Emperor of China, when he received George III's emissary, Lord Macartney, in 1793. China, the Emperor declared, had no need of any of Europe's products and even less of her bizarre religious doctrines. But the Europeans would be graciously allowed to establish *hongs* – small trading posts on the coast, similar to those to which the Japanese had confined European traders and missionaries, in order to give them access to the Chinese goods they needed.[39] Yet within half a century the gateway to the trade of China was to be blasted open in the Opium Wars.

The Industrial Revolution in Western Europe was based on a revolution in production: on the application of science to machinofacture and on new methods of organizing work:

> For the first time in human history, the shackles were taken off the productive power of human society, which henceforth became capable of the constant, rapid and up to the present limitless multiplication of men, goods and services.[40]

The new industries depended increasingly for many crucial raw materials upon colonial imports: rubber, oil and minerals. Growing prosperity also meant a revolution in consumption. Spices, silks and fine textiles, the historic luxury imports from the East, were now displaced by a new mass demand for sugar, tea, coffee, and other tropical commodities. Between 1850 and the First World War, real wages in England and France doubled. To meet this demand, political power was used to introduce new, capitalist forms of production in the colonies:

> It was a silent but far-reaching revolution that the plantation system introduced . . . Previously, the Dutch had only been merchants buying the spices and rice . . . and selling them at a profit. True, they used their

powers to establish a monopoly, but beyond this the trading activities did not interfere with the life of the people. But the change over into a plantation economy involved the actual exploitation of labour, a control of the economic activity of the population and an effective supervision . . . in fact 'estate management' over a whole country. The island of Java became a plantation of the Dutch United East India Company . . . The relations between the sovereign [the Company, *P.W.*] and its subjects were in substance those of planter and coolie, in which the former was not merely the employer of labour, but also the authority vested with the rights of life and death . . . A whole people was . . . converted by the excrcise of sovereignty into a nation of estate coolies, with their own natural aristocracy reduced to the position of foremen and super-intendents.[41]

Attempts to introduce Western technology – and not only guns – had begun as far back as 1520 in Ethiopia and in the eighteenth century in Western Africa. They had all been frustrated. In the nineteenth century, Turkey's attempt to establish a 'Turkish Manchester and Leeds' was blocked by Western interests. Mohammed Ali's efforts to modernize Egypt were brought to an end with the brutal invasion mounted by Palmerston to restore the nominal authority of the Sultan. Foreign debts, including the costs of military occupation, now became the first charge on treasuries and customs services often directly run by foreigners.[42]

Existing industry (notably textiles and ship-building in India) was now dismantled in order to eliminate competition with Lancashire and the Clyde. The colonies were *agriculturalized*: in 1891, 61 per cent of the population of India were working in agriculture; by 1921, 73 per cent.

Theories of Development

To nineteenth-century Europeans, the superiority of their culture was self-evident: it was a total superiority of 'civilization' over barbarism and superstition, not just an economic superiority. To Christians, it was attributable to their possession of the True Faith; the wretchedness of those they evangelized to their ignorance of the Word of God. But a more modern explanation was available: the doctrine of evolutionary progress through natural selection, which was soon transformed into *Social* Darwinism: the doctrine of 'the survival of the fittest'. For some, this meant the permanent inferiority of the 'unfit' races; for others, it was compatible with the notion that unlike animals or plants, human beings could acquire the prerequisites of social development, not just via religious conversion, but through learning European ways. Simple techniques (like how to work) might be acquired quickly; others (like how to govern themselves) might take generations. Either way, what was to be learned was what had already been learned in Europe.

These ideas have persisted through to our day, albeit formulated in more *Social* sophisticated ways. They still inform the aid policies of the industrialized *Darwinism* countries and of international agencies, as well as academic theories of development.

'Development' only became a distinct field of study after 1945, with the emergence of an ever-increasing number of 'new nations' which soon came to constitute a 'Third World' alongside the First and Second. The achievement of political independence, it was widely assumed, would now make possible rapid economic development. For most, this meant capitalist development. Hence the theory which best captured this mood of optimism and which drew, too, upon deep-seated evolutionist modes of thought: *Rostow* W. W. Rostow's *The Stages of Economic Growth* (1960) struck responsive *& evolutionism* chords outside academia. Though an economist, his was not an economistic theory. 'Economic forces and motives', he wrote, 'are not a unique and overriding determinant of the course of history.' Economic development required not only appropriate economic, technological and demographic conditions, but also appropriate social institutions and value systems. Development was a unilinear process. Though Rostow was one of the architects of the US policy of bombing Vietnam 'back into the Stone Age', even communism was a step on the road to development. But it was a 'disease of transition', since though State command over the economy might lead to economic expansion, it could never be as effective as a free-market, private-property economy, and would entail the sacrifice of political freedom. The model for underdeveloped countries, therefore, was the 'open' society of the West. Such was the arrogance of the USA, the greatest Power in human history, at this time, that even a distinguished liberal, David Riesman, could remark that 'it is not only Westerners who find it hard not to assume that the non-Western nations must either fail or follow one of the courses already marked out by the West'.[43]

And eventually, 'convergence' theorists argued, capitalism and communism as we now know them would both give way to a new, 'post-industrial' society: in the USA, the State was already playing an ever more important interventionist role, not only in the economy, but in all spheres of life, while the growing prosperity of the USSR meant that it would no longer be necessary for the State to control access to scarce goods. Both production incentives and the allocation of goods could be left more and more to the market. The cultural counterpart of this liberalization would be the relaxation of ideological controls.

Post-industrial society would necessitate the recruitment of vast numbers of skilled personnel, especially in the tertiary sector, who would be recruited on the basis of competence, via 'meritocratic' open competition, for entry into mass higher education. From their ranks, a new managerial élite controlling the economy, the State and civil society would be selected, replacing the older ruling classes whose power had been based on their monopoly of private property or on their political skills. The pyramidal social structure of the past, with few at the top, the vast majority at the bottom, and a small middle class, would be replaced by a diamond-shaped class structure in which most people would be in the middle, with only a small managerial élite and the unqualified at each extreme. All this, indeed, was *already* happening. Democracy, US-style, Lipset claimed, was 'the good society . . . in operation'.[44] Older sectional class interests, expressed in the ideologies of Big Business and of Labour, were becoming irrelevant: we were witnessing the 'end of ideology' and its replacement by rational technocracy.

To many, this optimistic evolutionism was not convincing. The most dominant theoretical school in the West, from the 1950s into the early 1960s, was that which became subsequently known as 'modernization theory'. All theories of development – or of any other field of social life – are necessarily particular applications of more general theories. In the case of moderniz- ation theory, it was the sociological functionalism of Talcott Parsons, in which roles, the atomic elements of institutions which together made up the social system, were informed by cultural value-orientations, cognitive, expressive, and integrative, which he then grouped according to a set of binary oppositions: between universalistic and particularistic value-orien- tations; between roles characterized by functional specificity as against functional diffuseness; roles based on ascription as against achievement, and roles charged with affectivity rather than affectively neutral; and with further systematic, not random, relations between these sets.[45]

These categories were then used by Hoselitz and others to develop a model in which roles in developed countries were seen as typically universalistic, based on achievement, and functionally specific; those in underdeveloped countries as particularistic, based on ascription, and functionally diffuse.

The solution to underdevelopment was *diffusion*: a simple idea shared by a rapidly-growing army of indigenous technocrats and by foreign technical experts and advisers specializing in development:

> You subtract the ideal typical features or indices of underdevelopment from those of development, and the remainder is your development program.[46]

Obviously what was needed had to be diffused from the 'centre' (particularly the USA) to the 'periphery'. For materialists, it was technology that was needed, or capital; the only kind of ideas that were relevant were scientific knowledge and technical know-how. For idealists, it was modern values and modernizing attitudes.

The idea that *social* change might be more important than any of these scarcely appealed to ruling élites or their First World patrons, since it would entail the erosion of their political and economic dominance. Most of the advice about social matters came overwhelmingly from economists. There had, in fact, been plenty of diffusion, during the imperialist era: the introduction of new colonial economic, political and social institutions. But it had always been selective: economic development which threatened the industries of the 'motherland' had been stifled, representative democracy refused. To the new intelligentsia, however, it was precisely these institutions and ideas, and later nationalism, socialism and communism, that seemed to offer solutions to the underdevelopment of their countries.

Functionalism is not, as its critics often assume, a theory which ignores the existence of conflict. True, it does not place much emphasis upon conflicts between interest-groups, and its adherents often seem to assume a degree of harmony between the component groups of society which is at variance with the facts. But it does recognize, in principle, that relations between the sub-systems of which society is made up are always problematic and can even break down, unless there is a shared belief that it is important to rise above these divisions in the wider interest of keeping society going. Unless such beliefs are effectively communicated and constantly, publicly reaffirmed as a coherent value-system, they will, as Durkheim argued, become ineffective. Those whose job it is to formulate and communicate values, especially intellectuals, are therefore of special importance. Conservatives like Shils argued that if they were poor communicators, or Westernized modernizers out of tune with the mass of society, who still cleaved to traditional beliefs and ways, or if suitable institutions where people could learn those values (schools, churches, etc.) were not available, they would not be adequately disseminated.[47] Those more concerned with development than with stability, such as McClelland, argued that what was needed were modern forms of achievement-orientation equivalent to the Protestant ethic which had supplied a dynamic of individual effort and reward during the formative period of capitalism in the West.[48]

The central assumption was the notion of 'dualism', that both economy and society were divided into two sectors: the 'traditional' and the 'modern'. In Africa, Arthur Lewis argued that the way to achieve economic growth was to shift resources – capital and labour – out of the traditional sector and into the modern, which would then make it possible to modernize agriculture. In Latin America, there was even a left-wing version, in which communists argued that national industrial capital had a 'patriotic' role to play, internally, in breaking the power of the traditional landed oligarchies interested only in agro-export; externally, in preventing the take-over of the economy by foreign multinational corporations.

The dualism of North American modernization theorists, however, was of a different kind. To them, underdevelopment was the consequence of deficiencies internal to the underdeveloped countries themselves, the heritage, not of their colonial, but of their *pre*-colonial past: feudal rulers interested only in maintaining their stake in archaic agrarian systems; cultural deficiencies, such as other-worldly religions or the irrational particularisms of tribal loyalties. It was not just a cognitive theory. Implicit in it was what Gouldner has called a 'metaphysical pathos'[49]: the *blame* for underdevelopment was laid upon the Third World itself.

It was not difficult for their critics to expose the inadequacy both of the categories and of their capacity to explain the world. In a classic essay, Frank pointed out that the model took insufficient account of *power*, since some social roles are more decisive for society as a whole than others. Empirically, too, oligarchies in underdeveloped countries controlled all areas of public life in a *very* 'diffuse' way, while mass movements of a thoroughly 'universalistic' kind were spreading everywhere. Conversely, particularism, in the form of interpersonal networks of legitimate and illegitimate influence, was a quite normal aspect of organizational life in large corporations.

As for the stages of economic growth, those countries longest subject to colonial control were still suppliers of primary goods to the developed world: they were no further along the road to 'take-off' than more recently colonized countries. All of them, too, had been so turned upside down that they had long ceased to be traditional, a term, in any case, which lumped together an immense variety of societies and cultures.

In the 1960s, C. Wright Mills, criticizing sociologists for their lack of a *societal* vision (most of them, he wrote, had only a 'middle level' consciousness), argued that the relevant unit of analysis, for modern society, was the nation-state. In the Third World, theorists had long been arguing a much more radical position, that the relevant unit of analysis was not the 'country' at all, but the colonial world, or, to some, the entire world. To Alavi, the Third World was shaped by a 'colonial mode of production'. To later 'globologists', the world as a whole was the 'primordial unit of analysis': a 'world mode of production'.[51] These were concepts with a special appeal to people in countries that had once been colonies, had long been politically independent, but which had experienced the limits of that independence. The reality was '*neo*-colonial', *economic* dependence. 'Dependency theory' therefore developed first in Latin America. It did not necessarily imply a radical political position. Most of its proponents were mostly quite unrevolutionary technocrats, aiming to promote capitalist, national development. Much of their conceptual equipment, however, was

borrowed from Marxists like Paul Baran and Paul Sweezy who had begun
the task of assessing the changes in world capitalism since the last major
Marxist critique, Lenin's *Imperialism*, written in 1916.

Lenin's model, Warren has argued, was seriously flawed: imperialism was
not a consequence of the rush to export capital from the developed world,
nor was there any special up-turn in the volume of capital exported in the
second half of the nineteenth century, the high-water period of political
imperialism. Capital, rather, actually flowed *in*. It was trade that grew, far
more rapidly, over most of this period:

> Lenin's *Imperialism* was obsolete even before it was translated into
> English, indeed as soon as it appeared. The great age of capital export was
> over by 1914 . . . Imperialism, far from being the product of a senile,
> decaying capitalism compelled to invest abroad the capital it no longer
> had the 'vigour' to absorb at home, was on the contrary the product of
> young and vigorous capitalist economies newly emerging onto the
> international arena to challenge their rivals in *trade*. The expansion of
> trade, rather than of foreign investment, was the logical conclusion of the
> accelerated industrialization of the nineteenth century . . .'[52]

Other Marxists began by rephrasing the notion of a world system, and of
the division of that world into imperialist and exploited countries, as a
division into centre and periphery. To even non-Marxist economists, the
conception of economic relations as of primary importance, and of other
institutions as epiphenomena and of ideologies as mere 'false consciousness', was perfectly acceptable. Using these ideas, a new strategy was
devised: of mobilizing national resources so as to replace dependence on
agro-exports by industry, which, in the first place, would meet the rising
demand for consumer goods in a more readily-controlled internal market:
the policy of 'import substitution'.

During the Depression of the 1930s and the Second World War, when
foreign competition was weak, the policy met with considerable success. It
was a phase of populist mobilization of the masses as well as of encourage-
ment to national capital. But it still left them dependent for more basic goods
on foreign imports. By the 1950s, the only way to avoid renewed head-on
competition with the foreign multinational corporations, and to acquire the
vast amounts of capital needed for the next stage of industrialization, was to
invite foreign investments. Ruthless authoritarian repression of organized
labour and of political opposition were the political prerequisites; the
results, industrialization at the cost of the loss of democracy at home and a
new dependency on foreign capital and foreign military support.[53]

Marxist theorists of dependency rejected both the populist-nationalist
solution to this situation and the policies of economic and political
collaboration with foreign capitalism of authoritarian governments. The

problem, they asserted, was not one of *poverty*; these countries were not poor. But the wealth produced in the periphery ended up in the centre. 'Aid' was a gigantic deception, designed to deceive humanitarians in the developed countries, but in reality a drop in the bucket compared to the *outflow* of capital. International capitalism was the problem, not traditionalism.

Marxists now embarked upon major historical studies of how the entire world had been integrated into a single world system, beginning in Eastern Europe and with the voyages of discovery outside Europe, and ending with the triumph of imperialism in the nineteenth century. The emergence of the Third World as a self-conscious political grouping after 1945 was only the end-product of a process that had begun half a millennium earlier. The Third World, as Frank showed for Latin America and Samir Amin for Muslim Africa, had a *history*. Together with Wallerstein and Stavrianos, they blocked out the general history within which that regional underdevelopment had taken place.[54]

The limits of this model were precisely those which gave it its strength: it was a model of a total system in which the parts, whether countries or types of countries,[55] were analysed solely in terms of political economy. Politically, to be told that 'for the underdeveloped parts of the world to develop, the structure of the world social system must change',[56] seemed a profoundly demobilizing counsel of despair not only to reformers striving to improve education or health – and sometimes succeeding – but even to revolutionaries for whom the only practical possibility was not to change the entire world, but their own society.

The very different kinds of dependence – from that of Bolivia or Chile to countries with very high living-standards for the masses but which were still producers of primary commodities, such as Australia, New Zealand or Canada, 'the world's richest underdeveloped country' – did not seem to be illuminated by a theory in which the term 'underdevelopment' was equally applied to the poverty-stricken *sertão* of Brazil's North-east and to oil-rich Venezuela.[57] More seriously, it was objected, industrial development *really was happening* in many countries. The vast differences of social structure and of culture in all these countries, moreover, called for a very different kind of theory from that which world-system theory provided. Some of the elements could be found in other varieties of Marxism; most had been developed outside Marxism altogether.

The Myth of Base and Superstructure: Dialectics versus Materialism

The problems of Marxist development theory derive from its wider theoretical underpinnings. Marxism, Engels insisted, was itself the product of the historical confluence of three pre-existing intellectual traditions: German philosophical idealism; French social theory; and British political economy. He and Marx, he over-modestly said, had contributed little that was distinctively new.[58]

A century later, Marxism can obviously no longer be thought of as a unitary thing. There are three main kinds of institutionalized Marxism: Soviet Marxism, Chinese Marxism, and Euro-communism: and fifty-seven varieties of neo-Trotskyism. The two largest are fiercely opposed to each other. As a body of theory, the variety is bewildering. To historians, Marxism is *historical* materialism; for some philosophers, historical *materialism*. To yet others, it is a dialectical *method*, which would still be valid even if all the specific predictions of Marxism proved wrong. For Gramsci, that was too intellectualist an approach. It was also too deterministic. The future was not something that unfolded itself in such a way that what was going to happen could be worked out theoretically in advance. Marxists were, therefore, not in the business of foreseeing the future at all, nor was Marxism merely 'theoretical praxis'. It was a philosophy of *political* praxis which enabled people to work out not what would happen, but what needed to be *done* in order to create the kind of future we wanted for humanity:

> Really one 'foresees' to the extent to which one acts, to which one makes a voluntary effort and so contributes to creating the 'foreseen' result. Foresight reveals itself therefore not as a scientific act of knowledge, but as the abstract expression of the effort one makes, the practical method of creating a collective will . . . To believe that one particular conception of the world, and of life generally, in itself possesses a superior predictive capacity is a crudely fatuous and superficial error.[59]

One intellectual tradition Engels did not mention was the newest one of all, one which affected the thinking of everyone in the nineteenth century from churchmen to revolutionaries like himself: positivist evolutionism, whose triumphs in studying and 'mastering' Nature, intellectually in the form of the 'laws of mechanics and biology' and in the material form of the achievements of modern industry, were taken as the paradigm for 'scientific' socialism too. Marxism also dealt in 'laws', both the general 'laws of motion' of political economy, and particular laws such as the law of the falling rate of profit. Today, even the labour theory of value has its Marxist critics. By the 1970s, a Marxist economist was urging not only that this 'last iron law of Marxism' be 'buried', but that the nineteenth-century conception of 'law' itself be abandoned.[60]

The limitations of these first attempts to formulate the central postulates of Marxism were apparent even to those who were the custodians of Marx's

archives and the official legatees of his ideas. Not long after the death of
Marx and Engels, Eduard Bernstein was arguing that 'peasants do not sink;
middle classes do not disappear; crises do not grow; misery and serfdom do
not increase'.[61] His name was to become a synonym, among Marxists, for
theoretical heresy and political betrayal. Yet eighty years later it had
become possible for a distinguished Marxist historian to go much further: to
argue that it was no longer obligatory to always look for an 'economic'
interpretation of history; that the model of 'base' and 'superstructure' did
not explain all 'dominance and dependence'; that class interests and class
struggles were not the only causal factors in history; and that belief in
historical laws and historical inevitability, or imputing the ideas of the
opponents of Marxism to class interest or bad faith were all merely 'vulgar'
Marxism – Marxism infected with nineteenth-century evolutionism and
positivism.[62] The trouble with that explanation is that Marx and Engels,
being creatures of their times, had themselves also absorbed these ways of
thinking, not merely their mistaken followers.

Some blamed the Second International inheritors of the Marxist legacy
for these misconceptions, not only Eduard Bernstein, Marx's literary
executor, but even Karl Kautsky, the major Marxist political authority after
Marx's death, and were able to invoke Lenin's authority for so doing. By the
1970s, it had even become possible to blame Engels for much of it. Though
Thompson loyally leapt to the defence of the 'poor old duffer',[63] the
problems the critics had seized upon were not peculiar to Engels' thought at
all. That 'scientific' socialism should give rise to predictions which were no
better and no worse than most other people's is not particularly damaging to
Marxism except for positivists, for whom the essence of science is its
predictive capacity. But the lacunae, inconsistencies, and mistakes are not
just particular, accidental misjudgements. Nor can they simply be converted
into assets: testimony to Marx's undoubted open-mindedness; his criticality
towards his own ideas; his readiness to change them in the light of fresh
evidence; his reluctance to jump to conclusions in the absence of adequate
data. All these are certainly aspects of Marx's genius, of his intellectual
honesty and craftsmanship. But even if he had finished more than one of the
four volumes that were to make up only one of the six-part study of political
economy he had embarked upon, he would still not have constructed a
sociology, a science of society. Further, though Marxists hardly ever
recognize it, these particular lacunae, inconsistencies and errors derive from
deep contradictions in the thoughts of Marx as well as Engels.

In the past, two main kinds of model of society have been used by
Marxists: the one-dimensional kind known in the 1930s as the 'economic
theory of history'; and the two-dimensional kind called 'political economy'.
Their limitations should not blind us to their achievements. The former was
an understandable and creative reaction to a bourgeois scholarship which

saw history either in terms of battles, kings and cabinets, or as a mere succession of events, without pattern or meaning, which could only be chronicled in narrative form, 'one damned thing after another'. In contrast to that kind of obtuseness, Marxism reinstated a holistic, Renaissance vision, akin to the thrill Keats experienced 'on first looking into Chapman's Homer': a blinding flash of revelation to those never before exposed to the idea that there were connections between Beethoven's symphonies, Romantic love, and the factory chimneys of Manchester. A similar sense of intellectual illumination and of the opening of new horizons was experienced by a whole generation of natural scientists when Hessen used 'historical materialism' to study 'the social and economic roots of Newton's *Principia*'.[64]

The second major contribution of the Marxism of the 1930s was that ordinary people, the classes hitherto ignored or confined to the intellectual ghettoes of 'social' and 'labour' historiography, were thrust onto the centre-stage of history. The more sophisticated, two-dimensional Marxism which emerged after the Second World War went beyond economistic reductionism by exploring the interrelations between the economy, the State and civil society, including studies of culture. But however often materialism was shown to be an inadequate framework for tracing out these interconnections, Marxists clung with religious devotion to the central dogma: the model of society as divided into an economic base, with the rest as superstructure. In its crudest forms, the complexities of relationship between economic and other social institutions, and between these and ideologies, were reduced to a set of simple, one-to-one correspondences; social structure was simply a synonym for class structure; and political parties, even when they patently cut *across* classes, were still held to represent the sectional interests of particular classes.

Political economy was also an advance. In a country like South Africa, for instance, it challenged deeply-entrenched assumptions that racial conflict was merely the expression, at the social level, of innate prejudices, or the inevitable consequence of contact between different cultures. Both prejudice and racism, Marxists showed, were constructs: instruments of a deliberate exercise in social engineering: the project of preventing the emergence of class-based solidarity by splitting the working class into sealed-off communities.

But neither kind of Marxism meets the requirements of a Marxist sociology, which necessarily has to be three-dimensional, and in sound and colour. The most notable attempt to formulate what was wrong with one- and two-dimensional Marxism, by Sahlins, focuses on several major 'antinomies' in Marx's thinking: the conception of thought as a Kantian *pre*-figuring v. thought as reflection; the treatment of wants, sometimes as culturally and historically specific (and therefore relative), and at other

times their reduction to system needs; the replacement of the cultural logics
which shape economic categories by an asocial calculus of practical reason;
the converse treatment of the production and reproduction of culture as a
mere epiphenomenal by-product of economic production; the expression of
all this in the form of the model of base and superstructure, rather than one
of a dialectical interplay between sub-systems and subcultures, not levels; a
positivistic stress upon laws, as against a historicist and culturalist conception of the emergence and disappearance of institutions and ideas as
society changes its general character; and the opposition between the
conception of prediction and the notion of the imposition of human values
on the natural world as the quintessential attributes of humanity. Taken
together, each of these sets of oppositions, Sahlins argues, constitute
different 'moments' within Marxism: the one, a naturalistic, utilitarian
theory; the other, a cultural version of historical materialism.[65]

To this considered critique, the Marxist response has been a resounding
silence. The replies it did evoke scarcely damaged Sahlins at all, and were
mainly effective only as criticisms of the weakness of his own structuralism.

A system of any kind involves relationships between component elements
such that change in one part necessarily leads to changes in the rest. Systems
of ideas are no different. But the degree to which all elements necessarily
change together and to the same degree varies considerably. Some
propositions, moreover, are central building-blocks, essential to the entire
structure; others subsidiary. Empiricists are reluctant to impose order which
they believe is not found in reality. Others, whose thinking is conditioned by
what Pareto called 'residues of combination', are given to over-systematiz-
ing. The central defect of Parsons' functionalist sociology, Gouldner has
argued, is that it fails to allow for the relative autonomy of the institutional
sub-systems of which society is composed.[66] The same is true of functionalist
Marxism.

In addition to the three main kinds of institutionalized (political)
Marxism, today, there are many other ways in which Marxisms can be
classified, each of these taxonomies illustrating different facets of these
varieties of Marxism. Each, too, contains within it a different set of
prescriptions for action, explicit or implicit, and a different conception of
historical agency. For some, capitalism is bound to collapse by virtue of its
internal contradictions; for others, its demise is not inevitable, it has to be
destroyed by collective human action. The problem then becomes one of
determining which class is to assume this world-historic role. For Marx and
Engels it was the proletariat in the advanced capitalist countries. For later
revolutionaries, it was the peasantry in the underdeveloped world. To
theorists like Marcuse, a century after Marx, it seemed that the working
class in the USA was no longer even potentially revolutionary: the forces of
change were not classes defined by their relationship to the means of

production at all, but such categories of the underprivileged as women and Blacks, in combination with a radicalized youth. This pessimism about the working class in the centres of world capitalism converged, paradoxically, with the optimistic Chinese view that the Third World was ripe for revolution and the Cuban 'spontanist' belief that all that was needed was a nucleus of dedicated militants, a *foco*, which would spark off and detonate mass revolution. Such models are therefore more than cognitive maps; they contain programmes of action.

Marxism, then, like any other system of ideas, is not a thing. It is constantly changing. Any system of ideas, too, deals in general propositions that have to be glossed before they can be applied to concrete situations. Thus, the criteria to be used in allocating people to categories such as 'proletarian' or 'bourgeois' are matters of considerable debate, and very fateful for the way people will be treated. Normative categories are equally problematic: 'from each according to his ability to each according to his means' might look like an unequivocal guide to action, but it leaves open how we are to determine 'ability' and 'need', and how we are to weight – if at all – different kinds of labour, mental and manual, skilled and unskilled. These are no mere intellectual exercises. They determine who gets what; sometimes, even the difference between life and death.

The variety of Marxisms, however, derives from a further set of *social* considerations: that like all theories, though they exist in people's minds, they are *inter*subjective modes of thought, shared by people who have common attributes and purposes. To understand the theories, we have to situate them socially: to understand the kinds of people, in different kinds of society and cultural situations who use them for distinct purposes. Thus, after Marx's death, despite its revolutionary content, Marxism became the official creed of the German Social Democratic Party, a huge party committed to an oppositional role not just in the Reichstag, where it had dozens of M Ps, but outside it; and there not only politically – in the shape of a large membership and the support of millions of trade unionists affiliated to the Party – but in the form of a whole institutional subculture of women's organizations, youth organizations, even holiday organizations, articulated to the Party and opposed to official bourgeois culture at every point: a degree of *Gleichschaltung* that has been called a 'state within a state'.[67] So profoundly national a party was fated to betray the ideals of 'proletarian internationalism', as it did in 1914. All Marxisms, however, necessarily bear the distinctive marks of the society and culture within which they flourish: in the Bolshevik case, the stigmata of an underground, highly disciplined and centralized machine. The elements in Marx's original synthesis were themselves national traditions which did not disappear with the emergence of Marxism, but continue to influence its national varieties to this day. Thus the Marxism of Germany is still stamped with the Hegelianism of the

Frankfurt School;[68] that of French structuralism by Cartesian dualism and systematics.

These intellectual Marxisms can be reduced to two types, which Sahlins traces to two different 'moments' in Marx's own thought: to a cultural strand and a utilitarian materialism respectively. The crucial distillation of these into different kinds of Marxism was the result of the social transformation of Marxism from a philosophy of revolution to its institutionalization as the official ideology of a state dedicated to economic growth. Soviet Marxism, Gouldner argued in 1970, was becoming a *functionalist* Marxism.[69] A decade later, that transformation had been completed.

The crisis came in 1953, when the orthodoxy imposed on world communism by the USSR collapsed with the death of its controller. Since that date, intellectual critiques and political heterodoxy have abounded. They can be grouped into two sets: systems Marxism, in which development is something determined independently of human agency (history, Althusser tells us, is a 'process without a subject'); and Promethean Marxism, in which history does indeed have a subject: 'the history of all hitherto existing society is the history of *class* struggles', in which people 'make their own history', though not under 'circumstances chosen by themselves' but 'given and transmitted from the past', or, as Childe put it in a pithy, if sexist phrase, 'Man Makes Himself'.[70]

The post-Stalin crisis of Marxism let loose such a barrage of criticism that some felt the need to make a stand in defence of what they took to be the quintessential propositions which had to be asserted at all costs if anything recognizable as Marxism was to remain at all. To Hobsbawm, the concept of contradiction was one. Most, however, joined him at another, singularly unfortunate, barricade: that of base and superstructure as distinct *levels* of social structure, a notion which Hall later declared to constitute a 'conceptual threshold and boundary-limit' without which a distinctive materialism could not exist.[71]

The image of base and superstructure *is* an image, a metaphor which uses extra-social analogies to describe social arrangements. All such images, whatever their value in illuminating the subject, are profoundly distorting as well. Society is not a machine; it is not an organism, nor does it follow sequences of gestation and birth (Marx's favourite, obstetric imagery) or of decay and death. Society is different *in kind* from any machine, rock or tree. The crucial difference, anthropologists have long insisted, is that human beings possess a developed consciousness and, collectively, a shared, cumulative culture.

The model reposes on the assumption that the economic base is material. It is not. We cannot even understand what material objects are unless we know the social uses to which they are put: archaeologists debate as to whether what they have found is a tool or a ritual object; whether a painting is a magical or purely aesthetic expression; even whether a building is a temple or a brothel. And for people to use tools, they literally need '*know-how*': skills, cognitive knowledge. The organization of production, moreover, involves internalizing or at least complying with norms of behaviour, such as the notion of a 'fair' day's work. The class struggle that is fought, in Beynon's words, 'every day of the year',[72] is a battle between workers and management over norms: norms of output and working conditions. But the system as a whole reposes upon even more fundamental concepts: of the *right* of some people to own the means of production and to appropriate the product and the profits made from the labour of others. The labour process itself is therefore saturated with what Godelier has called the *idéel*: not just ideals, in the normative or utopian sense (though those, too), but ideas – knowledge and beliefs – acquired and sustained outside work. The pursuit of naked self-interest, relationships of production based on the soulless cash-nexus, and relationships of exchange governed by market supply and demand are cultural values and institutions peculiar to capitalism. In other cultures and societies, production and exchange are conducted according to quite different norms, such as those of reciprocity or conceptions of a just price.

The most crass materialism, it is only fair to point out, is not that of Marxists at all, but of those who treat social relations as if they were determined by technology or biology. Thus, Marvin Harris' 'cultural materialism' (which has nothing to do with the approach of the same name developed by Raymond Williams, discussed below) is a nineteenth-century search for laws of history and 'the explanation of ideology and social organization' in terms of 'adaptive responses to techno-economic conditions';[73] its end-product the analysis of cannibalism or the veneration of cows by Hindus in terms of calorie and protein requirements and their economic utility. Even this one-dimensional materialism, however, is a healthy corrective to one-sided idealist anthropology, as Gamst's critique of Leach's structuralist analysis of traffic-light systems and Ross' refutation of Sahlins' culturalist analysis of meat-eating in US society demonstrate.[74]

Marx never intended, he said, that his 'historical sketch of the genesis of capitalism' was to be taken as 'an historical-philosophical theory of the general path which every people is fated to tread'. Yet many of his followers have done precisely that: they have 'installed one . . . cultural logic [that of capitalism, *P.W.*] as the definition of everyone's material necessity'.[75]

Structuralist Marxists have codified this culturally-specific logic of capitalism and turned it into a universalistic, invariant schema of base and superstructure, the base being the mode (or modes) of production. Having abstracted production from all other relationships, they then invest it with determinative significance. Neither step is usually explicitly justified; it is simply performed.

Production, Marxists argue, requires that people work with *tools* or instruments, from hoes to computers, upon *objects* (the soil, uranium ore, etc.). Together, tools and objects constitute the *means* of production. The means, together with the knowledge and technical *skills* needed to grow crops or make iron, are together designated the *forces* of production. (Though the latter are forms of knowledge, and have to be acquired and passed on through socialization, they are still designated part of the material base.) The complex social relationships entailed in the labour process are designated the *relations* of production: the co-ordination of the social division of labour that Marx called 'orchestration' – involving both co-operation and conflict, the internalization of work-disciplines, and the exercise of authority – and the further clash of interest between those who produce and those who direct and appropriate.

This is a useful schema, but for all its apparent clarity, it obscures the way in which extra-economic relations, vital if any production at all is to take place, are simply treated as economic, while even within the sphere of direct production, ideal elements, notably rights of ownership and inheritance, are labelled 'material' – which they are not.

Forces and relations of production, taken together, are said to constitute the mode of production, thus:

$$
\left.\begin{array}{l} \text{Objects} \\ \text{Tools} \end{array}\right\} \text{Means} \\
\left.\begin{array}{l} \\ \text{Skills} \end{array}\right\} \quad \underbrace{\text{Forces+Relations}}_{\text{MODE}} \quad \left\{\begin{array}{l} \text{Technical division} \\ \text{of labour} \\ \\ \text{Exploitation/} \\ \text{appropriation} \end{array}\right.
$$

The model, which was developed for capitalism, is, however, inappropriate to societies and cultures where quite different conceptions and practices of work, production, exchange and property obtain. Further, it is problematic even for capitalism, which no more operates according to the logic of this reductionist model than it conforms to the postulates of *laissez-faire* theory.

The concept of a mode of production, then, is by no means as straightforward as this schema would imply, as the sheer variety of ways in which it has been used indicates. At one polar extreme are those who restrict its use to the labour process; at the other, those who use it to designate whole systems of social and even cultural organization, which they take to be determined by economic relationships: feudalism, capitalism, etc. For some, the mode of production is an element in a theoretical kit, to be used in studying the variety of economic organization. For others, a mode of production is a concrete form of organization itself. The latter usage has inevitably spawned a growing number of modes of production, from wide usages: the 'colonial' or even 'world' modes of production: through the 'Asiatic' mode authorized by Marx and Engels, to the newer 'Arab',

'Andean' modes, to the 'peasant', 'lineage' and 'domestic' modes. Such is the diversity of ways in which productive activities and exchange are organized that there is virtually no limit to the number of modes of production that may yet be invented: 'each Andean valley', Foster-Carter has written, 'has its own mode of production, and individuals may change them two or three times a week like underwear'.[76] Even in societies with a limited technology, different kinds of work are organized in very different ways. The crisis inevitably came with the attempt to apply these categories, developed in the study of capitalism, to the very different societies studied by anthropologists. Thus Terray, re-analysing Meillasoux's study of the Guro of the Ivory Coast, distinguishes no less than five main branches of productive activity: agriculture, pastoralism, hunting, food-gathering, and handicrafts.

It could be argued that each of these is a distinct mode of production, since it involves different sets of people in distinctively different patterns of co-operation. But to Terray, they are only 'branches' of economic activity, which he then classifies into two categories: 'simple' co-operation at the level of the lineage, and 'complex' co-operation at the village level.[77] Yet these production relationships do not *determine* who gets what. Decisive authority in social life lies with the male elders. This does not derive from their monopoly of land or of instruments of production, or even of technical knowledge, for they have no such monopoly. Rather, their power derives from their 'privileged position' as *elders*. This, in turn, gives them certain kinds of economic power as well, but these economic prerogatives are culturally defined and limited. Though young people produce 'common-place' goods, they do not own them, and only certain kinds of goods can be exchanged against certain other kinds, and may be used only for specific purposes. Thus, the iron ingots and guns imported from abroad are 'matrimonial goods' which the elders monopolize but use as bride-wealth in contracting marriages on behalf of junior males. The elders' use of lineage herds is likewise confined to ritual purposes alone. These customs, moreover, are culturally specific: they are not typical of other pastoralists. Economic exchanges of this kind are quite different in kind from those involved in the internal production and exchange of 'commonplace' commodities. Nor is there a one-to-one relationship between the units involved in production and consumption respectively: hunting-units some-times do and sometimes do not consume what they catch. At the level of social organization as a whole, hunting-groups are, to use Terray's language, 'unrepresented' politically, while Guro ritual focuses not upon agriculture, which is their most important economic activity, but upon hunting and war – probably because the latter are culturally defined as the quintessentially *male* activities. Clearly, production relationships do not determine other social institutions. Rejecting the idealist view that the economy is simply contained within kinship, Terray recognizes, however, that it would be equally absurd to derive kinship relations from the economic base alone: that there is an 'unexplained residual element in kinship'. Relations between producers were not exclusively economic; there were non-economic bonds involved.

The attempt to preserve the model of base and superstructure, and to force it onto all cultures, inevitably involved resorting to Jesuitical casuistries and intellectual and verbal contortions of the kind pioneered by Engels. The base, it was admitted, was not necessarily dominant at all: in non-capitalist societies, political-juridical, religious, or kinship-based institutions might be. But the sacred central belief was preserved, by arguing that the base was still 'determinant' or even 'over-determinant' – a latter-day version of Engels' famous qualifications 'in the long run' and 'ultimately'. Kinship, Godelier argued, was 'both infrastructure and superstructure' (in other words, it was neither). Finally, Godelier reformulated the relationship as one of functions rather than levels. In different kinds of society, even different societies, *different* institutions could supply the dominant cultural idiom.[78] Deprived, now, of both levels and economic determination (except in the long run – which usually never came, and when it did, was still not determined by economic forces alone) nothing was left of base and superstructure except the words.

This multiplication of modes of production is avoided by those who take the unit of analysis to be far wider: e.g., Alavi's colonial mode of production; or the logical extreme view that the entire world now constitutes a single mode of production.

Living as we do in the midst of an economic crisis which affects Brazil and Poland, Britain and Mexico, we are only too aware that capitalism is not only a world-wide system, but still the dominant one. But we need not accept the views of those world-system theorists for whom the world has been 'capitalist since the seventeenth century', or that *everything* is simply capitalism. It is a view which implies, in economic terms, that capitalism is a form of exchange: of production for the market rather than a mode of *production*. The growing domination of the world market by countries which had reorganized their own production-systems along capitalist lines did not necessarily mean that the goods produced in their colonies or for which they traded were produced by capitalist methods. Rather, they were produced by slaves, serfs, peasant smallholders, and many other kinds of pre-capitalist workers, whose position, moreover, became consolidated precisely because of the articulation of the domestic economy to the world market. Capitalist wage-labour only became the dominant form, even in many of the older colonies, as late as the epoch of modern imperialism. Outright slavery only came to an end in Brazil less than a century ago, and even in the world's leading capitalist country only a couple of decades before that. Socially, in a country like Ecuador, a fully-fledged bourgeois State and civil society were delayed even later. Not until just before the First World War did the new agro-exporting commercial bourgeoisie of the Coast take political power out of the hands of the Sierran landowners, an oligarchy that had dominated national life since Independence, following the Liberal victory in the Civil Wars; not until the inter-War period were beginnings made on bourgeois political and economic institutions: a Central Bank and a modern bureaucratic machinery; not until after the Second World War was the administrative revolution completed under Galo Plaza; not until the military revolution-from-above of 1972 did the new industrial bourgeoisie establish control over the economy and not until the oil bonanza of the 1970s could land reform begin as landowners were assisted by the State to turn their haciendas into capitalist estates run on the basis of wage-labour instead of debt-peonage.

The spread of capitalist relations within the economy and their eventual domination, their further penetration outside the economy and the alignment or replacement of existing institutions in accordance, is, then, always a far more protracted and uneven process than schematic models of the bourgeois State and bourgeois society allow for. It is a transition which often takes centuries. Marxist conceptions of the mode of production, of the institutions of civil society, and of the State are, of course, all ideal types. Ideal types are abstractions, perfect models which rarely occur in reality. But they are not arbitrary: they are drawn from real life. The ideal type of the State most Marxists use draws – far too much – on Marx's analysis of the 'nightwatchman state' of nineteenth-century capitalist Britain, whose functions were restricted to what Radcliffe-Brown summed up as law and war. Internal 'social control': the protection of basic institutions and the regulation of disputes between citizens and corporate groups by monopolizing the administration of justice; externally, the defence of the society as a whole against attack.[79] Pre-capitalist forms of the State (about which Marx made copious notes in his ethnological notebooks) often controlled both narrower and wider ranges of social life, while the later capitalist State and the socialist State penetrate nearly every area of life, so much so that the word *étatiste* has been coined to describe them.

In recent years, Western Marxists have embarked upon the task of transforming Marxism from a political economy into a sociology by turning their attention to the relationship between the State, the economy, and the other institutions of civil society: the family, the educational system, etc. It is, of course, a perfectly scientific procedure to abstract economic, or any other relations, and to develop ideal type models of them. But they then have to be analytically related to the other parts of society, and, today, of world society. The major strength of world-system theory lies in its demonstration that the foundations of the Third World were laid nearly half a millennium ago, not in the 1950s, and that today development in any country is conditioned by its place in a world division of labour. The later the period studied, the less it becomes possible to take the 'country', or even Europe, as the main framework for the analysis of the growth of capitalism.[80]

The structuralist–Marxist model attempts to deal with the relationships between economy and society by postulating that any 'social formation' is a multiplex entity in which several modes of production co-exist, one of which, however, is dominant. It further recognizes that there are different 'instances' – political, legal, etc. – each of which has a certain degree of autonomy and is not therefore always or narrowly determined by the economic base. The economy, then, though not necessarily the dominant institution, is still said to be ultimately determinant. All these qualifications, however, do little to alter a model which, at bottom, is still one of base and superstructure, and still, therefore, fatally flawed. Thus, the conception of 'instances' is still a conception of *levels*, rather than dimensions of social life; the economic is taken to be the most fundamental and determinative instance, while institutions like the family, legal codes, or the educational system are labelled 'apparatuses' of the State (*sic*). The model, therefore, is scarcely any advance on Engels' attempts to rectify the patent inadequacies of the base/superstructure model by introducing qualifications about the relative autonomy of the non-economic, whilst still asserting that in the long run the economy was determinant.[81] Though there are many, often more sophisticated variations, the most common version of the structuralist model[82] looks something like the one below. It is a very crude model, drawn not so much from constructional engineering as from simple house-building.

Social Formation

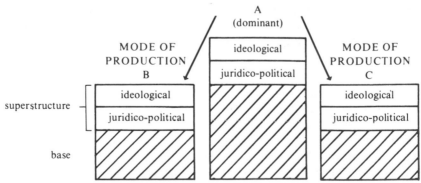

The larger size, and the arrows, are meant to symbolize the greater importance of the capitalist sector. In most models, the role of the State, and of the apparatuses attached to it, is taken to be the articulation of the different modes of production. Since the model is an analytical framework, and the mode of production is also considered to be a *theoretical* category, this conceptual framework can be applied to any actual society ('social formation'). Although the concept 'social formation' is just as much a theoretical category, in structuralist usage, for some reason, it has the status of a concrete historical entity.

There might well be more than the three modes of production represented in the diagram. In that model, the dominant one might be capitalist industry (mode of production A), co-existing with agriculture on traditional estates (mode of production B) to which the labour-force was tied by debt and by extra-economic compulsions such as the local power of the landlord or the central power of the State. Mode of production C might be the smallholder-peasant sector (though, strictly, they are considered incapable of generating an authentic ideology and political praxis of their own).

Bourgeois economics has long recognized that production in different fields (labelled 'sectors') involves differing forms of economic and social organization, at successive ranges up to the level of the world as a whole. It accepts class inequality as a necessary motor of enterprise. What it does not recognize is the contradiction of interest as between classes. The concept of the mode of production, by contrast, assumes that struggles between those who produce and those who appropriate are intrinsic and central. The label 'mode of production', though, is a misnomer, since production never takes place except as part of a wider set of extra-economic institutions and relationships. A mode of production, that is, is never just a mode of *production*. It is always a mode of production *and appropriation*. The economy is always a political economy. More than that, it is always contained within – and dependent upon – a matrix of structured social relations, of which the institutions governing property are the most important for the economy, and from which the economy can only be abstracted by an analytical act. There is no real-life economy-in-itself.

A more creative use of the concept of mode of production, which   *Wolf* recognizes these issues, is that used by Eric Wolf, who eschews the base/ superstructure model by expanding the concept of mode of production to include the social and cultural as well as the economic. For him, a mode of production is not a system of technology, nor a stage or type of society, but a heuristic tool which he uses to focus upon the strategic relationships of power and wealth. Production therefore includes the *re*production of social institutions and cultural values. This enables him to bring into his analysis not only the technoeconomic, but kinship, caste, the potlatch, oracles and secret societies. But it does so at the cost of blurring any distinction between the economic and the socio-cultural: for if everything becomes a force or relation of production, the notion of the extra-economic becomes redundant and vacuous. And if matrilineal descent systems or divine kingship are no mere epiphenomena of political economy, as they are in the reductionist models he rejects, neither is the conceptual problem solved by designating everything that bears upon, is affected by, or has consequences for the economy as 'production' relations. As he himself brilliantly shows, capitalism does not produce caste or the Aro Chukwu oracle, nor is Indian society today a carbon copy of British, capitalist though they both are. Capitalism works upon existing cultural materials, and often introduces new ones, but the dialectical synthesis that results is always culturally specific.

The economy, then, neither determines, alone or preponderantly – though economic considerations may, of course, be uppermost very often. It is, therefore, simply not true that man must eat before he can think. People would not find food at all if they did not think, while the search for food is not necessarily the only, the main or the perpetual preoccupation even of the technologically simplest hunting-and-collecting societies. What is true is that production is a *necessity*, in any society. In Sahlins' terminology, society has indeed to be 'provisioned'; and sets of people do have common interests by virtue of their relationship to the means of production – they constitute classes, whether 'in themselves' or 'for themselves'. But their allocation to a distinct place in production in the first place is itself often determined by factors other than considerations of skill or the technical requirements of production.

Of the four sets of classes, Marx singles out in the *Communist Manifesto* as the major paired antagonists of successive epochs, 'oppressor and oppressed'; three of them: freeman and slave, patrician and plebeian, lord and serf, are not categories determined by relationship to the means of production at all: they are extra-economic statuses into which people are born. It will come as no news to women or Blacks that their inferior economic opportunities are a consequence of their having chosen the wrong gender or colour – that their class position is a consequence, not a determinant, of their social being. Marx's familiar distinction between 'class-in-itself' and 'class-for-itself' is an inadequate one, because either way it abstracts economic relationships from the wider systems of structured social inequality of which economic inequalities are merely one form: divisions, in hunting-and-collecting societies based on age and gender; aristocratic and religious divisions; caste, estate and ethnic stratification. And it then (arbitrarily) invests economic relations with causal priority. Extra-economic divisions may coincide with class divisions, in which case they become doubly powerful. But they may also divide classes and link their members to people in other classes, vertically. Neither of Marx's categories, then, explains *social* class, even if he did use that adjective.

Weber

Better theoretical tools have long been available. Max Weber's concept of 'status groups' – groups to which people feel themselves to belong by virtue of believed common descent and/or shared culture – is usually thought to be directly antithetical to the concept of class as Marx defined it, and is usually taken to refer merely to subjective differences of rank or social prestige. In fact, Weber saw status groups as collectivities just as fierce in their defence of material as well as immaterial privileges as any class motivated by practical reason.[83] Indeed, where people who share the same cultural identity also occupy the same economic roles, a status group is *also* a class (or part of one), and a doubly self-conscious one because of this. More widely, Weberianism was seen by Marxists as incompatible with Marxism because Weber was a principled, life-long enemy of socialism; not only pessimistic about revolution as a liberating alternative to capitalism, but even cynical about the participation of the masses in politics. Many Marxists I know will admit, in private, to being closet Weberians. But never in public, since they do not wish to be pigeon-holed with enemies of democracy and socialism. Conversely, many who are very radical and engaged politically reject the intellectual crudities of dogmatic Marxisms, and their political counterpart – sectarianism. Yet Weber shared Marx's view that 'the factor that creates "class" is unambiguously economic interest, and . . . those interests involved in the market'. ' "Property" and "lack of property" ', he wrote, 'are the basic categories of all class situations'; 'the direct influence of social relations, institutions and groups governed by "material interests" extends (often unconsciously) into all spheres of culture without exception, even into the finest nuances of aesthetic and religious feeling.' But he had no intention, he insisted, of replacing Marx's 'one-sided materialistic causal interpretation of culture and history' by 'an equally one-sided spiritualistic one'. 'No economic ethic', he wrote, 'has ever been determined by religion – it is only one of the determinants of the economic ethic'. And the State, to him, was unequivocally an instrument used by those who claimed a monopoly of the legitimate use of violence.

Weber thus advocates not an idealist, not a materialist, but a dialectical sociology. Just as Marx over-emphasized the material in his struggle against the dominant German idealism, so Weber singled out for special attention what Marx had underplayed: the ideas and beliefs that informed capitalism, though carefully distinguishing, in the process, those institutions and relationships which were directly created or used for economic ends both from those non-economic areas which had *consequences* for the economy (say, religious bans on usury) and from non-economic areas *affected* by economic forces (e.g. the market value of Church property).[84]

The relative weight of economic and non-economic forces was always variable, and therefore a matter only to be settled by empirical investigation. Though there was always an economic *dimension* to every social institution – and even churches keep balance-sheets – churches are not economic organizations, but religious ones. Rather than conceiving of society in terms of levels, then, with the economy as the base, society was better thought of in terms of dimensions and of specialized institutions, the relationship between the component parts of the social system being variable, not uniform. Rejecting the language of determinism (economic or otherwise), Weber conceived of the connections between the institutions which constituted the sub-systems of society, rather, in terms of 'elective affinity', a phrase be borrowed from Goethe's novel of that name. The phrase reflects Goethe's interest in natural science: the idea that there are uniform and unifying principles in both society and Nature – which might seem to justify a determinist view of the world. But he qualifies it by stressing the dependence of human society upon Nature, which ought to be the object of reverence, and by a further, Kantian, distinction between choice and compulsion, which Weber picked up. This was the notion that there had to be *some* degree of fit between the various parts of society, but that this need not necessarily be tight or one-to-one: a conception of relative autonomy and of probabilities which functionalists and functionalist Marxists fail to grasp. It was also a pluri-causal model. Causal connections were often oblique and mediated: capitalism no more *caused* Protestantism than Protestantism *caused* capitalism. Religious ideas were important elements – but not all of them, only those which had a bearing on people's economic behaviour – not the theology, but the ethic, the code of conduct.

In Malraux's *La Condition Humaine*, a Chinese revolutionary prophetically remarks to a Soviet emissary of the Comintern that 'Marxism contains both the idea of determinism and an emphasis upon the will. Whenever determinism becomes more important than agency, I begin to get worried.' To those Marxists for whom Marxism is a self-contained system of scientific socialism, its central assumptions are beyond question, for all their protestations to the contrary. I have even known such extreme cases as the anthropologist who argued that it would be damaging to the entire Marxist theoretical edifice – and hence to socialism – to admit that Engels' belief that a stage of 'mother-right' had preceded the stage of patriarchal organization of the family was wrong. Such dogmatism and defensiveness was understandable in the days of McCarthy, and in those countries where Marxism has become a rigid State ideology. It is, however, a major obstacle to the further development of Marxist thought and to human liberation.

Creative Marxists have, in practice, if not in acknowledgement, deviated massively from the base/superstructure model. Amilcar Cabral, for example, begins his classic analysis of Guinean society by examining the economy and class structure. But he also recognizes the historical legacy of a variety of pre-colonial economic institutions: different systems of land-tenure and land usage; differences in the economic roles of peasants and traders in the different societies that were incorporated into the Guinean State; but also varying political forms: of State and stateless society; and of status differences: aristocrats and commoners, Muslims and 'animists'; varying forms of the family, of marriage, of the position of women, and so on. Laid on top of all this were the consequences of modern colonialism: the gulf between town and country, and, above all, the institutionalized superiority of European over African. His model of the colonial economy is also one of a *political* economy, with a major State sector as well as a private sector. His model of the stratification system, likewise, emphasizes the State-enforced colour-bar which kept Africans out of jobs reserved for Whites.[85]

Anderson's magisterial studies of the emergence of capitalism in Europe begin, likewise, with modes of production: slave, feudal, and capitalist.[86] But he then goes on – in a quite Weberian way – not only to describe the institutional specificities of each particular country, but also the persisting importance of two pan-European, trans-societal cultural institutions: the Roman Catholic Church, 'extraordinary in its persistence' and 'indispensable as a bridge between Antiquity and the Middle Ages', and the Roman law. Both of these existed long before either the Absolutist State or modern capitalism and persisted into the bourgeois epoch, the latter being adapted so as to strengthen the idea of absolute private property in land and to provide for the concentration of aristocratic power in a centralized State apparatus. The more creative Marxist anthropology, likewise, has grappled with such problems as class-variations in primordial structures of kinship and the integrative role of vertical, cross-class factions.[87]

Dogmatic Marxism, however, is much more widespread. Its persistence is not to be explained simply in intellectual terms. Engels' *Origin of the Family*, with its sequence, borrowed from the American ethnologist, Lewis Henry Morgan, of primitive promiscuity, followed by the so-called consanguine, punaluan, and pairing forms of the family, is no more convincing today than half a dozen other similar nineteenth-century essays in what Radcliffe-Brown called 'conjectural history'. (When he gets onto what he really knows about – the documented history of 'barbaric' society in Europe – he is much more impressive). But his appeal to a new generation of feminists does not rest on his scientific accuracy so much as his passionate conviction that relations between men and women need not be relations of superiority and inferiority. That aspiration – which I share – induces some to see primitive societies as classless and therefore more egalitarian in respect of gender relations. Classless they may be, others observe, insofar as everyone has access to the means of production; egalitarian they are not, since differences of age, gender and ritual status are converted into social divisions even more rigid than those of class society – which at least permits some degree of social mobility.

Marxism has survived despite theoretical weaknesses and political disasters because it is not simply an intellectual system – a cognitive schema or mode of analysis – but because it has normative and conative dimensions. This does not make it a religion, for it is a humanistic philosophy. Far less scientific, purely religious ideologies, it is true, have provided creeds adequate enough for the practical social purposes of the day in the past, from the conservative use of Catholicism to the revolutionary use of Protestantism.

The future of Marxism, if it is to contribute to, let alone lead, in the protection of the world against destruction and the elimination of inequality and oppression, is not improved by defending either its errors or its strengths in a religious way, but in improving it in order to improve the world. Its practical strength lies in that project: in present resistance to exploitation and in the dedication to working out better ways of living together in the future by getting rid of institutions and habits of thought developed over centuries. Marxism has regenerated itself despite disasters, and spread, not just because it offers a better material existence, but because it offers a wide vision: that of a better *society*. To those who arrogantly assert that it is already an adequately developed body of theory – even the only valid science of society – one can only urge a little humility in the name of the many millions who have died, from Stalin's Russia to genocide in Kampuchea, at the hands of people who were guided by their interpretations of Marxism. The notion that these horrors are somehow unconnected to Marxist ideas, or not authentic Marxism, implies an idealist, unsociological conception of Marxism as a body-of-ideas-in-itself. Inadequate forms of Marxism – institutionalized in the form of the State – have become part of the problem.

The very success of Marxism, paradoxically, has bred a new contradiction, the growing tendency to practise what anthropologists will recognize as avoidance and incest: reading nothing but the growing volume of specifically Marxist literature (except empirical, descriptive studies); avoidance of critiques of Marxism itself; sheer ignorance of other modes of thought; and the practice of talking only to the growing population of other Marxists in an increasingly esoteric private language, within the categories of an enclosed conceptual universe. And this rather than debating with opponents about the limits and strengths of Marxism and of non-Marxist science, and being prepared to borrow from the latter (and from where else, if Marxism itself lacks the capacity to innovate?) to fill in gaps, correct, complement, or innovate.

One dogmatic response is to dismiss the patent errors of Marxism as not really Marxism at all – as vulgar Marxist deviations, just as some Christians argue that Papal bastards and the Inquisition are not part of the Christian heritage; in extreme, that Christianity has never been tried. For me, Stalin and Trotsky, Gramsci and Togliatti, Lukács and Mao are all Marxists. Western Marxism, however, does have special characteristics. It is, in Anderson's words, 'a product of defeat', a revolutionary creed with an 'absent centre': revolution.[88]

Its failure to explain its major historical failures – its defeat by nationalism in 1914 and by popular fascism in the 1930s – was paralleled after the Second World War by the failure of Soviet Marxism to develop an explanation of the Stalin period. Marxist theories about the Third World have by now become bogged down in a seemingly endless multiplication of exercises in mode-of-productionism and world-systematics in which the distinctive features of each country simply disappear and all become look-alikes, only distinguished from one another insofar as some are central, others peripheral or semi-peripheral. Sociology, in these studies, is merely a kind of social economics, in which the peasants of European history only paid rent and never feudal homage or Church tithes, and those of contemporary India are a class of people who never belong to castes.

The basic theoretical blockage is a concept incompatible with a dialectical sociology: the materialist image of base and superstructure. It is time, now, to pay tribute, a century after Marx's death, to his own criticality as a man whose favourite slogan, he said, was *de omnibus dubitandum* – everything ought to be questioned (or, as we would now phrase it, everything is 'up for grabs'), by consigning that concept to the same place to which Engels wanted to consign the State: 'the Museum of Antiquities, alongside the spinning-wheel and the stone axe'.

Culture: the Missing Concept

The concept of culture has been virtually ignored by those social scientists who reduce the study of society to political economy or the study of social structure. The major exception has been cultural anthropology in the USA, and, in sociology, the functionalism of Parsons. (Malinowski's cultural anthropology was simply another form of biological reductionism.) For Parsons, a system of social action had *three* dimensions: the social system, the cultural system, and the personality system of the individual actor.[89]

Outside the social sciences, there is a rich line of literary criticism – one of the few distinctively English intellectual traditions, a preoccupation with the relationship between the arts and society – that runs from Coleridge and Southey, through Arnold, Ruskin and D. H. Lawrence to T. S. Eliot, F. R. Leavis and Raymond Williams. The only other contributions of importance have been the symbolic interactionists' studies of *sub*cultures, and, within the Marxist canon, the writings of Gramsci and of his Peruvian counterpart, Jose Carlos Mariátegui.[90]

Of these, only the notion of 'subculture' has passed into more general usage. To most people, culture still means only the 'fine' arts. Its wider connotations, when recognized, are designated by other labels, such as the Marxist term 'ideology'. Ideology itself means different things to different people. To some, it signifies *cognitive* disorder or incoherence; to others, the distortion of knowledge, especially scientific knowledge, by emotions and prejudices: ideology is something that *interferes* with cognition. Those who go further, and ask why irrational notions exist and persist – why truth is either ignored or rejected in favour of falsehood – are driven to conclude that the truth or falsity of propositions (their cognitive content) are not their only relevant properties, but that people espouse or reject ideas because they lead to conclusions that are *morally* unacceptable to them and are believed to lead to bad behaviour and conduct prejudicial to society and its institutions. They are then led to ask, as Marxists do, whose interests are served by maintaining both these institutions and these ideas; who it is that *uses* such ideas to legitimize, justify and rationalize their interests; and how alternative ideas are prevented from taking root. Such analysis, then, moves beyond pure cognition to normative and social issues. Questions of this kind inevitably led thinkers like Gramsci and Mariátegui beyond the term ideology to the conception of culture. In that kind of usage, though they retain the label 'ideology', it means much more than the logical systemiz- ation of ideas as sets of interrelated propositions.

Though they never developed an adequate theoretization of the concept, their work – whether that of Gramsci on intellectuals and on folk knowledge, or that of Mariátegui on Inca and Catholic religion – is informed implicitly by an awareness that any society always contains residues from earlier epochs, so that whilst some ideologies serve, organically, to buttress the contemporary social order, others are inorganic, and do not; indeed, may even constitute an actual or potential basis for dissent from the present order of things. Culture is therefore always *plural*, since not only classes, but professions and intellectual schools influence the way in which both their members think and behave and others. Implicitly, too, they recognized that culture has three dimensions: the *cognitive*, the *normative* and the *conative*: dimensions first recognized in eighteenth-century idealist philosophy, and labelled more recently, by Hannah Arendt, thinking, judging and acting.

Intellectuals are inclined by the nature of their occupation to emphasize the first of these: that culture provides us with a 'cognitive map', an intellectual, logical model of the world and of its constituent parts which supplies thereby both an ontology and a cosmology. A model of the natural world; of the place of humanity within that world; and a model of the relationship, physical or metaphysical, of that world to the cosmos. It also supplies a model of the social world and its components which tells us who we are, and how and why we differ from others, and which allocates us to social categories constructed on the bases of age, gender, descent, marital status, wealth, occupation, skill, power and so forth. The categories em phasized vary according to the world-view in question, some emphasizing personality-types, others classes, ethnic groups or religious affiliation.

But culture is not just analytical. It does more than tell us who we are or what is what: the components of the social world are also *evaluated*; arranged not according to some simple Manichaean or Lévi-Straussian binary opposition between good and bad, but in accordance with a complex hierarchy of values. The components of the world, then, are never purely cognitive: they are always also normative. They have values attached to them which invest them with social, not merely logical, meaning. Peoples whom we call 'primitive' often see themselves as *the* 'Human Beings' or '*The* People' (the name they use for themselves often means just that), not only different from all others, but superior to them. 'Barbarians', 'infidels', 'counter-revolutionaries', equally, are normative, not cognitive categories: they refer to ways of life we hold to be wrong, whereas true believers, the Chosen, or the class destined to end class society, have right (and history) on their side.

Such evaluations do not exist merely as *views*; they are institutionalized. Conformity to them is publicly rewarded in forms ranging from material rewards to medals, titles and other honorific expressions of social esteem; disapproved behaviour penalized by negative sanctions ranging in severity from raised eyebrows to torture. Individual behaviour which sustains social institutions is thereby endorsed; that which is not, discouraged.

Culture thus answers Chernyshevsky's famous conative question, 'What is to be *done*?'. It supplies a project, a design for living. In repetitive societies, the answer is simple: 'Do as your forefathers did and as the ancestors laid down.' But in more differentiated societies, the future is not such a self-evident reproduction of the past. Rival interest-groups espouse *alternative* projects. The definition of the future, and of what constitutes proper behaviour becomes, eventually, the terrain of what might be called cultural class struggle were the contending groups not necessarily always classes. Culture, then, supplies normative and conative meanings and not only cognitive ones.[91]

There are four ideal-type ways of conceptualizing culture: the élitist, the holistic, the hegemonic, and the pluralist. In the first, culture implies *superior* values, reserved for the dominant few; in the second, a whole way of life; in the third, a set of behaviours *imposed* on the majority by those who rule there. The last, a relativist sense, recognizes that different communities in the *same* society have distinctive codes of behaviour and different value-systems – which may even be opposed.

Though presented here as an abstract taxonomy, each of these conceptions of culture emerged at a different time in history and expresses changing attitudes on the part of thinkers largely of upper-class origins towards the masses. The oldest of them, the élitist, goes back, in the West, to the slave societies of Antiquity, where a leisured class dedicated themselves to studying mathematics, philosophy, music; in the East, to poetry, calligraphy, the classics: to anything, in fact, remote from the utilitarian, and, above all, from manual labour, a tradition consolidated in subsequent aristocratic conceptions of culture and cultural practices. Culture was the property of the few, the immaterial counterpart of their privileged monopoly of the material wealth of society and of political power, its symbol the long finger-nails of the mandarins who ruled Chinese society.

Culture, in this sense, implies both intellectual and social hierarchy: a set of *superior* values monopolized by a socially superior minority. It excludes the masses: culture is something the majority *lack*. There is also only one form of it. Yet is has to be acquired, either by intensive application (study) or via social osmosis, by exposure to milieux, notably a 'cultured' home, governed by the appropriate codes. Access to these, and especially to those institutions specially designed to formulate and communicate those values – from monasteries to 'good' schools – is, therefore, a jealously-guarded privilege. But *noblesse oblige* in a double sense: the nobility has duties towards its social inferiors; it must also defend culture against barbarism, against the *un*cultured: externally, the heathen and the savage; internally, the illiterate, uneducated, ignorant mass of the people, the peasants and urban poor to whom public notices are addressed in South America: '*Sea culto*' . . . they read, urging people not to put their feet on the seats of the bus or spit on the church floor.

Culture, in this sense, prescribes a complete code of manners, for these quotidian expressions of cultured conduct, which sociologists call norms of behaviour, derive from deeper ideas about the good and the bad: from *values* which, being ideals, are expressed, in their purest form, spiritually, in religion and art. This cultivation of the minds of the few necessarily depends upon the cultivation of the fields by the many, a primordial inequality which the Chinese rightly see as one of the 'Three Great Differences' that go back to the beginning of class society – between mental and manual labour; between town and countryside; and between industry and agriculture – a list which omits the oldest man-made inequality of all, that of gender.

Anthropology and Holism

In undifferentiated societies, wrongly called 'primitive', culture is not something ideal, set apart from the everyday material world. There is a dialectic between the ideal and the material, in which the individual, society, Nature and super-Nature form a whole.[92] In the Trobriands, Malinowski noted, 'there is no name for "work" . . . The distinction between technical or practical activity and magical activity cannot be made by the use of two mutually exclusive terms.'[93] In such societies, too, people produced not only their means of subsistence, but their own music and epic poems,[94] and expressed their most sacred values by decorating not only their shrines, but their bodies, their dwellings, and their cattle.[95]

The 'role inventory', in a society of this kind, often runs to no more than a few dozen roles of all kinds.[96] In more differentiated societies, this kind of generalized distribution of culture and social division of labour gives way to one in which art becomes separated from science and both, now in pure form, from mundane production. The production of culture becomes an occupational activity of specialists producing for consumers who were their wealthy patrons, initially, and later the sponsoring institutions of mass society. In Vienna, the two great museums, dedicated to the history of art and to the natural sciences respectively, stand opposite each other. The opposition between *Kunst* and *Naturwissenschaften* is built into the stones. And dominating the cultural life of the city, still, is the art-form of the upper classes, the Opera.

Anthropologists who have studied less complex societies have, therefore, tended to see culture as a whole. Reacting against the diffusionist conception of culture as a mere bundle of discrete traits, they took Tylor's classic definition of 1871 as their starting point:

> that complex whole which includes knowledge, belief, art, morals, law, custom, and any other capabilities acquired by man as a member of society.[97]

Culture was a whole, a *Gestalt*, with an overall pattern. It was also the collective, cumulative achievement of humanity over and above skills transmitted through the genes.

Eighty years later, Kroeber and Kluckhohn classified 164 subsequent definitions of culture into six types: descriptive lists, like Tylor's; historical; normative; psychological; structural; and genetic,[98] according to the different conceptions of the source of *content* of culture held by the various theorists. Bauman, on the other hand, concentrating on the *uses* of culture in drawing and maintaining social boundaries, reduces this complexity to three types: the hierarchical, binary distinction between high and low cultures; the differential conception of cultures, plural – differences between societies or between communities within the same societies; and the universalistic or generic conception, of Culture, singular, as that which separates human society from everything else: in his words, 'the boundaries of man and the human'.[99]

In the organic conception of culture, a close fit between the institutions of a society and its values is assumed. The causal relationship between values and institutions is sometimes expressed dialectically, as when Firth describes culture as the content of social relations:[100] neither determines the other. But the relationship is usually expressed in more nakedly idealist form: it is values which *determine* social structure. Values, then, are taken to be the basis of society, so fundamental that they have been variously labelled 'central', 'over-arching', even 'sacred'. It is further assumed that they form a coherent and binding ideological *system*, characterized by 'a high degree of explications of formulation . . . [and] an authoritative and explicit promulgation . . . Complete individual subservience to the ideology is demanded of those who accept it, and it is regarded as essential and imperative that their conduct be completely permeated by it.'[101]

This is plainly a limiting case only: for ideologues and for exceptional, closed total institutions like the monastery. Ideology, moreover, in this usage is reified; the contradictory interpretations even of the same ideology by competing interest-groups, and the social identities of those groups, are ignored.

Resistance to this dominant idealism has, alas, only replaced it, to paraphrase Weber, by an 'equally one-sided materialism', from Leslie White's 'scientific' theory of culture, in which the technological system was primary,[102] to Sahlins' and Service's view of societies as 'energy-capturing systems', whose level of progress could be measured in terms of 'thermodynamic accomplishment'.[103] Social systems and political forms were 'functions of technologies', together with the ideology 'appropriate' to each.

But since the number of kilowatt hours at the disposal of society (or those who run it) does not determine the uses to which that energy is put, who gets what, the nature of that society's social institutions, its conceptual apparatus and values, or the quality of life in that society, materialist evolutionists had as much difficulty in dealing with the non-material as idealists had in accepting the anthropological notion that lavatories, power-supplies, and banking-systems were every bit as much cultural artefacts as Bartok quartets or cathedrals. Since survival, moreover, is a minimalist, usually merely biological, concept which takes no account of changing output or changing wants, materialists have always had to resort to additional, non-material criteria in discussing progress. White's emphasis on tools and science was always counterbalanced, somewhat schizophrenically, by an equal and opposite emphasis upon culture as a supra-biological, collective product 'born of . . . and perpetuated by the use of symbols'. Human behaviour was *symbolic* behaviour.[104] Sahlins and Service rejected the holistic anthropology that stressed the unity of each culture in favour of a Spencerian emphasis upon *differentiation* as a central feature of progress and upon adaptability: the (Promethean) capacity to innovate, and the capacity of a culture to spread outside its place of origin, rather than mere adaptation to environmental determinants. The elements of materialist reductionism in their work were therefore contradicted, happily, by these more dialectical perceptions.

Literary Criticism: The Elitist Paradigm

Elitism and holism, being ideal types, do not mutually exclude one another. They can be combined in innumerable ways. In the nineteenth century, new syntheses emerged which retained some of the older aristocratic values. The more far-sighted responded to the arrival of the masses on the political scene with the realization that 'we must educate our masters'. Right-wing populism in contemporary Britain is thus rooted in a tradition of Tory democracy over a century old.

In the field of the arts, one response was to turn away from the world to a realm of pure art. More usual was the appreciation that the problem was one of 'culture *and* society'. The term 'culture' had long been used in varied, shifting senses: from the narrow senses of the creative arts or of a purely personal cultivation to the wider senses of a whole way of life, of civilization. The traditional exclusion of the masses from both education and political life was now replaced by the notion of a controlled, downwards hegemonic diffusion which would result in a *shared*, national culture.

Elitists continued to insist, as Leavis did from the 1930s to the 1960s, that civilization was embodied in a 'line' of great literature, in 'fine' art and in 'classical' or 'serious' music which expressed values conceived of as timeless, ineffable, but, now, precarious: under threat from the vulgar.

If the greatest threat, that from fascist barbarism, had been defeated, it had been achieved, at home, only via a massive liberation of popular energies and the expansion of popular political power; abroad, through alliance with the USSR. Writing in the new Labour Britain, T. S. Eliot took up the traditional defence of culture as a minority élite phenomenon.

> The education of too many people [leads to] the lowering of standards . . . There are some grounds for believing, too, that the elimination of the upper class . . . can be a disaster . . . Education should help to preserve [that] class and select the élite.[105]

His conception of the élite was thus much wider than Leavis' purely culturalist/intellectual notion. It was also pluralist. Like Pareto and Mosca, Eliot conceives of *various* élites of people outstanding in their respective social spheres:

groups concerned with art . . . groups concerned with science, and groups concerned with philosophy, as well as groups consisting of men of action; these groups are what we call the élite.[106]

These different élites together formed what we might call the élite-in-general. Though the special importance of the governing élite is clearly recognized, Eliot, like the Italian élite theorists, firmly situated it within this wider élite. Unlike Mosca, he does not go on to explore the downwards connections of the élite(s) with what Gramsci called 'subaltern' groupings at lower levels in the social structure. And he is too English to replace the concept of a ruling *class* completely with that of a ruling *élite*. For him, the élite is firmly connected to the dominant *class*.

Each of the vertical spheres dominated by its separate élite is horizontally divided into the creative minority who are producers of culture and the majority who consume the works of thought and art the minority produces. Collectively, they constitute the leadership of society; their function is to 'transmit the culture they have inherited'. The consumer's role is the traditional one of patron, audience, constituency.

But creativity, being an attribute of individuals, cannot be planned. On these grounds, Arnold's conception of culture as a purely personal search for perfection is as unsatisfactory to him as Joad's rationalism or Mannheim's advocacy of a meritocratic élite recruited on the basis of achievement rather than birth or wealth. Nor was a congeries of individuals dedicated to a purely expressive kind of intellectual/artistic creativity enough. The élite should be 'formed into suitable groups, endowed with appropriate powers, and perhaps with honours and emoluments'. The creative minority, though they might originate from classes other than the dominant class, must always serve society through being attached to '*some* class, whether higher or lower', though – he quickly adds – 'it is likely to be the dominant class that attracts this élite to itself'. Detached from the dominant class, they would ossify and deteriorate into an hereditary class or caste.

These are centuries-old themes. Yet there is a new, uneasy note, an awareness, over his shoulder, of the spectre of *popular* culture. The anthropological conception of culture as a super-organic whole, with a distinctive character greater than any 'mere assemblage of . . . arts, customs and religious beliefs', was acceptable and known to him. (He cites Layard, Mannheim and other social scientists.) Culture was 'that which makes a society'. It was a view quite compatible with his insistence on the need to institutionalize social mobility, since gifted individuals could emerge from many different walks of life, and there are many different *kinds* of competence, 'which will not all be transmitted equally to their descendants'.

Culture is here still a unitary conception: *the* culture of *the* society as a whole. The justification for the social superiority of the 'upper levels' is that they possess *more* of it than the lower orders, and that they are more conscious of it and have greater specialization in it. But since it is singular, it must never be allowed to become the 'property of a small section of society'; rather, 'the whole of the population should take an active part in cultural activities, though not necessarily in the same activities or on the same level'.

This unitary conception of culture was incompatible with the pluralistic notion that there might be more than one form of culture within the same society; even worse, that different groups might each have their own distinctive kind of culture. Turning from theory to reality was 'disturbing', for he realizes that 'Derby Day and the dog track' might be viewed as the religion of the people every bit as much as 'gaiters and the Athenaeum' might be seen as part of the religion of the higher ecclesiastics.[107] Culture, in England, was in fact extremely diverse both in its content and its social distribution. It included

> all the characteristic activities and interests of a people: Derby Day, Henley Regatta, Cowes, the twelfth of August, a cup final, the dog races, the pin table, the dart board, Wensleydale cheese, boiled cabbage . . . nineteenth-century Gothic churches and the music of Elgar.[108]

Williams has remarked that these are categories of 'sport, food, and a little art';[109] they stick close to the arts or recreational sense of culture and stay well clear of anything grossly economic. It is also class-bound: there is a note of surprise at his own daring in considering boiled cabbage and the dogs as *really* culture.

Eliot was on the verge of a pluralistic model of culture which would have threatened his assumptions about a shared, societal culture in the singular. He did, indeed, go on to discuss regional 'satellite' cultures, expressing 'local loyalties', within the 'common culture' of the British Isles, as well as national varieties of Christianity which expressed the 'local temperament' of each country. But he drew back from confronting the implications of the dart board and Henley Regatta: class differences.

Marxist literary criticism did not. Nor, in the hands of its more sensitive practitioners, notably Raymond Williams, was it confined to class, but rather entailed a wider vision of the complex relations between culture and society.[110] His assertion that 'culture is ordinary' challenged the fine arts (or even arts) conception of culture: his assertion that 'there are no masses; only ways of seeing people as masses' distinguished the culture produced *for* the masses from the variety of popular modes of self-expression. Cultural revolution was as integral a part of class struggle as political activity.

The relationship between culture and society, then, was a dialectical one. If literature expressed social values, it also shaped them: 'consciousness was no mere product of practical existence', but 'a condition of its practical existence'. His initial focus had been upon 'great' literature. But he became increasingly concerned with the culture supplied by the 'mass' media: with both the categories, attitudes and images which informed it and the relationship of these to the 'means and conditions' of their production – which are as thoroughly capitalist, in our culture, as the production of micro-chips or the marketing of fast foods.

This perspective, which he unfortunately came to label 'cultural material-ism', was quite different from the older anthropological conception of material culture, which signified everything produced by humanity in material form, as objects. However material these objects, for anthropologists, culture was not material: it was 'a pattern of significance which . . . artifacts have, not the artifacts themselves'.[111] Being *idéel*, it had to be acquired through consciousness; it was *learned* behaviour. Culture, there-fore, can never be reduced to the material. Commodities, Marx observed, embody so much congealed labour-power; conversely, even the most material of objects, a steel ingot or a long-playing record, embodies the *idéel*.

Yet the contradictory attempt to conceptualize culture by means of categories which assigned ideas to the realm of a superstructure determined by a material base was doomed to failure. Williams makes his own dissatisfaction with this reified metaphor – 'fundamentally lacking [in] any adequate recognition of the indissoluble connections between material production and cultural institutions and activity, and consciousness' – quite clear.[112] But in the absence of more adequate categories developed outside Marxism, his thirty-year-long struggle to escape the twin dead-ends of materialism and idealism is frustrated by his constant, convoluted worrying of the very categories – base and superstructure, relations and forces of production – that are the cause of the trouble.

From Hegemony to Pluralism: Subculture and Counter-culture

Marxist social historians, however, have not only accepted the concept of culture, but *used* it centrally in recent work. Foster's study of nineteenth-century England, for instance, constantly uses the word 'culture', and shows that what is designated as working-class culture was, in fact, a complex and contradictory amalgam, the resultant of class struggles every bit as hard fought as those in the economic and political spheres, in which the ruling class, to use Etzioni's terminology, used normative as well as coercive and remunerative sanctions.[113] In the proto-revolutionary situation of post-Napoleonic England, this meant the use of unbridled repression: savage laws against combinations of workers; the regular use of troops, police, informers and *provocateurs*; of deportation and imprisonment; as well as resort to less violent forms of traditional hegemonic social control: the established Church and the powers of a parliament composed of members of the ruling class. Later, it entailed the construction and use of quite new forms of political incorporation on the part of the ruling class: the extension of the vote; the eventual development of mass political parties; ultimately, even the legality of trade unions. It also meant new missions to convert the pagan urban working class, hitherto only evangelized by Nonconformists; new adult educational institutions to combat the influence of the secular Sunday Schools where Painite ideas flourished; temperance movements; chauvinist (anti-Irish) movements which split the working class; and Masonic and other social organizations in which the 'NCOs' of the working class could associate with their betters in their leisure hours. So strong, however, is the tradition of political economy that Foster devotes only two-thirds of one page to what he himself describes as the 'social base' of this 'mass subculture' and 'the most important one of all': the public house.[114] Working-class culture, Foster shows, did not conform to the holistic anthropological conception. In addition to occupational subcultures, there was an immense variety of social subcultures outside work. All of these were the loci of class struggle as bitter as those over the control of central and local government or over trade unionism.

Yet ruling classes have always presented their culture not only as if it were the keystone of the natural order of things but as the culture of the whole society. They have, to this degree, been thoroughly anthropological. But they also designated the mass of their subjects as *un*cultured, and ensured that they remained so by excluding them from access to 'high' culture. The 'twin revolutions', the Industrial Revolution in Britain and the political Revolution in France, however, made it necessary to resolve that contradiction by bridging the social gap between the classes with new political, economic and social institutions.

The analysis of these processes requires the use not just of the concept of culture, but also the notion of *subculture*, a concept developed not in the anthropological study of relatively undifferentiated societies, but in sociological studies in the heartland of modern capitalism. In 1850, Chicago had 30,000 people. By 1900, there were more than 1½ million, many of them new to America. Those who studied them in the 1920s and 1930s found that class was not as salient as ethnicity. There was a working class, but it was made up of Jews from the *stetl*; Orthodox Believers from Russia and Greece; Lutherans from Scandinavia; Catholics from Ireland and southern Italy; and Blacks from the South, who all lived in separate 'ghettoes' where they shared a distinctive, common culture and language.

Early attempts to make intellectual sense of these processes began with ecological maps of the ethnic districts of the city and with theories of urbanism as a generalized way of life. But it was in-depth studies of (mainly ethnic) communities which were to give rise to the notion of *sub*culture, of distinctive ways of life different in kind from the dominant w a s p culture. In exploring relationships within these communities, field-researchers found they were far from being disorganized or anomic; social interaction was guided by norms and values just as much as w a s p culture. Later, moving from studies of ethnic minorities to studies of deviant subcultures – from *avant garde* jazz musicians to marijuana-smokers – they found that new recruits went through secondary as well as primary socialization into the values and norms of behaviour required of the members of the group. Deviant subcultures were thus as structured and as principled as 'straight' ones. There were two logical extensions of this line of thought: the relativist one, which argued that *no* group could claim its values to be *superior*, only to be different or *as* good as those of other groups, and the more radical argument that superiority and inferiority were merely outcomes of power, of the capacity of a group to enforce its ideas and practices on others. The dominant class, which presented w a s p values *as if* they were synonymous with the 'American way of life', were simply engaged in a societal con-trick: the ideological project of *claiming* that what was in reality only their *sub*culture was the culture of the whole society.

These themes were developed, in more sophisticated ways, in later 'labelling theory'. Behaviour, it was argued, was not deviant in itself, deviance was not some quality inherent in the act: some kinds of killing were socially approved of, while criminals had strict codes of honour. What constituted a social problem depended on the value-system of the group making that judgement. Orthodox criminology had reified norms; in reality, norms did nothing: people did. They believed in norms, complied with them or rejected them, constructed legal and ethical codes and imposed them on themselves and others. Nor was it the case that deviant behaviour was simply the result of inadequate socialization in those norms: of poor teaching within the family, the school, or the community, or poor learning on the part of the inadequate.

The members of deviant subcultures, they argued, were themselves social actors, not inadequate, passive victims of social forces. They were subjects, agents in social life, their actions guided by adherence to alternative codes learned and sustained as members of subcultural communities. Those norms were as much expressions of consciousness, as moral, in Durkheim's sense, as any respectable ethic. Since values were general propositions, they had always to be interpreted when applying them to any specific situation. Further, changes in society always entailed the redefinition of old norms and the development of new ones. Norms and values, laws and customs, were therefore relative and changing, not absolute. They also varied situation-ally: nudity might be *de rigueur* on some beaches, but banned in the city centre. The more radical insisted that it was not enough merely to demonstrate that different groups adhered to different values and modes of behaviour, for some were more equal than others: the gatekeepers – from judges and policemen to priests and philosophers – who had the power and skills not merely to interpret the official codes but also to enforce them. Yet other subcultural groups criticized the dominant values, and some even sought to change them. At the very widest, Goffman argued, each one of us – the 'straight' as well as the deviant – was engaged in a constant series of performances designed to impress different others with different present-ations of the self. We were all social activists.

Yet these rich insights into the dynamics of interpersonal relations contained no adequate, explicit model of *society*: they were social, not societal in their vision – either micro-sociologies of life at its face-to-face levels or what Mills called expressions of 'middle-level' consciousness. The nearest approximation to a societal perspective was a fuzzy image of the 'wider society' as, at best, a mosaic or aggregate of subcultures; more often, society-wide institutions were simply an intellectually ignored, taken-for-granted backdrop known to everyone through a shared commonsense.

Cultural anthropology was no more satisfactory when it came to conceptualizing the structure of the world within which all these in-numerable cultures lived. The holistic concept of culture simply left each culture as a unique *Gestalt*. At best, one could merely typologize cultures, ahistorically, as 'Apollonian', 'Dionysian', or whatever other categories one chose to use. Marxism, conversely, strong on the societal (and even international) perspective, was virtually devoid of an adequate 'micro' theory capable of tracing out the connections and levels which intervened between the individual and the overall society.

Yet not all anthropologists accepted the holistic image of culture uncritically. Ralph Linton had great fun demonstrating that the things considered to be '100 per cent American' were the cultural products ('traits') of societies all over the world, often dating back centuries, even millennia, before Columbus. Cultural anthropologists also differed as between those who saw culture primarily as *learned* behaviour and as heritage – as a legacy handed down from generation to generation – and those like Leslie White who emphasized innovation and cumulation, the Promethean capacity to bring into being ideas and objects that never existed before. The former view lent itself to conservatism; the latter, though more sensitive to discontinuity and creativity, nevertheless rarely examined the differential distribution of culture within even the simplest societies and the existence, even there, of subcultures based on age, gender, occupation, etc.

For holistic cultural anthropologists, culture was assumed to be coter-minous with society. The holistic conception of culture therefore obscures the fact that culture is always plural: that there are subcultures and counter-cultures *within* any society, and cultural communities whose membership extends beyond the boundaries of any particular society. Culture is thus both wider and narrower than society; each group and category has its own *sub*culture, while all societies have always imported and exported ideas as well as material things from stone axes to computers. In today's 'global village', linked by the modern media of communication, youth cults, religious revivalism, consumerism, feminism, revolution, new and old ideas of every kind can be instantly diffused from one end of the earth to the other, when not blocked by those in power. Economic and political power are always backed by the exercise of cultural power to 'engineer consent' by implanting images which sustain material power and cut out unfavourable counter-images. Bismarck, usually remembered only as a man of 'blood and iron', was also the architect of the German Welfare State and the man who observed that you could do anything with bayonets except sit on them. Books can indeed be censored, radio transmissions jammed. But more positive justifications of the exercise of power are normally also resorted to.

Power

The exercise of power, Mills has argued, aways includes the possibility, in the last analysis, of resort to violence, the means of which, today, is legally monopolized by the State. But power is distinguished from mere force in that it involves the notion of legitimacy, of a *right* to exercise force; and for many such governments, the last analysis never comes. Though there are regimes which depend almost exclusively on gunships and tanks, as in Somoza's Nicaragua or present-day El Salvador, most regimes seek to *justify* their use of violence by appeal either to some kind of legitimacy, or, if not, on the pragmatic grounds that the system at least works, or pays off for most people, or that anything the opposition offers would be worse. Purely intellectual challenges may be managed through 'repressive tolerance' – the works of Marx are widely available and tolerated in many right-wing dictatorships as long as there is no connection between reading them and political *action*. And inactivity is positively encouraged, by spreading hopelessness and what the ancient Greeks called the 'idiotic' delusion: the notion that people should look for purely personal solutions to their problems and search for purely individual satisfactions in life; that there is no possibility of collectively challenging the established order of things, and that their interests are best served by vertically associating themselves with those above them rather than through horizontal solidarity with the underprivileged majority. But the diffusion of hopelessness and idiocy is rarely crude and total. People are also sold hope, taught that their humility will be rewarded in heaven, even the radical notion of *inversion*: that it will be easier for a camel to pass through the eye of a needle than for a rich man to enter the kingdom of heaven; that the mighty will be cast down and the meek raised up, and so on. But not here and now.

These messages are not mere direct expressions of ruling-class ways of thinking about the world imposed on other classes. Though they do embody class interests, they are aimed at *other* classes, telling those they rule not only what to do, but what can or cannot *possibly* be done. Mannheim's simple distinction between ideology – those ideas which legitimize the status quo – and utopia – those which express the dreams and hopes of the under-privileged – for all its utility, does not adequately capture this process of 'cross-class' spiritual co-option through which other-worldly hope is harnessed to ensuring that this world will remain as it is.

Those who experience discrimination, exploitation, and oppression react against a domination which always includes cultural domination by gener-ating their own forms of cultural self-expression. Even in classless societies, the underprivileged and the afflicted have their own special cults, such as women's cults, or what Turner has called 'communities of the afflicted'.[115] In a society like that of Rwanda before Independence – one based on caste inequalities, not just those of class – the *kubandwa* possession-cult offered the Hutu peasantry a freedom from the earthly distinctions of rank and caste imposed on them by their Tutsi overlords (against whom they finally revolted in 1959).[116] Roman soldiers – and officers – brought back the egalitarian 'mystery' cult of Mithras from the East.

Out of the collective, subcultural experience of sharing what E. V. Walter has called 'illth' as a way of life,[117] *counter*-cultures of many kinds emerge. 'Counter-culture' is a concept scarcely developed in orthodox social science. It came into use in the USA during the war in Vietnam when the radicalization of a hitherto apolitical youth culture gave rise to a wider critique of the values of US society and to a wide range of forms of rejection and resistance.[118] The new radicalism, however, often took forms that had little in common with traditional forms of class-conscious, atheistical socialism and more with older utopian religious sects or Bohemianism: resistance to war based on love, on flower power; communes based on transcendentalism or the quest for shared hallucinogenic or 'polymorphous' sex, rather than on community of goods or communal production.

But counter-culture is a phenomenon that had long been understood by many who never used that abstract term but were fully aware of concrete counter-cultures. In one of the seminal documents of modern times, Mao Tse-tung describes how, when he went to Hunan in 1926 to organize the peasantry, he found that they had already organized themselves into peasant associations with 2 million members and 10 million supporters, armed with spears rather than guns. He had already written a general sketch of 'the classes in Chinese society': the landlord and comprador classes; the middle class; the petty-bourgeoisie; the semi-proletariat (with five sub-divisions); the proletariat and the 'lumpenproletariat'. A year later, now with first-hand experience of peasant struggles, he described their economic actions: stopping speculation in grain, putting ceilings on rents, reducing the interest on loans, and establishing co-operatives; and their political actions:

breaking up landlord bands of armed thugs; exposing landlords and officials who embezzled public funds; overturning the political power of 'his excellency the county magistrate' and his bailiffs. The sanctions used ranged from public ridicule (being made to wear tall paper hats made landlords 'blue with fear') to shooting.

But he then goes on to describe, at equal length, peasant cultural revolution. In the Chinese countryside, he wrote, there were four kinds of authority: 'four great cords' that bound the Chinese people: the political power of the State, central and local, monopolized by the landlords; the authority of the clan; the 'theocratic' system of gods and spirits; and the subordination of women to their husbands. Though the peasants were principally engaged at present in political struggle, they were opposing landlord culture in every one of these spheres: women were being allowed into clan-temples, while Mao used the arguments of Li Ta-chao, for whom he had worked in Peking University's library, to deride the notion that the gods would protect them:

> Those who believe in the Eight Characters hope for good luck; those who believe in geomancy hope for the beneficial influence of the burial ground. This year the local bullies, the bad gentry and the corrupt officials all collapsed within a few months. Is it possible that till a few months ago they were all in good luck and all under the beneficial influence of the burial grounds, while in the last few months they have all of a sudden been in bad luck and their burial grounds all ceased to exert any beneficial influence on them?
>
> The gods? They may quite deserve our worship. But if we had no peasant associations but only the Emperor Kuan [the god of loyalty and war] and the Goddess of Mercy, could we have knocked down the local bullies and the bad gentry? The gods and goddesses are indeed pitiful: worshipped for hundreds of years, they have not knocked down for you a single local bully or a single one of the bad gentry!
>
> Now, you want to have your rent reduced. I would like to ask: How will you go about it? Believe in the gods, or believe in the peasant associations?

'These words of mine', Mao says, 'made the peasants roar with laughter.'

They had begun their own attacks on landlord culture long before Mao came along. They had burned idols in the clan-temples; banned opium-smoking and gambling (mah-jong sets were burned by the basketful). Luxuries typical of the lifestyle of the landlords were forbidden: sedan-chairs were smashed at first, then tolerated because they brought the carriers an income; the use of rice and sugar to make wine and spirits was prohibited, together with the keeping of pigs, chickens and ducks, and sumptuous banquets, and the slaughter of cattle which the poor needed as draught-animals but had often been forced to sell. To a landlord culture of conspicuous consumption, frivolous display, waste and idleness, they opposed a fiercely puritan peasant counter-culture of frugality and the husbanding of economic resources. There was to be no more 'flower drum' entertainment; no more chanting of New Year greetings to the accompaniment of castanets; no more praising of the local deities and singing lotus rhymes. The 'foolish' custom of paying New Year calls was to cease, together with festival processions in honour of the god of pestilence, the purchase of pastry and fruit for ritual presents, the burning of paper clothing during the Festival of the Spirits, the pasting-up of posters for good luck in the New Year, the smoking of water-pipes, letting-off of fire-crackers and firing shotguns, Taoist and Buddhist services for the dead, gifts of money at funerals, and other prohibitions, 'too many to enumerate'.[119]

Engels once advised people who wanted to know what the dictatorship of the proletariat would be like to look at the Paris Commune. Hunan in 1926 similarly illustrates what a counter-culture looks like. But this kind of head-on confrontation between class cultures is by no means typical of non-revolutionary situations. More often, subordinate classes are presented with several different ways of interpreting their underprivileged position in society. They are exposed, Parkin has argued, to the hegemonic ideas of the dominant value-system which justify their inferiority. They are also exposed to subcultural ideologies of two kinds: subordinate value-systems which promote 'accommodative' responses to the facts of inequality and low status and which commonly eschew any kind of preoccupation with society as a whole at all, but seek for satisfactions in life at the face-to-face levels of the community and family, and often of a purely personal kind – in religion, gambling, and a hundred and one other forms; and radical value-systems, which promote opposition.[120] The latter, he argues, usually finds expression in the working-class political party, whose ideology is usually articulated by intellectuals.

Theorists of mass culture see the working class as passive consumers in their leisure-time pursuits, too, whether in the home or in the pub or club, above all as audiences for literature and TV designed by others: culture *for* the masses, rather than culture *of* the masses. The popularity of this culture of the lowest common denominator is as indisputable as the political deafness of the working class in the countries of developed capitalism to those who urge them to revolt. But most people do also choose some at least of the better-quality programmes (not necessarily arts programmes, but the best in current events, sport, and comedy, too) some of the time, while there is an enormous variety of creative, sociable and active ways of using leisure-time, some old, some new, from gardening to making your own music, many of which are not to be recognized as culture by those who use that term only in the narrow, 'fine arts' sense.[121]

Radical political values also grew out of, and still persist at the local levels of working-class life. In one study of council house tenants in London, nearly half strongly condemned the ownership of more than one house and nearly three-quarters approved of sit-ins by workers, and over half believed that workers should have more say in running the factories they worked in – either 'a big say' or as much as the owners.[122] More widely, the majority held a dichotomic view of society, which they saw as a *class* system, divided into 'Them' and 'Us', in which the rich are also the powerful.[123]

Yet the working class is not homogeneous in other respects and other situations. Though most people do recognize a structural opposition of interest and status as between themselves and those who employ them, most of the time, in everyday life, for most practical purposes, they are not faced with such issues, and commonly operate with less societal views. Their reference-groups, as Runciman has shown, are usually much more proximate: they do not compare themselves with financiers or company directors, but with those of more immediate relevance in their home and work environments. Thus married men contrast their lot with that of single men without family responsibilities; night-shift workers with those on nine to five; and men with women ('working for pin-money', in one stereotype).[124]

The real working class, unlike Althusser's mythical proletariat – which is guided by 'science', not 'ideology' – is also subject to a plurality of historic cultural influences, many quite ancient, which influence the ways in which people see the world. Though the hegemonic culture (itself in various forms) of the bourgeoisie constitutes one pole, and the counter-culture of socialism the other, there are a variety of ideologies in between these. 'Upside-downers', for instance, rate doing a hard manual job or a socially valuable job highly. They put nurses and agricultural labourers high in their scheme of things, and company directors and university lecturers low.[125]

But culture, we have seen, is not just a societal phenomenon: it is often both wider and narrower than the bounds of any one societal formation. Nor are classes the only relevant units of culture. Ruling classes have the power to disseminate their ideas to those they dominate. Whether they succeed – whether these ideas are internalized – depends on so many variables that it has to be a matter for empirical investigation. Class, of course, is in any case a category, not an organized entity. Like other social categories, such as women or youth, classes may or may not perceive themselves as having interests in common: the protection of privileges, or protest against exploitation and stigma. Such categories are not structured wholes, but recruiting-grounds for organized groups which sometimes claim to represent the whole, sometimes to speak only for this or that segment of it. The rise and spread of student radicalism, of the Woodstock nation, the revival of Islam, the growth of women's movements across large stretches of the globe, are powerful evidence that a sense of common identity and of shared culture can give rise to social movements that quickly transcend the boundaries of any particular society and become supra-societal and international in scope. Many of the most important cultural identities of our, and any, time – from religion to nationalism – therefore cut *across* class, vertically.

The word 'culture', then, like that other major keyword, 'social', contains a variety of alternative, overlapping meanings accreted over centuries. Each of these captures some aspects of social life and omits others. For the cultural anthropology of the 1930s, 'culture' was a totalizing concept. Culture was a whole, a *Gestalt*, in which the various groups and institutions reinforced one another and contributed to the functioning of the whole. It was also an idealist conception, in which values were primary, and further concealed an idealist ontology, since Culture, with a capital C, was reified. It was Culture which did things: provided roles and allocated people to them, including even the role of deviant. The 'over-socialized conception of man', of which Wrong complained, thus had its counterpart in an over-societalized conception of society which omitted both trans-societal and intra-societal relations. Its modern descendant is structuralist anthropology.

The 'arts' conception of culture was equally idealist. Ideas were the motor of history; the institutions within which they were produced and the circuits through which they flowed were the heart and life-blood of social life. It is a view which has the virtue of emphasizing the content of social life: the values and projects which inform social institutions and structures. But ideas were conceived of as autonomous – as pure and unrelated to interests – while the historic monopoly of high culture by small élites blinded its proponents not only to subcultural differences and counter-cultural oppositions, but also to what Lévi-Strauss has described as *bricolage*: people's capacity to select bits and pieces of the systems intellectuals build and re-combine them for their own purposes in their own ways.

The word 'culture' cannot be divested of these complex penumbra of meanings by insisting on stipulative definitions, by fiat. The only alternative is to coin completely new terms. But to do so would be to lose sight of what all these historic usages do have in common: that they constitute what Wittgenstein called a 'family' of overlapping meanings which direct our attention to society as a whole and insist that it cannot be reduced to the economic or the political. This does not imply a new 'culturalism', in which 'culture' becomes *more* important than political economy: rather, it involves examining the interplay between economic and political institutions and the rest of social life.

Economists have long used the term 'social' in a residual sense: to denote relations other than those entailed in production and the market. In doing so, they necessarily conflate vast and varied domains of social life – religion, sport, sexual mores, art; as if these constituted some kind of outer space through which the space-ship of the economy floats. But 'social', in this sense, is just as problematic, for the economy itself is a zone of specialized _social_ relationships which obtain in the spheres of production and the market, and these are always informed by extra-economic interests and values. By drawing too rigid a boundary between the economic and the social and the cultural, these interrelationships are obscured. Nor does the term 'socio-cultural' solve the problem, for its meaning is still residual: that which is not economic or political (and it is clumsy, and deservedly, therefore, unpopular). What we need to avoid is not only the assumption that the 'cultural' is a _separate_ sphere, but that it is causally _secondary_ (merely 'super-structural'). It is, in fact, the realm of those crucial institutions in which the ideas we live by are produced and through which they are communicated – and penetrate even the economy.

Popular thought draws no such absolute boundaries. It recognizes that there _is_ an economy, and that there are institutions we all recognize as political. But the word 'culture', like the word 'social', is used in a whole variety of ways which overlap, constituting a family of meanings. No usage can be definitive, for all involve abstracting from the seamless web of social life. The main criterion has to be a heuristic one: whatever helps us _understand_ better. Even the fine arts conception of culture, we saw, is not without its value, for it focuses upon that central activity: the production and consumption of ideas. Rather than adopt a stipulative definition, therefore, I prefer to preserve some of the richness of popular ambiguity by using the term, at times, in the wider, anthropological sense of a whole _Gestalt_, and at other times, in the sectoral sense: that which lies outside the sphere of political economy. Which use is intended will either be made explicit or will be clear from the context. The positive value of using the word 'culture' in this overlapping fashion cannot be logically definitive; it can only lie in the demonstration that it provides a richer understanding of social life than those one-dimensional or two-dimensional approaches to the study of society which simply leave out most of human behaviour.

II The Undoing of the Peasantry

Before Agriculture

We suffer from a severely impaired sense of history. Creatures more or less like today's humans have existed on earth for over a million years. Recognizably human societies, where people make tools and produce art, go back many tens of thousands of years. But agriculture, the major technical break-through before industry, only goes back a few thousand years. And what we choose to call *the* 'Great Transformation', industrialization, only began about two hundred years ago, and is still incomplete over most of the globe. Even this brief period, Kumar has argued, has itself been misread in a 'premature', 'historical abbreviation', an 'unjustifiable fore-shortening' of the 'contradictory, uneven and long drawn-out' history of the industrialization process.[1] In 1851, the year conventionally taken as marking the triumph of industry in the first major capitalist country, Britain, the year of the Crystal Palace exhibition, he argues that the factory system was still in its infancy; industrial 'villages' were more common than modern cities; and the workforce was still heavily concentrated in agriculture and domestic service. Only at the end of the century did machinery displace seasonal travelling labourers in agriculture and a city proletariat homogeneous enough to give rise to a (reformist) party of Labour come into existence.

The wider the sweep of historical studies, the greater the temptation to use them to construct or buttress evolutionary cosmologies informed by metaphysics. These may be either optimistic or pessimistic. Most nine-teenth-century theorists were optimists, though there were gloomier 'social' interpretations of Darwin. Cosmic optimism was to receive its 'quietus' in 1914: 'the idea of progress', it has been said, 'was buried in the mud of Flanders.'[2]

Yet cosmic optimism is not entirely dead. Theorists aiming at 'future shock' confidently proclaim the end even of the industrial age: we are already living, apparently, in a '*post*-industrial' world, and have crossed a new Great Watershed in which micro-processors, nuclear energy, space technology and genetic engineering will soon render all previous history trivial. For pessimists, it is these very innovations that induce unease, reinforced by the knowledge that we may be on the point of exterminating ourselves altogether. To optimists, the millennia during which agriculture was the dominant mode of human survival seems so remote that it is an epoch of interest only as pure antiquarianism. To pessimists, its only interest is that we may need to return to those ways, or, more likely, to a way of life even more ancient: hunting and gathering.

For over 95 per cent of human history, Lévi-Strauss has pointed out, people lived not even by agriculture, but by hunting, fishing and collecting wild plants and fruits.[3] Furthermore, most of the key technical discoveries about the nature of Nature, from the domestication of animals to the unnatural selection of the wild varieties which became maize, rice and wheat and the transmutation of rocks into metals, were made by 'savages', either hunters and collectors or primitive agriculturalists. The distinctiveness of our own way of life can therefore best be seen by contrasting it with the principal historic mode of human existence: hunting and gathering.

Then, the rate of accumulation of knowledge was so slow that there was little difference between the life of one generation and that of its predecessors. Nor were they dedicated to the accumulation of material wealth. Hence their conception of time was not lineal. If we deny them any importance in history, they denied history as a category of the understanding. For Australian aborigines, human institutions were established in the Dreamtime, at the creation of the world, along with the things of Nature, through the actions of supernatural Beings. Time had a beginning, an initial Genesis. There is also the present. Those living in the present remember the recent past. But everything in between now and the Dreamtime becomes timeless; entire generations are 'collapsed' or 'telescoped'. The earliest names in the genealogies of lineage societies are therefore not the names of individuals at all, but of the constituent *groups* (or the eponymous ancestors of those groups) which make up contemporary society and have their traditional territories. Time, that is, is structural, not chronological. Even the most dramatic events – a famine, an epidemic, an invasion – get absorbed into the primordial and persisting framework of systems of descent groups like those of the Bedouin of Cyrenaica.

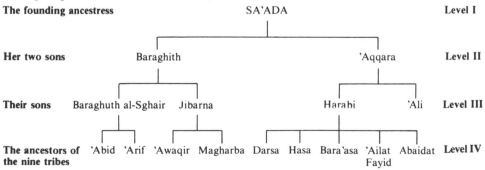

Such genealogies are maps of group relationships. The regular pattern of
segmentation into two ('sons') reflects the mythological nature of this
charter of descent. At level IV, however, irregularities begin, because the
nine ancestors of the present noble tribes are each associated with a
particular ecological zone of the country, whilst below this level, each of
these is further subdivided into primary, secondary and tertiary sections.
The last of these is the smallest unit of political, economic and social life. The
number of lineages within each therefore varies according to the precarious
balance between changes in social structure and the carrying capacity of the
land. At this level, then, the genealogies are less regular, but though some
groups become extinct and others are adopted into other lineages or become
their clients, the telescoping of the fusing of names allows the general fixed
shape of the genealogy to be retained.[4] The telescoping of generations and
the fusing of close relatives (especially where they have the same name)
means that most historical individuals drop out. Thus only **Peter 1** will
remain of the following:

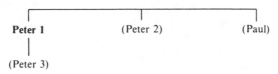

The wives and children of Peter 2, Paul and Peter 3 will also be assimilated to
Peter 1. In non-lineal systems, such as that of the Australian aborigines I
studied in the 1950s, there is no pyramid and no apex. As with ordinary
people in Britain (not aristocrats), it is an open-ended system: most people
cannot trace their descent beyond their grandparents, and there is no known
connection between the grandparents Peter and Nellie, John and Jill, and
James and Sheila. Once those who knew them are themselves dead, the
names of even the most important of these recent forebears will be
forgotten:

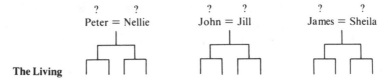

Such societies, Lévi-Strauss puts it, are 'cool' in their attitude to history, in
contrast to those in which history is 'hot': where chronology, continuity and
discontinuity, change and development, are central to their consciousness of
themselves. Even for agricultural peoples, history is significant only insofar
as it relates to *recent* events; it is mythology, rather, which legitimizes

institutions and gives the world meaning. For the Trobrianders, the original ancestors of their clans came out of holes in the ground at the beginning of time. And even for ourselves, history is *public*: the doings of important people and of the larger collectivities we belong to. Thus in our families, we only remember as far back as our grandparents or great-grandparents – unless we have more than a merely intellectual interest in preserving the historical record. Like our own aristocrats, Maori chiefly families which trace themselves back thirty-six generations to the Great Voyages which brought their ancestors to New Zealand do so in order to legitimize a privileged access to rank, resources and power that does not change with time.

The pioneer theorists of industrial society used time in a different way: to point to *change* and achievement both now and in the future. For the first time, as Thompson has shown, marking the passing of time became so important that it called for the mass diffusion of new instruments – clocks – by means of which its passage could be checked.[5] The past became chronology, and no longer mythology, once it was valued materially in a culture of infinite production. Mankind was no longer seen as having been called into being by some miraculous primal act of God, which laid down an eternal template for human institutions at the same time. By the time Condorcet came to write his *Sketch for an Historical Picture of the Human Spirit* in 1793–4, he was following what had by then become the accepted manner of looking at the past: as a sequence of *stages* (ten, in his model) through which society had passed. The arrogant lumping-together of everything not like us as 'pre-industrial' was a later deformation of thought.

It involved a moral as well as a cognitive blindness. Choosing to ignore most of history, the gap was filled with myths. To the evolutionists of the nineteenth century, and to most people still, the superiority of agriculture, however primitive, over hunting and collecting, and over pastoral nomadism, is a self-evident article of faith. 'Savages' dependent upon the chance of finding and then killing kangaroos or bison or running across patches of wild berries at the right time, must always, it is believed, be on the edge of starvation. In the poorer marginal zones, absolute scarcity was no doubt endemic. For marginal producers, like the Siriono of Bolivia, 'the supply of food is rarely abundant and always insecure'. Their frustrations are expressed in dreams about food rather than sexual fantasies.[6] But most hunters and gatherers did not live in such regions. They were only forced into the badlands – the Kalahari, the deserts of Central Australia, or the (to us) inhospitable Amazon – by more powerful late-comers, agriculturalists who wanted the favourable regions, such as South-eastern Australia or the Cape, for themselves. European colonialism was the last act. Thenceforth the survivors would have the choice between the desert, extermination, or a life of hand-outs on mission-stations. Finally, even the desert was to be denied to the nomads, once it was needed for its oil and minerals.

The idea that hunters and gatherers would eventually be labelled by an iconoclastic anthropologist as 'affluent' was unthinkable to most people; the proposition that 'the amount of hunger increases relatively and absolutely with the evolution of culture' scandalous,[7] for the cause of this man-made misery was attributed, in the minds of people saturated with evolutionist thought, to the shortcomings of hunting and gathering *per se*, not to imperialism.

Yet even today, in fertile parts where fish, game, and plants are abundant, life for hunters and gatherers has by no means been a struggle for existence. Hunters and gatherers, Sahlins calculates:

work less than we do; and, rather than a continuous travail, the food quest is intermittent, leisure abundant, and there is a greater amount of sleep in the daytime *per capita* per year than in any other condition of society.[8]

In capitalist terms, affluence, as Galbraith has classically observed, connotes those *private* goods we enjoy as part of a generalized culture of 'possessive individualism' which the more fortunate obtain through competition for scarce resources. Wants, in this culture, are infinite. It is a model, too, of a zero-sum economy, in which the gain of one occurs at the expense of the other. For hunters and collectors – 'the world's wealthiest people' – Sahlins argues, affluence has quite other connotations, for theirs is a 'Zen' economy, in which 'human material wants are finite and few, and technical means unchanging but on the whole adequate'.[9] Everyone has access to the principal means of production – the land – and can make or obtain the tools with which to work it. Living amongst abundance, they are often prodigal, at least when the salmon run and the wild yams are in season. Yet they accumulate little, because their livelihood depends upon moving on. In this economy, people, not things, are the crucial resource: one shares with one's relatives, and everyone is a relative, often in several ways.

Yet in the better-endowed regions, Australian aborigines worked for only four to five hours a day, Bushmen about two, and the Hadza of Tanzania even less. 'Hunters', Sahlins remarks, 'keep bankers' hours.' Or, as a !Kung Bushman put it: 'Why should we plant when there are so many *mongongo* nuts in the world?'[10] – so many that most of them are left to simply rot on the ground. It is the kind of question that many primitive agriculturalists have also asked.

For them, too, accumulation is not the cardinal principle, whether for the hard-pressed or the affluent. For them, as for hunters and gatherers, once basic needs are met – and there is only a certain amount one *can* eat – a different set of priorities comes into play. Hunters go out looking for luxuries rather than basic foods; they value the leisure in which to tell jokes or simply sleep or enjoy sex; or, like the Hazda nomads, to gamble for six months of the year (often losing their hunting arrows in the process). And seasonally, when there are large stores of food, they are able to gather in large numbers for religious rituals and secular ceremonies.

Enter Agriculture: the Domestic Mode of Production

The orthodox account of the Neolithic Revolution was not written by hunters and gatherers or by pastoralists. From henceforth, their achievements were to be denigrated. Agriculture, on the other hand, was depicted as making humanity free, no longer dependent on the vagaries of Nature, no longer compelled to keep on the move. Once food could be stored, some of the surplus could be exchanged for other material goods, and time was available for other things, including innovations in knowledge and technique, and for the arts.

It is a technological rather than a sociological account which counterposes a mythical scarcity among all hunters and collectors to an agriculture fantastically free from poor crops and the unpredictability of rain and sun, and from the inordinate amounts of back-breaking labour which it entails and which hunters never experience. Famine and poverty, moreover, are terms we associate with peasant life every bit as much as with nomadism, for the existence of surpluses attracts those who never produce themselves, but are all too ready to appropriate the products of the labour of others. To take the further step of not merely appropriating surpluses, 'booty' in Weber's terminology, but converting them into *capital*, required the prior replacement of an economy based on use-value by an economy based on exchange-value, the construction of class society, and the construction, too, of the State.

Primitive agriculturalists, in use-value economies, have more in common with their hunting ancestors than with the modern peasant producing for sale on the market. Like hunters, they sometimes suffer from problems of abundance. With finite wants and a finite market for surpluses, the yams the Trobrianders produced and the salmon the Kwakiutl shovelled out of the rivers satisfied no material needs above a certain threshold. But they could be used to satisfy immaterial wants by being converted into social status.

But not directly. Utilitarian trade existed: food could be exchanged for things unavailable locally, such as clay pots. Such trade responded to demand and supply. But the goods most highly valued in society could not be obtained in this way. They were exchanged in quite different fashion, and the most prestigious goods of all (those Malinowski called 'valuables' and likened to family heirlooms -- certain arm-shells and necklaces in the Trobriand case) were only exchanged between the leading men in different communities and could not be obtained in exchange for everyday goods at all.[11]

Such systems of exchange still operate side by side, but independently of each other and alongside modern capitalist trade-relations.[12] Even in the market for everyday commodities, however, a personal and social, rather than an impersonal, code regulates dealings, for each person trades with an established partner, a relationship elaborated by ritual and often consolidated by marriage. Such partnership trade links communities as well as individuals, groups which might at other times be enemies. Hence trade has political implications, and Malinowski wrote of the *kula* ring's implications for inter-tribal relations as an instance of 'the evolution . . . of primitive international law'.[13] In-laws are therefore not just kinsmen, but political intermediaries and at times peace-makers. Luxury goods constitute a third market distinct from those for utilitarian goods and valuables.

Unlike capitalism, there is no universal measure of value and medium of exchange – money in an economy of this kind. Values are incommensurable, plural, and unconvertible. But even utilitarian trade is regulated by customary not market norms. Prices are inelastic. Goodwill may be earned by giving good measure, even by being generous, but prices remain fixed. Greater supplies have to be obtained, not by offering higher prices, but by pressurizing one's trading-partner to produce (or mobilize others to produce) more, *at the same price*, or by going to other trade-partners, again at the same price. Permanent imbalance, of course, would drive the disadvantaged or badly-supplied partner out of the system altogether in the long run, but it is a system that permits inefficient producers or those who failed to innovate to survive because they are not exposed to the 'invisible' iron hand of a competitive market.

Yet production over and above any 'material' need is highly institutionalized, and at great cost in labour. Yams can be converted into prestige on one major condition, however: that they are not treated as having material use-value at all, but simply *displayed*, or given away in periodic giant splurges of conspicuous consumption designed to impress rival communities. Such contests augment the prestige both of the 'big men' who organize them and of the kinsmen they mobilize; the only way to outshine them is to stage an even more ambitious feast later.

More utilitarian uses of surpluses can be found in less privileged economies. Surplus grain, in the *jajmani* system of India, is given by each household to pay for the specialized services of barbers, priests, leather-workers, sweepers, and others who service the whole village but are not full-time cultivators themselves.[14] In societies where inequality used to be or is still institutionalized in the form of hereditary rank (aristocracies, chieftaincies, etc.), this hereditary superiority itself dictates a logic of *noblesse oblige* different from that of mere accumulation, a logic of

'centralized redistribution', to use Wolf's term, in which the superiors are
obliged to redistribute the tribute they received to clients and dependants
whose needs might not necessarily be those of hunger so much as 'social
wants' such as the necessity of finding the bridewealth with which to marry
off a daughter. Distributing surplus in this way builds up loyalty on the part
of the client, reinforcing established ties or building new ones. This moral
credit can later be cashed in in practical form, whether as reciprocal calls
upon material resources or in the form of social support, including military
service. It is a logic of the use of surplus different in kind from that of simple
instrumental exploitation, for wealth thus flowed through the hands of the
African chief or the Bedouin sheikh rather than ending there. As with the
assumption of expensive public offices, such as the *cargos* of Latin America,
wealth expended in the pursuit of high status had a certain levelling effect,
for even though its circulation was intended to reinforce status inequalities,
it entailed the dissipation of surpluses. For those without the wherewithal
could borrow it, and spend the next five years working in the plantations to
pay it off.[15] As a result, materially, the superior might often live otherwise in
a way little different from that of his subjects and fellows. Such obligations to
one's inferiors have often been symbolically expressed in dramatic 'rituals of
reversal', even of rebellion or degradation, such as those that accompanied
the installation of the Swazi king.[16]

The least utilitarian use of wealth, in the past, was to dedicate it to the
gods, whether to feed crowds of worshippers, or to feed a labour-force
building pyramids or cathedrals, or to supply armies which sometimes
campaigned to acquire material goods and sometimes mainly to acquire
victims for sacrifice, but always to maximize their ruler's glory.

Whatever the end-uses, wealth had to be produced over and above what
was needed simply for subsistence. There were two main ways this could be
done in agricultural society. The producer might work on land he owned,
using the labour of his family, and then be made to hand over part of the
product to a superior political authority: a lord. If the producer owned no
land, he would have to rent it, often paying with a share of the crop to a
landowner who played no part in production at all, but who claimed political
authority over the peasant. The State itself might even be the landowner.

But usually there was an intermediary class of those who owned large
estates. Smallholder agriculture was necessarily limited in scale by the
amount of labour the family could contribute, and even though kin and
neighbours could be called upon periodically, since they expected similar
assistance in turn, such reciprocal obligations also placed a ceiling upon the
scale of operation. Cultivation on large estates naturally involved the use of
larger supplies of labour. For most of recorded history it was obtained
through the exercise of political power by lords who obliged people to work
for them as slaves or serfs or kept them in bondage through debt. This kind

of landlord was not just a landowner renting out land to others who worked it; he was using the labour of others to work his own land as an agricultural enterprise. With the growth of capitalist market, corvée and other forms of unfree labour were increasingly displaced by the wage-labour of those who had lost their own small parcels of land and become a rural proletariat.

And over and above these structures of class exploitation, both independent peasants and lords had to pay 'tribute' (taxes) to the State, whether the State claimed to be the landowner, ultimate or proximate, or not.

Agriculture, then, can be ideal-typically conceived of in terms of two polar modes of production: small-scale peasant production (which may be primarily subsistence-oriented but more often is also involved in the market and sometimes wholly dedicated to selling cash-crops), and large-scale estate agriculture. Such estates were normally primarily oriented to the market, but also provided for most of the everyday needs of those who lived in them. Large haciendas, in nineteenth-century South America, could, at times of market recession, revert back to a kind of autarky, much as the peasantry could fall back on subsistence, and would shed their labour and leave it to grow its own food – or starve. Finally, with the commercialization of agriculture, those who provide capital, notably money-lenders (today banks and credit institutions), develop new ways of siphoning off peasant income.

The two types, in reality, are often interwoven in complex ways and there is much oscillation, over time, from one pole toward the other. Independent producers may supply corvée labour for so many days per year to estates; unfree serfs, even slaves, may be given small plots to grow their own food. The smallholding peasant is at the point of intersection between two systems which compete for his labour time. To understand one side of this equation we therefore need to examine the nature of the family farm; to understand the other, the peasants' involvement in the world outside it.

The Peasant Mode of Production

'Nothing we believe about peasants in the West is true', Rebecca West has written. For many people, peasant life still signifies what it did for Marx – 'rural idiocy': a nineteenth-century mental set established over centuries during which peasants were regarded as little more than animals:

> The *Declinatio Rustica* from thirteenth-century Germany had six declensions for the word peasant – villain, rustic, devil, robber, brigand and looter; and in the plural – wretches, beggars, liars, rogues, trash and infidels.[17]

For many people, development is still simply equated with urban, industrial life; underdevelopment with an agricultural existence. Progress is therefore deemed to consist either in moving people out of agriculture altogether or in creating 'factories in the field'. In the advanced capitalist countries, this has already happened. In Britain, the pioneer, only 2.8 per cent of the labour-force now work on the land. Even in France, where there were more people earning their living in agriculture, fishing and forestry in 1896 than ever before,[18] they now number only one in ten, though it was only in the 1920s that the majority of the population was to be found living in places with 2000 or more inhabitants, and only in the 1950s for the first time living in towns and cities of over 20,000 people. In the USSR, where the peasants had been sacrificed by Stalin to build industry, they had been reduced to a third of the population by the 1970s.

As a proportion of the entire world population, too, they are declining. Yet in absolute numbers the rural population is actually growing. In 1900, there were 213 million people working in agriculture; today there are 435 million – nearly double in seventy years – and the peasant population of a country like Mexico continued to grow throughout the 1960s, according to official data, and is probably still growing. In many countries, including such giant countries as India and China, the latter with over a billion people, the peasantry still constitutes over 80 per cent of the population.

But people working in agriculture are not necessarily peasants, and many who live and work in villages and country towns are not engaged in agriculture. Eighty per cent of those economically active in Mexican agriculture are still smallholders. But the term *campesino* has also been applied to those who have lost their own land ('landless peasants', in English, reflecting both the process and the contradictoriness of the term) and are now actually rural proletarians who dream only of getting a small parcel of land once more. The term 'peasant', like *campesino*, has been used even more widely, to refer to anyone who lives and works in the countryside: to tribespeople; to subsistence-producers and to those who produce surpluses which end up, wholly or in part, on the market; to feudal serfs and micro-capitalist farmers; and even, by some, to owners of highly-mechanized, large, capital-intensive farms in North America, still, however, worked by family labour.

The peasantry, Shanin has written, are an 'awkward class'. Awkward, because, despite all this heterogeneity, many of the categories grouped under the umbrella-term 'peasant' do nevertheless seem to have something in common. Awkward, too, because, despite two hundred years of determinist prophecies, they have not only refused to disappear, but have become the major revolutionary force of the twentieth century.

Yet the term seems to some to be so devoid of precision as to be of dubious scientific utility. For an anti-Marxist like Dalton the attempt to define 'peasants-in-general' is a 'dubious quest';[19] for some Marxists, 'peasantry as a theoretical category does not exist in Marxism' and should be regarded as a 'specific agrarian detachment of the petty bourgeoisie'.[20] Two classic modern attempts have, however, been made to render the term more heuristically valuable by constructing an ideal-type of the peasantry (though neither calls it that).[21] Both draw upon the theoretical writings of the Russian agronomist, A. V. Chayanov, from the earlier decades of this century;[22] he, in turn, from the pioneer *zemstvo* statisticians of nineteenth-century Russia.

For Wolf, the peasant is 'not in the business of farming', nor is he an individual entrepreneur. The unit of the peasant economy – and life – is, rather, the household. The peasantry thus defined involves smallholders under capitalism, serfs in feudal society and in bureaucratic empires, but excludes both the terms which make up the equation of capitalist farming: the farmer and those who work for him. Wolf also excludes those whom anthropologists have called tribal 'horticulturalists', since they are independent producers, who pay no *rent*. The peasant, for him, is involved in 'asymmetrical power relations' by virtue of which 'some superior power' . . . 'lays claim to his labor on the land . . . regardless of whether that rent is paid in labor, in produce, or in money', a claim, it should be noted, on the value produced by labour in any form, not just upon that labour which goes to pay for the use of someone else's land.

For Chayanov, peasant farming was a form of economic activity so distinctive as to merit being called a peasant mode of production; it was guided by a different logic both from that of 'pre-peasants' and a different logic, too, from that of capitalist production (including 'post-peasant' farmers who were simply capitalists operating in the countryside, on the land, instead of in the towns, producing boots or tables). The differences between peasant life and these other forms of existence, for Chayanov, had to be sought not so much in the relationship of the peasant family or village *vis-à-vis* the outside world, as in its internal constitution, dynamics and functioning. The peasant household was, therefore, the jumping-off point of his analysis, and though he concentrated on the economic relations between its members, for him it was not simply an economic institution, but a social one; not just a mode of production, but a *way of life*.

Shanin, like Wolf, takes family production as the first element in his definition of peasantry. Peasants, he then adds, are engaged in land husbandry (a point not quite as self-evident as it might appear, since social scientists have written about 'peasants in the cities').[23] Land husbandry provides their main means of livelihood, both for basic food needs, and for use in exchange (whether by cash or barter), as well as for payments to political authorities. Both writers then shift to the sphere of external relations.

A peasantry, as Kroeber first put it, was necessarily only a 'part-society'. The household, that is, is always part of a local community (whether concentrated in villages or dispersed in hamlets); while collectively peasant communities further constitute only a segment of the society as a whole. Redfield was to add that this distinctiveness was a cultural and not merely a structural phenomenon, the 'little community' having its own cultural forms, which were, however, always encompassed within or articulated to the 'Great Tradition' of the wider society.

We can distinguish, then, between primary peasantries, in which the peasants are a majority of the population, and secondary peasantries where they constitute a minority. Yet, either way, Shanin insists, marginal frontiersmen apart, peasants are always dominated by outsiders: economically, politically and culturally, they are underdogs. In earlier times, the most important external authorities were the private landowner, who might also be the land*lord* – the money-lender, the shopkeeper, the merchant who bought the crop, or the tax-collector; later, the banks, the commodity exchanges, and, increasingly, everywhere, the State, which sometimes performs every one of these roles.

But if the peasant household produces its own means of livelihood, it cannot *re*produce itself in isolation. Reproduction, of course, is here not a biological nor even an economic concept, for what is entailed is *social* reproduction.

The unit of production in peasant society is not the individual actor of classical economics. Nor are choices made according to an individualistic calculus. The central unit, rather, is the household, a multiplex entity whose collective productive activities, however vital, are only a part of its wider social activities. If the household is the core unit of production, it is also the core unit of consumption. Crops are grown primarily to satisfy the wants of the household's members, whether they consume what they grow directly or exchange part of what they produce on the market. The same people are both the producers and the consumers of the product.

Nor is the household only an economic unit of production and consumption. It is *the* crucial unit for *all* social purposes, economic and non-economic: a unit of residence, of marriage, and of kinship relationships; a unit for the purpose of worshipping the ancestors, the earth-spirits, and the Supreme Being. And it is always located within wider structures of corporate kinship, from segmentary lineages to consanguineous kindreds, which use various modes of tracing descent (matrilineal, patrilineal, etc) and patterns of residence (patrilocal, uxorilocal, neolocal and others). The forms of the extended family and the ways in which nuclear families are articulated to form parts of these wider structures, all vary greatly, as does the range of kin and non-kin with whom one may be obliged to co-operate in different situations.

But the household is there at the centre. In peasant society the farm is a family farm. In tribal society, the economy, Sahlins argues, is essentially a '*domestic* mode of production'. The household

> is to the tribal economy as the manor to the medieval economy or the corporation to modern capitalism; each is the dominant production institution of its time.[24]

The crucial resource the household holds in common, its source of livelihood, is the land; in Marx's terms, the chief 'object' of production. To work it, to transform inert earth into a source of life, tools – inanimate, material things (instruments of production) – are needed. But tools accomplish nothing on their own. Instruments need to be used by people equipped with the subjective, cultural knowledge: the material and the *idéel*, together, make possible the productive activity of growing plants.

The land, as the central requirement, carries a special value. It is, literally, _Land_ a sacred trust, for it has to be handed on to the next generation, in good heart, to provide for their subsistence as it was handed down to this generation from generations untold. The living, that is, are merely the present incumbents, a link in the Great Chain of Being which extends from the founding fathers to the unborn. The household is a transgenerational corporation; the present head merely its contemporary manager. Security, continuity, and risk-reduction are the principal preoccupations, not profit.

The land is thus essential to the survival of every member of the corporation. It must therefore be kept, and handed on, in good condition. It must also never be sold to anyone who is not a member of the peasant community, yet it does not necessarily continue forever as a single, indivisible patrimony in the way in which we have been accustomed in Britain (and have foisted onto much of the world). Land, rather, is commonly divided in accordance with the changing composition of the extended family. Impartible inheritance, whether based on primogeniture, ultimogeniture, or the personal decision of the household head, has often replaced other systems which provided for everyone: in Islamic law, even women received their due (smaller) share.

Where land is abundant, as in systems of shifting cultivation which require _Pop_ that anything from two to twenty times the area of land actually under _pressure._ cultivation be left fallow, the patrimony largely consists of *un*cultivated land, and there is enough for all. With growing population-densities (and static technologies), however, the system leads to fragmentation into ever-smaller, and eventually unviable, units, intensifying the pressure to change over to a system in which only one will inherit. The rest no longer have the option they once had of staying on and working under the new incumbent's authority. They have to get out.

Production for use means that the market takes second place. It is not a system like capitalism, where the chief factors of production – land, labour and capital – are all commodities that can be bought and sold on the market. Above all, the land is not a mobile factor of production, as it is under systems of juridical private ownership. Neither is labour a commodity. One does not pay one's children or one's husband for the labour they put in, and the hours worked are not checked by the clock and rewarded accordingly. The cash-nexus of capitalism – so many hours of labour in return for a given wage-rate – does not obtain. And there are no statutory limits to the working day when the harvest has to be got in. Disposable capital is the scarcest factor of production of all, for what surplus is produced finds its way into the hands or pockets of others. If there is any, it is reinvested in more land.

As long as land is plentiful, the prosperity of the household is thus a function, primarily, of its supply of labour. Yet not all are producers. The household contains children and the aged who can only contribute a little, but must be fed. Their existence is an extra fixed cost, over and above the necessity of feeding those who can contribute to production. But they cannot be ignored: the household is therefore also a miniature welfare state. The ratio of producers to non-producers, biologically determined by the stage in the life-cycle of its individual members, is, in its turn, a function of the stage reached in the cycle of development of the family as a structural unit. In one phase, there may be a high ratio of dependent non-producers to the able-bodied; in another, a favourable proportion of producers.

The family is not therefore a fixed structure, but one which changes over time. The two classic tables on pp. 76–7 illustrate the thesis. As an economic entity, a newly-wed couple setting up on their own would have only two full units of adult labour available. With the birth of successive children, the parents now have additional mouths to feed: the ratio of consumers to workers has deteriorated; the family is in a down-swing phase economically. But children grow up, and begin to help out, at first only in an ancillary way (by minding small animals and helping in the fields) but over time, more significantly. By the age of eight, they can be reckoned as contributing a half-unit of the labour contributed by a mature adult. A family with two teenage sons as well as the labour of the father and mother therefore disposes of four full units of labour. The family is now in the upswing phase.[25]

Over an ideal-typical twenty-five-year cycle, the family therefore experienced its greatest economic strain at the fourteenth year, when 1.8 workers were feeding 3.5 consumers: a consumer-worker ratio of 1.94. But thereafter, its fortunes improved. By year 26, the ratio had fallen to 1.32, for there were now 5.2 workers to feed 6.9 consumers. After that, the family would split, giving rise to new families that would go through the same phases. The parents would then become aged, dependent non-producers themselves, contributing to the adverse worker-consumer ratio of the family now supporting them.

As an economic unit, the peasant household thus reveals many character-istics shared in common with tribal 'domestic' producers. Yet, as Wolf insists, 'it is the production of a fund of rent which critically distinguishes the peasant from the primitive cultivator'. A peasant, that is, always exists within a wider system, in which asymmetrical relations of power mean that part of his production is handed over, by one means or another, to non-productive, powerful others.[26]

Chayanov's model deliberately concentrates on the internal dynamics of the peasant household and on its economic structure; non-economic relations and relationships outside the family are not part of that model. Yet even in tribal society, exchange is a universal and major process. Even in the most hard-pressed economies, surpluses can be generated, if necessary by foregoing consumption of food itself or by self-exploitation to produce more by working harder. And since the household produces most of its needs, it might appear to have no need of others; the domestic mode of production therefore is inherently predisposed to what Sahlins calls 'petty anarchy' and 'primordial incoherence'. However, reciprocity is a fundamental in primi-tive society, in all dimensions of life. In the economic sphere, from time to time, large inputs of labour or special skills are required in production: at times of planting, weeding, harvesting, or when houses have to be built. Common services such as guarding and pasturing the cattle, scaring the birds off the crops also entail co-operation. Quite basic requirements, too, like pots or stone axes, may have to be imported. From time to time, also, the worst does happen: typhoons, plagues of insects, or the failure of the rains; people and animals fall sick. Then help is needed from kin and neighbours.

But people are not only forced into sociation by economic necessity or by disaster. Just as there are centrifugal economic forces counteracting the centripetal tendencies of domestic production, centripetal social inter-dependencies are built into the social order: others are needed for marriage, for political security, for ritual purposes, and so on. And in the village, where all are kin, often through several lines of kinship connection, as well as neighbours; one can call on the services of others as a *right* by invoking these ties. Where they do not exist, one can build them, through fictive kinship such as god-parenthood.

This is not to romanticize the village. It was no idyllic *Gemeinschaft*, as Lewis' classic re-analysis of Redfield's study of Tepotzlán long ago demonstrated.[27] It was often necessary to scare not only the birds, but the neighbours from one's crops. But the relationship between the village as a whole and the wider society was fundamentally asymmetrical and exploit-ative. Of crucial importance was the market for the peasant's produce. The most systematic anthropological study, that of Skinner for China, follows

Table 1 Family Members by Age in Successive Years

Year of Family's Existence	Husband	Wife	Age of Children										Number of Persons
			1st	2nd	3rd	4th	5th	6th	7th	8th	9th	
1	25	20	—	—	—	—	—	—	—	—	—	2
2	26	21	1	—	—	—	—	—	—	—	—	3
3	27	22	2	—	—	—	—	—	—	—	—	3
4	28	23	3	—	—	—	—	—	—	—	—	3
5	29	24	4	1	—	—	—	—	—	—	—	4
6	30	25	5	2	—	—	—	—	—	—	—	4
7	31	26	6	3	—	—	—	—	—	—	—	4
8	32	27	7	4	1	—	—	—	—	—	—	5
9	33	28	8	5	2	—	—	—	—	—	—	5
10	34	29	9	6	3	—	—	—	—	—	—	5
11	35	30	10	7	4	1	—	—	—	—	—	6
12	36	31	11	8	5	2	—	—	—	—	—	6
13	37	32	12	9	6	3	—	—	—	—	—	6
14	38	33	13	10	7	4	1	—	—	—	—	7
15	39	34	14	11	8	5	2	—	—	—	—	7
16	40	35	15	12	9	6	3	—	—	—	—	7
17	41	36	16	13	10	7	4	1	—	—	—	8
18	42	37	17	14	11	8	5	2	—	—	—	8
19	43	38	18	15	12	9	6	3	—	—	—	8
20	44	39	19	16	13	10	7	4	1	—	—	9
21	45	40	20	17	14	11	8	5	2	—	—	9
22	46	41	21	18	15	12	9	6	3	—	—	9
23	47	42	22	19	16	13	10	7	4	1	—	10
24	48	43	23	20	17	14	11	8	5	2	—	10
25	49	44	24	21	18	15	12	9	6	3	—	10
26	50	45	25	22	19	16	13	10	7	4	1	11

Table 2 Ratio of Consumers to Workers in Successive Years

Years of Family's Existence	Married Couple	Children									Total in Family		Consumers ÷ Workers
		1	2	3	4	5	6	7	8	9	Consumers	Workers	
1	1.8	–	–	–	–	–	–	–	–	–	1.8	1.8	1.00
2	1.8	0.1	–	–	–	–	–	–	–	–	1.9	1.8	1.06
3	1.8	0.3	–	–	–	–	–	–	–	–	2.1	1.8	1.17
4	1.8	0.3	–	–	–	–	–	–	–	–	2.1	1.8	1.17
5	1.8	0.3	0.1	–	–	–	–	–	–	–	2.2	1.8	1.22
6	1.8	0.3	0.3	–	–	–	–	–	–	–	2.4	1.8	1.33
7	1.8	0.3	0.3	–	–	–	–	–	–	–	2.4	1.8	1.33
8	1.8	0.3	0.3	0.1	–	–	–	–	–	–	2.5	1.8	1.39
9	1.8	0.5	0.3	0.3	–	–	–	–	–	–	2.9	1.8	1.61
10	1.8	0.5	0.3	0.3	–	–	–	–	–	–	2.9	1.8	1.61
11	1.8	0.5	0.3	0.3	0.1	–	–	–	–	–	3.0	1.8	1.66
12	1.8	0.5	0.5	0.3	0.3	–	–	–	–	–	3.4	1.8	1.88
13	1.8	0.5	0.5	0.3	0.3	–	–	–	–	–	3.4	1.8	1.88
14	1.8	0.5	0.5	0.3	0.3	0.1	–	–	–	–	3.5	1.8	1.94
15	1.8	0.7	0.5	0.5	0.3	0.3	–	–	–	–	4.1	2.5	1.64
16	1.8	0.7	0.5	0.5	0.3	0.3	–	–	–	–	4.1	2.5	1.64
17	1.8	0.7	0.5	0.5	0.5	0.3	0.1	–	–	–	4.2	2.5	1.68
18	1.8	0.7	0.7	0.5	0.5	0.3	0.3	–	–	–	4.8	3.2	1.50
19	1.8	0.7	0.7	0.5	0.5	0.3	0.3	–	–	–	4.8	3.2	1.50
20	1.8	0.9	0.7	0.5	0.5	0.3	0.3	0.1	–	–	5.1	3.4	1.50
21	1.8	0.9	0.7	0.7	0.5	0.5	0.3	0.3	–	–	5.7	4.1	1.39
22	1.8	0.9	0.7	0.7	0.5	0.5	0.3	0.3	–	–	5.7	4.1	1.39
23	1.8	0.9	0.9	0.7	0.5	0.5	0.3	0.3	0.1	–	6.0	4.3	1.39
24	1.8	0.9	0.9	0.7	0.7	0.5	0.5	0.3	0.3	–	6.6	5.0	1.32
25	1.8	0.9	0.9	0.7	0.7	0.5	0.5	0.3	0.3	–	6.6	5.0	1.32
26	1.8	0.9	0.9	0.9	0.7	0.5	0.5	0.3	0.3	0.1	6.9	5.2	1.32

Source: Chayanov (1967), Tables 1–4 and 1–5, pp. 57 and 58.

the 'central place' theory developed by Christaller and Losch in Europe and Ch'iao Ch'i-ming, Martin Yang and C. K. Yang in China itself.[28] He shows how each village formed part of a local market zone – which he calls a standard market – at the centre of which was a market town, to which each village in its hinterland brought products for sale, and where goods not produced in the village could be obtained or the services of a carpenter secured. The majority of these standard market zones were 50 kilometres in size, and a peasant could walk the 4.5 kilometres from his village to town in a day. Each standard market, in turn, was articulated to a larger country town serving several such standard marketing areas. Finally, several of these intermediate level zones together formed a central marketing area which was both a wholesaling centre and an administrative capital.

At an even higher level, other writers have argued, the political divisions of China correspond to economic zones whose boundaries were set by topographical features.[29] Thus river valleys formed natural zones of trade with good communications, and became consolidated into economic regions with large cities at their heart. Conversely, the mountainous areas separating one such zone from another were the basis for provincial and other boundaries. Economically marginal, and distant from centres of political power, they were the classic 'no-man's-lands' where bandits and guerrillas could survive. They flourished, in particular, whenever central government was weak or inordinately oppressive. And periodically, when central government collapsed altogether, China flew apart into precisely these segments. But in times of stable government, Skinner observes, this nesting system of markets served to integrate 'myriad peasant communities into the single social system which is the total society'.[30]

Yet there were distinct differences in the functions of the towns at the different levels of the market system. At the lowest level, that of the standard market, markets were periodic rather than permanent, while the villages were further served by itinerant vendors and purveyors of services, such as barbers who toured the countryside on regular circuits. These market-areas were therefore well-integrated economic subcultures, composed, typically, of an inner ring of six villages surrounded by an outer one of twelve, all connected by six paths radiating out from the town. Any increase in trade could be catered for simply by having more market days ('doubling'). In those towns, landlords were paid their rents, and loans were contracted. The economic homogeneity of the area was symbolized by its distinctive system of weights and measures, and even dialect.

But it was not just an economic unit. By the age of fifty, the average peasant had visited his standard market town more than three thousand times. He had a 'nodding acquaintance with every adult in all parts of the marketing system', and 'at least one thousand times on the average, had been jammed into a small area along one street with the same male representative of every other household in that community'.[31] There, over tea, marriages would be contracted. The town, too, was the site of the ancestral halls of the composite lineage and of the temple and the lodges of the secret societies. It was also the centre for annual festivals and fairs and for organized recreation. There one would find '. . . professional story-tellers, theatrical troupes, blind singers, purveyors of games of chance, boxers, jugglers, performing medicine sellers, and magicians'[32] who never came to the villages. The basic unit of social life, therefore, was not the village, but the standard marketing area.

At higher levels in the system, the towns served other functions than those of the standard area towns, differences reflected in differences of structure. Whereas the standard area was a discrete unit in which a number of villages did business with only one town, the towns of each of these standard areas would have dealings, upwards in the chain, with *several* intermediate towns where the market was permanent and the dealers were specialized. In terms of socio-political structure, the standard area town was the level at which a few gentry families, backed by the landlord class as a whole, exerted direct social control over the peasantry, and acted as intermediaries between them and government officials. The intermediate level towns were controlled by gentry and merchants. Both the peasants and mandarins were excluded from this charmed inter-class circle where gentlemen, meeting in tea- and wine-houses, arranged the affairs of the entire district. Economically, they were towns which served this local élite and the artisan class. Industrial goods were only to be found in the central towns, as well as goods mainly of interest to the bureaucratic élite. Politically, they were the point of intersection between these officials and leading regional representatives of the gentry and merchant classes.

The market-system, with its various levels, by no means corresponded neatly, then, in some one-to-one way, with the units and levels of the administrative system, though as one moved upwards, the influence of officials became more and more significant. There were, however, two hierarchies, and if political power was concentrated in one, the market-system connected more deeply and at many more points with the institutions of everyday social life.

Peasant villages in China were thus enmeshed in political and social relationships as well as economic ones far beyond the confines of the village. In other parts of the world, too, interpersonal relations between villagers and traders and others in the towns are often elaborated by various kinds of social ties: they might be members of the same religious fraternity, or consolidate their relationship through marriages, or by sending children to live in the city with relatives. Debt itself is even a mode of continuing relationship, for the shopkeeper by no means wished to see his customers pay off their bills completely: to do so would liquidate the debt that bound them to each other. Credit ensured that the tie endured.[33] And towns were also cultural centres, where children went for advanced schooling, where the family would go once a year to the fair, or the devout on pilgrimage, as well as political centres, where they would interact with the representatives of the State – the tax-collector, the police and the army recruiters.

Chayanov's model was especially strong in explaining the operations of what he called the 'production machine': the family household unit of production. It explained much not only about the economic behaviour of peasants, but also about their psychology that classical economics did not explain. But it shed comparatively little light on extra-village relationships.

The Russian village was much more of what Wolf has called a 'closed corporate' community[34] than the Chinese village. Significantly, the word for village – *mir* – also means 'world', for village life was organized within a very strong corporate institutional structure, quite capable of resolving its own internal disputes without resort to outsiders specialized in the administration of 'justice', from judges to policemen. *Mir* therefore also means 'peace'.[35]

But the Russian village was no 'natural' unit. Such was the cohesion of the Russian village that, over time, it became the basic administrative unit of the State. The Russian countryside thus differed considerably from the Chinese. So great are these differences, from country to country and epoch to epoch, that some commentators have concluded that to talk of 'peasants' in general is futile. A few have relapsed into total empiricism: each peasantry is unique. Most attempt to construct a typology: of *types* of peasantries, plural. Some Marxists attempt to abolish the 'peasantry-in-general' by subsuming them within wider modes of production: they are part of the feudal mode of production, the capitalist mode of production, etc. But this then generates further problems. It still denotes a distinct class of small farmers, but refuses them the same kind of general identity that it freely bestows upon 'feudalism-in-general' or 'capitalism-in-general'. Lenin, for instance, recognized *two* capitalist alternatives in agriculture: the 'Prussian', in which the smallholders become labourers on large estates, and the 'American', in which they become prosperous family-farmers. 'Feudalism', likewise, is a label that has been applied not only to its place of origin – the societies of medieval Europe, and to Japan (where it seems appropriate) – but even to the highly centralized autocracy of Tsarist Russia and the bureaucratic empires of Asia. The Chinese Communists, for instance, still describe Imperial China as a feudal society.

Much of the confusion stems from a confusion of levels: by 'relations of production', some understand the structure of the polity and society as a whole; others the processes and relations or the internal dynamics of Chayanov's production machine of the smallholding peasantry. In reality, there must always be a dialectical interplay between both levels, for all peasant households necessarily conduct their activities within overlapping sets of wider social relations, of which the widest, today, is the international market, and the most politically relevant no longer the lord, but the State.

In Chayanov's Russia, the basic unit of economy and society was the household. It was, to this extent, literally a domestic mode of production. As in primitive society, the well-being of the members of this unit was the main priority. But it was the commune which was the land-owning unit. A commune might include more than one village, and a village might have two or more communes within it. It was the commune which allocated land to the different households in accordance with their needs, estimated by taking into account age and sex composition, numbers, and consumer–worker ratio. Succession to the headship of the family was patrilineal, the eldest male generally being responsible for the management of the household economy. Though he possessed great authority, he had to use it in ways that did not threaten the security of the household's members, and all males possessed theoretical equality which they could use in extreme circumstances, to remove him on grounds of mismanagement. Neither he, then, nor the family, were owners of the land.

Each family was given strips of land in several different fields belonging to the village, and was obliged to cultivate the same crops in the same way at the same points in the year as other strip-owners in the same field. There were two main systems of land tenure: hereditary tenure, in which each household owned a house-and-garden lot, plus strips of ploughland and meadow, and repartitional tenure, in which, by a two-thirds vote, the land in the fields around the village, owned by the community as a whole, could be reallotted, usually every twelve years, in order to take account of changes in family composition and circumstances, since some now needed more, others less. Four-fifths of the peasant lands were held under repartitional tenure, involving three-quarters of all peasant households. But there was considerable overlap between the two systems. Even in the hereditary system, each household was made to follow a common, three-field crop-cycle and plant and harvest the same crops at the same time alongside their neighbours as part of a common operation, after which all could pasture animals on any part of the fields. All, too, had access to common pastures and woodland elsewhere.[36]

The Russian peasantry thus possessed very special characteristics – as do all peasantries. But they are singularly important in one other way: more is known about them, in quantitative terms at least, than any other rural population in history, for despite the recent information explosion in every branch of human knowledge, there is nothing to compare with the no less than four thousand volumes of economic and statistical data on peasant economy that were collected in Russia between the ending of serfdom in 1861 and the First World War.

The analysis of that mountain of information reaches us today mainly via Chayanov, though his intellectual pedigree goes back to pioneers such as Vasilchakov and Engelhardt who wrote at the turn of the century. (Chayanov was arrested under Stalin in 1930 and died in a prison-camp in 1939.) Chayanov, however, must be given the credit for the distillation of the basic principles informing this mode of analysis. The economic behaviour of the peasantry, it was found, followed quite different laws from those assumed by bourgeois classical economic theory. Orthodox economics ('formalist', as we would now say) assumed that the categories it had developed were universally valid and applicable, therefore, in the study of *any* kind of economic system, from primitive hunting to large-scale capitalist industry, slave-plantations, or feudal serfdom. Their critics, the 'substantivists', argued that they were forcing these categories onto reality in a Procrustean way. They might be appropriate in analysing capitalist society, but not for other economic systems which were governed by quite different logics. According to the logic of capitalism, the economic behaviour of the peasantry often seemed to be sheer irrationality. On closer inspection, it turned out to be quite rational, but based on fundamentally different assumptions from those which governed capitalist market calculus, nor could these patterns of behaviour be explained by differences in the size of the farm-unit. Higher prices, for instance, resulted in *lower* production on the part of the peasants; poor peasants bought land at high prices more readily than rich; and so on. The explanation seemed to be, Chayanov concluded, that peasants were guided by a different set of priorities from those which were the motors of capitalism: accumulation, competition, and profit. For them, the top priority was to satisfy the wants of the members of the household, not to make profits. This they could do either by producing for their own consumption directly, or by marketing enough to enable them to buy whatever else they needed. Over and above their fixed wants, however, they did not invest further effort in producing more. Like the tribal domestic mode of production, it was, in Sahlins' words, 'intrinsically an anti-surplus system'.[37]

In Chayanov's analysis, labour was usually a more significant constraint on production than land. But even given more labour, peasants did not produce over and above a culturally-defined norm: in his terminology, they preferred to limit consumption rather than face further drudgery. Drudgery can, of course, be diminished in principle and in practice, by extra inputs of technology or by rationalizing production methods. Such increases in production and productivity, however, do not necessarily lead to improvements in living-standards; landlords and money-lenders may cream off the increase, or, as Geertz' classic study of colonial Java has shown, increased output may be absorbed by rising population. The result is neither progressive improvement of living-standards nor Malthusian disaster, but agricultural *in*volution: more people are enabled to live, but at static consumption levels.[38] In China, the introduction of early-ripening varieties of rice, which made possible more than one crop per annum, and the subsequent introduction of the new American crops – maize, sweet potatoes, Irish potatoes, and peanuts – from the eighteenth century onwards, led to an even more spectacular explosion of population: from 60 million in 1290 to 179 million by 1750.[39] The subsequent slowing-down of both agricultural and industrial growth has been attributed by Elvin to the emergence of a 'high-level energy trap', though Needham's alternative explanation of the general slowing-down of Chinese science as a whole in terms of wider rigidities of social and political structure which set limits upon economic innovation and enterprise seems more convincing.[40]

For Russia, authoritarian social and political structures were such as to make even technological innovation impossible. Most landlords were uninterested in modernizing estates run on serf labour; the minority who were did not have the capital. And for peasants themselves to expand their scale of operation required not just capital, but the abolition of both serfdom and the village commune.

The preconditions for the transformation of agricultural production, then, were political changes at the societal level: at the level of the State. Only then could change in civil society come about. There had to be change in the so-called superstructure, therefore, before changes in the so-called base were possible. In the West, these changes were to eventuate in the victory of capitalism in agriculture, then in industry; in Russia, in the emergence of a State-owned and State-run agriculture and industry. The peasant smallholder, resist as he might, was doomed to extinction one way or the other; a victim of the market or a victim of the State.

To understand the different outcomes in West and East – the road to agribusiness, on the one hand; the road to the collective farm, on the other – we need to examine the historical conditions out of which each emerged; firstly, the nature of the social system out of which capitalism emerged in Western Europe – feudalism; then the very different political culture of Tsarist Russia, where serfdom lived on into the middle of the last century, and royal autocracy only ended in this one.

The Road to Capitalist Agriculture

Modern capitalist agriculture grew up, initially, only in the interstices of a far more widespread manorial system which had lasted hundreds of years, and in which agricultural production took place within a completely different structure of both State and civil society from that which succeeded it in the bourgeois epoch when capitalist relationships had transformed not just the economy but the polity and the entire cultural order of society.

The manorial system was far older than feudalism. It had two wings to it, like most historic forms of agriculture. The large estate-owners were not just economically powerful but dominated local society in all its aspects. They administered justice in their courts; they patronized the church; and they supervised the moral life of the community. Collectively, as a class, they dominated national life, too, though rivalries between the greatest of them inhibited the consolidation of a coherent ruling class at the national level, and to periodic civil wars.

Their estates were worked by peasants who were obliged to give their labour in return for the use of a plot of land which they could cultivate for their own uses. In this dual system, the peasant was, schizophrenically, both smallholder on a family farm and a unit of labour on the lord's estate.

As a whole, the system is generally labelled 'feudalism'. It was thus an economic system, with distinctive institutional arrangements which governed how work was done and who got what. But no economy exists in itself. Production always takes place within political structures. Yet the concept of 'political economy' is still inadequate as a model of the context of agriculture, for the organization of labour and the appropriation of the product were not resolved by force alone, but by reference to cultural conceptions of rights and duties held by the different classes.

Most bourgeois authorities on feudalism have seen it primarily as a political system, a form or 'method of government, not an economic or social system',[41] and where they do discuss social classes do so primarily with reference to the distribution of superior and inferior statuses, and the ways in which they are articulated so as to form an overall system of personal dependence, with particular reference to the ideologies of rank, nobility and estate which inform these structured social inequalities. The crucial units of social structure are not social classes, but estates, while the distinctive political characteristic of feudalism, for them, is what Anderson has described as the 'parcellization' of sovereignty.[42] The feudal State, that is, was a weak State, in which authority was fragmented in several ways: between the Church and the secular polity; between the different estates; between the great nobles; and because, as we will see, several lords claimed authority, often, over the same peasants.

Others, including most Marxists, have insisted that it was primarily a system of *economic* relations between classes. At the end of his classic study of *Feudal Society*, Marc Bloch makes a fundamental distinction between manorialism and feudalism:

Though an essential element in feudal society, the manor was in itself an older institution and was destined to last much longer. In the interests of sound terminology it is important that the two ideas be kept clearly separate.[43]

In that book, he had been concerned primarily with feudalism as a set of overall political, legal and judicial structures and relationships. 'Ties of dependence among the lower orders of society' occupied only thirty-eight pages of that volume. Yet the distinction he insisted upon has commonly been ignored, notably by the protagonists in the great debate as to whether Asian societies were feudal or not.

The debates were of more than terminological importance, indeed, more than academic interest, for they involved differing conceptions of the nature of feudal society. Those who thought of feudalism primarily in economic terms, as a system in which a landlord class extracted rent from peasants by the exercise of extra-economic compulsion, insisted that Asia was feudal. Those who thought of feudalism primarily in terms of political structures simply pointed to the differences between the weak state of medieval Europe and the huge centralized bureaucracy of imperial China, the Ottoman or the Inca Empire. Those for whom European culture was a unique whole simply pointed to the differences between the system of estates in the West and the cosmically-ordained caste-system of Hindu India.

We need, therefore, to take Bloch's advice: to keep clearly in mind the distinction between 'civil society' at the level of the local community, with the village and the lord's estate as its crucial components, and the other level of the State. At the same time, as we will see, these levels are not discrete spheres. The manor and the village were articulated to the lower levels of a State-wide political system, and it was the latter, in turn, which guaranteed the social order of the village. It was a dialectical relationship. Informing the whole were cultural values which justified it as being rational and just not merely in secular but also in religious terms. Yet there was never consensus about rights and duties, and the vision of the peasantry included notions which were quite antithetical to the hegemonic ideology of their lords. Finally, those ideologies themselves were plural. The Roman Catholic Church was itself a house with many mansions, and what the Papacy announced from Rome often carried little weight even within religious orders, which interpreted the word of God in their own way. Venal bishops and ascetic monks were both members of the same Church, and that Church itself the greatest landowner, and its Head a potentate. As for the peasants, their Christianity contained egalitarian as well as millenarian elements that were anathema to the Christianity of the Church and State. There was, moreover, no neat correspondence between the economic, political and cultural spheres, however much they overlapped: it was not a congruent system so much as a field of forces in opposition. The search for a pure form

of feudalism in the historical record is therefore almost as futile as the attempt to find a pure ideal type of Catholicism in reality.

Feudalism, moreover, underwent major changes. From the time when it jelled, the epoch of the 'first feudal age' to the 'nationalized feudalism'[44] of the Absolutist monarchs, both State and civil society changed radically. Some basic components, notably the manorial estate, went back to the *villae* of ancient Rome; others, such as the tenements of land owned by free peasants, to Germanic society. With the break-up of the Roman Empire, former slaves and tenants were now able to convert themselves into independent farmers. But there was a price to be paid for this social freedom and the crumbling of State power: anarchy. Locally, justice often became reduced to the exercise of force. But organized authority on any significant scale was quite inadequate to defend society as a whole against the periodic waves of nomad invaders who swept through Europe, and the more sustained incursions of Norsemen, Muslims and Magyars. It was this *political* insecurity that led people to seek the protection of well-armed 'knights', horsemen who were then the armoured equivalents of the tanks of modern times, much as Japanese villagers hired the services of *samurai* professional fighters. Over time, these relationships grew into a more permanent dependence. The model was a military one, that of a warrior who became 'vassal' of a powerful man who needed fighting men and their political support ('counsel'). He would then bestow upon them a grant of land, usually for life, in order that they could be provided for. Similarly, in principle, peasants freely 'commended' themselves, by entering the service of another free man who thereby became their lord.

Yet these military relationships were principally only significant at the higher levels of the political system, and were notionally limited to forty days per annum in Norman England. The peasant might, indeed, be required to fight, at times. But the fundamental obligation, in time, became that of paying *rent*, either in kind, or in the form of labour services on the lord's demesne estate or in his household. Eventually, only the superior fighting ranks continued to be designated as vassals. But even for them it was no longer principally a military-political status. Great magnates sought to become vassals of the king because of the economic benefits this entailed. Whereas land had been bestowed, originally, to enable the fighting man to do his military service, now vassals would only serve because they expected, and received, a *benefice* in land. The word *benefice* now became increasingly replaced by *fief*, which had originally signified moveable property (usually cattle), and now came to be applied to all kinds of obligations entered into by virtue of holding land from a lord, and even to the obligations due to various kinds of holders of public office, such as mayors or priests, who might, for example, hold the right to levy tolls. By now, as Ganshof puts it, 'services were being rendered only in return for a benefice instead of the other way round',[45] and the crucial obligation was that of paying rent. 'A social structure founded on service', Bloch concludes, had given way to a 'system of land rent'.[46] Unpaid labour was exacted from the peasants in innumerable forms: the duty of working on the lord's estate, of course, but also the provision of chickens, beeswax, firewood or corn. The lord also strove to monopolize commercial opportunities, making the peasants grind their corn at his mill, or reserving to himself the right to sell beer. Rent and its extraction had become the *raison d'être* of the system; the struggle over rent its central contradiction.

Formal reciprocity, Gouldner has shown, can become a mystification of *de facto* inequality.[47] The ideology of vassalage was that of a contractual relationship, freely entered into, symbolized in the ritual act of homage, in which the vassal placed his hands between those of his lord and swore an oath of fealty, sealed with a kiss. And the vassal was still a free man with the right to seek justice in courts other than that of his lord. The reality, for the powerless, was one of increasing subordination. Class struggle took place between lord and peasant mainly over rent in all its forms. At times of labour shortage (exceptionally so following the Black Death) lords sought to increase labour obligations, and used their power over the State to discipline their workers. In 1349 and 1351, for instance, legislation was introduced in Parliament to restrict wage increases and prevent the mobility of labour. Later, as agriculture became more commercialized and money was needed to purchase commodities the estate could not supply or to finance trading ventures, there was pressure to pay in money.

There was also class struggle over the ownership of the land itself, or over access to the use of it. Vassals tried to convert the lands they were granted into their own private property; lords attempted to resume land. A singularly favourable opportunity presented itself whenever a tenant died, for the ideology of lord–tenant relationships was that of a *personal* contact. In principle, the relationship ended with the tenant's death, and the lord might then bestow the land upon another, or retain it for his own use. Yet in practice benefices became hereditary as both peasants and vassals of higher rank clung to what had become customary rights. Lords were still able, though, to use the occasion of investiture to exact a special payment. Despite these attempts to maintain control over the disposition of the fief, land often fell into the hands of others, especially when the heir was a minor. The unscrupulous would then get themselves nominated as their representatives, particularly in the case of rich heiresses, who, despite their rank, were minors in law *ob imbecillitatem sexis*. Class struggle now took the form of competing conceptions and interpretations of kinship rights and duties and rules of inheritance. Lords might try to insist that vassalage was 'a relationship that dominated all other human ties',[48] but peasants gave priority to more primordial loyalties of kinship, especially the bonds between parents and children, partitioning their holdings between several children in defiance of the lord's attempt to keep the fief in one piece. Several children would now be responsible for the holding of the land, a situation which obviously allowed for evasion and conflict over who was responsible for what. These attempts to maintain feudal obligations, and the resistance they encountered, were paralleled by the struggle over free allodial lands, which the lords constantly tried to convert into fiefs. By extending the doctrine of *nulle terre sans seigneur*, jurists in Germany even argued that since, in principle, all lands, even allodial lands, were fiefs, the latter were fiefs 'of the sun' (*Sonnenlehen*)![49]

Feudal theory thus postulated a consistent hierarchy in which a graded system of rights over land corresponded with differences of personal status and in which political power was exercised at each successively higher level over those below, culminating in the king at the apex.

These ideological conflicts were expressions of very material basic conflicts of interests. In a forty-acre Mecklenberg farm in fourteenth- and fifteenth-century Germany, for instance, over half the grain harvested would be reserved for seed and for feeding the horses; of the remaining 4000 lb, more than half (2700) would go to the landlord. Only about an eighth (1300) was left to feed the family.[50] Under such pressures, evasion of obligations to one's superior at all levels, the search for ways of adding to the land available for cultivation, and, in the extreme, more open forms of resistance were built into the system.

One strategy was to hold land from several lords at once. A man might also hold land from a variety of *kinds* of superior: from religious institutions as well as secular lords, together with some allodial land all of his own. This plurality of allegiances resulted in a fragmentation of power and loyalty which was easily exploited. It was no longer a system in which authority formed an unbroken and unambiguous chain. One solution was to define a *liege* lord, superior to the rest, a role particularly sought after by the king.

But kings sought this pre-eminence precisely because of the limits on their own power. Indeed, Anderson has argued, it was precisely the apex that was the weakest point in the system.[51] This parcellization of sovereignty was the reality that contradicted those images of society portrayed in medieval paintings, in which society is represented as neatly divided into estates and ranks which are the earthly counterparts of the angels and archangels, the seraphim and cherubim of the heavenly order, with the king as the point of intersection between both worlds.

In fact, he could normally only rely on the resources of his own estates and followers. Tolls, fines, levies, payments at investiture, plus less legitimate exactions, were intermittent and inadequate. The great bankers, in the end, had to be paid. These resources apart, the king could only *request* his vassals to supply men, money and services. His authority was qualified, below, by the political power of the Estates, which had to approve major taxation; above, by the immaterial power of the Church. Legitimate succession to the throne, confirmed through the religious rituals of anointment and investiture, therefore by no means meant that the juridical position of the monarch as *primus inter pares* could be translated into command over the material resources of great magnates as rich as himself, who exercised powers normally attributed to the State in their own domains, and who could call upon their vassals to back them up with armed force if necessary. It was a weak, segmented State founded on a relationship so *personalized* that a vassal did not recognize that he had any obligations even to the lord of whom his own lord was a vassal.

Thus however much kings might claim ultimate authority, or to be the only true allodist, there was scarcely any independent State apparatus, whether of finance or military force, which could enable them to convert these grandiose claims into reality.[52] In his own domains, the feudal lord might or might not have the right delegated to him to exercise judicial functions. But whether he did or not, larger princes and counts established and strengthened their jurisdiction – often in the name of the king – and lesser lords imitated them.

But feudal society was not exclusively agrarian. Ancient trading towns and cities in the Mediterranean, as well as those founded under the Roman Empire, survived the collapse of Rome, albeit weakened, since Europe, by that time, was a very undeveloped zone when compared to the gigantic civilizations of the Near and Far East, of Central America and the Andes, and of Africa. The revival of trade was only a gradual process, contingent not so much upon technological innovation as upon the establishment of political security. In the absence of a strong State, towns and cities often had to provide that security themselves by developing into powerful city-states. Yet even those which formed part of a wider feudal polity were such valuable sources of revenue to monarchs with no permanent source of regular finance that merchants and guilds were able to secure charters from the king that effectively delegated control over the affairs of these urban enclaves to their collective authority as municipal corporations. Though the strengthening of the State and the revival of internal and international trade thus went hand-in-hand, the merchant class won considerable political autonomy in the process.

Capitalism also developed in agriculture. Far from maturing only in the sixteenth and seventeenth centuries, Macfarlane has argued, capitalism – or what he more often calls 'individualism' – can be found already flourishing 'as far back as the "golden age" of European peasantry . . . the thirteenth century':

From at least the thirteenth century the majority of ordinary people . . .

were rampant individualists, highly mobile, both geographically and
socially, economically 'rational', market-oriented and acquisitive, ego-
centred in kinship and social life.[53]

He claims that, 'There was a very considerable land market . . . from at least
the late fourteenth century', and 'in certain areas . . . most land was
transmitted by sale rather than by inheritance'. Multi-generational households were probably only an ideal or a phase in the life-cycle of some kinds of
family, which, by the fourteenth century had become atomized. The
connection between family and land had gone 'by or soon after the Black
Death'. The rules of patrilineal inheritance and the norms of kinship were
therefore often flouted: fathers disinherited their eldest sons (often by
selling the property); children failed to support their aged parents; women
and not only males could and did inherit. Nor was the village community a
'self-sufficient, self-contained, natural unit'. Production was not domestic,
either. By the thirteenth century a body of landless or almost landless
labourers had emerged; by the later fourteenth century, well over half the
adult able-bodied male population in East Anglia were servants or
labourers. The pattern of class differentiation therefore began to resemble
that of the classic capitalist profile. By the later fourteenth century 'the
peasantry had . . . vanished', and 'About one-third of all English land was
. . . copyhold in the early seventeenth century'.[54]
    It is a scintillating attack upon virtually every major authority on medieval
Europe from Marx and Weber to Vinogradoff, Maitland, Kosminsky, and
contemporary Marxists such as Hilton and Hill.
    No one escapes his lash as he denounces their central mistake: the notion
that medieval Europe was a peasant society. Unfortunately, they never said
it was. What they did say was that it was a *feudal* society. What he is
attacking, therefore, is a straw man created by himself out of materials
provided by Chayanov. The value of his outline of the growth of capitalist
relations within feudal society is particularly vitiated by the disappearance
from the scene of the most important figure in the medieval play: the feudal
lord; and by the omission of any serious discussion of the central class-
relationship: that between lords and peasants, or of the central mode of
exploitation built into that relationship – rent.
    Yet he points to trends that were to become ever more pronounced, and
ultimately dominant: the disappearance of serfdom, as lords commuted
their rights in return for cash; the consequent emergence of a sizeable class
of prosperous yeoman farmers, engaged in production for the market; and
the transformation of large estates worked by serf labour into techno-
logically-advanced enterprises managed according to capitalist rationality
and worked by wage-labour. None of this could be accomplished without
sustained class struggle, in which the attempt to introduce new modes of

relationship met with resistance not only on the part of an entrenched landowning class struggling to maintain its traditional powers, but also by peasants leaving the loss of their traditional access to common lands and other rights embodied in customary law. In Eastern Europe, the nobility were successful in restoring a 'second serfdom'. Even in the West, new manufacturing or mining activities on the lord's estate were often developed by serf labour. But the main growing source of labour, in both town and countryside, was the 'free' labour of those who had lost their land altogether.

Many of them dreamed of getting it back, and were even prepared to fight to do so. Those who still had their smallholdings also resisted the growing exactions of lords in bloody *jacqueries* and even large-scale peasant wars. Counter-violence was equally freely used to contain them. But the manipulation of cultural belief was another mode of social control, notably through the intervention of a Church which identified with other large landowners and saw itself as the spiritual guardian of order, but also because, over the centuries, peasants themselves had internalized ideologies which formed part of the cultural hegemony of the ruling class. For John Ball and his followers, the anointed king was the source of justice. If one could only reach him, he would understand and respond to his subjects' genuine grievances at the disturbance of traditional norms. Richard II acted his part to perfection. Facing the rebels at Mile End, he first consented to abolish serfdom, and promised an amnesty. Then, when one of his squires had cut down Wat Tyler, he persuaded the peasants to depart, crying, 'Sirs, will you shoot your king? I will be your chief and captain, you shall have from me that which you seek.'

The fragility of the State when faced with threats of this magnitude could only be overcome by fundamental change in the entire institutional structure of State and civil society. The key changes were classically defined by Weber[55]: the definitive centralization of political power in the hands of the monarch; the establishment of a new and efficient machinery of administration; the breaking of opposition and the marshalling of the nobility behind a king who was now Absolute Monarch.

These changes took centuries to introduce and consolidate, and occurred at different times and at different tempi in different countries. The legacy of the past was a crucial variable. In England, where the last private battle between great lords took place in 1470 and where the last great private castle was built in 1521, the royal power established at the Conquest made the task of constructing a centralized bureaucracy by Thomas Cromwell less difficult than in France. There, it was a process stretched out over centuries from its beginnings in the reign of Louis XI to its further consolidation by Colbert and Richelieu, only reaching its climax in the reign of the Sun King. In Germany, where the princes retained their autonomy, a centralized nation-state was not to emerge until the nineteenth century.

The construction of Absolutism began in all the pioneer countries in the fifteenth century: under Louis XI in France, Henry VIII in England, Ferdinand and Isabella in Spain, and Maximilian I in the Holy Roman Empire. The crucial institutional innovations were the establishment of standing armies by recruiting and paying mercenaries, in place of feudal levies; the construction of a permanent bureaucratic machinery from sale of offices; and the elevation of secular Roman Law over Church and customary legal codes so as to guarantee the inviolability of private property and the fulfilment of contracts – a legal framework which extended beyond the bounds of the State to provide an umbrella for international as well as internal trade. The growth of inter-state relations further required a new machinery of diplomacy.

None of this took place without widespread resistance, especially on the part of provincial lords who led movements of regional revolt backed by peasants who also feared the loss of their traditional rights. But despite fears over the commutation of rights over labour into money-rents, the nobility was eventually won over, and consolidated as a class, through the endorsement by the State of their local political authority over the peasantry and the strengthening of their economic title to absolute ownership of the land.

Under the Absolutist monarchy, capitalist enterprise thus flourished in both town and countryside. The urban bourgeoisie grew in size and power and moved into manufacture, employing wage-labour in enterprises of increasing size and technological sophistication. Now textile and coal-mining industries could grow up precisely because they were not subject to the monopolies of the guilds granted by the State that inhibited similar expansion in other branches of industry. Commercial agriculture and the expansion of international trade provided increased scope not only for owners of large estates but for the numerous class of small farmers.

The interests of all these classes now became increasingly incompatible with that of an authoritarian monarchy that sought, on the one hand, to limit their growth and autonomy, on the other, to siphon off as much of their new wealth as possible. In England, the clash came with the civil war of 1641–9. With the king's defeat, central power, together with taxation, became the prerogative of Parliament. The dismantling of the machinery of royal bureaucracy through which the king had controlled society was, in Hill's words, 'the most decisive single event in the whole of British history'.[56] Internally, the central government did away with manufacturing mono-polies, thereby opening the economy to competition. The excise, a tax on commodities in general use, replaced levies on manufacturing and royal tributary dues, together with the assessment, a tax on landed estates. The poor were made the responsibility of local authorities, leaving labour at the mercy of those who employed them. But overseas, State support for trading companies was strengthened, notably in the charter granted to the East India Company in 1657. The way was now open for the expansion of overseas trade. Under the Navigation Act of 1651, the colonies were brought under the authority of Parliament, and trade to them made a monopoly of British shipping. From then onwards, the expansion of England's colonial activity was to steadily outstrip that of the Dutch, and eventually of France too.

Parliament now governed the country, but the gentry governed the countryside. 'The Middle Ages were brought to an end' in agriculture, Hill writes, 'in 1646 by the abolition of feudal tenures and the Court of Wards.'[57] Now it was no longer possible to levy arbitrary death-duties; estates were no longer subject to despoliation through wardship. It was now worth while investing capital in the land and preventing the fragmentation of the patrimony. 'Strict settlement' according to primogeniture was now established so that the eldest son could inherit, maintain and develop the estate.

But downwards, there were no such new freedoms. Copyholders did not acquire absolute legal security of tenure and remained liable to arbitrary death duties, and therefore even eviction, as determined by their landlords. Freeholders were equally insecure. Regressive excise taxes ensured that it would be the less affluent who bore the brunt of supplying the State's revenues, rather than a land-tax which the propertied would have paid. Finally, the gentry controlled the militia and rural local government.

Society was now controlled by a bourgeoisie with two wings: the merchants of the towns and the bourgeoisified aristocracy, an economic and social intermarriage of rank with money, in which landlords invested in land. The restored constitutional monarchy was the embodiment of this class compromise in which the power to elect and be elected to Parliament was made contingent upon property qualifications as the only way to keep the common people at bay.

The history of each capitalist country, Moore has shown, was fundamentally conditioned not merely by the way industrialization took place (with advantages of backwardness going to the late-comers who were able to introduce the latest technology), but also by the way agriculture was modernized, particularly whether it occurred from above, via State action, in response to market opportunities, or as a result of social and political pressures from below.[58] In France, it came about through the revolutionary dispossession of the landed aristocracy. So many peasants acquired land that their existence seemed to Marx to provide a key to the strange phenomenon of Bonapartism, for the persistently revolutionary urban working class was counterbalanced by a mass of peasants who lacked *class* organization and revolutionary consciousness (so many 'potatoes in a sack'), but repeatedly provided mass support for leaders who promised to act on their behalf.

This view of peasant inability to take class action is, of course, misguided.

Nor was the experience of the English peasantry paradigmatic for other European peasantries – even less for the peasantries of colonized countries. Even as early as the thirteenth century, 40 per cent of the arable land in central England had been held by *free* tenants, of whom half were smallholders, while the unfree paid more than half their dues in *money*. The by-laws, the customary rules which regulated 'the gathering of the harvest, including times of reaping, entitlement to gleaning, pasturing of beasts on the stubble [as well as] blocking of ditches, repair of fences and harbouring of strangers';[59] were made by the village community, not imposed by the lord's steward. They indicate a flourishing peasant political subculture, capable of mounting the kind of defence of its rights which reached its high-water mark in 1381. But the subsequent spread of capitalist relations in agriculture divided the peasant community, opening new market opportunities which the more fortunate and entrepreneurial seized but which left the rest exposed to the winds. The last peasant revolt occurred in 1549. By the seventeenth century, the English peasantry had 'ceased to exist as a homogenous class'. Increasing numbers of yeoman farmers and the better-off husbandmen, producing food for the market on farms they owned or rented, and taking the profits, existed side by side with larger capitalist farmers who employed a large labour-force made up of those who had no option but to work for others. But the situation was to change dramatically between 1760 and 1830. By 1830, the peasantry had been replaced by an agricultural proletariat in a thoroughly unfeudal countryside. By 1780, Hill notes, 'we are in the world of *urban* radical discontent'.[60]

Nemesis for the peasantry involved the use of both the violence of the State and landlord violence.

Laissez-faire ideology postulated (and celebrated) the gradual displacement of the less efficient by the more efficient producer as a purely economic process, the consequence of the small producer's inability to compete by reducing his production costs. Nothing could be a less appropriate description of the process by which the capitalist agricultural revolution was brought to its climax in Britain, for it was the political use of the State's monopoly of the means of violence and the domination of that State by the bourgeoisie and the landed aristocracy which were central. In the 1770s, in Arthur Young's phrase, 'open war' was launched against the cottages: social violence so extreme that it 'was easier to emigrate than to resist'.[61] Where there was opposition, resort to extra-legal coercion went hand in hand with legal eviction and legal enclosure through Acts of Parliament, a process that had been going on for hundreds of years, but which was now speeded up. From the end of the seventeenth century, lower prices drove freeholders under in the competition with new capitalist estates formed out of land formerly rented but now consolidated by landlords, and by the taking over of common land.

The new consolidated estates could now be transformed into modern enterprises by introducing the latest scientific techniques and rational capitalist management, forcing the labourers to work every day of the year. More labour might be needed on these new estates, but wages began to fall from about 1765. The majority of the dispossessed had little alternative other than to move to the cities. There, for freeborn men and women, the factory represented not only a new and more vicious form of exploitation, with not merely an unfamiliar work discipline, but a loss of customary freedoms: 'to go to a factory was to surrender their birthright'.[62] Their frustration and resentment at 'wage-slavery' took the form of what one historian has called 'collective bargaining by riot', attacks on the implements and symbols of the new urban system – plug-riots and machine breaking.

In the countryside, resistance to dispossession was often fierce and protracted, organized class war rather than class struggle which continued long after the defeat of Napoleon. Rural terrorism – rick-burning, 'Captain Swing' threatening letters to landlords, and attacks on their agents, were met with counter-terror.[63] In the towns, Jacobin conspiracies and illegal 'combinations' were crushed by the use of police, troops, the bourgeoisie in arms (the militia) and spies.[64] Significantly, the urban resistance looked back to the countryside from which people had come only recently: to the world they had lost. As long ago as the civil war, Gerald Winstanley, the communist Leveller, had expressed the traditional pre-industrial world-view 'that wage-labourers had no share in their own country, and that wage-labour should be abolished'.[65] A century and a half later, the special significance of the loss of the land, and hatred of the landed aristocracy by ex-peasant workers in the towns manifested themselves in the Chartist Land Plan and in urban support for the Tolpuddle Martyrs.

Both rural and urban resistance were broken. But though the economic revolution wrought by capitalism had been an 'agricultural revolution in the first instance',[66] Britain, replacing manufacture by machinofacture, was to become the workshop, not the granary of the world. By 1770 grain was being imported to feed the cities. After the repeal of the Corn Laws, it was the USA which was to become the new world source of cheap grain.

By the time the new urban working class was emerging as a political force, the peasantry had been abolished.

The Road to the Collective Farm

Russian art at its greatest has been a societal art. From *War and Peace* to *Doctor Zhivago*, its writers have presented a vision of society as a whole and of the gigantic social transformations it has undergone, within which individuals struggle to express themselves and maintain some autonomy. In music, the great operas are, similarly, massive canvases. Moussorgsky's *Khovantschina*, for instance, opens with the Streltsy Guardsmen terrorizing the citizenry in the streets of Moscow, brutalizing women, Germans, priests, a scrivener: the innocent and defenceless. There is little here of the individual 'bourgeois' hero of Western Romantic novel or the quiet voice of a purely personal poetry. These differences of cultural theme and style are not, then, accidental: they are part and parcel of societal differences which go back centuries, probably to the Roman Empire.

The division of Europe into West and East that we are so conscious and fearful of today is not something that came about in 1945. It is, of course, possible to exaggerate these differences. In both regions, the landowning class was given control by the State over the mass of small peasants. But the peasantry in the East remained not just peasants, but serfs; in Russia, until 1861, ten years after the Crystal Palace Exhibition. Further, the State was a 'service State' which enforced obedience and service upon the nobility as ruthlessly as the latter exercised their power over their serfs. It had not always been thus: ties of feudal dependence and authority had been weakly developed East of the Elbe. The subjugation of the nobility to the autocratic power began, with barbarous cruelty, under Ivan the Terrible in the sixteenth century. Under Peter the Great, the nobility was reorganized into a system of fourteen ranks, in which duties were more important than rights, and every nobleman made to serve in the army, the navy, or in civil administration. Those who failed to do so, even those of highest rank, might be beaten or flogged into submission: they were servitors, not vassals.[67] Rank depended not on the size of one's estates but on the position occupied in the hierarchy of State offices. Since the Tsar also controlled the towns and international trade, a substantial and autonomous urban bourgeoisie never developed. Where serfdom disappeared in the West, then, it was consolidated in the East.[68]

But the consolidation of these 'hyper-centralized' Absolutisms cannot simply be attributed to these economic relationships. The 'second serfdom', Anderson points out, occurred in Russia and Poland *before* the growth of autocratic power in those countries, while in Poland, where the aristocracy was particularly unrestrained in its power over the peasantry, their numbers and their power of *liberum veto* enabled them to control a State which resembled a 'nobiliary republic' more than an Absolutist monarchy.

 World-system theorists connect the rise of Absolutism in the East to the growth of an international division of labour in which Eastern Europe became a colonial zone, underdeveloped in the interests of the West, as a source of grain and other raw materials. Yet this trade *caused* neither the Absolutist monarchy nor the second serfdom, and in Russia, in any case, was of limited size.

Far more significant than such economic factors was the political necessity of sustained military resistance, over centuries, in enormous regions without obvious natural boundaries, against the threats from Asia – from the Tatars to the Turks (which still underlies Russian attitudes to China today) – and the very different threat from modernizing countries on the western frontiers, notably Sweden. Extreme militarization was therefore characteristic of Eastern Absolutism, from Prussia to Russia: the drill-sergeant and the knout.

Secondly, the frontier provided the possibility of escape from the lord's oppression analogous to the role played by the city in the West, where the air of the city, it was said, made men free (*stadtluft macht frei*). The Russian peasant, Maynard has written, was therefore

> . . . a peasant with a difference, a peasant in whom the nomad survived until yesterday, as much at home in Asia as in Europe . . . There is something in him of the land-sailor, with a range of Minsk to Vladivostok, and with some of that flexibility of mind which a sailor acquires. The land led him on, as the inland sea led on the sailor, from headland to headland.[69]

'Beyond the last stockade', Robinson writes, using several American analogies,

> there was a no-man's-land that drew out to itself many a free-hearted peasant who had no taste for the obligations of the serf. Here, with an admixture of Tatar nomads, these adventurers formed the wild self-governing communities of the Don, the Dnieper, and the Volga, and attacked with almost equally good will the manorial estates to the northward and the Tatar towns to the south. It is here among these Cossacks of the open border that one must look for the Daniel Boones and the Davy Crocketts of Russian history.[70]

Their ready resort to arms, he writes, was as 'natural as [it was] that the Sioux and Apaches should attack the wagon-trains of the American frontier'. But when they made common cause with peasants who had already been enserfed on the other side of the frontier, the threat to the State was serious. It was as 'if the Indians of the American west [had] formed an effective alliance with the Negro slaves of the South'. To prevent that happening, the Cossacks were converted, with difficulty, into élite mounted regiments, and let loose, when required, on the peasantry.

Since labour was by far the scarcest factor of production, not land, control over that labour, whether on the frontier or elsewhere, became the *sine qua non* of the system of exploitation. Though the external threat diminished, the hyper-centralized State was to remain in existence as the instrument that guaranteed that control. The aristocracy, in consequence, despite the control exercised over them, rarely revolted, for their interests as a class were protected, and during the imitative Enlightenment of Catherine the Great, their obligation to serve the State was finally removed in 1762. Not until the younger nobility was infected with the liberalism of the French Revolution, in the Decembrist conspiracy of 1825, when the flower of the aristocracy was cut down, was there to be any serious challenge from the aristocracy. Land could not be sold without serfs, nor serfs without the land they were tied to. The peasantry, by contrast, periodically shook the regime to its foundations in revolts of gigantic scale, disaffected because modernization, to them, meant the loss of customary rights and the intensification of landlord oppression. In 1666, the very Church itself was split in a Schism which expressed itself in disputes over ritual but was rooted in social antagonisms. The Old Believers, predominantly peasants, clung to the practices and beliefs of the past, and saw the Tsar, the source of all this innovation, as Anti-Christ. But they dreamed of a future earthly kingdom which would be ruled by a *just* Tsar, a notion found in so many times and places, of which the English Peasant Rising of 1381 or the procession of workers led by Father Gapon to the Tsar which sparked off the 1905 Revolution (and was bloodily dispersed) are only two of the better-known and more significant historical examples.

The violent rebellions, notably the great Pugachev Revolt of 1773–5, were stamped out in blood; Pugachev himself was roasted alive in a red-hot cage like the Anabaptist leaders of the communist Reign of the Saints in Münster during the German Reformation. But the dissenting sects survived and flourished. Schisms, however, now took place among the schismatics. The Old Believers split into two wings, and one of these into further subdivisions. Enthusiastic sects now multiplied: newer and more intransigent bands of zealots like the Doukhobor 'Spirit-wrestlers', the Stranniki 'Wanderers', or the Molokany 'milk-drinkers'. Though some might primarily emphasize unorthodox ritual practices (the Molokany, for instance, drank milk on fast-days), others went in for ascetic denial of the flesh; the Khlysti flagellating themselves, the Skoptsy practising self-mutilation, with castration for the truly devout. In doing so, they brought down upon themselves the wrath of the Orthodox Church and invited the intervention of the State. But some went further, and deliberately challenged a State which they regarded as having *no* rights over true Christians. The distinction between the things of Caesar and the things of Christ, for them, had no meaning. There was only one true law, that of God. The State had no right to conscript people for the army and require them to kill other human beings, or to oblige them to pay taxes or carry passports. Many withdrew into separate communities; extremists advocated the abolition even of fixed places of abode. Some were even forced into exile.[71]

But most stayed, and their numbers increased. By the time of the

Revolution of 1917, they constituted no less than a tenth of the population. Among these peasants, millenarian dreams of creating an egalitarian society made up of spiritual communities of the faithful were infinitely more widespread than the Western doctrines of liberalism and socialism which appealed to the intelligentsia and the growing, secularized working class.

A Diversion: The 'Asiatic' Mode of Production

The profundity of these economic, political and cultural differences as between Eastern and Western Europe impressed all those who moved between the two regions as deeply as the differences between the agrarian order of the English countryside and that of continental countries had impressed travellers who knew both in the early modern period.[72] For those who first visited the real East in person, or confronted it intellectually, Asian societies seemed different in kind from those of Europe, so different that a theory of Asiatic society-in-general began to emerge and swiftly became the reigning theoretical orthodoxy. It has been a diversion in three senses: it was an intellectual blind alley; politically, it misdirected, and continues to misdirect intellectual energies; thirdly, it is diverting in that the conceptual inflation and slippage involved, to use Anderson's terms, have assumed comic rather than tragic proportions.

Though the theme goes back to the Greek encounter with the Persian Empire, it became of renewed importance to Europe with the Ottoman thrust which was only halted at Vienna in 1683. Enlightenment thinkers like Voltaire, Diderot, and Montesquieu subsequently drew upon both classical Antiquity and upon the descriptions of societies encountered by European explorers in the eighteenth century, to develop a comparative sociology which tried to distinguish between the special attributes of European society and those of other times and regions, providing at the same time a critical vision of alternative cultural arrangements and possibilities. If Montesquieu formulated these differences in terms of a generalized model of 'Oriental despotism', others, such as Hegel, were to suggest significant variations on that theme, notably the difference between the undifferentiated despotism of China and the hierarchical despotism of the Indian caste-system. But both of these despotisms were different in kind from despotism in the West. In the East, 'only one person was free, and even that one, being given to the exercise of caprice and not freedom, was a despot and not a free man',[73] whereas the European State was to reach its apogee in a Prussian monarchy embodying Reason exercised in the interests of the whole of the body politic.

This untrammelled concentration of power itself, however, was merely an epiphenomenon, the consequence, it was thought, of the lack of private property, particularly in land. It was also the cause of stagnation: of an *unchanging* society and polity. An alternative explanation, proffered by Adam Smith,[74] replaced the geographical determinism of Montesquieu with a technological determinism: the State's political power was the result of its central role in building, maintaining and regulating the use of enormous hydraulic systems – 'tanks' in India, canals in China – which were central to irrigation-agriculture and, in the latter case, constituted major transport-routes.[75] A later generation of economists, basing themselves on contemporary reports written mainly by officials of the East India Company, did not add much to these notions, but were to be of special significance because they influenced the thinking of Marx and Engels and thereby that of their intellectual and political descendants. They have remained important, too, because they have seemed, to some, to offer a non-Eurocentric explanation for Asian backwardness. Yet the model is quite compatible with the arrogant ethnocentric chauvinism expressed by Macaulay, himself a member of the Supreme Council of the East India Company, for whom 'the history of England' was 'emphatically the history of progress' . . .,

> . . . the history of a consistent movement of the public mind, of a constant change in the institutions of a great society. We see that society, at the beginning of the twelfth century, in a state more miserable than the state in which the most degraded nations of the East now are . . . We see the most debasing and cruel superstition exercising boundless dominion over the most elevated and benevolent minds. We see the multitude sunk in brutal ignorance, and the studious few engaged in acquiring what did not deserve the name of knowledge. In the course of seven centuries the wretched and degraded race have become the greatest and most highly civilized people that ever the world saw, have spread their dominion over every quarter of the globe.[76]

'A single shelf of a good European library', to him, 'was worth the whole native literature of India and Arabia.' When the news reached him of the performance of an operation on a human body by a European-trained doctor for the first time, he ordered the guns of Fort William to be fired as a salute to the triumph of Western science over Eastern superstition.

Serious scholars like Weber were to attempt to invest the theory with a more rigorous content by postulating a relationship between the eventual universal dominance of the Western spirit of capitalism and its failure to develop as the dominant ethic East of Suez. A modern disciple expresses it well, but far more arrogantly:

> Only in advanced Western societies is the detached and systematic approach to social (and perhaps also to natural) phenomena at all commonly adopted – or adoptable.[77]

The image of the backward East is lodged as deep in the European subconscious as it is in scientistic ideologies of this kind. It calls for a mighty intellectual leap: the omission of the evidence that the cultures of Central America, China and the Near East were far more advanced, for centuries, than anything Europe had to show:

> The Islamic Empire of the Abbasid Caliphate had . . . been the richest and most powerful civilization in the world, in the 8th and 9th centuries; the Chinese empire of the Sung epoch was unquestionably the wealthiest and most advanced economy on the globe in the 11th and 12th centuries . . . It is possible that Chinese iron output in the 11th century was approximately equivalent to total European production at the start of the 18th century . . . By 1100 China possessed perhaps as many as five cities with a population over 1,000,000.[78]

Nor was this lead anything new. Yet Europeans of the imperialist epoch asserted their new-found superiority by creating an image of the world outside Europe as devoid of history. 'Hydraulism' was never popular as an explanation of the causes of what they conceived of as '2000 years of stagnation'. It was the payment of rent to the *State* that seemed to Richard Jones the clue to the whole thing, an idea which appealed mightily to minds saturated with *laissez-faire* ideology. The absence of private property in land, especially in India, had its logical complement in the belief that the land had always been collectively *cultivated*. Some dissented from this view: private property in land, they showed, had existed for millennia; the unit of production, typically, was the family household. A Select Committee noted of India as early as 1810 that, 'The land in general appears to have constituted a clear private property, more ancient, and probably more perfect, than that of England.'[79]

But Mill expressed and popularized the view which was to win out, both because it fitted Europe's stereotypes of the East they had conquered and explained that conquest. It was not just intellectually appealing, but was consonant with British colonial interest, in that it provided a rationale for the Company's authorities to levy their own taxes on the peasantry, and justified the intervention of the State, not just to maintain the existing socio-economic order, but, now, to change it along new, capitalist lines. In order to stimulate production and productivity, agrarian relations were fundamentally re-structured. Under the Permanent Settlement of 1793 in Bengal, *zamindars*, originally Mughal military officers with armed followers who were licensed to collect taxes from the conquered peasantry, were converted into land*owners*. But it was to be a colonial form of capitalism, replacing Mughal political controls by British ones. There was to be no enrichment or autonomy for the smallholding peasants, for the *ryots* were turned into tenants with no permanent title to the soil, but with the obligation to pay greatly increased taxes.

Marx and Engels, saturated with the evolutionary schematism of a century mesmerized by Darwin's victory in the field of natural science, swallowed these 'authoritative' accounts wholesale. Yet there were so many different versions, that they, too, naturally oscillated, inconsistently, between a materialist (actually technological-reductionist) emphasis on hydraulism, an economistic model of the village, a theory of the State in the East as a phenomenon of conquest, and so forth.

By now, the model of the village had taken on new dimensions and was becoming more salient in models of Asiatic society. In the remote past, it was now argued, the land had belonged neither to thc State nor to the individual cultivator, but to the village *community* as a whole, as a corporation. The claim of the sovereign to ultimate rights was therefore merely a rhetorical or ideological one. Though Marx did know, and admitted, that private title in land had existed in India, and certainly in Japan, he put all that to one side.

The village community, obviously, was not just an agrarian entity; every village contained its specialist artisans and providers of services. Politically, it might be democratic or despotic in its internal constitution. But economically, all these occupations only constituted separate branches of an overall division of labour. Both peasants and craftsmen, however, produced mainly for their own immediate needs. It was a self-sufficient economy of use-value, which would have produced little for exchange, had it not been for the intervention of the State, which levied taxes, in grain and in the form of handicraft goods, which it then fed into the wider market via the cities. Without the State's pressure the surpluses would not have been produced, let alone reach the market. Politically, it was the State, then, that connected villages – each a 'separate community or republic' – which otherwise would have remained 'disconnected atoms'.[80]

The cities therefore differed in kind from Greek and Roman cities, which had bccn seats of landholders, and from the medieval towns of Europe which had been centres of trade under the privileged authority of the merchants and the guilds. They were, rather, central places of *political* authority, in which the only interest in and connection to the villages was the periodic exaction of tribute. These agricultural surpluses and craft goods could then be exchanged for luxuries and exotica. It was a system of *political* exploitation that inhibited innovation within the village, since any increase in rural production only benefited the rapacious tax-collectors, and, in the towns, the merchants and manufacturers were similarly at the mercy of the class which controlled the machinery of State power. But whereas urban manufacturing in Europe involved continuous production for the market, Indian craftsmen, it was thought, only produced when a customer placed an order; and even the demand for industrial goods stimulated by State-initiated large-scale public works was intermittent, the bulk of the wealth of society, in any case, going into the State's other major activity, war, which like taxation, was essentially a form of plunder. Marx was aware of the lengthy history of cities like Dacca as centres of textile industry, but, once more, these awkward facts were set aside in the interests of intellectual schematism.

Engels eagerly seized upon another theme: that of the role of the State in constructing and controlling irrigation-works. Marx, at times, cautiously demurred: irrigation-works had, he noted, been developed outside Asia without any necessary association with despotism. But the idea lived on, and was to be revived in the twentieth century by Wittfogel as the key to the contrast between the decentralized, conditional sovereignty of medieval Europe that Anderson has characterized as 'scalar' and 'parcellized', and its subsequent bourgeois democracy, as contrasted with the centralized despotisms of the East and their subsequent colonial fate. To build dykes, bridges and dams, to install machinery, to see to their upkeep, and to control the use of the water, called, he argued, for a permanent, specialized army of civil servants: a bureaucratic apparatus of the State of a size, and ruthlessness, unknown in the West.

We know today that it is a distorted model of the complex processes by which these great works were constructed. We also know that they were often, initially, not necessarily massive systems, but were built in stages, added to piecemeal, century after century, rather than at one blow; constructed, too, under the aegis of local kings and authorities rather than rulers of gigantic imperial states, and maintained by local initiative.[81] The economies of the enormous successive empires of Turkey, Persia, or India, moreover, had *not* been based on this kind of irrigation-agriculture; while in the one outstanding case where this was true, China, private property in land and a market in land were highly developed, rather than the State or village forms of ownership that the theory (variously) required.[82]

In certain respects, as Anderson observes, Marx and Engels even 'regressed behind their ancestors'. Marx was unequivocal in his denunciation of British rule in India, especially during the Indian Mutiny. The 'interference of the British tax-gatherers and the British soldier . . . , English steam and English Free trade' was 'brutal' and 'sickening'. Nevertheless, 'men of "Property, Order, Family and Religion" ' had unleashed 'the only social revolution ever heard of in Asia'.[83] It was not of course. Yet there was a note of special exultation, too, for this 'revolution wrought by a victorious ruling class would, in time, result in the emergence of a proletariat, and therefore issue in a very different kind of social revolution: the displacement of a capitalism now triumphant in the East as well as in the West.

The work of regeneration has begun . . . The political unity of India was the first condition of its regeneration. That unity, imposed by the British sword, will now be strengthened and perpetuated by the electric telegraph. The native army [is] the *sine qua non* of Indian self-emancipation . . . The free press . . . a new and powerful agent of reconstruction . . . From the Indian natives . . . a fresh class is springing up . . . Steam has . . . revindicated [India] from the isolated position which was the prime law of its stagnation . . . The introduction of railways may easily be made to subserve agricultural purposes . . . [and] . . . will provide [the villages with] the new want of communication and intercourse . . . Modern industry . . . will dissolve the hereditary divisions of labour, upon which rest the Indian castes . . . The Indians will not reap the fruits of the new elements of society scattered among them by the British bourgeoisie, till in Great Britain itself the now ruling classes shall have been supplanted by the industrial proletariat, or till the Hindus themselves shall have grown enough to throw off the English yoke altogether.[84]

In China likewise, 'the bales of calico of the English bourgeoisie' had 'in eight years brought the oldest and most imperturbable empire on earth to the threshold of a social upheaval'.[85]

But in contrast to his careful and extended economic researches, he devoted little attention to the cultures of India already well-known in the West via the pioneer Sanskritic scholars.[86] The note of contempt for millennial 'stagnation' now being swept away includes a perfunctory dismissal of the great world-religions of India in a few grunts and caricatures: 'man the sovereign of nature', under Hinduism, 'fell down on his knees in adoration of Hanuman, the monkey and Sallala, the cow.' It was 'at once a religion of sensualist exuberance, and a religion of self-torturing asceticism; a religion of the Lingam and of the Juggernaut; the religion of the Monk, and of the Bayadere.'[87] The persistence and deep-rootedness of Islam he found baffling. 'Why does the history of the East *appear* as a history of religions?', he asked Engels.[88]

The deformations led him into political misjudgement of an almost cosmic scale: the denunciation and stigmatization of the most important nineteenth century mass struggle of exploited classes in an exploited country, the Taiping Rebellion, as a reactionary barrier to capitalism's onward march. He called it a 'reign of destruction' which was 'a still greater abomination for the popular masses' than Manchu imperial rule. Only the 'lumpen-proletariat' of Europe was more savagely castigated than this horde of 'lumpen elements, vagabonds and bad characters'.

But it was his economism that led him to most seriously misunderstand the nature of Indian society. The village, he believed, being self-sufficient, was incapable of co-operation with other villages, externally, and was only linked to the rest of civil society by the State. Internally, it was self-sufficient. Being religiously 'tone-deaf', to use Weber's phrase, he assimilated the division of labour by caste to a European model of the guild system, thereby divesting it of what was unique to it: that this *economic* division of labour was only a part of a much wider social system of inter-caste relationships, and that the whole was grounded in a religious cosmology and philosophy, not in a utilitarian secular culture. He only saw castes as instances of a general tendency, in earlier forms of society, for occupations to become hereditary, and thereby 'virtually ignored the whole massive structure of the Hindu caste-system – the central social mechanism of class stratification in traditional India'.[89] And, one should add, not just the structure, but the rationale. His rejection of Judaism and of religion in general thus had its intellectual costs, for nothing can be more bizarre in the analysis of Indian society (the designation of the village as 'communal' apart), than to represent as some kind of Eastern version of the medieval guild system an asymmetrical social order in which 'Untouchables' are stigmatized in every sphere of life and where the 'twice-born', conversely, are privileged, all in accordance with a cosmic necessity; where the proximity, let alone the actual touch of a member of a lower caste is polluting to members of higher castes; where the whole social order is based on *varna* and *jati*, and the entire edifice underpinned and informed by religious belief in *karma* and *dharma*.[90] Only by an act of supremely economistic intellectual violence can a mode of production be thus wrested from its social and cultural matrix, and, by fiat, given the status of a causally prior social sub-system.

It is important, however, to note what Indian Marxist philosophers have been arguing recently: that our image of the essentially other-worldly nature of Hindu society, and the conception of spirituality and cosmology as the supreme forces in Hindu social life, are products of Brahmin idealist revisionism, *claims* to pre-eminence which were strongly disputed for centuries; that thoroughly materialist thought is a rich part of the legacy of Hinduism; and that the entire structure of caste, both at the overall level of the *varnas* and at the local level of the interrelated *jatis*, is articulated to and validates a much more prosaic, secular opposition of classes, in which the 'twice-born' are usually landowners, urban entrepreneurs and profes-sionals, and the lower castes tenants, smallholders and rural or urban proletarians.[91] It is also important to remember that the poor are kept in their place, under control, and exploited, by more than religious authority or internalized belief. Force, in the form of landlord 'goon squads', is an historic, and rapidly increasing, mode of social control.[92]

The dismal consequences of economistic thinking, non-Marxist as well as Marxist, can be seen from one economist's awareness of the necessity to remind his colleagues of the obvious in our own times:

Caste stratification, which is the basic characteristic of the Indian villages, is generally ignored by economists in their analysis of rural problems . . . even though . . . mostly the dominant upper castes have command over the supply of land and other material resources. A majority of them are capitalist farmers . . . so a point of convergence exists between caste and class.[93]

In one part of Karnataka, Mishra shows, where Brahmins were *not* the principal landowning caste, and complete landlessness was uncommon (3 per cent of all households), 82 per cent of the dominant Vokkaliga caste nevertheless owned big farms, while 70 per cent of the Scheduled Castes (sometimes popularly called 'Outcastes' in the West) had no land at all. The Vokkaligas, though only 53 per cent of the total population, therefore had 72.32 per cent of all village income from agriculture, dairying and sericulture, and the rich farmers among them over 90 per cent of big-farm income. The Scheduled Castes, by contrast (15 per cent of the population), plus the tribal peoples (14 per cent of the population) 20 per cent *in toto*, had only 13.62 per cent of all income and were dependent on wage-income to supplement what they could grow on their tiny holdings.[94]

At a higher, societal level of culture, Hindu cosmology has been conflated as 'Asian' together with a this-worldly Confucian world-view. In Fairbanks's words, 'to a Westerner the most striking thing . . . is that three of the five relationships . . . [between ruler and subject, father and son, elder brother and younger brother, husband and wife, and friend and friend] . . . were within the family, and four of the five were between superior and subordinate'.[95] This is almost as astounding as the subsuming, under the general label 'Oriental despotism', of the political structures of India or Persia with the Chinese State – which was administered by a millenial system of meritocratic selection by examination in the classics, and which permitted large-scale social mobility by recruiting, at times, even those of modest family background, into the service of the State.

The theory of Oriental despotism has undergone several phases of revival in this century. In the 1930s, Wittfogel breathed new life into the hydraulic version in an attempt to generate a distinctively Marxist materialist interpretation of Asian history. Though he then abandoned the Comintern, and became a leading anti-communist during the McCarthy era, he stuck to the same theory, though he now used it to attack the USSR. Hydraulism, it seemed, even explained Stalin's terror and the monocentric Soviet state.[96] Even more absurdly, hydraulic societies were discovered in Peru (the Inca State, which some saw as 'Inca Socialism'), in East Africa, in ancient Sumeria, Pharaonic Egypt, Aryan India, and in Hawaii. The next wave of theoreticians took it up after Stalin's death in an effort to explain how it was that a Party led to power by a theorist who claimed that 'every cook could rule the state' could have laid the foundations of a totalitarian regime in which democratic centralism had turned into the victory of centralism over democracy. Previously, Marxists who had dared suggest, prematurely, that this was because the ruling class was not an economic class which owned the means of production but a *political* class which controlled the economy only because it controlled the State, were likely, like Djilas, to end up in jail and/ or be denounced as enemies of socialism.[97] After Stalin, one still had to be careful, but an oblique, 'Aesopian' critique of State power and discussion of its basis could be developed by discussing the seemingly thoroughly academic, even esoteric, issue of the nature of society in pre-colonial Asia or medieval Russia. In the 1950s, Hungarian and Italian communists became surprisingly interested in Asia overnight.

There was renewed interest within Asia itself and the Third World generally. The rise of China as a revolutionary force of the greatest magnitude, and the groundswell of revolution and decolonization in three continents, revived an interest in a theory that seemed to give the Third World a pre-colonial identity and to explain its conquest and subsequent underdevelopment, together with the likelihood of revolution in the Third World. The theory is still spreading. Its attractiveness is its simplicity and its amorphousness. As fast as one of its several heads is cut off, another revives. But it is possible because the model of the State as the 'committee of the whole bourgeoisie' is an inadequate one, not just in respect of non-capitalist society, but for capitalism, too. Despite its shortcomings and ambiguities, in communist countries, the twin concepts of the Asiatic mode of production and Oriental despotism have become a cryptic way of talking about polities in which the State dominates civil society, including communist states; and which is able to use Marx to criticize not only the official theory of the State, but to covertly criticize the State itself. Outside those countries, it has been used by writers like Samir Amin to describe societies in which rent goes primarily to the State, not the landlord. The precise relationship between the landowning classes and the class which monopolizes political power is, of course, highly variable, and can only be established by empirical investigation. The State's claim to own the land is often a legalistic one, or only an ultimate right, while peasants may pay dues to both the landholder and the State. Either way, Amin's conception of the 'tributary' state seems preferable to the confused theory of 'Oriental despotism'.[98]

The concept has been creatively extended by Eric Wolf who treats Western feudalism and Oriental bureaucratic despotisms not as qualitatively different kinds of society, but as variants of one single mode of production, in which the decisive factor in extracting the surplus from the producer is political power, not the operation of the market. The difference between European feudalism and Asiatic society is then seen simply as the difference between those tributary societies in which power is decentralized as against those in which it is concentrated in the hands of the class which controls the State. This approach has the virtue of concentrating upon the 'rational kernel' in the concept of an Asiatic mode of production which has kept it alive despite romantic but contradictory myths about idyllic rural communities and hydraulic totalitarianism: the use of political power as a means of economic exploitation.

The Great Debate: Russia

After the tide of liberal revolution receded from Russian soil with Napoleon's armies, absolute resistance to change was developed into an anti-progressive social philosophy by theorists of reaction such as Maistre and Bonald and a political praxis applied both within the country and as the basis of a universalistic foreign policy. Russia, with Austria, now became the chief guarantors and reservoirs of practical and moral support for the reactionary regime and forces which Metternich built into a system of continental reaction.

After the crushing of the aristocratic Decembrists, who were more often the service nobility than the landowning aristocracy, three decades elapsed during which any change within the congealed social order of Russia seemed hopeless. The frustrated predecessors of the 'interior refugees' of today took refuge in art, philosophy, music, drink, love, the private life. But in the 1850s, the peasants stepped onto the stage of history once more.

Just as the Indian *comunidades* of the New World went back to pre-colonial times, the Russian village communes went back to an epoch long anterior to the Absolutist State. Many of them could trace their continuity back over centuries. But some were the result of more recent economic growth and political expansion; others quite novel constructs, though based upon traditional principles of village social organization. But for all of them, their functions and powers were specified, and limited, by the State. Ancient rights had been lost, and new obligations laid upon them.

The famed solidarity of the village was thus a two-sided phenomenon: in part, deriving from the legacy of the past of the commune as the collective owner of the land; in part, as a consequence of another historic heritage, its responsibility to the State for, since 1742, seeing to it that its members paid their taxes, and, in some areas, ensuring that they performed corvée labour on landlord estates.

Over much of northern and Asiatic Russia, the State was also the landlord. Yet, *pace* theories of Asiatic despotism, it often proved a less onerous landlord than private proprietors who, by the mid-nineteenth century, were making the peasants spend three days per week working on their estates (*barshchina* labour), and supplying their own implements. A third of the peasantry, however, paid their dues in kind (*obrok*), and only later in money. As in feudal Europe, in the richer black-earth country, labour dues were heavier and peasant allotments smaller; in the poorer lands to the north, landlords only kept a quarter of their land, and leased the rest to peasants who earned a larger share of their income from handicrafts and town industry, from which they paid the rent. But landlord authority went far beyond the payment of rent. Labour services were so extensive that the lot of the serf was often indistinguishable from slavery. By 1792, 34 out of the 36 million peasants were bondaged serfs: 19½ million to landlords, and another 14½ million on State lands; and until 1861, a landlord could flog his serfs, send them into the army or to Siberia, separate children from their banished parents and even exercise the *droit de seigneur*.

There were two main categories of serf: 'bound' peasants, theoretically supporting themselves on their own subsistence-plots, and landless 'court-yard people' who were the servants in the manor-house. A liberal landlord might give them gardens, cattle and their own dwellings. Yet even on the gigantic estates of the largest landowners like Count Seremetiev, who lived in a mini-Versailles where, like most of the aristocracy, he spoke French at home and surrounded himself with poets, musicians, architects, actors, and ballet dancers, *all of these were serfs*. There were 100,000 male serfs alone. Count Orlov-Davydov owned 'considerably more than half a million of acres', and the Strogonovs' estates would have formed 'a good-sized independent state in Western Europe'.[99]

Yet the majority of landed proprietors were poor. In 1861, out of 100,247 of them, 41,000 possessed less than twenty-one serfs; only 3803 had more than 500. The great majority of them were of 'the old school', quite uninterested in modernizing their properties. Those of the 'modern school' could earn far more in government service.

Politically, the Russian nobility had been so dependent on the State for centuries that it never became an independent force. Social status had depended upon one's position in the State bureaucracy. Most landowners therefore lived in the towns and cities leaving their estates to be managed by bailiffs and the peasants to the control of the commune's elders: 'the country *dacha* was a vacation home not an administrative centre'.[100] By mid-century, the controls were breaking down. Peasant discontent expressed itself in mystical rumours of an imminent New Jerusalem, which would come when the century reached its mid-way point; then, with the Crimean War, in rumours that the Tsar would give those who fought for Russia their freedom – or that the British or the French would. The number of serious peasant disturbances increased yearly. By the time mid-century was reached, there were six times as many as there had been thirty-five years earlier.

There was strong support, too, amongst the younger landowners, and in the cities, for change. Controlled instalments of reform had already been tried out in regions such as the Baltic provinces. But as in the Third World today, there had been fierce debate about what direction reform ought to take. One school – the Westernizers – had advocated following models pioneered in the capitalist West, notably England. The other – the Slavophils – pointed to the negative side of that experience: the slums, the pitiless exploitation of the new working class and the elimination of a whole, and valuable traditional form of life in the countryside. In any case, it was neither possible nor desirable, they argued, for Russia to copy the West. Instead, they should build a new, more humane society, *better* than that of the West, as an 'organic' development of *Russian* social institutions, notably the commune.

But one ancient traditional institution would have to go: serfdom. The end of the post-Napoleonic Ice Age came with its abolition in 1861, overnight, in the aftermath of the disasters of the Crimean War. Economically, it seemed, the Westernizers had won out, for the intention was to give a decisive impulse towards the modernization of agriculture along capitalist lines. Yet politically, the government's policy was to preserve the autocratic central power intact, while mobilizing the nobility in a new relationship to the State, via their participation in novel political organs, the *zemstvos* at the local level. 'Better,' the Tsar had decided, 'that the emancipation came from above rather than from below.'[101]

'The right of bondage over peasants settled upon the landlords' estates, and over the courtyard people', the General Statute of Emancipation proclaimed on 19 February 1861, 'is forever abolished'. By 1867, State peasants, too, were freed. But to have simply freed the serfs without giving them the means of supporting themselves would have been a sure-fire recipe for mass starvation and mass discontent. They were therefore to be given enough land, in principle, for their subsistence needs. At that time, there was little hope that any significant breakthrough to commercial agriculture could be made via modernizing the landlords' estates.

Peasant agriculture was very small-scale indeed. Moreover, they did not get the land for nothing, but had to pay redemption dues over a forty-nine-year period for land over-valued at 40 per cent above market prices. They themselves had to put down 20 per cent of the value of the land; the State the other 80 per cent, which they had to pay back at a 6 per cent rate of interest per annum. It was to be a model for land reform under capitalism that was to be replicated in many countries in subsequent decades. To ensure that they did pay up, the commune was not only retained, but strengthened, since it was now charged with ensuring that its members paid their redemption payments as well as their taxes.

It was now made very difficult for anyone to leave the village, or to sell the land they had been given, while joint economic activities were encouraged.

Pasture and woodland remained in common as before, but new collective activities were now added: the purchase and renting of land by the village as a whole; the extension of co-operation in agricultural work, in ploughing, sowing, harvesting, threshing, and building barns; in the infrastructural sphere, in the joint construction of bridges, roads and threshing-floors; and even in non-agricultural co-operative enterprises (*artels*): handicrafts, breweries, grist-mills, brickyards, and so on.

The powers once shared between the landlord and the elders of the *mir* were now exercised by the latter institution on its own. For key decisions, two-thirds of the heads of households had to agree. Elders thereby exercised control over the women and the younger men, and the latter had to have passports in order to leave the village, and when they were allowed to go to find work, could even be recalled from the towns and the estates. Stratification within the village thus entailed structured inequalities of sex and age, not of property alone. It was a social and not merely an economic stratification. The civil status of all peasants, moreover, was different in kind from that of the urban classes. Like the nobility, they were not just a *class*, but a *status-group*, whose rights and duties were specified by legislation and custom, not merely by their position in a system of market-relationships. They were an *estate*, not just a class (or set of classes), living within 'a distinctive structure of social interaction':

> . . . a single peasant estate (*soslovie*) . . . moulded [and] reinforced by specific peasant legislation, distinct from national law.[102]

Being a peasant, then, meant that one married according to a different legal code from that which governed the life of townspeople; was subject to special controls on residence, mobility, and property; and came under different official institutions. It was not just a relationship to the means of production.

Economically, the situation, for the majority, was little improved. Only one in five hundred had farms of over 270 acres. The great majority lived on tiny pocket-handkerchiefs, a quarter of which were less than fourteen acres in size, with only the most primitive equipment and no capital with which to improve their farming practices. Even as late as 1917, half the peasant households had only one horse, the principal draught-animal, another third had no horse at all, and half of them broke the soil with the primitive wooden *sokha*, and the situation was getting worse. The buying and renting of more land became essential to survival. In 1883, a Peasant Land Bank was established by the government to help them do so, and it was readily used to buy land off impoverished landowners. Those of the old school had often simply thrown up their hands, once they lost their serfs, and resigned themselves to selling the cherry orchard to the new upstart capitalists from the towns, or renting the land to the rising class of *kulak* would-be capitalist farmers. Between 1877 and 1905, the landed nobility lost a third of their land, and despite the establishment of a special government bank to assist them, one which gave them twice as much as the peasant got, a third of the land that remained was mortgaged by 1905. The average size of estate shrank from 538.2 dessiatines in 1887 to 488 in 1905, and the ownership of horses fell by 8.5 per cent. Eighty per cent of the newly-acquired land passed to the communes, which now owned nearly a half of the country's farmland.[103]

Some successes could be recorded among the landlords of the new school, ready to modernize along capitalist lines. Grain exports actually went up from 1½ million tons in 1860 to over 6 million tons in 1900. But there were great variations from region to region, and the general pattern was so complicated and uneven that enormous debates raged both about what *was* happening and about where Russia *ought* to be heading.

The enlightened gentry, fired by the hope of creating a new, liberal and scientific Russia, threw themselves into using their privileged membership of the *zemstvos* to make them work. Their energy, and that of the statisticians, generated the data which was now drawn upon to yield very different conclusions. The economic debates were only part of wider differences of conception about the nature of Russian society and on the left, the nature of socialism. It was not just an intellectual analysis, but a moral critique. The Populists (*Narodniki*), intellectual heirs of the Slavophils, took as their starting-point the peasant household and the peasant village community. Socialism, they believed, had, in Russia, to be built upon these traditional foundations. Ninety per cent of the population in the 1850s, they argued, were peasants or pre-capitalist artisans or merchants. Development policy should therefore aim at strengthening not eliminating them, whilst building ties between the hitherto isolated villages. Society would be a union of prosperous, democratic, diverse self-governing communities in place of a repressive State and a ruling class whose *raison d'être* was the exploitation of the peasant majority.

The central economic themes in populist thought in the West have been traced back to Sismondi and Proudhon early in the century. For them, the most desirable way of producing wealth is one based on the *small* producer; large-scale production, on the contrary, leads to proletarianization and the ruin of thousands of peasant cultivators and artisans who cannot compete with larger firms or survive the manipulation of the market by middlemen. 'More lace, more pins, more threads', wrote Sismondi, 'but how dearly we have purchased them if it is by this moral sacrifice of so many millions of human beings.' Populism therefore favours a society composed of self-sufficient small producers, preferably associated via the community or some form of co-operative linkage, which enables them to constitute themselves into a force powerful enough to ensure that they will receive the just reward for their labours. It distrusts large size, centralization, and the power of money, and often has an anti-urban bias.

The classic populist themes can perhaps best be grasped by turning to the most impressive twentieth-century expression of them: the Ujamaa socialism of President Julius Nyerere of Tanzania. *Ujamaa* means 'familyhood'. It is a form of socialism, he argues, that is distinctively *African*, not a European import. It is 'tribal socialism' brought up to date, opposed both to the capitalism introduced by colonialism and to 'doctrinaire' European socialism which postulates the inevitability of conflict between man and man. Class war is something unknown before colonialism. Differences, in those days, were resolved by rational debate. The class differences that exist now are destined to be eliminated under Ujamaa socialism. African socialism sees society as an extension of traditional tribalism and the African extended family unit, founded upon the principles of mutual respect for the rights of other members of the family; the sharing of property and income; and the obligation that all work for the general good. Nyerere does recognize that women were to some extent treated as inferior in the pre-colonial past, and that the general standard of living was low. The future, too, in a country where over 85 per cent of the population were peasants, can only be an agricultural future. National capital should therefore be invested in the countryside, to modernize agriculture, not in industry based in the towns. Real development would consist in contributing to production by hard work, not in accumulating money (which tended to get siphoned off abroad anyhow). The main aim of the educational system should be to raise the standards of the masses, not to give advanced education to a small élite. Overall, African socialism meant fairness in the *distribution* of wealth, though there needed to be increased production before there was much to distribute.[104] These principles were put into effect, eventually, in the nationalization of most foreign-owned enterprise – plantations, factories and banks – as well as indigenous enterprise of any size, and in the Programme of the Arusha Declaration of 1967 under which government servants were prevented from enriching themselves in the private sector and their salary levels were strictly controlled.

The idea of developing peasant agriculture as the basis of a future socialist society seemed to Russian populists, on the other hand, not so much an ideal, as the only realistic possibility. Once serfdom had been abolished, the commune, they thought, could now come into its own. Russia could move straight from village communitarianism to socialism without going through the horrors of capitalism which evolutionist theorists, including Marxists, declared to be inevitable. The peasants, the soul of Russia, would be the social base for the regeneration of the whole society, a natural bulwark against the emergence not just of capitalism in agriculture but of an over-centralized State-socialist agriculture too. In the famous summer of 1870, thousands of dedicated, idealistic, and militant young people, mostly sons and daughters of the rich, 'went down' to the villages to take this message to the peasants. The latter, scared at these bizarre intruders, ignored them, drove them out, and even turned some of them over to the police, who completed the work of smashing the movement. Thereafter, young revolutionaries were to turn to terrorism, of which the assassination of Tsar Alexander II was the most famous instance. When that strategy also failed, some of them turned to social democracy (i.e., Marxist revolutionary socialism, not the contemporary Western reformist version), which had long opposed terrorism.

One such was Lenin, whose brother had been executed for terrorism. Lenin had no time for the romantic individualism of the terrorists or the idealistic illusions of the populists. He took his lead from Marx, who had dismissed their programme with characteristic pungency:

> They . . . want competition without the lethal effects of competition. They all want the impossible, namely the conditions of bourgeois existence without the necessary consequences of those conditions.[105]

In his *The Development of Capitalism in Russian Agriculture* (1899), he launched a central attack on populist agrarian theory. He paid little attention to the persistence of *pre*-capitalist relations: these were dying. Whereas the populists emphasized the family household and the village commune, he stressed capital, class and the market.

Capitalist relations were penetrating the village so rapidly that the populist notion of preserving the egalitarian commune was a pipe-dream. Class differentiation, class polarization, and class conflict already existed in the Russian countryside. The richer peasants were already buying up the land of others and hiring the poor and landless to work it. The majority, totally lacking in the capital needed to hire labour and purchase inputs, would have to sell and cease to be peasants at all. The most successful would become a class of 'farmers'. In the long run, class differentiation would be succeeded by class polarization, and in the very long run, agricultural capital, like industrial, would become concentrated and centralized in the hands of a few large corporations, either directly engaged in production, working enormous tracts of land with hired labour complemented by modern machinery and using managerial methods, or indirectly controlling formally independent farmers through the banks and the commodity markets.

The socialist alternative would grow out of this legacy of capitalism. It would retain large-scale production-units, which need not necessarily be owned or managed directly by the State itself, but rather through various forms of social ownership by the producers themselves, but which would be able to call upon the capital in the hands of the State to finance their operations and the modernization of production-methods.

The evidence, drawn from the tomes of the *zemstvo* statisticians and others, was overwhelming and self-evident. The figures spoke for themselves. They showed, for 1905, one and a half million capitalist farmers with farms, on average, of about 125 acres; at the other pole, 10.5 million pauperized peasants on plots of less than 20 acres. The consolidation of classes, and the sharpening of class contradictions, was obvious: the richer 20 per cent of the peasantry were using between 35 and 50 per cent of the land plus a half of all commercial industrial enterprises and used most of the hired labour; the middle peasantry (30 per cent of the peasant population) were using 20–45 per cent and the poor peasants (50 per cent of the peasant population) only 20–30 per cent.[106]

To Lenin's opponents, the figures said something very different. As Thompson has remarked, classes are not things, but relationships.[107] For Lenin, it was axiomatic that the relationships that mattered were those between classes: the class-*system*. But for his populist opponents whose ideas remained very influential even after the collapse of the militant populist movement called the 'People's Will' in 1887, it was not class but the family that constituted the relevant framework for analysing peasant relationships. The categories 'rich', 'middle' and 'poor' made social as distinct from statistical sense only when it was understood that several quite distinct processes were going on at the same time within peasant households, processes which often cancelled each other out: polarization and levelling *within* the peasant sector; aggregate shifts, upwards and downwards, in the prosperity of the peasantry as a whole; the extinction, partition, and merger of some households and the emergence of other newly-created ones; and the effects of emigration.[108] Lenin, they argued, was misled and misleading. Dynamic studies, tracing the fortunes of *specific households over time*, showed that the *same* household might be in the rich peasant bracket at one phase of the family-cycle, on the up-swing, when the ratio of workers to consumers was favourable and permitted more land to be brought under cultivation, and ten years later, having lost the labour of sons and daughters, might be at a downwards point of the cycle, and have contracted in scale of operation to middle peasant status. Classes, according to this time-series analysis, were not polarizing, nor was access to capital the key determinant; rather, households expanded and contracted in accordance with the phases of the family-cycle, and moved into and out of different class brackets over time. It was a model not of progressive, unilinear economic class differentiation and polarization, but of the oscillation, over time, of the social unit of the family. What Lenin's analysis failed to grasp, they argued, was cyclical change within the family, over time.

By the standards of developed capitalist agriculture, even a rich peasant was miserably poor. But he did have enough land to support his family and even to produce a marketable surplus, and might even rent or share-crop additional land from larger owners. But 90 per cent of the peasantry hired no labour even as late as 1912, the peak year for hirings. A 'poor' peasant might, in fact, have no land at all, certainly not enough to support his family, even when agricultural income was supplemented by handicrafts. He would therefore have to rent or share-crop land or work off-farm for wages, normally for the rich peasants. Paradoxically, a rich peasant with a horse might be hired by a poor peasant without one. The middle peasantry were those who could manage to feed themselves without having to hire labour or work for others themselves. But they were permanently on the margin between viability and disaster. Where the consumer–producer ratio was adverse they would hire temporary labour or merge with another household. The fragility of their situation was expressed in the saying: 'Today I am a middle peasant (*serednyak*), tomorrow I become a poor peasant (*bednyak*). If the horse dies, I'll have to hire myself out.' They were at the mercy of the slightest chance fluctuation of Nature, of human biology, of social misfortune, and of the market: A successful contract, a hard-working son, a useful merger, or, conversely, the illness or death of a working member, a fire, the death of a horse, the obligation to provide a dowry, or even a family quarrel culminating in partitioning, could lead to a complete change in the socio-economic position of a household.[109] Disaster was extremely common; in 1929, it was recorded, 400,000 peasant houses caught fire every year. There was not a single peasant who had not been burned down at least once.[110]

'Rich' and 'poor' were therefore not discrete taxonomic categories; they were related to each other, supplying labour and services to each other. Economic disaster was intimately contingent upon social and even natural factors; and innumerable households experienced upwards and downwards mobility that prevented their becoming consolidated into a permanent class status. The most radical of them were likely to be those that had a marginal stake as middle peasants, for whom hopes of maintaining themselves, and the greater hope of even moving up a little, were constantly dashed by failure. It was they who controlled the communes. It was they, not the poorest peasants, who became the most radicalized, just as it was to be in Asia half a century later.[111]

Revolution, 1905

By 1905, agriculture was in crisis. Yields were a third of those in Germany and a quarter of those in Britain. Industry, on the contrary, was growing rapidly and on modern lines. By the time of emancipation a quarter of all workers were employed in factories with a workforce of more than 1000; by the end of the century, a half. As in the other late-comer capitalisms of Germany and Japan, the State, in alliance with foreign capital (which owned some three-quarters of banking, mines and railways), backed the installation of new plants based on the latest scientific technology, such as the famous Putilov works in Moscow, which were as advanced and large as anything in Western Europe.

The working class naturally grew with industry, though at first not as a class-for-itself. In the first post-emancipation decades, two-thirds of urban workers still owned allotment-land in the villages, and half sent money home. Gangs of men from the same village lived in *artels* in the towns, working for starvation-wages, and went home for the spring sowing and the harvest. But by the end of the 1890s, half the industrial workers were children of fathers who had themselves been industrial workers. Revolutionary ideas spread rapidly among them, in part through the dialectic of inter-generational family life experience, for the young experienced the contradiction not only between the explosion of urban industry and the rigidity of political despotism, but between the extension of mass education and resistance to even modest instalments of democratic reform. By 1914, a quarter of all university students were children of workers or artisans, and 14.5 per cent of them even children of peasants.[112]

But agriculture lagged behind. The nobility were steadily abandoning the lands they had retained in 1861. By 1905, one peasant in twelve owned some non-allotment land. But not enough, in most cases. The population had shot up by two-thirds between the middle and the end of the century, but the price of land had increased *tenfold*. Though a million went to the towns, and another 2½ million to the zones of colonization in Asiatic Russia (at one point, 400,000 a year), the majority faced starvation. The traditional methods of social control – 'beating out' the taxes, and, now, the redemption payments – were no longer adequate.

They were replaced by short-term responses, such as the writing-off of peasant debt, and, between 1899 and 1903, the more radical abolition of the village's responsibility for taxes and redemption payments. But peasant revolt could not now be stopped. It began in 1902, with villagers seizing grain (often in the name of a ruler believed to have replaced the Tsar, and who had authorized the distribution of the landlords' goods and establishments). By 1905, mansions were being burned down and taxes and rents refused. The explosion then spread to the cities, when the working class began to strike as well. The Japanese victory in the East, where 'this most Asiatic of European powers [had] finally blundered and blustered its way into war with the most European of Asiatics – the Japanese', was the final blow to stability and legitimacy.[113]

Faced with revolution, the more far-seeing of the Tsar's advisors such as

Witte and Stolypin, saw the need for change and not brutal repression alone. In past centuries, change in Russia had come about in manic bursts of energy on the part of despotic rulers, from Ivan to Peter and Catherine, great enough to found a Petersburg out of the marshes, followed by decades of exhaustion. In the nineteenth century, a new class of politicians took over the role of modernizers. The Tsar might still claim that

> . . . to the Emperor of All the Russias belongs supreme autocratic power. Submission to His Power, not only from fear, but as a matter of conscience, is commanded by God himself.[114]

But he now made that claim on the occasion of the announcement of a major programme of social reform to a newly-constituted Duma, in 1906. Both the programme and the pseudo-parliament were reluctantly conceded. Of the two principal social institutions on which Russia's agrarian order had been based for centuries, one – serfdom – had been abolished only forty-five years ago. Now, with equal decisiveness, it was the turn of the commune. Capitalism had failed to develop successfully on the landlords' estates; now the entrepreneurs among the peasantry were to be given their chance. The commune, which stood in the way of private property and investment for modernization, was to go. Peasants would now be allowed to convert their repartitional holdings into hereditary ones, to consolidate their strips, and to buy and sell land. But Stolypin, the Prime Minister who announced the legislation, made it clear that these social changes were designed to strengthen the State, not to weaken it. In words that every conservative land-reformer has since echoed, the government, he said, had

> . . . placed its wager, not on the needy and the drunken, but on the sturdy and the strong – on the sturdy individual proprietor who is called upon to play a part in the reconstruction of our Tsardom on strong monarchical foundations.[115]

Only limited village functions were to be retained: some kinds of land could still not be alienated, and where the strips remained, so did common cultivation. The legislation now rained down. Yet by 1915, only 200,000 individual holdings had been physically consolidated. After 1909, there was actually a sharp drop in the number of enclosed farms and in the number of households choosing to leave the commune. 'The majority of Russian peasant households,' Shanin remarks, 'were still living within the framework of the traditional commune when the 1917 revolution came.'[116]

For all this decisiveness, the changes had come too late. In 1917, the entire archaic machinery of State collapsed under the strain of war, as peasant armies, demoralized by revolutionary propaganda for Peace, Land and Liberty, literally voted with their feet. They went home, and took over the land they had shed so much blood to defend.

The Moral Economy of the Peasant

The finest summary of the nature of peasant society and its values and institutions – its culture – has been written, not by a social scientist, but by a creative writer and interpreter of art who brought that quality of imagination to the understanding of the life of the French village he lived in. 'The peasant economy,' John Berger writes, 'was always an economy within an economy. This is what enabled it to survive global transformations of the larger economy – feudal, capitalist, even socialist.'[117] Like all economies, it is embedded in a matrix of social institutions informed by cultural values.

Peasantries are Janus-faced. Insofar as they support *themselves*, peasants are 'a class apart'. But since they also produce a surplus, they are integrated, too, into the environing society and State. Their culture, therefore, like their economy, is never totally independent, nor does it remain static. They are Christians, Muslims, Hindus. But they also have their 'little traditions': distinctive sets of principles and attitudes, which include resignation and despair, suspicion, resentment, even contempt *vis-à-vis* the outside world, but also pride in their own culture, heresy and subversion, amusement at the gullible and ignorant city slicker, and rituals and millenial dreams of an *inverted* social order: what Wertheim has called 'counterpoint'.[118]

Their economic priority, as we have seen, is not to make profits, but to *survive* both the natural disasters, 'bad seasons, storms, droughts, floods, pests, accidents, impoverished soil, animal and plant diseases, crop failures' as well as the man-made ones, 'social and political catastrophes – wars, plagues, brigands, fires, pillaging', and to come through alive.[119] But this is only the subsistence half of their economy: *before* they can eat they have to work for their masters, 'often at the price of going hungry themselves'. The extraction of the surplus, so drily analysed in theoretical treatises, is singularly stark and transparent: the fruit of one's labours had to be carried, sack by sack, to the landlord's granaries, a directness of exploitation that the modern industrial worker rarely experiences. For them, survival becomes the main consideration. Hence, in South-east Asia, they often prefer what Scott calls a feudal relationship in which they get a *fixed* minimal return, but where the landlord takes both the losses as well as the profits, over a system in which they would have to gamble on a loss of profit, but where they would have to pay a fixed rent come what may. Their second preference is for a share-cropping arrangement where landlord and peasant each gets a fixed proportion of the whole.[120]

For the peasant, then, life is not thought of as *progress*, but as a cycle, of seasons, generations, lives, a philosophy carried to its logical extreme in the great Asian peasant cultures which see this life as a mere speck in an eternal cosmic process, and regard the attribution of supreme importance to earthly existence as a mere Western anthropocentric illusion. The object of human effort ought to be to escape from the wheel of the material world altogether, from the bonds of the body and of society, of change and reincarnation, into a plane of timeless, pure being. Any particular life is therefore merely an interlude.

Peasants everywhere also have a survival psychology: they *expect* scarcity, predicate their lives upon its probability. Their principal strategy, then, is the minimization of risk. Tradition – the accumulated wisdom of generations – is the best guide, the safest insurance; innovation a gamble one should not take lightly. This is not conservatism in the sense of the defence of privilege or deference to the powerful. In an economy subject to the vagaries of Nature and of the market and to the superior power of outsiders, the future is unpredictable. One therefore follows tradition, Berger writes, as one follows a track in a dangerous environment (as guerrillas do), relying on local knowledge. Routines and rituals offer the best chances of success: doing things as they always have been done.

It is an intrinsically tragic view of life. Peasants do not look forward to a better future, unlike workers, who hope and often expect, within capitalism, to enjoy more as consumers, or, if revolutionaries, to construct a better alternative society. To the peasant, the future is the future, not a time upon which dreams of improvement are projected. The revolutions of peasant life are the rhythms of the seasons, which they attend to with the most minute observation. But they do not expect this world to give way to something else, whether through social revolution or scientific innovation. But it is a world so bad that it cannot always have been like this. A better world must have existed in the past, or must exist somewhere now, out of this world, in heaven. '[The peasant's] ideals,' Berger concludes, 'are located in the past; his obligations are to the future, which he himself will not live to see . . . he will return to the past.'[121] Even the most apocalyptic visions of an alternative world are therefore dreams of the revival of a lost Eden.[122]

But in the real world, one had simply to endure and suffer. Only in extremes of desperation were peasants driven to pick up their scythes, flails and pitchforks and use them as weapons, departing from their basic philosophy by risking all, even life itself, in desperate *jacqueries*.[123] More often, they trusted their lord or their king to give them justice, and to be reasonable, in times of distress, in the demands made upon them for rent or taxes.

They were not necessarily met with reasonableness, for their lords and kings did not see them as reasonable beings themselves, but as cunning, secretive, hidebound by tradition, lacking in enterprise or effort, and probably concealing the wealth they had in their socks and mattresses, and hiding their real hostility behind a mask of deference. Overall, they were untrustworthy, incomprehensible, even irrational. Twentieth-century students of the peasantry have often reproduced some of these historic stereotypes in more academic language, in the concept of the 'amoral familism' of the peasantry,[124] or the notion of the peasant 'image of the limited good'.[125]

There are only a limited number of options open to peasants beset by endemic poverty or by sudden crisis. One can try to *produce* one's way out of the situation by intensifying the self-exploitation of the family: working longer hours, switching to risky 'starvation crops' or to new 'miracle' strains of wheat or rice instead of the lower-yielding, but tried and true ones. Or one can simply cut back on consumption: eat less. Where the source of one's misery is social oppression rather than of natural provenance, it has sometimes been possible simply to leave: to light out for the frontier, for new zones of colonization where land was free. In the eighteenth century, Thai kings had to be careful how far they went in exacting tribute from their subjects, for if they became too demanding the peasants would simply disappear into the jungle.[126] In the early nineteenth century, the big 'squatter' landowners who imported English labourers to Australia found that, on arrival, they soon took off to establish themselves as small 'cocky' farmers, for land empty (or emptied) of aboriginals was freely available. (The capitalists, Marx wrote, were in possession of the two main factors of production – the land and capital – but had forgotten to export the social *relations* which governed production.)[127] But there were few countries with conveniently available frontiers, and by the twentieth century even the American West had been filled up. To move to another country altogether, as most of the pioneers of the West had done, was always a tremendous undertaking that few could face, and sometimes too expensive for the very poor. For them, it was only possible as indentured labourers whose passage was paid for by mortgaging years of labour into the future, during which time they were tied to their employer-importer by savagely enforced laws.[128] Emigration to a nearby city was more likely, though once there, ex-peasants were only fitted for occupations involving hard manual labour, begging apart.

Better, then, to stay in the village and ride out the storm until better times came. This meant finding more land or more money. Landowners themselves were often only too ready to rent land and even to lend money, advanced, usually, by securing a lien on the future crop or the peasant's chattels, including house and tools. For money-lenders were in business not just to lend, but to *make* money. At the end of the day, the indebted peasant might still find himself and his family living on the same plot, and working in the same way, but now as workers for the landlord/money-lender rather than as owners of the plot. In China, by the 1930s, Tawney reported:

. . . a 'good' money-lender, described as a blessing to the village, has been known to charge only 25 per cent, but such restraint is exceptional. Interest at 40 to 80 per cent is said to be common; interest at 150 to 200 per cent to be not unknown. Goods are pledged at two-thirds of their true value. As far as the poorer peasants are concerned, permanent indebtedness is the rule rather than the exception; they pawn their crops in the summer, their farm implements in the winter, and their household belongings through the whole twelve months'.[129]

The end of that road is beggary. Even in the 1960s, 60 per cent of the aptly-named Ecuadorean *precarista*'s cash income went in interest repayments, plus another 10 per cent for the use of the land as a share-cropper, and more for the use of water, as well as further payments to rice-mill-owners.[130]

The best way was a social solution: the help of those in the community, above all kin and neighbours whom one could call upon for assistance as of right, by virtue of extra-economic ties, in return for similar, reciprocal aid in the future when disaster might (and almost certainly would) strike the donor in turn. Welfare might also be provided by religious institutions, such as temples, shrines and brotherhoods, and by secular associations ranging from the clan and the lineage to secret societies and rotating credit-institutions.

But agricultural disaster does not usually select just individual families. It strikes whole crops, villages, even regions at the same time. Then everyone has to resort to someone with sufficient reserves of capital and stores of grain to feed them all. It is for this reason that peasants build and nurture relationships, not just horizontally, with their peers, but vertically, with their superiors. Where no natural relationships of kinship exist, Wolf has shown, kinship still provides a model for fictive relationships such as god-parenthood *modelled* on kinship. Historically, there have been two forms of ritual co-parenthood (*compadrazgo*): vertical and horizontal. In the latter, the relationship is between equals; in the former, between a poor person and a wealthy or powerful individual. The shift from blood brotherhood to ties of ritual kinship during the feudal epoch in Europe was closely connected with changes in systems of land service and inheritance.[131] In most years, *compadrazgo* largely takes the form of ritual services: acting as god-parent, giving and receiving gifts, the formal expression of mutual respect. But in a crisis, these ties can be cashed in for hard material assistance: food and money.

The vertical integration of entire strata rather than of dyadic pairs of individuals has been classically studied, unfortunately, by cultural anthropologists for whom the 'primordial' bonds of the family, of ethnicity or of religion are 'assumed givens of social existence' and therefore 'ineffable', not to be explained, but necessary themselves in any explanation of human behaviour; not caused, but causing; not situated, but absolute, 'unaccount-able', 'natural', 'overpowering'.[132]

For Java, Geertz has argued that the most important of such 'primordial' identities and bonds are those which derive from the several religious traditions within that culture, generally termed *aliran*, literally 'streams', which are vertical associations or alliances of believers. Two derive from Islam: one, the more purist, the other a more popular variant. Two derive from pre-Islamic forms of Javanese religion: the *prijaji* form, which used to be the religion of the Javanese court, embodying Hindu and Buddhist elements; and *abangan* religion, which contains many elements of folk-religions which existed before any of these three great world-religions arrived in Indonesia. Each is associated with particular social classes: *santri* Islamic purism with traders and entrepreneurs; *prijaji*, today, with the new governing class, the bureaucratic élite; while the peasants espouse *abangan* beliefs and rituals. Modern political parties, moreover, draw their follow-ings from the different *aliran*. Thus Muslims support either conservative Nahdatul Ulama or the more popular Masjumi, and the peasants the Communist PKI. These class constituencies are further mobilized through the women's clubs, youth and student organizations, trade unions, peasant unions, and religious and charitable associations attached to each party. But though each has its primary constituency in one class, *aliran* also cut across classes to varying degrees, and parties try to win support outside the primary base of their *aliran*.

Marxists have argued, convincingly, that insofar as class relations are assumed, uncritically, to be merely epiphenomenal instances of religious affiliation, the model is simply a form of ideological mystification current in the society under study which idealist social scientists have simply reproduced as the framework of their own analyses. Reacting against this idealism, however, they have sometimes been tempted to lapse into a reductionist denial of the reality of significance of the *aliran*. Hence reminders that there is no isomorphic correspondence between *aliran* and the complex relations of classes involves no denial of the reality of the *aliran*, nor are the real-life effects of such religious identities any less real than what Kahn terms the 'underlying reality' of class relationships.[133] To this extent, the critique replaces Geertz's idealism with a reductionist materialism which a dialectical sociology would avoid.

Geertz's claim, in fact, is a different one: not that there is no relationship between *aliran* and social class – for he elaborates these connections at length – or a one-to-one relationship, but a causal-methodological one: that the *aliran* are 'phenomenologically real', that is, ideas which have real consequences. The debate is thus marked by much methodological fuzziness in distinguishing the concepts used by the religious believers from the analytical categories projected onto the material by the social scientists, and by failure to clearly tease out the degree of fit – or of looseness of fit – as between beliefs and behaviour.

The integration brought about by the *aliran*, it would appear, is primarily effective at two levels: at the level of diffuse confessional identification, and at the face-to-face level of interpersonal relationships similar in kind to those of the patron/client relationship, though the latter is devoid of any necessarily religious rationale. The most important element is the provision of mutual obligations. Despite the protestations of idealists and materialists, the patron/client model is therefore perfectly compatible with even the most spiritualized relationship between worshipper and deity or saint:

> At the core of . . . peasant 'theology' is an all-powerful God who is at the center of all occurrences . . . and to whose will each individual must submit . . . Yet the Brazilian peasant's resignation is not complete, and through an ongoing exchange relationship with one or another saint, he undertakes to mitigate some of the harsher circumstances of his life. These saints take on the aspect of mediators between the secular and sacred worlds. Each individual devotes himself to the personal saint whose name he bears and with whom he closely identifies.[134]

The relationship between both saint and devotee and between secular patron and client are therefore suffused with the *same* 'extraordinary . . . submissiveness to authority and obligation to meet debt . . . in both the sacred and secular domains'. The basic principles of *both* sets of relationships are *congruent* (my italics).[135]

The peasant search for security thus goes on in many forms, from the sphere of practical mutual aid to the religious domain. It is never purely economic, since a purely economic world does not exist. What does exist is a world peopled with kin, landlords, fellow-sufferers, and other social categories of persons.

Security can be sought, at times, by entering into relationships that are not predicated at all upon any material pay-off, but which are sought as spiritual experiences in themselves, however much they are usually provoked by some incident or disaster. In Turner's terminology, *comunitas* has therefore to be distinguished from *societas*, since it derives its very power from the fact that it brings together people looking for identity and seeking for spiritual compensations in an unsatisfactory world. Religious relationships of this kind are therefore charged with a singularly powerful and often hitherto untapped emotional charge. Thus, those afflicted by illness may join communities of the afflicted, in which they receive moral support from people with whom they have no necessary previous connection but with whom they share the common pains of illness or stigma.[136] Such associations need not necessarily be religious in nature: Alcoholics Anonymous is not. Nor are they peculiar to peasants. But they have flourished in peasant societies, where religious sodalities and brotherhoods have constituted alternative worlds for those afflicted not only with illness, but any kind of misfortune. They are voluntary associations, in the technical language of the social sciences, suffused with both hope and resignation; whose boundaries and memberships cut across the established structures not just of religious life, such as congregations, but also those of the secular order of society. The search for *comunitas* thus takes the believer out of accustomed frameworks of place and time and may lead him or her to go on pilgrimage in the search for grace in sacred places; in the extreme, even to abandon conventional life altogether, by retiring from 'the world'.[137]

These are forms of response to insecurity that seek relief, not through material improvements, but in personal or collective catharsis, in the discharge, the spiritual release of the suffering. We have seen them among the Russian peasantry. But they can be found in other cultures, too. At the end of the day, the lot of the peasant on this earth is not changed, however. The alternatives, then, may only be illegitimate ones: for the women, prostitution or being sold into marriage; for the men, begging or banditry. The poor provide the largest constituency for the bandit, and are freely preyed on, but it is more rewarding to rob the rich, and bandits, from Robin Hood to the twentieth-century Brazilian bandit, Lampião, soon pass into song and legend as courageous rebels who redistribute wealth from the rich to the poor. Yet many of them equally readily work *for* the landlord, who uses them as extra-legal strong-arm squads to keep the peasants in their place. The line between banditry and 'social' banditry is a fine and shifting one.[138]

Rebellion against the system as whole is a last resort, for it involves not only the exhaustion of other possibilities but demands being prepared to lay down one's life and to risk that of one's family, as well as the formulation of an attainable objective. Revolution involves even more: the destruction of a whole social order, some vision of an alternative one, and the construction of the machinery or the use of existing institutions through which this can be realized. In totalitarian societies, where there are no safety-valves, no escape routes, no enclaves, no social ties between exploiter and exploited cutting across class divisions, violence may become endemic, force the only means of ensuring the continuity of the social system. In the Spanish Colonia, rebellions recurred in the major zones of Indian population, Mexico and the Andes, from the Conquest to the eve of Independence, culminating in the great Rebellion of Túpac Amaru in 1781.[139]

But assistance, or relief, may come from the landlord himself and become institutionalized 'tradition'. Not all landlords exact the maximum, or are totally, inflexibly, predatory, and landlord–tenant relationships have commonly included more than naked exploitation: a paternalistic interest in the welfare of the people off whose labour the landlord himself lives;

expectations of help over the life crises; acting as godfather; helping with the marriage payments; or with the costs of that greatest occasion for conspicuous expenditure on the part of the poor – a once-in-a-lifetime magnificent funeral.

Such calls on landlord generosity may go unheeded. Then, violence can erupt. But it is not usually directed, at first at least, against the system so much as against those who deviate from customary norms or 'reasonable' behaviour. The right to subsistence is the most basic of these primordial expectations. For this, one will fight. It is a duty not only for one's kin but also for one's landlord to make it possible for the family to survive. *Noblesse oblige*: and in ritual and song even the king could be humbled and reminded of his obligations to his subjects.[140] These expectations are moral norms of exceptional power. A good landlord may be expected to do much more quite routinely. In economic terms, to give loans before harvest, to allow access to wood and water; to help out when times are bad, and at specific social crises, notably during illness, if only by modifying his usual demands. If, 'throughout his life, the Brazilian peasant or agricultural labourer *submits* to a series of acknowledged dis-equal relationships in which he *obligates* himself in a variety of ways', and 'the patron's word is law and not to be questioned', it is also axiomatic that a good patron must command respect and deference if he is to build up a following:

> The ideal patron is a rich and powerful figure who can and does protect his dependants and intervenes for them in their dealings with the world at large. While his attitude toward them more often than not contains a degree of condescension, he is expected to treat them with affect and respect . . . to solidify the . . . bond by accepting the additional obligations of godparenthood . . . to be concerned with their health and well-being and with that of their families, loaning them money, and even providing them with food and medical aid when need arises. He might also facilitate the education of their children, and, occasionally [enable] . . . a dependant to get started in some limited entrepreneurial activity.[141]

Only when such entrenched customary norms are suddenly or wilfully abandoned, when landlords fail to respond to disaster by lowering rents, does rebellion begin. If the crisis affects everybody, what begins as rebellion against a person or a class, locally, can end as revolutionary struggle to overthrow an entire social system. For that to come about, several conditions have to be fulfilled.

By 1917, these conditions had been fulfilled in Tsarist Russia. Lenin, who knew a good deal about revolution, summed it up pithily: revolutions occur, he wrote, when, 'not just the "exploited" and oppressed masses understand the impossibility of living in the old way and demand changes but when the exploiting classes also are no longer able to live and rule in the old way'. In expanding what that meant, Trotsky remarked that 'the mere existence of privations is not enough to cause an insurrection; if it were, the masses would *always* be in revolt'. His own analysis of the Russian Revolution, therefore, begins not only with the economy and the two revolutionary classes, the proletariat and the peasantry, but also with the 'peculiarities of Russia's development', the War and with the Tsar and Tsarism as well.[142] The collapse, that is, was not merely economic, but a *total* collapse of the social and cultural frameworks of the society. Defeat in war, in particular, destroys the State's authority as 'protector' as well as its physical capacity to control a deteriorating situation.

On one side of the political equation, the ruling classes lose control, not only because they are unable to ensure at least a tolerable living for the mass of the people, but also because the explanations they normally use to explain away injustice or misery, that these things are either inevitable or just, are no longer credible. Nor are their explanations for a crisis for which they are now *blamed*. The political legitimacy of the ruling class and its wider cultural hegemony, already greatly eroded away, now suddenly cease to be effective. The classes which normally constitute the bulwark of the regime withdraw their support, or propose concessions. The government, caught on the horns of a dilemma it cannot resolve, either gives in to those demands – and thereby invites more radical ones – or, if it resorts to force, fails to deal firmly enough with opposition, or over-reacts by brutal repression, thereby arousing even greater hostility. The instruments of repression themselves often become ineffective or unreliable: the army revolts, or sits with folded arms.[143]

On the other side of the equation, the masses abandon any hope of resolving the crisis through traditional channels or via gradualist reforms, and create or turn to more effective radical alternatives, notably political parties, and organize themselves, initially often for self-defence which soon turns into an armed revolutionary offensive.

By 1917, the Russian State was in collapse, not because of the maturation of the internal contradictions of capitalism, but because it was unable to maintain a war effort that had cost the lives of millions of soldiers, nearly all of whom were peasants in uniform. Infected by Bolshevik demands for peace, they now simply stopped fighting and started off home, often with their rifles.

But Lenin's policy won out, when, in November, the Bolsheviks, who had won the support of the urban working class and the backing of army and navy units, seized power not in a mass revolution, as in 1905, but in a two-city *putsch*.

The Bolsheviks now controlled the cities and the State machinery, though shakily, with only one division of Latvian riflemen and 7000 Red Guards in Petersburg and Moscow. But only 17 per cent of the population lived in the cities, and as late as February 1917 there were only 30,000 Party members in the entire country. In the countryside, the Party scarcely existed: by 1916, there were only *four* rural branches; in the Smolensk *guberniya*, a year later, with a population of over two million, they had only 128 members.[144]

Yet the really decisive Bolshevik slogan proved to be that of 'land to the peasant'. In March came the Revolution that finally brought down the Tsar. It was a revolution in the cities. But it could never have survived without the far more extensive revolt of the peasants not in uniform who now started to attack their oppressors directly:

> Finally the desired moment . . . for which poor peasants had waited for ages [had arrived]. All the rage seething in their hearts against the accursed landowners' nest, against the fat bellies and bloated mugs of the squires fed on peasant labour – was now, at long last, released. The hungry crowd of peasants and labourers descended on the manor. It seemed that no power on earth could stop these enraged peasants, who grabbed, dragged away, broke, threw into the river, and carried away the lord's property . . . The peasants also got at the shopkeepers. A noisy crowd came into the shops, and when the owners tried to put up a fight, infuriated peasants seized everything they could find.[145]

Two revolutions were thus going on side by side. In the cities, the Bolshevik leadership saw the accession of the moderate Kerensky to power in March as the beginning of a period of bourgeois democracy and capitalist economic growth. Lenin had different ideas. An eye-witness records the astonishment of his comrades who heard him, on arrival back from exile at the Finland Station, advocate the amazing policy of the seizure of power by the working class, led by the Bolshevik Party, and the establishment of a socialist system. Few of them, at first, could believe what they heard, let alone accept it! A non-Bolshevik writer who was present, N. Sukhanov, described the impact of Lenin's words: 'I shall never forget that thunderlike speech, startling and amazing not only to me, but also to the faithful, all of them . . . Nobody had expected anything of the kind. It seemed as though all the elements and the spirit of universal destruction had risen from their lairs.'[146]

Though the Bolsheviks had seized control of the State, the political base of their opponents was far wider. The Social Revolutionaries, successors to the Populists, had the largest bloc of seats in the *Duma*. The revolution that ended Tsarism took place during the five days between 23 and 27 February. At that time, 'Bolshevism . . . was still only simmering in the depths of the revolution . . . The official Bolsheviks represented only an insignificant minority'.[147] The subsequent 'ten days that shook the world', in October, when the Bolsheviks seized power, was decided by the adherence to the Bolshevik cause of over 150,000 soldiers in Petrograd alone, where they outnumbered workers by over four to one.

The defection of the 10 million peasants in uniform had been decisive throughout. But peasants had not been interested in seizing State power. What they had been interested in seizing was the land. The despoliation of the landlords had begun in 1861. They had won the second instalment under Stolypin, when 2½ million peasants got their hands on another 46 million acres. In 1917, they finished the job and seized over 400 million. The Bolsheviks had won the cities and controlled the State; the peasants had won their war in the countryside.

They were still anything but rich. Three-quarters now lived on plots of up to twelve acres, but a sixth had only about two acres per family, and four out of five households had only one horse or none at all. As a result of the dreadful years of civil war and the counter-revolutionary invasion and sealing-off of Russia that followed, by 1920, only three-quarters of the land that had been under cultivation in 1913 was sown to crops; a third of the horses, half the cattle, and a quarter of the sheep and goats had died or had been killed in Russia and the Ukraine.

In the cities, the Bolsheviks clung to power ruthlessly. The Red Army swiftly grew into a large and efficient fighting-force. In the process, 40,000 former Tsarist officers were used, though carefully watched over by political commissars. The latter, and the bulk of the first rank-and-file cadres, were working-class and Bolshevik revolutionaries, most of whom were to die during the subsequent civil war. The rest were absorbed into new Party and Government apparatuses, and into industrial management.[148] By that time, an entirely new – and thoroughly unproletarian – working class had come into existence: a working class of ex-peasants.

Meanwhile, opposition parties were outlawed. In March 1921, the sailors at the Kronstadt base near Petrograd, who had fought for the Bolsheviks and had been described by Trotsky as the 'pride and glory of the Russian Revolution', came out in support of strikers demanding better rations and free speech. For this, they were labelled 'anarchists' and 'counter-revolutionaries'. But the Bolsheviks did not stop at verbal stigmatization. At the end of this much less widely-known ten days, during which they had machine-gunned and shelled the sailors into submission, 18,000 of them lay dead.

Peasant opposition, over large areas, was suppressed by shooting the leaders, with or without trial, and peasants became as numerous as bourgeois enemies of the regime in Soviet gaols by 1920. Their opposition was not bourgeois, however, though the Bolsheviks clung to the Leninist belief that social differentiation in the villages would eventuate in polarization into two hostile forces and end in class war in the villages, analogously to the struggle between proletarians and bourgeoisie in the cities. In fact, the opposite happened. The predictions made by the leading Marxist authorities on agriculture, from Kautsky to Lenin, had therefore been falsified.[149] The proportion of peasants without any land at all dropped by half (from 15.9 per cent in 1917 to 8.1 per cent in 1920). Nor was there any significant strengthening of the richer peasantry. The much discussed *kulaks* (a term meaning 'fists', i.e. what we might call land-grabbers), a mere 3 per cent of the population as late as 1925, were more competent and entrepreneurial peasants, rather than capitalist farmers proper. They used the methods of those who – like the publican or the usurer – had always exploited the villagers, to lay their hands on more land. But the dominant trend was very different from that portrayed in Bolshevik ideology: towards *levelling*. At the end of the revolution, there were 25 million agricultural units where there had been 16 million before the War. The average household of 5.4 persons now had to support itself on a mere six acres of land. Only one household in a hundred employed *any* permanent labour at all. The rural proletariat upon which the Bolsheviks pinned their strategy for socialist advance in the countryside scarcely existed. Neither did capitalist exploitation.[150]

Such a discrepancy between ideology and reality was bound to end in disaster. But it was not just a contradiction at the level of theory: it was institutional confrontation between an unstoppable force and an immovable object.

The Soviet government had been acceptable enough to the peasantry when it had endorsed their seizure of the land. After the landlords had gone, peasant wrath turned against the 'opters-out' (*otrubniki*) whom Stolypin had encouraged to leave the commune and set up as individual proprietors, a struggle acceptable to the Bolsheviks, too. But the Committees of the Rural Poor, the political organs which the latter had tried to establish in the countryside, had to be disbanded after only a few months, and the subsequent Rural Soviets fared no better. Peasant membership of the Party had increased to 14.5 per cent by 1918, and by 1924 to nearly 25 per cent, but the rural branches were mainly composed of administrative officials working in the countryside and ex-soldiers. Real economic power lay with the communes, which now controlled two-thirds of the land, and underwent a veritable renaissance. The interests of the peasantry and of the Bolsheviks now began to diverge.

Bolshevik political strategy was not restricted to the analysis of class differentiation and class struggle under capitalism. It also contained an alternative project: the socialization of the economy. For them, as for their revolutionary predecessors, the peasantry had been the indispensable mass force, the battering ram, which was to dislodge Tsarism. But economically, they were destined to disappear. In the cities, Lenin had argued, even the working class, by itself, would never attain more than an economic, trade-union consciousness concerned with the defence of its living standards, wage levels, and working conditions. They could be infused with a revolutionary political consciousness only by a vanguard of professional revolutionaries. Socialist economic development, following the smashing of the capitalist and landowning classes would, however, retain the forms of production developed under capitalism. Socialism was to be 'electrification plus soviet power'. For the countryside, it meant the conversion of farms into factories in the field.

Under capitalism, the concentration and centralization of private capital followed the same logic in both town and country. Under a socialist government, the modernization of the productive forces would still call for the investment of State capital in large-scale enterprises. In agriculture, this would mean, eventually, the establishment of new, large-scale units, based on industrial inputs, notably, agricultural machinery, and with a labour-force of wage labourers. But it could not be done overnight. The restoration of large-scale capitalism was impermissible, but so desperate was the economic situation that for a while at least, during the New Economic Policy, small workshops and shopkeepers in the city and *kulaks* in the villages were encouraged to 'enrich themselves'. If the workers were to be fed and the factories supplied with raw materials, nothing must be done that might alienate the vast majority of the population. The full socialization of the economy was thus deferred – but only deferred.

In 1925, agricultural taxes were reduced; it was made easier to rent land and to hire labour. Now it might seem worth while investing one's savings once more. Those who, like Preobrazhensky, advocated 'milking' the peasantry as the way to accumulate the capital needed to pay for industrialization seemed to have been defeated. But a basic contradiction of class interests remained, which, given Bolshevik ideology and reliance upon the working class, was to be resolved at the expense of the peasantry: low-priced food for the urban workers meant low prices for the producers, too.

The peasants had other ideas. So did the intellectual descendants of the Populists, notably Chayanov, who argued that the best way to increase output was to give the peasants the resources they lacked. Despite his emphasis upon the household, he recognized that the family was not the sole determinant of farm size and that capitalist forms of agriculture had undoubtedly been developing in the countryside, especially in densely populated zones of surplus labour for a long time. Long before 1917, he wrote, the cotton grown on 'Sidor Karpov's farm, lost in the Russian forests, was now bound to the London banks and the London Stock Exchange' via firms in Moscow which advanced credit for food, seeds, and other inputs, and bought the crop at harvest-time. A major part of Russia's chief export crop, flax, had come from peasant holdings. They were, then, responsive to market inducements.

More and better inputs would increase production only if the circulation process were improved, through better marketing, modern processing and packing facilities, etc. The best instrument for this purpose was the co-operative, which would serve the peasants of a given locality and link them to the wider national market. Once the rural economy had been revived through the establishment of a co-operative network, it would become possible to move on to the creation of large-scale production units.[151] But only then, for at present the USSR lacked the army of agricultural specialists and farm administrators which would be essential. Better, for the moment, not to go over to new forms of production overnight, but to persuade the peasants of the advantages of the new possibilities of co-operation, so that, eventually, without pressure, they themselves would see the virtue of voluntarily grouping themselves into larger units. Otherwise, even the exiguous output of present-day peasant agriculture would be lost.

The debate went on for many years, but the resolution of the peasant problem started to become urgent with the 'price scissors' crisis of 1922 onwards, when prices for manufactured goods began to rocket. In 1913, a plough had cost the peasant the money he received for 10 *puds* of grain; by 1923, he had to pay 36 *puds*. Stalin, now in power through his control of the Party machinery despite his second-rank status during the Revolution, had always been a cautious, middle-of-the-road opponent of both those like Bukharin who advocated going 'at a snail's pace' and people like Preobrazhensky and Trotsky on the Left who called for all-out industrial-ization and 'exploiting' the peasantry like an 'internal colony', and all-out struggle against the increasingly 'capitalist' peasants.[152] The peasants, Stalin said, were an 'ally', an 'active and conscious participant' in the construction of socialism. Moreover, any 'easy leap' from individual smallholdings to large-scale agriculture was 'out of the question'.[153] When, in 1929, he finally turned his back on this policy of moderation and launched the very campaign that he had denounced when the Left had advocated it, there was little effective opposition. Unable to use the hard-line methods he had used in organizing the Red Army and in dragooning the trade unions, Trotsky proved an incompetent organizer of resistance to the wily Stalin. By 1921, the Party had changed radically, as had Soviet society. The half million Party members were mainly ex-peasants; the Red Army was made up of conscripts; and half the working class had just come from the villages, where one in five of them still held land.

For the peasantry it meant the end. Bukharin had predicted that the policy would lead to uprisings which would have to be drowned in blood.[154] Lenin had thought the same. They were to be proved right.

Within a short time, rural Russia became pandemonium. The over-whelming majority of the peasantry confronted the Government with desperate opposition. Collectivization degenerated into a military operation, a cruel civil war. Rebellious villages were surrounded by machine guns and forced to surrender. Masses of *kulaks* were deported to remote unpopulated lands in Siberia. Their houses, barns and farm implements were turned over to the collective farms.[155]

The response of the peasants was typical of peasants over millennia, faced with overwhelming superior force:

The bulk of the peasants decided to bring in as little as possible of their property to the collective farms which they imagined to be state-owned factories, in which they themselves would become mere factory-hands. In desperation, they slaughtered their cattle, smashed implements, and burned crops. This was the *muzhik*'s great Luddite-like rebellion . . . In 1929, Russia possessed 34 million horses. Only 16.6 million were left in 1933 – 18 million horses had been slaughtered. So were 30 million cattle . . . about 40 per cent of the total . . . and nearly 100 million, or two-thirds of all sheep and goats. Vast tracts were left untilled.[156]

In the establishment of capitalism in the first major capitalist country, over a century earlier, the smallholding peasantry had been wiped out. Now they were to be eliminated in the first socialist state.

Collectives and Communes

The specific crisis had arisen over grain deliveries. With prices kept low by the State in the interests of the working class, the peasantry simply voted with their feet for immobilism – doing nothing – hiding their grain and eating their animals, since it was not worth their while marketing their surpluses. The cities were faced with starvation.

The peasants, now forced into the huge collectives, found that they bore little resemblance to the factories in the field that the advocates of modernized agriculture had envisaged. They had imagined that the ex-peasants would work on large farms as wage-workers who would be every bit as much proletarians as their urban counterparts. Management would be entrusted to new, Red, professional cadres drawn from the ranks of the workers themselves. But this form, the state farm, was only adopted in a minority of cases, and then thoroughly divested of any element of workers' control. It was the collective farm which was to be the principal form, controlled, overall, by the State planning machinery, and locally by a management appointed in order to rationalize agriculture so as to ensure the maximization of output by relating the interest of the individual both to his or her work and to the collective success of the enterprise. The farm was required to make a profit by selling its surpluses to the State. Higher output therefore meant more income to be shared all round, calculated for each individual on the basis of work-points awarded for the number of hours spent in each kind of labour. Payment on the basis of nationwide standard wage-scales would simply have allowed peasants unused to quasi-industrial work discipline, and brimming with resentment, to do – and produce – as little as possible, merely to put in time. Finally each family was allowed a small plot on which to grow their own food and raise a few small animals.

Even in the pioneer countries of industrial capitalism it had taken long enough to instil an appropriate work ethic in urban workers, and had entailed the establishment of a whole panoply of institutions from schools to churches. In the USSR, the internalization of an appropriate work ethic was impossible, given peasant hostility to an employer which was also their political oppressor. Rhetoric about the dignity of labour or service to State or society could scarcely have fallen on deafer ears. But technological innovation did afford an opportunity for a new form of political control.

There had only been 7000 tractors in the entire country when collectivization began. In 1929, Stalin secured another 30,000 through superhuman efforts. They were concentrated in the countryside in giant machinery parks, Machine Tractor Stations, manned by reliable cadres, and driven from there to work in the fields. Rather than being at the disposal of the new collective farm-members, the MTS personnel, under rigid Party control, were themselves a new arm of the State in the countryside through which it imposed its will on the peasantry.

With all the opposition crushed during the years of the Great Terror, when 20 million people died,[157] these draconian measures ensured that industrial production was pushed up by 6–10 per cent in 1930 and to 13–14 per cent during the years of the Second Five-Year Plan (1932–7). In agriculture, compulsory procurements brought in half as much grain again as in 1928. But only because the peasants were eating less. The prices paid by the State for key items – wheat, potatoes, cattle and pigs – only rose between 1.9 and 2.09 times from 1929 to 1952, during which time the overall retail price index rose by 10.76 times.[158] And as late as 1960, the average member of a collective farm was only getting 40 per cent of the wage of an average industrial worker.

But the disparity was not merely to be measured in cash terms. Peasants received none of the new welfare services which were provided for workers in the cities. In the countryside, education, health services, and other social needs had to be provided out of the income of the collective farm – which meant that they existed in rudimentary form, the family bearing the brunt in the early years. Without an internal passport, peasants could not leave for the cities on their own but labour was needed in ever-increasing quantities for a rapidly-growing industry. The political culture of the new working class was light-years removed from that of third-generation children of urban workers. Hence although they experienced the authoritarian rule of Stalin along with everyone else, they reacted to it differently. For people whose grandparents could remember serfdom and whose parents had lived through the break-up of the commune and forced collectivization, even the Great Terror was only different in its scale and intensity. Materially, they gradually became better off, as the epoch of famines gave way to one of rapid economic growth. Many moved into the middle ranks of Party, government and management; some even into the top élites. The successful therefore often looked on Stalin much as their parents had looked up to an all-powerful Tsar, as a superhuman, stern father-figure.

These inequalities between town and country persisted right into the post-Second World War era. The economic outcome was low productivity on the collective farm's own land, and remarkably high output on the peasants' own plots. The latter – only 3 per cent of all land – produced four-fifths of the vegetables, two-thirds of the potatoes, over a half of the eggs, and a third of the milk and meat consumed in the country,[159] and provided the peasants with two-thirds of their total incomes even as late as 1952. They therefore spent a third of their work-time (mainly at weekends and in the evenings) on their plots, with the help of children and old people.

After Stalin's death, there were huge increases in the prices paid for agricultural products. Between 1952 and 1964, the price paid by the State for wheat rose by 8.5 times, for potatoes by 16.3 times, and for cattle by 15.8 times.[160] By 1964, the income received from the kolkhoz had begun to equal that from the private plot. By now, the peasantry was also a minority in the population numerically as well as sociologically. The collective farm population had shrunk to a mere quarter (22.3 per cent) of the total. Overall, productivity had improved within the collective farm sector, and the collectives, in any case, were steadily losing ground as the principal form of agricultural production. Today, there are 21,000 state farms alongside the 26,000 collective farms and the 9000 interfarm enterprises which supply both.

Yet agriculture remains the Achilles heel of the Soviet economy. Its periodic deficiencies have to be made good by importing grain from the West, notably the USA and Canada. The weakness no longer derives from the opposition and resentment of a conquered peasantry. Today's peasantry is two generations and half a century removed from the trauma of forced collectivization. Nor can it be explained solely in terms of the undoubted problems created in many regions at least by geography: short growing-seasons, farming on marginal, virgin lands, etc. – explanations which the Soviet leadership itself no longer accepts. Rather, the decisive factor, today, is the low priority accorded to agriculture by economic planners. Top priority is given to defence, which is equal in quantity and quality of its output to anything the West can produce, as the Soviet sputnik proved nearly a quarter of a century ago. Second is heavy industry which is very efficient, often better, than its Western counterpart. Third is industry supplying consumer goods, from clothes to typewriters, the output of which, being quantitatively inadequate, results in the notorious queues for such goods, and, being qualitatively inferior to Western goods, to a black market for Western jeans for ordinary people and a network of shops containing Western goods in which only the élites or those with access to Western currencies can shop.

The reasons for the low efficiency of Soviet agriculture therefore derive from the urban bias of a political ideology which devotes less capital to agriculture than to industry, allots inadequate scientific resources, material and human, to agriculture, and leaves the supremely difficult management of such a variable productive activity as agriculture in the hands of those considered not good enough to run industry.[161]

The socialization of agriculture in the USSR had been carried out in the worst possible way under the worst possible circumstances. However, despite the dominance, ideological and political, of the USSR over the new Second World, there was no re-run of Soviet disasters in agriculture, *pace* theorists of the 'natural history of revolution' school. Critics of this approach have emphasized the advantage of backwardness which enables late-comers to start with more advanced or more appropriate technology. But it also means that they can learn from the mistakes as well as the achievements of their predecessors.

Given the dominance of the pioneer communist country, large-scale collectivized agriculture was the goal in the newer communist states. But given the trauma of collectivization in the USSR, implementation of that project was to vary from country to country, in accordance with historical and cultural legacies of each, and to be marked by caution and experiment in pushing and leading the peasantry towards collectivization. In Poland, it was even abandoned. If the USSR provided a model, then, just as the United Kingdom and later the USA had done for the First World, it was a negative as well as a positive model.

The most gigantic task of all was that which confronted the Chinese communists when they took power in 1949 in a country of 500 million people, four out of five of them peasants. The course of revolution there had been fundamentally different: it had been based on a peasantry that had been involved in revolution and social upheaval for over a century. The greatest mass war of the nineteenth century was not the US Civil War, but the Taiping Rebellion of the 1850s and 1860s against the foreign Manchu (Ch'ing) dynasty. That national struggle expressed in the traditionalist slogan 'Overthrow the Ch'ing; restore the Ming', overlapped with a much more radical and novel utopian project, ideologically compounded of both new Christian and older Buddhist millenarism. But its social content was a peasant one: the dream of getting rid of the mandarins and the gentry and distributing the land so that each family could support itself. Women, who 'held up half the heavens', were to be freed from foot-binding, concubinage, arranged marriages, polygyny and prostitution, and brought into public life. The drugs, from opium and alcohol to ancestor worship and the great religions of Confucianism, Taoism and Buddhism, which had reconciled the peasants to their lot, were denounced.

It was a vision, and a regime, powerful enough to move millions in a struggle that lasted over a decade and cost the lives not of millions, but of tens of millions. The role of revolutionaries like Sun Yat-sen in the collapse of the Empire half a century later was, in comparison, of minor importance.

Hence there was no social revolution of the kind that had occurred in Russia. Politically, China was a semi-colony, in which the real power lay with the various imperialist Powers that had already chopped off the outer parts of the country and now each had their own sphere of influence within it. Effective government lay in the hands of warlords ruling their own countries within a country. But in the 1920s, Chiang Kai-shek set about re-unifying the country, and with the aid of a modernized army and the political support of the rapidly-growing Left, was soon in control of most of the country. He was to use that power to keep China firmly within the capitalist world.

To observers like Tawney, in the early 1930s, it was clear that the revolution begun in 1911 had been 'a bourgeois affair'. The 'revolution of the peasants' was 'still to come'. In an oft-quoted image, he described 'whole districts' in which 'the rural population is [like] a man standing up to his neck in water, so that even a ripple is sufficient to drown him'.[162]

During the Northern Expedition of reunification, Chiang's Nationalist Party had been supported by the much smaller Communist Party. As we saw earlier, Mao Tse-tung, one of the young Communist cadres sent to Hunan province to mobilize the peasants, found that the peasants had already mobilized themselves; co-operatives were springing up everywhere, roads and embankments were being repaired and evening classes organized. Women and poor people marched into temple feasts and sat down to eat and drink. In this struggle between the 'peasants' cultural movement' and the 'bad social customs' of the 'culture of the landlords' more had been accomplished than all the efforts of the 'so-called "educators" for "popular education" ' (which we would call 'community developers') put together.[163]

Mao's rich peasant background enabled him to grasp peasant behaviour in a way that eluded a city intellectual like Lenin. Though he continued to use the language of base and superstructure throughout his life, he showed the peasant's counter-cultural challenge to landlord cultural hegemony to be no mere superstructural phenomenon, but an integral counterpart, in the struggle between classes, of economic and political struggles. But this was no mere peasantism, and the analysis of culture was a complement to, not a substitute for, the analysis of economic relationships. At the societal level, indigenous landlords and compradors had become the 'vassals of the international bourgeoisie, dependent upon imperialism', and representatives of the 'most backward and reactionary relations of production'; the 'national bourgeoisie', on the other hand, had an interest in developing capitalism in both town and countryside, and might, at times, resent competition from foreign capital. But they would never tolerate a militant proletariat. The petty bourgeoisie – owner-peasants, master handicraftsmen and 'petty intellectuals' – could be divided into those who were doing well economically, those who just got by, and those who were losing out. Mao's knowledge of the life of the mass of the population is reflected in the detail of his breakdown of what he then called the semi-proletariat (i.e., the rural working population) into no less than five categories: semi-tenant peasants, poor peasants, handicraftsmen, shop assistants, and pedlars, the first two categories containing the vast majority of the population. Since there was hardly any capitalist farming proper, the rural proletariat were simply poor peasants hired by the year, the month or the day; the urban proletariat was a mere two million, together with a sizeable 'coolie' and 'lumpenproletarian' population.

Mao was to modify these categories in subsequent years, though he continued to cling to the dogma of the city proletariat as the 'leading force of the revolutionary movement' and the belief that poor peasants were more revolutionary than middle peasants.

The first idea was understandable in a country where the Communist Party, only founded in 1921 with fifty-seven members, was able to lead a general strike in Canton only a few years later. But two years after that, the workers' movement had been smashed and the Communist leaders forced to take refuge in the countryside. There they built up military forces in rural Soviet zones which they finally came to see as the new base for the revolution. So did Chiang Kai-shek, who launched five successive extermination campaigns against them. In 1934, they retreated again, in the Long March of 6000 miles to the border zone of Yenan in the North-west where they proceeded to establish a state within a state.

The Soviets in the South had been too short-lived to generate a large mass base. Often, so-called lumpenproletarian ex-soldiers and unemployed had to be recruited and turned into good communists through 'ideological remoulding'. In Yenan, the Communists, unlike bourgeois parties, had no economic resources with which to buy peasant support, through patronage or other inducements. They had no outside power-base either, so their own military strength depended upon local peasant volunteers and peasant supplies. Persuasion had to be the main way of developing a mass base rather than the exercise of force, as in Stalin's Russia, but support could not be built out of abstract propaganda about the dialectic or a socialist future. It depended on improving the life of the peasants here and now:

> We must go among the masses; arouse them to activity; concern ourselves with their weal and woe; and work earnestly and sincerely in their interests and solve their problems of salt, rice, shelter, clothing and childbirth . . . If we do so, the broad masses will certainly give us their support.[164]

The most crucial problem of all was the question of the land. It was the hope that the Communists would give them the land which was to transform a population habituated to resignation in the face of ruthless landlord oppression into the greatest mass revolutionary force of the twentieth century. Before then, 'the peasants', Hinton has written, 'seldom resisted the demands of the gentry', knowing full well what would happen to them if they did.[165]

In the South, they had gone too far too fast, taking land not only off the landlords, but also from rich and even middle peasants, who turned against them and used their influence to whip up the poorer peasants against the Reds. Now, faced with Japanese fascist invasion, it was crucial to retain the support of a wide coalition of classes. Land reforms were therefore restricted to the taking over of land belonging to collaborators with the Japanese, unutilized land, and that of exploitative landlords and rich peasants, but not the land of the middle peasants and other categories who engaged in little or no exploitation, since the development of agricultural production and rural industry was now the central economic necessity.

But in 1947 came the show-down with Chiang Kai-shek:

> The military offensive . . . was accompanied by an equally important political offensive. The heart of this second offensive was the Draft Agrarian Law . . . With sentences as abrupt as the strokes of a fodder-chopping knife, the new law proclaimed the death of landlordism:

> *Article 1*——The agrarian system of feudal and semi-feudal exploitation is abolished. The agrarian system of 'land-to-the-tiller' is to be realized.

> *Article 2*——Landownership rights of all landlords are abolished.

> *Article 3*——Landownership rights of all ancestral shrines, monasteries, schools, institutions, and organizations are abolished.

> *Article 4*——All debts incurred in the countryside prior to the reform . . . are cancelled.[166]

If they had stopped there, they would have brought into being a mass base for capitalism in the countryside in the shape of many tens of millions of micro-capitalist smallholders. Already highly acquisitive, individualistic, competitive and self-regarding, the more entrepreneurial and ruthless would have swiftly driven the poorer peasants to the wall. Stolypin's conservative dream would have been turned into reality – by communists.

But they had not fought for decades to develop capitalism. Instead, they proceeded, rapidly, to socialize agriculture. Once war-time destruction had been made good, they began to build upon other more positive elements of what Simmel called 'sociation' which were also intrinsic to peasant life. In the South, lineage property had been extensive and the income was often used to finance public works or leased to poor lineage members at low rents. Village associations also undertook such activities as crop watching or raising money for schools. Labour was also pooled, though usually only two or three households would work together in ploughing, planting, or harvesting. Larger groups would co-operate to maintain the dykes or form labour gangs to work on landlord estates.[167] At first they simply extended and encouraged traditional co-operation, gradually building up the number of households involved and designating them 'mutual aid teams'. Those blessed with a buffalo or a plough were encouraged to make them available to their neighbours and were often paid for doing so. In the mid-1950s came the first co-operatives, based on larger units, usually the village. By the time of the next phase of co-operation, not only had payments been phased out, but the separate pieces of land were being farmed jointly, though the product still belonged to the owner. Finally, in 1958, came the Great Leap Forward, when the 'relations of production' were brought into conformity with the reality of a socialized organization of work. Private property in land was now replaced by giant new farming units. The communes had made their historic appearance.

The model for these large-scale entities, divided into Brigades, and those into Teams, was, like so much else, borrowed from Soviet experience (though the Chinese do not acknowledge it) – the only model then available. So was the reward system based on work-points. But they had no intention, Mao was to privately remark, of doing what the USSR had done: 'drain the pool to catch the fish', ruin the rural economy and alienate the peasantry in the process of stepping up agricultural output.[168] Yet the formation and reorganization of the communes within the space of three or four years reflected their own bureaucratic shortcomings.

The marketing system discussed earlier changed considerably over the centuries. As population grew, people hived off to colonize new areas. Existing markets were held more frequently and their functions expanded; new ones were established. The decisive change came with the intensified commercialization of agriculture in the nineteenth century. As railways and roads penetrated the rural areas, many of the traditional markets were killed off and replaced by direct trade with the modern centres; whole villages now shrank back upon themselves.[169] Yet by 1948, the year before Liberation, only 10 per cent of the traditional systems had been supplanted by modern ones and when the Communists came to power in the following year, there were still some 58,000 of them. They were rapidly replaced by State trading companies and by co-operatives which both purchased the peasant's crops and supplied his consumer needs. The area they covered still corresponded to the 'natural' (historic, economic) boundaries of the older system with townships at their centres. By 1958, 30 per cent of the old markets had been modernized.

Then followed thc Great Leap Forward. In the drive against private traders, established markets were closed down and enormous new ones established that soon proved unworkable. There followed a period of serious empirical research to determine just what the natural boundaries of the trading zones of the countryside were, and a return to smaller, traditionally based areas. By 1964, there were still six to seven traditional markets for each modern one.

A similar process took place in production. The cautious progression from land reform, through mutual aid teams, to lower-level co-ops, and then to collective farms or advanced co-ops, reached its climax in 1958, when the leadership decided to group the villages which had become 750,000 collective farms into much larger units. At first, it seemed that this would be done in accordance with natural systems. But fear of local particularism, and of the domination of the countryside by local leaders who could readily mobilize ties of kinship and friendship to re-establish their control, led the Communists to incorporate the village within a very much larger unit in which such networks would be ineffective. The criterion of progress now became one of *size*: to make the new units, the communes, as big as possible. The 750,000 collective farms were now fused into only 24,000 gigantic communes often bigger even than Skinner's intermediate marketing areas. It was a system which could not work. The cadres were totally inexperienced in management of this kind at this level, and their ideological hostility to trade, plus the cult of self-sufficiency and egalitarianism, soon produced disaster. The whole system, constructed so rapidly in 1958–9, had to be dismantled in 1960–1 and reassembled by splitting the 24,000 communes into 74,000 new ones – a third of their former size. Unlike their predecessors, these now corresponded more to the natural standard marketing areas with their townships.

It had been a double dislocation, but it had laid the basis for steady expansion subsequently. Prices for grain were favourable and stable; the prices of consumer goods and agricultural inputs made in the city were kept cheap; taxes were low, and personal taxes non-existent; and.the peasantry kept and ate much of what the commune produced as well as the produce of their private plots. Non-economic benefits included a welfare fund for the needy (usually those households with a high worker:dependant ratio);

improved social services, from schools to clinics, at successive levels in the commune structure; and a high degree of local autonomy overall. Though the Party was still the decisive political authority, and classically Leninist in its democratic centralism, the commune was a unit of local government and not merely a farm, exercising important judicial, administrative, and even military functions, running its own schools and hospitals, and filling in an historic gap as the successor to the *hsiang* (township) which had always been the weak, lowest level of administration.

It was a development strategy which did not sacrifice agriculture to industry, nor give agriculture a privileged priority; a policy of 'walking on two legs', developing industry as well as agriculture. Between 1958 and 1975, 58 million new workers went into industry. But workers were absorbed within agriculture, both into traditional activities such as planting and trans-planting, and in newer, but still labour-intensive activities such as irrigation construction and maintenance and the techniques involved in developing multiple cropping and inter-cropping. Industrial inputs into agriculture came both from the urban factories and from developing local resources, notably fertilizers, nearly half of which came from small commune units by the mid-1970s. At the national level, it was the industrial sector which provided the bulk of State capital-formation; in 1950, agricultural tax receipts made up 29.6 per cent of national budgetary receipts; in 1958, only 8 per cent.

The Peasantry: Persistence, Transformation, Disappearance

In the first communist society, as in the leading capitalist countries, the mode of life followed by the majority of humankind since the Neolithic Revolution had been superseded. In Western Europe, however, it was usually a much more gradual process than it had been in eighteenth-century Britain. In Eastern Europe, the peasantry not only obstinately refused to disappear, but became an important force in political life.

After 1918, when the great archaic Empires of Austria-Hungary and Turkey were broken up to form new states, Yugoslavia, Czechoslovakia, and Romania, alongside Bulgaria, Greece and other pieces already hacked off the body of the Ottoman Empire, there was even a revival of peasant populism. Large landed estates, owned by those who had previously been the economically as well as politically dominant classes, were taken off them and divided amongst the peasantry. In Romania, the landlords lost 15 million acres and received only minimal compensation in return; at the end, the peasants' share of the arable land had risen from 55 to 88 per cent. In Bulgaria, all land over 75 acres was taken, and those who did not cultivate their holdings were only allowed to keep 25 acres. By 1926, four in every five peasant households owned their own land. But they lacked the capital and the expertise to develop agriculture, and the State, dominated by dis-possessed landowners who had moved into business and banking, directed capital into industrial development. Agricultural output declined and peasant discontent increased, taking the political form of peasant parties. In Bulgaria and Czechoslovakia, they actually participated in government for a time; in the Ukraine, during the chaos of the civil war, an autonomous peasant republic, with its own army based on the villages and inspired by a revived national consciousness, was established under the leadership of Nestor Makhno. A Green International of peasant movements and parties was even established.

Their social programme was classically populist. It denounced the exploitation of the countryside by the towns and by the financial middlemen. It was no longer possible to resist the march of industrialization, but it was possible to put forward an alternative to the concentration of industry in large plants located in the cities. Instead, labour-intensive industry, in smaller units spread across the country, should be developed. These ideas were actually put into practice. In Bulgaria, co-operative factories were established to can and export fruit; in Poland, a similar trade in meat. The Croat Peasant Party, the largest of all, with 5000 village branches and nearly a quarter of a million members, undertook road construction, irrigation, electrification, price-control, and extensive educational work.[170]

These movements were wiped out by fascism in the 1930s. As a class, the smallholding peasantry was to disappear altogether, Poland apart, after 1945.

But in the rest of the capitalist world, in the colonies and in neocolonial Latin America, soon joined by the newer dependent states established after the Second World War, peasants were still the majority of the population in most countries, even increasing in absolute numbers. Their influence on history was therefore quite different and much greater. Instead of being displaced by the new working class, as had happened in Britain, they co-existed with them.

The most dramatic irruption of peasants onto the stage of national life in a backward country, Russia and China apart, was the Mexican Revolution of 1910, under the leadership of Francisco Villa in the North and Emiliano Zapata in Morelos. Villa's men were mainly cowboys from the gigantic, often foreign-owned ranches of the North, where the presence of US-owned industry as well had led to the savagely repressed textile-mill strike in Cananea in 1908 and therefore to a higher level of anti-*gringo* nationalist sentiment than further South. Villa, indeed, was to achieve the distinction of leading the only foreign invasion in modern times of the US homeland. Zapata's followers were smallholders whose Indian ancestors had been pushed out of the fertile valleys into the surrounding mountains from whence their descendants came down to work on the sugar estates and in the mills.[171]

More than a million people died in that revolution – one in fifteen of the population, and one in three in Morelos. At its end, the two armies met in Mexico City. State power almost literally lay in the street. It was in their hands. But neither wanted it. Villa had little conception of an alternative social order beyond using the huge ranches to support his veterans, some of whom became landowners themselves.[172] The southerners' aims were quite different; they also knew exactly what they wanted: the restoration of the land that had been lost. When hc went off to the revolution in 1909, Zapata buried the sacred land titles of the village under the floor of the church in his village. At the end of it, the peasants were to turn to these documents, the *mapas*, in reclaiming the lands taken from their forefathers. The southern programme was violently anti-*hacendado*: the monopolist of all the lands, the usurper of nature's wealth, the creator of national misery, the infamous slave-trader who treats men like beasts of burden; an unproductive and idle parasite. But urban capitalism was acceptable: the manufacturer, the merchant, the mine-owner, the businessman, all the active and enterprising elements which open new paths for industry and provide work to great groups of workers. The programme was therefore very simple: 'War to death against the *hacendados*. Ample guarantees for all the other classes of society.[173] Even less were the Zapatistas interested in State power. When they met in Mexico City in 1914, Zapata symbolically let Villa sit on the Presidential throne while their picture was being taken. But neither was to become Head of State. Instead, power fell into the hands of a third force, the Constitutionalists led by Carranza, whose successors were to create a new capitalism controlled by a new class of politicians who brought together under the umbrella of a single party all the major power-blocs in society. Their mass base was the new working class, which they were even able to use in the shape of 'Red battalions' of workers against the Zapatista rebels who continued to fight for the land. After several more years of bloody fighting, and the treacherous murder of Zapata, and then (after he had long laid down his arms) of Villa, the peasant dream was realized in a land reform more analogous to the system of land-tenure of the Russian *mir* than to that of the small-holder under capitalism, since though each household was entitled to a plot, the land belonged to the village, designated an *ejido*.[174]

Eighty per cent of Morelos households now had fields of their own, mostly just enough for subsistence. But they had no capital, and the sugar economy was in ruins. If title was communitarian, individualistic farming, on a capitalist market, was a recipe for poverty. For decades, they struggled to get more land, and often had to pay high prices when they did. Meantime, the population grew by leaps and bounds. By the end of the Second World

War, they were surrounded by booming towns filled with immigrants from other Mexican States. By the 1960s, Zapata's own village, Anenecuilco, was poverty-stricken and in debt.

The heroism of the Mexican peasantry had been a tragic sacrifice, contradicted by the narrowness of their own social vision.[175] They had succeeded in restoring social forms based on the past which could only result in economic disaster. Unlike the communists, they had no alternative project with which to resist the growing competition of urban industry and agribusiness elsewhere in Mexico.

Reds, the film of John Reed's life, is, in one way, an astounding instance of Euro-North American ethnocentrism, in that it devotes no attention to Reed's involvement in the Mexican Revolution. Yet there is justice in that silent judgement, for the Mexican peasant revolution failed in its social project. Hence it had only minimal significance as a model for other countries, and only minor influence even on adjoining countries. In contrast, the Russian Revolution was an event of world significance, for, despite the way in which the Bolsheviks won power, they used it to establish an entirely new social system.

Reform:

(i) Community Development

The response of peasants to their oppression has only rarely been a revolutionary one, for that can only come about under a very special concatenation of conditions, as is also the case with regard to revolution amongst that other major exploited class, the proletariat. Only in the fantasies of romantics are peasants – or workers – intrinsically and endemically revolutionary. Most of the time they try to solve their life-problems by far less drastic and dangerous methods. Nevertheless, the peasant revolution of 1917 and the collectivization campaign afterwards cast an ominous shadow over Europe, as did the more limited peasant revolutions in colonial Ireland and ex-colonial Mexico.

After the Second World War, the lessons of China seemed even more threatening, above all in the world becoming known as the 'Third World'. The need for reform assumed urgency. The first sizeable, but cautious initiative took the form of what was called 'community development'. Ideologically, it drew upon a de-politicized version of Mid-West populism mixed with a vulgarized North American psychology from which any vestige of conflict theory had been removed. The central theoretical notion was that the farmers' problems were basically problems of knowledge (i.e. ignorance) and of communication, and could be solved via education and by discussing their difficulties with other members of the local community and with the local representatives of government. The wider vision, and class militancy, of traditional Western populism, which had seen the banks, the commodity exchanges, the railroads, and government as the main enemies, were thus expunged, and group therapy put in its place. If the blockages to the spontaneous expression of the peasants' basic needs could be overcome, it was assumed, popular energies would be released on a gigantic scale. And the whole thing would be democratic.

In India, where the largest experiment took place, the Ford Foundation played a major role in its implementation, with the co-operation of the Indian government.[176] The main effort was devoted to injecting new life into the village councils, the *panchayats*. The key catalyst was to be a new kind of representative of government whose function is best expressed by the French term *animateur*. He was to stimulate and mobilize latent reservoirs of initiative and talent which would set the development process in motion. It was a project, as Moore points out, based on the 'absurd' assumption that it was possible to 'democratize the villages without altering property relationships'. Moreover, even a revivified network of *panchayats* could scarcely be effective when the real centres of power lay outside the village altogether. Thirdly,'bringing resources and techniques to the peasants' doorstep through bureaucratic procedures, while generally refraining from making or even trying to make any change in the social structure and general situation that prevents the peasants from adopting better methods' was doomed to failure.

Land reform proper has still to be undertaken by the State to this day (Vinobha Bhave's *Bhoodan* Land Gift movement being a limited substitute relying on religiously-activated charity). The Community Development Programme was launched in 1952 with considerable energy. By 1963, development blocks covered the whole country. But since the programme steered clear of such sensitive problems as caste, land ownership, and labour relationships, it could not be expected to get far, and didn't. The Nagpur Resolution, adopted by Congress in 1959, envisaging a future of co-operative joint cultivation, was to remain an even more abstract asseveration. CD, in Moore's terse verdict, turned out to be an 'out-and-out failure'.[177] Seven years after it had been launched, more than three-quarters of India's food production never reached the market, and 85 per cent of the villagers' credit still came from money-lenders and the richer people in the village, at exorbitant rates.

The administrative shortcomings were a consequence of the programme's ideological underpinnings. At the macro-level, a national bureaucracy famed for its standardized methods of administration applied uniform methods across the immensely varied terrains of a subcontinent, making a mockery of the notion of responsiveness to local 'felt needs'. At the local level, the dominant castes, resisting any weakening of their control over labour and rent, effectively blocked change. Working among Canadian Indians at about the same time in similar group discussion workshops, I also observed that the poor were fearful of openly expressing any criticism of the village oligarchs in public, and that when controversial positions were taken, the result was not resolution of the problems, but the sharpening of class hostilities.

(ii) Co-operatives

Agrarian reform necessarily entails a dialectical interplay between peasant aspirations and the intentions of those who control the State and the economy. By the 1960s, the search for a non-radical way of achieving the twin objectives of alleviating peasant land-hunger and raising productivity had led to a recognition that reliance on technological innovation or upon education alone was not enough: new forms of economic and even social organization were needed. Though such ideas remained anathema to landowning dinosaurs, for whom 'co-operative' was a synonym for socialism, to the more far-sighted the co-operative seemed the ideal solution. It was eminently social, but also perfectly compatible with the maintenance of private property. Under socialist auspices, as in China, it had been a step on the road to socialized agriculture. But co-operative movements could also be steered in other directions more acceptable, too, to peasants whose main aim was to maintain and even extend their independence.

By the 1960s, co-operativism had become quite acceptable to the Inter-American Development Bank, the ILO, and other development agencies.[178] The co-operative form of organization, it was now appreciated, was intrinsically neither socialistic nor redistributive: firstly, because it was based upon the private enterprise (however small) as the key unit of both ownership and production; secondly, because it was a form of mutual association in which inequalities of land-holding were not threatened, for the two principal ways in which farmers benefited by joining together were through the sharing of jointly-owned resources (orchards, grazing lands, etc.), or via access to common services such as those of a veterinarian or the use of a tractor. The most important benefits, however, were in the sphere of marketing rather than in the sphere of production. Yet the costs of production could be lowered, too, by extending the classical pattern of the pioneer consumer co-operatives introduced in Rochdale a century ago: via economies of scale entailed in bulk-purchase, and the more radical bypassing of profit-taking middlemen. Not only household necessities, but farming inputs (gasoline, fertilizer, seed, machinery) could be purchased in this way. In Saskatchewan, by the 1960s, co-operatively owned supermarkets in the big cities had emerged alongside the smaller rural retail outlets for consumer goods, and a vast network of co-operatively-owned services, from gas stations to bus companies and even insurance, had grown up.

But the basic unit was still the private farm, and it still had to compete on the capitalist world-market. The very success of the co-operative, paradoxically, strengthened the private farm and private farming. Further, though the Rochdale principles were politically egalitarian (and under inegalitarian colonial conditions 'one man – one vote' could become a revolutionary slogan), economically, the more you purchased, the larger your dividend. Even if the rate of dividend was the same for everyone, those who purchased the most got more back in absolute terms.[179] It was also they who made more use of the co-op's jointly owned facilities, such as tractors. This contradiction between *de jure* political equality and *de facto* economic inequality – the classical bourgeois contradiction – inevitably resulted in the domination of the co-op by the larger farmers, Their economic predominance enabled them to build up networks of patronage, and they also possessed the social skills – minimally, at least, literacy and numeracy, but also managerial know-how – with which to run large-scale organizations.[180] Control over the funds and over the machinery of communications of such large-scale organizations also became a basis for the exercise of even national-level political power, since they could be used to deliver votes, and their funds to finance enterprises often in no way related to the direct improvement of the farming operations of their members. In modern, *étatiste* societies, especially in the mobilizatory states of the Third World, co-operative organizations are far removed from their origins in small-scale, voluntaristic associations, and are often not only controlled, but even initiated by the State:

> The State intervenes not only via technical and extension assistance but also by providing credit; by organizing co-operative marketing . . . that replaces the private middleman by State marketing boards or marketing co-operative monopolies, by subsidizing transport and storage facilities; [it also] underwrites subsidies and price stabilization agreements, and by forward trade agreements seeks to ensure a guaranteed market . . . to protect the small producer from the vagaries of fluctuating demand and the uncertainties of Nature.[181]

(iii) Land Reform

Taking land off large landowners and giving it to those without enough to live on is, at first sight, the most radical alternative of all. Since the Second World War, populist and radical regimes as well as socialist ones have, indeed, introduced such reforms. But so have many governments of impeccably reactionary complexion: South Korea, Taiwan, MacArthur's Japan or the Shah's Iran, to name no others. There has often been fierce resistance, as in Guatemala in the 1950s, when the moderate reforms proposed by the Arbenz government were enough to plunge the United Fruit Company into panic, even though, despite the fact that 2.5 per cent of the population owned 70 per cent of the arable land, it was only proposed to take over uncultivated land. Within four years, the government had been overthrown by an invasion stage-managed by the CIA. It was an old-fashioned response. Within seven years, the Alliance for Progress was proposing not dissimilar reforms.

For land reform, properly managed, did not have to threaten the future of the propertied classes prepared to alter their mode of operation. To governments, it offered the prospect of political reprieve: damping down peasant discontent which might induce them to listen to leftists; and economically, the likelihood that peasants on their own land would produce more, thereby assisting the balance of payments, feeding the cities, soaking up unemployment, easing the pressures on the urban areas, and extending the tax base. Landowners could unload their marginal lands, and use the compensation they received to modernize their operations on the best lands, or invest it in industry and business, in consumption or retire to Florida.

Pressure from below, though a key ingredient, is not necessarily decisive. Nor is the misery of the peasant population. The ideological orientation of government and its flexibility are equally important variables. Two case studies, one of land reform under a leftish military government in Ecuador, the other under a newly-independent African government inheriting an agricultural economy dominated by white settlers, illustrate the interplay of these forces.

An Agrarian Reform Institute (IERAC) had been established in Ecuador as early as 1964, its objective being the modernization of agriculture by replacing 'feudal' relationships by farms run as modern business enterprises. In fact, even in the traditional Sierra, capitalist relations had long been dominant, though traditional ways of mobilizing labour, such as the *huasipungo* system, in which the worker received the use of a small plot on the landlord's estate in return for his labour, were still common. Those who owned land had, on average, less than five hectares. Over a third of the land was owned by 0.2 per cent of the population in estates of over 1000 *has.*; two-thirds belonged to owners of 100 *has.* and over who often did not bother to farm it.[182] Hence, though four out of five peasant farmers on the Coast owned their plots, they were so small they had to go and work for others and were endemically in debt to money-lenders.

Extensive pastoralism had become the dominant type of farming in the Sierra. But on the Coast, which had been virtually unpopulated throughout most of the nineteenth century, a new class of landowners, oriented to export agriculture, had come into being at the end of the century, and in the civil war of 1895–1912 under Eloy Alfaro, had broken the dominance of the older landowning class in the Sierra. The way was now open for the cocoa boom which began in the 1920s and ended with the World Depression of the 1930s. By the 1960s, multinational banana corporations, faced with crop diseases in Central America (and, some say, fearful of a re-run of Arbenz) turned to Ecuador. The Coast now became a sea of bananas as the 'green gold' replaced the 'golden bean' (cocoa).

The multinationals rarely owned the plantations themselves. Half the land was in large units (over 100 *has*.), the rest worked by peasants, whose average holding was 50 *has*. Four out of five owned their own land; the rest rented it in a variety of ways, some (*precaristas*) paying rent in kind; others (*arrendatarios*) in cash. The large plantations were owned by or, via contract arrangements, closely articulated with the major export houses who oligopolized the export trade controlled by the major fruit corporations in the USA.

By 1967, Ecuador was importing £7 million worth of food per annum (though the Coast alone, it is estimated, could feed 20 million people). Three years later, the bill for food imports had doubled. Yet the small peasants could not survive; in the rice-growing areas, the average size of the smallest holdings was only one (*sic*) hectare. Many fled to the city: Guayaquil grew from a small port at the turn of the century to an industrial city of over a million by 1975. Two out of three of the inhabitants were first-generation immigrants.

The Land Reform Institute, and the first Agrarian Reform Law, had no radical intent. In Catholic language, it saw the 'social function of property' as the productive use of the land, and to this end, encouraged new zones of colonization in the jungle, a policy which did not conflict with existing rights of ownership (except those of the few remaining Indians). Conversely, redistribution of land, which did threaten private landowners, went on at a snail's pace. Then, overnight, the two crucial constraints were removed. In 1971, Ecuador became an oil-rich country. A radical military government then launched across-the-board capitalist modernization, including the new Agrarian Reform Law of 1973. Brigades of young *técnicos* now descended on the Coast to appropriate and distribute the land. Yet a campaign of this kind, by now, could have impeccable capitalist sponsorship: the Canadian government backed the research, and the US AID added the new element: the co-operatives. The numbers of coastal owners of land now shot up from 5000 to 15,000 in two years. Nevertheless, only 7 per cent of the land had been scheduled for redistribution, for the larger landowners fought a fierce rear-guard action, fearing that the reform might be extended to their better quality land and their more efficient and profitable estates. With the arrival of a more right-wing military government in 1976, that trend disappeared. For the peasants the crucial constraint had now become credit, which the government now also provided. In 1972, the Banco de Fomento had authorized a mere £8000 in loans in Guayas Province; two years later, nearly

£4 million. For if the great bulk of this went to the 2.5 per cent who still owned a third of the land, the peasant had now been liberated from the grip of the money-lender. The tenurial changes had also been real, nevertheless: former tenants were now owners. But they faced new kinds of dependence. Increasingly organized into co-operatives, party political, religious and personalistic movements competed for their allegiance. But their key dependence was now upon the State, through its crucial control of credit. Control of the State had now become decisive in society as a whole, for neither the feeble industrial/commercial bourgeoisie nor the traditional landowning class had proved capable of launching capitalist modernization. In one crucial respect the situation was atypical of the Third World as a whole, for reform had become possible only because of the miraculous arrival of the income from oil. For most of the world, the State did not have such vast quantities of capital to draw upon. In the newly-independent countries of Africa, the main source of income for the State had been the profits it made by establishing monopolistic control over primary-product exports, including oil. In countries dependent on agricultural exports, monopolistic marketing boards purchased the peasants' crops and sold them on the world market, the peasants receiving a price well below that for which the crop was sold, the State keeping the rest. In Ecuador, income from oil made that kind of extraction less necessary, but marketing – like most things – was still regulated by the State. The peasant organizations which now sprang up therefore had little real autonomy.

They were also divided internally. The poorest of them, with on average only 1.5 *has*, even after the Reform, had to seek wage-employment with their more successful neighbours, often members of the same co-operative. Others swelled the ranks of the urban poor in Guayaquil. Thus class differentiation split the co-ops down the middle, the poorest, indeed, favouring collective farming as the only solution to the chronic shortage of land.

The dilemma facing governments which had to respond to popular demand for land reform was a severe one. Repression was out of the question, in particular, in the newly-decolonized states which had been swept to power on a wave of nationalist enthusiasm and now had to meet expectations that life would be improved for everyone. Paradoxically, the distribution of the land to the poor was often to prove easier to manage in countries where the best land had been appropriated by foreign settlers than in countries where it involved removing an indigenous landowning class. Moreover, the finance to buy the settlers out was available, since the colonizing Power was equally sensitive to the need to protect the interests of its nationals who had come as colonists.

Britain's experience in rescuing its colonists went back to the American Loyalists. More recent was the bailing out of the English settler class in its oldest, European colony, Ireland. Despite forty-eight Coercion Acts between 1830 and 1875, after the Land War of 1879–82, in which rents had been refused and mansions burned down, the writing was on the wall. The land, by then, was, in any case, rapidly losing its value on the market. Hard on the heels of the limited Land Acts of 1870 and 1881 came the more radical Land-Purchase Act of 1903. The central objective was to ensure that the landlords were compensated. The sheer scale of the operation meant that only government had the resources and the political commitment to its historic supporters to put up the £112 million needed. But they also needed to recoup that outlay. The obvious solution was that the new owners should pay for the over-valued land at an average of 3.5 per cent rate of interest over twenty-five years. At one end of the class spectrum, the preservation of the large estates was encouraged, by reducing the interest-rate; at the other, tenants were given special inducements to purchase the land they presently rented.

This pattern was repeated, sixty years later, when an African settler state, Kenya, had to be decolonized. Kenya had only come into existence at the end of the last century, when the Highlands were handed over to European settlers, and a labour-force brought into being by making Africans pay taxes in cash which could only be earned by working for White men. Some found themselves 'squatters' on land which had originally been theirs; they were soon joined by the impoverished of the Reserves. An initially vigorous growth of African cash-crop production was swiftly suppressed by legislation which reduced African farmers in the Reserves to the level of subsistence-producers, while their taxes paid for government administration and for massive subsidies to European farming. By the 1920s, half the able-bodied men from the two largest tribes, the Kikuyu and the Luo, were working for Europeans.

The first nationalist movements began soon afterwards, but they were not to become mass movements until after the Second World War, in the shape of an orthodox nationalist party, the Kenya African Union. To a new generation influenced by wartime experience in the army, especially overseas, more radical methods were called for. Backed by the landless *ahoi* and the unemployed, they launched the Mau Mau Rebellion in 1952, in which families with even a little land often became 'Loyalist' home guards.

By 1954, the Rebellion had been crushed. But the more forward-looking elements, half a century after Stolypin, realized that further conflict could only be avoided by tackling 'the basic problem of low living standards, so that there may rapidly emerge from the poorer majority people having similar interests and similar ideals to those economically more advanced'.[83]

Even before independence, the Swynnerton Plan had advocated 'African advancement' via the consolidation of the land and the issuing of freehold titles. 'Able, energetic or rich' Africans should be given their head. But the opposition to the majority of the settlers had to be broken before this could happen on a national scale. Independence, in 1964, made that possible. As in Ireland, the settlers were bought out by the British government, now assisted by the Commonwealth Development Corporation and the World Bank in putting up the £7.5 million needed, which the 7800 peasant and yeoman farmers were to pay back over twenty-five or more years. But the need for land was so great that further settlement schemes had to be rapidly improvized. By 1970, 35,401 families had been given land in the Million Acres scheme, and a further 18,000 on 'squatter' settlement schemes. By now, a fifth of the old White Highlands was in the hands of small peasant proprietors and output increased impressively by 4.5 per cent per annum between 1964 and 1969. But the poorest farmers soon found themselves unable to hand over the 70 per cent of their income required to meet debt payments, and to develop the land they would have needed even more capital. By 1970, 44 per cent of the scheduled repayments were in arrears. There were then attempts to both enforce payment, and to ease the terms. But foreign governments and international agencies were not prepared to tolerate default on this scale. Though there were now increasing numbers of landless once more, further settlement projects had to be abandoned and those who had no land now began to resent the privileges of those in the settlement areas.

The decisive shift, however, was the creation of a new ruling class, to which political power had been handed over at Independence (not, as in Algeria, including any of the leaders of the armed struggle in the field), who now used their control over the State to forge new links with international capital, and, in the process, enrich themselves. In agriculture alone, they were able to borrow £3.2 million from State agencies between 1963 and 1969. Though the rate of default was high among this new élite, the British government, in contrast to its stance *vis-à-vis* the smaller peasants, stepped in to bail out the large farm sector, since these people were their new neocolonial allies. The latter, drawing on development loans like their White settler predecessors, also used their political weight to win favourable prices for maize and milk. At the top, now, was a class of very large landowners, plugged into the ruling political party and to foreign capital; at the bottom, micro-enterprises lacking the capital to improve their farming practices. But the major pickings were in business. Nationalization, a term which hitherto had had socialist connotations, now became a synonym for Africanization. To operate locally, foreign corporations now needed to put Africans on the board. A year before Independence (1963), even among the Kikuyu, there had only been 645 with over thirteen years of education. By 1971, 41 per cent of all management posts were held by Africans. African entrepreneurs further received government assistance in favourable loans or credit, reserved markets and sources of supply, and prices which enabled

them to move into small-scale retail trade, transport, and construction, and
bring to an end Asian dominance of these sectors. But it was foreign capital
which now flowed in on a massive scale – £10 million a year by the late 1960s –
and was to dominate the commanding heights of the economy. The
dispossessed European farmers who had invested their compensation in
industry and commerce were swiftly eclipsed by the multinational corporations, who, a few government-foreign ventures apart, soon controlled the
entire urban sector of the economy.

In socialist Tanzania, the vision, at Independence in 1961, of a participatory society, with a minimal repressive apparatus – of a country without an
army – had been rapidly destroyed. Amin's brutal invasion, seventeen years
later, had to be met by counter-force. Internally, the ideals of Ùjamaa were
used to legitimize the 'villageization' of 5½ million people in three years
enforced by bureaucrats ignorant of the agricultural realities. The benefits it
brought in the social field, such as improved access to education, were
negated by the alienation of most of the peasants, while progress in
agriculture was held back because the towns were receiving three times as
much capital investment as agriculture.

The Varieties of Capitalist Agriculture

The variety of forms of capitalist ownership and ways of organizing
production, then, can be reduced to a limited number of types, for
agriculture is shaped, under capitalism, by the same forces – the concentration and centralization of capital, and the optimization of return on capital
investment – that govern the development of industry. One taxonomy of
Latin American agriculture thus classifies the present-day successors of the
hacienda and of the Indian closed corporate communities of the past
together into decentralized estates; more modern centralized ones, run
according to the logic of rational (capitalist) management, together with
commercial estates and plantations; and peasant family enterprise.[184]

Another approach is to focus on the economic consequences of these
arrangements for people who work on the land, rather than on property
relations and production arrangements, distinguishing units run by family
labour from those too small to absorb the labour of the whole family, and
from those needing additional, non-family, labour.

Capitalist relations in agriculture can thus take many forms in respect of
the organization of agriculture, in terms of forms of ownership and use of the
land, and in the ways crops are marketed both nationally and internationally. The increasing control over agriculture by the State, and the increasing
involvement of producers everywhere in a market where the prices for their

Table 3   **Relative Number and Area of Farm Units by Size Groups in Seven Latin American Countries**

(Percentage of country total in each size class)

Countries	Sub-Family[a]	Family[b]	Multi-Family Medium[c]	Multi-Family Large[d]	Total
Argentina					
No. of farm units	43.2	48.7	7.3	0.8	100.0
Area in farms	3.4	44.7	15.0	36.9	100.0
Brazil					
No. of farm units	22.5	39.1	33.7	4.7	100.0
Area in farms	0.5	6.0	34.0	59.5	100.0
Chile					
No. of farm units	36.9	40.0	16.2	6.9	100.0
Area in farms	0.2	7.1	11.4	81.3	100.0
Colombia					
No. of farm units	64.0	30.2	4.5	1.3	100.0
Area in farms	4.9	22.3	23.3	49.5	100.0
Ecuador					
No. of farm units	89.9	8.0	1.7	0.4	100.0
Area in farms	16.6	19.0	19.3	45.1	100.0
Guatemala					
No. of farm units	88.4	9.5	2.0	0.1	100.0
Area in farms	14.3	13.4	31.5	40.8	100.0
Peru					
No. of farm units	88.0	8.5	2.4	1.1	100.0
Area in farms	7.4	4.5	5.7	52.4	100.0

a *Sub-Family*: Farms large enough to provide employment for less than 2 people with the typical incomes, markets and levels of technology and capital now prevailing in each region.

b *Family*: Farms large enough to provide employment for 2 to 3.9 people on the assumption that most of the farm work is being carried out by the members of the farm family.

c *Multi-Family Medium*: Farms large enough to provide employment for 4 to 12 people.

d *Multi-Family Large*: Farms large enough to provide employment for over 12 people.

Source: Barraclough (1973), Table 1–2, p. 16.[185]

produce are governed by world commodity markets in New York, Chicago, or London, rather than by local flows of goods and movements of prices, has resulted in programmes which seek to grapple with all these problems at once. But they are never purely technical or purely economic, for they always involve a social and political calculus as well. Under such conditions, peasants often experience a new lease of life, on terms, however, over which they have little control. One of these major innovations was the Green Revolution, the development of 'miracle' strains of wheat, rice and other basic grains, which was immediately seized upon by governments and ruling classes as a means of pre-empting the Red Revolution and sometimes built into programmes of colonization or land reform. The package involved usually entailed much more than seeds: inputs of irrigation-systems, fertilizers, pesticides, and machinery which were beyond the reach of the poorer peasants without access to cheap credit. The outcome, for them, was inevitable: those with the necessary capital succeeded, whilst those without sold out or went to work for their richer neighbours. As so often before, the cultivator often found himself working the same land, but no longer for himself. And even where ceilings were established upon the amount of land that could be legally owned, as in the Gezira Scheme in the Sudan, ingenious entrepreneurial peasants soon found ways round these obstacles, installing their kin and dependants as dummy owners.[186] In India, these 'unprecedented changes have enabled that country to come near to self-sufficiency in food supplies. They have also greatly strengthened the political power of the rich peasants and the capitalist farmers.'[187]

In Mexico, research into new varieties of potatoes and other crops, developed locally by Rockefeller Foundation scientists, produced disease-resistant, high-yield varieties that were already widely in use by the time of the boom of the 1960s. The boom, which had begun during the Second World War in cotton, cereals, coffee and sugar, was bringing in nearly half the country's foreign earnings by 1966. But most of the $8 billion generated between 1940 and 1970 went to develop industry (leading to a negative balance of payments). In agriculture, government investment was mainly restricted to irrigation projects. The new Green technology, originally conceived of as appropriate only for the larger farms, considered more receptive to innovation, was now made available to others not only because of the urgency of greater production, but also because of the political dangers of discontent among 40 per cent of the population. Through marketing organizations, price guarantees, and a host of State and parastatal institutions, the Green Revolution, backed by international credit agencies, banks and other bodies (the FAO, IDB, etc.), had brought about the transfer of $2 billion worth of capital and technology per year to Latin America alone by this time.[188] It was profitable business, for rates of profit of US food corporations abroad averaged 13 per cent on capital invested as against only 7.8 per cent at home, apart from income from patents, technological services, and payments for the use of brand-names.

Beginning in the 1960s, agricultural expansion slowed down. In the towns, food became dearer; in the countryside, people began to leave in larger numbers than before for the cities and the USA, and in some zones virtual guerrilla war broke out. By 1975, Mexico was importing 8 billion pesos' worth of cereals and grains a year. The government's response was not simply one of repression, but to stimulate production and strengthen CONASUPO, a State distribution network established to bring cheap food to the urban population. Its budget grew from 5 billion pesos in 1970 to 40 billion by 1976. By 1975, there were 2,185 urban outlets, many of them huge supermarkets, offering clothing and other consumer goods as well as food. To ensure supplies, guaranteed prices, and a network of 'people's granaries', were established, together with credit agencies, training facilities, and even touring theatrical troupes and TV shows aimed at the peasants.

The crisis was averted. Peasant production had been revived. The costs were increased dependence upon technology owned by the multinationals, and an increase in new irrigated zones of agribusiness in the North far greater than the increase obtained in the peasant sector. To achieve this, the water supply of whole new valleys was used to irrigate what had previously been semi-desert. Most of the production went to the USA, notably meat, luxury and tropical vegetables and fruit – a trade Feder has called 'strawberry imperialism',[189] funnelled through centres like Nogales, Arizona, where ninety US distributors purchased half the incoming supplies. Internally, growing flowers for Mothers' Day once a year was far more profitable than growing food.

The peasants, too, become a source of enormous profits. Despite government price controls, and support for purchasing and marketing organizations, these themselves often make gigantic profits, and often become the major source of government revenue. Rather than protect the peasants, they constitute enormous systems of governmental exploitation, which feebly organized peasants or those in bureaucratically controlled unions are powerless to influence. In the interstices, private enterprise often persists. Independent 'coyotes', who advance credit to peasants in return for half the crop, make excellent profits. All the costs of transport, chemical inputs, and the labour costs involved, are split between the two parties, before the balance is divided. The middleman thus pays nothing for the peasant's labour or for the use of the land. The seeds are monopolized by a few large agricultural firms, who are themselves crop-producers, who also sell fertilizers and insecticides at high prices. Production on the smallest plots (less than half a hectare) brings in half what a peasant working and selling on his own account receives for the same volume of output. Lacking experience of the new varieties and techniques, poor-peasant production is inferior in quality and quantity. The poorest share-croppers end up with half the price for which wholesalers sell their crops to retailers in Mexico City's central market; retailers then sell to their customers at double the price they paid. The middleman's profit in staking the poorest category of share-croppers, Oswald estimates, reaches 1414 per cent.[190]

Agribusiness

The elimination of the peasantry is usually defended, on economic grounds, as progressive. Peasants, it is argued, are inefficient, cannot compete with modern capitalist farming, and therefore *ought* to disappear, and even some of their greatest defenders, like Chayanov, accepted this as a long-run perspective. Others fought a rear-guard action on social and political grounds, arguing that otherwise millions would be underemployed in the countryside or miserable unemployables in the cities. Only a minority of 'peasantists' asserted that smallholder production could be, and was often, as efficient or even *more* efficient than capital-intensive farming, even by strictly economic (i.e., market) criteria.[191] Peasant production can, indeed, be highly productive in favourable environments.

The often despised shifting cultivation, for instance, can outstrip permanent farming, even in arid zones; in Tepotzlán, Mexico, equalling the best yields achieved by plough cultivation and double the average of the latter. With irrigation, astounding levels of output are found: in some areas of Java, nearly 5000 people can be supported on a square mile.[192]

The limiting factors are clearly, in part, technical: the amount and quality of land available, length of growing season (and therefore the number of harvests and types of crops possible), etc. But high productivity can also be achieved by using high inputs of labour rather than capital: in the extreme, what Wolf calls 'inordinate' inputs of labour, an acre under 'palaeotechnic' cultivation in Tepotzlán requiring 18 to 24 man-days of labour per acre in South-western China 178.2 man-days. But few peasant societies can live by agriculture alone. In the 'dead season' of winter they have to turn to handicrafts, usually textiles: weaving in the Andes; silk-production in China. In pastoral societies, carpet-making has become the major source of cash income, rather than a seasonal 'ancillary' activity, for the nomads of Central Asia.

Peasant cash-crop production can thus become a crucial source of supply and profit. Smallholders on Brazil's Amazonian frontier and in the Coast of Ecuador are used to clear the jungle, in colonization areas, then dispossessed, often by force, by companies who cash in on their labour. Peasant production is turned off and on, and abandoned when no longer needed. When world prices decline, the smallest peasants go to the wall. Yet as with industry deemed essential to the national interest (e.g., defence), or costly developments which are uneconomic at present, the calculus can never be purely economic. In the Third World, there is always the spectre of peasant revolution, more salient, hitherto, than that of proletarian revolution. Purely economic calculations of the efficiency of peasant as against large-scale farming do not count the social costs: the self-exploitation of efficient peasant production; the lack of inputs which would allow the poorer to increase their yields; or price structures which favour the big producer. Critics of peasant farming as *intrinsically* low both in productivity and in production usually fail to recognize that its shortcomings are usually due to external factors beyond the peasants' control such as the starving of peasant agriculture in Poland by withholding needed inputs. Under these conditions, Stavenhagen has written, 'comparing the *ejidatario* with the large agricultural enterprise is like comparing an unskilled worker with a business-school graduate in their ability to run a factory'.[193] Under optimal conditions, peasants can compete with extensive farming quite spectacularly, for the family growing a few acres of coffee can get to know each bush by name, where giant machines cull the bad and the good berries together.

But the smallholder will remain poor nevertheless. Hence they, and governments, seek new ways of raising the living-standards of the household, via the intensification of agriculture, or its extensification, and by shifting labour into the urban-industrial sector (rarely into small-scale rural industry). If the limitations upon peasant agriculture have never been purely technical, today this is even less the case. Cotton, coffee, tea, even rice, can be cultivated by machinery instead of by hand. Whether they are depends upon an economic, not a technological calculus: the relative costs of labour as against capital embodied in things, and the relative rates of return on each of those capitals. Inputs into agriculture also vary considerably. Thus, though both are capitalist agriculture, Japanese agriculture is fertilizer-intensive, but uses far less machinery than US agriculture. Conversely, the US farmer uses much less fertilizer per hectare, but ten times the horsepower. The yield per hectare in the USA (in wheat units) is therefore only 0.87, but the yield per male worker is extremely high: 123.5.

In India, where the amount of land available per worker is about the same as in Japan (1.7 *has.* as against 1.9), but where inputs of both fertilizer and horsepower are very low (0.02 h.p. per worker; 0.003 tons of fertilizer per *ha.*), the yield per male worker is only 2.2 wheat units and the yield per hectare 0.01. Give India seventy times its present fertilizer input and 300 times its present tractor horsepower, Omvedt writes, 'and its land could yield six to seven times its present output . . . [while] either maintaining present numbers of workers on the land or releasing them for industrial employment'.[194]

Yet whatever the technical differences as to the kinds of inputs and ways of organizing production, both are capital-intensive forms of agriculture. It is capital that is the prime mover. The process has naturally gone furthest in the leading capitalist country, the USA.

Agriculture there grew up on the basis of the small, independently-owned family farm in the North, and on the slave-plantation in the South.[195] The pioneering ideology and practice generated in the North was to be given an enormous impetus during the westward expansion and to become hegemonic after the Northern victory in the Civil War. The colonization of the West is commonly attributed either to the spur of poverty in the urban East, including mass immigration, or to the entrepreneurial energy of the pioneers, myths that took definite form in the celebrated Turner thesis. What these versions of history neglect is the central role played by the State, which provided the military force to break Indian resistance and dispossess them of their lands; sold them to would-be farmers for virtually nothing (the high-point being the Homestead Act of 1862, after which 10 to 20 million acres per year were allotted); used income from land to finance the construction of the railroads and townships without which commercial farming would not have been possible; and established a network of land grant colleges, today often very distinguished universities, but then popularly known as 'cow colleges', because they were dedicated to research into varieties of plants and animals best suited to Plains conditions, educating people not only in these new techniques but also in farm management and running farms as business enterprises (and, for the women, home economics).

Then, and only then, could the enormous tracts of land be divested of the 30 million buffalo. By the end of the 1870s, this had been done; by the turn of the century there were only eighty-five left. The prairies were then turned into seas of wheat, soya and alfalfa so large that the standard unit of measurement used, the section, is 640 acres, a piece of land whose size is almost inconceivable as a farm to peasants in Asia and Africa, whereas anything under four sections is scarcely viable in Prairie wheat farming.[196]

The historic poles of large-scale estates and small-scale peasant holdings which, together with those who had no land at all, provided the labour for those estates, have existed throughout history, and persist today. Where the renting of land to tenants no longer proves profitable, two polar forms remain: extensive capital-intensive farming – agribusiness – and family farming. The main outputs of the first range from meat production on gigantic ranches[197] to vegetable production on the vast tracts of irrigated land owned by corporations in California and Florida. Traditional lands of historic agriculture, such as the North-eastern United States, by contrast have now become economically unviable and are reverting to woodland.

The labour agribusiness requires is largely seasonal, and typically supplied by immigrants from underdeveloped countries, many of whom are undocumented and can therefore be paid less. Unionization is difficult, due to cultural problems and the use of violence. In the 1980s cases of virtual slavery have been brought to the US courts, but the pressures of poverty are the more normal mechanisms which keep labour tied to the employer. Between 1942 and 1962, Mexico alone supplied 4 million workers under the Bracero Program; today, the annual net inflow of illegals fluctuates between

100,000 and 200,000 a year; the stock has been estimated at between 3 and 6 million people. The number of illegal *apprehensions* reached 900,000 by 1977. Legal migration, per contra, ran at a mere 71,000 in 1974. Newer immigrants come from Haiti, Jamaica, and the Dominican Republic.[198]

Since the yearly income of the *bracero* was often twenty times what they could earn in Mexico, their savings – some of the highest rates of saving in the world – go back home to keep peasant farming alive by injecting capital into smallholdings. In the villages of South-central Africa, for generations, as much as 75 per cent of the able-bodied men have been absent on mine-labour. The labour for the farms had been provided by women, old men, and children.

It is a system which avoids any responsibility or cost for the social reproduction of the worker (bringing them up and educating them to the point of delivery to the labour-market), or their continuous support. It began to displace the earliest form of large-scale labour-intensive agricultural production-unit, the slave-plantation, only when the costs of buying and maintaining slaves became uneconomic.

Corporate agribusiness has not, however, displaced an even older form of capitalist agriculture: the farm owned and run primarily by the family. Well over 4 million such farms have disappeared in the USA since 1929, but well over 2 million still exist, many of them in large acreages, but operated with only a handful of seasonal labourers. For this reason, they might be regarded as high-level technology peasants. But they are highly capital-intensive, the key inputs being machinery, fuel, seeds, fertilizers, pesticides, irrigation-systems, not payments for labour. Today, farms operated only by family labour are worth millions of dollars.

In 1910, there were 100 tractors in use in US agriculture; by 1940, nearly half a million. 22.5 million hours of labour had to be used in 1910 to produce only two-fifths of the production achieved with just over five million hours of labour in 1975, on less land.[199] The crucial requirement, therefore, was the capital with which to purchase these inputs.

For this reason, farmers in the USA have often become very radical when they have suffered at the hands of those who set the prices of those inputs, control credit and determine the prices they receive for their crops. Agrarian radicalism, which goes back at least to Andrew Jackson, became a serious national political force at the turn of the century when farmers, combining at times with workers in the western mining zones and in the logging industry, sometimes even with urban labour, organized themselves, firstly in the Grange movement of the 1860s, later in the Farmers' Alliance of the 1890s – 'the most belligerent farm organizations in American history' – and eventually backed William Jennings Bryan's Populist Party, which polled a million votes in the Presidential Election of 1892. By 1896, they widened their appeal by adopting a classically populist 'silver' platform (restoring silver as the basis of the coinage), thereby attracting non-farmer support, a coalition which McKinley only defeated by half a million votes.[200]

They could command that support because the expansion of agriculture, which was beginning to dominate the world market, brought little improvement to the farmer. The experience of early capitalism in England had been that 'whilst the living standards of men and women fell catastrophically, the living standards of sheep improved equally remarkably'.[201] Now it appeared that the farm machinery firms, the banks, and the grain exchanges were making the money, but still not the farmer. The major world recession of the 1930s saw a great resurgence of militant populism in the left-wing form of the Co-operative Commonwealth Federation in Saskatchewan and the right-wing form of Social Credit in Alberta, parties which were to dominate the political life of each state right through to the 1950s, and in the case of the CCF, to lay the groundwork for the New Democratic Party in alliance with the labour unions. As Lipset observes,

> Agrarian radicalism has rarely been *socialist*. Yet it has directed its attack against big-business domination. In certain economic areas farmers have openly challenged private ownership and control of industry, either through governmental or co-operative ownership, to eliminate private control of banking, insurance, transport, natural resources, public utilities, manufacture of farm implements, wholesale and retail distribution of consumers' goods and food commodity exchanges. The large measure of socialism without doctrines that can be found in the programs of agrarian political and economic organizations is in many respects more socialistic than the nationalization policies of some explicitly socialistic parties.[202]

But radicalism stopped short of collectivism. The basic unit was still the privately-owned farm, which only co-operated with other like units to the extent that the private advantage of each could best be secured by joint activities which, however, stopped a long way short of joint production and even further away from joint ownership.[203]

Radicalism declined as the Depression receded. From then on, market competition took over. Today, an average of 2000 farms go out of business each year, a system some describe as 'agrarian cannibalism'.[204] Since the price of food to the consumer declined by a half between 1929 and 1970 – wage-rates having quadrupled while prices for farm products only doubled – the tax-payer became the source of the 23.7 per cent of farmers' incomes received in the form of government subsidies. The smallest farms often survive only because the farm is not the only source of income. This solution, which in both Western Europe and in Poland has taken the form of worker-peasant/farmer combinations of occupation,[205] often meant, for the USA, combining a small urban business with the farm, or renting it or leaving management to others, often residing, at least seasonally, in the city.

The large corporations effectively control whole commodity sectors: 100 per cent of sugar production; 98 per cent of milk; 97 per cent of broiler chickens; 93 per cent of processed vegetables; 85 per cent of citrus fruit; and 36.2 per cent of livestock, either through vertical integration or contract production. Medium-sized firms, though the most efficient, have to compete with firms that determine the prices they will receive, and often compete with them as producers too. Ninety-three per cent of egg production comes from 5.5 per cent of all farms; one corporation operates an egg factory with a million birds; another grows 10,000 acres of potatoes. Vertical integration means not only large-scale production, but forward links: the processing and finally the selling of the product in supermarket chains owned by the same corporation. Such firms are usually involved in much more than agriculture. Thus Tenneco, Inc., a Texas conglomerate with $11 billion sales in 1980, owns and runs over a million acres of rangeland in California and Arizona. But it also made most of that income from oil, natural gas, ship-building and farm machinery. Farming is a good investment for smaller non-farmers, too, a type of investment described as farming by 'one thousand three hundred dentists'. Perhaps a half of all farmland is owned by non-farming operators and investors.[206]

But in most cases, it has been said, 'the corporation does not need to become a farmer; it rents one'. Individually, there may still be over two million farms employing 20 per cent of the workforce, but most of them earn little and lack any real independence.[207] Under contract production agreements, they produce for and sell to processors and dealers who determine not only the prices they will get, but what seeds they will use, when they will plant and when they will harvest, ready for the crop to go direct to the canning plant within hours. Electronic machinery calculates the moisture content and the appropriate moment for harvesting; large specialized firms do the grain harvesting, moving North with the ripening crop from the Mexican to the Canadian borders.

If Charles Bodrey, 'winner of numerous crop production awards and twice featured on the cover of Progressive Farmer magazine', could not survive on his 994 acres of prime land (though he used 'the most advanced irrigation system available'), and had to sell out after twenty-seven years,[208] the chances of survival for the small peasant producer in the Third World, now competing on a world market, are minimal. Even on the internal market he faces competition, not only on the market, but for the land itself, for agribusiness now operates in Third World countries as production-enterprises, the extreme being represented by the 6000 square mile property carved out of the Amazonian jungle at Jari, in Brazil, where Charles Ludwig, one of the world's richest men, operated one of the world's biggest agro-enterprises, a timber-growing plantation that supplies a processing plant producing 750 tons of pulp a day, which, together with a 55,000-kW generating plant, was floated from Japan by sea. Criticism by ecologists and nationalists, and economic downturn, finally forced the government to establish a consortium of financiers to buy him out, but other large corporations are still moving into the frontier zones, alongside the myriads of small colonists who have also flocked into these zones, where the capacity of the soil to keep bearing crops for more than a few years is low, whilst enormous stretches of privately-owned land in the older zones of agriculture in the South and the South-east are under-utilized or not farmed at all. As a development model for countries with a superabundance of labour, but a chronic shortage of capital, giant agribusiness ventures like Jari are irrelevancies. For poor peasants, lacking all the essential ingredients, from capital to know-how, competition with them is impossible.

The efficiency of large-scale agriculture of the kind classically developed in the American West on the basis of intensive mechanization, and now in the irrigation-agriculture of the sunbelt, especially Florida and California, based on the use of masses of cheap labour, cannot be judged simply by using capitalist criteria of profitability. The high prices which are so 'disastrous for countries that depend on American grain for their margin of safety' are pushing more and more marginal land into production in many parts of the USA.[209] As a result, at least one-third of American farmland is eroding at a rate that causes declining crop-yields, though the effects are masked by the use of fertilizers. The larger farms also use more herbicides and insecticides than the small, though it is the plantations of Central America which experience the highest rate of saturation of plant, animal and human life with noxious chemicals.

The social consequences have long been noted; not simply rural exodus and the decline of rural communities, but deterioration in the quality of life for those who do remain in the countryside. One well known study of California's Central Valley in 1974 analysed two communities, one dominated by large corporate holdings, the other a community of small farms:

> The latter enjoyed a higher living standard, more parks, more stores, with more retail trade, superior physical facilities such as streets and sidewalks, twice the number of organizations for civic improvement and social recreation, and two newspapers where the other community only had one.[210]

The often-quoted statistic that one American farmer now feeds forty-eight other people also ignores the economic costs, especially now that the epoch of cheap oil is over; the equivalent of 80 gallons of fuel to produce an acre of corn, and an even more wasteful use of energy to produce meat. Paradoxically, while farm exports pay for more than half US oil imports, for every dollar's worth of farm exports in 1980, American agriculture used the equivalent of 25 cents of imported oil. To this global irrationality, then, has to be added energy-production ratios which make Western agriculture 'one of the least efficient in history':

> Asian wet rice cultivation yields 5 to 50 food calories for each calorie of energy invested. The Western system requires 5 to 10 calories to obtain one food calorie.[211]

Globally, the ecological costs include deforestation, soil erosion, the salting and silting of irrigation systems, the decline of fishstocks and the elimination of whole animal species: disasters attributable to modern farming methods rather than to population growth *per se*. To those familiar problems, the cost of the Western know-how, from patents to machinery, have to be added, as well as the newer cost of buying new varieties of seed every year or so before they become susceptible to biological attack once more. The Third World further faces the 'other energy crisis': the growing shortage of firewood with which to cook the food which, for half of them, is less than the daily intake of food calories and other nutrients which the WHO regards as minima.[212] Yet Indians in the most remote headwaters of the Amazon, serviced by fleets of light airplanes, and Asian peasants in the 'golden triangle' now form part of a chain of production whose final destination is the United States of America, where the cocaine and heroin will fetch tens of millions of dollars when it hits the street in Chicago or Los Angeles. Within the USA itself, too, marijuana (though a very different kind of drug) is now probably one of the five major crops.

The elimination of the smallholding peasantry took centuries in the world's pioneer capitalist country, Britain; in the rest of Western Europe, what Franklin calls 'the last phase' only began after the Second World War: between 1957 and 1979, some 10 million farmers left the land. In today's leading capitalist country as a result of the westwards expansion of the frontier up to the late nineteenth century, there still remains a large but declining population of small farmers (though they constitute less than 5 per cent of the population).

In the Second World, the brutal destruction of the peasantry in the USSR was too disastrous to be repeated elsewhere in Eastern Europe, but more humane forms of collectivization, Poland apart, have everywhere resulted in the elimination of the small proprietor and in the maintenance of output with a far smaller labour-force. In the newer communist states outside Europe, while co-operatives are strongly encouraged, no attempt has been made to replace the smallholder even in countries as highly-organized and as ideologically influenced by the USSR as Vietnam and Cuba. China, which began its own NEP following the defeat of the 'Gang of Four', has allowed the private sector in agriculture to revive in the shape of the marketing of produce from the peasants' tiny private plots, which, as in the USSR, are now an important source of output and profit. With the eclipse of Maoism in recent years, however, the system of remuneration has also changed; now the individual producer receives cash at the end of the day's work, while the hiring of labour has appeared once more in disguised form: those who make their living outside agriculture pay others to work their private plots. But the main institutions of farming, the communes (the central internal policy, insofar as it is there that 85 per cent of the people live and work) remain, just as the central plank of foreign policy (hostility to the two Superpowers) has not been abandoned.

In the capitalist Third World, the smallholders are now under strong pressure from agribusiness. Their absolute numbers remain large. At the beginning of this chapter we noted that there are more people living in the rural towns and villages of Mexico than there were in 1910. There are also some four million without land at all – more than there were at the time of Zapata and Villa, before land reform. In those giant countries, India and China, the vast majority of the population are still peasants.

Their final elimination will obviously take a very long time. But the trend is unmistakable. The world has never been a place where the peasants have held power, even when they constituted nine out of ten of the population. They will have even less political influence in the future, when they will cease, in one country after the other, to be a majority at all.

At the global level, more and more Third World countries are now importing food, while exporting tropical products and meat to the First World. In the leading country in that world,

the American economy is absolutely dependent on agricultural exports. Not steel, not transistor radios, nor even old armaments, but wheat, corn, rice and soya beans are the major products it has to sell to the world. In 1973, US exports of $17.7 billion overcame a trade deficit of $7.6 billion in other areas. . . . About half of these exports go to Third World countries: grain imports by non-oil-producing developing countries jumped from $2,800 million in 1972 to about $7 billion in 1973 . . . most being from the US and Canada. . . . In 1972–3 the US share of world food exports had risen to 43.9 per cent of wheat, 57.1 per cent of animal feed grain, 58.1 per cent of oilseeds. . . . The US is also the major seller on the world market of . . . that pre-eminently Asian crop, rice.[213]

In the last ten years, American farm exports have almost tripled in volume; in the last two years alone they have grown by 25 per cent. The old system of imperialism, based on the export of manufactured goods to the underdeveloped world, and the converse movement of food and raw materials from the colonies to the centre, has clearly changed radically. The changes on the industrial side of the economic equation we shall examine later. On the agricultural side, it means tremendous new power in the hands of those who control world food surpluses in a world where most people do not get enough to eat.

III The Making of the Working Class

The Urban Explosion

Migrations gigantic in scale, over immense distances, have occurred throughout human history, long before the emergence of industrial society, even before agriculture. Since it was agrarian society, however, which ultimately came to dominate world history, and gave birth to industrialism, we usually forget that nomadic hunters and collectors, and peoples anthropologists usually called 'horticulturalists' rather than 'agriculturalists', pioneered the colonization of the world's empty spaces. Such societies were still predominantly subsistence economies; politically acephalous, 'stateless' societies (a term that only negatively, residually defines what they were not, rather than the positive variety of their modes of social organization). But societies without kings or even chiefs were able to organize themselves, often on a large scale, using such mechanisms as the 'predatory' segmentary lineage[1] or by throwing up messianic leaders, either in order to move into unoccupied lands, or to conquer or resist neighbours competing for scarce resources. Polynesian navigators colonized the islands dotted across the immense expanse of the Pacific; the people we call aborigines arrived in an empty Australia only 40,000 years ago, when the ancestors of the Amerindians crossed the Bering Strait and started to move southwards.

Equally ignored is the historic contribution of pastoralists, of whom tens of millions still exist in Africa and Asia. In Europe, they are often forgotten altogether. When I asked an old French peasant why the mountains near the Spanish border bear the name Mont d'Alaric (after the Visigoth king), he had no idea. Where there is a folk-memory, it is a memory of fear and horror, of wave after wave of fast-moving horsemen pouring across Europe from the steppes, even from Central Asia; crossing from North Africa at the rock named for their leader, Djebel-el-Tarik (Gibraltar); or descending from Scandinavia upon defenceless farmers. Their names – Huns, Vandals in Western Europe; Tatars in Russia – still reverberate with overtones of plunder, death and destruction. Such negative images of culture of the Other reflected a conception of the superiority of one's own culture that was not just a political or economic superiority, but a total one. The Others were 'infidels', 'heathens', 'pagans', 'barbarians'; 'Christian', to a Russian or Spaniard, was the normal term for a civilized human being.

The horsemen who wheeled off after a meteoric sweep of a few years, and those defeated, repulsed, or ejected, could be written off as self-evidently lacking in favour in the eyes of the Lord.[2] With the halting of the Muslim advance from the south at Poitiers in 732, their ejection from the Iberian Peninsula in 1492, and the ending of the later threat from the East at Vienna in 1683, the history of eight hundred years of Muslim rule in the West and a briefer interlude in Central Europe could be written off as Dark Ages during which nothing happened except oppression. After Lepanto, when Muslim naval power was destroyed, Islam was to remain significant militarily only as a chronic irritant – as pirates preying on Christian ships and cities for loot and slaves. To expunge the memory of centuries of Islam in Europe required more than the rewriting of history: to fabricate the myth of Athens as a purely Greek city, the Turkish buildings clinging to the side of the Acropolis had to be dismantled.

The reality was that the defeat of the Moors in Spain was a massive cultural loss, for it was a culture light-years removed from that of the first Muslim explosion out of Arabia into the Fertile Crescent and Asia Minor.[3] Descendants of the Hilalian invaders who swept across North Africa brought to Spain a culture far superior to anything they found there, opening Western Europe to the science and urbane civic culture of the world of Islam,[4] just as Babar's victory at Panipat in 1526 ushered in the epoch of Mogul civilization.

Where the invaders encountered superior civilizations, the conquerors themselves were absorbed. The barbarian conquerors of Rome became Christians, and created new states based on a synthesis between Roman institutions and their own. In China, the successive pastoral conquerors – Tungus, Mongol, Manchu – court and army apart, became thoroughly sinicized, being only a microscopic minority in a Chinese sea.

The denigration of pastoralism on the part of sedentary agriculturalists, over centuries, has persisted into the industrial epoch. Evolutionists have treated it as if it were a form of life which has either disappeared already or is doomed to do so. Yet today there are more than 8 million nomads in West Africa, 6 million in East Africa, and 5 million in the Near East (apart from those in Sinkiang and Mongolia and numerous smaller groups elsewhere). Even within industrial societies, tiny groups like the Gypsies try to preserve a nomadic way of life in the face of unrelenting and atavistic hostility (which only recently included the gas-chambers). Everywhere, governments try to sedentarize nomads, arguing that their way of life is culturally incompatible with modern society and economically irrational, contributing nothing to national income. Comparisons are made, to the nomads' disadvantage, between the yields of Holstein cows in Cheshire and scrawny animals in the Somali desert, making no allowance for the vast differences in inputs of grain and pasture such as the 2½ tons of hay each cow consumes per annum in England, or of labour inputs, let alone the ability of Somali or Fulani herds to survive in arid and semi-arid zones which would otherwise be un-productive, and where no European animal would survive at all. The prices they receive for their leather and milk are so derisory that there is indeed little incentive to participate in the money economy. Their best lands are taken from them for agriculture, and they are forced into restricted, marginal areas where their traditional economy, based on movement and on intimate knowledge of the land and its resources, inevitably degenerates into a vicious cycle of over-stocking and soil-erosion. This is then held up as evidence of their incompetence: the self-fulfilling prophecy has come true.

 Where these unfavourable conditions have not been present, throughout history great civilizations and vast empires have flourished in which the pastoral-nomadic economy has either been the dominant sector of the economy or a major one.

Cultures with their roots in ancestral pastoralism could not accept a reading of history that saw nomads only as pillaging savages. One of the earliest attempts outside the West to construct a general theory of social change, Ibn-Khaldun's *Muqaddimah*, therefore saw human history as an interplay between the steppe and the sown, the crook and the flail, between sedentary agriculturalists and dwellers in cities on the one hand, and desert nomads on the other, each with its distinctive cultural strengths, each with its limitations, and engaged in a continuous dialectic in which the city was by no means always dominant. When the urban centres lost their dynamism, they succumbed to the superior vitality of the nomad tribes.

Modern Muslim scholars have demonstrated important differences and the changing functions of Islamic cities since Ibn-Khaldun's day. In the Maghreb, while they were centres of regimes of conquest, symbolized by the governor in his citadel, dominating the city,[5] they were also centres of craft production and trade with the surrounding countryside and of long-distance caravan trade across the Sahara to the Guinea coast. Some pre-industrial cities were predominantly administrative capitals and ritual centres;[6] others centres of industry – which, in the Chinese case, were already mechanized by the thirteenth century. Under the Sung, the iron industry was 'not to be surpassed until the creation of the Urals iron industry in Russia in the eighteenth century'; while 'the state armaments factories operated on an even greater scale'. At the beginning of the dynasty, 16.5 million arrow-heads were already being turned out annually at the Bow and Crossbow

Department's workshops in the capital. By 1160, the yearly output of the Imperial Armaments Office, not including provincial production, was 3.4 million weapons a year, supplying an army of one and a quarter million men.[7]

Leaving aside the ancient cities of Mesopotamia, the Indus Valley, and China (notably Ch'ang-an, whose markets were larger than the entire area of medieval London), the Asian cities Europeans first encountered outstripped anything in the West. By the time of Marco Polo's visit, in the thirteenth century, China had become 'the most urbanized society in the world'.[8] Edo, the capital of Japan, had nearly a million inhabitants a century and a half before Commodore Perry's arrival.

As well as large-scale migration, and large cities, rapid population-growth was by no means unknown long before the epoch of Western imperialism. The population of China rose from 200 million in 1580 to 410 million in 1850, as a result both of the introduction of new crops and of social changes, notably the disappearance of manorialism and of serfdom, which had transformed China into a 'world of smallholders' by the beginning of the nineteenth century.[9]

The result was steady expansion southwards and eastwards at the expense of less numerous and less developed peoples. Those who were not culturally absorbed remain today, in the South, in Sinkiang and Tibet, as 'national minorities'. Where the existing inhabitants were hunters and collectors, pastoralists or horticulturalists, the land was defined as 'empty' and the property rights of the indigenes treated as of no or little account. At worst, they were exterminated; in Tasmania, the pampas, South Africa, cleared off the land like wild game or vermin in genocidal battues, hunts and sweeps. Elsewhere, they were pushed or retreated into the margins: the mountains, jungles, swamps and arid plains unsuitable for agriculture which Aguirre Beltrán has called 'regions of refuge'.[10]

There was always 'primary' resistance, even on the part of tiny bands of hunters and collectors. In Chile, it took more than four and a half centuries to subdue the Araucanian (Mapuche) Indians who, in the process, learned to use fire-arms and horses and developed skills in positional warfare.[11]. The advance of the frontier was no mere nibbling into empty lands on the part of innumerable small pioneers, as the myth of the frontier would have it. It required an apparatus of genocide: 'Indian fighters' and *bandeirantes*, backed by the State and by commercial capital.

In the extreme, the State itself was the agent of conquest, in wars for booty, land and slaves. Foreign wars provided an answer to internal social and economic contradictions, while the psychological compensations of glory in victory abroad contributed to social peace at home. In ancient Rome, landless peasants soon found that even the capital city could not provide all of them with work. Those who contributed nothing to society and had no other possessions than their children – and were therefore known as *proletarii* – were destined to lend their name to another class, centuries later, who, separated from the means of industrial production, had nothing to sell but their labour-power. Their discontent might be partially alleviated by State wheat-doles and circuses. But the army provided a more substantial alternative, not so much through the appropriation of land abroad as through the appropriation of people. As Rome became one vast fighting-machine organized for foreign war, slaves in increasing numbers were brought back to provide both rural and urban labour. 'Roman peasant soldiers, in effect, were engaged in capturing their own replacements.'[12] Ex-soldiers invested their booty in land, while the State established colonies of a quarter of a million more between 80 and 28 BC alone.

But the permanent occupation of conquered territory was the other alternative – colonization abroad – and the colonists could double as military reserves: a policy adopted by the Incas with their frontier *mitimaes*; by the English, who planted Protestant Scots in Northern Ireland and drove the native Irish 'to Hell or Connaught'; and by the Tsars with the Cossacks. The interests of the State and of the dispossessed could thus be reconciled at the expense of other peoples.

The size of even the greatest cities of the world before capitalism, and the scale of even the most massive movements of population pale into insignificance, however, when compared to the urban explosion that has taken place under late capitalism, for the flight from the land to the cities is taking place today on a scale which is not only global, but exponential. *Laissez-faire* theory saw labour as a mobile factor of production, like land and capital, responsive to market supply and demand. The reality was that when labour was scarce, the labourer remained tied to his employer by a variety of extra-economic mechanisms from debt-peonage to indenture. Landless peasants have existed throughout history. But they had a place in the rural economy as smallholder and labourer. But today, the peasantry is finally being separated from the means of production – the land – and not only in terms of ownership.

So they quit the land altogether, or are driven off. The scale of this migration is such, today, that it is changing, irreversibly, what has always been thought of as the natural and immutable order of things: that society and civilization depend for the subsistence of all and the wealth of the few upon the cultivation of the land. Beginning with the Great Transformation (the capitalist modernization of agriculture and the rise of machinofacture) the city has triumphed over the countryside, and the industrialized countries over the agrarian ones. In the world's first major capitalist country, Britain, there were already more people living in towns and cities than in the countryside as early as 1861. A century later, the flight from the land had been completed all over Western Europe: between 1957 and 1979,

10 million of the remaining farm population left for the cities.

That flight is being repeated, now, in the Third World. Today, there are more people alive than have ever died. And within our lifetime, we will be crossing another watershed in world history: the majority of us will be living in towns and cities, not in the countryside. The future is an urban future.

This fact has long been obvious to tens of millions of people who, for generations, have been leaving their villages. Not all were absorbed into industry. Many went as settlers on agricultural frontiers in the New World, in Canada and the USA, Argentina and Brazil, others to Australia and Siberia. Between 1850 and 1914, no less than 40 million of them had left Europe – about a tenth of the population and a quarter of the labour-force. Between 1812 and 1914, Britain alone exported 20 million people. But the majority of the emigrants went to towns and cities, not to the countryside, and for every two of them, another three left the rural areas for towns and cities in their own country.[13] Nevertheless, emigration was an important safety-valve, often forgotten today in explanations of the capacity of the capitalist ruling class to maintain its rule despite mass poverty – explanations which usually only attend to repression, civic incorporation and ideological mystification.

In the first phase of colonialism, the shift from commercial capitalism to the capitalist organization of production necessitated new and massive supplies of labour for the plantations and the mines. To bring that labour-force into existence, brute force, whether private or that of the State, was freely used, in forms ranging from slavery to forced labour and debt-peonage. Millions of Chinese peasants left for the lands of the Nanyang to the South and around the rim of the Pacific and Indian Oceans from South Africa to California and Peru; hundreds of thousands of Tamils were recruited in South India for plantations in Malaya, Fiji and further afield under an indenture system that has been described as a 'new system of slavery'.[14]

But 'push' factors: shortage of land, the fragmentation of holdings, declining productivity, technological displacement, and the exactions of landlords, money-lenders and tax-collectors; as well as 'pull' factors: new wants, for clothing, kerosene lamps, bicycles, were soon able to draw African workers to the mines of the Rand and the Copper Belt, year after year, as effectively as direct compulsion had previously done. Even a Marxist government like that of Mozambique had to tolerate tens of thousands of its citizens still working in the mines of South Africa.[15]

The flow, then as now, whether within the country or abroad, whether in the newly-colonized areas or the old centres, was inevitably towards the dynamic poles of the world economy, and within the First World, from depressed rural areas to the prosperous cities. By the 1930s, when Steinbeck's Okies began to abandon the dustbowl for California, Blacks had been heading North, after the First World War and the arrival of the boll-weevil, for a generation. The industrial boom of the Second World War sucked in millions more, until today their descendants demographically dominate many of the major cities of the North. The attraction, today, remains the same: the value of both the subsistence and cash components of his crop to a Zambian peasant in 1968 was about 145 *kwacha*; a wage-earner in the towns earned 4½ times as much: 640 *kwacha*; and a mine worker nine times as much: 1300 *kwacha*.

Globally, the flows across borders have accelerated even more dramatically. Immigration from Mexico and the Caribbean to the USA is on such a scale that the political potential of the huge underprivileged Hispanic population, and their higher rate of natural increase, has been called 'America's biggest time-bomb'. In Western Europe, over 11 million Turks, Algerians, Portuguese, Italians, Moroccans, Greeks, Yugoslavs, and Spaniards flocked to France, Germany, Sweden and Switzerland in the 1960s and 1970s to supply booming economies with cheap labour.[16] In an oil-rich Third World country like Kuwait, the majority of the labour-force similarly came from poorer countries like Egypt, South Korea and Pakistan, relieving the indigenous population of the necessity of doing any serious work.[17]

Between 1945 and 1947 – *before* the Communist liberation of China – the population of Hong Kong tripled, from 600,000 to 1,800,000; by 1978, it had more than doubled again, to 4,606,000. The rate of growth of the urban population of the Third World, indeed, has long outstripped the rate of growth of the world population in general. Between 1800 and 1850, world population increased by 29.2 per cent, but the population in agglomerations of 100,000 and over grew by 76.3 per cent. Between 1900 and 1950, when world population grew by 49.3 per cent, the urban population grew by 254.1 per cent. But the highest urban growth of all was in the Third World: 444 per cent in Asia; 629 per cent in Africa.[18]

The great majority, however, are internal migrants. Thousands of people arrive every week in Cairo, 2500 every day during the mid-1970s in Mexico City, which is now racing São Paulo, where nearly a million people arrived between 1951 and 1968, to become the largest and worst polluted city in the world. These last two cities now rival New York, London and Tokyo in size. Long delayed in India, the flow is now in full spate in that enormous subcontinent. In the last ten years, hundreds of Indian cities have grown by around 40 per cent; some smaller towns have tripled in size; and there are now twelve cities with more than a million people, three added during the last decade. Virtually a quarter of the entire population is now urban.[19]

The world is therefore no longer divided, as it was in the colonial epoch, into an agrarian 'periphery' and an urbanized 'centre', for the great cities of the world are growing most rapidly in the Third World:

Table 4   **Top Ten Cities (by population size)**

17,180,500	New York – NE New Jersey, USA
11,540,283	Tokyo, Japan
11,339,774	Mexico City, Mexico
11,308,800	London, Britain
10,041,132	São Paulo, Brazil
9,863,400	Paris, France
8,925,000	Buenos Aires, Argentina
8,328,784	Rio de Janeiro, Brazil
8,049,233	Osaka, Japan
8,632,000	Moscow, USSR

Source: *Times Atlas of the World*, Bartholomew/Times Books, London, 1980, p. xvi.

In some small countries, a sizeable proportion of the entire population has gravitated to the primate city, usually the capital.

In nineteenth-century Europe, despite endemic mass poverty and cyclical boom and slump, industrial output increased spectacularly overall and absorbed millions into productive employment. Where it did fail to provide a viable livelihood, other mechanisms, from repression and incorporation in the political sphere to emigration and the Welfare State in the economic, were developed to avert mass misery turning into militant discontent. The situation in the Third World today, however, many argue, is different in kind: one of urbanization without industrialization.

It is a description scarcely applicable to the so-called 'NICS': the newly-industrializing countries such as Brazil or Mexico in Latin America, or, in Asia, Singapore or Hong Kong, which latter ranks number 18 in world trade and number 9 in value of trade *per capita*. But most Third World countries have achieved no such spectacular growth and are unlikely to, especially now that world capitalism is in recession. Hence more of the new urban population has to be absorbed, not just within the tertiary sector, but in the so-called informal sector; a process less of tertiary development than of hyper-tertiarization: the unnecessary and unproductive involvement of hundreds of thousands in street-hawking, petty retail trade and low-productivity backyard workshops. To damp down discontent and build loyal clienteles, bureaucracies, police and armed forces absorb hundreds of thousands more. But service occupations absorb the majority, including the armies of ill-paid and unskilled who provide personal services in the homes of the middle classes.

Many of these ways of making a living were equally characteristic of the pioneer capitalist countries in the last century. But there were significant differences, too: the State provided very little employment, and the patterns of movement to the city today often differ greatly from those typical of nineteenth-century Europe or North America. In 1885, Ravenstein described the classical pattern of what became known as 'chain migration': the step-by-step migration from the English village to a nearby small town; from there to a provincial city, and perhaps, eventually, to the primate city. Today, it is more often than not direct, as migrants board the buses in the bus-stations of the provincial city and go straight to the big industrial centres, where they join their kin who went before them. Direct or indirect, two-thirds of the population growth of São Paulo between 1900 and 1960 was due to immigration. And with growing numbers born in the city itself, the cities are inevitably growing at a rate faster than the rate of increase of the population as a whole:

	1940	1950	1960
Total population of Brazil	41,236,000	51,944,000	70,967,000
Urban population	12,880,000	18,783,000	31,991,000

Source: Berlinck (1975), Table 4, p. 48.

Rapid urban growth is thus not, as is often thought, mainly a post-Second World War phenomenon. Though São Paulo grew into one of the world's largest cities only between 1934 and 1970, when it expanded from just over a million to nearly six million, the fastest *rates* of increase were actually between 1890 and 1920, when it grew from 64,934 to 579,033.[20] And though it is the giant conglomerations that strike the visitor, in countries like Argentina, the smaller cities and towns have often grown even faster:

Average annual rate of growth	1940–50	1950–60
Total	3.8%	5.5%
Cities of 10,000 and above	5.2%	6.6%
100,000 and above	4.5%	6.8%
1,000,000 and above	4.5%	4.0%

Source: Berlinck (1977), Table 5, p. 48.

In the extreme a boom town like São José dos Campos, in Brazil, grew by 75,000 people in less than a decade. In 1940, two-thirds of the working population had been employed in the primary sector; by 1970, half were working in secondary industry, the other half in tertiary. The primary sector had shrunk to a mere 1.74 per cent.[21]

Many of the immigrants had no alternative but to congregate in places where they threw up temporary, ramshackle housing made out of packing-cases, canvas, flattened petrol-tins and corrugated iron, bamboo and matting. In the literature about them which has grown almost as rapidly as the reality it describes they are generally called shanty-towns.[22] The vernacular terms are often more vivid: in Chile, they are called *callampas*, because they grow like mushrooms; in Turkey, *gecekondu* because they were built overnight; in Panama, *barriadas brujas* because they seem to be conjured up as if by witchcraft. In Mexico, the new arrivals are described as *paracaidistas* (parachutists) because they seem to fall 'out of the blue'. In North Africa *bidonvilles* because they are built out of *bidons* – petrol-tins.

Their sheer size makes them difficult to ignore: a highly visible quarter of the residents of Manila and Djakarta, a half of the population of Ankara, Bombay and Lima. Such estimates vary wildly, for no one really knows how many there are. But it is the quality of life rather than the mere size or rate of growth of the settlements that amazes the casual observer and provokes scholarly and public debate.

They are naturally perceived as a *problem* by the rich and by the urban authorities. The rich are terrified that a mass of frustrated and poverty-stricken people will one day burst out of the ghettoes they are presently confined in and invade the territory of the bourgeoisie in an explosion of rage: they are perceived as what nineteenth-century France called *les classes dangéreuses*. Social theorists often see them as people set apart from normal society, including even the established working class, who, however poor they may be, at least have jobs and live in houses or apartments. In this view, they are analogous to the Outcastes of the Hindu caste-system, below even the lowest of the recognized castes proper: not a *class* at all, but an *under*class or a *sub*-proletariat. To city planners, they are primarily an administrative problem, a problem of inadequate dwellings and inadequate urban services – water, electricity, and sewage: a *housing* problem.

To the visitor who enters one of these settlements, which commonly grow up right next to the luxurious apartment blocks and villas of the outrageously rich, it seems as though he has penetrated down into the lowest circle of the Inferno:

> . . . There are vast numbers who . . . have nowhere else to go. They are to be found late at night and every morning throughout the centre of the city, lying under the arcades of Chowringhee and besides the standpipes of Bentinck Street. There are squadrons of them around the approaches to Howrah Station across the river, in addition to the platoons who sleep inside the station itself . . . You have to step over their bodies as you move out of the dancing lights of the Ballygunge crossroads . . . And wherever a fire is, bodies are huddled beside it. Sometimes they lie still there during the day and they are so reduced that they do not even sweat any more; they lie in some shade from the blistering sun, almost and sometimes totally naked . . . their skins bone dry and very dusty. They die like that, eventually . . .
>
> Sometimes these inhabitants of the streets construct lean-tos . . . of any material they can find. There is a particularly awful series of them . . . at the bottom of Bepin Behary Ganguly Street . . . For five hundred yards or so there is a confusion of packing cases, straw matting, odd bricks and wads of newspaper arranged into a double-decker sequence of boxes. Each box is approximately the size of a small pigeon loft, with room in it to squat and only just to kneel . . . The rest of their life is conducted on the pavement where they cook and play and quarrel together; and in the

gutter, where they wash themselves and their rags in the gush of fractured standpipes.

There are other forms of slum in Calcutta . . . They stand in terrace rows, and they are made of the same glazed brick as the factory, a couple of storeys high. They contain a total of 630 rooms and 1,500 people inhabit them. One room on the ground floor is 10ft. by 6ft. and three men share it; there is space inside for nothing but them, a string from one wall to the other with clothes hanging from it, half a dozen metal cooking vessels and a few religious pictures . . . an open drain runs within two feet of . . . a short bamboo porch added to give them a little extra space for a kitchen of sorts. Once a year these men return to their families for two months' allotted leave, a fortnight of it paid. Each collects *Rs.*200 a month for a forty-eight hour week and absolutely no chance of overtime. He has six per cent of his wages deducted for an unemployment benefit scheme. He spends *Rs.*70 per month on keeping himself alive. The rest he sends home to his family. These three men have lived like this since they came to Calcutta in 1965. By the norms of the city, they are not too badly off, even though the pumps of unfiltered water supplied by the company work out at one for every hundred people, even though the solitary latrine for the whole colony of 1,500 is so foul that most people instead take to the Hooghly.

. . . The nuns have a refuge specifically for dying destitutes . . . It is crammed with stretcher beds, row after row of them, and their moribund occupants. There are people in here in their twenties, but hardly anyone looks less than sixty years old. They lie very still, blinking and clawing at food, but otherwise not moving at all . . . The nuns move perpetually down the rows of stretchers, dishing out food to those who can eat, cropping the heads of those who are lousy, dressing the sores of those who are rancid, mopping up the ones who are squittering incontinently. There are moments . . . when a visitor believes he has reached the backside of hell.[23]

Systems Theory, Interactionism, and Dialectical Sociology

The causes of this extreme spatial expression of the social distribution of 'illth' was a matter of fierce debate in countries like Britain which experienced the first wave of mass urbanization. It was a search for blame as well as cause, a political and moral debate, not solely an economic one. Sociology in Britain, indeed, emerged precisely as a part of that debate. On the one hand, there were those who regarded poverty as the consequence of individual inadequacy: improvidence, idleness, or ignorance; on the other, those who blamed the system. A third alternative, today, is to introduce a third term between the individual and the total society: rather than cast the blame on either, the individual is said to be *socialized* into a '*culture* of poverty'.

Individualistic explanations aside, sociological analyses of how it is that millions are condemned to this kind of marginal existence still conform to one or other of two metatheoretical polar types: systems theories and interactionist ones.[24] System theorists concentrate on the functioning of the economy at societal and world levels: with systems as wholes whose structural components and sub-systems are governed by the aggregate requirement of multinational and national enterprises for labour. The only social attributes taken into account in such models, normally, are the formal educational experience and technical skills of the various cohorts that make up the labour-force. People, that is, are seen as labour in a market: collectivities whose meaning is their significance for the economic system. The kinds of questions such analysts ask, then, are system questions. They may be economic: What is the effect of migrants' savings upon inflation rates? Do they create a downwards pressure on wages? What are the consequences of the movement to the city for agriculture? Or political: Do they divide the working class? Are they conservative, revolutionary, or neither? For macro political economy of this kind, the individual is simply a digit, an atom, a unit, a component. The implicit metaphysical pathos of such models is that he or she is a mere victim, of inexorable system forces.

Interactionist theorists ask a different kind of question, not about the logic of the system at the societal level or the level of the world-system, but about the ends people pursue and the strategies such individuals, groups and categories use in order to satisfy their social purposes: ends and means generally seen as distinct from those of the powerful and rich. The accent is upon human agency, not system. It is an approach summed up in the title of an outstanding study of Mexican shanty-town dwellers, Lomnitz's *Como sobreviven los marginados?* (How do the marginals survive?).[25] The answer to that kind of question calls for a sociological as distinct from a purely economic analysis. It cannot be answered, either, purely at the system level. People survive, she shows, because they mobilize the social networks they are involved in, both older, established ties of kinship and *compadrazgo*, and newer ties of neighbourhood to find employment and to cope with the entire range of social problems they face outside work, too, housing, schooling and health being the most important. This kind of model, then, is necessarily concerned with social action and with the subjective: with strategies for survival, with the cultural equipment, the knowledge, ambitions and values of real, existential individuals, households and communities which react to the pressures of the system upon them, and are not merely acted upon.

The way in which shanty-towns are thought about, the kind of explanatory model adopted (often uncritically), therefore determines the way research is carried out and the kind of data considered relevant. Each model has its strengths and relevances, and its weaknesses. Neither is inherently necessarily more progressive than the other. There are radical inter-actionists who show how people fight the class struggle every day of their lives; idealist interactionists who carry that notion too far by asserting that,

> . . . individuals are . . . able to shape their own destinies and the destinies of others. Social structures and social systems as far as they are the analytical constructs of anthropologists and sociologists are also the creations of the individuals and groups these social scientists observe.[26]

For most systems theorists, from functionalists to functionalist Marxists, this is unacceptable. Their models depict an all-powerful ruling class or the impersonal logic of the system determining all, inexorably; class struggle, resistance, alternative projects get short shrift.

Yet systems analysis and interactionism are not inherently mutually exclusive. In a dialectical sociology, indeed, *both* are needed.[27] The demand of the economic system for labour *is* the prime cause of the gigantic movements of immigrants from the Mediterranean to Western Europe. The rationale of the whole enterprise, from the standpoint of the Turkish State, has to be explained, too, in system terms, for it was the $740 million remitted back home by migrants in Germany which balanced the deficit of $678 million between Turkey and the rest of the world.[28] It is therefore the West German and Turkish *States* which regulate the volume of the flow and even ensure quality-control by having German doctors in Istanbul stamp the product fit for export.[29] Analysis in terms of political economy is thus a *sine qua non*. But to understand the variety of responses of the millions subjected to those pressures involves cultural, subjective elements which systems models restricted to political economy cannot provide. And to explain the striking failure of that volume of capital to generate economic growth one has to examine the ends to which that capital was devoted: not investment in capital enterprise, but the improvement of living conditions and the enhancement of social status via expenditure on both traditional and modern consumer items; a half of all savings (from two-fifths of all migrants) went on houses and on consumer items, mainly clothes and radios.[30]

The very decision to migrate in the first place is necessarily informed by these same wants, which are social and not exclusively economic. The intentions of migrants and their value-systems are therefore crucial, for not all are like these Turkish emigrants. The majority of *internal* migrants to the *gecekondu* of Istanbul[31] and 85 per cent of Rio *favelados* had 'no intention of returning to the village'.[32] Neither did Pakistani immigrants to Britain in the

1960s. Though the idea that they would return is in fact a myth or ideology, it nevertheless affected the economic strategies they adopted in England as well as the nature of community life there, for the values they brought with them included a strong preference for investment in land as a source of income and prestige, while the status of tenant, conversely, was a negation of traditional values. The high cost of land (£4000 to £6000 an *acre*) in Pakistan made the UK a much more attractive proposition in material terms. Before recent racist legislation, kinsmen and fellow-villagers already in Britain sponsored others, raised the cash for their travel to the UK, and lent them capital, interest-free, on arrival.

Investment in low-cost, multi-occupancy housing, which British sociologists have seen simply as something forced on immigrants by racial discrimination, was a preferred strategy since it solved the two main problems of income and accommodation, while culturally, these ghettoes provided identity and support for people to whom British ways of life were alien.[33]

This is nothing new. Most of the millions who crossed the Atlantic to the USA in the nineteenth century, from the poverty-stricken regions of Europe, from Ireland, Poland, Russia and Italy, were on one-way tickets. They were not going back (though a surprising 30 per cent did from North America and over 40 per cent from Argentina). There were also the millions of *golondrinas* (swallows) who could pay for their round-trip passage to Buenos Aires in the 1890s with only two weeks' labour.[34] Labour migration in the form of movement between the village and the mine and back again, has also been a permanent way of life, not a 'transition to industrialism', for decades, for miners in southern Africa and the Andes.[35]

The majority of even those who originally intended to return, however, never did, in part because they could never save enough, but more often because, over time, they adapted to a new, urban life-style whatever their original intentions. Their cultural project changed. Over a century later, there was a clear distinction between the 'Red' migrants and the 'School' people in East London, South Africa. 'Red' not because they were revolutionaries, but because they were traditionalists who smeared ochre on their clothing in accordance with custom. Raised in rural ways, they dreamed of going back home eventually, to the village. The School people, educated in rural mission schools, were modernists, readier to adapt to the life of the city, which was soon accepted as their *real* home. Neither they nor most of the Reds would ever go back to live in the village. It was a dream, a *myth* of return, an aspiration never to be realized; at best, a place to visit, but where they often felt uncomfortable.[36]

They were tied to the city, not just by poverty, but because they had become, culturally, urbanites, their goals for the future more often to obtain city education for their children than buying land in the countryside.

The migrants' projects and their socialization into a new culture are therefore as essential in understanding their behaviour as is political economy to an understanding of their aggregate (and class) behaviour as labour – which they undoubtedly are. 'Target' mine-workers, who came to 'raid the cities for cash', and who, under *apartheid*, were in any case prevented from staying permanently in the cities, oscillated between town and country. Originally they had had to be forced into the labour-market;[37] later, growing land pressure in the Reserves ensured that they would go back, on contracts of one or more years, several times in a lifetime, until their physical strength gave out. The rural economy now depended upon the miners' remittances, even for sheer subsistence. And all had developed new wants. The psychology of the miner therefore differed from that of a permanent proletarian and that of a peasant. Nor could it be schizophrenically split in two: as long as there remain ties to people and land in the village, it is not true that 'an African townsman is a townsman, an African miner is a miner; . . . only secondarily a tribesman'.[38] He was what he was; a *migrant* worker, with a foot in both worlds, but whose overall fate, like everyone else's, was determined by the dominant classes and the State, and the responses these evoked.

Long before the First World War, the countryside had been transformed into a labour reservoir, one vast rural slum servicing the mines and the White-owned farms. Hence theoretical debate about the relative importance of push as against pull factors became increasingly irrelevant in a capitalist society where the logic of the market celebrated in *laissez-faire* theory had been displaced by the intervention of the State, not only in the operation of the economy, but in the construction of a totalitarian racist social order after the Second World War. It had always been fatuous to represent entry into the labour-market in terms of a voluntaristic reduction of the social to the level of abstracted individual choice, as a matter of preference schedules and a range of equally available ends, or as the consequence of values acquired through membership of primary groups, for both ends and choices were sharply restricted and largely imposed, determined by poverty and pass laws. The mines, the city, and the State were no longer a backdrop to a largely rural African society. Rather, the village was itself a dependent variable, its culture thoroughly transformed by urban influences. The dichotomy tradition/modernity therefore no longer made sense. The analysis of labour migration as a modern substitute for traditional *rites de passage*, similarly, no longer carried conviction. And attempts to use 'traditional' institutions in the urban mining compounds could only be reactionary: the 'Elders' installed as 'representatives' of each 'tribe' by the mine authorities carried little credibility, for there was no pre-colonial precedent for the authority structure and political culture of a mining town. On the Copper Belt, trade unions and political organizations soon displaced such puppets of management;[39] on the Rand, they were rigidly proscribed.

Systems Theory: Functionalist and Marxist

After the Second World War, functionalism was the dominant theoretical system in both Western sociology and anthropology. Its unit of analysis, the total society, made its vision singularly holistic: one which was societal, not just social. Its most rigorous and influential version, that of Talcott Parsons, further stressed the crucial integrative role played by a society's value-system: the cultural system which supplied the meanings that, through socialization, became internalized within the personality-system of the individual, within the psyche.

Underdeveloped societies, in areas which had experienced the imposition of colonialism, faced special problems of integration: those entailed in reconciling values inherited from pre-colonial times with newer ones diffused by the dominant Western countries during and after the colonial epoch. It was a model of a dualistic, rather than an integrated society, with two distinct sectors, each with their typical institutions and value-systems.

These theories, elaborated in the journal *Economic Development and Cultural Change*, reached a much wider public in a book that quickly became the major statement of what became known as modernization theory, W. W. Rostow's *The Stages of Economic Growth* (1960), though in a rather special form; that of a revived unilineal evolutionism. All these variants, however, shared the common assumption that development consisted in diffusing modern elements from the already developed centres of the world-economy to the backward countries, thereby displacing traditional elements. The models for modernity, of course, were the developed countries, above all the USA. Exuding an optimism similar to that of its nineteenth-century forebears, this new evolutionism postulated that the backwardness of traditional societies was only a temporary condition: after an initial phase culminating in the investment of savings of some 10 per cent of GNP, the pre-conditions for 'take-off' would have been created; compound interest would then have been built into the economy. The drive to maturity, when 10–20 per cent would be saved and invested, could be expected within about twenty years, followed by sustained economic growth and the transition to high mass consumption.

Critics of the model, notably Frank,[40] challenged it on empirical, theoretical and policy-related grounds. The number of people who made their livelihood, not in the modern sector, but in what came to be called the 'marginal' sector, they observed, was growing, even in countries such as those of the southern cone of South America, where import-substitution, during the Depression of the 1930s and the Second World War, had resulted in marked industrial growth. According to zero-sum models, the growth of the modern sector should have led to the diminution of the marginal population. Unfortunately this category seemed to be growing precisely in those places where modern industry had been implanted. They were growing *together*. And far from benefiting from the spin-off of modern industry, not only the marginals, but the regularly employed workers were still poor.

Third World social scientists trained in US functionalism nevertheless continued to treat development primarily as a problem of integration, both in institutional terms and in terms of the coherence of a society's value-system. The problem of marginality, for the pioneer functionalist sociologists, notably Gino Germani,[41] was not simply a question of economic under-development (nor had it been for Rostow either). It was a problem of *social* development. Marginality was a *multi*dimensional problem: immigrants were people who were not just poor, but incompletely urbanized, culturally unassimilated and spatially segregated: cut off, in every way, not just from the middle and upper classes, but from the working class, too.

Yet the separation was not total: marginals were still part of the society. The various dimensions, too, might vary independently. One could not assume, *a priori*, that they would necessarily overlap. Marginality was therefore both a plural and a relative condition: one might be marginal in one respect and not in another (e.g. belong to the same ethnic group as the ruling class, but be a street-pedlar). The degree of congruence of these different dimensions was therefore something which could not be established by empirical investigation.

The principal dimensions of marginality were economic marginality, political marginality, cultural marginality, and inadequate integration of the individual personality. The economic position of the immigrant worker we shall examine in more detail below. Politically, a person was held to be marginal when he or she did not participate in party, electoral, or other modes of decision-making. They might be cut off from the mainstream culture of the society, further, by differences of language and customary life-style. Psychologically, they were often held to lack the personality attributes appropriate to life in modern society, from work-habits and consumption-orientation to scientific ways of thought and rational conceptions of the self and of society.

Germani's solution to the problem of multidimensionality was to measure each dimension separately and to combine the results so as to form an overall profile of marginality, both for individuals and groups. They *might* all be found to occur together, but might equally vary from society to society, from group to group, and from person to person:

It is convenient to think of marginality as a multidimensional phenomenon . . . although in certain cases it may be possible to identify a
common (phenomenological and explanatory) base.[42]

As for causality, no *absolute* formula concerning the degree or mode of fit,
or as to which aspect of marginality was the most important, could be arrived
at:

It would appear impossible to determine the temporal or causal priority of
one or the other in the abstract . . . [for] this will vary with different
historical and social conditions and contexts.[43]

This did not exclude the empirical possibility that generalized marginality
– in which there was a congruent inferiority on *all* dimensions – might be
found, each reinforcing the other: for instance, low educational level leading
to the inability to get skilled jobs. Further, however much the different
dimensions needed to be separated out analytically, marginality in one
dimension, he recognized, *necessarily* had implications for other, different
sub-systems. The separation of the different dimensions of marginality was
thus, in practice, a methodological precept and recommendation to caution
rather than a common empirical finding:

Although it is convenient for analytical purposes to analyse [class, status
and power] separately, one must always bear in mind that they are all
directly or indirectly related . . .[44]

For Germani, marginality was not a purely 'objective', structural
phenomenon. Rather, it entailed a contradiction between the objective facts
of role and social structure and the subjective: the normative ideals which
were supposed to determine how role occupants ought to behave and groups
function. But there was often a contradiction between values and norms and
reality: role occupants were inadequately socialized; expectations not
necessarily fulfilled. He therefore followed writers like Marshall and
Bendix[45] who emphasized the 'tragic gap' between ideals of citizenship in
European bourgeois society, that everybody ought to participate, and had
the right, even the duty to participate, in principle, whilst noting that even if
progress was a feature of capitalism, these ideals had taken a long time to be
realized even in the most developed societies. In underdeveloped societies,
the conflict between ideal and reality was far more severe, owing to the
'asynchronic' existence of an unincorporated marginal mass.

Other theorists found this all too open-ended, too pluralistic. Economists
began, naturally, by focusing upon the analysis of the labour-market.
Keynesians emphasized the incapacity of the system to maintain full
employment, but believed that this could be corrected by judicious fine
tuning, and followed Bairoch in attributing much of this malfunctioning to

demographic and technological change. Rates of population increase had been much lower, they pointed out, in late eighteenth-century and early nineteenth-century Europe: around 0.5 per cent per annum, i.e. 30–40 per cent over fifty years, whereas they were now running at 2.2 per cent per annum: 300 per cent in fifty years. Europe's population-growth, moreover, had been counterbalanced by massive emigration to new countries.

On the technological side, whereas an artisan could transfer his skills to factory work a century ago, today there was no compatibility between the skills needed in the village to produce handicrafts and those called for by assembly-line work, let alone by the computerized factory. Technology, today, was intransitive. Nor could backward countries simply copy the design of machines built in more advanced countries, as Japan had once done. Illiteracy-rates were far higher in the contemporary Third World, yet modern industry necessitated much higher levels of technical training than did the industry of a century ago. The upshot was that local industry was unable to compete with that of the advanced countries; instead, they had to import technology from abroad, and diminished costs of transport made this ever more feasible. Like Myrdal, Bairoch concluded that the Third World was caught in a vicious circle; and that the system was under the control of the developed countries. The only way out was to develop industry behind tariff walls, a policy which would require much higher levels of economic and political independence than existed in most such countries.

This emphasis upon the displacement of labour-intensive industry by capital-intensive industry was perfectly acceptable to those who saw it as something inherent in the logic of *industrialism*. But for Marxists, it was caused by the competitive nature of the *capitalist* market. For them, Marx's general theory of the changing organic composition of capital, and his specific categories – the 'lumpenproletariat', the 'labour aristocracy', and the 'industrial reserve army of labour' – provided starting-points.

Lumpens, Aristocrats, and the Reserve Army

In *The Eighteenth Brumaire of Louis Napoleon*, Marx had written some very nasty things about what he called the 'lumpenproletariat' of nineteenth-century Paris: the

> . . . vagabonds, discharged soldiers, mountebanks, *lazzaroni*, pick-pockets, *literati*, organ-grinders, rag-pickers, knife-grinders, tinkers, beggars – in short, the whole indefinite disintegrated mass, thrown hither and thither, which the French term *la bohème*, . . . this scum, offal, refuse of all classes . . .

Engels was no less contemptuous: they were 'the "dangerous class"', the social scum, that passively rotting mass . . . for the most part a bribed tool of reactionary intrigue . . .', 'the worst of all possible allies . . . absolutely venal and absolutely brazen . . . Every leader of the workers who uses these scoundrels as guards or relies on them for support proves himself by this action a traitor to the movement.' These shameful insults to the wretched of the earth were *political* denunciations: they were castigated for their reactionary political role as hit-men for Louis Napoleon (though there is something, too, of patrician disgust, rather than sympathy, felt by two Victorian gentlemen contemplating the life of the underclass). The categorization of them as intrinsically reactionary was, however, a metaphysical position. A better Marxist analysis, because more dialectical and situational, had to wait another century, when Mao Tse-tung described what he called the '*éléments déclassés*' as 'brave fighters, though apt to be destructive'. But, he added, given proper guidance they could become a revolutionary force. Large numbers of them were recruited into the early Red Armies in China, subjected to 'ideological re-moulding', and became sturdy revolutionary fighters.

A more serious approach to the urban poor was Marx's characterization of them as a part of the 'reserve army' standing outside the factory gates, ready to take any kind of job for low wages if necessary and thereby undermining trade union power and working class solidarity. The 'relative surplus population', he wrote, was made up of three components (though every worker belonged to it when out of work): the 'floating', the 'latent', and the 'stagnant', and the last of these could be divided into those able to work (but lacking it); orphans and pauper children; 'the demoralized and the ragged', and those unable to work (the aged, victims of industrial accidents, etc.).[46] It is this last category, the 'lowest sediment of the relative surplus population', living in pauperism, that most commentators have emphasized in developing the concept of the marginal worker, though for Marx it was only one part of the reserve army of labour.

At the top of the social hierarchy within the working class stood the labour aristocracy: in Marx's day, the skilled craftsmen who defended their privileged status through strong trade unions. All ruling classes, of course, endeavour to divide and rule, and to recruit subaltern allies. Patron-client, master-journeyman/apprentice relationships, and other forms of vertical integration are by no means restricted to capitalism. Lenin's attribution of the emergence of a bourgeoisified stratum within the British working class to imperialism was therefore quite unhistoric. The process had been going on since the Industrial Revolution and the privileges included not only superior economic rewards, but social association with their masters, and cultural assimilation into respectable circles, Church, school, and voluntary associations.

The Marxism developed after the Second World War in what were then the major centres of social science in Latin America – Argentina and Chile – paid little attention to these socio-cultural processes. It was an austere form of systems-Marxism, which took production as primary. Moreover, it was, dialectically, strongly influenced by its major enemy, functionalism, to which all had been exposed during their professional training.

The pioneer Marxist study of marginality was undertaken by José Nun. Surplus population, he argued, is necessarily a *relative* concept, and a surplus only exists in relation to a given type of productive system (mode of production). The relationship of surplus labour to the system may be functional, dysfunctional or afunctional: functional, when the growth of the labour-force benefits both employer and employed (as, for instance, in estate-systems where the owner uses the labour of serfs who receive in return the right to use plots of land for their subsistence needs); dysfunctional, as when there is an absolute limit on resources beyond which more people simply cannot be supported; and afunctional, when the existence of an excess population (such as the vagabonds of medieval Europe) has no significance for the functioning of the system one way or the other. Only that part of the surplus population which has consequences for the system is a reserve army. In Marx's day, capitalism was characterized by rampant competition not only between firms, but within the working class itself. The reserve army competed for jobs not only with each other but with those at work, too, and exercised a downwards pressure on wages. But today, under managed capitalism, advanced technology meant fewer workers; those with jobs, conversely, were paid *well*, in order to promote loyalty to the firm and thereby lower turnover. But a considerable part of the surplus population today, Nun argued, has no functional role at all for the monopoly-capitalist enterprise. Hence they do *not* constitute a reserve army, and are not part of the working class, but a 'marginal mass' – and a growing one. Since this mass no longer competes for jobs it no longer exercises a downwards pressure upon wages, either. It is 'afunctional'.

This novel theme of afunctionality was taken up later by Aníbal Quijano, another Marxist theorist, whose initial model, however, was not specifically restricted to capitalist societies only, but applicable to any kind of society. Following Althusser, for whom, as we saw, history is a process without a subject, Quijano insisted that marginality has to be studied in terms of the integration *of* society, not in terms of integration *within* society: with the logic of the system as a whole, and with its constituent parts, the 'institutional sectors', rather than with the purposeful action of the members who constitute society.

In any society, one has to distinguish between the basic structure that determines the fundamental characteristics of the society as a whole, and secondary institutions, which, while not defining the basic structure, nevertheless help to support and extend it. But, he argues, there is a third level of structure only indirectly connected – marginal – to the basic structure. Yet since the different parts of the system are interdependent, by definition, even this marginal sector is a part of the capitalist economy and society.[47]

In a later attempt to strengthen the Marxist content of this rather general and abstract mode, and to relate it more specifically to the Third World, Quijano took up the theme of dependent capitalism introduced by Nun.[48] He now argued that the 'marginal pole' had become a *permanent* feature of dependent capitalist economies, concentrated in low-productivity sectors of the economy where backward techniques were used. An unskilled labour-force of this kind, however, only produced low rates of surplus value, and was therefore of little interest to the big bourgeoisie who left these workers to be exploited by the petty bourgeoisie. Later Marxist writers then simplified this scheme by reducing it to one of three sectoral levels: advanced multinational industry; less-developed national capital; and the marginal sector. Since demand for their labour was declining, the main economic role of the marginals, increasingly, was not so much as producers, but as consumers: as a market for the products of the leading sector. Their life was therefore a Hobbesian nightmare: precarious, unstable and incoherent. To avoid total impoverishment and consequent social unrest, governments then had to bring into being minimal welfare services for people who lacked any purchasing power at all.

What is striking about all this theorizing is its disconnection from any examination of the now-voluminous data accumulated from numerous field-studies.[49] Research of that kind was categorized, not as *empirical* work, but as mere empiri*cism*. Theory, on the other hand, was something constructed in the study, by assiduous re-reading of Marx's writings of one hundred years ago. The search, often, is for some hitherto overlooked obscure passage, usually in the *Grundrisse* or Volume 3 of *Capital*, which might provide the required revelation. Out of this reading, a model is constructed and then applied, like a template, to reality, which is itself constructed out of common knowledge backed by figures drawn from censuses and other economic surveys (however these latter were constructed, for whatever purposes, and under whatever theoretical auspices). The dialectical conception of a continuing interplay between concept formation and the observation of reality is notable by its absence. One hunts in vain through such texts for anything so mundane as a fact – or even a datum.

Such metatheoretical procedures reflect the insulated position of intellectuals in such societies, drawn as they are, overwhelmingly, from upper-class backgrounds, with minimal knowledge of or involvement in the daily life of the poor. They are, in a word, élitist theories, whatever the identification in principle, and often in practice, sometimes with great courage, of their authors with the cause of the working class. It is a view from the penthouse and the university office – or the beaches restricted to the upper classes.

The Culture of Poverty

The intellectual raw materials of a radically different approach had been available for a long time. They went back to nineteenth-century debates about the nature of the new industrial society in Europe: about changes in the division of labour; about demographic transformations; about the decline of community and the growth of the city; the growth of the State, of bureaucratization and mass democracy; secularization and rationalization.[50]

It was one of the least likely – because most austerely formalistic – contributions to this debate, Georg Simmel's classic discussion of 'The Stranger' that was to be taken up by social scientists in the United States who were trying to make sense of the consequences of massive immigration into a city that had only come into existence within living memory: Chicago.[51]

For the pioneer theorists in the 1920s and 1930s, notably Robert Park and Everett Stonequist, marginality was a general concept applicable to any situation of cultural transition which resulted in inadequate personal adjustment, whether that transition was caused by migration, educational mobility, marriage, or external influences, and across the boundaries of *any* kind of social group: from country to country, from one Church to another, or from one occupation to another. They have been subsequently criticized as being individualistic and psychologistic since Park emphasized the *mind* of the marginal man as the most relevant focus of study, and Stonequist insisted on marginality as 'a core of psychological traits'.[52] Yet they did see these personality attributes as consequences of membership of structured social groups and categories: the marginal man was a 'cultural hybrid', in Park's view, precisely because he lived on the margins of two cultures and two societies, but was a full member of neither. Those who cleaved to their culture of origin experienced no problem of marginality. The real problem arose when, as Merton was later to classically express it, they came to accept the values of the dominant culture, but lacked the means to achieve them or were prevented, for instance, by institutionalized reaction, from doing so: a situation he labelled 'anomie'.[53]

In American society, the principal cleavage was between the dominant WASP culture and the various ethnic sub-cultures of the newer immigrants, divisions much wider than the purely economic dimensions of class. The pioneer theorists often retained the optimism of their nineteenth-century predecessors (though many were Social Darwinists). Park saw the marginal man as a source of innovation[54], just as Israel Zangwill wrote of America as a giant melting-pot in which the original European cultures would dissolve, but provide the elements for a new, rich American synthesis.

This Dream had never seemed convincing to those in sweat-shops or to radicals who fought bitter class struggles before and after the First World War. By 1921, the boom had been lowered on further mass immigration. By the 1930s, the world economic Depression was reflected in a new metaphysical pathos, a mood of pessimism in social thought, which emphasized not only the persistence of older ethnic identitities, but the erection of new barriers designed to stop traffic across cultural boundaries: prohibitions upon intermarriage, and taboos upon social intercourse at the everyday level of eating and drinking together. Rather than resulting in assimilation, the outcome was a *permanent* cultural pluralism, with each ethnic group living its own life in its own ghetto. The more pessimistic commentators, such as Louis Wirth, believed that not only the life of the marginals, but urban life *per se* was disorganized: that individuals only related to others impersonally, in segmented roles and via 'secondary' associations, rather than as members of primary groups, and therefore lacked any meaningful cultural identity: urban life was 'anomic', a 'social void'; urbanites manipulable 'fluid masses'. So deep was the pessimism that Wirth believed the city could not even reproduce itself biologically.[55]

Chicago sociology had not, however, been dominated by pure theorists. Its practitioners, whatever their differences, all paid close attention to the empirical reality around them. In a succession of rich studies, the dominant techniques and methods employed were those of intensive, small-scale, qualitative, participant observation, similar to those used in anthropology. Anthropologists raised on the study of tribes, and who themselves later turned to the study of the burgeoning towns and cities of the Third World, found Chicago-style sociology acceptable, not only because of its research methods, but because both sets of social scientists shared in common a further central conceptual category: the concept of culture – or, more precisely, in the case of Chicago urban sociology, of subculture.

Economists saw these urban populations primarily as so much labour. For sociologists and anthropologists, they possessed many other significant social characteristics: ethnic affiliation and identity, religious and political outlooks and memberships, and ethical values which they acquired often through informal socialization within the family and the neighbourhood rather than via formal schooling. Such institutions and networks, moreover, formed an overall and local subculture, different from the hegemonic W A S P culture.

Their culture was stigmatized: it was only a *sub*culture: and commonly spatially separated off, within ghettoes. Sociologically, Glass has written, a minority, ethnic or otherwise, is not a quantitative, but a qualitative and political concept: it expresses inferiority and superiority, not number.[56] Thus ethnic groups which are less numerous than the rest of the population may be minorities in both the sociological and the quantitative senses. But Blacks in South Africa, who number eight out of every ten in the population, are a sociological minority.

Economic and social marginality, the Chicago School discovered, usually went hand-in-hand. But it could not be assumed that economic marginality *caused* social marginality: it was as often a *consequence* of social inferiority. The degree of overlap, therefore, was something that had to be taken as problematic, as a matter for empirical investigation. Over-integrated models, as Germani warns, not only fail to establish distinctions, but falsely impose themselves on reality by reifying it, suppressing inconsistencies and contradictions. Fieldwork-based research is no more immune to the disease than systems theory, however, for immersion in the life of the people is no guarantee against over-systematization, since researchers both interpret their findings in the light of theories and concepts they bring to the data (often without being aware of doing so), and their conceptual apparatus even determines what is to count as data in the first place.[57] The 'view from the barrio', then, can be quite as distorted as the view from the penthouse.

C. Wright Mills, long ago, pointed out the defects of 'Grand Theory', spun out of the head by pure cerebration, in offices and libraries, ungrounded in first-hand knowledge of the world outside. But he also warned against the opposite: 'abstracted empiricism' from which anthropologists and historians so often suffer.[58] The shortcomings of that kind of approach are twofold: it provides no model of the wider society, of how the shanty-town, for instance, fits into and is, indeed, a product of the overall social system, and it is casual about the problem of representativeness.

These defects are classically present in the work of Oscar Lewis, who constructed a 'culture of poverty' out of interviews and tape-recordings made amongst poor people in Puerto Rico, Mexico and New York. Unlike previous urban anthropologists, he postulated the existence not of various subcultures of this or that ethnic group, but of a generalized culture of the poor.

Outcast from orthodox culture, he argued, the poor had evolved a coherent life-style of their own, distinct in every particular from the dominant culture, which was handed on from generation to generation. But the values and skills children were taught disqualified them from participating in the mainstream society. At the societal level, they had no experience of participating in the social institutions of formal society; in the community, apart from the family, they had little social organization of their own other than ephemeral informal groupings and voluntary associations; and at the level of the family, childhood as a protected and protracted phase of life was absent, sexual activity began early, and instead of the stable nuclear family, mother and children were often abandoned, resulting in a matricentral family organizationally and emotionally focused upon the mother and her close kin. Discipline was authoritarian, privacy non-existent.

Lewis' schematic proclivities led him to construct not only a culture of poverty, but to revive the notion of a rural-urban continuum elaborated by his mentor, Redfield, in which urban society was seen as the polar antithesis to 'folk' society. Like Wirth, Redfield further considered the city to be disorganized. Yet the culture of poverty, Lewis acknowledged, was a distinctive alternative culture, not a disorganized one. It differed from the hegemonic one (a term he did not use) across the board, though what he often actually revealed from his field-data was not two compartmentalized cultures, sealed off from each other, but the penetration of the hegemonic culture among the poor, for whom, however, bourgeois norms of family solidarity were contradicted by the absence of the father, competition for maternal affection and for scarce household material resources, and by the necessity to seek support from relatives outside the nuclear family and from non-kin.

Lewis' vivid accounts of the life of the poor in *Five Families*, *The Children of Sánchez*, *La Vida*, and *Pedro Martínez* sent a *frisson* through the bourgeois reading public. The culture of the poor was shocking: negatively, because to be poor was to be wretched and because most of the traits Lewis listed were unrespectable ways of behaving; positively, because a repressed *nostalgie de la boue* lurked within the breast of the materially privileged: the poor seemed to have a capacity for spontaneity and adventure, and for sensual (especially sexual) enjoyment missing in 'straight' society. Being poor seemed to have some compensations, and could even be fun at times.

Social scientists were less impressed.[59] Firstly, they criticized his methods. How had his informants been selected? Were they typical of the poor? On what basis was the information they gave him organized – by them or by him? And though the data were voluminous, on such crucial matters as economic, religious, political and ideological beliefs and institutions they were quite inadequate. How had the traits – around seventy altogether – been defined, abstracted from life histories and converted into a culture?

These were no trivial questions. But the critical issues were the political assumptions and the attribution of cause and of blame. Lewis shifts his ground from time to time, but overall, the 'psychological and social core' of the culture, for him, was its values and consequent norms for behaviour; the crucial institution through which they were communicated, the family. It was here, then, that the *cause* of poverty was to be looked for, as Glaser and Moynihan were later to argue, without ambiguity, with respect to Blacks in the USA. In reality, the behavioural and attitudinal traits of Lewis' poor

were not so much 'emic' cultural proclivities as *responses* to *externally-*
imposed conditions, for which those who controlled the commanding
heights of the polity and the economy were responsible – as he often shows.
Poverty was a product of the total system. Lewis, in the end, for all his
closeness to the lives of the poor, responded with middle-class ethnocentrism. He blamed the poor for their poverty. They were hopeless,
impotent, apathetic, and dependent. What he recorded, he remarked,
revealed not only a culture of poverty, but the poverty of that culture; the
failure of the poor to conform to conventional standards of respectability.

    The culture of poverty was thus an observer's construct. Yet the poor, like
any other class, were very heterogeneous in respect of the ways they made a
living, their membership of different Churches or of none, their varying
levels and kinds of education, and so forth. Cross-culturally, Lewis himself
recognized this: the culture of poverty was only typical of people coming to
the cities from the countryside in colonial or newly-developing capitalist
societies. It was not to be found where the poor felt themselves part of a
wider cultural whole – whether the caste-system of India, the corporate
descent-groups of Africa, or socialist society in Cuba. Moreover, it had an
adaptive value, helping people to solve problems of life in the lower depths.
The culture of poverty was only one form of culture among the poor.

The Variety of Poverty

It is time to turn from theorizing to the world out there, firstly by questioning
whether it is a world, for the heterogeneity of the poor, both within any
given country and from one country to another, at first appears to defy all
classification.

For many important areas of the world, the data we would need is
qualitatively and quantitatively poor. The sheer diversity of occupations
alone is reflected in Mexican official statistics, which label as 'marginals'
street-hawkers, sellers of ice-cream and ball-point pens; people who polish
shoes or mind cars, or sell lottery-tickets; concierges, doormen, waiters,
hairdressers' assistants, traffic wardens and ticket-collectors; servants,
cooks, gardeners, drivers, cleaners, and watchmen in private homes;
stevedores and unskilled labourers in the mines and on the docks, in the
metal industries, in paper manufacture, in the timber industries, in textiles,
food, tanning, tobacco, in garages, in the building trade, and, in the
countryside, field labour and cowboys on estates, and peasant producers of
very little who work for themselves.[60] In Rabat, Morocco, twenty-two
different categories of occupation were distinguished within the shanty-
town areas alone.[61]

Some of these occupations are highly visible to those who are not poor, firstly because many of the poor work in the homes of the middle and upper classes as resident maids and other servants, whilst others come there seeking work as fixers of radios, cobblers, or door-to-door pedlars. Others they encounter on the street: the boys who try to sell them cigarettes, sweets, ball-point pens or chewing-gum while their cars are stopped at the traffic lights; the girls hawking plastic gew-gaws or cheap magazines in the city-centre; the kids who mind or polish their cars (and threaten to damage them if not hired) while they go off for lunch; the women who carry baskets on their backs which middle-class ladies load with their purchases, like so many beasts of burden.

Others are less visible: the women who work in their own homes in the putting-out rag trade in the huge working-class district of Nezhualcóyotl, Mexico City, or the army of prostitutes who cater to the lusts of men of all classes. All, in one tragic sense, are on the margins, not just of the economy, but of society. As workers, they are poorly-paid for long hours of work, often in impermanent, hard-labour, dirty and dangerous occupations which do not make them eligible for whatever meagre social security benefits exist. Residentially, they live in one or another kind of inadequate housing: old slums, new tenements, shanty-towns. As consumers, they lack the purchasing power to purchase the goods and services enjoyed by the rest of society. Socially, their státus is that of the 'insulted and the injured'; culturally, they lack formal education, sometimes even the ability to speak the national language.

Yet this is a very varied list of occupations alone, more exactly, of kinds of occupation. Nor do other social characteristics necessarily go hand-in-hand with occupation. It is an aggregation of different kinds of sub-populations which socially and culturally often share little in common beyond their poverty. Questions of representativeness and size are therefore important, for the tendency is to assume that visible occupations, or those selected for study, are typical. Yet the most extensive survey yet conducted for any Third World city, that by Muñoz and his colleagues in Mexico City, showed that a third of all migrants were working in manufacturing industry, albeit in menial jobs as labourers, messengers, porters, cleaners and the like. Nor do they only work in workshops and small factories: 82 per cent of new arrivals to Bogotá did work in enterprises employing less than twenty workers, but so did 74 per cent of earlier immigrants and 67 per cent born in the city.[62] And only 2 per cent of those classified as marginals in Mexico City were in street-trading, one of the most visible occupations, commonly thought to absorb vast numbers.

Though they range from street-sellers to workers in large industrial plants, a quarter of the labour-force in Mexico City are officially classified as marginals, on the grounds that these are all low-pay, low-skill, low-security and low-status occupations. But this is to define them negatively, by what they lack; it is a residual, aggregate category which does not take into account any features other than a common poverty. It tells us, therefore, more about what they are not, than about what they are and what they do.

Classifications of occupations used by economists are of limited use sociologically, whether they be the classification of the economy into primary, secondary and tertiary sectors, or by branch – metals, pharmaceuticals, etc. As in all countries, the largest single occupation for women – housework – does not, of course, get socially recognized as formal employment at all, let alone rewarded by a wage. Many of these women also fall into one or other of the following categories, which means that they have two jobs, one of which they are not paid for. Furthermore, many of the following occupations also employ children in large numbers, also at very low rates of pay. For sociological purposes, the following occupational categories seem to be of most heuristic value:

(a) Firstly – because they are usually neglected – there are the urban poor who work in manufacturing industry;
(b) workers in sweat-shops which only compete by paying their workers low wages;
(c) putting-out work in the home;
(d) self-employed artisans: shoe-repairers, service technicians of all kinds;
(e) domestic enterprise using family labour;
(f) street-vendors, pedlars, hucksters, lottery-ticket sellers, itinerant salesmen of all kinds;
(g) a huge personal service sector (over 60 per cent of working women in Mexico City are maids, and 1,748,000 women recorded in the 1970 Brazilian Census);
(h) casual wage-labour: porters, car-washers, etc;
(i) the 'hunters and collectors of the urban jungle' to use Wolf's phrase: refuse-collectors, etc;
(j) criminals and other deviant occupations, notably prostitutes;
(k) beggars and unemployed.

Let us discuss each of these in turn.

(a)   workers in manufacturing industry

One of the commonest assumptions in dependency theory is that high-technology monopoly capitalism, being capital-intensive, does not need large supplies of labour and will need even less in the future.[63] In reality, despite the increased use of technology during the boom of the 1970s, manufacturing industry in Mexico 'maintained higher rates of growth per annum in employing labour than other economic sectors, apart from . . . finance and banking'. A third of the capital's labour-force (30.2 per cent was working in industry (though the scale is not specified), almost a third (29.0 per cent) of all migrants among them.[64]

To the extent that modern industry does dispense with labour, the determinants, however, are not necessarily technological, but often economic. In the great ABC industrial belt south of São Paulo, Volkswagen employed over 42,000 in 1980 (since severely reduced), Ford over 11,000, and Mercedes-Benz over 15,000. Most of these jobs were unskilled and impermanent because modern technology, computer-designed and controlled production-flow systems, was used precisely in order to maximize the employment of that kind of labour, not because of any technical necessity, but because it made it possible for employers to avoid the social security payments required by law as well as annual cost-of-living and inflation adjustments for workers employed for longer terms. Before the arrival of the general recession of 1973 onwards, the decline of employment opportunities for the unskilled was not highest in modern industry at all, but in the handicrafts sector and in agriculture.[65]

Large-scale multinational engineering, pharmaceutical and electronics corporations, moreover, contract for the supply of often quite sophisticated components from smaller firms, some of which do operate with simpler technology. And even in the older capitalist industrial countries, such as Britain, industry is polarized in respect of its labour profile: at one pole, one out of every six workers in manufacturing industry work in establishments employing 100 or less workers; at the other pole, two workers in every six work in establishments employing more than 10,000 workers.[66]

(b)   sweat-shops   *THE GAP*

A branch also of manufacturing, but where wages are so low that rates of profit double and treble those of industry in general are normal, and working conditions are so bad that the bribing of government inspectors is essential. Labour legislation, which can be quite good on paper, is therefore never put into practice. In Hong Kong, it is not even good on paper. The 'economic miracle' in that country, whose economic performance outstrips every Asian country except Japan, depends, to a significant degree, on low wages and poor working conditions: one worker in every four is an under-age child. There are no legal restrictions on hours of work for men over eighteen, who work the longest working week in South-east Asia (60 per cent of them seven days a week in 1968); no minimum wages, and trade unionism is very weak. Improved legislation in 1971 (unlikely to be enforced, since 6000 industrial undertakings were unregistered with the Labour Department a year later, and because the workers themselves try to evade these controls since they need the income) still allowed children of fourteen and fifteen to work up to forty-eight hours a week.[67]

(c) putting-out work in the home

In Nezahualcóyotl, Mexico City, there are 3000 women who make a living working with their own machines in their own homes, sewing up ready-cut cloth supplied by their employers, who pay them wages below the official minimum wage for a working day of over twelve hours and pay no social security contributions. The women have to pay for the materials and the upkeep of the machines.

In Hong Kong, because of low wages, wives and children complement the husband's earnings by working at home, where there is no control over hours worked, threading plastic beads on necklaces, or, as I have seen, making up plastic holly for happy English Christmases. A child can bring in 10 cents an hour: a tenth or less of the average daily wage of male workers. But components for much more sophisticated products like radios, calculators, watches and so forth are also made in the home or assembled there. Multinational corporations contract out such operations to subcontractors who then farm the work out to home-workers, even in Japan. They and workers in sweat-shops are therefore part of a pyramidal structure controlled by the large corporations. Being unorganized, they are paid very low wages. Governments from Sri Lanka to Mexico connive in the process by setting up 'free production zones'; in the latter country, a whole zone on the US border is filled with foreign-owned (mostly US) 'maquiladoras', factories attracted by cheap, usually female,[68] labour, the absence of trade unions, investment grants, tax holidays, customs privileges and the ready repatriation of profits. Modern industry thus has plenty of room for the small enterprise and even reaches into the home. Even in Hong Kong, where 47 per cent of the labour-force work in industry, the vast majority of firms are still tiny family or partnership affairs, with little capital and only simple machinery.

From Malaysia and Thailand to Egypt, 'offshore' manufacturers exploit cheap local labour in these zones and export their output to the First World where they are sold at greatly profitable prices. In the US, most of the radios and TV tubes, and a growing proportion of automobiles, books, toys, even *haute couture* from French fashion-houses, are now made in countries like South Korea, Taiwan, and the Philippines. Whole countries, from Singapore to the Dominican Republic, become dependent satellites of this kind.[69]

(d) self-employed artisans

With rarely more than one assistant, these workers fall outside the net, such as it is, of social security legislation, from unemployment benefit to severance, sickness and other payments, and do not benefit from statutory wage increases or adjustments for the cost of living, inflation, or laws concerning holidays and working conditions. Nor do those who work for them. Their skills are often acquired informally, their capital minimal, and their earnings exiguous in the extreme: two-thirds of those working for themselves in Monterrey were in the lowest income bracket. It is not the case that they necessarily work very long hours. Some of the self-employed are able to compete with larger firms only by working inordinate hours, but others are unable to find enough customers, and hence work short weeks; most work between forty and sixty hours.[70]

(e)   domestic enterprise using family labour

Here the home is a centre of production, using the labour of the household's members. For this reason, it has been variously called 'subsistence urbanization' and the people 'urban peasants',[71] the analogy being Chayanov's model of the peasant family as a self-exploiting economic unit of production and consumption, and, further, as a social and residential unit. The home, for instance, may be the place where ice cream or cooked foods are produced for sale, using family labour in the making and selling, often on street pitches or in the local market. Even more sophisticated operations can be quite peasant-like: the father may own a second-hand truck, and the family members load, service and drive the vehicle. Urban peasants commonly mobilize kinship, ethnic and other ties in drumming up business and securing cheap supplies, often from rural relatives or connections, and commonly sell, too, to their neighbours. Others raise chickens or pigs for sale. They both produce and trade.

'Urban peasants' is thus a more apt term than 'penny capitalists' for these micro-entrepreneurs,[72] for they are capitalists only in the most Pickwickian of senses, since they have only the most minute quantities of money or goods. Not for nothing is the coinage in Third World countries subdivided into the equivalent of small portions of a British penny, since the scale of operations may be the sale of a cup of water or a split match-stick, with commensurate profit levels. These minuscule operators have to buy dear and sell cheap, because they lack withholding-power and cannot obtain credit, except in exchanges with kin and favoured customers, relationships which deviate from the pure capitalist rationality of the cash-nexus. They are capitalists who hire no labour and end up with incomes often inferior to wage-workers, after working all the hours God sends.

(f)   street-vendors

Unlike the last group, these people do not produce what they sell, but they resemble them insofar as they often acquire their stock-in-trade via extra-economic ties (though often from wholesalers, too), and often sell, too, to kin and neighbours. Thus vegetables may be bought on preferential terms from kin or most-favoured partners in the villages, or are produced on fields they own themselves, or they may act as urban sellers of produce belonging to relatives in the village. They are often not so numerous as commonly thought, though a city like Cali, with over a million people, has nearly 10,000, leaving aside the very numerous shoe-shiners, ticket-touts, queue-standers and suppliers of other services, as well as those working in bus-stations, football stadiums, official markets and other places where the street-traders are not allowed. They are subjected to constant harassment by police officials.[73]

(g)   personal service

For instance, 200,000 women in Mexico City, 72 per cent of whom live in, usually in small, ill-furnished, often windowless rooms, on call twenty-four hours a day, with one or two days off a month. It is almost impossible for them to have a normal social life, and they face the usual risks of sexual harassment by the males of the household. Three-quarters are illiterate, from rural villages; 80 per cent get less than half the official minimum wage. Four out of five are less than twenty years of age; 60,000 between eight and fourteen.[74] In addition, are the gardeners, the cleaners and washerwomen, the chauffeurs, concierges, and hall porters in condominiums, and other service workers. Models like Quijano's, focused upon industrial production as the main source of surplus value, neglect cheap domestic labour, which may not produce surplus value embodied in commodities, but makes possible not only for the rich, but even for the lower middle classes, standards of living which people on the same income levels in the USA could not afford. In the upper class suburbs of the Third World, the rich live in a state of siege, surrounded by high walls, and guarded by entryphones and TV monitors in the corridors and at the entrances, and by floodlights, Alsatians and security-men with walkie-talkies in the grounds. Security – the protection of the rich – gives employment to thousands of the poor.

(h)   casual wage-labour

Such jobs range from temporary work on construction sites to portering in markets, running messages in offices, night-watchmen, etc. They may last a few hours, a few days or weeks.

(i)   'hunters and collectors'

Graphic though the above phrase is, strictly, very few such jobs are pure individual, casual, scavenging. It is systematic in every respect. Those who live on the rubbish dumps of the city of Guayaquil, Ecuador, the *chomperos*, do so in a double sense: they live *off* the rubbish by picking it through and sorting different kinds of rubbish: bottles, metal, rags, paper etc., and they also literally live *on* the rubbish, for they build their bamboo-frame dwellings there. The *gallinazos* (vultures) of Cali, Colombia, acquire their supplies from the garbage-cans left out on the pavement for the official city garbage-collectors. Others buy from houses (often from the maids.) They may specialize in certain kinds of rubbish, like paper, and even buy it from shops and offices. Their forward linkages are to small buyers with whom they deal direct, and who sell in turn to a satellite warehouse which, in its turn, supplies a central warehouse, from where the scrap materials go to a factory. Though the *gallinazo* 'appears to work for himself . . . in fact he is part of an industrial organization', in Birkbeck's words, an 'informal factory'.[75] In Cairo, the carts of the 25,000 Zabbaleen, members of a Coptic sect, provide the only household-refuse collection-service in a city of 14 million. Their Muslim 'Wahiya' (bosses) contract with landlords and tenants to collect the refuse, then sell the rights to pick it up and keep it to the Zabbaleen.

(j)   criminals and deviants

A very large category indeed, by its very nature unamenable to precise quantification. The red-light districts near the bus-stations and the lobbies of the big hotels are two extremes of locale, some of them relatively secure, others dangerous, when heroin addicts can only ensure their daily fix by selling their bodies or stealing. In New York City, it will cost them $100 a day; in the Third World, it comes cheaper, but it is a habit which brings them into contact with professional criminals. Crime and deviance is by no means restricted to the self-employed, individual petty entrepreneur, however, for the logic of the centralization and concentration of capital and of power works as inexorably in this sphere as in the steel industry or the garbage industry. The machinery of articulation extends from the individual burglar or mugger, through the small gang, to large-scale organizations. Protection money is extorted at every level, by police, pimps and other intermediaries. The individual producer is thus either linked to or part of larger organizations, while prostitution may also be concentrated in larger houses and call-girl networks. Like straight business, those who begin as workers on their own account commonly end up working for organizations which may even be international in their scale of operations, and own legitimate businesses – hotels, gambling casinos – and even perfectly conventional factories as well.

At the top of the hierarchy of prostitution are women whose role and talents as elegant and cultured mistresses of government leaders and businessmen or as entertainers moving in high society brings them closer to the eighteenth-century courtesans of France or Violetta Valéry than to the street-walker peddling 'quickie' sexual services.[76]

Separating illegitimate occupations from respectable ones is, therefore, a normative rather than an economic classification, but is justified sociologically insofar as these occupations are not merely illegal, but regarded by respectable society as deviant and illegitimate, as offences against morality and not just the law, attitudes which are real in their social consequences for those so stigmatized.

But the attitudes of people who are themselves poor are not necessarily the same as those of the respectable bourgeoisie (who nevertheless patronize both the street-walkers and their more expensive sisters). The poor in the slums of Manila, who do not share the values of the hegemonic subculture, treat sexual deviants, including prostitutes, 'with tolerance and accommodation', drawing a distinction between a woman's 'calling' and her personal character. Prostitutes are socially accepted, for their motives are understood to be purely economic. They are Matza's 'disreputable poor'. But *malandi* – sexually 'hot' and restless women, who are gold-diggers and ruin honest husbands, often running away with them – are detested.[77]

Similarly, criminals who provide patronage, especially jobs and other material favours such as mediating with authority and protecting the poor against the depradations of the rich and the police, are popular – like social bandits throughout history. As with the sex industry, crime is highly specialized: pick-pockets, sneak-thieves, fountain-pen-stealers, muggers, etc, etc. In Cali, *caimaneros* steal purses; *carteristas* specialize in wallets.

(k) beggars and the unemployed

At the bottom of the heap, one would imagine, are those who do not earn, but can only beg. Begging is not, however, necessarily the ultimate in anomie. In Europe, writers from Villon to Balzac, Dickens and Brecht, have described their highly organized economic practices: the territorial pitches, the systems of recruitment and of social control over their members. Similar guilds of beggars, and the strong subcultural codes, have flourished in West Africa for centuries. Very different are the beggars in San Cristóbal de las Casas, Mexico, two-thirds of whom are physically handicapped people, many of them old or alcoholics, 'passive, pessimistic and even fatalistic', alienated from society, 'without established associations with their peers' and even lacking family links.[78]

Yet, so badly-paid are the unskilled among those who do work that one in ten of a sample of beggars in Bahia declared that they were better off than when they were working![79]

The Myth of 'Marginality'

Of the categories used by Marx to analyse divisions within the working class, the description of the urban poor as 'lumpenproletarians' has been the most damaging, since it misled whole generations of subsequent Marxists not only into condemning them politically for their supposed lack of class consciousness and of revolutionary potential, but also into disconnecting them in economic terms from the working class. Yet an examination of categories (*a*) to (*j*) above reveals that, far from being marginal to capitalism, or economically significant only as a reserve of labour for manufacturing industry, and though family labour predominates in some of these modes of making a living, the majority work for wages in a variety of thoroughly capitalist relationships and institutional contexts, producing goods and services for the capitalist market. If they are 'reserves', they are not sitting on the touchline, but playing in positions from which they will be the first to be dropped.

That hundreds of millions of people in these kinds of occupations are very poor indeed is beyond contention. Sixty-seven per cent of the population of Africa, Asia and Latin America are designated as 'seriously poor' and 39 per cent as 'destitute' by the ILO; in Latin America alone, in 1969, 153 million were 'without employment' and another 75 million 'underemployed'. 'Unemployed', however, does not mean that they are not working. If they were not, in the absence of assistance from others, they would die. Yet, as a Filipino researcher notes of the slum he studied: 'poverty is only one of the many pressures slum dwellers have to contend with, but so far no one has yet been reported to have died of starvation!'[80]

Many, it is true, do die, either quickly, or more slowly, of diseases of poverty. As the Second Declaration of Havana put it, the value of the flow of capital from the Third World to the United States was $4000 a minute; but the social cost was '$1000 per corpse and four corpses a minute'. The unemployed, in fact, do work – in the kinds of occupation which are very often omitted from official statistics, along with the contribution of housewives to the economy via unpaid domestic labour and the repro-duction of the labour-force. The label 'unemployed', then, is a managerial category, constructed for bureaucratic purposes according to bureaucratic criteria. What it normally means is 'not counted by government agencies as working for more than forty paid hours per week'.

But the label 'marginal', if taken to mean 'afunctional' *vis-à-vis* the economy, is just as misleading as 'unemployed'. As Lenin remarked:

> . . . capitalism would not be capitalism if the 'pure' proletariat were not surrounded by a large number of very mixed transitional types, from the proletarian to the semi-proletarian (and petty artisan, handicraft worker and small proprietor in general), from the small peasant to the middle peasant, and so on, and if the proletariat itself were not divided into more or less developed strata, divided according to territorial origin, according to trade, sometimes according to religion, and so on.[81]

Of the ten categories given above, workers in manufacturing industry and those working in sweat-shops ((*a*) and (*c*)) are clearly directly involved in mainstream industrial production as classical factory proletarians, while putting out work ((d)) merely involves a difference in locale. Personal servants, equally, work for wages, though for employers who normally only employ one or two workers, and in their own homes. The self-employed and domestic producers produce goods and services, either individually or as families, and sell the product of their labour or their services on the market in a perfectly capitalist way. Casual labourers are equally paid, either for short-term work or by piece-work, for the work they do. Street-vendors, again, are usually the last link in a chain of distribution or commercialization which begins when commodities are produced in a capitalist factory, are then sold wholesale, and thence go to retail outlets, the point of intersection between the ultimate seller and the customer being sometimes a street-vendor. 'Hunting and collecting', as we have noted, is, for the most part, organized on thoroughly capitalist lines; criminal and deviant occupations no less so, despite variations in the scale of operations. About the only category below the line, thoroughly marginal to capitalism insofar as no value is created and no wages are paid, are beggars. The economic relations of all others are capitalist relations.

The myth of economic marginality has been most vigorously refuted by Perlman for the *favelados* of Rio, a third of whom, in 1969, though commonly thought of as non-productive, worked in manufacturing industry, transportation and construction (and only one in ten in the local community) albeit in unskilled jobs, with three-quarters of them in dire poverty (17 per cent unemployed and another 26 per cent earning less than the legal minimum wage – then only US $10 a week). Three in ten were doing odd jobs.

They are, for the most part, not just a reserve; they are a part of the working class, hired or fired as needed, and very badly paid when they do work. In relation to them, those with steady jobs are usually better-off. But in backward economies, this is not necessarily the case. In Accra, the army of wretchedly paid low-level public servants (messengers, porters, cleaners, clerical workers, police, road workers, drivers, servants) often have to supplement their meagre wages by moonlighting or working land within the city.[82] But in newly-industrializing economies, skilled workers are indeed a labour aristocracy while the 830,000 production workers of all grades of skill in the Brazilian automobile industry earned, on average, six times the minimum wage in the late 1970s, and a third more than workers in older industries such as textiles, glass, printing and railways.[83] In the labour-force as a whole, the proportion earning more than five times the minimum wage increased from 2 per cent in 1960 to 8.3 per cent in 1976; the proportion earning less than the minimum decreased from 70.1 per cent to 46.7 per cent.[84] Further evidence of growing prosperity among the working class (eagerly seized upon and distorted by the military President) was the increase in the number of households with refrigerators (from a tenth in 1960 to half in 1978), while over half had TV (a considerable proportion of them rented, second-hand or on hire-purchase). Yet only 35 million people in a working population of 80 million received more than the minimum wage; two-thirds less than three times the minimum wage, and three-quarters less than five times. The purchasing-power of the minimum wage may be estimated when it is realized that even the élite workers only got a tenth of the pay their US, Swedish, Belgian, Dutch, or German counterparts would have received for the same work; WHO recommended levels of milk consumption would have required 4.8 million litres per day for the Greater São Paulo area, but only 1.9 million were actually consumed, and where there had only been three *favelas* in the ABCD industrial triangle fifteen years earlier, by 1980 there were 184 with 200,000 inhabitants, most of them employees of Volkswagen, Brastemp, Scania-Vabis, and Mercedes-Benz.[85] Those at the top of the wage-scale get twenty, fifty, even a hundred times more than the poorest-paid workers. A sixth of the country's labour-force, however, either work less than forty hours a week or earn less than the minimum wage, especially rural workers who still constitute nearly half the labour-force.

Such low wage-rates, and the gap between the élite and the mass of unskilled and casual workers, are not, however, simply a consequence of market competition for scarce jobs – the classical downwards pressure created by the existence of a reserve army of the unemployed. Indeed, the reverse is often true: in order to hoard supplies of scarce skilled labour and to keep that labour from becoming politically militant, the labour aristocracy is not only given decent wages, but job security, largely through 'closed shop' agreements operated by the skilled workers' trade unions. Nevertheless, those in all but the highest brackets have the greatest difficulty even in keeping up with inflation-rates that rarely sink below 70 per cent a year and often exceed 100 per cent. Divisions within the working class are thus the result of conscious policies, not simply of the price for labour as determined by the free play of the market, and are designed to separate the tiny élite from the impoverished mass, whose dissatisfactions are kept under control by State repression. Yet poverty is always relative. In the UK, the official measure of poverty is twice that used by Rowntree in 1899; yet the poor in Britain are seven times better off than the poor in India. The relevant reference-group, however, for immigrants to Third World cities, is not any class in the First World, not even the rich or the privileged workers in their own country, but more often those in the villages and towns they have come from. What looks like the 'backside of hell' to the outsider, indeed, is often experienced by the shanty-town dweller as *improvement*. Measures of absolute poverty, such as the WHO's standard of 3000 calories per day as the minimum required by a moderately active man and 2200 for a moderately active woman, are therefore thoroughly non-sociological, since they not only omit differences in work intensity or environmental conditions, but crucially fail to take into account the *social* environment. For notions of what constitutes an adequate diet, let alone adequate pay, or an adequate standard of living in general, are culture-specific norms, defined by people in specific societies according to *their* criteria of what constitutes want or plenty, not standards deemed appropriate for them – often arbitrarily – by social workers, statisticians or nutritionists and measured against some universal biological yardstick. Social wants, not asocial, biological needs, define health and wealth. And today, wants are changing with ever-increasing rapidity, due to greater social mobility and exposure to new values, particularly through the mass media.[86]

In a country like Brazil, commonly taken to be an outstanding instance of Third World industrialization – even a miracle – the strategy for satisfying these new wants is to go for growth, not redistribution. The richest 10 per cent continue, therefore, to receive 54 per cent of all income, leaving only 9.7 per cent to be shared by half the population. Economic growth, under these conditions, only reinforces economic disparities, which are further consolidated as differences of generalized class culture by virtue of differential access to most other social resources, such as education.[87]

The so-called marginals, then, are not a class apart; they are part of the working class, many of them ex-peasants or people from provincial towns, with all the cultural attributes that that implies. They aspire to become workers or to set up in business, though any strategy for self-advancement will do. But they do not necessarily succeed in any of these projects. 'Urban poor' is therefore the most appropriate term to describe them – and the term 'marginal' should be dropped.

So far, we have discussed the urban poor largely in terms of the size and sources of their incomes. But income is by no means the only significant aspect of work. Industrial sociologists have also emphasized the differential status accorded to different occupations and the importance of job security. Stability of employment – security – deserves far more attention than it normally gets in discussions of the life of the urban poor, for though, analytically, jobs can be classified into categories, as I have done above, the existential reality is that any individual moves in and out of many different kinds of occupation. In a Mexican shanty-town, Lomnitz has written, a man may be 'one day a gardener, another a bricklayer or a driver's assistant'. In emergencies, when he falls ill, his wife has to go out 'selling *tortillas* or *nopales*, or doing washing or ironing. The children go out selling lottery-tickets or chewing-gum or begging for bread. The use of rubbish can become systematic: one resident who works as an independent rubbish-collector raised pigs with the scraps he picks up on his daily round'.[88]

If one man in his time plays many parts, so do the women and children.

Miguel Durán, at thirty-eight, has been rubbish-collector, thief, drummer in a band, burglar, marijuana-seller, mugger, cake and sweet vendor, newspaper-seller, night-watchman, horse and cart dealer, and had a dozen other jobs, respectable and disreputable.[89]

A major attribute of the urban poor, then, is the volatility of their occupations. Under such conditions, they are unlikely to develop a distinctive class-consciousness, for though they are would-be workers or in the process of becoming workers, it is a process that does not necessarily get consummated. Since they are the endemic casual poor,[90] it is as the poor, rather than as members of the working class, that they are likely to see themselves. This is not false consciousness; it is a realistic appraisal of their situation.[91]

Since they normally live in households which are complex and unstable, and not as isolated individuals, their survival depends on the support of kin (pejoratively labelled *parasitisme familiale* in some African studies) outside the nuclear family, on ties with members of other primary groups and networks within the local community, and on connections with influential individuals outside the community. Kin speak for their relatives in their places of work; women help each other with food preparation and child-minding; families combine to form rotating savings clubs and to share ritual expenses, notably by entering into godparent relationships.[92]

These extra-economic ties are thus a safety-net substituting for the non-existent Welfare State, but also act as a drag on the more successful. In Dakar, in 1965, 188 industrial workers were found to be supporting no less than 1802 others (800 of them distant kin).[93] Civil servants take children sent by kin in the rural areas into their homes as unpaid servants, and sometimes pay for their schooling. It is thus prosperity that is shared, not poverty. The poor survive only because they are self-reliant and exercise initiative, both individually and as groups, by mobilizing available relationships and creating new ones.[94]

Yet the belief that they are not merely economically, but psychologically depressed, and lacking in social skills, is still widespread. A sociologist in a country that boasts the largest slum area in Asia, Tondo (Manila) in the Philippines, refutes that view:

> Nobody questions the stress of the negative aspects of slum life. [But it] is not totally bleak nor filled with unrelieved misery as often portrayed. . . . Slum dwellers are far from what most people say they are. They are far more pragmatic [and] more intelligent, and psychologically attuned to take advantage of changing conditions and available opportunities. . . . Happiness is hardly the attribute of life we, the outsiders, would ascribe to the existence of people in this neglected part of the city. [But] happiness is a part of slum life, of the people's own view of everyday existence and of their strategies in carrying out the business of everyday life. . . . Even conflicts can be satisfying, provided positive experiences result from them.[95]

Scattered studies suggest that even in India, living in slums does not necessarily mean being without work.[96]

People would be fools if they abandoned subsistence and came to the city to suffer even more miserably. A generation ago, pioneer studies of the urban poor in Argentina showed that migrants from both the rural and urban areas of the more developed provinces tended to find better jobs than those from the more backward regions; twice as many immigrants as city-born were semi-skilled and unskilled workers (27.3 per cent as against 14.9 per cent); and immigrants provided nearly all the domestic servants. Yet no less than half who had come to Buenos Aires as migrants were in semi-skilled and skilled non-manual jobs or in skilled manual work, compared to three-quarters (76.3 per cent) of those born in the city.[97] A later study of Monterrey, in Mexico, followed by a study of Mexico City, showed that during the first decades of rapid industrialization after the Second World War those who had spent more time at school or who were artisans, and who had often been living in smaller towns and cities before moving to the big city, were over-represented among the immigrant population.

During such periods of rapid industrial growth, immigrants often actually take a higher share of the better jobs than the city-born. More of those who came as migrants to Mexico City started work in low-level non-manual jobs than people born in the city (23.8 per cent as against 19.1 per cent) and their share of even the higher non-manual jobs was also higher (4.9 per cent as against 1.6 per cent). They also got promotion faster: 48.5 per cent moved up one or two grades from their first job as against 29.2 per cent of the city-born.[98] The less-skilled, certainly, were not so fortunate. They started lower than the city-born, and have poorer promotion records. In recent years, these less-educated and skilled people have begun to make up a larger proportion of the newer contingents. The superior educational facilities of the capital, moreover, have meant that the city-born school-leaver is now twice as likely to find a low-level non-manual job as the migrant educated elsewhere. So if nearly a half of the youngest age-group born in the city still find themselves in unskilled manual jobs, this is the fate of two-thirds of the immigrants. In the early stages of industrialization, then, it was those with a few years of education or some skills who moved to town. Today, those who follow them are likely to have lower levels of education and skill.

The picture is still far removed from that of the 'backside of hell'. Nearly half of all immigrants into Mexico City in the early 1970s were in fact able to find a job within a week; 30 per cent of the rest within a month. Only 4 per cent were still unemployed after six months.[99] Around half had acquired a TV set, gas-stove and even a sewing-machine since they arrived. It is not surprising, then, that 80 per cent of them said that they would never go back even if they could.

Though they live in slums, they are slums of hope, not slums of despair.[100]

Even with the austerity enforced after the military *coup* in Brazil in 1964, over two-thirds of the *favelado*-dwellers felt that their lives had 'improved in the past and [were] going to improve in the future'. Far from being locked into a hopeless culture of poverty, they valued 'modern forms of accomplishment, [were] anxious to secure well-being for themselves and their children, [and strove] to be integrated into the society at large. . . . The aspirations of the marginals', Perlman wrote, 'do not differ from those of the middle class.'[101] The long-despised lumpenproletarians, it now seemed, were petty-bourgeois – in their aspirations at least!

Though most remain desperately poor, and know that they will stay that way, a minority do acquire stable jobs with good prospects, and become role-models for the less fortunate. If the dream of individual upwards mobility is only realized for a few, the majority not just hope, but *believe* life will be better for their children. Even among the 4½ million in more than 500 settlements in Mexico where there is no piped water and no sewage system, 84 per cent, in one sample, thought that life would become better or much better, a third thought it possible to move to a higher social class; a half thought it likely that their children would be middle class and 60 per cent thought it possible that they would get university (*sic*) level education.[102]

It is often forgotten, too, that those who come to the city are by no means all poor or unqualified. The literacy rate among Turkish male migrants was 84 per cent ; in Lima 86 per cent, in Caracas 75 per cent, and in Delhi 42 per cent,[103] while in 1970, four out of every ten who had migrated into Mexico City were professionals, technicians and sub-professionals, owner-businessmen and managers, civil servants, legislative staff or administrative workers, or petty traders and salesmen. Only a quarter of all immigrants thus fell into the categories most people have in mind when they talk about marginal immigrants![104]

The most ambitious and qualified, of course, move even further afield. They are part of the international Brain Drain. Between 1962 and 1966, no less than 57,595 professional, technical and kindred workers were admitted to the USA alone. Though some go back, there is usually a sizeable permanent loss to the country of origin which, by financing their initial education, thereby provides aid, free of charge, to the First World. Some countries export large numbers: 44 per cent of the junior medical staff in the British National Health Service came from overseas in 1967, and over 55 per cent of the senior grades were born outside the UK and Eire. For smaller countries, the loss of small numbers – 13 doctors in the case of Ethiopia – is very serious in a country which had only one doctor for every 62,000 people – virtually a large First Division football crowd. For Ecuador, which only had 51,900 professional, technical and related workers altogether in 1962, it is a tragic haemorrhage of human capital.[105]

The 'Informal' Sector

Sociologists, Sorokin has written, suffer from 'discoverers' complex'.[106] These 'new Columbuses' are constantly discovering what has been discovered before, even hundreds of years ago. A more sociological interpretation would be that they confront a similar reality; that information retrieval-systems fail to acquaint them with the exponentially growing work of others, from which they are further cut off by linguistic barriers and by membership of discrete scientific networks. Independent invention is therefore not only endemic, but likely to increase.

The analytical separation of the marginal sector from mainstream capitalism by Latin American theorists overlapped in time with the development, in Africa, of a parallel theory: that of the 'informal' sector, but the anglophone theory grew up quite independently of that in the New World. The concept of the informal sector, introduced by Hart in 1971, was classically dualist: in underdeveloped economies, there were *two* sectors to the economy: the dominant, capitalist sector – now dubbed the 'formal' sector – and an informal one,[107] distinctions later codified by the ILO as a set of attributes thus:

Informal	Formal
(*a*) ease of entry	(*a*) entry is difficult
(*b*) reliance on indigenous resources	(*b*) dependence on imports
(*c*) family ownership of enterprises	(*c*) corporate property
(*d*) small scale of operation	(*d*) large-scale
(*e*) labour-intensive and adapted technology	(*e*) capital-intensive, imported technology
(*f*) skills acquired outside the formal school system	(*f*) skills often acquired abroad
(*g*) unregulated and competitive markets	(*g*) markets protected by tariffs, import and exchange licences[108]

The history of Hart's model provides a fascinating study in the diffusion of ideas, for though his work owed nothing to others, similar ideas had been adumbrated by various writers, but had attracted little attention.[109] Hart's formulation, however, had an extraordinary impact. To international agencies wrestling unsuccessfully to develop the Third World, it offered new hope. The ILO's World Employment Programme, begun in 1969, had got nowhere. The new strategy, based on the informal sector, offered the best of all possible worlds: the promise of new income-generating activities which would help the poor 'without any major threat to the rich'.

A conference at the Institute of Development Studies, Sussex, England, in September 1971, provided the launching pad. The idea was fed to experts from forty-nine countries, who thereupon leapt into action. Within months, the ILO had a Mission in Kenya (including ten people who had attended the Sussex conference). Earlier policies, based on Bairoch's view of the problem as one of *rural* underdevelopment and of an over-urbanized city, logically implied policies of stimulating rural development and reducing rural-urban drift. Now, the answer seemed to lie in the very sector that these earlier studies had seen as the problem: in the despised informal sector where the urban poor actually made their living. Country studies in Colombia and Sri Lanka quickly followed the Kenya one, complemented by city studies of São Paulo, Jakarta, Calcutta and Abidjan.

No sooner had the new theory taken wing than the critics opened fire to shoot it down. The objections were both methodological and substantive: Why assume that there were two (and only two) sectors? Might 'informal' and 'formal' not be better thought of as poles at either end of a continuum? Why had there been no multivariate analysis to test whether the attributes listed as identifiers of informality were *causally* connected or not? Were the two sectors really independent of each other? Was it wise to advocate a unitary policy for such a diverse range of activities? Was there not an informal sector in the countryside? How were the two sectors related to the State and other sectors (and what were the latter)? Was not a model of the overall system needed? Could informal units be converted into petty capitalist enterprises merely via government intervention? What would happen to those involved, and would established firms tolerate new competition and lost dependencies? Was the individual, the household, the locality, or the enterprise the unit of the informal economy? Were all informal workers really poor, and all in the formal sector aristocrats?[110]

Answers to these questions were not to be found by reading Althusser or volume 3 of *Capital*. They called for empirical research informed by theory, the most substantial studies coming from MacEwen Scott in Peru, Middleton in Ecuador, and Bromley in Colombia.

Using Marxist categories creatively, and focusing on the border between the self-employed and wage-workers rather than that between casual and stable workers, MacEwen Scott rejected the 'excessive individualization' of what are, in reality, *social* relations of production – built in, for example, to statistics of personal income or consumption-oriented studies of the sharing of poverty. 'Self-employment', she wrote, is not a Marxist concept, since it does not specify how the producer relates to others either in production or via the market. Most enterprises, moreover, employ *some* labour, whether family or wage-labour (and often both). Her starting-point and her unit of analysis, therefore, is the *enterprise*, since it is here that labour and capital are brought together. Those who are (i) juridical owners of the means of production, who (ii) directly appropriate the profits, and (iii) control the decision-making processes involved can then be distinguished analytically from those who work for the profit of others. Yet existentially, many people do both, or move from one kind of employment to another.

Marx saw petty commodity production not just as an element in most historic modes of production (usually subsidiary to the dominant one), but as part of an evolutionary *process*, in which capitalist industry would eventually drive out the petty producer. Much of what these people produce, today, takes the form of services – 'intangible commodities' – rather than material things. The first major type of petty enterprise in Lima – traditional artisanal industry supplying luxury goods (jewellery, footwear, clothing, leather goods, carpentry) to a small wealthy clientele – still flourishes, and some even expand, the master-craftsman then becoming an employer of labour. But in a declining and fiercely competitive market, even accidents like a fire, a death, or a robbery can drive them under, so that they end up doing detail work for others, or as dependent sub-contractors. Thousands work in construction, a notoriously unstable industry, and though they may think of themselves as working for a fee rather than a wage, despite such illusions, self-images and aspirations, the reality is often one of gradual proletarianization. The transport sector, likewise, presents opportunities to make money for hundreds of owners or renters of taxis in which the ground can be seen through the floorboards. But they can also be quickly driven out of business by fleets of superior modern vehicles. Street-traders, commonly thought of as the epitome of independent self-employment, are often selling on commission or dependent on suppliers.[111]

 The independence of the majority of petty entrepreneurs, whether producers or traders, is thus illusory. Control over the latter's output, production decisions and prices is often effectively out of their hands. Most of them do not become petty capitalists in a city like Lima in part simply because there are too many of them for all to survive. But they are also victims of the volatility of the market. For three decades (1940–72), the self-employed did manage to keep their share of the market, at about 22 per cent, since they colonized specialized occupational niches as suppliers of jewellery to the rich, of cheap, non-factory goods as well as repair services and second-hand goods, to the poor. Hence even in a world where the world price of oil or of gold is unstable, and inflation rampant, like peasant smallholders, petty enterprises survive because they are willing to occupy these insecure niches, to pioneer the less profitable and risky areas which the big firms leave alone. The latter, however, profit by selling to the petty producers and buying their output. The workers in these industries – on low wages and for whom no social security need be paid – can be dropped when business declines.

The fortunes of petty enterprise thus vary in accordance with the state of wider national and international markets. In an uncertain economic climate like that of Peru under the radical military regime of Velasco (1968–72), domestic and foreign capital was nervous about investing, and world-prices for metals, on which the economy depends, were shaky. Increased tertiarization resulted, for despite the increase in the numbers of the self-employed, the rate of growth of petty commerce was far greater, and the rise of manual and non-manual wage-labour greater still.[112] Self-employment in the tertiary commercial sector grew both relatively and absolutely, while the small *producer* sector lost ground. Yet under the very different conditions of rapid economic expansion in adjoining Ecuador at about the same time, the very same pattern was repeated. There, the discovery of oil in 1971 led to a veritable bonanza; the country probably changed more in five years than it had done in many decades. GDP increased by a third in four years. The result, however, was not the postulated transformation of petty enterprise into small-scale capitalism, but the Peruvian experience repeated: the expansion of wage-labour manufacturing at the expense of the petty producers and a large increase in the number of artisans in the sector which expanded fastest of all – services.

The informal sector, then, is a greatly reified concept.[113] Analytically it fails to distinguish between capitalist production – where a non-owning producer works for a non-producing owner; empirically, it conflates the very different spheres of production and trade under the rubric of 'petty enterprise'. Yet the two vary independently. In petty production, where skills are required, 43 per cent of the Quito labour-force in Ecuador were wage-workers; in trade, 85 per cent were either self-employed or used unpaid family labour. But production was so little truly *capitalistic* that 40 per cent even of the wage-workers were related to the head of the enterprise, and since two-thirds of these micro-producers used only hand tools (often handed down or second-hand), they could scarcely compete with the multinational firms that now moved into fields like textiles or shoe-production, where one firm displaced 1000 artisans in two years. For the petty producer, the prospect was not that of becoming a small capitalist, but of being driven out of business.

The Poor in Action

For liberals, poverty is a tragedy, its victims deserving of sympathy and assistance. Radicals go further: they condemn the *structural* causes of poverty. But many people blame poverty on the poor: it is, they say, a just reward for their idleness, lack of enterprise, skill, energy, courage, etc. Yet it is the exercise of initiative, both individual and collective, that keeps the poor alive, and even the least-privileged do make a living:

> The rate of employment is very high in nearly all the shanty-towns of
> Turkey, Latin America, India and North Africa surveyed. . . . In the
> Turkish shanty-towns, 93 per cent of the men; . . . in Lima . . . 99 per
> cent; . . . in Caracas . . . 72.5 per cent; . . . in Delhi 81.2 per cent; . . . in
> Algeria 92 to 94 per cent.[114]

Hence, though, like all poor people, most of their income goes on food
(75–80 per cent of it in Istanbul), they do have some disposable income:

> . . . the squatter's income, although below the average of the established
> city dwellers, was substantially above that of the rural inhabitants, and
> definitely much higher than that of many of their friends and relatives left
> in the native villages.[115]

The first thing they do with their earnings is to improve their housing. Piles
of bricks are one of the commonest sights outside the temporary dwellings
people erect when they first come to the *barriadas* of Lima. But they also
organize themselves as pressure-groups to obtain water, electricity, a
school, paved roads, sewerage, usually by invoking the aid of powerful
brokers for whom their votes become the basis of their own standing within
the political party. If they do not get these things, they simply *take* them
wherever possible, and others show them how to do it. A wealthy colleague
of mine in Mexico City, having failed to get the electricity corporation to
connect his house to the mains, was rescued by his poor neighbours, who did
for him what they do for themselves: hooked him up to a *telaraña*, one of the
spider webs of illegal cables plugged into the city's electrical supply-system
which festoon the dwellings of the poor from Mexico to Hong Kong, and
provide free electricity for rice-cookers, fans, TV sets and radios.[116]

Since they often pay no taxes at all, and usually have no rent, or low rents,
to pay, living-costs are so low that even those who do increase their earnings
often continue to live in the shanty-towns but invest in home improvements.
Though some do move out to better accommodation elsewhere, over time a
variety of types of housing comes into being within the shanty-town itself, so
that quite solid middle-class residences may be found cheek-by-jowl with
shacks. Though most of them are wretched dwellings, the rate of home
ownership in shanty-towns is high: between 93 and 96 per cent in Caracas;
81–93 per cent in one Indian study; and 75 per cent in Rabat. Class
differentiation is thus a feature of shanty-town life. Nearly one in ten of the
population of such settlements in Ankara were government officials.[117]
Some of the more entrepreneurial achieve upwards mobility not through
their jobs, but by becoming resident slum landlords, renting plots and
accommodation within the shanty-town and even speculating in building
land.

But collective initiatives are more typical of the early phases of the life-cycle of the shanty-town. The basis of joint activity varies. Common origins are a ready-made basis of association in the city, though formal voluntary associations are much rarer than they are often thought to be.[118] People from the same region or ethnic group keep their rural connections alive through visits and by feeding money into the rural economy. The persistence of pre-colonial culture, even after half a millennium, is by no means simply an expression of conservative, backwards-looking traditionalism. It is a *modern* reaction, sometimes involving even the revival of ancient customs which had been abandoned. The interplay of the old and the new is thus a dialectic which invests ancient cultural heritages with quite new significance. After colonial conquest, such beliefs and rituals acquired a new significance as modes of cultural resistance. Today, peasants in Bolivia who honour the Christian saints also sacrifice to Pachamama, the deity associated with the earth; miners organized into militant trade unions not only hold masses underground, but also sacrifice to Supay, the deity who lives with them in the mine and the mining-encampments, and whom Christianity has wrongly equated with the Devil, so that he will protect them in their highly dangerous work.[119] Similarly, the worship of the ancestors, which is losing ground in rural areas, is finding new adherents in Soweto, for it is now being taken up, by some, as part of an assertion of a distinctive *Black* identity,[120] just as American Blacks turned 'Back to Africa' in their rejection of White culture.[121]

The poor are therefore culturally as well as economically differentiated before they arrive in the city, and become more so. Settling is a gradual process which can take a lifetime. It is the second generation that grows up fully urbanized. For their parents, the rural connection remains important as long as significant Others are there, or until land is disposed of. Some retire to the village. But most of them are no longer really comfortable there: they feel like outsiders, and to the villagers they are modern people, city slickers beside whom they feel like rural 'hicks'. But new institutions, such as ethnic associations, emerge in the city, catering to a demand for cultural forms rooted in the countryside. Radio-stations in Lima – which has been described as 'the first Indian city in South America' – now play modern versions of Highland music, not just imported rock. Dislodged from their cultural bearings, immigrants turn to religions which are new to them, or new to the country: Protestantism in Catholic countries, or new syncretic religions like Umbanda in Brazil which attracts not only the poor but others who feel left out of the hegemonic culture.

But new identities also develop in the city – conceptions of oneself as a worker or as middle class. The housing situation of the poor, like their job, market and status situations, also varies. Though we have concentrated, deliberately, on shanty-towns, since they have been seen as the spatial manifestation of a supposedly distinctive new class, shanty-towns are by no means the only places where the poor live. They inhabit a variety of locales and types of housing, from run-down city-centre multi-occupancy slums to whole new satellite dormitory cities, such as the settlement blocks of Hong Kong.

By the 1950s, the housing situation in that colony had become so threatening that government reacted decisively. Many of the 300,000 squatters had been evicted from tenements; others were looking for cheaper accommodation, or preferred areas without electricity and water to sleeping in cocklofts in shifts in spaces little bigger than that taken up by a coffin, despite the fire risk, the gangsters, and the mud-slides in the shanty-towns which took 100 lives in June 1972 alone. Motivated by the desire to avoid social disorder, to free potentially valuable land of squatters, and to avoid squatter settlements being seen by visitors, a fifth of the population was evicted between 1962 and 1965 alone and decanted into gigantic estates of 40,000 people, each with twenty massive buildings, at densities ten times those in Britain and eight times those in similar estates in Latin America. A third of the blocks have now progressed to the level of providing each person with 'twice the area of a grave' – less than WHO minimal standards, for to have satisfied even that low standard would have cost HK$47 per person.[122] (At the time, profit tax was only 12½ per cent, income tax 15 per cent, and firms expected to recoup the capital they invested in five years, many in two or three.)

The blocks, with communal toilets flushed automatically every fifteen minutes, are the nearest approximation to the life of a battery hen that one can imagine.[123] Even with all this new housing there were still 1½ million people in tenements, and probably around half a million squatters.

Capitalist imperatives not only constrain the plans of colonialist governments, but frustrate dedicated socialists like Oscar Niemeyer who designed Brasília as a democratic city in which people from different social classes would live side by side, and as a city to walk in. Market forces and military dictatorship have left it a city of immense distances, large, fast cars, and poor bus services, inhabited by civil servants, with the lower grades housed in an outer ring, and the construction and service workers in a belt of shanty-town often twenty kilometres from the centre.[124]

But the poor have often taken things into their own hands. In South America, collective 'invasions' are typical of the early phases of the life-cycle of the shanty-town: carefully organized occupations in which thousands, overnight, invade unoccupied land in ravines, sand-pits, swampy areas, hillsides, vacant lots, privately or publicly owned, setting up largely symbolic temporary structures of tin, wood and straw (in order to establish a legal claim to have a dwelling), and skilfully manipulating, too, the symbols of the hegemonic culture in their own interests. They therefore put up national flags and sing the national anthem, and call in TV, radio and press reporters, thereby making it very difficult for governments, municipal authorities or landowners who would love to unleash the riot police and send in the bulldozers to do so, since this attack on patriotic poor people would not only get blazoned across the country, but even become international news.

The heroic phase does not usually last long. Community leaders become co-opted and corrupted, and popular energies channelled into 'carefully controlled, officially sanctioned channels'. The obdurate face physical violence, prison, torture, even death.[125]

Internal class differentiation within the slum often results in the monopolization of leadership positions by the self-employed and professionals who live there because rents and taxes are low or non-existent, and who are usually readily bought off or co-opted. Communities and individuals who co-operate get favours in return for political conformity; others do not. But some degree of community organizations remain in being as long as schools, electricity and other services are still needed, even when invasion has been legalized. More far-sighted governments replace repression with incorporation. They realize that it is far cheaper to let the poor provide their own housing, and that if they provide stand-pipes or even electricity in the streets they may win a modicum of popularity. In São Paulo, 75 per cent of all working-class housing is built by the people themselves in their leisure-time, after a full week at work. The State is thereby able to save vast sums which it can then spend on projects closer to its own heart, from improving upper-class residential areas (which have very many times more spent on them than the working-class zones – though over half the houses in the city lack piped water) to expenditure on the armed forces.[126] Site and service schemes, in which an infrastructure of roads, gas and electricity supply and water is installed by the State, while the residents build the houses, often with simple materials and with assistance from specialists, are attractive not just to reactionary governments but also to humanitarian agencies and international bodies such as the WHO and the ILO, which argue that otherwise the poor will get nothing; *this* way they will at least get a roof over their head, and are actively involved in running their own lives. (Ultra-radical groups denounce such schemes as a 'cop-out' which relieves an exploitative State of its responsibilities.)

Victims as they are, the poor are also agents, active in history. The direction of their activity, however, is so ambiguous that while some see them as aspiring bourgeois, others, like Fanon, have regarded them as a potential revolutionary force, indeed, *the* revolutionary force in the cities. That the vast majority find life in the city a great improvement is incontestable. 'With due exceptions', Karpat writes, *gecekondu* in Turkey

. . . centres of crime, prostitution, juvenile delinquency, economic drain, and radicalism, but associations of optimistic people aspiring to reach a higher standard of living. . . . The overwhelming majority appear to be satisfied with their life. . . . Village migrants . . . express in general a feeling of satisfaction and optimism. They seem very confident that their situation will improve in the future, and that their children . . . will have a better life than their parents.[127]

But their wants are by no means wholly satisfied; rather, they increase, to an extent that is truly a revolution of rising expectations, however un-revolutionary they may be politically. Their values and aspirations are commonly individualistic, deriving in part from peasant backgrounds; in part from the need to help oneself in a viciously competitive world; in part, from the internalization, in bourgeois society, of its hegemonic values. The outcome is a philosophy best captured by Mangin:

Work hard, save your money, trust only family members (and them not too much), outwit the State, vote conservatively, if possible, but always in your economic self-interest; educate your children for their future and as old-age insurance for yourself. [They also] aspire towards improvement of the local situation with the hope that their children will enter the professional class.[128]

Or, as Perlman puts it, they 'have the aspirations of the bourgeoisie, the perseverance of pioneers, and the values of patriots'.[129]

The dream of owning property is real enough, but, for most, only as real as dreams are. In Turkey, two-thirds even said they would like to own their own businesses, but their expectations were that the only way this could be achieved was by getting a steady job, which would enable them to save for that house or for land in the village. But those who do have houses even benefit from rising property values, and, as Karpat observes, house ownership inhibits the spread of radicalism. The rest have to pay rent, sometimes just for the use of the plot, but rarely more than a sixth of their income. There are thus *grades* of poverty even among the very poor.[130]

Preoccupied with problems of immediate survival and individual better-ment, the poor perceive and treat the political system as another resource to be exploited. If politicians are to get votes, they expect favours in return. They also have a surprising knowledge of their legal entitlements to welfare. Their attitudes to the system are, however, more than instrumental: they are commonly quite positive. The system is not just taken for granted, but endorsed, and populist rhetoric (the government as the ally of the ordinary people) as well as development rhetoric (growth as the prerequisite for prosperity) is widely accepted. A study of working-class opinion by a Mexican left-wing writer is particularly illuminating. There, the political class, the politicians and civil servants, not the bourgeoisie, were seen as the real power in society – and, people believed, *ought* to be! The vast majority believed in a mixed economy managed by the State and the dominant party and approved of US investment. To them, Mexico was a class society, but an egalitarian, open one in which the classes were not mutually antagonistic and mobility was possible. Having experienced real improvements in their lives, both manual and non-manual workers evinced an almost total absence of independent class consciousness or of their own potential power as a class. Lacking any 'ideological shield', they fully internalized the ideology of the dominant class.[131]

'The prevailing political ideology in the shanty-town', then, 'is not hate and aversion toward the system, as romantic revolutionaries have speculated and hoped for';[132] and Fanon's belief that lumpenproletarians were 'one of the most spontaneous and the most radically revolutionary forces . . . rebels by instinct',[133] whereas the proletariat had a stake in the system (if not property, then job-property) and were in any case only a tiny minority, clearly overestimates both the appeal of revolution to the poor and the benefits enjoyed by those who do have jobs. In 1964, when the military seized power in Brazil, the nightmare of the bourgeoisie that the *favelados* would come down from the hills had, it seemed, finally come true. But the poor had come not to loot, to riot, or to protest against the dictatorship. Exasperated by inflation and chaos under Goulart's populist regime, they 'descended from the hillsides and marched alongside businessmen and housewives in support of law and order, tradition, the family, and private property'. For many left-wing intellectuals 'the double shock of the *coup* and its popular celebration pushed them into psychic breakdown'. Others were to suffer imprisonment and torture.[134]

The shanty-town dwellers themselves are also constantly subjected to threats. Opposite a rubbish dump where the garbage-pickers of Guayaquil live is an army barracks with the slogan 'The Army is with the People' on the wall. So it is, and the people know only too well why it is there, for hundreds of thousands, from Rio to Manila, have been bulldozed out of shanty-towns. Their leaders end up dead, tortured, or in gaol. Faced with State violence on this scale, 'any signs of radical ideology, or propensity to revolutionary action . . . are completely absent'.[135] Instead, the poor make a 'rational adaptation to the rules of the political game, distinguishing which kinds of political action are rewarded by the authorities and which kind are likely to be ignored or violently repressed'. Though they continue to fight for their own interests, they have to do so 'within a wider framework . . . carefully fashioned and maintained by the ruling élites'. The limits of orthodox politics are therefore defined by the powerful: associations created by the poor are tolerable as long as they remain confined to the level of the community and channelled into 'carefully controlled, officially sanctioned activities'.[136] Corruption is one omnipresent fact of political life everyone has to reckon with. So is repression. 'The political subculture of the *favela*', Perlman has remarked, 'cannot be understood outside of the context of political repression.'[137] After the military take-over in Brazil in 1964, hundreds of thousands of *favelados* were forcibly removed. They dared not protest, since those who had tried it in the past and been burned out of their homes, fired upon by the police, and gaoled – even tortured – if suspected of being leaders.

Repression, though, is not reserved for political meetings or demonstrations. It is a normal part of everyday life for Mexico City's urban poor who, like Blacks in Britain, expect harassment from the police whenever they encounter them.[138] To overstep the limits of the permissible by trying to link up community organizations on a city-wide basis (let alone a national one), is to invite repression, or decapitation of the movement by removing its leadership. Yet movements rooted in local networks of sociation and fuelled by the experience of disprivilege are not easily broken. They then have to be incorporated by turning them into appendages of the ruling party or by converting their leaders into dependent clients. The poor are thereby disarticulated, divided, even individualized, made to compete with each other for favours. Traditional patterns of deference are given new life in the city. Lacking time, organizational skills and experience, autonomous popular organizations survive only with difficulty.

In Turkey, Karpat concludes, the poor are 'conservative and middle of the road'.[139] In fact, the poor, like the established working-class, do not respond to poverty ideologically, but instrumentally: their main aim is to stop being poor. They are therefore vulnerable to a variety of demagogic and hegemonic appeals, promises, blandishments and deceptions.

Yet the urban poor are not apolitical. In Mexico City, the vast majority are 'at least minimally cognizant of the political and governmental activities that impinge on their lives'; most vote with great regularity; and over half have engaged in political activities other than elections.[140] Where elections exist, their sheer numbers make them a valuable resource. Historically, they have been organized by the Church, by criminals and by parties of the Right which convert them into the kind of urban mob Marx and Engels denounced; more recently, by populist movements. Yet there is no evidence that the casual poor are any more (or less) susceptible than organized workers to the demogogic appeals of the Right or of the populists, or intrinsically deaf to socialism. They are not, as mass society theory would have it, simply a 'disposable mass'.[141] Rather, they persistently pursue their interests, as they see them, within the limits of the structures available to them. In the elections of 1973 in Turkey, the vote of the 3½ to 4½ million *gecekondu*-dwellers (one in ten of the population) was crucial in the victory of Bülent Ecevit's victory, who had promised them land deeds.[142] Similarly, the Argentinian working-class has remained the solid mass power-base of Peronism for nearly half a century.

Neither segment of the working class has been notably revolutionary in social terms. Yet in the struggle for *national* independence, they have been as active as peasants. In Algeria, the urban base of the anti-colonial revolution (albeit crushed by Massu's *para* torturers) was the poor in the Casbah, symbolized in the character of Ali La Pointe in Pontecorvo's film, *The Battle of Algiers*.

The spurious thesis that the urban poor are politically different in kind and supposedly lacking in class consciousness because they are sociologically distinguishable from those in regular work was given its most distinctive expression, both theoretical and practical, on the Right, in the work of Roger Vekemans, a Belgian Jesuit living in Chile, who saw them as a potential mass counterforce to a working class unshiftably committed to socialist and communist parties. The theoretical underpinnings of his project were pure Oscar Lewis: the marginals were *rural* people, living in the city physically, but not socially integrated into urban life. If not incorporated soon, their present resignation would be replaced firstly by frustration, then by aggression; isolation, withdrawal, and non-participation would give way to 'availability' – to revolutionary appeals.[143]

Under the general rubric 'Promoción Popular', a vast network of mothers' centres (serving half a million people), of neighbourhood groups; of centres for male heads of households; of youth centres and sports clubs was then rapidly brought into being, all attached to Eduardo Frei's Christian Democratic Party.[144] When Allende's Popular Unity socialist government replaced Frei in 1973 they inherited this network of organizations and changed its political direction.

The abandonment of the Marx-Engels view of the lumpenproletariat was by now acceptable to many kinds of Marxists. On the far Left, the Chilean MIR, outside the government coalition, moved into the shanty-towns with the aim of realizing Fanon's vision of a revolution whose urban wing would be the lumpenproletariat. The sharpest theoretical reformulation (without criticizing Marx and Engels) came from a revolutionary movement which finally achieved its revolution. In ultra-imperialist, under-urbanized Guinea, Amilcar Cabral distinguished between *two* categories of what he called the 'rootless' people in the towns:

One of these two groups does not really deserve the name of 'rootless', but we have yet to find a better name for them. The other group is easily identified and might easily be called our lumpenproletariat, if we had anything . . . we would properly call a proletariat: they consist of beggars, layabouts, prostitutes, etc. . . . . It is upon the first of these . . . that we have concentrated particular attention, and . . . they have played an

important part in our liberation struggle. They consist of a large number
of young folk lately come from the countryside, and retaining links with it,
who are at the same time beginning to live a European sort of life. They
are usually without any training and live at the expense of their petty-
bourgeois or labouring families.[145]

The Established Working Class

The notion of a labour aristocracy recurs with increasing frequency in the
later writings of Engels, who lived to see more of the final consolidation of
world imperialism than Marx, as well as significant improvements in
working-class living standards (even if Rowntree still found a third of York's
population to be living in poverty at the turn of the twentieth century). Even
as early as the 1840s, in the conclusion to *The Condition of the Working Class
in England*, Engels had already noted the beginnings of provision of
working-class housing, however inadequate. A decade later, Marx was
ruefully writing to him about the rise of a 'bourgeois working class' alongside
the bourgeoisie and the 'bourgeois aristocracy' (letter of 7 October 1858).
Though they believed the growth of a labour aristocracy to be a new
phenomenon, there had always been a sizeable stratum of craft workers and
foremen who very strongly distanced themselves from the unskilled and the
unrespectable. The labour aristocracy was actually no bigger in the 1860s
and 1870s than it had been in the 1850s. Half a century later, Lenin tried to
explain the spread of reformist illusions and even of jingoism among the
British working class by projecting the notion of the labour aristocracy as a
global phenomenon, in terms of imperialist super-profits extracted from the
workers in the colonies, part of which was now used to buy off a significant
segment of the working class in the West.

Two World Wars later, Lenin's global explanation of the spread of
revolution in the Third World and its absence in the West was given a radical
new twist by Fanon. The *whole* working class in the First World, he argued,
had become a labour aristocracy living off the backs of the Third World.
'Economically, the proletarians of Europe', Senghor brutally put it, 'have
benefited from the colonial regime.' Embittered by French Communist
support for the war in Algeria, Fanon concluded that, politically, organized
labour in the West as a whole was not only non-revolutionary, but effectively
condoned imperialist repression of Third World liberation movements.
History, he declared, would henceforth be made by the people of the Third
World. As for the West:

> . . . one can say of the European democrats in Algeria what one has had
> to say repeatedly of the French parties of the Left: for a long time now

history has been made without them. . . . The Left has done nothing for a long time. . . . But it has prevented some things happening.[146]

Even within the Third World itself, he further argued, the working class was similarly privileged – and was therefore interested not in revolution, but in preserving its privileges.

Academic theorists of revolution have been less immanentist: the working class has been seen as neither *inherently* revolutionary nor conservative, but as likely to change in accordance with the capacity of the system to satisfy culturally-established expectations. Davis' famous 'J-curve' theory of revolution thus rejected both the notion that people were driven to revolution through misery and de Tocqueville's belief that revolution occurred when familiar constraints were suddenly removed. It was not deprivation, but *relative* deprivation that was involved: a dialectical interplay between the subjective – what people believed they were entitled to – and the objective – what they actually got. When traditional expectations, including customary levels of exploitation, were suddenly no longer in force, discontent would be maximized, and once traditional standards were abandoned the emergence of quite new kinds of wants and methods of satisfying them was likely. Revolution might therefore as readily occur during periods of economic expansion as during recession. The relationship between expectations and the system's capacity to satisfy them might result from changes either in values or on the 'delivery' side. Values might remain quite 'steady' ('traditional'). They might suddenly be transformed, while the productive system failed to expand. *Either* situation could lead to revolution.[147]

Such models were more flexible than the Lenin–Fanon type which simply assumed that a class would defend its economic interests and that the relevant framework of analysis was a global one, for they introduced wider elements and conditions, adding changes in cultural expectations to economic expansion and contraction.

Yet they still reduced the complexity of society to only two terms: the values of the oppressed and the delivery-capacity of the system. The complex sets of cultural and institutional forces which shape any revolution, from available ideologies of the desirable and possible (political, religious or whatever) to the efficiency and variety of the mechanisms of social control and the contrary possibilities of crystallizing discontent into organization, were omitted.

Whereas classical Marxist theory assumed that the trade union consciousness of the working class – its solidarity *vis-à-vis* the employers over wages and work conditions – would ultimately give way to a revolutionary challenge to the capitalist system, reformist theorists argued that compromise between capital and labour was not only possible but necessary if economic growth were to benefit all. The power of labour, they argued, had historically forced change even upon the ruthless capitalist class of the nineteenth century. With the Welfare measures of Bismarck in Germany and Lloyd George in Britain, wealth had begun to be redistributed to those in need. But the Welfare State, both camps agreed, was only possible in advanced capitalist countries. It therefore came as a shock when a Marxist, Bill Warren, in 1980, not only credited imperialism with diffusing 'the greatest cultural and material achievements so far attained by humanity' to a hitherto benighted pre-colonial world, but discerned substantial improvements in both material and general welfare in the contemporary Third World, invoking Marx's remarks about the revolutionizing of 'the whole relations of society' by capitalism as his authority.[148]

Grand Theorists, whether revolutionary or reformist, are so little inclined to look at the empirical fact of the growth in *some* Third World countries of systems of social security that we might well describe it as the *secret* Welfare State. Yet in every major country in Latin America state systems of social security had appeared before the Second World War.[149] Provision for retirement pensions and sickness benefits, indeed, go back before the First World War. But they were only available then to privileged upper and middle class groups, notably the military and civilian servants of the State. Concessions to the professions, and then to sections of the working class in key, usually State-run industries like electricity, petroleum and the railways, and organized into powerful unions, came later. Today, the insured often enjoy a range of benefits so extensive that it is fatuous to call them 'fringe' benefits, while in countries like Uruguay and Chile, by 1970 the social security coverage was only surpassed by some developed Western and Eastern European countries. In Uruguay, there was one pensioner for every two active members of the labour-force.

The gulf in both earnings and fringe benefits is especially marked between blue- and white-collar workers. In the mines of Peru, a white-collar *empleado* not only earns far more than a miner (*obrero*) but has better working conditions and is provided with a decent apartment, for rent, while the miners live in insanitary dormitories. The *empleado* may well retire on full pension at the age of forty-three; the miner is as likely to die in an accident or from the slow poisoning he endures every day.[150] Yet economic analysis still commonly only takes wages into account, rather than the total social wage.[151]

By the 1970s, over a quarter of the Mexican population was covered by the IMSS social security system. For Federal civil servants (including staff in Federal schools and some academic institutions) ISSTE provides even more: subsidized housing, cheap housing and other loans, statutory paid holidays, medical services, maternity care, life insurance, funeral aid, day-care centres, sports and recreational facilities, even department stores *à la russe* where cheap consumer goods, from household appliances, clothing and groceries to cars can be bought at 40 per cent of market prices. In addition, firms pay Christmas bonuses, and the large corporations and the trade unions may provide social benefits which sometimes include luxurious vacation, recreational, cultural, sports and training centres, and theatres.

But the vast majority are not eligible, notably peasants and unorganized workers in the countryside, and the unorganized, self-employed and domestic servants in the cities. The gulf is so dramatic that Mesa-Lago's careful study does not hesitate to describe the insured workers as a labour aristocracy (and he does not include the highly-developed social security system of Brazil).

In the First World, we generally associate welfare with liberal and social-democratic regimes. In Latin America, social security systems were also expanded most radically by populist regimes courting labour. Thus the 'Ten Rights of the Workers', which gave most of the Argentinian labour-force pension rights between 1944 and 1954, built a loyalty to Perón and his *justicialismo* which lasts beyond his death. Vargas' more corporatist regime in Brazil introduced a social services scheme in 1945 that had to be abandoned under pressure from the Right, but which enshrined him in the hearts of the people as the *pai dos pobres* (father of the poor). Even today, he is still the best-known political figure to poor people. It was a later populist government, that of Goulart in the 1960s, which announced a series of reforms that, like Peronism, frightened the ruling class. The overthrow of his regime by the military in 1964 began with the abolition of democratic political rights. But this was a new kind of technocratic military, its dominant ideology shaped within an institution, the Superior War School (ESG), significantly known as 'the Sorbonne', which civilian policy-makers from the right-wing Institute of Social Research and Study also attended. Anti-communist, pro-US and pro-capitalist (ESG courses included a twenty-day tour of US industrial and military establishments), it had a place for 'social peace' programmes as well as a paranoid preoccupation with subversion and security. Only two months after the *coup*, a new housing agency, BNH, was established, since 'a person with a house', the Minister of Planning declared, 'would not destroy someone else's'. A new adult education agency, MOBRAL, designed to counteract Paulo Freire's radical 'conscientization' movement of the 1960s, followed, together with a new, integrated system of social security. Guaranteed job security, which carried with it rights to high compensation on dismissal, was replaced by a fund provided by employers which could be drawn upon by workers on dismissal and which was used by the State to finance private housing, a system extended in 1970 in the Plan for Social Integration, under which workers would draw on a fund built up out of employers' contributions and taxes for specified social purposes.[152] In 1966 the present social security scheme for the urban population began, and

in 1971 even the rural population was provided for through the creation of
FUNRURAL. By the late 1970s, even in a remote small town in the poverty-
stricken North-east, two-thirds of the over-sixties were in receipt of state
retirement pensions set at 50 per cent of the minimum wage and little worse
than the lowest rural wage-rates.[153]

Such schemes might stave off immediate starvation, but scarcely offset the
general decline in living standards in a society where the poorest half of the
population got 17 per cent of national income in 1960 and only 13.7 per cent
ten years later, under the dictatorship; where malnutrition and diseases of
poverty killed off 100 out of every 1000 children before they were a year old;
where over half the population of São Paulo had no piped water supply and a
third no access to public sewerage; where the average daily intake of calories
was between 1400 and 2100 per day (the FAO-recommended minima being
between 2300 and 3200); and where the rural pension only amounted to
US $1.50 a day.[154]

Welfare, moreover, in such newly-industrializing countries, is usually not
progressive, as in Western and Eastern Europe, but regressive. Even where
workers do not have to pay direct contributions, they pay indirectly through
taxation and higher prices – which even the non-insured have to pay. The
most powerful groups pay less in proportion to their income and receive
more; while the State has the use of the funds for investment. Urban
facilities, which include Mexico's National Medical Centre, one of the
world's finest hospital complexes, contrast with inferior, often primitive,
rural services and a vastly-superior and profitable private-hospital sector
which, in Brazil's case, profits out of contracting its services to the State
system. In the North-east, male sisal workers are forced systematically to
deprive their wives and children of food, as workers were in Britain before
1939; 'if they did not they could not function as wage-earners'. Their homes
are 'practically devoid of furniture'; clothing consists of rags and sacking.[155]

In an expanding economy like that of Mexico, where there is a
revolutionary political heritage and a history of close government association between government and organized labour, radicalism is contained by
incorporating potential opposition. Most trade unions, like peasant
organizations, are attached via a union *central* to the dominant political
party which has run Mexico ever since the Revolution that straddled the
First World War. Unions are, however, allowed to operate legitimately in
defence of their members' interests, even unions not connected to PRI, the
governing party, including some with nominally anarchist or communist
affiliations. Jobs in a boom industry like automobiles, which increased
output twenty-eight times in twenty-nine years between 1950 and 1979, are
valuable property. Wages are high, and over half total earnings come from
fringe benefits. Powerful unions are therefore under strong pressure from
their members to defend their interests by maintaining comparability with

other plants, and some readily resort to the strike weapon. Jobs even become virtually hereditary through union contracts which favour hiring sons of existing workers, while control of the unions themselves – some democratic, others oligarchic – becomes a source of economic and political power fiercely competed for.

The workforce, however, is deeply split between workers on *planta* contracts for an indefinite period, only liable to be fired with due cause and entitled to compensation based on length of service; and casual workers (*eventuales*) on short-term contracts of less than one year. Seniority and promotion, on the whole, therefore seem to preoccupy the leaderships more than control over the work-process or defending workers' grievances in industrial tribunals. After several years, *eventuales* may get up-graded to *planta* status, but they are more likely to be laid off during recessions. Typically, on reaching eleven months of service, they are fired, then re-hired a month later for another eleven months, so as to avoid legal obligations to pay bonuses, compensation, etc. Not only are union officials, who may be professionals or workers themselves, allowed to do union business during working hours, but union dues are deducted from the pay-packet, and sizeable subsidies are regularly paid to the union itself by the firm (often to be used at the discretion of the officials) and sometimes even the salaries of officials who do not work in the factory![156]

Such privileges are unthinkable in countries under dictatorial rule, like Brazil, where union officials cannot enter factories to organize, and militants lose their jobs. They are completely absent, too, in the major newly-industrializing countries of East Asia, which Halliday describes as 'not merely military *regimes*', but 'militarized *societies*'.[157] While much of this military weight is directed against other countries, it is also routinely used to break up any opposition, especially from organized labour. Optimistic unilinear theories of economic growth, whether of the Right (Rostow) or the Left (Warren), which postulate the emergence of bourgeois democracy together with capitalist industrialization, culminating in the emergence of a Welfare State in the Third World, thus ignore both the regressive nature of what welfare exists, as well as its restrictions to privileged segments of the population, thereby reinforcing rather than countervailing class inequalities. Though there has to be *some* provision for minimal health and educational services in urbanized societies, and a supply of skilled, semi-skilled and supervisory personnel to industry, for the majority these services are only rudimentary enough to avert starvation and act as a safety-valve for discontent that might otherwise build up into an explosion. For the wealthy, *per contra*, private health-services and tiny élite universities of international standing are available.

Modern political theory, in its classical beginnings, recognized, with Machiavelli, that rulers have a choice between reliance on force, on the one hand, and fraud on the other. These variations, however, are not random or matters of pure choice; they have to be made within the context of political culture: the historical experience of whole societies crystallized into institutions and idea systems which persist, often, for centuries and which are ignored in most global dependency theory. Theories which focus exclusively on material factors in their attempts to explain social stability – on incomes and welfare benefits – either omit these political and cultural dimensions altogether, or assume that political democracy will *inevitably* develop in the wake of capitalist economic growth.

Yet welfare has no necessary association with democracy. It can take many forms and is readily manipulated by authoritarian regimes to limit mass discontent and to deliberately create a labour aristocracy. But in many cases, it is a subsidiary, even non-existent strategy. In 1967, a working party in Hong Kong described social security provisions as 'conspicuous by their absence', even by Asian standards, since the colonial government only spent 1 per cent of its budget on the social welfare of four million people – three times as much as was spent on the few thousand students at the two universities. Apart from those in Public Service, a local expert concluded:

> . . . workers in Hong Kong had no old age pensions, no medical insurance, little protection against loss of earnings due to sickness, no unemployment benefits, and no guaranteed redundancy payments. Female workers have not been entitled to maternity benefits. As the Financial Secretary said when presenting the 1969 Budget, the Government has been 'more concerned with its distribution'.[158]

Many governments do rely predominantly on force. The military hardware trundled out on Independence Day to impress the citizenry is light equipment designed for counter-insurgency – for class war against their own people, not some foreign enemy. It is understandably only the nurses and fire-fighters who evoke a cheer from the people lining the pavement. Preeminent among such repressive regimes is South Africa, which has succeeded in transforming itself from an agricultural and extractive economy to one with a large manufacturing sector without making any concessions to bourgeois liberalism, let alone social democracy, while East Asian countries, Halliday remarks, 'have endured unprecedently long reigns of unbroken repression against popular organizations of any kind: 140 years in the case of Hong Kong: nearly a century in Taiwan and South Korea. Nowhere in the world, except South Africa, can compare with this record.'[159]

But force is hardly ever the only strategy. Ideological appeals to ancient identities, usually national or religious, are invoked to counteract class solidarity and attempts to build alliances between exploited classes and segments of classes. To the menace of historic enemies on the borders is added, today, the menace of rival world-ideologies.

In East Asia, not only has the working class in the newly-industrializing countries of South Korea, Taiwan, Hong Kong, and Singapore experienced unprecedented economic growth, but they live in countries split off from larger societies which have undergone revolution. Their attitudes to socialism, therefore, are quite different from those which obtain in Europe (East European refugees apart); or in Latin America, where Marxism is the normal language of the intelligentsia and Cuba a Utopia; or in Africa, where Soviet aid has been vital in revolutionary decolonization and where White Communists hold leadership positions in the African National Congress of South Africa. In East Asia, Halliday observes, with millions of refugees from socialism, 'anti-socialism . . . has acquired an ideological sanction and degree of mass support which has been absent in most other post-colonial states'; millions are ideologically deaf to the project of class struggle as the key to social betterment, and hostile to the institutionalized socialisms they are constantly reminded of.

They readily internalize the hegemonic alternative: the appeal of capitalist materialism, which, as Marcuse emphasized for the USA, has long ago shifted from a Protestant emphasis upon work to the celebration of consumption. Work is now merely instrumental: a means to an end, something to be endured, despite its monotony, because it makes possible TV sets, refrigerators, stereos, gas-stoves, and record-players that almost every Mexican car-worker's family owns.

In the modern global village, consumerism is beamed night and day into the homes of even the poorest, who may still lack direct water and electricity supplies but who all have transistors, and many, TV sets. The prime target for the advertisers is the newly-rich middle class. Their style of life, however, becomes a model for millions who can only afford cheaper versions of that life-style: jeans, hamburgers, liquor, rock music, sex. More insidiously, the same messages are more obliquely conveyed through cash-games, chat-shows, and soap-operas, or, as Dorfman and Mattelart have shown in their 'How to Read Donald Duck', through the 'harmless entertainment' of Disney's World: of competition for status in a world of immutable hierarchy; of nostalgia for rural peace as an escape from urban frenzy; of astute cowboys and easily-duped Indians; of simple savages who live in Inca-Blinca, Sphinxland, Aridia, and 'Inestablestán' (Unstableland); above all, of the search for *treasure* in a world where nobody *works* or wants to; where there is no production, only consumption; where the villains are those who sit on their money or steal the property of others; where money, status and virtue are randomly distributed, individual, good or bad luck; where there is no God, only an innocent mouse and a cunning duck. Not so much the American Way of Life as the American Dream of Life.[160]

Modern capitalist ideologies have no monopoly of working-class consciousness, however. Older cultural values persist deeply, especially among first-generation urbanites. Just as British workers retained established Christian identities and developed new ones during the Industrial Revolution, so workers in Northern Nigeria belong to Islamic brotherhoods such as the Tijaniya or Qadiriya. Their children go to Western schools by day and Koranic schools in the evening, or study with peripatetic *mallams* who often work in factories themselves and frequently act as the workers' spokesmen. From them, they acquire Islamic ideals of justice, legitimacy, rights and equality which are often quite at variance with Western bourgeois values. The traditional term *talakawa* (commoner) is now applied to anyone who lacks wealth, skill, Western education, or access to public office or patronage; to small tradesmen as well as wage-workers. But a new term, *leburori* (labourers), has emerged, and industrial workers (a low-status group) further distinguished. New class identities and relationships are therefore mediated via Islamic categories and institutions old and new. Class conflict thus tends to be more than merely economic confrontation and is thereby charged with greater social power. The 'Yat Tatside uprising of 1980, during which the Friday Mosque in Kano was occupied by members of a new Muslim millenarian sect, in which between 100 and 1000 people died, artillery was used, and mass suicides occurred, has been described as an 'overt critique of the materialism that accompanied the petroleum boom in Nigeria',[161] and was followed by a second eruption in Maiduguri in 1982. Industrial class consciousness and militancy are thus perfectly compatible with older Islamic values and institutions, which supply wider meanings than those of purely materialist ideologies and also express a radical reaction to Western imperialist conquest and capitalist penetration – better known in the West from the coming to power of the Ayatollah Khomeini in Iran and the occupation of the mosque in Mecca by a quite different kind of Islamic fundamentalist.

Political economy analyses of the working class are silent on such cultural issues. Economists' analyses at best deal with their effects on the economy, but leave the question of how these effects (treated as *ceteris paribus*) come about to others. Both modes of analysis involve the elimination of crucial causal agencies, for it is not only bankers and industrialists who take decisions of strategic societal significance, but politicians and generals and those who control the machinery of communications and opinion formation.

The working class does not just *come* into being, then. It is *brought* into being – 'made' – but only in part as a consequence of the purposeful decisions of those who dominate society. The English working class, Thompson has written, 'did not rise like the sun at an appointed time. It was present at its own making'; not just the *product* of the factory system; 'the working class made itself as much as it was made'.[162] The working class, everywhere, 'makes itself', that is, generates a set of counter-cultural responses, some Promethean, some accommodative, which are not those produced for working-class consumption by the hegemonic class.

The omission of such dimensions results in a purely abstract and mythological image of the working class as a culture-free, economic universal. How concrete, historical working classes actually think, their goals and organizations, is treated simply as determined by a unitary, inexorable, global capitalist process which in the end produces the working class which will bury capitalism and class society with it.

This metaphysic of the working class as the privileged agency ('bearers') of social change is supported neither by the experience of advanced capitalist society – where no successful revolution has been made by any working class – nor of dependent capitalism, where none of the successful revolutions have been made by the working class.

This is not to say that the working class never can or will overthrow capitalism, or that, short of actual revolution, is never militant or committed to socialism. Being an exploited class, it will always strive to defend itself and to improve its life-situation. In the last few years, the Brazilian working class, for instance, has played precisely the role assigned to it in nineteenth-century Marxist theory, paralyzing São Paulo in a succession of enormous mass strikes that began over bread-and-butter issues but which in the end forced the military to make major political concessions, notably the restoration of a measure of authentic party-political life.

Yet since the working class has no monopoly upon exploitation, it has no monopoly of militancy, of revolutionary potential, either – or of reformism, as anti-Marxists assert. Neither have peasants. Which class will play the decisive part in the struggle for socialism is therefore not some ahistoric, metaphysical absolute: it is a function of the history and resulting social structure of each society. Nor is there necessarily *a* leading class. Exploited classes – industrial workers, the urban poor, smallholding peasants, the agricultural proletariat – have parallel interests and to reject any one of them is to invite them to give their allegiance to the enemy. Political philosophies which given unique preference to the urban proletariat, the agricultural proletariat, or the smallholding peasantry are ideological blockages impeding the kind of alliance between different exploited classes which provided the guerrillas in the Sierra Maestra, in Batista's Cuba, with the crucial support of the working-class underground in the cities, just as the romanticism that dismisses anything short of armed struggle as reformism neglects opportunities for social advance and invites uninhibited State terror.

In some countries, the issue is clearer. A 'second edition of the peasant war' is scarcely likely in Britain, while it would be difficult to base a revolution on the working-class of Black Africa, since nine out of ten people still live in the countryside and most of the industrial proletariat is in extractive industry rather than manufacturing, and much of it still a periodic labour-force. In the really underdeveloped countries, like Guinea-Bissau, there is hardly 'anything', Cabral remarked, that 'we could properly call a proletariat. . . . We are careful', he wrote, 'not to call [such casual workers as dock-labourers, domestic servants, porters, etc.] a proletariat or working class'.[163] These people – in transition from a peasant existence to an urban one – have as much revolutionary potential as the working class proper or the peasantry. Each class, of course, has particular modes of life which give it a distinctive political character: the culture of class inherent in factory life is of a different kind from the solidarities built into a peasant mode of living. It is true, historically, that it was the working classes of the West which first took up socialism as their major alternative project. But they have no continuing monopoly on it any more than the bourgeoisie has had over liberal democratic principles and practices. The myth of the proletariat as the privileged agent of revolution has often only been preserved by the 'substitutionism': the jesuitical devices of re-labelling other revolutionary classes 'proletarians'. Thus the Vietnamese Revolution has been called a 'proletarian' one, even though 95 per cent of the FLN forces were peasants.[164]

Exploited classes, then, are not inherently revolutionary, nor reformist . . . or *anything*. What they become is a function of the institutions and values available to them. They can be captured for conservatism, even fascism. But the rational kernel of Marx's ascription to the working class of the role of grave-digger of class society is that there is a structural contradiction of interests between *all* exploited classes and those who exploit them. The transformation of that common class situation into a project for an alternative society, however, only comes about as a consequence of bitter historical experience (which can be lengthy or highly compressed), and which is only transformed into revolution under the exceptional conditions of social (not just economic) collapse.

Exploited classes can be set against one another, as when Mexican workers were induced to fight revolutionary peasants, or when rural youngsters in Western Europe are recruited into riot-control forces for use against urban workers and students. But the natural elective affinity is one of common opposition to classes and governments which unjustly exploit both. If the struggles of organized labour sometimes only principally benefit a labour aristocracy, they can also raise minimum wages, win welfare concessions, and extend political rights that benefit the poor in general, and even the middle classes.

The final immanentist myth is that all that is required to generate revolutionary consciousness is the right theory, and that Marxism somehow provides an unambiguous key which will enable those who possess it – the vanguard armed with scientific socialist theory – to provide the needed leadership: in its most millenarian (and disastrous, asociological) form, the belief that the exploited are like dry grass, ready to burst into flames once the spark, the *foco*, is there.

One of the factors inhibiting class militancy, however, has been the involutionary multiplication of *soi-disant* Marxist *groupuscules*, each claiming leadership of the working class, which could often hold their annual congresses in a telephone-box. Fiercely asserting a monopoly of the truth, they denounce not only reform of any kind, but their revolutionary rivals too; the less risible outcome being the wars of mutual annihilation waged, for instance, in Argentina between rival Montonero (Peronist) and Marxist guerrillas, whose main enemy, for a time, was not the dictatorship, but each other. With enemies like this, ruling classes need no friends.

In today's global village, these divisions are usually introjected into local labour movements by rival world-claimants to possession of the authentic interpretation of revolutionary doctrine, from the adherents of Bakunin and Marx in the nineteenth century, through the Stalinist-Trotskyist schism of the 1930s, to present-day attempts to yoke working-class and nationalist movements to the Soviet or Chinese camps, the competition between brands of Islam, or the nationalist competition between Taiwan and China for control of the trade union movement in Hong Kong (which concentrates almost entirely on that external issue and does little to defend the working class against extremes of exploitation, neither country wishing to rock the Hong Kong boat they benefit from too hard).

Given such misleadership, the difficulties facing Third World workers are immense, and the potentially great material and moral resources of the socialist Powers become forces for political demobilization.

A final illusion of immanentism is the optimistic, unilinealist, belief that the marginal population will inevitably disappear, as it did in the West. By far the most exhaustive and vivid account of a massive underclass we possess comes not from a contemporary Third World but from Henry Mayhew's account of the street folk of nineteenth-century London[165] – a circumstance which renders the attribution by some theorists of the existence of similar large underclasses today to dependency impossible to sustain, since Britain was at the time the 'workshop of the world'.

The rapid growth of an urban population which cannot find regular employment in modern industry or commerce is natural enough during the early growth of a capitalist market economy, as is the subsequent absorption of this population into mainstream employment in those countries which did make the take-off. But many today will not, and capitalism still remains a system characterized by boom and slump, a truth only obscured during the long prosperity after the Second World War but which scarcely needs to be defended today. During those years, the contention that there was an 'other America' was a last-ditch, dogged assertion, ignored by the trendy apocalyptic theorists of 'post-industrial' society.[166] Yet even in the heart-lands, throughout the boom, the poor remained with us, and when the supply of cheap labour was insufficient, it was imported – introducing new cultural divisions within the working class and within the nation to which we must now turn.

IV Ethnicity and Nationalism

→ RECENT
PHENOMENA.

- How to resolve the problem of ethnicity + nat^n.
- Nat^m + Pop^m, Cap^m, Soc^m, Auth^m.

Ethnicity, Class and Culture

So far, we have discussed workers predominantly in terms of their economic attributes, as generalized labour, as if their position in society was solely determined by their place in a system of production, their relations with their fellows and with those who employed them determined by a purely economic logic of the distribution of property and the operation of the market. All other *social* attributes of workers are excluded from this kind of model. Yet they have kept forcing their way in. We have seen Indian workers finding jobs for fellow caste-members, Nigerian workers expressing militancy through Islam. Even within the sphere of production itself, then, there are many different kinds of relationships, many different kinds of labour, and people get allotted to one type of job or another not simply by virtue of individual qualities such as skill or strength, but because whole categories of people are believed, by those who employ them, to have desirable or undesirable qualities over and above any purely technical aptitudes.

Such beliefs, though *prior* to class, become a basis for class membership. Thus the primordial cultural assumptions which transform sex into gender have determined the restriction of women to domestic labour and the raising of children inside the home, and prevented them from dedicating themselves to career specialization outside it for millennia; secondary rationalizations confine them further to ill-paid jobs. Nimble fingers, throughout history, have been invoked as the reason why women and children are peculiarly fitted for tending looms and picking tea, just as male strength fitted men for digging coal. But whole peoples, too, are perceived as being naturally suited for distinctive roles in the division of labour, and these 'natural' differences often include cultural as well as physical differences. Thus in colonial India, some peoples were regarded as martial, others unwarlike.[1] In the American South and the West Indies, some tribes were considered less likely to rebel or try to escape from slave-plantations; to accept their lot. In the mines of colonial Rhodesia, workers recruited by force were organized into gangs and housed according to their ethnic origins,[2] practices which still continue in the mines of southern Africa today, partly because it is natural to want to live with people who literally speak the same language; partly because tribal differences are deliberately encouraged to divide and rule. Thus White audiences are entertained with 'tribal' dances which are modern modifications of a wide variety of types of indigenous dance, some from secret societies, others associated with victory, the curing of sickness, and the like.

Those who operate such policies may become victims of their own myths. In East Africa, in the Second World War, I discovered that whole tribes were regarded as only fit to be 'sweepers' – to clean out lavatories. Others, like the Kikuyu, were also considered to be unwarlike but fitted for non-combatant duties because many of them had school education. They were therefore recruited mainly as clerks. When, seven years later, these same unwarlike Kikuyu mounted the Mau Mau Rebellion, it took well over 50,000 troops, including two British brigades, plus a squadron of Lincoln bombers, as well as torture, hooded informers, and the incarceration of 40,000 people, to defeat them.[3]

The cycles of expansion and contraction built into capitalism have also resulted in the periodic importation of massive amounts of labour into the heartlands themselves. In addition to the half million who crossed the US border as legal immigrants from Mexico alone during every year of the 1960s, another quarter million entered illegally. During the 1970s, net immigration from all countries exceeded 7 million, with another 1.7 million from Puerto Rico.[4] In the boom decades of the 1950s and 1960s, no less than 11½ million workers emigrated to Western Europe from the poorer circum-Mediterranean countries. Though their jobs in factories and offices were working-class occupations, they were brought in to do the dirty, dangerous, monotonous and badly-paid jobs the indigenous working class rejected. The working class was thus split down the middle by a geological fault which separated the new immigrants from their more privileged workmates – a split so marked that some academic analysts designated the immigrants an underclass rather than part of the working class proper.

In official usage, neither their racial nor their national origins were emphasized; rather, they were given a supra-ethnic, supra-national collect-ive and purely economic identity, that of 'guest-worker', a term which, for all its clinical neutrality, soon acquired, in popular usage, a connotation of stigma. On the streets, more racist categories could be heard: 'Wog' in Britain; 'snake-eater' or 'camel-rider' in Germany; 'spic' and 'greaser' in the USA. Yet overt and organized racism as a generalized practice of hostility in every domain of social life has remained a minority reaction. Massive institutionalized discrimination (racialism) was perfectly compatible with the absence of, or overt, organized mass racism.[5]

The main reason for this is that the immigrants were not a threat, but an asset. They were not a mass of cheap labour in direct competition with natives for jobs. Thousands of them, rather, took over the jobs the natives did not want. But far more of them (four out of every five in Germany) were employed in manufacturing, notably in metal-producing and engineering. In 1973, they made up 45 per cent of the workforce in the Volvo plant at Göteborg; 40 per cent at the Paris Renault works; and 40 per cent at the Ford plant in Cologne.

The whole system reposed upon a set of myths. Governments declared it to be a system of short-term *migrant* labour, a flow which was seen as something which could be turned on or off by bureaucratic fiat, whether carefully organized, as in the bilateral government-to-government agreement between West Germany and Turkey, under which every applicant was medically examined by German doctors in Istanbul before being stamped fit for export,[6] or left to market forces, as in France, where 82 per cent of the migrants entered illegally, smuggled across the border by guides who, with corrupt officials, relieved them of anything up to a year's savings in the process. Germanic *Gleichschaltung* made it easier to control the flow at source; by 1973, a ten-year queue of would-be immigrants had built up in Turkey. But these objective system-models did not allow for illegal immigration or for subjective changes in the minds of people who might have originally come as target-workers, aiming to stay only a year or two while they saved up enough money to marry, to buy a piece of land, to build a house, or to invest in modern status symbols and consumer durables like cars and refrigerators. Save they certainly did, prodigiously. But the $740 million saved by half a million Turkish workers in Germany and remitted home did virtually nothing to modernize Turkey's economy: only *three* enterprises employing 100–200 workers proved viable.[7] Instead, wage-labour migration became a self-perpetuating cycle. Individuals now accustomed to high standards of living, but unable to find suitable investment opportunities at home, could only keep up those standards by going abroad once more. Migration in Mexico, one authority writes, 'tends only to breed more migration'; overall, 20 per cent of the country's population were dependent on wages earned in the USA, and, in some small towns, as much as 80 per cent of the population.[8] During the annual fiestas of the patron saint, pride of place goes to the messages sent from Los Angeles; it is the remittances sent from abroad that make possible the finery of the statues and the lavishness of the fireworks. So they go back, again and again, many never to return at all.

The myth of return, however, is subscribed to by migrants as well as governments. While abroad, they talk about 'home' incessantly, and spend their leisure time with people from their home areas. Their second-class status fuels this nostalgia. Yet as time goes by the likelihood, increasingly, is that despite their inferior social status in the 'host' country, they are never going home. Germany, Great Britain or the USA is now their home, especially for the children born there. Though they may continue to talk of a place thousands of miles away as their real home, their actual home is a shared room or a dormitory for the bachelors, a room in a run-down multi-occupancy building for the family. Whatever the needs of the system, then, whatever their original intentions, they have become changed people, with new aspirations and identities.

From the point of view of the employer in post-war Europe, they make admirable labour. They put up with low wages, bad working conditions, and long hours because, as aliens, they are often liable to deportation. In Switzerland, they could not even change their jobs or hold trade union office. For those in charge of the economy, they cost nothing to train. The poor countries were thus contributing £2000 work of social capital, embodied in the person of every worker, to the rich countries: the costs of producing him or her up to the point of being ready for delivery to the labour-market. It was a form of cost-free aid from the Third World to the First.

Though they paid social service contributions and taxes, immigrants were often only entitled to minimal benefits, particularly the majority who were single men. Politically, they were made malleable and compliant by the degree of social control and their isolation from the native-born in ghettoes and barracks;[9] their insecurity; their immemorial habits of deference; their lack of relevant social skills, organization and collective identity; their orientation to another society and culture altogether. Communal solidarity provided by ethnic identity and neighbourhood associations might provide a degree of self-defence and moral support, but also served to isolate them further from the indigenous population. Though they generally supported their indigenous work-mates when they did get involved in trade unions (and in Germany, one in three joined unions, about the same proportion as for indigenous workers), their solidarity was rarely reciprocated either by their fellow-workers or by trade union officials.[10]

The economic segregation of the dual labour market is thus reinforced by a wide range of social and cultural barriers consolidated by spatial segregation in ghettoes. What one anthropologist called 'the biggest Berber village in the world' was to be found just outside Paris:

> From a high vantage point, the *bidonville* looks like a rubbish dump. . . . There are no sanitary amenities of any kind. . . . Toilets do not exist either. . . . At Nanterre, one *bidonville* of over 1000 North Africans shares a single water tap with a nearby Portuguese 'village'. . . . Health risks are compounded by the risk of fire. The frequent blazes spring from shack to shack like in medieval towns.[11]

Rather than live there, many turn to the *marchands de sommeil* who sell space in city slums, cramming ten beds into rooms intended for one double bed. People often sleep by shifts.

The cumulative effect of all these congruent forms of segregation is the consolidation, over time, of a generalized culture of ethnic inequality, in which immigrants are perceived in stereotypical terms by the indigenous population, whatever their actual attributes, as a race apart, as primitives. In Switzerland, in 1970, 46 per cent of the voters wanted to expel them altogether. That they were not expelled was because the presence of the Italian immigrants actually made life significantly better for many Swiss. Since 40 per cent of the factory work was done by immigrants – a sixth of the population – the better jobs could now be reserved for nationals. Only one in five of the children of labourers in Geneva followed in their fathers' footsteps and became labourers; only one in ten became unskilled or semi-skilled workers. The rest moved up the pay, skill and status hierarchies to become part of a labour aristocracy.

The immigrants, conversely, who tended to be the more educated or artisans (the really poor could not afford the journey) became deskilled on the assembly-line in Western Europe. In the long run, their presence helps to hold down wage-rates; it is this, rather than prejudice in some immanent and generic form, that is the chief factor underlying trade union antagonism to immigrant labour. But in the short run, as in Switzerland, skilled and white collar workers may gain from the presence of cheap labour. In such a situation, prejudice – which may well exist in abundance – never gets translated into organized racism as long as jobs remain plentiful and the best ones go to nationals. When there is direct competition for *any* kind of work, let alone the best jobs – a zero-sum game – the situation can be very different. In 1922, on the Rand of South Africa, the army, backed by artillery and aircraft, had to be used against White workers who were in open rebellion (during which 230 people were killed) under the slogan 'Workers of the World Unite to Defend a White South Africa'.[12]

To understand immigration, then, a dialectical sociology has to take into account both the objective logic of the system and the subjective intentions and responses both of those who run it and of their victims. There are methodological precepts which many pay lip-service to but fail to observe in practice. Because ethnicity has often been used to divide and rule, some theorists treat all forms of ethnicity as reactionary, forgetting that it has also been a mode of resistance. Analyses which take economic exploitation of workers as their starting-point fail to recognize that workers have other significant social attributes, notably ethnic, and that only certain categories of people are selected to be made into workers in the first place. Their class position, and the niches they occupy in the hierarchy of occupations within the working class, are consequences of historical relationships of inequality and conflict between ethnic groups. Though exploitation is the *raison d'être*, ethnicity is never merely a random epiphenomenon.

Many theories fallaciously assume an *invariant* relationship between class and ethnicity. Class divisions, however, may be related to ethnic divisions in three different ways. They may *overlap*, reinforcing each other in a congruent or isomorphic manner (as when all workers in a given factory, industry, town or region are of the same ethnic background). If the employer is of a different ethnic background, this solidarity is further reinforced. Ethnicity may, however, cut *across* class, vertically, when members of the same ethnic group are to be found at various levels as workers, clerks, or managers, and the employer may also be of the same ethnic group. Thirdly, classes may be *segmented* by ethnicity with skilled workers drawn from one ethnic group, unskilled from another, and so forth; one segment may be of the same ethnic affiliation as management; others may not.

Stereotypes about ethnic groups, however they originate, whoever codifies and fosters them, and whatever their interest in so doing, are not necessarily to be explained simply in terms of some rational hyper-intentionality on the part of a conspiratorial group, such as a calculating capitalist class consciously promoting divisions among the workers. This *can* be the case, but the possibility of such a strategy depends in the first place upon the *prior* existence of shared assumptions about peoples seen as inferior both to management and to labour aristocrats seeking to transform 'job property' into an hereditary monopoly. Whatever their origins and sponsorship, once such myths become grounded in material self-interest, justifying differential access to rewards, they take on a new and more powerful significance. Ideas, that is, become significant social forces, not because of human fallibility or irrationality – some immanent propensity to prejudice – but because they legitimize, ideologically, the privileged position of those who profess those beliefs. Over time, the beliefs, and the practices associated with them, harden into a total system of social and not merely economic relations, often backed by legal discrimination: *apartheid*. The labour aristocracy becomes a caste.

In South Africa, the earnings-gap began to rise with the establishment of a legal colour-bar in the mines in 1926, under which skilled jobs were reserved for Whites. By the time *apartheid* was enacted as law, after the Second World War, the gap had increased from 11.7:1 before the First World War to 20:1 by 1969. African miners' wages, in real terms, were probably lower than in 1911, while those of Europeans had increased by 70 per cent. Asociological economic models neglect these matters.

Under such circumstances, to argue that such privileged strata have objective interests in common with those subjected to *special* exploitations, to social exclusion from all forms of prestigious status, and even from eating or sleeping with their fellow-workers, makes a mockery of the word 'objective', for institutionalized prejudice and privilege are facts as real in their social consequences as the fact that even labour aristocrats may be said to be objectively exploited by the bourgeoisie, because the value they create is also appropriated by the latter. But it is the segmentation of the working class, the social distance between Whites and Blacks, not just in status terms, but in the quite material terms of wages and occupation, rather than the opposition between workers as a class and those who employ them, that is the prime, brutal social fact, a quite objective one that both White and Black workers are subjectively aware of. In societies based on mass racism, the significance of institutionalized inequality within the working class is very consciously understood both by those who benefit from the existence of a cheap labour-force, and by those who constitute that specially exploited and oppressed segment of the working class. The morality of those who benefit is false, but their consciousness is not.

Classical *laissez-faire* theory assumed a market in which a culturally neutral seller of labour power found a buyer interested only in the worker's productive potential, who then entered into a contract in which each was bound to the other only via the cash-nexus. Functionalist sociology likewise assumes the rational recruitment of those technically best fitted to fill a given role. Yet labour has a habit of coming from somewhere, that is to say it possesses qualitative, socio-cultural and not merely economic attributes. The 11½ million 'guest workers' in Western Europe, or the Mexican 'wetbacks', are not mere units of labour, as economists perceive them: they are people, with complex social identities.[13]

Their national identity is especially important. National identity entails much more than legal disabilities, for immigrants have to face a whole range of informal social barriers which indigenous workers do not have to reckon with. They are more likely to work in non-union firms, especially when working for agribusiness. Their lack of command of the spoken language, their inability to read, their lack of experience of the local social institutions and mores disarm them further. Their funny clothes and bizarre customs alienate them socially from indigenous people. They then react to this social exclusion – which Parkin terms 'closure'[14] – by falling back on ethnicity, but using it in a way which is quite different from the way management uses it to divide, manipulate and rule. To protect themselves, they build ethnic organizations, sometimes trade unions and political parties, more often multi-purpose voluntary associations, sometimes primarily cultural or recreational, though usually with a strong welfare component. This is a response of the victim, not the hunter: a recovery of the self via a redefinition of the group, in reaction to being treated as 'Blacks' or 'greasers' by officials, by the boss, and even by their fellow-workers.

Yet, South African *apartheid* is an extreme, limiting case, firstly because it is a Weberian ideal type of *total* separation and inequality, in every domain of social life, from the economic and the political to what Weber called connubium and commensality, prescribing and proscribing who you can and cannot work with, who you can and cannot live with, who you can and cannot sleep with, the whole underpinned by a hegemonic ideology and by the power of the State: by law.

Few societies, however racialist, approximate to this degree of *Gleichschaltung*. Racialism is usually more informal and unofficial; more partial, applying only in certain areas of social life; and often ideologically 'shamefaced', to use Engels' term, nobody admitting publicly to racist beliefs ('some of me best friends are . . .'). Rather than a total, congruent system, it flourishes in the social space between public rhetoric and private practice.

In public rhetoric, the Olympic Games and the World Cup are occasions for the assertion of internationalism, of 'sportsmanship' and a purely technical individual and team rivalry. The reality is that the medals are totted up in order to establish a *national* hierarchy or prestige, while on the football terraces, frustrated British supporters are only too easily transformed into mobs howling for the destruction of the 'dirty Spanish bastards'.

 Ethnic and racial identity thus takes on quite different meanings in different contexts, depending on who uses them for what purposes. They are relative, situational categories, not absolutes. Kashmiri Brahmins, who think of themselves not merely as White in contrast to the despised dark-skinned South Indians, but as cosmologically 'twice-born', are shocked, on coming to Britain, to find themselves classified as 'Black' or 'Coloured', together with West Indian Negroes – and treated accordingly. Nigerian aristocrats and Muslim *hadjis* are reduced to the same global inferiority; a legacy of British imperialism, which divided the world into the 'Lords of Humankind' and their coloured subjects.

The distinctions drawn by social scientists between race, ethnicity and national identity are unknown to those who use such stereotypes as weapons of social struggle and who would reject these intellectual distinctions if they knew them. During the anti-fascist struggle, liberal anthropologists like A. H. Haddon, crusading against Nazi race theory, found a more receptive public; a generation later, liberals might react furiously against more subtle and 'scientific' theories of Negro inferiority, but in a Britain nostalgic for lost supremacy – Falklands Britain – these debates have no resonance at all in humbler walks of life. The racism that flourishes there is of a quite different, more atavistic order, rooted in the fear, on the part of those at the lowest levels of the class hierarchy, that their social status will now be reduced to that of Blacks. It has a life of its own, grounded in the very ascriptive and deterministic fallacies the academics denounced: allocating people to categories of generalized superiority and inferiority on the basis of *either* their physical or their cultural characteristics, or both (whatever their other attributes), and imputing causal priority to these as determinants of social behaviour. Distinctions between racialism and racism are pedantic irrelevances to those for whom a Wog was a Wog whether they could produce a coherent rationale for that belief or not.

If race and ethnicity are commonly conflated in vulgar consciousness, no clear lines are drawn, either between these and national affiliation. Such distinctions are irrelevant to people for whom racial and ethnic categories are part of a social praxis rather than objects of intellectual analysis. Social differences of supreme importance that do not fit these categories are therefore unknown or matters of indifference. If the differences between Muslim and Hindu; between Sunni and Shi'a; between the 'twice-born' and the Untouchable *are* perceived, they are treated with indifference or as barbaric superstitions, thereby reinforcing the stereotype of inferiority.

Yet only obsessional racists treat race as an absolute by the side of which everything else pales into insignificance, conducting inquisitions into the ancestry even of people whose physical appearance enables them to 'pass'. Only the ultra-fanatic makes no concessions to other considerations, by failing to distinguish between the Ghanaian Ambassador and the Haitian fieldhand. Even South Africa could create a special category of 'honorary' Whites for important Blacks and Japanese businessmen.

The danger of clinging to absolute stereotypes is that they divide the world into crude categories which blind their users to other significant characteristics of the people they are dealing with. They are therefore profoundly misleading.

It is not only illiterate poor Whites who become victims of such stereotypes. Politicians and newspaper editors, though they may not subscribe to ideologies of physical racism, are singularly ignorant of other cultures. In a country like the USA, where two million have been 'born again', it might seem strange that the appeal of religious revivalism in Iran should have been so seriously underestimated by US governments which backed the Shah. Yet the domain assumptions of the great majority, and especially of the ruling class, are still secularist and bourgeois: public life follows the norms of a civic culture in which one's social personality is defined as an economic actor and one's prime political identity is that of citizen. The ignorance comes home to roost. Cultures which give priority to other identities – religious or ethnic – cannot therefore be understood or handled. Force has then to be used to overcome their obstinacy and one's own ideological short-comings. Material things are used to counter ideas, to prop up regimes threatened by religious radicalism: helicopters sent to Iran, AWACS to Saudi Arabia.

On the Left, Marx's own inability to understand the appeal of Hinduism or of Islam to the faithful is reproduced today in the puzzlement of contemporary Marxists in the face of modern Islamic movements which draw, as Islamic society has always done, on *sunna* (custom) and *hadith* (the narrative statements of usages set by Mohammed himself) as well as on the Koran, not in order to resist change, but in order to promote it.[15] 'Islam', Halliday writes, 'retains a spectacular vitality that cannot be attributed merely to the economic level of the Arab world'. The very accusation of atheism indeed 'can seriously damage political work'. Yet though it is therefore 'essential to supersede Islam with materialist thought, it is extremely difficult to do so'.[16] To radical and revolutionary Muslims, however, Islam supplies religious authority not only for the militant rejection of Western materialism, but for the assertion of new conceptions of cultural identity and of social solidarity which draws upon, but re-interprets traditional conceptions of the community of believers so as to justify struggle. In the words of the theorists who guide the armed left-wing Islamic opposition to Ayatollah Khomeini, 'when we speak of "submission" . . . we do not mean the reactionary view of silent submission to social injustice and oppression'.[17]

Ethnic Group and Nation

Theoretical confusion about the relationship between ethnicity and race, or the persisting appeal of religion, is only equalled by the nigh-universal confusion that exists with regard to the nature of the nation, which, though in Hobsbawm's words, 'probably the most important political phenomenon of our century', has been remarkably unstudied as a theoretical category. If 'the theory of nationalism', as Nairn has remarked, 'represents Marxism's greatest historical failure', he rightly immediately adds that other traditions of Western thought have not done much better.[18] And 'virtually everything written by nationalists [themselves] (at least about their own nations)', Hobsbawm further notes, 'is question-begging and therefore negligible'.[19] Most writers have been more concerned to evaluate nationalism as good or bad than to analyse what it is. The paucity of the academic literature, too, is almost as striking as its theoretical poverty.

The historian, Butterfield has said, has a

> . . . distrust of disembodied reasoning. . . . His training and habits of mind fasten him down to the particular and the concrete and make him essentially an observer of the events of the external world. . . . [Historians] have been content to make rather facile analyses from the other arts and sciences. . . . They are not happy when they leave the concrete world and start reasoning in a general way.[20]

Nowhere is this truer than in the study of nationalism, where the riches of innumerable case-studies have contributed little to theoretical clarification of the nature of the nation. What generalization there has been has largely consisted either of chronological periodization for particular countries or regions, often assuming too neat a fit between successive types of nationalist ideology and social formations (Charlton Hayes); or of abstracted intellectual history which concentrates on ideas and their diffusion (Trevor-Roper, Kedourie) at the expense of the other term in the dialectic: the social seedbed without which these ideas would simply never take root; or dubious taxonomies such as Kohn's distinction between Western and Eastern variants of European nationalism.[21] The major sociological study, unfortunately, turns generalization into veritable taxonomic intoxication, creating a bewildering plethora of types and sub-types.[22]

Though there is a large anthropological literature on ethnicity, it rarely discusses the nation at all, focused as it is, for the most part, on social rather than societal identity, and on tribal part-societies within the nation-state. It starts, therefore, with the dynamics of interaction at face-to-face, small group and community levels, emphasizing the situational relativity of identity, and how identities are learned and managed, rather than on how they are structurally generated, organized, ascribed, sustained and sanctioned.

Methodological individualists focused on motivation, on individual choice as between different identities, and on the motives informing such choices: from the 'need to belong' or to establish a coherent self-image to the maximization of material advantage.

Early cultural anthropologists saw identity as a primordial imperative, which, like murder, would 'out', imposing itself on the individual. With the arrival of a *political* anthropology in the 1960s, concentrated upon 'public power' at the level of the 'social group as a whole', the time seemed ripe for confronting the national question.[23] Yet that step was never taken. Nor did the later arrival of a 'new ethnicity', which treated ethnicity not as a cultural imperative, but as a strategy in the struggle for resources, result in an anthropology of nationalism. The society as a whole, it seemed, was not the nation; struggles over resources did not include competition for resources at the level of the State, or competition between states. True, even the most abstracted approach of all, formal sociology, did illuminate some aspects of reality: at a high level of abstraction, there are clearly similar processes of boundary-definition and boundary-maintenance involved whether the entity concerned be a cocktail party, a band of hunters or a large nation-state. Simmel's theory of play as pure sociation, for instance, does illumine the phenomenon of rivalry between teams within the same city whose supporters do not otherwise differ significantly in their social characteristics: Sheffield Wednesday *v.* Sheffield United; Notts Forest *v.* Notts County. The assumption that there *must* be other, prior bases of solidarity, that factional identity is always an *epi*phenomenon, is a disease of overly-sociological thinking. Only in special cases such as the ethnic/religious basis of Celtic/ Rangers antagonism, or the upper-class associations of a few Brazilian teams (symbolized by throwing rice-powder, in mockery of ladies' face-powder, when they come onto the field) is this the case.

Formal sociology's insistence that consciousness of Self necessarily implies distancing oneself from the Other, however true, does not explain why only certain kinds of groups or categories become reference-groups in certain kinds of societies. Tribal football, for instance, flourishes at club level in mass societies which provide no meaningful *foci* of group loyalty, and where international contests are the only regularly available opportunities for participatory expression of identification with the society as a whole.

Many interactionist studies of ethnicity at the level of the community are vitiated by a liberal metaphysic developed in open societies, where a degree of choice exists for the individual to consciously decide whether to assimilate or not, and where social mobility is permitted and significant. The individual is thus taken as the jumping-off point in the analysis, and choice is assumed to be the crucial social fact. Life, it would seem, is a market, or cafeteria.

It is a singularly inappropriate model for caste or estate-based society, for slave societies, for those based on indentured labour, for contemporary apartheid, and to a large degree, for most class societies – in other words, for most of recorded human history. It ignores the *in*voluntary nature of most socially significant identity, that closure is *ascribed* not just by 'significant', but by *powerful* others, including the ever-growing power of the modern State, which permits or insists upon certain identities and refuses others. To do so, a whole battery of negatively and positively sanctioned modes of social control are used: frontier patrols, passports, Ellis Islands, Berlin Walls; as well as modes of socialization: national languages, established religions, obligatory public affirmations of loyalty to the motherland. The State may further impose ethnic identity at levels lower than the society as a whole, designating some of its subjects 'Jewish', 'Caucasian', 'Hispanic' and so on.

But many ethnic identities are maintained, too, in and by civil society, and it can be every whit as difficult to evade these (to 'pass') as those sustained by policemen and officials. The State may even draw upon civil racism in constructing its own, official racism. Passing, of course, is at least possible when stigma and inferiority are not a mere 'uniform of colour' (for a uniform can be taken off)[24] but indelibly stamped on the body itself, as the White man, Griffin, found when he dyed himself black, and experienced for a short while what truly Black people experience every day of their lives.[25] In the extreme, escape from enforced identity was refused even for those among the six million Jews who were gassed and burned to death who were not religiously Orthodox at all but culturally assimilated. Their crime was a common one: of 'objectively' belonging to a stigmatized social group.

Ethnicity, then, is not a unitary thing: it is both wider and narrower than nationality, and takes on different forms at different levels. Different ethnic groups co-exist within the boundaries of the nation-state while cultural and racial identities such as Pan-Arabism and Pan-Africanism transcend it. Ethnicity, as De Vos and Romanucci-Ross rightly say, supplies answers to the questions 'Where are we from?' 'How are we different?' and 'What must we do?'.[26] Answering these questions locates the individual and group in time and space, but the answers vary at different levels. The cognitive, normative and conative answers supplied by ethnic communities which transcend the State, whether the Great Traditions of the major world-religions or newer secular ideologies, notably communism, are ideologies charged with singular power precisely because they are cosmic.

But the State level of ethnicity has proved far more important and the effective maximal unit for the focus of human loyalties. In comparison, 'Pan' nationalisms, which profess (or call for) Arab or African unity, have never been seriously effective. Despite its rhetoric, Panislamism has proved incapable of rallying together the Arab states even in the face of Zionist expansionism. Supra-national ideologies have equally failed to prevent war between Muslim states, between African countries, or today, between socialist states. Islam alone was unable to hold together the ethnically distinct regions of West Pakistan and Bengali East Pakistan (now Bangladesh). Indeed, rather than inspiring a universalistic gathering-in of the world between Morocco and Indonesia, Islam has instead injected the special passion of religious fanaticism into inter-state conflicts. That between Iraq and Iran tragically demonstrates that the focus of attachment of religious loyalties is in fact the nation-state, not the universal community of believers.

Before the level of the State, narrower levels of ethnicity still flourish, and retain a very special potency since they are existentially grounded in a way that the Great Traditions are not, in organized communities of people who live together in everyday life and trace their descent, through a series of levels, from the lineage ancestors and the earth-shrines, back to the eponymous founding heroes of the Dreamtime and even to the gods.

Nationalism is also a form of ethnicity, but it is a special form. It is the institutionalization of one particular ethnic identity by attaching it to the State. This was clear to the doyen of historical studies of nationalism, Hans Kohn. Nationalism, he wrote, 'centres the supreme loyalty of the over-whelming majority of the people upon the nation-state, either existing or desired.'[27] Ethnic groups do not necessarily act together except when they have special interests to secure. When those interests are to obtain a State of its own (or part of a State) the group becomes a *nationality*. Those which are successful become *nations*: the unsuccessful remain 'nationalities' – nations without a State'.[28] National*ism* refers to movements to activities and ideologies developed in order to acquire or sustain a State of one's own.

The modern nation-state, however, only emerged in Western Europe a few centuries ago, and is only being brought into being in those new countries where nation-building and development go hand-in-hand as the two main items of today's agenda. The State, though not the nation-state, is a much older phenomenon; ethnicity even older; coterminous, indeed, with social life, as old as society.

Anthropologists (especially those concerned with stateless, or in Wolf's more positive term, kin-ordered societies) have therefore often concluded, formalistically, that national forms of ethnicity are no different in kind from those attached to other forms of polity or group. Conflating all these different levels of ethnicity, they have concluded, wrongly, that the differences between the tribe and the modern nation are quantitative rather than qualitative. 'Tribalism and nationalism', Lewis writes, 'differ only in scale.' 'Tribalism', Bennet asserts, 'represents in Africa what nationalism represents elsewhere.' The very distinction between tribe and nation, Argyle concludes, is therefore invalid.[29]

Ahistoric formalism of this kind is perfectly compatible with another apparently opposed strand of anthropological thinking, that which insists upon the *relativity* of ethnic identity at different levels and in different situations. Evans-Pritchard's analysis of Nuer fission and fusion provides the classic demonstration of the logic of the Arab proverb 'Mÿself against my brother; my brother and myself against our cousins; myself, my brother and my cousins against all others' – a system which makes effective co-operation possible when needed, for political (including military) purposes, between hundreds of thousands of people otherwise lacking permanent, specialized central political institutions.

Formalism and relativism are compatible because although they entail distinctions in levels of ethnicity they do not recognize distinctions of kind. Yet when contrasted with that kind of cultural anthropology which sees ethnicity simply as the expression, at the level of group organization, of underlying shared values and behaviour patterns conceived of as primordial tradition, handed down unchanged over millennia, relativism had its value. The Lue of Thailand, Moerman notes, distinguish themselves from neighbouring peoples by pointing to cultural traits they in fact often share with others.[30] In pre-colonial times, Leach has shown, hierarchical *gumsa* societies ruled by hereditary aristocracies became transformed into *gumlao* egalitarian polities – and back again – without changing the rest of their cultural baggage.[31] And the tribe, Colson demonstrates, was a recent colonial construct, not a survival from the pre-colonial epoch.[32]

The *ethnos* (or *etnia*) – we lack a word in English – far from being the natural unit that Romantic thought proclaimed, a thing-in-itself, is always the product of relationships with other ethnic groups. The process of ethnogenesis, the consolidation of ethnic identity, is best illuminated by Evans-Pritchard's classic analysis of the Nuer, for the group with which the Nuer identify themselves varies, depending on whom it is they are dealing with.[33] Rival sub-lineages, when faced with hostility from members of other lineages, draw together, now, as a *lineage* in the face of this new common threat to both. That identity is thus not only situational and relative, but a function of opposition, is a dialectical phenomenon familiar enough in Britain during the Second World War, when Tory and Labour parties suspended electoral competition for the duration and formed a Coalition government in order to promote national unity against the Nazis, or when Shona and Ndebele (who had been conqueror and conquered before both fell victims to colonial rule) co-operated in the guerrilla war against the Smith regime (though each with its own Party and army) only to resume their private quarrel after Independence.

The boundaries of the polity do not necessarily coincide with those of culture. Cultural attributes are not so much unambiguous determinants of political identity as *resources*, used selectively and situationally, according to their utility, rather than absolute borderlines marking one culture off from another (whether sharply or, to use Nadel's term, diacritically). Co-operation for common purposes might be limited to specific, intermittent kinds of activities: on ritual occasions, for instance, among the Gusii. Though a 'moral community with political *potential*' (my italics), their culture did not normally unite them. Only when – exceptionally – united against non-Gusii did they appeal to common language and culture.[34]

In rebutting the culturalist myth of ethnicity as some primordial need, the Marxist concept of *interest* has therefore to be introduced. Cultural traits are not absolutes or simply intellectual categories, but are invoked to provide identities which legitimize claims to rights. They are strategies or weapons in competitions over scarce social goods. What is mistakenly often seen as tradition – attachment to the past as a value in itself – is better viewed as a way of maintaining title to power, wealth and status in the present, or as a nostalgic spiritual contrast to present disprivilege. Affirmations of ethnic identity become particularly passionate when claims to rights are contested by others. Established identities then become infused with new force, providing solidarity, support and bases for organization in the face of a common threat: archetypically in ghetto situations from that of the Jews in medieval Europe to that of immigrants in modern Chicago.[35]

Management also appeals to tradition for its purposes. On the Copper Belt of Northern Rhodesia in the 1930s, the purpose was to divide and rule and to resist the rise of class-based trade unions by backing, instead, tribal elders, a policy doomed to failure since the role of tribal elder in a mining compound is no part of rural tradition.[36] The tribal categories were themselves novel, urban constructs – what Parkin calls 'super-tribes' – for they reduced the complexity of scores of tribal identities to a few simple categories, Bemba, the name of the largest tribe from the Northern Province, being applied to all the various ethnic groups from that province.[37] Smaller ethnic groups, only large enough to provide a clientele for corner shopkeepers or local politicians, can persist in the city. But this is a limited social base. As Grillo's study of political factions in an East African railway trade union shows, to be more successful, one has to transcend the limits of any particular ethnic group, even the larger ones.[38]

Ethnic identities, tribal or national, may be retained or shed, old ones invested with new meanings, new ones may emerge and become readily adopted; the crucial consideration being whether they are useful. 'Changing one's language', Gellner has remarked, 'is not the heart-breaking or soul-destroying business which it is claimed to be by romantic nationalist literature.'[39] But it is rarely total: nearly half a century after their arrival, Ware reports, Tammany Hall machine politics had become an integral part of the lives of Italian immigrants – but hardly any other part of American culture had – and this vote-mobilizing machine was itself the creation of an earlier immigrant group, the Irish.[40]

If the economic system is the force which sucks in or keeps out foreign labour, it does not determine the intentions of those who become immigrants, the subjective component essential to a dialectical analysis of ethnicity.[41] Short-term target-workers differ basically from those with one-way tickets. For the latter, before the First World War, the USA was a land of opportunity: the past connoted memories of poverty, oppression and stigma. For generations, many immigrants were ready to drop their cultural baggage overboard and become Americans. Most simply wanted to become better off, but not necessarily to Americanize themselves. Others came because they wanted the freedom to maintain and develop religious and cultural identities denied them where they had come from. The great majority, whatever their motivations and their attitudes towards their cultures of origin, were poor. For them, ethnic solidarity provided social support in finding jobs, during sickness and unemployment, occasional splurges of community festivity and – above all – the assurance that they would leave this earth with a magnificent display of conspicuous consumption for the first and only time in their life – at their funeral. For all this, they relied on those with whom they had pre-existing ties – usually of kinship – which entailed obligations they could not deny, and who, like them, were forced into tenements and exploited as cheap labour. Cultural separateness, forced on them, generated in its turn a counter-culture of collective self-defence.

By the second generation, many of them had made it economically, as individuals. But they still needed a social identity wider than 'rich' and 'successful'. Deprived of acceptance into the hegemonic w a s p subculture, they could now compensate by becoming heroes, role-models, and patrons for their less successful fellows. For their children, upwards social mobility was more likely to come about through the school than through the support of their ethnic association. For them, Sicily or the *stetl* were places they only knew of from the interminable boring stories their parents told them, places where their elders dreamed of buying land one day. But the dream of becoming a big man 'back home' had no meaning for children brought up in Brooklyn. Home was not some village back in Europe, but America.

The third generation had often experienced the limitations of the American Dream. Many had failed to make it. For them, the ethnic community often still provided support, though now more often moral rather than economic. But even those who had made it were not culturally accepted. They reacted to the exclusiveness of the w a s p subculture by asserting the validity of their own culture in the very terms in which culture was usually talked about: the arts. A new pride in language and in rediscovering what was written in that language now grew up amongst the educated, together with the reappropriation, as theirs, of Chopin, Liszt, and other creative artists whose cultural products had been appropriated by the upper classes and incorporated into their culture every bit as much as the material wealth created by others. Cultural hegemony was thus more than a matter of *imposition*; it also entailed appropriation and exclusion of 'high culture' in the opera and the concert-hall. To remind the world that Chopin was Polish involved a cultural reassertion; to assert that Shevchenko was as great as Dickens, paradoxically, involved inviting the admiration of others as well as reappropriation. But the underlying logic was the same: a new pride in minority culture. By the third generation, the grandson, in Gellner's phrase, was busy trying to remember what the son had tried to forget.[42] For the 20 million Americans who had been the most brutally stigmatized of all, the recovery of pride in being Black, in having roots in rich cultures and in the distinctively Black contribution to American culture, was inevitably harder and slower. When it did come, it came with a singularly explosive emotional force.

The Three Modes of Nationalism

New ethnic identities are not, then, simply older ones writ large. Where they are not novel constructs, they entail the transmutation of older categories to meet new needs in new ways. If I concentrate here on that special kind of ethnicity that we call nationality – ethnicity institutionalized at the level of the State – this is not to say that other modes and levels of ethnicity do not exist or are not important. But they will be considered only insofar as they impinge upon that meta-identity which one acquires as citizen of a State.

Historically, there have been three main ways in which the relationship between the State and its constituent ethnic groups has been resolved. They emerged in different epochs, and therefore embody different conceptions both of society and of the State. The older ones, however, did not simply disappear, but lived on, now overlaid and synchronic with the newer ones.

The first, the *hegemonic*, recognized only one ethnic identity as legitimate: the national culture is the culture of the dominant class and its region. The second, based on *uniformity*, is informed by liberal values and assumes that older ethnic identities are now *dépassés*, and that a new synthesis, either of physical type, or of language and culture, or of all three, has emerged in their place. Once this new nation has established its own State, oppression ceases to exist. Since society is the aggregate of its citizens, there are, or should be, no groups, ethnic or otherwise, separating the citizen artificially from the political community as a whole and impeding the free exercise of the rational judgement of each individual citizen. The third mode – the *pluralist*, involves the recognition by the State, in addition to the master-identity of citizenship, of secondary nationality, sometimes in the form of the status of a minority. This mode emerged only in the twentieth century, when a whole series of ethnically compound nation-states were brought into being.

The term 'nation' has, of course, been used in many different ways. Evans-Pritchard used it to refer to large cultural communities like the Nuer or Shilluk which were able to act politically in concert when they needed to, but which lacked permanent specialized state institutions. In this sense, Lewis has written, the problem for the Somali, at Independence, was 'to make the nation a state, not the state a nation'.[43] I will argue that it is more heuristically useful to restrict the term 'nation' to that mode of ethnicity which only emerges with the modern centralized State, and which therefore entails not so much continuity with older ethnic identities as their supersession, if necessary, their repression. Nation-building, then, goes hand-in-hand with the formation of the State.[44]

Before Nationalism: The Segmentary State

The states and ethnic communities that existed before the Absolutist epoch were segmental polities: castes, estates and ethnic communities being the main kind of segment.[45] Only the great men of the realm had a direct relationship to the State. For the rest, an individual's primary identity was as a member of such a segment, determined by the primordial fact of birth, and buttressed, usually, by other-worldly cosmologies. Movement from one segment to another was, in theory, precluded; it was an absolute condition. Thus in Hindu society, caste was the primary segment, determining not only the totality of one's rights and duties, from rights in land to rights in marriage; from the giving of rent to the physical distance to be observed when in the presence of members of other castes, for the touch of inferior castes was polluting, even their shadow. In feudal Europe, one was born into an estate, and fulfilled one's earthly duties accordingly: the knights fought for all; the clergy prayed for all; the king ruled for all; and the peasants worked for all.

This neat fit of function and boundary was only perfect in ideology: in reality, even in Hindu society, women could move upwards individually, through hypergamous marriage; collectively, whole castes, by adopting the customs of superior castes – by 'Sanskritizing' themselves – could, over time, move upwards in the hierarchy.[46]

Externally, the State's boundaries were not absolute or all-decisive either: the nobility of medieval Europe shared a trans-societal culture in common with their peers in other countries, and their domains, too, might lie abroad. The powers of the State were neither absolute nor defined by secular criteria alone, for feudal society postulated a duality of Church and State in which Augustine's City of God – in its earthly form, the Papacy –took precedence over any merely secular polity. Ideologically, the stratification of earthly society, with its horizontal estates and the monarch at the apex, was projected onto a cosmic plane in the iconic imagery of paintings which represented the earthly order as merely the inferior part of a cosmological whole whose superior part was a heavenly realm similarly stratified into archangels, angels, seraphim and cherubim. Below were the nine circles of Hell, the last 'round' of which, according to Dante, was reserved for those who betrayed their masters and patrons.

States of this kind were thus composite affairs, incorporating different ethnic communities, and arose either out of royal inheritance or marriage, or by conquest. Conquest states commonly incorporated the conquered by simply replacing the defeated king or chief by a member of the royal house of the victors or someone loyal to him. A more devious policy was to be magnanimous: to re-install him, or to install one of his sons in his place, though now as a vassal – thereby avoiding the cost of creating and maintaining new apparatuses whilst appealing to traditional legitimacy.

The unit round which this kind of policy was constructed was not the individual. The Ottomans recognized

> . . . Every religious sect as a social and administrative unit of public law, called *millet*. . . . Each *millet* maintained its social and family relations according to its own law, administered and controlled its own schools and

social institutions and had its own political chief and representative in the person of its religious head. The very broad autonomy of the *millet* was based not on territorial divisions but on personal allegiance to a church or creed.[47]

This segmentary structure, dating back to Fatimid times, was still spatially visible in nineteenth-century Cairo. Below an ethnically distinct class of Mamelukes, headed by the Governor in the Citadel.

Each ethnic group occupied its own quarter [*harah*] . . . which was both a place of work and place of residence [entered] usually through a street terminating in an open square, . . . [and] equipped with walls and a gate. . . .

Socially the *harah* is a group of persons usually unified by ethnic and/or occupational characteristics as well as by vicinal ties. . . . The physical city was an accretion of cells . . . through whose representatives the directives of the State were channelled downwards and the responses channelled upwards.[48]

Archbishop Makarios was able to lead his people to Independence in the twentieth century because he was the last of these Ethnarchs, for despite the natural assumption of the superiority of Islam (Muslims belonging to no *millet*, but only to the universal community of the True Faith) other ethnic communities and their religions were not only allowed to persist but even strengthened, just as, in the economic sphere, the State's abstract juridical claim to ownership of all arable land left the large proprietors free to exploit the peasants as they wished. The State simply insisted that the landlords hand over some of their rents as taxes and that the army and civil service were periodically supplied with recruits.

This kind of State was not so much compatible with pluri-ethnicity as founded upon it. The model developed by Furnivall to describe colonial South-east Asia is therefore illuminating here, even though its validity for the societies to which he applied it has been questioned. It was, he argued, a dual economy, with pre-capitalist and capitalist sectors, in which the different racial groups occupied distinctive economic niches. But only their individual economic needs were satisfied in the market. Socially,

. . . each group holds by its own religion, its own culture and language, its own ideas and ways. As individuals they meet, but only in the market place, in buying and selling. . . . [It is] a plural society . . . different sections of the community living side by side, but separately, within the same political unit.[49]

The Absolutist Nation-state: Hegemony

In the 1930s, Marxist writers saw the centralization of the State in early modern Europe primarily in terms of the centralization of the market. Trade carried with it the necessity for security of property; efficient communications; uniform laws, courts and apparatuses through which to enforce the courts' decisions; standardized coinage, weights and measures; and central institutions, from private credit banks to State systems of taxation. The causality was largely seen as one-way: the economy determined changes in the polity. With the growth of merchant capitalism, cities like London and Paris emerged as capitals because they were riverine centres of communications for rich agricultural hinterlands and well-located for overseas trade.

More recently, Anderson has argued that economic integration and capitalist growth were dialectically *contingent* upon concomitant *political* integration through a whole range of new institutions: standing armies; a permanent bureaucracy; a system of national taxation with which to pay for them; and a codified system of law: the Absolutist State of the New Monarchies of Henry vii, Louis xi, Maximilian i, Ferdinand and Isabella.

The period between 1450 and 1550, in England, Hill writes, thus saw a 'decisive rupture' with the pattern of oscillation between periods of household government (Weber's 'prebendal' and 'patrimonial' systems) under strong kings and periods of bureaucratic baronial power under weak kings or kings who were minors.[50] '*All* government was now national government, the king's government', and even the great builders of the new Absolutism, Wolsey, Thomas Cromwell, or Richelieu, were themselves victims of the new royal power.

Yet a key element needs to be added, for the modern State entailed not merely economic and political, but also cultural integration. Externally, this meant break with the claim of the Catholic Church to universal authority over secular monarchs. Religion, as Namier put it, therefore became 'a sixteenth-century word for nationalism',[51] as monarchs consolidated their power by appeal to the doctrine *cuius regio, eius religio*. Religion was therefore nationalized by attaching it to the State. The individual, too, Hobsbawm writes, was 'no longer definable as the locus of a complex of multiple loyalties, but overwhelmingly in terms of a single one, his nationality'.[52]

The persistence of autonomous ethnic cultures was equally intolerable. A single national political culture was now imposed on the whole country, if necessary by bloody repression, as in Ireland. Even those who, like Oliver Cromwell, undertook the destruction of the political tyranny of the Absolutist monarchy in his heartland, drowned the struggles of the Irish for their independence in blood. Political centralization was reinforced by cultural hegemony: the imposition of the subculture of the ruling class and its region upon the rest of the country. Just as the Parisian French of the Isle de France became Standard French, in England the dialect of the 'home counties' was to become Standard English. The dialects in which the York and Wakefield mystery plays had been written gave way to the King's English of Chaucer, the South-east Midland dialect. Six centuries later, the BBC's 'Guide to Preferred Usage', prepared by the chief editor of the Oxford English Dictionaries, takes as its ideal the 'form of speech' of 'a person born and brought up in one of the Home Counties, and educated at one of the established southern universities, for example, those of Oxford or Cambridge'. The creation of a new ideology of the nation-state involved the use of the national tongue to invent a new past, even inspiring great art: in England, Shakespeare's celebration, in his history plays, of the glory of monarchy and the evils of national discord.[53]. When Queen Isabella asked, in 1492, what his new Castilian grammar was for, its compiler replied, 'Your Majesty, language is the perfect instrument of empire'.[54] The political significance of culture had been obvious a millennium and a half earlier to Tacitus. Agricola, he wrote,

> . . . used pleasurable inducements to accustom [the British] to quiet and ease. . . . Soon a people who had spat upon the Roman tongue began to strive for fluency in Latin. Our dress became a mark of honour, and the *toga* became a common sight. Gradually men succumbed to the corrupting charms of colonnades, baths and elegant dinners. They are a part of the process of subjugation, but to men who had not known them before they bore the name culture.[55]

In States that emerged as a result of dynastic fusion rather than conquest, as in the union of England and Scotland in 1603 or the earlier union of Castile and Aragon, the constituent ethnic groups might be allowed to retain some of their own political, legal and other cultural institutions. But though Catalan or Basque *fueros* might be entrenched in constitutional law, secession was out of the question. When the Jacobite Rebellion of 1745 showed that the Highlanders had not given up the struggle to separate Scotland from England, despite their defeat thirty years earlier, they were left to the mercy of Butcher Cumberland. By 1805, 'England' and 'Britain' had become synonymous: '*England*', Nelson signalled the Fleet at Trafalgar, 'expects that every man will do his duty'.

The Bourgeois Nation-state: Uniformity

The centralization brought about by the Absolute monarchs was not undone when power was taken out of their hands in the new bourgeois epoch, though it was now, in principle, in the hands of the people. Liberal democracy involved a new conception of the relationship between the individual and the State: the individual was now a citizen with rights, not just a subject with duties. The State, the body politic, was the organic community of free citizens as a whole.

A whole gamut of novel concepts concerning the individual and the individual's relationship to society now came into being: possessive individualism[56] and *laissez-faire* in the economic sphere; Romantic notions of personal sensibility in the arts of understanding the world in other than purely intellectual ways; and the political idea that 'man does not possess citizenship in virtue of prior membership of some organic sub-part of it. He possesses citizenship – if he possesses it at all – *directly*'.[57] Both the traditional groups which had hitherto provided individuals with their primary identity, estates or ethnic groups, together with newer sectional interest-groups such as classes, were now impermissible. The individual had become the building-block of both the State and of civil society.

The most thorough-going expression of this new political philosophy naturally came from the country that experienced that most radical recasting of all its social institutions as a result of revolution. Each citizen, Rousseau argued, 'should speak his opinion entirely to himself'. The politics of the State would be determined by the *general* will: the 'grand total' of individual opinions. Discovering what the general will was, it was assumed, would be unproblematic; differences between one individual's opinion and another's would be a 'trifling', technical problem, and the ensuing resolution of what differences there were, it was equally assumed, would always result in the good of all.[58] But a new machinery would be required for ascertaining the general will by adding up the sum of millions of individual opinions: the plebiscite. The equality of each individual citizen further implied that their relationship to the State should be *uniform*: in education, it has been said, the ideal that each school-child of the same age would be turning over the same page in the same textbook on the same day at the same time in every school in France.

Any kind of corporate 'intermediate interests' separating the citizen from the public weal, Le Chapelier argued in the Constituent Assembly in 1791, ran counter to Reason and Justice, since they impeded the free expression of individual opinion. Rights of religious association, a major non-economic exception to the doctrine of the illegitimacy of intermediate interests were, however, permitted, as was the joint-stock company in the economic sphere. But organization by working people, above all 'combinations' (trade unions), represented a singularly vicious form of intermediate interest, since they interfered with the fulfilment of contracts freely entered into by the individual worker and the individual employer. They were therefore properly forbidden. Those who perversely continued to combine were visited with the full rigours of the law. And ethnic differences, too, were supremely irrational and archaic kinds of intermediate interest now that all were not only free and equal, but *Frenchmen*. The final codification and diffusion of the new uniformity across Europe was to be the work, ironically, of a Corsican who was to repress the national liberation struggle of his own people in the name of France. These were indeed revolutionary ideas. For a Croatian nobleman, the notion that he shared a common nationality with his peasants was more preposterous than the notion that his horse was a member of the Croatian nation.[59]

These ideals might be presented as univerals and imposed on Europe by the Code Napoléon, but their political and totalizing quality is in fact peculiarly *French*. The end of the *English* Revolution, a century and a half earlier, had left the bourgeoisie dominant economically, but the aristocracy still had their lands as well as their heads, and the King still reigned. Bourgeois thought, in England, was therefore singularly economic. 'Manchestertum', the theory of *laissez-faire*, according to which anything extra-economic had to be justified in terms of market rationality – otherwise it should be abolished – prevailed. In the eyes of the manufacturers, with their philosophy of 'produce as cheap as you can and do away with all the *faux frais* of production', the House of Lords, the standing army, the State Church, the legal system, and foreign wars were all '*faux frais*' of production.[60]

Following Weber, Bendix has argued that this language of *utility* (*Vergesellschaftung*), of material advantage irrespective of personal or social responsibility, neverthless left a gap often filled by ancient popular conceptions of community and of social rights and duties. As late as the eighteenth century, class oppositions were still expressed in the folk categories of a conflict between a 'Norman' landed aristocracy and the 'Anglo-Saxon' inhabitants they had conquered.[61] The word 'class', indeed, only began to replace older collective designations – 'orders', 'ranks', 'degrees' – as late as the 1830s.[62]

Such categories of social thought survived precisely because they filled a spiritual gap left by *laissez-faire* theory just as the workhouse and the Friendly Association were to fill the gap left by an economic theory that postulated that the master had no responsibility whatsoever for the fate of the families of his workers, or even for the workers themselves outside the workplace. The language of utility had therefore to be complemented by a new language of *affinity* (*Vergemeinschaftung*). In part, this was supplied by the ideology of citizenship: all were equal before the law. In time, all were to become equal before the ballot-box. But civil society required a more social interpretation of freedom: the notion of *fraternity*.

Decolonization: The First Wave

Liberty, defined as freedom *from*, meant a good deal not only to Philadelphia merchants and lawyers but also to tens of thousands of small farmers in the North American colonies who had likewise suffered from British taxation and control over the colonial economy. For rich and poor alike, the right to one's land, to the harvest painfully won on that land; to personal property and personal savings; were sacred. Locke's limitation of the legitimate powers of the State to the guarantee of life, liberty *and property* therefore evoked as strong a response in the USA as it did in Mexico, from Morelos:

> Freedom means the enjoyment of equality, security, property and liberty on the part of the people as a whole and by every citizen.

But fraternity was another matter altogether. Those in Europe who had extended its meaning to the sphere of property and production relationships, like Babeuf, were struck down as savagely as their Leveller and Digger predecessors had been in revolutionary England.

The revolutions in the colonies also stopped short of a radical *social* interpretation of fraternity. The European doctrine of universalism, rather, was interpreted as implying political internationalism: relations between States, not classes. Men like Kosciusko, Tom Paine or Lafayette, therefore, were no narrow nationalists: they drew no distinction between the fight for freedom in America, Poland, or France. To countries fighting for self-determination, the rights of others to do likewise were self-evident. Each particular struggle was merely one part of a general, world-wide process of universal emancipation which would usher in a new era in which free people would live at peace with one another. 'Man' would become an historical reality for the first time, and all 'men' citizens of the *world*.

Just as the State was an association of free individuals, so each state could freely choose to associate with others. 'Liberty and Union' were compatible. In North America, thirteen states had chosen to do so. Bolívar hoped that the Spanish ex-colonies would not only follow suit but that this might lead to an even wider new harmony between nations. In his *Letter from Jamaica* he wrote,

> We are a microcosm of the human race . . . neither Indians nor Europeans, yet we are part of each. . . . How ineffable it would be if the Isthmus of Panama should become for America what the Straits of Corinth were for the Greeks. May God grant that we can some day enjoy the good fortune of a congress of republics, kingdoms and empires that would discuss peace and war with the rest of the nations of the world.

A creation of the liberal intelligentsia, political nationalism in Europe had been infused with a 'strong democratic and egalitarian element'.[63]

The peasantry, on the other hand, clung to the ancient solidarities of ethnicity and class. In Galicia, they rejected the nationalist intelligentsia even when the latter advocated also the abolition of serfdom, just as Italian peasants rejected nationalist advocates of agrarian reform because of their age-old suspicion of the upper class gentlemen who were the bearers of these new ideas.[64] Politically, liberal nationalism was directed against reactionary regimes, notably the Austro-Hungarian and Russian Empires, those prison-houses of nations, which denied rights of self-determination to peoples who were, as Herder had shown, the 'natural, primordial divisions of mankind'.

Looking backwards, it is easy to see this simply as error. In Gellner's words, 'The central mistake committed both by the friends and the enemies of nationalism is the supposition that it is somehow *natural*'; in Nairn's more sardonic language, 'the ideology . . . that human society consists essentially of several hundred different and discrete "nations", each of which has (or ought to have) its own postage-stamps and national soul'.[65] It is easy to point to the disappearance of the Scythians, the Catuvellauni or the Goths. Easy too, to demonstrate how *un*natural, artificial and ambiguous the boundaries of the nation-state often were through the ideas of Mazzini, the great theorist and leader of revolutionary nationalism, who envisaged a future Europe composed of united Iberia; a united Scandinavia; a United Kingdom of England, Ireland, and Scotland; an Alpine confederation of Switzerland, the German Tyrol, Carinthia and Slovenia; a Balkan federation including Greece, Albania, Macedonia, Rumelia, Bosnia, Serbia, and Bulgaria; a Danubian federation of Hungary, Romania (including Herzegovina) and Bohemia; Germany (including Holland and Flanders); Russia; and Poland – entities which correspond to virtually no subsequent nation-states.

There were two basic positions on the national State. The Serbs argued that nationalism involved a struggle for the right to one's language, customs and culture, and for 'enough self-consciousness to use them',[66] requirements which could be satisfied even where the nation was divided under different governments or where several nations co-existed within the same state. Kossuth, the great Hungarian revolutionary, argued, *per contra*, that each nation must have its own *government*. Ethnic and political boundaries should coincide.

It was the latter conception which was to win out during the heroic age of nationalism between Mazzini and Garibaldi. In the North American colonies, freedom meant, first and foremost, freedom from external, foreign control; social differences, whether of gender, class or ethnicity, were of subsidiary significance, and in any case part of the natural order of things. Since private property was the basic source of a rational interest in the proper ordering of society, class differences were both natural and legitimate. The 'first new nation' therefore emerged politically as a union of states, economically as a capitalist society. But not of *nation*-states; there was only one nationality: American.[67] The ethnic *origins* of Americans were not relevant in a New World. Other ethnic groups simply had no rights.

Indians were simply savages, useful as allies in the wars against the French and the British, but destined to give way to the progress of civilization. Their very presence united Whites in a frontier society. Blacks were disqualified as members of civil society, for, far from possessing property, they *were* property. Fraternity might be thinkable, even for Blacks, in the minds of those who did not rely on their labour. But Jefferson struck out a passage proposing the abolition of slavery from the draft Declaration of Independence. Ninety years were to elapse, and over 600,000 men had to die, before that deletion was rectified. It could scarcely have been otherwise in a country whose leaders, George Washington among them, included owners of vast slave-plantations.

In the southern states of the USA, and in the newer colonies of nineteenth-century Africa, the problem was resolved by denying equality altogether and dividing people into one of two categories, White or Black, a social frontier which could never be crossed because it was defined by physical characteristics. 'Negro' was anyone who could be proven to have any trace of Negro blood. It was to remain in force as a system designed to keep the workforce in place long after the removal of the formal extra-economic controls of slavery. Today, it only persists in South Africa.

The leaders of the other great wave of pioneer colonial revolutions, in Hispanic America, were like their northern counterparts, men (and some women, notably Manuelita Sáenz) steeped in liberal thought. Even the richest of them suffered from metropolitan control of the State, of the economy and of the Church. The principal social distinctions were thus the outcome of a double equation. On the one hand, they reflected the policies and ideologies of the colonizing Power; on the other, the interplay of class and ethnicity within colonial society. For the Spanish conquerors, *Tierra Firme* had proved to be a very different proposition from the islands populated by Caribs: vast lands with populations of millions of people, notably in the advanced civilizations of Mexico and the Andes. Labour was therefore available in abundance for the mines; slaves were only needed in the coastal sugar-plantations. As we saw in Chapter 1, for centuries the mines were the heart of the economy, sources of gold and silver even more valuable than spices had been and sugar was to become. To funnel them to Spain, ruthless exploitation was backed by a powerful administrative machine firmly controlled from Madrid by the Council of the Indies. Within his colonial Audiencia, each Viceroy might be as powerful as the monarch he represented, but he was always answerable to the King. To prevent the inordinate consolidation of his power or the growth of too close an identification with a particular colony, officials were rotated between Audiencias regularly, and the key positions were reserved for appointees from Spain, usually Spaniards, not local-born *criollos*. Resentment at metropolitan control alienated even churchmen and bureaucrats in the colonies who wanted to run things their way. Evasion and foot-dragging became a major political strategy, expressed in such formulae as *obedezco pero no ejecuto* and *se acata, pero no se cumple* (instructions acknowledged, but not carried out).

To prevent association between the colonies, trade and political traffic between them were forbidden. Once the mines had begun to decline, agriculture and manufacturing became the main sectors of the economy, with agriculture based on large estates worked by unfree labour. In North America, farmers working their own land had developed political forms that drew both on European forms of democracy and on new, home-grown American institutions from *habeas corpus* and the freedom of speech to the town-meeting and the election of representatives. No such developments occurred in the Spanish colonies. There, from the beginning, it had been a political culture of conquest, not freedom. Conquest had meant wealth and social status for the Conquistadores, ennoblement for the few, and, for the majority, the status, at least, of *hidalgo*, a person of consequence. A person of consequence did not work with his hands. Where there was no one to do that work, they would live in squalor rather than demean themselves by labouring. Buenos Aires, as late as 1852, was a large squalid village, where the carcasses and bones of animals that had died were left in the street, since there were no Indians left to do the work of removing them.[68]

In most of the southern cone, the indigenous population was virtually wiped out and replaced by immigrants, mostly from Southern Europe. In the other South America, notably the Andean countries, Indians still constitute the majority of the population.[69] Once the Conquest was over, a new social order had to be constructed. The main relationship was the artefact of conquest: the defeated Indians worked the lands the Spaniards had appropriated. To legitimize this exploitation, they were made into juridical inferiors. The category 'Indians' – a purely colonial construct – had to be invented.[70] Because the Spaniards were few, and needed legitimacy, they had used indigenous nobles and lower level *caciques* (chiefs) as instruments of the new colonial administration. But all others were reduced to a total, common inferiority. Colonial society was a new society: the outcome of an interplay between indigenous structures and cultural systems and those imposed by Spain.

Spain itself was a recent state-formation. The union of the royal dynasties of Castile and Aragon had only come about in 1469. The reconquest of the Peninsula had been a struggle not merely between two states, but between two cultures. Victory over the Moors clearly signified that Spain had an historical, divine mission to implant the Word of Truth in new worlds. Unlike Alexander, who wept because there were no more worlds to conquer, Spain set out to find a New World and then conquer it. It was a world-view suffused not with the spirit of toleration, but with a belief in a national destiny, the conviction of absolute truth, and a commitment to the extirpation of heresy.

To learned friars soaked in a theoretical literature of millenarianism, the New World was either the real site of the Garden of Eden, or the place where a completely new Kingdom of God on earth might be brought into being. Less apocalyptic idealists like Las Casas strove, too, to emancipate the Indians once they had been Christianized. But the dominant relationship that was to prevail was one of extremes in exploitation, not one of heavenly brotherhood. Laws to improve the status of the Indians were resisted, at times in open revolt, by settlers despite their own lack of feudal privileges or representative institutions, or simply ignored.[71] For the secular conquerors, brotherhood with Indians was not in the nature of things. Those who lacked noble birth could at least claim racial purity and this could only be total when it was bred in the bone. To hold public office in the motherland, one had had to prove that there was no trace of Moorish or Jewish blood for four generations and no forebears who had converted. In the colonies, *limpieza de sangre* – purity of blood – was elevated even more strongly to the status of a cardinal principle. To this day, Brazilians use the language of race as a compliment to a football team's drive and energy where the British use terms of class, nobility, aristocracy or gentlemanliness: '*raça*', in place of 'first class' or 'the King' of players.

If the exploitation of human beings as slaves requires that their humanity be denied, the cultural forms available for doing so vary. For the Greeks, a slave was philosophically reduced to the status of a thing, an instrument or tool, which only differed from inanimate tools in that slaves had the faculty of speech:

> In Roman theory, the agricultural slave was designated an *instrumentum vocale*, the speaking tool, one grade away from the livestock that constituted an *instrumentum semi-vocale*, and two from the implement, which was an *instrumentum mutum*.[72]

In the New World too, serious debate took place as to whether Negroes had souls. Though it was decided that Indians did have souls, their conversion to Christianity was not to bring them freedom.[73]

Before the Conquest, there had been Zapotecs, Mayans, Aztecs, Tlaxcalans, and scores of other ethnic groups, some organized into states, others acephalous tribes. Now they were all given a new, overall, common identity: 'Indian', just as the term 'Oriental' was to be coined, in a later, imperialist epoch, to express the colonial relationship between the Western capitalist countries and the peoples of Asia as a whole.[74]

In the beginning, the social and cultural gap between the conquerors and the conquered was as obvious as the physical differences between them. Colour was a self-evident, ready-made indicator of that gap. Cultural differences corresponded with physical differences. The gap was never absolute, however, for Doña Marina, Cortés' mistress and right-hand, was not the only Indian who established political alliance with the Spaniards through intermarriage.[75] Spanish conquistadores and Aztec and Inca nobility intermarried freely, among the rank-and-file on a very large scale, since the Spaniards brought few women with them. Outside marriage, they exercised their sexual will over Indian women freely.

Contradictions now developed between the Manichaean simplicity of the division into Indian and Spaniard and the reality of children who fitted into neither category. Even successive children of the same father and mother could look very different. Socially, fathers wished to free their children; culturally, to hispanicize them and bring them up as Christians. Many who were not children of mixed parentage also obtained education, and went on to occupy low-level posts in the Church and the bureaucracy. Economically, Indians and even slaves who obtained manumission became smallholders, traders, and artisans. With each generation, the physical, social and cultural complexity became even greater.

There were two ways in which this growing discrepancy between social and physical attributes could be resolved. One was by *multiplication*, the other by *simplification*, of the categories. In the former, the physical criteria for social classification were retained, but the simple binary opposition between Indian and Spaniard was replaced by the elaboration of new distinctions and sub-distinctions. There now ensued a veritable frenzy as new *castas* were invested to try to keep pace with the mixture of physical types. Initially, only two had been needed: *mestizo* (children of White and Indian), and *mulato* (children of White and Negro). Now they began to snowball. The ultimate in racist lunacy was reached in Haiti in the eighteenth century, where Saint-Mery developed a classification of physical types based on the notion that each individual was divisible into no less than 128 separate parts (rather like genes):

> Thus a *blanc* (white) had 128 parts white, a *nègre* (Negro) 128 parts black, and the offspring a *mulâtre* (mulatto) 64 parts white and 64 parts black. In addition, he also listed *sacatra* (8 to 23 parts white), *griffe* (24 to 39 parts white), *marabou* (40 to 48); *quateron* (71 to 100); *metif* (101 to 112); *mamelouc* (113 to 120); *quateronné* (121 to 124) and finally a *sang-mêlé* (125 to 127).[76]

Given the additional presence of Indians as well as Negroes, Mexican *castas* were even more complex.

It was a race that could not be won. Such physical mixes could not be distinguished in daily practice; they could only be tracked down through genealogies. The obsession was not without practical consequences. In the USA, mulattoes, quadroons (one quarter Negro ancestry), octoroons (one eighth), and 'musties' (near-Whites) were considered more intelligent and therefore fetched higher prices in the slave market. But when two individuals who looked quite dissimilar could be assigned to the same category, and two individuals who looked alike could be assigned to different categories only by genealogical criteria, the system was open to considerable manipulation, and permitted people to whiten themselves.

Today in Brazil, the inter-mixture of physical stocks has been so extensive that there is a continuum from Caucasoid through various degrees of mixed physical appearance to Negroid, and only a minority at either pole. The poles therefore provide reference-points, but most people fall into the intermediate area between them. Yet though there are no social groups formally marked off from each other by colour, few Blacks are to be found in the upper classes, and most Blacks are poor. As in eighteenth-century Mexico, more elaborate distinctions are drawn, however, in the local community, between *degrees* of 'colour' (*côr*). The word subsumes, in fact, a whole range of physical features (shape of nose, lips, type of hair, etc.) of which colour is only one. Thus people are labelled as *preto* (dark, Negro), *mulato*, *pardo*, *sarará*, *moreno*, and so on. Yet the adjoining categories are so close that as a person becomes more successful, his physical features can be re-defined: thus a dark, Negroid-looking professional will be labelled a *pardo* or a *moreno* rather than a *preto*. They are categories of what Wagley calls '*social* race', a function of one's class position.

Racial distinctions are thus very much alive. Yet constitutionally, they do not exist. In Mexico, their abolition was part of the very programme of Independence. Meeting at Chilpancingo in 1813, the revolutionary Congress announced in ringing words what the North American revolutionaries had shrunk from granting:

> Slavery is forbidden for ever, likewise distinctions between *castas*. All will be equal, and only vice and virtue will distinguish one American from another.[77]

It was a promise of social freedom, over and above political freedom from Spain. It was those who hoped to benefit from it, and who believed that it could only be won if Independence was won first, who responded in largest numbers: the armies that followed Hidalgo and Morelos, often described as 'Indian hordes'. Symbolically, it was an Indian miner, Pipíla, who, with a stone slab on his back to deflect musket-bullets, set fire to the great door of the Spanish grain-depository, the Alhóndiga, in Guanajuato.

In Peru, San Martín declaimed the same message in the same grandiloquent tones:

> From now on, the indigenous people are not to be called Indians or natives. They are sons and citizens of Peru and should be known as Peruvians.

The political dream of a League of Hispanic-American States was soon dispelled, and the more limited union of Gran Colombia soon disintegrated. Bolívar himself only escaped the fate of Sucre thanks to Manuelita Sáenz.

The new states that did emerge were the outcome of hundreds of years during which the different Audiencias had been sealed off from each other by the Spanish authorities. Their main external relationships had been with Spain. Internally, they had become increasingly integrated economically, politically and culturally. Hence once the grid-iron of Spanish bureaucracy was removed, there was little to hold them together. The Empire now flew apart into its constituent units, which became the independent states of Venezuela, Ecuador, Peru and the other countries of today's South America. Underlying these divisions consolidated during the Colonia were older political and cultural divisions, such as that between the Inca heartland and the more recently-conquered North – which became, respectively, Peru and Ecuador.

Within the new states, ethnic differences were not recognized in the constitutions. Not only were there no longer any Indians – but a new ideology of *mestizaje* now took hold, best expressed in the modern plaque attached to a ruined building in the archaeological site of the former Aztec city of Tlatelolco, in Mexico City:

> On the 13th of August 1521, heroically defended by Cuauhtémoc [the Aztec Emperor], Tlatelolco fell to Hernan Cortés. It was neither a victory or a defeat, but the painful birth of the mixed people of contemporary Mexico.

Brazilian nationalism today celebrates a similar fusion, not of White and Indian, but of White and African. It has the unique distinction of being the only nationalism which uses the vibrating buttocks of the *mulatas* not just as sexist tourist attractions but also as national symbols.[78]

The ethnic reality, after Independence, was very different from the public rhetoric. All were not even citizens, for as in Europe qualifications were introduced debarring the illiterate and unpropertied from the exercise of civil rights. Indians were either marginalized in remote villages, in 'regions of refuge', where, even though their aboriginal cultures had been radically changed over hundreds of years, they lived a way of life very different from that of the Whites, or they were bound to the *haciendas* by debt, sometimes living in villages apart from the estate, sometimes having the use of a small parcel of land on the estate. In reality, contemporary observers noted, there were *two* nations with opposed interests: Indian Mexico and Westernized Mexico,[79] while a cynical jingle in post-Independence Ecuador expressed the popular mood:

> Ultimo día del despotismo
> y primero de lo mismo
> (The last day of despotism;
> the first day of the same thing).[80]

Indians, it seemed, were bound to disappear culturally where they had not been wiped out or assimilated physically. The great Indian President of Mexico, Juárez, was to prove one of the strongest opponents of Indian-ness.

By the turn of the twentieth century, power had been wrested from the traditional ruling class, the great landowners, by new commercial and industrial bourgeoisies: in Ecuador, by the victory in civil war of an agro-exporting Liberal bourgeoisie; in Mexico, by a new 'political class' which won control of the economy because it had won control over the State first, during the Revolution of 1910. By then, Indian communities were no longer the main source of labour. As their economic importance declined, and since they were not a serious political force, Indian-ness could now be found a new place in nationalist ideology, even glorified. After the Revolution, important families changed their names to those of Aztec heroes. Today, monuments to the Conquistadores are virtually non-existent – even Cortés' burial-place is marked only by a small plaque in a church wall – whereas monuments to Moctezuma and Cuauhtémoc, the last Aztec ruler, abound.

Indian communities still survived, and communitarian systems of land-tenure were even strengthened in Mexico, where *ejidos* were the corner-stone of the revolutionary land reform: the land belonged to the community, and the individual had rights to land as a member of that community. But the tiny plots they received were scarcely viable; now the crucial shortage was capital, not land, and what wealth there was in the community went into the hands of non-Indians.[81]

Though not recognized constitutionally as culturally distinct minorities, the existence of large and distinctive Indian communities in Mexico was the *raison d'être* of special institutions, notably the Instituto Nacional Indigenista, catering for Indians via special welfare projects, schools, health centres, etc. In contrast to these instruments of State policy, the Indians themselves had no autonomous machinery through which to express their interests. The beginnings of country-wide Indian organization in the 1970s reached only a minority. By the 1980s, it seemed all too likely in many areas that the disappearance of Indian culture, including language, which four centuries of Spanish rule had failed to accomplish with all their genocidal brutality, might well come about within a generation or so under the impact of schools and the mass media.

The four thousand remaining nomadic Indians in the Amazon are treated in even more brutal fashion; for their lands are being steadily invaded by settlers. Only a few years ago officials of the Brazilian governmental agency responsible for administering the Indian reserves, the FUNAI, were proved to have been engaged in genocide themselves. Paradoxically, in these countries where genocide had been most thorough, in the southern cone countries, Indian music, suitably Europeanized, but played on traditional instruments, has now become the national folk-music, its most expert practitioners often of Italian or Spanish descent. On the Left, it could become an anti-gringo symbol of South American opposition to Yanqui cultural hegemony.

Pluralism: Internationalism and Multinationalism

The values of the Enlightenment had been expressed as metaphysical absolutes: 'We hold these truths to be *self-evident*, that all men are *created* equal, that they are *endowed by their Creator* with certain *inalienable* rights . . .' yet whole categories were, in fact, excluded from their provisions. 'Men' meant, literally men, not women. Slaves were, of course, unfree, but those who lacked the central prerequisite of personal independence and social responsibility – property ('a stake in the country') – were also refused many civic rights. As groups, ethnic minorities were simply not recognized, even in federal States.

Despite the language of Enlightenment universalism, those who set about building the new states built them as *nation*-states, in accordance with a newer body of doctrine: the Romantic notion that there should be an isomorphic fit between nation and State, that each people should have its own State. But not all peoples had national potential. There were 'historic' peoples and 'non-historic' peoples. The former *deserved* their own State: they were *nationalities* which thereby became fulfilled *nations*. The others were doomed, by history or later, by evolution, to extinction or assimilation. But a third possibility, that of the co-existence of several nationalities within a wider polity, had been reluctantly recognized, during the liberal epoch, even in Empires like Austria-Hungary, hitherto held together by brutality and the dynastic principle, but now facing nationalist revolt. Only archaic, pre-bourgeois states like the Tsarist Empire stuck to the traditional segmentary tactics of divide and rule: the repression of nationalist revolt, the exploitation of inter-ethnic animosities, and chauvinist *pogroms*. Elsewhere, the idea of the multinational state began to take root. Even hegemonic ethnic groups saw in it a way of preserving their traditional superiority by according the secondary status of national minority to the others.

Pluralism, in the form of the multinational state – advocated most vigorously in the nineteenth century by the Serbs – was a model not translated into reality in Europe (Switzerland apart) until the Treaty of Versailles, with the coming into existence of a Czechoslovakia made up of Bohemia, Moravia and Slovakia, and a Yugoslavia (South Slavland) made up of Serbia, Bosnia, Montenegro, and Slovenia.

The adoption of this policy by the victorious Powers was no sudden conversion to liberal principles. Rather, it was *Realpolitik*: a way of dismantling the defeated Ottoman and Austro-Hungarian Empires and putting smaller, weaker states in their place.

The doctrine of multinationalism, however, still assumed the persistence of the State and the nation. It was therefore the socialist movement, rather than liberalism, which went beyond multinationalism to internationalism, since the proletariat 'had no Fatherland', and under socialism, the State would 'wither away'.

Under Stalin, international repression was, of course, directed against any individual or group of any kind that stood out against conformity. It was to result in a new phenomenon, *Soviet* nationalism, expressed in language redolent of Ivan the Terrible and Peter the Great:

> Those who lag behind are beaten. We do not want to be beaten. . . . [In] the history of old [Russia] she was ceaselessly beaten for her backwardness. She was beaten by the Mongol Khans, she was beaten by Turkish Beys, she was beaten by Swedish feudal lords, she was beaten by Polish-Lithuanian *Pans*, she was beaten by Anglo-French capitalists, she was beaten by Japanese barons, she was beaten by all – for her backwardness. For military backwardness, for cultural backwardness, for political backwardness, for industrial backwardness, for agricultural backwardness. She was beaten because to beat her was profitable and went unpunished. . . . We are fifty to a hundred years behind the advanced countries. We must make good this lag in ten years. Either we do it or they crush us. (Speech to business executives, February 1931.)[82]

That Stalin's prediction proved right immensely strengthened Soviet nationalism. The common trauma of 1941–5 became, and is still officially designated, not the war against fascism, but the 'Great Patriotic War'. Soviet nationalism, then, is not simply Great-Russian chauvinism up-dated, but the product of a period which had seen the backwards Tsarist Empire transformed – at the cost of the lives of the millions who died in Stalin's camps – in only thirty years, into the second greatest power on earth and the number 1 socialist country. The loss of another 20 million people through foreign invasion in the Second World War reinforced the determination above all to prevent any intrusion into the Soviet heartland.

For communists, the principle of internationalism had always been sacred. The major debates had been over tactics, not principles. Rosa Luxemburg advocated the translation of internationalism into organizational form there and then, via a revolutionary Party for the whole Russian Empire; others, the majority, argued that each nationality should have its own workers' Party. Paradoxically, Lenin, who opposed her, was to be the 'lone voice [in 1914] proclaiming the defeat of his own country as a socialist aim and crying treason against the "social-chauvinists" '.[83]

After the Bolshevik seizure of power, the right to national self-determination was translated into practice when, in 1917, Finland was allowed to secede and become a separate, and implacably anti-Soviet, independent Republic. But self-determination had always been viewed as a conditional, not an absolute right. It must not be allowed to threaten the Revolution. The subsequent trajectory of Soviet policy *vis-à-vis* the nationalities was inevitable. Building socialism in only one country, under the pressures of Allied blockade, subversion, and actual invasion from Baku to Murmansk and Vladivostok, soon led to the designation of movements of self-determination in Central Asia, led by nationalist mullahs and backed by the Allies, as counter-revolutionary and to their suppression by the Red Army. The low point was to be reached during the Second World War, when whole nationalities, from the Volga Germans and the Crimean Tatars to the Chechen-Ingush of the Caucasus, suspected of disloyalty, were deported, like the Nisei (US-born) Japanese in the USA.

Disgust at these tragedies has led many to dismiss Soviet policy towards component nationalities as unworthy of serious attention. They are quite wrong. Firstly, from its inception, the USSR was built upon the multi-national principle. It was a federation, not just of Socialist Soviet Republics, but of *national* republics. The largest of these, the Russian Federated Soviet Republic, today contains 130 million inhabitants; the second, the Ukrainian SSR, 41 million; between them, 70 per cent of the entire population. The rest live in thirteen other Republics ranging in size from Uzbekistan (9 million) to Estonia (1 million).

The state the Bolsheviks inherited was a singularly diverse collection of peoples, ranging, politically, from remnants of Polish, Ukrainian and Lithuanian states in Europe to khanates, emirates and acephalous tribes conquered during expansion into Central Asia and Siberia. Economically, they included agriculturalists, hunters, and pastoral nomads; culturally, Christians, Muslims, Buddhists and pagans.

Stalin's definition of the nation, in 1913, was to be the basis of Soviet policy towards the nationalities. 'A nation', he wrote, was an 'historically evolved, stable community of language, territory, economic life, and psychological make-up manifested in a community of culture'. But it was an historically-specific *emergent*: a 'category of . . . rising capitalism'. Some nations, however, were more 'backward' than others: what they needed was the helping hand of a 'higher culture'. To give autonomy to backward peoples was to condemn them to isolation and to cultural stagnation. 'Tribes' were not even an 'historical' category, but an 'ethnographical' one.

It was a thoroughly evolutionist and paternalistic model. Forms of ethnicity reflected levels of development. No explicit recognition was given to the value of any specific aspect of backward cultures: they were simply to give way to more modern modes of life. The very structure of the Soviet policy was based on these ideas. Firstly, everyone was a Soviet citizen. But everyone also belonged to a cultural group, a 'nationality' (*narodnost,* today; more usually, *nationalnost*), or some lower-level kind of ethnic community.[84]

Translated into political structure, this meant that the Republics were the highest level of organization; below them, the Autonomous Regions, and below them, the Autonomous Areas. The largest Republic by far, the RSFSR, thus contains within its boundaries no less than sixteen Autonomous Soviet Socialist Republics, five Autonomous *oblasti* (Regions) and ten Autonomous *okruga* (Districts), while the other SSRs include four additional ASSRs and five further Autonomous Regions. Some of these ASSRs are themselves pluri-ethnic. Daghestan ASSR, in the RSFSR, for instance, contains no less than twenty *narodnosti* (nationalities), within which even smaller recognized groups are consolidated. The outcome, then, was not all that dissimilar from what would have resulted had the Romantic distinctions between 'historic' and 'non-historic' peoples been applied. But Soviet evolutionism was not used to justify the oppression of the less-developed nationalities; rather, the opposite. Evolutionary differences, it was believed, would disappear over time as *all* came to share equally the same high living-standards once socialism had been constructed. Under communism proper, not only would political and economic national barriers disappear, but a common culture would emerge, ultimately over the entire world. In the meantime rights to cultural distinctiveness – even to *special* privilege as objects of what a later generation was to call 'positive discrimination' or 'affirmative action' – were entrenched in the 1935 Constitution in the shape of a second Soviet of Nationalities flanking the Supreme Soviet.

The usual Western response to such things is a cynical dismissal of all this as ideology or institutional window-dressing. The non-Russian nationalities, the conventional wisdom has it, are the Soviet Union's time-bomb, growing in numbers, and resentful of Great-Russian chauvinism. In reality, despite continuing disparities such as those between Tashkent and Riga, the nationals of the Central Asian Republics are increasingly taking over the key administrative and professional posts in their Republics. The more appropriate contrast is that between Soviet Central Asia and the misery across the borders.[85]

Nationalism and Myth: Inventing a New Past

The association between liberalism and nationalism developed during the struggle against reactionary regimes in Europe and the Americas did not survive the First World War; thereafter, nationalism was seen as a problem, even a catastrophe; a reason for pessimism, not hope.

To intellectuals, it had now become supremely illogical and supremely irrational.[86] The subsequent emergence of fascism, which launched upon the total elimination of dissent at home and military expansion abroad, seemed the final confirmation of the *inherently* evil nature of nationalist thinking pushed to its ultimate extremes. The things done in the name of the nation – from Auschwitz to Kampuchea – seemed confirmation enough.

Exposing nationalist claims as myths was not difficult. The objections were both logical and sociological. Internally, there are always many kinds of divisions within any ethnic community; externally, clear national boundaries often do not exist. Thus the mountains which separate the maritime provinces of the Basque country from the inland provinces of Navarra and Alava also mark distinctive economic and cultural boundaries; the boundaries between what eventually became the Netherlands and Germany were exceedingly ambiguous in the seventeenth century;[87] while even where people live in communities with distinctive cultural features such as language, villages may be intermingled in a mosaic which, as in Western Poland before 1945, do not correspond with political boundaries.

The activities of those intellectuals who created national historical myths is best described by the word 'forging'. The Greeks pioneered the prototype for liberal nationalism the world over: the idealized selective amnesia, immortalized by Byron, of an ancient world of democracy and shining white temples under blue skies, that omitted war and slavery. By the end of the nineteenth century, Greeks scattered across the eastern Mediterranean since the Byzantine Empire – so that their King was eventually to call himself King of the Hellenes, not King of Greece – had to be persuaded to join a new state of Hellas centred on the heartland of southern Europe. Jews dispersed across Europe for two millennia had to be persuaded, firstly, that they *were* Jews, and not Germans or Frenchmen, and secondly, that their real home was in the Middle East, where no more than a handful of actual Jews lived (though only after such unlikely national homes as the Highlands of Kenya and Uganda had been canvassed by the Zionist pioneers).

A common language – often carelessly assumed to be quite essential to national identity – sometimes did not exist. Ancient tongues then had to be resurrected and new vocabularies coined, from Hebrew to Swahili; regional dialects elevated to the status of national languages. At the unification of Italy, only 2.5 per cent of the population spoke the Florentine dialect, the new national tongue. But even in France, long politically unified, cultural homogenization was far slower. As late as 1863, 'French was a foreign language for a substantial number of Frenchmen, including about half the children who would reach adulthood in the last quarter of the century'.[88] Instead, at home, they spoke various *patois*. In Norway, *Ny-Norsk* (New Norwegian) was adopted as the official form of the language after separation from Sweden in 1905, and only a minority speak it in the home even today. In countries where ethnic divisions ran so deep that no one of the indigenous languages was acceptable to the rest, the solution was a national language that was the mother-tongue of nobody. In India, it was English. The Chinese speak dialects so different that they can only communicate via a common *written* language.

The project of the in-gathering of the nation was most successful in two tragic situations: the expulsion of the Greeks from Asia Minor, due to their chauvinistic attempt to seize Western Anatolia as part of a new Greece, and the extraordinary return of Jews to Israel. Yet those who did take part in the Return were a minority who did so only under the extreme conditions of the trauma of the Holocaust and the fear of resurgent Islam. The rest – the majority by far – stayed in Leeds, the Bronx, and Moscow, for nationalism has little appeal to people who were tolerably comfortable where they were and often much better off there. The negative face of nationalism, 'chauvinism', could easily be whipped up (as with Armenians in Western Turkey) when the victims' possessions were available for distribution to the ethnic majority. Being a member of an ethnic minority might thus carry with it the constant fear of death and despoliation. More usually, it meant a less dramatic second-class citizenship in which one was condemned to lower-class occupations not necessarily by force or by law, but because one did not command the resources of the hegemonic culture, the language or the social connections, rather than because one wore different clothing, ate uncivilized foods or worshipped bizarre gods at unbusinesslike times.

To define the culture and the boundaries of the nation, it was not enough to create a new consciousness of the nation here and now. A new past had to be invented. Written history had to be rewritten; archaeology, linguistics, even palaeontology taken up with enthusiasm in search for roots and fore-fathers. To demonstrate the *Volk*'s lineage, folklore exploded into a new industry in the nineteenth century as scholars ransacked Greek, Norse, Celtic and Nibelung myths in their effort to create new ones. After Independence, the Founding Fathers provided more up-to-date and direct symbols: monuments and memorials to Washington, Jefferson and Lincoln, the tombs of Napoleon and Sun Yat-Sen, became national shrines, even the very bodies of Lenin and Mao. Historical sites mark the events associated with the emergence of the nation (even when there is nothing to be seen except a memorial). The institutional calendar of national political life – 7 November in Red Square, the State Opening of Parliament, Independence Day everywhere – provide other apt occasions. But quite non-political occasions of societal sweep, from the Cup Final to the World Series, are also fit occasions for the affirmation of sacred *représentations collectives* through the singing of the National Anthem or the presence of the Head of State.

Though these themes are universal, they necessarily draw upon personages and events taken from actual history. But they project the values of the present onto a past which does not always sustain them. Thus Brazil celebrates real political martyrs like Tiradentes and creative artists like Aleijadinho. But the monument to Brazil's war dead on the waterfront at Rio celebrates the opportunist last-minute switch of a pro-fascist regime to the side of the winning Allies in 1944 as if it were an authentic commitment to democracy.[89]

Museums the world over present the achievements of individual artists and scientists as if they were the achievements of their countries. Museums of national culture and history, like Mexico's Anthropology Museum, may even serve as secular shrines. More chauvinist present-ations depict their contents not just as achievements but (by implication at least) as achievements *as against* the lesser achievements of other countries, or as achievements of *world* significance. Thus, in Stalin's day, Russian scientists were claimed to have invented virtually everything first. The initial discovery by one or other colonizing Power of foreign territories is thus usually taken to be the starting-point of its history, even though the Indians had discovered America long before Christopher Columbus. The theme of connection to the developed world is even occasion for more modern celebration, as in the Aeronautical Museum of São Paulo, where the plane which Santos Dumont (who lived in Paris) flew from Europe to Brazil is displayed as evidence of Brazil's modernization. In more chauvinist popular versions, it seemed that the outside world was fortunate in being connected up to Brazil; in the words of a popular song of the time:

> Europe bowed before Brazil
> Rending homage in gentle tones
> Another star shone in the sky
> As Santos Dumont appeared.

> He honoured forever the twentieth century
> The hero who astounded all the world
> Higher than the clouds, almost God
> And Santos Dumont is a Brazilian![90]

Folk heroes and heroines, from Pelé to Bobby Charlton, readily become symbols of the nation because they are believed to reflect their country's institutional strengths, its values, or its national character. The body of Carmen Miranda, after her success in Hollywood, was given a lying-in-state in Rio's legislative buildings, where tens of thousands filed by to pay their last respects. Later, a museum was erected.

A more intellectual form of national myth-making came from anthropologists. In true functionalist fashion, Roger Bastide dismissed both the notion of cultural survivals and the over-emphasis on the Portuguese contribution by writers such as Gilberto Freire by insisting that what had been created in the New World was a rich synthesis of African, Portuguese and even Indian cultures, different in kind from any of those original constituent elements,[91] against which a later generation of colour-blind Marxists have further reacted by treating class as the only significant reality and thereby denying the existence of any special 'Black Problem'.

Nationalism and Socialism

For Marx, nationalism was a double-edged phenomenon. At one level, insofar as it postulated a community of interest between exploiter and exploited, it was a form of false consciousness. By purporting to transcend class, it mystified the reality of exploitation. Modernizing Jews who assumed that they could escape from stigma and social marginalization by abandoning their religious-ethnic identity were deluded, he wrote, for the abandonment of religion, or success in passing socially, would do nothing to eliminate inequalities of wealth and property. Jews, like Gentiles, would remain unfree until private property in the means of production was abolished and social ownership put in its place. To the proletariat fell a world-historic task: not just its own liberation from bourgeois rule, but the ending of class society altogether.

In more archaic societies, the proletariat Marx thus celebrated was only small and recently-formed out of dispossessed peasants, and therefore gave its support to bourgeoisies engaged in struggle against landed aristocracies and feudal monarchical regimes. The ideological form in which these alliances was normally couched was that of liberal nationalism, of the rights of freeborn Englishmen. Those they fought against sought to divide them by appealing to older, more atavistic forms of ethnic chauvinism, diverting the resentment of the oppressed onto other exploited groups by encouraging a sense of cultural superiority over those lesser breeds.

In the bourgeois democracies, intellectuals, drawing upon Darwin, developed more modern, scientific forms of racism, which eventually trickled down to the masses as in the form of the law of the survival of the fittest. But older forms of chauvinism were more widespread among the uneducated. In Britain, the historic ethnic group against whom prejudice was most easily whipped up, both as aggressive Fenian terrorists and as drunken, stupid figures of fun, were a colonized people, the Irish. (Marx observed, even in his day, that comic books and jokes were one of the chief ways prejudice against them was kept alive.) By the end of the century, with imperialist expansion, aggression was to be directed against newer enemies of Britain outside rather than inside the country, and fanned into mass jingoism. With the arrival of large numbers of these outsiders, seeking for jobs in Britain itself, the ashes of the jingo era were readily fanned into flame once more. Today, the cultural counterpart of Marx's comic books is the working-class racist comedian on TV, the butts of whose jokes are – still – the Irish, but now, also, the 'Pakis' and the Blacks.

Marx therefore distinguished between nationalist movements which would further the development of bourgeois society (and hence make possible the subsequent transition to socialism), and the reactionary manipulation of ethnic hostility by Tsar and feudal landowner. The unification of Germany as a new, bourgeois state would therefore be a progressive step, likewise the detachment of Poland from the Tsarist Empire.

Scientific socialism no more enabled him to foresee just what future nation-states were eventually to emerge than Mazzini's theoretical equipment had helped him to anticipate the formation of such unlikely entities as Czechoslovakia or Yugoslavia. Marx and Engels, being creatures of their time, were also unduly influenced by evolutionist and Hegelian distinctions between historical nations and history-less peoples. In general, Smith notes,

> [they] favoured large-scale, even multinational, political units, since only they could provide an adequate framework for effective industrial capitalist production and so generate a class-conscious proletariat. Small, underdeveloped peoples were a barrier to economic progress: Montenegrins were 'pious freebooters', Mexicans *'les derniers des hommes'*; and the Chinese [characterized by] 'hereditary stupidity'.[92]

Hence it would be better for the Slavs to be absorbed by Germany or Austria-Hungary; the Mexicans by their more dynamic capitalist neighbour to the North.

For Marx, it was class, not nation, that was ultimately significant. The proletariat had a *universalistic* mission: to abolish class society everywhere, and to abolish itself in the process. To do so, it would have to abolish the irrational divisions that had grown up historically between the proletariat of one country and its brothers in other lands. It was an internationalist vision: the proletariat 'had no fatherland'. Proletarians in each country should defend and assist their brothers in every other country because they faced a common enemy. National workers' parties themselves were only transitional historical accommodations to a world divided into capitalist nation-states which the world proletariat would replace by world socialism.

To the Marxists who came after Marx, and who experienced the unification of the entire globe under imperialism, his prophecies seemed to have been thoroughly confirmed. The class struggle was now internationalized on a world scale. Proletarians everywhere faced transnational corporations who, with their local 'comprador' accomplices, operated not just in one country, but on every continent. Even the reformist Social Democratic parties of Europe – notably the huge German SDP – still cleaved to Marxism as their official creed, and still called on the workers of the world to refuse to fight in wars between states governed by capitalist classes competing with each other for profits across the globe. The reality of proletarian internationalism was put to the ultimate test in 1914, when millions of French, German, British, and Italian workers went off, under the command of their national bourgeoisies, to slaughter millions of their fellows.

Internationalism – their 'objective' interest – seemed to have collapsed, and after 1918, the revolutionary tide in Europe soon receded, leaving the USSR as the only socialist state. The USSR's attitude toward nationalist struggles abroad was no longer based on the contribution they made to the struggle between modernizing capitalism and feudal reaction, as in the nineteenth century, but on the role they played in the new world-wide battle against the leading capitalist Powers. Newly-emerging capitalist classes in the colonies, struggling to wrest control of their countries from the imperialist Powers, might therefore play a progressive role. The expansion of the advanced capitalist Powers in the colonial world reflected the exhaustion of the historical mission of the bourgeoisies in their homelands. With the proletariat ready to replace them, they sought to resolve the problems of the economy by enslaving, not freeing other peoples. It was a reactionary form of nationalism, the nationalism of a dying social system.

Lenin therefore distinguished in 1916 between 'bourgeois-progressive national movements' in the leading capitalist countries which had achieved their victory long ago; those in the countries of Eastern Europe and Russia where they had become significant only in recent decades; and those in colonial and semi-colonial countries where they were only beginning.[93] Within the USSR, the principle of national self-determination now gave way to the reduction, *de facto*, of the constituent national units, the Republics, the ASSRs, the Autonomous Regions and Districts, to organs of administration controlled from Moscow. Abroad, proletarian internationalism was redefined: the unconditional defence of the Soviet Union was now the *first* duty of every foreign communist and the first of the 21

Points required by the Comintern, under Lenin's guidance, of every foreign workers' movement before it could become recognized as a Communist Party.

Totalitarian conformity could be effectively imposed on the USSR and on European Communist Parties. It was to prove far more difficult to control revolutionary movements in societies outside Europe. The moral authority conferred upon the Bolsheviks by virtue of having accomplished the first successful socialist revolution in one of the largest countries in the world reinforced the traditional assumption that socialism would come about first in Europe, even though it had not happened in an *advanced* capitalist country. But the expectation of further revolutions in Western Europe seemed to be confirmed by the disturbances of the immediate post-War years. In 1919, the Comintern was still telling the workers and peasants of Annam, Algiers and Bengal that they 'would gain the opportunity of independent existence *only* when the workers of England and France have overthrown Lloyd George and Clemenceau' (my italics).[94] By the Second Congress in Baku, a year later, the doctrine of the priority of revolution in the West was – in effect, if not in explicit principle – abandoned for ever.[95]

Lenin had long been aware of the revolutionary potential of the East and mistrustful of the reformism of Western working-class movements. But he was far too steeped in traditional Eurocentric Marxism to accept M. N. Roy's heretical reversal of that doctrine: the strategy of giving priority to revolution in the East. Yet Roy himself clung to another element in that orthodoxy, the notion that the revolution would be led by the working class. Lenin saw the leadership as coming from the bourgeoisie Roy despised, and the mass force, in countries with only microscopic working classes, from the peasantry.

The strategy of alliance between working-class anti-capitalist revolution and nationalist anti-imperialism led by revolutionary bourgeoisies was put into practice most significantly in China. It was there, however, that the doctrine of working-class priority was to be abandoned in practice – though not, even to this day, in words. After the Northern Expedition of 1926, when the infant CCP had helped Chiang (who had even spent six months in Moscow) establish his authority over most of the country despite his earlier *coup* in which he had turned on the Left in Canton, he now turned on the workers of Shanghai in 1927, butchering those who had made his victory possible. Most of the Communist leadership were wiped out in the process. The remainder fled the cities. Some of them now came to the totally heterodox conclusion that the revolution could only be won, thenceforth, from a rural, rather than an urban base.

Within a few years, internal class struggle had ceased to be the main priority. The singular brutality of Japanese fascist invasion threatened both the national bourgeoisie and the communists alike. This was now the 'principal contradiction' which justified a new attempt to re-establish the alliance with the Kuomintang despite the successive extermination campaigns which Chiang launched against the communists. He finally agreed only after he had been captured by the Young Marshal, one of the more patriotic warlords whom he had not been able to subdue. But he remained too preoccupied with holding off the internal communist threat to offer effective resistance to the invaders. The communists, meanwhile, had established themselves in their own state within a state in Yenan, in the North-west, from whence they developed a vast network of anti-Japanese guerrilla bases among the peasantry, thereby building the political support that was to bring them to power.

Chalmers Johnson has argued that the communists came to power not so much because of their social policies as because they became effective leaders of a militant *national* resistance.[96] Yet the communists did far more than protect the peasantry against the invader. Given landlord domination, too, nationalist appeals to unite against the Japanese were ineffective. Resistance, rather, involved social struggle *against* landlords who often co-operated with the invaders and who always maintained their ruthless exploitation of the peasantry. Yet it was, in fact, extremely difficult to mobilize peasants so imbued with a 'deep, almost instinctive reluctance to mount an offensive against the power of the gentry' that 'only the most severe provocation could overcome the peasants' great reluctance to act'.[97] National resistance became a mass phenomenon because it meant radical social change – not the revolutionary dispossession of a ruling class, but the elimination of immemorial injustices. The Red armies behaved as no army had ever done in Chinese history, with scrupulous honesty and consideration towards the peasants. The eight rules of military conduct towards the people required the soldiers to actually pay for goods purchased, return things borrowed, and replace anything lost or damaged. But over and above all this, they put into effect rudimentary policies that benefited the poor: building bridges in the villages, providing medical attention, teaching the children, and, above all, improving the peasants' economic situation.

This did not necessarily mean extensive land reform. Such policies had alienated rich peasants and even middle peasants when they had been introduced in the Red Soviets in the South years before. During the war, they were soft-pedalled. But rents were reduced by at least 25 per cent and interest-rates to 10 per cent; unused land was also taken over and distributed to the poor and landless. But the intention for the future was clear: the promise of land redistribution on a scale which would necessarily mean taking it from those who had plenty. It was that promise which was to bring them to power.

Communist nationalism was obviously not an instrument of reaction. Nor was it a purely liberal struggle for progressive civil rights in an independent but still capitalist China. It was a strategy designed to lead to an egalitarian socialist society. But communism and nationalism had become compatible; alliance with patriotic segments of the bourgeoisie a legitimate policy. It was a strategy whose success in the world's most populous country was to make it a model for other movements of national liberation, notably Vietnam.

China's liberation from Japan was swiftly followed by liberation from bourgeois Nationalist rule. By 1949, socialism was no longer confined to one country. It also existed in the states of Eastern Europe, implanted by the Red Army, where Soviet hegemony was therefore unchallenged. The situation of China was quite different, for the Revolution there had been achieved without Soviet assistance and in defiance of Soviet advice. Even in countries closer to the USSR, Soviet hegemony was soon challenged. Within only three years, the state with the strongest tradition of its own *communist*-led resistance to Nazi occupation, Yugoslavia, came into open conflict with the USSR, and developed its own, national version of communism. Poland, which had also put up a bitter resistance to Nazi genocide, continued to assert its national identity in a very different way through the Catholic Church and peasant economic resistance to Soviet-style collectivization. Though both retained classic democratic centralism internally, Albania broke completely with Moscow in 1961, while Romania operated an increasingly independent foreign policy.

Other attempts at national self-expression were less successful: the revolt in East Germany in 1953, where eventually a third of the population left for the West, and a Wall had to be built to prevent the rest from following them; in 1956, the attempt of the Hungarians to assert their independence, which was drowned in blood; the Prague Spring of 1968, which turned to winter when Soviet tanks moved in. Bulgaria alone, loyal to Russia since the nineteenth century, never offered the USSR any opposition.

The degree to which these different countries displayed a readiness to resist Soviet hegemony thus varied in accordance with the strength of their historical traditions of self-determination and of a more recent praxis of mass resistance during the Second World War.

Outside Eastern Europe, the new communist states emerged as a result of national struggles against the domination of foreign capitalist powers. In Korea, there had been a powerful communist-led resistance before the arrival of the Red Army in 1945. In Cuba, a very bloody struggle for national independence only half a century ago had been aborted, as was the first nationalist anti-colonial revolution in Asia, that of the Philippines, both ending in formal independence but *de facto* US control. The cost of revolution was high. Vietnam was to suffer the loss of millions of lives in its wars of national liberation against Japan, France and the USA. But there were other losses and casualties besides the mountains of corpses. To achieve that degree of self-sacrifice, organizational control and ideological commitment had to be as total as possible. The democratic centralist party was the instrument. In the economic sphere, the price of even a needle or a box of matches was fixed by the State; in the village, each purchase was recorded in a booklet kept by every family and inspected and stamped by the local Trading Committee.[98] In the political sphere, total dedication was expected of cadres:

> To get a footing amongst our national minorities our political workers have not simply learned their languages, but have pierced their ears when the minority in question pierces its ears, filed their teeth when the minority files theirs. . . . The [cadres] . . . scarcely ever leave their villages. They know the terrain, the people, their own families. We have political workers who have lived for years like this, hidden underground by day and only coming out at night. Some of them have become blind through never seeing the light.[99]

The outcome was a set of singularly monolithic forms of national communism, sealed in blood, that emphasized the unity of all classes apart from the handful of comprador accomplices of imperialism. Like all nationalisms, and every bit as much as demagogic populism, it thus asserted a poly-class ideology of vertical integration and solidarity.

Internally, after liberation, the rights of national minorities were recognized in principle. How far those rights extended was far more ambiguous and contentious. The evolutionist denigration of minority cultures as backward, across the board, and the early frontal Soviet attack on Islam as reactionary, have been replaced by more flexible policies in newer revolutionary regimes. Cultural autonomy clearly involves the right to use one's own language in schools and local government; now, even the right to religious freedom is recognized, though counterbalanced by the Party's adherence to a materialist philosophy. But the minorities and the State were still often in conflict over much more material issues, particularly the ownership of land. In Nicaragua, recognition of the cultural distinctiveness of the peoples of the Atlantic coast did not extend to awarding them the status of national minorities. Their rights to the lands they cultivated and built their houses on were accepted, but not rights to the whole national territory; while sub-soil resources (potential mineral wealth) were deemed to be the patrimony of the State. The result was disaffection so severe that it pushed the Miskito Indians, initially well-disposed to the Sandinista regime, into the arms of the CIA.

The monopolization of riches found on the territory of tiny minorities cannot be justified. For they are entitled to more than equality; they are entitled to *equity*. In Marx's words, they have a 'right of inequality',[100] to *un*equal 'positive discrimination', firstly because it is *their* territory; secondly, because they are entitled to what US Blacks call 'reparations' for hundreds of years of oppression and in order to bring them up to the levels of living-standards the majority already enjoy. That revolutions do not follow from an immanent ahistoric logic, but learn from their own experience and that of others is shown in the recognition by the Guatemalan Guerrilla Army of the Poor (EGP) that their movement is a movement of no less than twenty-three different *ethnic groups*, symbolized by the twenty-three stars on their flag, and including some that have actually been wiped out or are in the process of disappearing. Two of the stars are for the non-Indian, mixed Ladino people. And in the centre are two large stars for *classes*: the workers and peasants. It is a historic, dramatic iconography of the long-delayed recognition on the part of Marxists, that class and ethnicity are separate but interacting phenomena.

The external relations of socialist states involve relationships with two kinds of nation-states, capitalist and socialist, on the part of states which are themselves nation-states. Yet socialist internationalism is by no means dead, either in principle or practice. The most principled recent assertion of proletarian internationalism was the military assistance given by Cuba to Angola when that country was threatened by South African invasion (an involvement itself conditioned by the historic origins of most of Cuba's population in Africa). The extension of that involvement in the form of the support given to Ethiopia in the face of Somali invasion of the (ethnically-Somali) Ogaden could also be justified because of Somalia's resort to armed force and as defence of a regime which, though it had come to power via a military *coup*, had smashed Haile Selassie's autocratic regime and its social base by giving the lands of his feudal supporters to the people. The unacceptable face of this regime internally, in the ruthless massacre of Marxist rivals for leadership, had its external counterpart in the continuation of the pre-revolutionary Amharan policy of crushing movements for independence in Eritrea and for autonomy elsewhere. Patently embarrassed, the Cubans avoided directly fighting Eritrean guerrillas some of whom they had once trained themselves. Yet their presence behind the lines freed the Ethiopian army to hit back when the Eritreans had seemed on the brink of victory.

The two largest communist countries, Russia and China, have stopped short of full military conflict, but are still deadly rivals. In their competition for political support abroad, the USSR was easily able to control Eastern Europe and could outbid the Chinese in supplying military and economic aid to the newer socialist countries and to liberation movements. Cuba, cut off by the USA from her former markets and sources of supply, invaded once and constantly threatened with further US destabilization, inevitably fell into dependence on the USSR. Vietnam, which had performed miracles during the war with the USA in walking the tightrope between the Soviet Union, which had supplied the bulk of its war *matériel*, and China, through whose territory much of it, notably oil, had had to pass, soon also found itself dependent on the USSR, when confronted with the heartbreaking task of rebuilding a devastated country. The Chinese invasion of Vietnam, reviving millennial enmities, was the tragic outcome, followed by Vietnam's own invasion of Kampuchea to free her borders from the menace of a genocidal regime.

Socialism, as an ideal, involves not just a commitment to the material equality and improvement for individuals, but to cultural equality and tolerance between groups, internally, and, externally, solidarity with the struggles of other peoples. It has, in reality, all too often been submerged by the necessity of defending socialist states from destruction. The experience of decades of *cordon sanitaire*, of containment, invasion, surveillance and, now, nuclear encirclement, has induced in the USSR a hypersensitivity which has led that country to intervene freely by force whenever its borders seemed threatened: in East Germany, Hungary, Czechoslovakia, Afghanistan, and Poland. The consequence, for countries immediately on its borders, has been the constant repression of movements seeking to assert independence of Soviet control.

But the USSR has also been the main source of arms and training for anti-colonial guerrilla movements from Vietnam to southern Africa. For a time, China also sought to build support in the Third World for her brand of communism by giving assistance to Third World regimes and liberation movements, armed and otherwise, a policy replaced after 1964 by one of nationalist *Realpolitik* in alliance with any country which was anti-Soviet, whatever its political complexion. Its logic was a distinctively nationalist, rather than a class logic. In a country whose very name, Chung-Kuo, means 'Middle Kingdom' (represented by the written character 中 in which China is represented by the line which situates her at the centre of the (square) world), the continuity of ethnocentrism, in the most populous country on earth, was scarcely surprising. Chinese policy *vis-à-vis* her numerous non-Han national minorities is not fundamentally dissimilar to Soviet policy: though it is dedicated to reversing historic 'Great-Han chauvinism', any threat to control from the centre, or from outside the borders, is fiercely resisted.

Abroad, Chinese policy, today, is pure state *Realpolitik*. Alliances with repressive regimes in Asia and with Conservatives like Mr Heath or Mrs Thatcher in Europe, rather than with regimes and parties further to the Left, have outraged socialists and mystified most people. The logic informing Chinese foreign policy is actually very simple. It is the 'Nuer' logic of the saying 'the enemy of my enemy is my friend'. The preservation of the Chinese Revolution in the shape of the Chinese *state* is the top priority, as it is for the Soviet Union. Once the USSR became defined as an enemy, even the main enemy, one therefore allied oneself with enemies of the USSR.

The social system in those countries is a secondary matter; what matters is that they are states, wielding power, and that power must be harnessed, if not in direct support of China, at least against the USSR.

Socialist internationalism remains a powerful ideal, inspiring millions. In China, it inspired Mao's vision of eliminating not just the legacy of capitalist inequality, but the 'Three Great Differences' which have persisted throughout successive epochs of different kinds of class society: differences between town and country, between mental and manual labour, and, most primordial of all, between men and women; cultural assumptions which legitimize differential access both to wealth and to illth, and different kinds of socialization and of social opportunity. But it is contradicted by the fact that the structural unit of socialism is the nation-state. National sensitivity is particularly strong in those countries that have only just won their freedom from capitalist domination and poured out blood to do so.

The newer communist states depend for political and military protection on the USSR. Cuba's economy, still based on the export of sugar – now to the USSR – and Vietnam's reconstruction, still depend on Soviet aid. In the older communist countries, Soviet hegemony is still decisive at the military level in the Warsaw Pact. But there are no over-arching, collective political institutions transcending and superior to the separate nation-states: the unit of the socialist economic planning is also still the nation-state. COMECON has provided a framework for the successful industrialization of each country along Soviet lines, but only at the cost of accepting Soviet political hegemony. But the setting-up of joint economic organs to plan a frontal assault on the historic inequalities between nation-states by integrating their economies, which a *socialist* international community – as distinct from a capitalist one – ought to imply, has never come about, and COMECON probably wields less effective authority over its member-states than does the EEC.

Nationalism in the Capitalist Third World

Uneven development, the material legacy of the world division of labour established during the imperialist epoch, is much harder to overcome in countries whose economies were distorted by direct or indirect colonialism, and where, politically and culturally, there are no supra- or trans-national institutions and ideals comparable in range and power to socialism. Islam, the most important, is limited in geographical range, and, when it comes to the crunch, has been more often yoked to the nationalisms of separate states than a force for unity across the Muslim world.

The most virulent forms of the nation-state hark back to forms which

existed elsewhere only before the bourgeois epoch. Liberalism was never for
export to the colonies. Like Cromwell in Ireland during England's
Revolution, Napoleon tried, unsuccessfully, as did Britain, to crush Haiti's
struggle for independence – though, unlike Britain, in the name of the
French Revolution. The Dutch also swiftly stamped out any idea of
extending the revolutionary principles of the Batavian Republic to the East
Indies.

Under colonialism, politics existed only as domination. The colonial state
was an *administrative* state; the notion of national identity simply a subject
of mockery by colonial officialdom. These were neither states nor nations:
they were simply political dependencies and ethnic aggregations of tribes,
sultanates, princedoms, castes, and so forth, with no shared heritage and no
contemporary interests in common.[101] The constituent unit was the ethnic
group; the colonial state was therefore a segmentary state, often fragmented
into many dozens of ethnic segments. Democratic political rights were not
even extended to the ethnic group of the colonizers, the settlers. Despite
occasional attempts (in Ireland and Kenya) to seize control by force, the
settler never won out, with one major exception: South Africa. The
national/ethnic situation in that country is therefore thoroughly aberrant,
for the majority of the people are not allowed the status of individual free
citizens under *apartheid*, but are treated as members of ethnic segments,
Bantustans, imposed and manipulated through a State dominated by a
single ethnic minority which reserves to itself the monopoly of political
rights and political power. To seek for analogues, therefore, one has to go
back before the bourgeois epoch of liberal democracy to the epoch of the
segmentary state. Unlike the hegemonic, Absolutist state, the ruling class,
in order to maintain its political and economic domination, seeks to preserve
the purity of its culture from contamination, as something eternally
separate, not to impose it. The other aberrant settler state came into
existence much later. In Israel, initially seen by many as a force for
modernization in the Middle East, 'gun Zionism' and the myth of 'a land
without people' soon displaced 'binationalist' and socialist rivals.[102] By the
1970s, the racism and genocide practised against the Jews by fascists who
glorified war had spawned a political culture of Zionist racism and a praxis of
continuous military expansion.

Colonization has frequently been justified by appealing to notions of
progress. This was seen as the diffusion of a superior culture to backward
peoples, or the extension of technical and economic rationality: the
incorporation, for instance, of the economies of the numerous groups living
in different niches at different ecological levels in the 'vertical archipelago'
from the Amazonian jungle to the moorlands of the Andes and down to the
tropical coast into the Inca Empire.[103] But the process has still always been
hypothecated upon conquest and exploitation. Some conquerors hardly

bothered to develop a justification of conquest. In the epoch of high
imperialism, economic transformation was uninhibitedly brutal. Whole
countries, we have seen, were converted into coffee-estates, sugar- and tea-
plantations and sources of minerals, whole peoples into workforces obliged
to labour by various forms of extra-economic compulsion, including slavery,
the poorest zones supplying labour for the plantations, the mines and, later,
the factories; others into zones producing cash-crops for export and to feed
the labour-force.

In the process, pre-colonial polities were simply smashed and reassembled to form a new, colonial jigsaw. Only Japan saved herself from
colonization. A few other states, Siam, Afghanistan, Persia, China and
Ethiopia, remained formally independent, effectively semi-colonies. Some,
like the Amhara monarchy in Ethiopia and the Ch'ing dynasty in China,
were still engaged in asserting their domination over other peoples when
they had to face a new, Western threat. The Afghans proved capable of
defeating two British expeditions; and Menelik's armies actually defeated
the Italians at Adowa. But they were the exceptions. Even the Ashanti and
Zulu states, powerful enough to defeat British armies in pitched battle, in
the end went down to defeat.

Over most of Africa, the countries that were brought into being by
imperialism corresponded to no pre-colonial polity. 'Tanzania' and 'Nigeria'
were colonial constructs, and even countries which, on Independence, were
to take their names from ancient empires – Ghana, Mali, Zimbabwe – were
composed, in fact, of different peoples in different places. Yet the past could
be drawn upon to create ideological resistance to imperialism, by 'a certain
sort of regression . . . looking inwards, drawing upon indigenous resources,
resurrecting past folk heroes and myths', appealing to conceptions of the
community which were far 'wider, older and superior to . . . a still
rudimentary class consciousness'.[104]

Yet colonies were *European* creations, carved out of geographical zones
inhabited by a variety of societies and cultures. Their viability, after
Independence, was therefore problematic. 'Tribe' was a colonial category
loosely applied to a wide variety of units. The larger of them – super-tribes
rather than tribes – vied with each other for control of the new state. In a
country like Nigeria, the mosaic of ethnicity might be reduced to three broad
regions. In Tanzania, the existence of over 300 pre-colonial tribes ensured
that no one of them was able to exercise political hegemony. (Its President,
significantly, was to come from a people, the Zanaki, numbering only a few
thousand and therefore threatening nobody.) The rhetoric of citizenship
suited super-tribes like the Kikuyu whose members got the majority of the
new posts. Cases like Fiji and Malaya, where the colonial Power only
handed over on the strict condition of entrenched constitutional clauses
giving special rights to indigenous peoples who were no longer an effective

majority in their own country and were threatened by competition from entrepreneurial descendants of immigrants (Indians in Fiji, Chinese in Malaya), were exceptions.

With the removal, overnight, of the colonial authority during the 'winds of change' of the 1960s, there was a distinct possibility that these fragile and recent political formations might fly apart into their constituent components, as Spanish America had done over a century earlier. This was particularly likely in areas on the borders, where whole ethnic groups had sometimes been cut in two (the Ogaden, the Northern Province of Kenya) and whose defection therefore especially threatened the security of the State. It might also invite further movements of secession, not just in other frontier regions, but anywhere. These were particularly likely in areas that were extremes in uneven development: at one pole, the zones where most of the country's wealth came from; at the other, the backlands, smouldering with the resentments born of deprivation. The advanced regions like Katanga, the centre of mining in Zaire; Biafra, the oil-rich part of Nigeria; Bougainville, in Papua New Guinea, site of the world's richest copper-mine, were highly desirable properties. The new élites were as anxious to keep that wealth in their hands as others were to hive it off for themselves by creating independent statelets. Normally, the power of the central government, and the stake of the decolonizing Power in the post-colonial settlement, were sufficient to frustrate attempts at secession. Nor was support necessarily forthcoming even from neighbouring countries which were political enemies or whose borders split people in two, since support for secession was a policy that might well backfire on them at home. The crucial support therefore came from multinational corporations, such as the Union Minière in Katanga, which sought to install a puppet regime in a mini-state effectively under its control, and from foreign governments which hoped to replace governments of a militarily anti-imperialist neo-colonial regime.

The political destabilization of unfriendly regimes, including the use of savage mercenary Europeans, presented as the struggles of submerged nationalities fighting for their independence against traditional tribal enemies and new-style dictators, resulted in the wiping-out, in the minds of central governments, of any vestige of tolerance for the rights of ethnic minorities to cultural, let alone political self-determination. In some marginal regions of the world, where local resistance might be more easily contained without drawing down the wrath of international anti-colonial movements, old-style direct colonial control could continue over such valuable pieces of real estate as New Caledonia, the major source of the world's vanadium and other minerals, or the Marquesas, used by France as a nuclear testing-ground.

But uneven development also entailed the opposite: the 'development of under-development' in peripheral zones whose boundaries were often congruent with some kind of older ethnic boundary.

The concept of 'internal colonization' has been coined to express the political aspect of these regional inequalities. It was a respectable enough concept in nineteenth-century Marxism, but has been more recently criticized by some contemporary Marxists as giving 'unwonted' prominence to 'ideological and political inequalities . . . thereby depriving the economic level of any autonomy whatsoever' and leading to the erroneous conclusion that 'there is no possibility of the white working class or any fraction of it ever entering into an alliance with African workers in the struggle to overthrow the capitalist state'.[105] As Parkin has remarked, if such a conclusion is reached, 'this would . . . illustrate its soundness rather than its deficiency'. Yet the theory has been found useful by Black Power militants in the USA and by academic writers such as Hechter in analysing the overlap of class exploitation and ethnic/national discrimination and oppression in certain geographical zones. 'The preferred response to the fact of racial or communal strife, in this kind of Marxism', Parkin comments, 'is to ignore it.' It results in analyses of Nazism solely in terms of 'political economy' which are quite incapable of explaining the Holocaust.[106]

In Britain, the major zones of underdevelopment were the 'Celtic Fringe': Scotland, Wales and Ireland, zones of historic colonial conquest and domination still officially designated as Depressed Areas until the Second World War.[107] In Uganda, the contest between Buganda, the most developed part of the country, and the poorer Nilotic North, was to be typically complicated by the irruption onto the scene of a force hitherto kept out of history: the peoples of the northernmost and most backward zone of all, from whence came Idi Amin.

In all these struggles, rival economic and political groupings appealed to the very same doctrines of national self-determination made sacred during more than a century of liberalism and now an accepted part of socialism. Regional autonomy was the compromise solution painfully conceded, in Spain only after centuries of struggle between the central State and the provincial nationalities on the periphery. In the Africa of the 1960s, regional autonomy was an unlikely option, for the State was far too fragile. Recognizing any of the constituent ethnic groups as nationalities threatened governments whose authority was new and legitimacy weak. The doctrine that prevailed was the opposite: the sacrosanct nature of the former colonial boundaries. The basic principle of the Organization of African Unity, after anti-colonialism, is the immobilist doctrine that colonial boundaries are not to be tampered with.

Despite the ghastly brutalities practised by Idi Amin upon the people of Uganda, his government continued to be recognized by the OAU and he even became President of that organization. Only when he invaded Tanzania was he brought down. Similarly, Pol Pot's genocidal regime was tolerated – and still receives overwhelming international recognition from even the most virulently anti-communist governments – because Vietnam, in invading Kampuchea, broke the fundamental rules: that frontiers are sacred and what goes on inside them are internal affairs. In the name of the same doctrine, West Irian and Timor were denied independence and deemed to be part of Indonesia, a Dutch colonial creation, Timor being visited with genocide. The only legitimate identity, in these new societies, is that of citizen of the State – 'Nigerian' or 'Kenyan'. As Eric Williams declared at Independence,

> There can be no Mother India for those whose ancestors came from India. . . . There can be no Mother Africa for those of African origin. . . . There can be no Mother England and no dual loyalties. . . . The nation, like an individual, can only have one Mother. The only Mother we recognize is Mother Trinidad and Tobago.

Majority peoples can even maintain their *de facto* dominance and opposition from their smaller rivals by labelling the claim to any other kind of ethnic identity as 'tribalism'. District boundaries may be exactly the same as the 'tribal' boundaries of the colonial period, but now they must not be called 'tribal', but 'district'. Groups which claim cultural, let alone political autonomy in any degree are denounced for their regressive atavism, 'regionalism', 'secessionism', 'provincialism', 'traditionalism', and innumerable other perjorative labels. In India, the autonomy of even small ethnic groups such as the Nagas of Assam, the loss of whose numbers would scarcely be very significant for the economy of a great country of nearly 700 million, is, however, violently resisted, since to allow *them* to secede might spark off demands for national autonomy on the part of other so-called 'linguistic provinces' numbered in hundreds of millions. In Tamilnad, a powerful separatist movement, the DMK, already exists. Whether the ethnic minorities are recognized or not, they are still there. When the word 'tribe' was banned in Somalia, people started using the term 'ex-tribe', until this, too, was banned.[108]

Some suppressed nationalities, like the 15 million Kurds in Iran, Iraq, Turkey and Syria, are very large minorities indeed. Claims to national autonomy, however, involve far smaller groups, for whom the knowledge that Suriname (population 448,000), Fiji (596,000), or Lesotho (1,213,960), and even islands like Kiribati (70,000), Dominica (80,000) or Nauru (8000) are formally independent and members of UN, is carried into the most remote corners of the globe, instantly, by TV and radio. Resort to terrorism, therefore, is by no means necessarily simply a response to chauvinist terror of the State, or imitation of successful armed revolution in Cuba or Vietnam. As often, it reflects the impotence of minuscule movements which, by hijacking a plane or kidnapping a prominent politician, win instant prime time publicity for their cause. The greatest problem for these movements is not always that they will be crushed by military and police repression; it is that they will be ignored, or laughed to death, for the very idea that even large, developed societies like Scotland or Quebec could be economically self-sustaining and politically viable is often greeted with scorn and disbelief. Terrorism is a violent challenge to such complacency, without which the minority will be ignored.

The nightmare of the unifiers is based on the realization that there is no logical lower limit on the size or number of groups which can legitimately claim to possess a common culture or subculture. The possibility of infinite regress opens up, for any sizeable group can always be further decomposed into regional subcultures, each with its distinctive territory, dialect, history, and so forth, and into further sub-divisions within the region. They are often communities far larger than many nation-states. If they have achieved independence, the argument runs, why not us? When Uganda became independent of Britain, the Kinzo and Amba of Uganda – less than 150,000 people – came together to fight, from 1962 to 1967, for a new state of Ruwenzururu, which would finally free them both from the domination of whoever ruled Uganda and from a far older foreign domination, that of the Toro.

Nationalist movements have multiplied by fission in recent decades. But their numbers have also increased because 'extinct' nations have been re-born. One of the most horrific cases of genocide known to history is the extermination of the Tasmanian aborigines. Everyone knows that they were wiped out in military battues across the island, and that Truganini, the 'last of the Tasmanians', was – despite her requests – disinterred in 1876 and her body sacrificed to science.[109] But what 'everybody knows' is wrong, for today there is a militant movement among the thousands who proudly trace their mixed, but nevertheless partly Tasmanian descent to their slaughtered forebears.

National revival, however, is often far larger in scale and therefore in political effect. Nor is it confined to the new countries of the Third World. The military conquest of Wales was accomplished centuries ago by Edward I. Wales was joined to England over four hundred years ago, and today, there are less than a million Welsh speakers. Yet there is a powerful Welsh nationalist movement. The effective revival of Celtic nationalism began with the Irish Revolution, victorious in 1921, if incomplete. Today, nationalism in Scotland has become strong enough to force the British government to hold a referendum, and in Quebec to bring a party committed to independence to power. In North America, 'Red Power', dramatized at Wounded Knee, has broken down divisions of ancient culture and modern reservations. The new movements among the 30 million Indians of South America, rooted in living communities, are infused with a similar pan-

Indian consciousness.

Psychologistic theory often assumes that national and ethnic conflicts are simply epiphenomenal manifestations of a natural human propensity to dislike people different from ourselves. Culturalists, likewise, take differences between cultures to be the primordial bases of political boundaries, ignoring the fact that there are always cultural differences within groups as well as between them which do not necessarily become socially emphasized, and that people of markedly different culture have been able to co-exist – even when they had little positive love for each other – so long as there was little material reason to convert prejudice into actual conflict. The problem, for social science, therefore, becomes that of defining the conditions under which that translation gets made or does not get made.

The basic requirement is inequality. Both the survival and revival of culture are grounded in uneven development. Today, the names of the villages in the rich valleys on the borders of Wales are English; those of the hill villages, fit only for sheep-farming, are Welsh. The legacy of the past is not preserved only in history-books. It has a tangible presence in the shape of rural underdevelopment and of modern industry in zones – Wales, Scotland, and Northern Ireland – of exceptionally high levels of unemployment.

Economic inequalities are not the only ones and they themselves are often consequences of prior social stigmatization and the denigration of whole cultures. (The Vice-Chancellor of a British university told me how he was forbidden, at school in the 1930s, to speak Welsh even in the play-ground.) Individuals may respond by 'passing': by denying their cultural identity; economically, by a purely individual upwards social mobility. The majority are more likely to have to rely on each other, on a collective solidarity which under conditions of repression and hopelessness, expresses itself in withdrawal from national life. Such is the stereotype of Indian passivity and resignation, which are, in reality, neither conservative commitment to entrepreneurial tradition nor a lack of the entrepreneurial spirit, but *refusal*: refusal to become plantation-workers, to learn Spanish, to promote oneself at the expense of one's fellows or at the expense of losing one's cultural identity and memberships.[110]

When hope – and organization – become possible, refusal becomes resistance, resistance protest, and protest eventually turns into positive demands for alternatives which involve selectivity both *vis-à-vis* the indigenous culture and the White. Neither 'revivalism' nor the evolutionist project of becoming White men, it involves both the exploration, recovery, and development of elements of indigenous culture, and the demand for access to valued, and therefore withheld aspects of White culture. It is not a search for purely economic opportunity, but far wider: a struggle for the reassertion of the wholeness of the human personality and for the reinvigoration of community life at every level, and a cultural reassertion, too, of the value of long-despised forms of knowledge, from traditional medicine (actually always innovative) to modes of experiencing the world and conceptions of the relationship of humankind to Nature which are often far richer than those either of the West or of a Second World hell-bent on socialist accumulation, meritocratic mobility, and cultural modernization.

Nationalism, as we have seen, has no *necessary* social content. It is, as Nairn remarks, 'Janus'-faced: 'by nature ambivalent'.[111] Historically, it has been compatible first with liberalism, later with socialism. But in the absence of an effective *inter*nationalist ethic, it degenerates all too rapidly into chauvinism, from a pride in Self to a contempt for the Other, the result, in the extreme, the genocidal brutality of Kampuchea or the endless expansionism of Israel. Even the socialist ideal proves quite incapable of preventing the transformation of nationalism into chauvinism insofar as it remains an ideal which is not grounded in an institutional praxis of internationalism.

The nationalist mystique, on the other hand, *is* grounded in an institutional praxis, that of mobilization for development: 'part', as Nairn puts it, of the 'great compensatory drive to catch up'.[112] All nationalisms are mystifications in that they postulate the immanent and absolute priority of the interests of the whole, usually defined by those who dominate society, over any merely sectional interest. During the phase of anti-imperialist struggle, it tells people that they are all, say, Tunisians and that if they come to govern themselves, the nation will flourish. How the governing is to be done, and which Tunisians will govern which others, is left unclear. After Independence, when development becomes the main priority, those crucial interest-groups – classes – are dismissed as the main threat to the success of the nation. The image of society is one of vertical solidarity.

The states which emerged during the epoch of a world system dominated by multinational corporations and Superpower rivalries had acquired experience of mobilizing the masses during the Independence struggles. After Independence, they try to continue that mobilization, for the possibility of developing capitalism along classic *laissez-faire* lines is a pipe-dream, since its major prerequisite – capital – is missing. Not much capital gets generated in the first place, and much of what there is, gets exported. What does exist, in abundance, is labour. For these very late-comers, then, the only possible development-strategy is a labour-intensive one.

The outcome is the emergence of highly-centralized state systems, either one-party states or military ones. Mexico's aptly-named Partido Institucional Revolucionario (the Party, one might say, of the 'Institutionalized Revolution'), still in power after forty-five years, was a notable pioneer of the monocentric system in which all major interest-groups – women, youth, workers, peasants – are articulated to the Party. It is not, however, an authoritarian system, since elections take place and even rival parties are tolerated.

In Mexican political rhetoric, the Party is the legatee of the Revolution of 1910 and the guarantee that what was won during that Revolution will be defended. Populist parties often appeal to a more radical version of this doctrine: not just the defence of the interests of the *people* as a whole, but especially of the less-privileged majority of the people.

Populism and Authoritarianism

Nineteenth-century Russian populism was an ideology of intellectuals *about* the peasantry. In North America, it was a movement of farmers, miners, and, sometimes, urban labour; in inter-war Europe, a real peasants' movement. The appeal of populism, therefore, is not to any particular class, but to the 'small man' in all classes: at times, the smallholders, at other times and in other places, the city poor. Its most skilful proponents turned its vagueness into an asset, its open-endedness into a generalized ideology. The most successful populist in history, elected as President of Ecuador no less than five times between 1933 and 1968 and as regularly removed by the military, was José María Velasco Ibarra.[113] Though he spoke with particular affection of his beloved urban *chusma* (city mob), he purported to embody *all* interests. The theme of the common interests of the people became, with him, became, for him, an occasion for windy rhetoric:

> In this revolution all Ecuadoreans are united; in this revolution conservatives join with reds; the monk with the soldier; men and women; academics and workers.[114]

He would lead them, *all*, on a voyage across 'the infinite sea of all that is noble, to fundamental justice and ultimate humanity'.

More radical versions of populism are explicitly hostile to class differentiation as a strategy for development. Purely agricultural development programmes, President Nyerere declared at the time of Independence, were socially repugnant:

> We in Tanzania reject the creation of a rural class system even if it could be proved that it gives the largest overall production increase.

When the 'villageization' programme was launched ten years later, the negative side of this opposition to class was revealed, for in this, the oldest populist regime in Africa, no serious analysis of the very real degree not only of colonial and post-colonial, but of pre-colonial class differentiation had been made. The concept of *Ujamaa* was no substitute.[115]

Vagueness on the subject of class is no accident; it is intrinsic and necessary to populism. But the main emphasis is still on the poor, not the rich. It underlay the success of Evita Perón, who appealed to the *descamisados* – the shirtless ones – as the twentieth-century equivalent of the *sansculottes* of the French Revolution, who not only lacked shirts on their backs, but had never been listened to by anyone before: the insulted and the injured, the wretched of the earth, the 'little people' (*menu peuple*) who had been left out of history, but who were now about to inherit their birthright.[116] Admired by the poor not only for her social work, but also for the rooms full of shoes that expressed the popular aspirations always projected on those who rise from obscurity, but usually reserved for stars of sport, theatre, or film, her eventual canonization in a musical was therefore utterly appropriate.[117]

The relationship between the people and their leader thus becomes a quasi-mystical bond, one of direct empathic understanding of their interests on the part of the paternal leader, in whose heart and in that of the Party the poor are said to have a special place. The usual outcome was the gradual forfeiture of popular support and legitimacy as the populist leader failed to deliver on his promises. But in a few cases, such as Perón in Argentina, or Goulart in Brazil, they did actually embark upon measures of social justice which entailed a degree of redistribution of wealth from the rich to the poor which induced panic among the privileged. Then the army had to be called in, or stepped in, to stop the rot before the rights of property were more fundamentally infringed.

For socialists and communists, by contrast, class was the decisive structural unit. For all their efforts to build poly-class alliances out of the different segments of exploited classes, old and new, in town and country-side, they were unable to compete with the populists in countries where class consciousness was only incipient. Yet the populist regimes were themselves replaced by authoritarian, monocentric – mostly military – regimes. Those who showed leftish inclinations, like Rodríguez Lara in Ecuador or Velasco in Peru, were soon overthrown by right-wing generals, or died in mysterious airplane accidents, like Panama's Torrijos or the social-democratic civilian President Roldós of Ecuador.

But in the Third World, nationalism has become much more than merely a way of maintaining the boundaries of new nation-states, or monopolizing access to resources. It also concerns the creation of resources. The conversion of a whole country into a kind of private estate or deer-park in which the inhabitants can be freely exploited and hunted down by the proprietors of the State if they resist is still practised: the style of a Somoza, a Trujillo, a Stroessner, or a Duvalier. But they are a dying breed. So are those regimes which are not seriously interested in development at all, like the rulers of Kuwait or Saudi Arabia, for whom modernization means introducing levels of luxury living for the élite which far outstrip the West, with a little trickle-down for the masses denied the most elementary political rights. Their concern is not with development, but with preparing for the day when they have to flee to California or Zurich. But most regimes are dedicated, verbally at least, to *developing* their countries. The new military regimes which have come to power in Latin America are therefore a totally different species from the oligarchies and *caudillos* of the nineteenth century.[118] They are technocrats in uniform, a new species of military trained in modern business management, impatient to modernize their countries and thereby enhance their power, not by the old-fashioned methods of wars of expansion, but by the planned modernization of their economies as fast as possible, along capitalist lines. Hence they rely on the most advanced form of capitalist organization, the multinational corporation, and on modern methods of the 'management' of society as a whole.

Politically, both fascism and the new military dictatorships resort to unrestricted torture and massacre of their opponents – which is why most people call them 'fascists'. Yet, as Borón has put it, classical fascism 'was born at Sarajevo and died at Stalingrad'.[119] The fascisms of the 1930s were *popular* movements (the Nazis got 17,200,000 votes, 44 per cent of the total, in 1933), dedicated to the revival of *national* industry, whereas the new military relies on the foreign multinationals as their central instrument of economic policy. The Nazis militarized the entire society in order to lead it to war. The new military, *per contra*, use the armed forces primarily against their own civilian populations. Both share a contempt and hatred for democracy and the liberal institutions of parliaments, parties, and trade unions; yet the new military prefer the legitimacy conferred by a controlled party-system, for they are parties of order, not regimes bent on war.

The populist movements they displaced were compatible with nationalism in a way that neither socialism nor capitalism are, since they promised benefits to *all*, whereas capitalism openly favours a few, and socialism gives priority to those who produce the wealth, and promises, ultimately, to abolish classes altogether. The heroic age of Third World populism was the 1960s, when an earlier wave of South American populisms overlapped with a second wave in the newer independent countries of Africa and Asia. Since then, in all but a few countries, the reality has been the abandonment of even the rhetoric of 'serving the people' and its replacement by an all-out, nakedly capitalist, inegalitarian and usually authoritarian development strategy.

v One World or Three?

Decolonization

The first major wave of decolonization – in the Americas – was the consequence of the collapse of *anciens régimes* in Europe under the impact of the French Revolution. Its dominant ideology, inevitably, was the new, triumphant liberalism. But it did not triumph everywhere, and where it did, was quite compatible with a later wave of expansion on the part of the leading industrial powers. Progress meant (and justified) the elimination of barbarism. By 1884–5, they had parcelled up Africa, the last uncolonized continent, between them. But they had also completed the process, begun five centuries earlier, of creating a single world-wide social system.

Both direct resistance and attempts to exploit inter-imperialist rivalries had failed. The French might make common cause with Tippoo Sultan against the British in India – and even supply him with a mechanical tiger which went through the motions of eating an East India Company officer, from whom terrible groans emerged – but both were defeated, in the end, by the superior might of the world's first industrialized country.

Yet the epoch of high imperialism lasted a remarkably short time. No sooner had primary resistance been broken than a new wave of revolt against imperialist domination broke out in China, Persia, Turkey, Mexico, South Africa, Cuba and the Philippines. Even as late as the 1930s, many of these movements, like the great Indian Mutiny nearly a century earlier, still looked to a restoration of the past. The Saya San Rebellion in Burma, in which 9000 were captured and 350 hanged, despite the magical amulets they wore, drew upon the millenarian tradition of folk Buddhism for its ideology. Saya San claimed to be the *Setkya-min* avenging king of Burmese legend, the *Buddha Yaza*, the 'divinely sent creator of a Buddhist utopia'.[1] He went to the scaffold defiantly: 'In all my future existences', he swore, 'may I always conquer the British.'

The generation that followed remembered the dead and the cause they had died for. In the 1930s, in a country whose independence struggle had been strangled by the USA, a Filipino schoolboy, asked to write an essay on 'The Cow', wrote: 'A Cow is an animal with one leg at each corner. It has horns and gives milk, but as for me, give me independence.'[2] By that time, primary resistance and backward-looking revolt had given way to new kinds of anti-colonial movements which looked forward to the construction of new kinds of society after independence, the models for which were no longer, as they had been in the nineteenth century, the liberal democracy of the West, but more often some kind of socialism. The Western sequence, in which liberalism had been followed by the emergence of social democracy, was not duplicated in the colonial world.[3] There, Western-style democracy hardly took root, for after 1917 a new, more revolutionary social alternative was available. The overthrow of capitalism in a major but 'backward' European country injected a quite new, social element into what had hitherto been a purely nationalist resistance to foreign rule. To many radical young people, the scenario for the future was not necessarily simply to be a re-run of what had happened in the heartlands of capitalism – the triumph of the bourgeoisie.

Yet socialists, though often influential, never succeeded in winning the leadership of anti-imperialist movements before the Second World War, in part because they addressed themselves to a working class which doctrine identified as *the* revolutionary force, but which often scarcely existed. The leadership of even the revolutionary anti-imperialist movements remained in the hands of modernizers who saw the future of their countries as one of capitalist development. The linking of nationalism with socialism was only successfully to be achieved during the Second World War, with the Soviet defeat of Nazi invasion in 1945 and the communist-led liberation of China four years later.

Many colonies achieved independence without traumatic struggles. The independence which was granted to Ceylon, India, Syria, Lebanon, the Philippines in the years immediately after the Second World War was to be the prototype for the last major wave of decolonization in British and French Africa during the 1960s.

Most of these countries soon came to realize that they were now involved in a new, neo-colonial relationship with the West, one in which political independence was combined with continuing economic dependence and with participation in a world-wide anti-communist front. For those un-prepared to accept that position, the only major alternative, inevitably, was capitalism's major rival: Soviet-style communism. But few were prepared to see it implanted in their countries. In those countries where mass revolu-tionary communist parties did emerge, notably China, those parties came to power not only because of the leadership they had given on social issues, but because they had played a leading role in the struggle against foreign invaders. Inevitably, they soon developed their own, national forms of communism.

Non-communist revolutionary nationalist movements in countries like Indonesia were even more resistant to Soviet influence. They had not struggled to free themselves from capitalist imperialism simply in order to fall under the domination of a new Superpower. Within less than a decade from the end of the War, this mood was to translate itself into a new concept: the notion of a *Third* World – well-expressed in the old Trotskyist slogan, 'Neither Moscow nor Washington' – and in a new political praxis: 'non-alignment'. Co-existence with communism abroad, however, was perfectly compatible with the massacre of hundreds of thousands of communists at home.

The leadership came from Nehru in India, independent only since 1947; Indonesia, where armed revolution had triumphed in 1949; from Nasser in the United Arab Republic, whose confrontation with the West culminated in the Anglo-French invasion at Suez in 1956 and in the acceptance of aid from the Soviet Union; from Ghana, where Nkrumah had come out of gaol to lead his country to independence in 1957 and to inspire anti-colonial movements across Africa; and from Tito in Yugoslavia, the first Eastern European country to break with the USSR. Practically all of the leading members of the new groupings – which insisted that they did not constitute a 'bloc' – had only recently been colonies. Their fierce assertion of the right to independence excited little enthusiasm in Latin American countries, which had been politically independent for over a century, however qualified that independence was by the economic and political domination of the major capitalist states, firstly Britain, later the USA, including regular military intervention in the countries closest to the US borders: Mexico, Central America and the Caribbean. Nor, for Latin America, was the integration of the nation-state a major problem.

The prime interest of the newer states was the liberation of the remaining colonies, and, internally, the decolonization of their own societies and cultures. In the 1930s, Mariátegui had called for the 'Peruvianization' of Peru; now, African leaderships called for the 're-Africanization' of Africa.

There now began a whole series of explorations of common interests, in Afro-Asian Conferences, meetings of Heads of State, etc., which were to culminate in the Conference of twenty-nine African and Asian countries in Bandung in 1955.[4]

Anti-colonialism necessarily brought them into confrontation with the West. But *vis-à-vis* the Second World, the 'first great failure' of the new grouping was their 'mealy-mouthed evasion' and 'sickening . . . timidity' when faced with the Soviet invasion of Hungary, in contrast to their vigorous denunciation of the invasion of Egypt.[5] This was not due to pro-Sovietism so much as to the preoccupation of the new nation-states with their own major initial problem, that of holding the country together. What countries like India feared was that UN intervention in Hungary would, in Nehru's words, 'reduce Hungary to less than a sovereign state . . . [and] . . . set a bad precedent', i.e. for Kashmir, where UN intervention might well mean the loss of India's control over that territory.

To the new states, in any case, the actions of the Soviet Union in Europe, whatever they thought about them, were no immediate threat to *them*. The principal external danger they faced was from *revanchiste* attempts by ex-colonial Powers, smarting under the loss of Empire, to restore control in ways that might stop short of actually re-establishing colonial rule, but certainly involved the manipulation of internal divisions and, in the extreme, support for secession movements, as in Katanga.

One of the most widespread hyper-intentional current myths among the more conspiratorially-minded proponents of underdevelopment theory is the belief that independence was simply a controlled transfer of power to reliable local bourgeoisies on the part of the former colonial Powers and the classes they represented. It was by no means so controlled. Even in countries where the transition to independence occurred without armed struggle, leaders like Nkrumah, far from being seen as reliable, were regarded as dangerous Reds. Like Kenyatta, Nkrumah emerged from gaol to form a government and soon after to become the President of an independent country. These were by no means the ideal sound successors colonialists would have preferred. But their preferences were not decisive. Rather, these leaders were the choice of the people. Nor was power simply handed over. It was wrested from the hands of those who tried to cling on to it, bitterly, particularly in settler territories: in Algeria alone, the struggle to dislodge the *colons* cost the lives of a million people. That war was only one in a protracted series of last-ditch efforts to maintain imperial rule, from Indonesia at the end of the Second World War through to Vietnam and Algeria. Those two wars, however, signalled the end of the line. France's ignominious defeat at Dien Bien Phu in 1954 did not mean the end of French intransigence and repression elsewhere. Indeed, France managed to crush the urban guerrilla movement in Algiers through the unbridled use of torture. But the costs, material and moral, were becoming intolerable at home. By the 1960s, both France and Britain realized that fundamental concessions had to be made. Decolonization was the order of the day.

Holland had been the first imperialist country to throw in the sponge, by granting Indonesia her independence after years of vicious, large-scale warfare. Britain and France fought on, at first with some success, in Malaya and in Kenya, where 'Mau Mau' was defeated, but with the increasing realization that what they were engaged in was little more than the Canute-like project, without any visible end in sight, of sweeping back the sea. Under Macmillan and de Gaulle, in the early 1960s, the die was cast. In 1960, seventeen new countries appeared on the world scene. The power vacuum that resulted was, however, swiftly filled by the greatest Super-power in history, the USA, which now assumed a global role as the world's policeman. Increasing military intervention and destabilization, from the

Planned
Neo-Col?

Dominican Republic to Vietnam, and the mobilization of their dependent allies in a crusade against communism, were, however, only one side of the coin, for military-political involvement was underpinned by a new set of economic arrangements: control over world-prices, aid, and investment by multinational corporations. Indirect neo-colonial control, first pioneered in Britain and then by the USA in Latin America during the nineteenth century, now became the new global strategy.

The notion that the ruling élites in the new states were all conscious agents of international capitalism from the beginning is a view which deprives them of any independent interests or autonomous action. They were scarcely a bourgeoisie proper, most of the leadership being at best petty-bourgeois, usually low-level, government functionaries. They were, rather, a 'new class', a political élite who used their control of the State to turn themselves into a propertied class. Frank has called them a 'lumpen'-bourgeoisie, a class incapable themselves of undertaking the bourgeois project of creating a capitalist society. Fanon called them a 'caste', 'good for nothing' except their 'historic mission' as intermediaries – as junior partners of foreign capital – a role they readily accepted since it brought them personal riches and a measure of dependent development to their countries.[6]

Many of them had no clear project at all, in the first place. Only those with the strongest commitment to creating a more equitable kind of society, and who also had a very clear idea of how to go about it, would have been able to withstand the intolerable pressures which the small, poor, agrarian societies they inherited faced. There were very few such people or parties. Many of those who by no means shared his socialist convictions would have agreed with Julius Nyerere's later frank admission that 'if you had asked me what I intended to do after independence I would have given you only the vaguest idea of a programme'.[7]

Most, faced with circumstances over which they had no control – especially the prices they received for their exports – and which left them only minimal room for manoeuvre, simply gave in to those pressures which were the most immediate, those from the capitalist world whose markets were vital to them. They positively welcomed the prospect of finding the capital needed for development by inviting in the multinational corporations. The possibility of development, of any kind, over-rode any worries about what kind of development it would be.

The new governments had been swept to power on a wave of nationalist enthusiasms which was often channelled into one main mass party. In others, like Ghana or Kenya, sizeable smaller parties existed, mostly with an ethnic/regional base. Colonial governments had made it very difficult for class-based parties or movements to survive, even if the peasantry in the Reserves of Kenya and the landless proletarians ('squatters') on the settler estates of the White Highlands had provided most of the fighters in the Mau

Mau forces. The urban proletariat usually generated trade unions rather than parties.

After the honeymoon period following Independence, the new governments faced serious economic and political problems that their opponents were not slow to exploit. They therefore set out to break that opposition, though not necessarily by force. In many countries, a mix of incorporation and 'legal' authoritarianism was used. Thus in socialist Tanzania, the trade union federation, the TFL, which had supported the main party, TANU, against its smaller pre-Independence rival, the UTP, was brought under close party-government control even before actual Independence in 1962. Two years later, it was replaced altogether by a new federation, NUTA, 'firmly controlled by the Minister of Labour, who was designated by the President as the Union's first general secretary. This represented marriage under duress.'[8] The trade union movement had become merely one wing of single-party government in an *étatiste* society: 'the modern form', Fanon called it, 'of the dictatorship of the bourgeoisie'.

The elimination of opposition took different forms in different countries, but everywhere the trend was in the same direction. In countries like Kenya, where the preservation of a Westminster type constitution and a parliamentary regime had been one of the conditions for the transfer of power by Britain, the elimination of opposition was a complicated process. In Kenya, the main opposition was led by Oginga Odinga, backed by the large Luo ethnic group of western Kenya, who soon found themselves outnumbered and outmanoeuvred in parliament, and their party, the KPU, together with the Coast-based KADU, was banned in 1969. Most of the defeated were later allowed to join KANU, the now-dominant single-party, as even Odinga himself (who had been detained) eventually did, only to be expelled in 1982. But more and more frequently, there was simply a *coup*, either on the part of a section of the armed forces or in which parties called in the army to crush their opponents. By the late 1960s, most of Africa had fallen under one form or another of monocentric regimes, either 'no-party', military regimes, or single-party ones.[9] Where the parliamentary trappings were preserved, or where a tiny opposition was tolerated, it became what Macpherson has called a 'quasi-party system'.

Westminster constitutions, in countries which had been ruled by colonial officials since their creation, and which, in many if not most cases, had had no more than one or two years of experience of operating a system in which opposition was legal and constitutional, were doomed to wither on the vine. The social bases which might have breathed life into a multi-party system were themselves silenced.

The elimination of opposition inside and outside parliament was generally justified on the grounds that national unity was threatened by tribalism or separatism. It is, of course, true that many opposition parties were parties which spoke for ethnic minorities (sometimes large ones), though class-based opposition was similarly denounced as divisive, even in a socialist State like Tanzania. The desire to create a united country was real enough, but it was all too easily exploited by the new classes which were able to use their numerical strength as leaders of the larger ethnic groups while using the slogan of anti-tribalism and the power of the State they now controlled to squeeze out their rivals.

In these struggles, both government and opposition parties looked abroad for support. Foreign Powers, including the Superpowers, were only too happy to take on board as allies these ready-made mass parties. In Kenya in the 1960s, the Luo opposition, reacting against a nakedly pro-capitalist government, took on a leftish tinge; in Zimbabwe, two decades later, it was the government which pre-empted the radical, anti-imperialist position, denouncing the opposition as pro-South African. Under such conditions, the adoption of what looked like class politics couched in terms of Western ideologies and social programmes became a rhetorical code through which ethnic domination and ethnic resistance were expressed. But class interests and party affiliations do not fit neatly with ethnic divisions. Thus ZAPU is not just a party of the Ndebele and ZANU the party of the Shona. It is an opposition party which attracts those whose main concern is not their ethnic affiliation but the fact that they never obtained land before or after Independence; those who worked on White farms, where increasing rationalization has meant the loss of their jobs; as well as those who never experienced the politicizing effects of the guerrilla war for whom older ethnic categories do remain more salient. Even the latter, however, appeal to new conceptions of Shona identity, or as speakers of Shona languages, that have no counterpart in any of the political entities of the past.

In the 1960s, the populist governments had also talked a good deal about 'socialism', wishing to distance themselves from the colonial Powers, which were capitalist Powers, and to emphasize their identification with the masses. Though it was difficult to see it at the time, in retrospect it now seems that there was perhaps an inverse relationship between the amount of socialism talked and the amount practised. Even Kenyatta's Kenya, soon to become a 'sub-imperialist' bastion of Western investment, published a famous red-covered document in 1965 – entitled *African Socialism and its Application to Planning in Kenya*. The word 'socialism', though, always had a qualifying adjective attached to it: 'African' or 'Arab' socialism or 'people's' socialism, labels which disguised the reality of supremely nationalist regimes to which the class struggle was as threatening as ethnic rivalries.[10] They were purely verbal forms of socialism, and never went beyond words.

Nearly all the new countries, too, drew up national Development Plans. Most of these were 'little more than public relations exercises for foreigners', who, it was hoped, would fund one or another of the projects.'[11] Most Plans, in fact, were simply lists of particular projects, of diverse kinds and very varied in their scale and in their implications for the use of resources. Such 'Plans' were then hawked around various Western governments in the hope that they would fund this or that project. Most never were funded. These procedures, however, did give funding agencies considerable and demeaning influence over the internal affairs of poor foreign countries, for they naturally insisted on 'pre-investment surveys' before parting with their money and monitored the progress of their chosen projects from time to time. Since there was no way the governments of poor countries could avoid such humiliating conditions and controls any more than they could control world prices, and since the technocrats and the advisers who formulated the Plans (mainly foreign economists) did little to involve the middle and lower-level administrators who would have to carry them out, let alone the people whose interests they believed they could best evaluate, many even of the projects that were funded never got off the ground.

It was axiomatic, too, that no fundamental structural changes in the distribution of political power or economic resources would be involved, and that those in power would have to endorse whatever was proposed. The Plans, that is, were inherently conservative. Given this formidable set of constraints, deceptions and self-deceptions, it was scarcely surprising that most Plans lacked coherence and omitted to mention the key problems that were to make it impossible to translate aspirations and intentions into actuality. The reasons for these failures were basically political, because in all but a handful of oil-producing countries the Plans depended upon foreign aid, and because, internally, for all their monopoly of power and the highly-centralized machinery of the single party (often modelled on the 'democratic-centralist' parties of the Second World), these new parties and administrative machines were hollow shells, partly because they were hastily and poorly organized, but more fundamentally because they lacked mass support, attracting instead a mass of opportunists of all kinds. In a country like Kenya, the ruling class had become so unpopular by 1983 that when a military *coup* was attempted, the poor of Nairobi rushed out into the streets, cheering.

Everywhere, whatever their relationship to ethnic movements, those who were seriously committed to democracy and to socialism were defeated, replaced by one kind or another of monocentric regime, including such bizarre despotisms as that of Emperor Bokassa of the Central African Republic. By the 1970s, Tanzania apart, radical-populist governments and parties had been virtually eliminated in Africa. Most of them did not fall; they were pushed, and much of the muscle used was applied by foreigners. The radical young hero of Zaïre's independence struggle, Patrice

Lumumba, was beaten and murdered, and his body stuffed into a refrigerator. The man who replaced him, Colonel Mobutu, is still President. Foreign mercenary soldiers and hired hitmen were also freely used to kill leading individuals and to spread terror by massacring whole villages. And everywhere the CIA – with 16,500 personnel and a budget of $750 million in the mid-1970s – was energetically engaged in 'destabilization', especially in countries where Soviet or Chinese influence was suspected.[12] $550 million of this was earmarked for 'Clandestine Services', which included 'Health Alteration' programmes, such as murdering or helping to murder individuals like Lumumba and Trujillo, and attempting to murder Fidel Castro, and promoting the massacre of whole populations and the destabilization of whole countries. Nearly 40,000 Latin American students have been trained in counter-insurgency techniques at the School of the Americas in the Panama Canal Zone, among its alumni a galaxy of subsequent dictators, of whom General Pinochet of Chile is the best-known. One million policemen from 41 countries and over 500 high-level military trained at the Inter-American Defense College on the Potomac also help to keep order. First World intervention, however, is much more varied and usually much less dramatic: European Social-Democracy, especially West German, supports its counterparts in Latin America; the CIO-AFL and international 'free' trade union organizations act as a Labour arm of the State Department.[13]

The task of all these organizations is made easier because they are able to exploit internal divisions in the Third World, for conflicts such as that between the Nilotic South and the arabicized North in the Sudan, between Iran and Iraq, or between Ethiopia and Eritrea are not creations of the CIA. They arise out of differences rooted in history and culture. Neither is the exploitation of those differences by governments inflamed by irrational chauvinism, or, more often, seeking to head off popular discontent by calculated appeals to historic enmities, something that is masterminded by the giant Powers. But today, in a global society, all such disputes cease to be private quarrels. US governments see revolutions, even in tiny countries like Nicaragua, El Salvador or Guatemala, as military threats to their southern defence perimeter and potential detonators of regional revolution.

But older spheres of influence, and many of these local historic animosities, have been increasingly subsumed within a global neo-colonial strategy in which the former imperial Powers now play only secondary roles. Recent anti-colonial revolutions have also been infused much more emphatically with a new social content because they have had to turn for assistance to the only countries that could and would provide it: the Second World.

Earlier, there had never been any great sympathy for communism even on the part of leaders often believed by the more paranoid Western politicians to be closet communists. Those who had visited Moscow, like Kenyatta and

Nkrumah, who were not Marxists, as well as those like George Padmore and C. L. R. James, who were, had been impressed, above all, by the way Russia had, to use the title of one of Padmore's books, 'transformed her colonial empire'. They were therefore attracted by the idea of reproducing the institutions which had been the organizational foundation of that transformation and the machinery of mobilization: the democratic-centralist Party and the State planning apparatus. They do not seem to have been particularly concerned that it had been an authoritarian development strategy which had achieved industrialization only at the cost of the lives of tens of millions of workers, peasants, and intellectuals and of the great majority of the leadership that had made the Revolution. Their eventual disillusion with the USSR, rather, was due to what they saw as the USSR's attempt to subordinate national liberation movements across the world to its own national interests and to impose Soviet models and strategies upon those movements.

After 1945, by which time the USSR had emerged as the second most powerful state in the world, Stalin's political caution, and the need to allocate all available capital to the rebuilding of the shattered cities of the USSR and to the communist bloc, precluded the provision of assistance to colonial liberation movements or the governments of newly-independent countries. By the 1960s, however, the end of Stalinism, and the expansion of the Soviet economy, made possible the beginning of a new era of 'forward' policy *vis-à-vis* the Third World. Military equipment, training and military advisers were made available to national liberation movements and friendly states, while the Aswan Dam became the symbol of the emergence of the USSR as a major source of capital for non-military development projects. Up to 1960, the bulk of China's foreign aid had come from the USSR. Vietnam's triumph over the greatest Power in world history was primarily due to the expenditure of Vietnamese blood, but they could not have fought without Soviet weapons. Without Soviet materials, too, Cuba's revolution would probably have been crushed.

In Angola, Mozambique and Guinea-Bissau, the most archaic colonial Power of all had rejected the new strategy of decolonization and even tried to solve its domestic problems and at the same time inject new life into these ultra-colonial possessions by encouraging a new wave of settlement by poor Portuguese immigrants. The result, inevitably, was bitter armed struggle, which ended in the victory of revolutionary movements which had depended heavily upon Soviet and Second World assistance. By the 1970s, then, a new set of underdeveloped countries, indebted and sympathetic to the Second World, had emerged within the Third, while Soviet aid, including military, was being extended on a large scale to such anti-communist countries as India.

Models of the Third World

The emergence of the Third World, world-system theorists have argued, goes back to the beginnings of capitalism in Europe and the beginnings of European expansion overseas. At that time, it was only a Third World in itself. A Third World for itself – a group of countries conscious of their common colonial history and of its legacy: underdevelopment – only emerged five centuries later, after the Second World War.

The Afro-Asian grouping of the 1950s began as a coming-together of countries that had reached different points in the decolonization process. Some had just achieved their independence; others were still struggling to win it. Yet others, like Cuba, had been politically independent, but had only just succeeded in establishing a true economic independence of the capitalist world, while countries like China had never formally lost their independence, though they had become semi-colonies. Chou en-Lai, who played a major role in the building up of the original Afro-Asian grouping, was not simply a representative of communism. He was the spokesman for the world's largest *underdeveloped* communist state. By then, the USSR, by contrast, was no longer eligible for membership of a grouping of underdeveloped countries, for it was not only a developed country, but a Superpower.

The unity of such a diverse set of countries, extremely varied in their cultural heritages, with very different historical experiences and marked differences in the patterns of their economies, whatever their common history of subjection to colonialism and their common underdevelopment both as colonies and as independent states, was inherently problematic. It was increased by the subscription of some to forms of Marxism, and by the unapologetic invitation, by many more, to multinational corporations to come in and develop their countries along capitalist lines. But the closest elective affinity between the political search for a 'third way' or 'third force' internationally and its counterpart in internal policy was the economic strategy of a mixed economy, in which private ownership would be under the firm control of the State. Its socio-political counterpart, populism, purported to reject both capitalism and communism in their classical Western forms.

 The coherence of such a group was necessarily dependent on the presence of a common enemy. It was a negative unity: politically, against colonialism; in economic terms, a solidarity between the 'proletarian nations'[14] in opposition to the developed ones.

The notion that the countries which were now coming into being were different in kind from both the First and the Second Worlds seized the imagination after the experience of global Cold War and a major conflict in Korea. The term 'Third World' did not even originate in the Third World at all but in post-war France. Some have therefore assumed that it reflects Gaullist thinking, since that movement saw itself as the major opponent of the powerful Communist Party at home, and sought to avoid French and European dependence on the United States by rallying Western Europe in the face of the new threat from a non-communized Eastern Europe.

The term, in fact, emerged in a very different political milieu, that of the non-communist Left, which had played an heroic and militant part in the Resistance and which now continued to espouse a militant socialism despite being overshadowed by the much larger Communist Party. One major focus for those for whom neither social democracy nor the Soviet Union were synonymous with socialism was the newspaper edited by Claude Bourdet, *L'Observateur*. They naturally saw parallels between their own search for a 'third way' between capitalism and Stalinist communism and the struggles of a new wave of militant anti-colonial movements which opposed imperialism but were by no means pro-communist.

The analogy was a peculiarly French one: the '*tiers monde*' was the analogue of the *tiers état* of pre-revolutionary France: the estate of the bourgeois, the petty bourgeois, the artisans, the peasants and workers who lacked the privileges of the first two estates, the clergy and the nobility. The first public use of the term came in an article of *L'Observateur* on 14 August 1952 by Alfred Sauvy, the demographer, entitled *Trois Mondes, Une Planète*. The Third World, he declared, '*ignoré, exploité, méprisé, comme le tiers état, veut lui aussi être quelque chose*'.[15]

The term was quickly taken up in academic circles, but soon became diffused outside those confines in an epoch when it looked as if the Second World War would be followed only too quickly by the Third, as the Cold War in Europe – symbolized by the eyeball-to-eyeball confrontation of the Berlin airlift – threatened to turn itself into the very hot kind of anti-communist war being fought in Third World countries like Korea and Malaya.

The search for a 'third way' in Europe, on the part of weak socialist movements overwhelmed by the hysteria of McCarthyism and by the construction of a new anti-communist alliance, NATO, was doomed to failure. It was to leave traces in the association of figures like Aneurin Bevan with those who now emerged as the leaders of a 'non-aligned' grouping of countries, most of which had only just won their independence. The term 'underdevelopment' first seems to have been used in an official UN document in 1951.[16] Since some Third World countries objected, either on the grounds that they *were* developing or even that they were already developed but in ways different from those of the West, various euphemisms were later substituted: 'less-developed' or 'developing', '*en vie de développement*', 'late-developing', etc., etc. It was not a question of whether they were or were not developing, but rather an exercise in what Gunnar Myrdal called 'diplomacy by terminology'. From that year onwards, UN documents began classifying countries into three categories. The first two were categories of political economy in that what were labelled as 'economically developed countries' (sometimes, more accurately, as 'developed market economies') were the 'free enterprise' countries. (Even though by this time the USSR, despite war-time devastation, had emerged as the second major industrial country in the world, it was excluded; Western Germany, while equally devastated, was included.) The second category, the 'centrally-planned economies', lumped together, on political grounds, the industrialized USSR and the still agrarian Eastern European countries. The rest, however, in the third category, were simply classified according to economic criteria, whatever the differences in their social systems or cultures, as 'primary producing countries'. The criteria used were, therefore, a mix both of the political and the economic, different criteria being invoked in different cases. Logically, there ought to have been four boxes: the developed capitalist world; the underdeveloped capitalist countries; the developed communist world; and the underdeveloped communist countries. Yet at this time there was only one industrialized communist country. The rest – Eastern Europe, China and North Vietnam – were so economically weak and backward, and apparently so dominated by the USSR, that they were assumed to constitute a solidarity bloc and simply lumped together with that country as the Second World.

From the very beginning, then, there were two different bases, albeit inconsistently used and rarely spelt out, for conceptualizing the components of the modern world-system; 'political economy', a two-dimensional concept, was, in fact, usually decomposed, some stressing political criteria, others the economic. The result was very different conceptions of the Third World.

The concept of the Third World also necessarily implies the existence of two prior worlds. (It is also stipulative in that it assumes there to be three and only three.) It is important, therefore, to spell out also what the characteristics of the first two worlds are; an operation, again, that is all too rarely performed. They are of course not only political and economic.

The First World emerged as, and remains, an economy based upon private property in the means of production and characterized by its necessary concomitants, the existence of a supply of exploitable wage-labour, and competition between firms seeking to maximize profit in a market economy. All of these institutions and structures are legitimized by assumptions so deep that they are scarcely ever inspected, let alone questioned: property by the theory of possessive individualism;[17] competition by the *laissez-faire* belief that the good of the majority is best ensured by institutionalizing the search for private gain; while politically, individualism means the equality of all citizens before the law and before the ballot-box, the separation of powers, and the existence of a legitimate opposition, including socialist and communist parties. The absence of social equality, which left poverty to be catered for by religiously-inspired charity and by public assistance based on a biological conception of basic needs and a punitive conception of deserts, has subsequently been replaced by newer conceptions of *rights* to social justice based on customary levels of minimal wants, as a matter of entitlement. In place of the older solidarities provided by religion, the Welfare State thus supplies a dimension missing in the older ideology of citizenship and countervails and damps down the worst effects of the theory and practice of possessive individualism.

The power of the State has also grown immensely, both in terms of its intervention in the economy and in terms of its involvement in all areas of social life.

The contrast with the Second World could scarcely be more striking. There, the economy is based upon collective, above all State, ownership of the means of production and upon the planning of production, rather than on private property and the market. Both economy and society are controlled by a ruling class whose power is based, not upon private property, but upon control of the State in the shape of the democratic centralist single party. Access to this élite is based upon meritocratic competition and upon the internalization of the official culture, including the ideology of the State, or, more precisely, of the class which controls the State apparatuses. With the passage of time, political domination has ceased to depend principally upon the exercise of terror, as it did during the Stalin era, but rests upon the control and manipulation of the media of communication and socialization, through which the hegemonic culture is diffused and public opinion shaped.

The nature of the Third World seemed so self-evident in the 1960s that in a book on *The Third World* I published in 1964, I saw no need to define it any more precisely than that it was the world made up of the ex-colonial, newly-independent, non-aligned countries. Nor did I trouble to define any more rigorously the characteristics of the First and Second Worlds.

Yet the problems of how to reconcile the conception of a *single* world-system with the conception of *three* distinct worlds was there from the beginning. Many writers continued, (and continue) however, to use both without confronting these problems. Their definitions of the three worlds, in consequence, are usually descriptive, often arbitrary, and at times so loose as to be casual. Horowitz, for example, described the Third World reasonably enough, as made up of the ex-colonial, non-aligned countries, 'thoroughly dedicated to becoming industrialized', but then went on to assert – in a quite cavalier manner – that they drew their technology from the

First World and their ideology from the Second.[18]

The central notion was the notion of *dependency*. Third World countries did not have a distinctive economic system (or mode of production) different in kind from that of the capitalist world; politically weaker, and with a lower level of development of productive forces, they are exploited by the latter as sources of cheap labour, of raw materials, and latterly of manufactured goods, while the West specializes in advanced technology.

But dependency is not a purely economic concept. It is a category of *political* economy, since it describes inequalities of power as between states, economic institutions and actors operating on the world-market. Cultural dependency was usually simply omitted from most models.

There is no necessary opposition, of course, between political and economic models. In reality, most people use a mixture of both, but usually inconsistently, and without providing justifications for doing so. I present them in the following table, however, in opposed pure, extreme form – as Weberian ideal types – even if, in the real world, only certain ideologies fit either extreme, because the procedure points up important differences.

The first, the *political*, sees the world as divided into two opposed political camps, characterized by differences of social system and ideology: capitalism and communism. The second takes levels of economic development as the crucial criterion; the world is therefore divided not into capitalist and communist countries, but into developed countries and underdeveloped ones. These two models are diagrammatically represented in the meta-model below (which only gives the more important countries or representatives of each category).

Moving across the rows, horizontally, the world is divided *politically* into

ECONOMIC

		DEVELOPED	UNDERDEVELOPED	
P O L I T I C A L	CAPITALIST	1 USA, EEC countries, Japan, Australia, South Africa	3 Rest of capitalist world, e.g. Bolivia, Botswana, Bangladesh	**W E S T**
	COMMUNIST	2 USSR, East European countries, North Korea	4 China, Cuba, Vietnam	**E A S T**

NORTH   SOUTH

two sets of capitalist and communist countries respectively. This model prevailed during the Cold War. It classifies together the USSR, Eastern Europe and North Korea (cell 2) with underdeveloped communist countries such as China and Cuba. The former is sometimes called the 'West' (in its widest usage, though, of course, that label is often reserved for the advanced capitalist countries alone).

Conceptions of the Third World in *economic* terms read vertically down the columns, thereby combining industrialized capitalist countries like Japan or the EEC (cell 1) with industrialized communist countries like the USSR or North Korea (cell 2), but separating both of these from that other half of the world, the world made up of both underdeveloped capitalist countries like Bolivia, Botswana or Bangladesh (cell 3) and underdeveloped communist countries such as Cuba (cell 4). The first half is what has now come to be called the 'North' (cells 1 and 2); the second, the 'South' (cells 3 and 4).

Economistic models naturally attracted economists, both on the Left and the Right. The level of development of productive forces was the key causal factor, though there were differences as to what the main element was; for some, it was the accumulation of capital; for others, the presence or absence of the entrepreneurial spirit. Political institutions, social arrangements, and cultural differences were usually treated as irrelevant in these models, or subsumed under the phrase *ceteris paribus*. It was a reductionist, economistic conception of development and of its causes and impediments.

To some people, taxonomies like these are merely academic exercises. Yet they clarify the distinctive political praxis which each of the various models both justifies and expresses. Ideas, as W. I. Thomas observed, are 'real in their consequences', and the names we give things – the taxonomies we construct and then impose on the world – have, as Hobbes noted, consequences not just for the way we think about the world but also for the way we act in it. The real-life implications of the Chinese conception of the three worlds for instance, differs from any of the foregoing, and – surprisingly for a Marxist regime – treats the distinction between capitalist and communist countries as a subsidiary matter. Far more important, in their view, are the differences in *levels* of development of the productive forces, whether in a capitalist or a communist society, which enable the rich countries to exploit the poor. The most powerful of all are two only – the Superpowers – which 'compete' with each other for world hegemony, but 'collude' to prevent any challenge to the world balance of power which they have created and which they jointly maintain. Central to that competition is the struggle to win over Second and Third World countries to their side. The Second World they see as a set of countries with relatively advanced levels of economic development – which again puts communist countries like Hungary or Czechoslovakia in the same bracket as capitalist countries like

Italy or Brazil, despite differences of ideology and social system. The Third World consists of the least economically developed countries, including China herself. As the majority of underprivileged mankind, they have a common interest in bringing the domination of the Superpowers to an end.

At one level, this is an economistic or technicist model, one in terms of levels of development and forces of production, not a class model, in which the nature of the social system is the primary criterion. But it has clear political implications. Since the principal contradiction is that between the Super-powers and the rest, the precondition for development on a global scale is the ending of their joint domination of the world. For a time, both the Superpowers were jointly condemned, but by the mid-1970s, the USSR, rather than the leading capitalist Power, had been identified as the greater menace.[19] The Chinese model of the three worlds thus requires a modification of our original diagram.

	DEVELOPED		UNDERDEVELOPED
	SUPERPOWERS	OTHER	
CAPITALIST	USA	Japan, EEC, Australia, South Africa	Rest of capitalist world
COMMUNIST	USSR	Eastern Europe, North Korea	China, Cuba, Vietnam
	FIRST WORLD	SECOND WORLD	THIRD WORLD

Starting from the same basic theoretical assumption that countries are to be classified according to their level of economic development other theorists have arrived at quite different conclusions – and policy implications. Wallerstein, as we saw, rejects the notion that there are three, or even two worlds. For him, there is only a *single* world-system, which is a capitalist one and has been so since the seventeenth century.[20] Hence it follows that, according to him, 'socialist systems do not exist in the contemporary world'. The communist state is merely a 'collective capitalist firm as long as it remains a participant in the capitalist market'.[21] Since any system, by definition, is made up of parts, however, he takes the 'country' as the unit of the world-system. Countries are then classified into three types: those at the centre of the system ('core countries'); countries on the 'periphery'; and 'semi-peripheral'

countries. In this model, communist countries do not constitute a distinct type of society: the Second World is decomposed and divided into one or other of the three categories, the Soviet Union, for example, being a core country and Cuba a peripheral one. Since the model is predominantly an economic one, it ignores such institutions as the Warsaw Pact or the military assistance given by the USSR to Cuba, Vietnam and other regimes and movements. Yet paradoxically, it ignores the existence of such economic institutional realities as COMECON, or the post-revolutionary aid supplied by the USSR to Cuba and Vietnam.

Institutionalized state socialism, in this basically neo-Trotskyist view of the world, is not socialism at all. Socialism is seen as a system of production which can only be realized when collectively organized at *world* level. It is hard to see how the transition to that level of organization could ever be made at all since the world, as the model recognizes, is composed of nation-states, and revolutions have occurred and can only continue to occur in real-life countries, not via some kind of global orgasm. Further, whatever one's reservations about and criticisms of Soviet and other forms of State socialism, and the distortions caused by the struggle to survive and grow in a world in which capitalism is still far stronger materially and militarily, the socialism that has developed up to now – however authoritarian – is fundamentally oriented to establishing not only a collectivistic, but an egalitarian alternative to capitalism, and draws its ideas and ideals from the Marxist founding fathers. It is, therefore, a *variant* of socialism, and to refuse it that title, even when it does damage to socialist values, is simply an arbitrary, dogmatic and stipulative judgement.

The other kind of economic model differs fundamentally from both the Chinese and neo-Trotskyist versions in its value-assumptions. The aid-lobby, which advocates massive redirection of world resources in order to develop the presently impoverished regions of the globe, is made up of people of varied political persuasions, the majority probably Christian and humanists to whom capitalism and communism are equally repugnant ideologies which merely legitimize the rule of two different kinds of political élites.

One of the most influential political models of the three worlds, naturally, has been that promulgated by the communist Superpower. Since Soviet policy is usually seen in the West simply as one of brutal expansionism, it becomes important to examine the assumptions which inform Soviet policy, as expressed by Soviet theorists themselves – an operation only too rarely performed.

The Soviet model of the world reflects the duality of interests of a country which is both a nation-state whose first priority is the consolidation and preservation of its social system at home, and a Superpower supporting movements of national liberation and socialist states outside Europe. Like any other nation-state, it is particularly sensitive to threats to its borders – with particularly good reason after invasion and destruction on a gigantic scale twice in less than a quarter-century. That sensitivity is most acute with relation to those countries of Eastern Europe whose socialism was designed in the USSR and implanted by the Red Army. There, mere friendship between states is not enough. The entire social system, with its distinctive political institutions and ideology, has to be kept in being, by force if necessary.

These considerations scarcely explain Soviet involvement in Ethiopia or even Afghanistan (even though that country does have common borders with the USSR). Nor does the paranoid assumption that the USSR simply moves in wherever it can. From Stalin's abandonment of the Greek communists at the end of the Second World War to the very limited support for the Allende government in Chile, the USSR's record has not always been one of unequivocal support for socialist or even communist movements. Conversely, she has traded with Argentina, despite its ultra-Right military regime, and helped a (Marxist) Ethiopian government to contain Eritrean independence movements which also claim to be Marxist.

Many who would defend the protection extended by the USSR to Cuba because that country was threatened by US invasion (though not Krushchev's provocative installation of rockets), or Cuba's assistance to Angola, find no such justification for Soviet (and Cuban) military involvement in Eritrea, or, now, for the use of counter-insurgency methods pioneered by the USA in Vietnam to impose socialism by gunship on Afghanistan. The dilemma of the USSR in the face of Marxist-led regimes that came to power via *coup d'état* (without the mass involvement in the revolution that occurred in Angola and Mozambique) is a very real and tragic one, for to have failed to intervene would have meant abandoning Marxist revolutionaries (whose arrival in power was not brought about by the USSR) to their fate, and the installation of ultra-reactionary regimes. In the Ethiopian case, the removal of the feudal ruling class and the distribution of their lands did initially generate an *ex post facto* popularity among the masses. But the utter ruthlessness of the regime towards any opposition, even on the Marxist Left, itself owes much not only to Soviet conceptions of the one-party state and of the necessity for ideological conformity, but to the military and security organs which Soviet advisers directly helped to create.[22]

The wider theoretical underpinnings of these Soviet policies towards the Third World are scarcely ever studied. In contradistinction to Chinese policy, the Soviet model of the three worlds is not based on *levels* of development. It is a *political* model, which discriminates between *kinds* of states according to the nature of their social system, the primary distinction being that between the socialist and capitalist societies. Though the objective interests of the Third World are, in their view, to detach themselves from capitalism and take the socialist road, most of these countries are tied by authoritarian governments to the Western chariot. Yet some do strive to preserve a degree of independence of the Western embrace, and others even to extend their autonomy and their room for manœuvre. They are, in Soviet parlance, 'progressive' countries, which have embarked on a 'non-capitalist path', which constitutes a 'transition to socialism' in terms of the internal structure of those societies, and is anti-imperialist and anti-capitalist at the global level.

Soviet theorists explain this contradiction between internal and external policy in terms of an analysis of the class structure of such countries: having only a weak indigenous bourgeoisie, no strong party has emerged to represent its interests. Since the working class, likewise, scarcely exists, a significant workers' party is equally absent. The class struggle therefore takes place between quite different classes than those characteristic of advanced capitalism. Apart from the rich comprador accomplices of Western imperialism, the majority of the propertied classes are landowners, small peasants, and urban petty bourgeois. The most exploited elements are mainly non-proletarians, notably those without any work at all. Where these progressive forces are effectively mobilized – usually by petty bourgeois and intellectual elements – they sometimes come to power on a platform of 'national democracy', and then use the power of the State to curtail foreign monopolies and to limit exploitation, to extend state ownership, and to plan and diversify the economy, especially agriculture; and to democratize hitherto dictator-ridden societies.

On the Left, outside the USSR, this strategy has been criticized because it has resulted, in practice, in subordinating the task of creating a Marxist, workers' party and a revolution based on mass involvement to reliance on dictatorial and authoritarian methods; secondly, because it under-emphasizes class struggle, especially the opposition between the interests of the exploited classes and those of the élite who control the State and the dominant Party; and finally because it places too much emphasis upon external considerations – the global struggle between imperialism and socialism and pro-Sovietism in foreign policy – at the expense of internal class struggle, including struggles over different strategies of development.[23]

From Politics to Economics

With the passage of time, the ideas that had informed the Third World's own conceptions of itself shifted, as new kinds of problems became more salient within those countries; as relations between them and the developed world changed; and as important changes took place in the Second World.

In its formative period, the Afro-Asian grouping had been primarily a political grouping, concerned with the independence of the State and with internal decolonization, the replacement of foreign personnel and the creation of a national culture. It was only later, after the euphoria of political independence had subsided and the reality of economic dependence had been experienced, that the emphasis shifted to the problem of neo-colonialism, an experience distilled in a book with that title published by Nkrumah in 1965. The discovery of just how little control small, under-developed countries had over institutions whose power set limits upon the decisions they could make – and which seem likely to do so for the indefinite future – was only slowly borne in upon governments which had been swept to power on a heady wave of mass enthusiasm and were confident that this new energy of the masses could be harnessed for development.

Djilas' conception of the governing élites in Eastern Europe as a 'new class' inverted Marx's image of the State as the mere 'executive committee' of the bourgeois class: by virtue of their control of the State, he argued, they also controlled the economy.[24] But they did not *own* the means of production. Others therefore argued that they should be labelled an 'élite', not a class. But in the new, *étatiste*, post-colonial countries, the new élites used the power of the State to turn themselves into a propertied capitalist class, albeit as junior partners to the multinationals. They are therefore both a political élite *and* a new *class*.

Yet whatever the degree of their monopoly of local power in single-party states, the class that owned the mines, the plantations, the factories and the banks was not even in the country, but outside it: in the First World.

The nation-state is still a significant unit in international politics, depending on the political weight of the country – which is not entirely a matter of economic or even military strength. It still remains significant, too, insofar as the political decisions governments take (tariffs, tax laws, etc.) have consequences for the economy for both foreigners and natives. But even major countries like Britain today belong to the wider political and economic communities and military blocs of the EEC and NATO; and most Second World countries belong to COMECON as well as the Warsaw Pact. The newer communist states depend heavily on the Second World for both protection and for assistance with their development plans, while the influence of the smaller Third World capitalist countries upon world affairs scarcely extends beyond the use (or sale) of their UN vote. Economically, a government like that of Botswana has less to spend every year on ensuring the survival, let alone the development, of the country than people in Britain spend on deodorants and slimming foods or on their gardens or their pets. But far more important than even the larger governments are the

Multinatls.

multinational corporations.

These operate, by definition, at a new, 'transcendental' global level, and can shift their operations and investments from one country to the other depending on profitability, political stability, etc. This does not mean that they have no national affiliations. They are, indeed, based in one or other of the leading capitalist countries, of which the USA and Japan are the most important. But their operations are worldwide. The largest, Exxon, has some 300 subsidiaries in over fifty countries. Political influence apart, the sheer scale of their operations means that the decisions they take are often more important to the economy of a country than those taken by its government, and not only in the case of the smaller countries. Even large, developed countries are losing the capacity to control their own economic future. Today, General Motors spends more than the Japanese government (and Japan is the world's fourth largest industrial Power); Ford spends more than the French government's defence expenditure; and Imperial Chemical Industries has a budget larger than that of Norway. In the Third World, in 1970, only three Latin American countries – Brazil, Mexico and Argentina – had a GNP superior to the annual sales of General Motors, Standard Oil, Ford and Royal Dutch Shell.[25] The capacity of governments in societies with a GNP of less than US $450 *per capita* per annum to exercise sovereign choice is thus extremely limited. Even where the State has taken over the ownership of major economic enterprises, world commodity prices are beyond its control, while the operation of those enterprises is usually still carried out by expatriate organizations (often the former owners), which charge heavily for management services. Where they still retain ownership, limits set on dividends or on their repatriation can readily be compensated for. The profits retained permit further expansion, while novel forms of income such as payments for technical know-how, patent rights and licences, are quite as rewarding as old-fashioned dividends, while transfer pricing enables the parent company in the developed centre to charge their local subsidiaries abroad inordinately high prices for components, chemicals, and other sophisticated products from the First World. Even in Tanzania, where practically everything had been taken into State ownership, the haemorrhage was debilitating.[26]

The vulnerability of Africa, by far the poorest part of the world economy, to capitalist world economic crisis, was reflected, in 1982, in outbreaks of protest in Morocco, the Sudan and Tanzania at drastic increases in food-prices as a result of IMF pressure. Africa's external public debt had grown to more than four times what it had been nine years earlier, and whereas only two African countries had credit agreements with the World Bank four years ago, twenty-one of the forty-eight African members had called on the Bank for credit by the end of 1981.[27] Globally, the debt burden grew from $19 billion in 1960 to $376 billion in 1976.

The shock of surprise at realizing just how limited the power of the State was in economic matters expressed by Robert Mugabe in 1982 was no news to leaders of an earlier cohort of the new nations of Africa. At the time of Independence, Julius Nyerere has said, they had 'assumed that political liberation would take care of the economic problem'.[28] Two decades later, he had learned differently:

> Most of Africa is now free from colonial rule. . . . I know that we were right in our united demand for freedom from colonial rule. I know that we are right to support the demand for political freedom which is still being made by the peoples of southern Africa. . . . Our mistake was not in our demand for freedom; it was in the assumption that freedom – real freedom – would necessarily and with little trouble follow liberation from alien rule. . . .
>
> A new African government which tries to act on economic matters in the interests of national development, and for the betterment of its own masses . . . immediately discovers that it inherited the power to make laws, to direct the civil service, to treat with foreign governments, and so on, but that it did not inherit effective power over economic developments in its own country. [Hence . . .] to a very large number of Africa's peoples, independence has brought no change in economic conditions, and very little – if any – social change. Progress is very slow when considered in the light of what we know to be possible for life on earth. And injustice – even tyranny – is rampant in a continent whose peoples demanded independence as a remedy for those same evils.
>
> . . . If deliberate countervailing action is not taken, external economic forces determine the nature of the economy a country shall have, what investment shall be undertaken and where, and what kind of development – if any – will take place within our national borders.
>
> Neo-colonialism is a very real, and very severe, limitation on national sovereignty. . . . Our countries are effectively being governed by people who have only the most marginal interest in our affairs – if any – and even that only in so far as it affects their own well-being. That, in fact, is the meaning – and the practice – of neo-colonialism. It operates under the cover of political colonialism while that continues. Its existence and meaning becomes more obvious after independence.[29]

One response to neo-colonialism, Nyerere notes, was not to resist it, but to adapt to it, even to glory in it:

> Some of our people identify their own personal interests with the existing neo-colonial situation . . . the local agents of foreign capitalists, and . . . the local capitalists who have developed in the shadow of large foreign enterprises. Such people may feel that their wealth and status depend upon the continued dominance of the external economic power. . . .

They point to the statistics of their Gross National Product as an example of what can be gained from it – rather in the manner of a high-class prostitute glorying in her furs and jewels![30]

Nyerere thus recognizes that capitalist development (as in adjoining Kenya), which he, as a socialist, rejects, is nevertheless a fact in certain of the new states.

In the nineteenth century, Marx had feared that socialism would be established first in the older centres of capitalism (Europe), but then find itself threatened by dynamic new capitalism in the colonial world. Since this did not happen, some dependency theorists have argued that growth, especially industrial growth, is not possible in countries dominated by the capitalist First World. The fact is that the annual rate of growth of manufacturing industry in recent years has been higher in Third World countries than in the First World – 11.2 per cent between 1960 and 1970; 8.7 per cent between 1970 and 1979 – albeit from a low initial base, and with rates as low as 3.7 per cent in very low-income countries. Warren's attack on the 'illusion of underdevelopment' was the first challenge on the Left to dependency theory. The evidence, he argued, showed that Marx had been right after all – capitalist development *was* taking place in the Third World rather than the development of underdevelopment,[31] to which his critics replied that this was only growth, not development, since it still left those countries under the domination of the multinationals centred in the First World; others called it 'dependent development'.

Whatever the words used, it was abundantly clear that very rapid industrialization had taken place and was taking place in a number of formerly agrarian countries. Because labour-costs were very low, especially in countries where authoritarian governments kept trade unions firmly under control or actually abolished them, foreign capital flowed in, expecting a far higher rate of return on its investment than it would get in comparable industries in the First World. The textile industry was one of the first to shift its operations to the Third World. Automobile assembly, then automobile production, followed; then shipbuilding. A whole range of new, light but modern, sophisticated industries, producing transistor radios, plastics, chemicals, cameras, TV sets, components, now employ millions of people in a growing number of Third World countries. In enclave countries like Hong Kong or Singapore, and in the 'free production' zones' within larger countries such as Mexico, most of this is for export. Such zones have even been established inside China, mostly in the form of joint enterprises. Countries with huge internal markets like India or Brazil have developed very large industrial and manufacturing sectors which flourish side-by-side with vast zones of peasant poverty. India possesses several of the world's largest and most advanced steel plants; those in Brazil produce 12 million tons a year and feed her automobile industry and her factories. In Mexico, industrial growth, as in Brazil, began as early as the 1930s, followed by the import substitution of the Second World War. But during the 1950s and 1960s, manufacturing industry nearly quadrupled and the workforce doubled.[32]

A very different kind of massive increase in national income has occurred in the OPEC countries, which were formerly impoverished client states of the West or actual colonies. But whereas Mexico and Venezuela have used their increased income from oil to import the means of industrialization and of the modernization of agriculture along agribusiness lines, the ruling classes in those Near Eastern countries which are the biggest producers in the world are not seriously interested in modernization, while their appetites for luxurious living can be satisfied from only a tiny percentage of their oil-revenues. Even such major oil-producers as Mexico and Venezuela are therefore merely included among other 'middle-income' countries in World Bank tables, and are now having great difficulty in servicing their foreign debt, whereas countries like Saudi Arabia, Libya or Kuwait, with so much income that they cannot use it all at home and who invest it in the First World – with major consequences for the economies of that World – now constitute a separate category in World Bank statistics as 'capital surplus oil-exporters'.

Two-by-two tables such as the ones we have used to classify models of the three worlds enable us to understand the logic – and therefore the foreign policies – of those who use them. But they also have their limitations. The categories 'underdeveloped' and 'developed', 'communist' and 'capitalist' do explain a great deal about real-life international groupings because countries with those kinds of characteristics have interests in common. But they do not explain everything, and were not intended to. Since they are timeless, synchronic models, with only four categories, they cannot, inherently, capture relationships other than those built into the model: whether relationships which cut across those categories, such as political ties between countries in different cells (India and the USSR; the US and China), or relationships between countries in the same cell. Thus Czecho-slovakia and the USSR may both be developed communist countries (and the former country even has a higher GNP *per capita* than the Soviet Union) but that does not tell us that the USSR *dominates* Czechoslovakia politically. Since the basic unit is the country, relationships between the major groups within the country (classes, ethnic groups, religious com-munities, etc.) are left out of the picture.

Nor can such schemas capture change, whether it be economic change of the kind we have just discussed, or shifts of political allegiance at world level. Internal social change, in many countries, has been very rapid and very uneven. They therefore display contradictory economic mixes (developed industry, but low living-standards, as in Turkey; high living-standards, but a limited industrial sector, as in New Zealand or Uruguay) which makes for disagreement about how to classify them. There is dispute, too, on political grounds: whether to put South Africa and Israel into the First World, to which both are firmly attached politically, or into the Third, because of the persistence of the colonial syndrome of racial exploitation and oppression. These disputes are generally resolved 'by fiat', to use Cicourel's term, and in different ways by different people: by stipulating that one criterion or the other will be used and others ignored.

Such considerations have induced many theorists to abandon the notion of three *worlds* altogether. Goldthorpe, who retains the overall label 'Third World', which he defines simply as the poor countries, proceeds, firstly, to separate out the communist countries and then to further sub-divide them into the old and the new communist states. The capitalist world is broken down even further: into the better-off poor, the middling poor, the poorer and the poorest (apart from anomalies and unclassifiable small countries and territories); nine groupings in all.[33] Others, in the spirit of V. S. Naipaul's sardonic designation of the Caribbean as the 'Third World's Third World' describe the really poor countries as the *Fourth* World.[34]

One logical end-product of this multiplication of worlds would be the abandonment of the concept of 'world' and its replacement by a purely *linear list* of countries ranked in order of level of development. The World Bank goes farthest in this direction, ranking each country from the lowest, Kampuchea, to the highest, the United Arab Emirates, on the basis of a set of indicators of levels of development: GNP *per capita*, food production, annual growth of production, adult literacy and life-expectancy-rates. Even if we ignore the technical problems of compiling such figures, the use of indicators of this kind often obscures important social issues. The richest country on earth, in terms of GNP *per capita*, for instance, is, as already stated, the United Arab Emirates ($26,850 million, 1982). Yet only a few 'heads' monopolize the great bulk of this wealth; the vast majority of the population get the rest – as in any other capitalist country. Most of the wage-earners, moreover, are *foreign* immigrant workers. Half a million non-nationals from the two Yemens, Jordan, Palestine, Syria, Lebanon, Iran, South Korea, Turkey, Pakistan, and elsewhere worked in Kuwait, Bahrain, Qatar and the United Arab Emirates in 1975, outnumbering nationals by more than two to one. Figures of income *per capita*, again, do not tell us that Whites in the mines of South Africa get eight times more than Black workers.

And as with earlier UN statistics, political criteria are smuggled into economic language. Thus the 'non-market' industrial economies (a category which does not include Yugoslavia, China or Romania) are ranked in a league-table of their own. The underdeveloped communist countries, however, are merely listed together with capitalist underdeveloped countries as 114 'poor' countries, which are then divided into even more categories: 'low income', 'middle income', 'industrial market economies' and 'high-income oil-exporters' (formerly known as 'capital surplus' oil-exporters). The line dividing the highest low income country, Togo ($410 *per capita* per annum) from the lowest in the middle income group, Ghana (with $420), is purely arbitrary, while Israel, the highest of the middle income group of countries, with $4500 *per capita* per annum, is similarly separated, again by fiat, from Ireland, the lowest of the group of industrialized countries, which has $4880 *per capita* per annum. This classification also results in such strange bed-fellows as the adjacent pairs  Malawi and Mozambique, Yugoslavia and Argentina, Romania and Portugal, India and Haiti, Cuba and South Korea. Using these criteria, Hong Kong and Brazil are excluded from the list of industrialized countries, while Portugal, South Africa and Ireland are included.[35]

Third Word: Resistance and Change

These intellectual attempts to abolish the Third World have been paralleled by political scepticism about the existence of a Third World both on the Left and the Right. Régis Debray, for instance, has written that,

> 'Third World' is a lumber-room of a term, a shapeless bag in which we jumble together, to hasten on their disappearance, nations, classes, races, civilizations and continents as if we were afraid to name them individually and distinguish one from another: it is the modern version of the Greek *barbaros*, whereby all those who did not speak the language of Pericles were lumped together in a single word. . . . Yet what is there in common between Saudi Arabia and the People's Republic of Vietnam, between Israel and Yemen, between Cuba and Brazil?
>
> . . . The term 'Third World' . . . indicates a certain backwardness in economic and social development [but] the real meaning of the 'Third World' is that it presents the concept of a world apart, equidistant from the capitalist first world and the socialist second world, whose sole inner determining principle is that of underdevelopment. . . . It conceals – and this is its main usefulness – the paradoxical unity of the capitalist mode of production all over the world . . . in which the lower level of 'under-development' is maintained and continued by the 'development' of the upper. . . . The 'Third World' is in fact an annexe of the first world, an enclave in the international system of market relations. . . . It is an astute piece of stage-management . . . to distinguish as merely a statistical gap something that is the necessary result of an international *and national*

system of exploitation . . . everyone in the poor countries is poor, everyone in the rich countries is rich, even the poor. . . . What 'Third World' means in the last analysis is to reject or evade the capitalism/ socialism dilemma . . . Anyone who uses the latter term will inevitably tend, whether consciously or not, to isolate any actual 'national liberation' movement from the international socialist movement. . . . True, there is a certain solidarity among the 'three continents': but it comes more from outside than from within: they share the same economic exploiter, the same political opponent – imperialism – but it is a hollow unity, a kind of negative community. . . .[36]

The demolition job on the Right was terser. The Third World, the then US Secretary of State, Alexander Haig, declared in January 1981, is a 'myth'.

The rationales underlying these two rejections of the concept of a Third World could not have been more different. Debray was criticizing the proposition that these countries possess economies and social systems different *in kind* from either the First or Second Worlds (e.g. the notion of a mixed economy, or the populist conception of a State run in the interests of the people rather than any particular class). To him, they are all either socialist or capitalist countries. There are capitalist Third World countries and socialist ones. All of the capitalist countries are exploited dependencies of the First World; an integral part of world capitalism. Politically, too, these countries align themselves with either the capitalist or communist blocs.

Behind these verbal wrangles then, there are serious differences of political position. To understand them, we need to distinguish more carefully between international economic and political relationships (which may or may not overlap) and differences in internal economic and social systems.

The accusation that the concept of the Third World is only a piece of mystification, designed to persuade people into asserting an equal independence of both the First and Second Worlds, is an accurate one. That was exactly what the pioneers of non-alignment intended. On the Left, however, that perspective was never accepted by all; some identified themselves politically with the Second World. But the majority of countries, most of which were non-communist, also saw the Third World as a grouping of poor countries with a common interest in ending *First* World exploitation. But other radicals and revolutionaries, Marxists included, had no difficulty in using the term 'Third World' in exactly the same sense that caused Debray to reject it: to express the existence of a world system in which the capitalist First World dominates and exploits the capitalist Third World. Robin Jenkins, for example, described the Third World as a world 'owned, managed and underdeveloped by the First World'.[37] Pierre Jalée, a Marxist, for whom the world is 'sliced into two', into the socialist and capitalist 'groups', and the latter into the 'imperialist zone' and the 'Third World', uses the term not with the intention of mystifying his readers as to the reality of First World exploitation, but precisely in order to draw attention to it.[38] And the country with which Debray has identified himself so closely, Cuba, strongly stresses the common interests of the 'Tricontinental' countries, the exploited continents of Asia, Africa and Latin America, and plays a major role in the Non-Aligned Movement.

On the Right, however, the rulers of many Third World countries have indeed used the language of non-alignment, and of themselves as spokesmen of the wretched of the earth, in precisely the demagogic way to which Debray objects: internally, in order to present an image of common interests as between themselves and the people they exploit, and externally, to project a pretence of non-alignment that disguises the reality of very aligned – normally pro-First World – policies. Their rhetoric is a rhetoric of 'national unity' and 'independence' even of the 'sacred revolution' (which means the day they seized power), and of 'solidarity' with other poor countries. The reality is that, every day, they sell their countries into an ever-deeper dependence on the multinationals.

After the 'Bandung' honeymoon period of the 1950s, the Afro-Asian grouping consolidated itself as a force independent of both the blocs. A sympathetic observer who was perfectly aware of the self-seeking character of many of the new élites could nevertheless still refer to the Third World in 1963 as a 'vast fellowship of the dispossessed'.[39]

But the gap between the rhetoric of a non-aligned neutralist Third World and political reality, present from its beginnings, steadily widened. A careful study of UN voting patterns shows that whereas in its early years the non-aligned did 'reach an impressive degree of coherence and were clearly identifiable as a distinct group', by the end of the 1960s they were 'no longer clearly identifiable as a group that behaved distinctly in East-West relationships'; 'as a voting bloc', there had been 'complete collapse'.[40] By contrast, a virulently anti-communist group of Asian countries, ASEAN (Indonesia, Malaysia, Singapore, Thailand and the Philippines), which only voted the same way on a third of all issues in the late 1960s, did so nine times out of ten a decade later.[41]

The doctrine of non-alignment, of course, was never an absolute. It always included not only alignment against colonialism, but the right to side with one or other of the Superpowers in any particular dispute, where that Power adopted a justifiable position. What was precluded, in Nyerere's words, was 'any *permanent* diplomatic or military identification with the Great Powers' (my italics). But politically today, the great majority of the non-aligned are actually *very* aligned. As an independent political grouping, the Third World has been split down the middle by the attachment, *de facto,* of most of its members – the capitalist Third World – to the First World, and of a minority to the Second World. No country was more aligned than the host country in 1979, Cuba. The counterpart of this external polarization has been the internal disappearance of the populist governments of the 1960s. In Africa Nyerere's Tanzania is the sole survivor, faced with desperate economic difficulties. A victim of the one-party system, which Nyerere defends, Oginga Odinga, in neighbouring Kenya, lamented that the one-party system was 'fast becoming a commandist institution . . . a source of political instability'.[42] To Ben Bella, one of the founders of the Non-Aligned Movement, who had been imprisoned for sixteen years, non-alignment died in 1965, when Colonel Boumédienne seized power in Algiers on the eve of the Afro-Asian Conference. Internally, since then, the consumerist society and 'development . . . in terms of GNP' had displaced cultural priorities and self-management.[43]

Those who had done the fighting were shut out. In Algeria, the armies that had sat out the war in Morocco and Tunisia were in power while the guerrilla commanders of the *wilayas* occupied only very minor posts. In Kenya, Mau Mau fighters found themselves living in the shanty-towns of Nairobi while Kenyatta became a very wealthy man. He was succeeded by Daniel arap Moi, a Muzorewa-type former government appointee in the colonial legislature. The Minister for Constitutional Affairs, Njonjo, had, as Crown Counsel and Public Prosecutor, administered the State of Emergency under which thousands had been herded into prison-camps and many executed.[44]

The decay of the original principle of non-alignment was dramatically symbolized at the 1979 meeting of the non-aligned countries in Havana, with the marginalization of the eighty-seven-year-old Tito, one of the founding fathers of the movement, who tried, without success, to prevent the adoption of resolutions which laid the blame for underdevelopment primarily on the capitalist world and who tried to reassert the Movement's independence of both East and West:

> To many observers, it sounded like the last will and testament of the only surviving member of the movement which he created with Nehru, Nasser, Nkrumah and Sukarno twenty years ago. Tito sat alone at a table as though becalmed in the eye of the hurricane which had been whipping round the conference hall. As the conference reached its climax, it became increasingly clear that Yugoslavia had . . . become isolated.[45]

A year later, Tito was dead.

In the 1961 non-aligned meeting, at Belgrade, there had only been twenty-five full members, plus three observers from Latin America and thirty-five representatives of national liberation movements. By 1979, at Havana, there were ninety-five full members and only nineteen observers, most of them representing independent states, plus representatives from

eight European countries and many international agencies. The organization had become the major forum of the Third World. In 1961, Cuba had
been isolated in Latin America. In 1979, Cuba was the host country, and
there were eight Heads of State from Latin American and Caribbean
countries, plus five Foreign Ministers. Their main concern was North
American influence and the power of the multinationals. The Arab
countries were preoccupied with oil and with Israel, issues which brought
them into conflict with the West. New revolutionary governments were also
present from Africa. Only India, Egypt and the fiercely anti-communist
countries of South-east Asia put up any consistent opposition.

The paradox is that these radical resolutions were passed by an assembly
in which the majority of Heads of State were from countries in which they
had seized power from populist governments which had claimed, verbally at
least, to be the spokesmen of the common people. The rhetoric of the new
regimes was usually that of stamping out the corruption of their predecessors
and the inauguration of efficiency in government. They usually claimed, too,
to represent the *whole* nation and to reject the divisive class-biased policies
of the past. What it added up to in practice was the defence of property and
the elimination of opposition. In reality, at the level of foreign policy, there
was little unanimity except on the two issues of Israel and South Africa – the
last important residues of colonialism.

 Culturally, of course, Debray is right: the Third World is only a 'negative
community'. All that it has shared in common has been the colonial
experience, and even that legacy has left quite different systems of
education, of public administration, even modes of thought in countries
which had been subjected to the very different cultural hegemony of
England or France. The apparent paradox is readily resolved, however, for
what these governments were concerned about, now that most countries had
achieved their independence, were economic rather than political problems.

The political meetings had continued throughout the 1970s. In 1964 in
Cairo; in 1970 in Lusaka; in 1973 in Algiers; in 1976 in Sri Lanka; and in 1979
in Havana. But even these meetings were increasingly focused on economic
issues. The turning-point had come in 1962 when seventy-seven countries
had succeeded despite opposition from the industrialized world in winning
UN backing for a World Conference on Trade and Development. UNCTAD I
took place in Geneva in 1964; UNCTAD II in New Delhi in 1968; UNCTAD III
in Santiago in 1972; UNCTAD IV in Nairobi in 1976; UNCTAD V in Manila in
1979; and UNCTAD VI in Belgrade in 1983. Over that period, the
non-aligned also held their own meetings on economic issues at Dakar,
Lima, Delhi and elsewhere. But by 1979, they were becoming increasingly
frustrated and divided by the foot-dragging of the West, by the Sino–Soviet
dispute, and by divisions within the Third World itself.

OPEC, the very Third World organization which had demonstrated the power of Third World producers to co-operate in raising the prices of primary commodities, now proved to be far more damaging to the economies of the poorer countries. Even the more industrialized, like Turkey or Brazil, were now having to spend a third to a half of their foreign earnings merely in order to pay their oil bills. For the very poor, it meant disaster, especially as world recession affected their exports. The establishment of a sizeable OPEC fund to help non-oil-producers in the Third World, at favourable terms, did little to counterbalance these losses. UNCTAD V had been especially disastrous: the more industrialized Third World countries, strongly dependent on the multinational corporations, blocked proposals for a code of conduct for multinationals; the developed capitalist countries fought off proposals to discuss world energy problems; and no progress was made on attempts to establish a common fund to control stocks of raw materials in order to stabilize prices at present controlled by the operations of the market in the commodity-exchanges of London and New York.[46]

Though manufacturing now constitutes a fifth of the GDP of the underdeveloped countries as a whole, over half of this comes from nine newly-industrializing countries, mainly in Latin America and East Asia. Primary commodities, which were two-thirds of the exports of the underdeveloped countries at the beginning of the 1970s, are now only a half. Leaving aside the spectacular NICs, over half of the exports even of countries like Bangladesh and India are now manufactures. Some of this goes to other Third World countries. Poor/rich and agricultural/industrial, then, no longer neatly overlap. But the older pattern of centre/periphery trade persists: 84 per cent of the imports of the developed countries from the Third World in 1978 still consisted of primary commodities, mainly agricultural products and minerals; 82 per cent of the imports of the Third World from the developed countries were manufactures.

Many countries are still dependent on one or two commodities for their foreign earnings in a world where prices for 33 such commodities, which varied by an average of 5 per cent during the 1950s and 1960s, fluctuated, on average, by 12 per cent during the 1970s. Cash-crops – rubber, cocoa, jute, tea, coffee, etc. – are still the main exports for most countries: tea constitutes half of India's exports; bananas, two-thirds of Costa Rica's; rubber, a half of Malaysia's; cocoa, two-thirds of Ghana's, etc., etc. Minerals, including petroleum, constitute over four-fifths of the exports of Chile, Zambia, Bolivia, Venezuela, Iran and Iraq, while the Third World provides the developed world with nearly all its tin and chrome, three-quarters of its petroleum, two-thirds of its iron ore, half its phosphates, bauxite and copper, and two-fifths of its zinc and lead.[47]

In agriculture, as we saw, the drive to industrialize and to increase cash-crop production for export has led to increasing dependence on imports of food. Between 1955 and 1970 Third World food imports doubled. Though prices for oil increased greatly after 1973, between 1950 and 1982 the terms of trade for exporters of agricultural commodities and minerals deteriorated, making attempts to plan national economic development difficult in the extreme. Third World countries, too, have to compete with each other for a share of the same market. Hence attempts to build organizations similar to OPEC which could control world prices for other primary commodities have met with very little success, since although the First World may not be able to survive without the oil, the tungsten, or the manganese of the Third World, it can certainly live without bananas and can produce substitutes for sisal.

The most vital strategic resources of all, which the West must have at all costs, were identified recently by ex-President Nixon: oil and minerals. It is this which explains the gap between the rhetoric of commitment to defence of the free world and the reality of shoring up archaic and repressive monarchies and sheikhdoms in the Arab world, as well as America's special hatred for Iran's revolution. The power of the Zionist lobby inside the USA is certainly a major factor in US support for Israel, but that country also plays a major role in destabilizing and dividing the Middle East and the Maghreb, for all the talk of the 'brotherhood' of the Islamic community. It is not because of covert racism, either, that the West avoids any actions which might seriously endanger the stability of South Africa despite the unpopularity support for this racist regime brings. The increasingly militaristic South African and Israeli regimes, and the sheikhs, receive support because 'from the American viewpoint South Africa is to strategic materials what Saudi Arabia is to oil'.[48]

Suppliers of those materials are in a position to demand political support as well as high prices. But those dependent on less crucial commodities, even reactionary governments, find themselves frustrated and resentful at their economic disadvantage *vis-à-vis* the West, and join in the demand for New International Economic Order. It is these common interests, independently of other differences of social system or ideology, that are emphasized in the newest image of the Third World. The non-aligned movement, it asserts, has not only become the authentic voice of the overwhelming majority of the countries of the Third World, but the main object of its common hostility is now the First World. At the UN, the Third World has long had a majority, which frequently votes with the Second World to successfully carry motions denouncing the West. No less than eighty-seven Third World countries even risked US disapproval sufficiently to attend a conference in revolutionary Nicaragua in January 1983 to denounce US policy in Central America and the Caribbean.

In this triumphalist version of the Third World, consolidated under Cuban leadership at the Havana meeting of the non-aligned in 1979, the socialist countries are seen as the allies of the poor countries, which 'objectively' are playing a 'progressive' role, at the international level by virtue of their participation in the movement of the poor majority of mankind, whatever the nature of the social system within those countries. The analysis inevitably soft-pedals some aspects of the unacceptable face of the Third World: such ruthless regimes as Uganda, Singapore, Kampuchea, Saudi Arabia and Pakistan are included, whereas China, the largest country in the world, let alone the Third World, is not recognized as a Third World country at all. This is because the criteria, in the final analysis, are not just economic, but political: only countries which are members of the movement are included. China, despite its major role in the formative days of the Afro-Asian grouping, is no longer a member of such organizations (and also has a permanent seat on the Security Council). Hence while the Open University 'Third World Studies' course takes Turkey as one of its first case-studies, in this political model, Turkey is not a Third World country at all, since she belongs to no Third World organizations, and is a member of NATO and OECD.[49]

Yet the underlying divisions remain. The First World is not just the USA. The ex-colonies of Britain and France in Africa have been given special status under the Lomé Convention which carries with it free or preferential access to the markets of the EEC for their agricultural products, and some measure of price-stabilization. It is a huge market, since Western Europe's political consolidation has brought together not only rich countries like France, whose GNP is greater than that of forty-one countries south of the Rio Grande, but 'newly-industrialized' ones like Spain, which produces nearly as much as Brazil. Germany and France together outstrip the USSR in output by nearly a fifth.

The Western European image of the Eastern countries as a military threat to their security carries no weight, of course, in countries like Vietnam, Angola or Mozambique which owe their independence to Soviet and other Second World military assistance and which, together with Cuba, now depend on those countries for development aid as well as continued military protection and diplomatic support. ('Have you any idea what modern arms *cost*?' I once heard Amilcar Cabral ask a public meeting of sympathizers.) Hence even the destruction of the Polish workers' movement evokes no significant criticism in these countries. But after Soviet military intervention in a Third World country, Afghanistan, 111 countries voted against the USSR in the UN; only 12 of the 22 votes she could muster were from Third World countries.

The Soviet record in the Third World is neither one of consistent success nor of a deliberate 'forward' policy. In the Arab world, the balance, Halliday concludes, has been a 'net deficit'.[50] As well as supporting mass revolutions, she has found herself dragged along in the wake of Marxist-led revolts and *coups* of various kinds. Support for a popular revolution like that in Cuba has long been a debilitating drain on the Soviet economy, but has been a political asset. Ethiopia, where popular support for land-reform was displaced by horror at sectarian butchery at home and repression in Eritrea, and the invasion of Afghanistan, have proved both economically burdensome and politically even more embarrassing. And despite Western paranoia, Soviet military assistance was as non-existent in Nicaragua's revolution as it had been in Cuba's. The brutality of the Batista and Somoza regimes brought together in one broad front a coalition of parties, classes and, in the Nicaraguan case, even much of the Church. In Guatemala, as we saw, the alliance is based on a struggle for self-determination on the part of many different ethnic groups as well as class struggle. Marxists, though very influential and well-organized, by no means exercise unquestioned control over their allies in such situations. They also face continuing opposition. In post-revolutionary Zimbabwe Marxist cadres are a distinct minority in a government which came to power as a result of armed struggle in which there were two guerrilla armies, each based on one of the two major ethnic groups, and which had inherited a flourishing, White-dominated, capitalist economy, heavily dependent upon South Africa and the capitalist market. The party the USSR backed, Nkomo's ZAPU party, and its military wing, the ZIPLA guerrilla army, failed to win power.

The revolutionary experience in these countries, and the ensuing regimes, are vastly different from those of Eastern Europe four decades ago. They differ profoundly, too, from the revolutionary regimes of China or Vietnam, where the authority of a powerful centralized Communist Party is unchallenged, or even those of countries like Angola and Mozambique (leaving aside the most centralized of all, North Korea). Geography and history also make post-revolutionary Nicaragua highly vulnerable to US economic pressure and destabilization, and render Soviet assistance highly problematic.

By comparison with the USSR, the other major communist country, China, has been unable to exercise anything like the influence, even within the Third World, that her size would seem to warrant. In terms of numbers at least, she has been called 'half a Superpower'. That she was herself an underdeveloped country was also an asset in her relations with other Third World countries. China, the Chinese have constantly insisted, is part of the Third World. Her very underdevelopment, however, explains part of her failure to build a network of allies, for she simply lacks the resources with which to assist them. Despite that, she did win many friends in the 1950s, initially because of her active role in the Afro-Asian movement, then after the *rapprochement* with the USA when the opening of China to the noncommunist world in 1972 brought the amazed realization that all this time she had been pioneering a revolutionary development strategy that differed, obviously, from the classical pattern of the capitalist Industrial Revolution, but also rejected its Soviet counterpart of sacrificing consumption (and a whole generation) in the interests of building a heavy industrial base. Nor had the peasantry been brutally destroyed. Instead, they had been formed into self-governing communes.[51] Industry 'walked on *two* legs' like everything else. A Soviet-style heavy industrial base had been built, mainly in the North-east; but there was also a more primitive industrial sector, symbolized by the backyard iron-foundries of the Great Leap Forward period. To many in the Third World, that kind of technology seemed, indeed, 'appropriate'.

Chinese aid, inevitably limited in size, was, however, aid without strings. Its high-water mark was the building of the railway between Tanzania and Zambia, which China not only financed but built with the labour of tens of thousands of unskilled volunteers and technicians, all of whom lived at the Third World standards of living which the people of China share with the people of Tanzania.

Chinese support for movements of national liberation, too, won her friends among revolutionaries. But in the 1960s, her readiness to back any kind of movement or regime so long as it was anti-Soviet quickly lost her most of these friends on the Left. The friendship of rightist generals in Pakistan or of authoritarian figures like Mrs Bandaranaike in Sri Lanka, who had just slaughtered tens of thousands of young rebels, was no substitute. By the seventies, China was isolated both in the Second and Third Worlds. Finally, she invaded socialist Vietnam, after all that country's sufferings. More concerned with trade and with assistance from the West in modernizing her economy and in building an anti-Soviet front, her Third World activities lapsed. By the late 1970s, only small sects and micro-Communist Parties in countries like Paraguay or New Zealand still claimed to be Maoist.

The communist world today, then, is clearly no longer a bloc. These rivalries between different communisms, too, have had divisive effects on revolutionary movements in the Third World. Those who make successful revolutions always protest that they have no intention of exporting their ideas – and then proceed to do so. In the 1930s, Brazilian workers spent their energies in bitter disputes about the relative merits of the rival projects of Bakunin, Trotsky, and Stalin.[52] By the 1970s, disputes between Maoist and other revolutionary groups were being fought out not only with words but with sub-machineguns. The arrogance displayed by Che Guevara towards the local Bolivian communists and the peasants he fought for not only cost him his life but set back revolution in a whole continent.[53]

The First World has exhibited much more cohesion than either the Second or the Third, and has had the economic resources with which to bring refractory Third World governments into line. Where that proved insufficient, force was used, either directly or indirectly. Resistance to that repression cost such a high price in blood that the prospect of turning their country into another Vietnam or of facing the genocide being practised in Central America today is one that people are driven to only in very special circumstances: when no other alternative seems viable.

Until the beginning of the world recession in 1973, economic expansion in many Third World countries had in fact presented millions with new opportunities for individual social mobility. Nineteenth-century imperialism had been based on contempt for native cultures and the belief that they would be replaced by Western culture. The economic and political hegemony of the First World was to be complemented by establishing its cultural hegemony. To nineteenth-century colonists, the superiority not just of Western technology, but of Western social institutions and cultural values, was self-evident. Even Marx had been impressed by the alchemy as well as the horrors wrought by capitalism:

> It has accomplished wonders that far surpass Egyptian pyramids, Roman aqueducts, and Gothic cathedrals. . . . [Its] expeditions . . . put all former migrations of nations and crusades in the shade, [its] productive power [is] more massive and more colossal than . . . all previous generations put together. . . . As in material, so in intellectual production. . . . All that is solid melts into air, all that is holy is profaned. . . . The bourgeoisie . . . draws all, even the most barbarian, nations into civilization. . . . It creates a world after its own image.[54]

The culture of the West was equally impressive to its victims. The 'comprador' allies of imperialism were naturally the most responsive to Western influence, the paradigm, in this century, being the Soong dynasty of inter-War China with the Christianized family of Chiang Kai-shek, the political controller; T. V. Soong, the banker; and Madame Chiang. The upper classes, increasingly, were actually educated in the West; Pandit Nehru, for example, went to Harrow. Even the radicals took their ideologies, first liberalism and positivism, then nationalism and Marxism, from the West.

Cultural Imperialism, Cultural Resistance, and Cultural Revolution

But the messages which emanate from the Second World rarely reach the majority of those living in the capitalist Third World. For them, economic and political domination and penetration are accompanied by a new, more intensive and more extensive cultural imperialism. For the rich and the middle classes, the dream is no longer that of visiting Lourdes, or to do the Grand Tour of Europe. It is to visit the Middle Kingdom itself. The rich send their children to be socialized in the First World: to prep schools, and then to

Cornell or Oxford. Middle-class students go to the State Universities or spend a year as an *au pair* in the Mid-West learning the English that will be vital to their futures. For the less affluent, the great dream beamed at them night and day on TV is to visit the secular shrines of Western culture in person at least once in their lives – a new version of the Muslim *hadj*; be it a holiday in Miami, which is fast becoming the Mecca of South America, or in Las Vegas, where they can live like millionaires for a few days, and dedicate themselves in playing as well as working (though in quarters and not thousands) at acquiring money; or in Hollywood, the apotheosis of the dream of becoming a young, sexy star; or a family holiday in Disneyland, where they are given (in a state which, until a century ago, was at the margins of Western civilization) a plastic, comic-book reduction of the world's cultural diversity, from cannibals to Western pioneers, to the level of a hi-tech fun-fair in which, ironically, it is the cardinal American values of enterprise and individual freedom that are emphasized.[55] Today, the tourist flow from the Third World to the First, or to First-World-style cultural enclaves within their own country, has become a mass phenomenon. The First World even meets the Third World face-to-face in playgrounds such as Tijuana or Hong Kong, where, paradoxically, Americans go to experience the mysteries of the East or to buy sombreros or mushrooms while the locals go to live it up American-style. But all can enjoy the symbols of modernity: brothels, ballet, hard rock, hamburgers, whisky, jeans and bikinis. Those who have to stay at home have TV or their transistors. Even the illiterate can 'read' strip-cartoon booklets. From the soap-operas, the chat-shows, the money-games and the romances they absorb Western culture vicariously, though mainly the ideal of the life-styles of the rich. They can even experience a more collective identification with something greater than themselves by watching the national team on the screen, even if they cannot afford to go to Maracanã, the Aztec stadium, and Wembley, the great shrines of the new world-religion of soccer, themselves.[56]

Meanwhile, back in the First World, more and more people are experiencing disillusion with the Western dream, some because world recession is now depriving them of the steady rise in material prosperity they had become accustomed to since 1945; others, because they reject capitalist consumerism. During the Vietnam War, vast numbers of American youth were 'turned off' by a culture which meant death on a genocidal scale for the Vietnamese and on a lesser scale for those drafted into the American army. From that, they progressed to a wider critique of materialism. Many dropped out, temporarily at least, of mainstream society, some into various forms of the culture of narcissism, others escaping into a separate reality provided by hallucinogenic drugs, or into new forms of sexual experience, in the attempt to recover the primitive or the natural, the 'world we have lost', usually within small groups, from life-style communes to Californian versions of Hindu ashrams.

That movement largely degenerated, after Vietnam, into a preoccupation with the Self and with purely interpersonal relationships, a mere 'do-your-own-thing' lifestyle devoid of any societal, let alone political content, which soon degenerated into health fads and religious cults that were perfectly compatible with the materialism of the 'Me society'.

If the rejection of consumerism remains widespread, not surprisingly it is strongest amongst those who are not poor. In the form of the ecology movement, it has actually grown into a major force in Western Europe. Such people (mainly young) are no more attracted by the materialism of the Second World. Socialism, for them, means the transformation of human relations, now, not mobilization to increase production so as to bring about abundance and freedom in the future. A generation traumatized by the prospect of nuclear extermination and by the slower destruction of the environment on which human life depends find the largely technologistic Soviet imagery of a communist future, quoted with approval by Luis Corvalán, the leader of the Chilean Communist Party, no more attractive:

> To lengthen the life of man to between 150 and 200 years, to end contagious diseases . . .
> To put at the service of man all the forces of nature . . .
> To apply atomic energy to industry, transport and construction . . .
> To foresee and prevent the consequences of natural disasters . . .
> To manufacture all the substances known in the world . . . and others that nature does not possess . . .
> To obtain new breeds of animals and varieties of plants . . .
> To modify and make habitable the barren areas of the earth . . .
> To learn to control the weather . . .[57]

For all these dreams, the Second World is a negative Utopia for most people in the First in material terms. For them, Eastern Europe means queues, shortages and bureaucratic inefficiency. The media of the Western world ensures that these are the only aspects of the Second World they get to hear about. Soviet living-standards have in fact risen far more than is realized by most in the West. Between 1965 and 1980, the monthly wage rose from 96.5 roubles to 168.5: by 1980, 85 per cent of all families had TV sets, as against 24 per cent 15 years earlier, and 84 per cent now also have refrigerators. Whereas they were eating mainly bread and potatoes two decades ago, they now eat a lot more meat and vegetables. The number of doctors has doubled.[58] Visitors from Eastern Europe, too, for all the seductions of Marks and Spencers and the Beatles, are genuinely shocked, even dismayed, by the naked inequalities, the advertising and the decaying public services of the West.

But the strains of life in a rigidly controlled society and the drain of military expenditures are reflected in the Second World in the deterioration of health conditions which have hitherto been exemplary in rising infant mortality, alcoholism, and death by trauma (suicide, murder, and fatal accidents).[59]

World-system theorists are right to remind us that economic conditions within the Second World are affected by the crisis of the capitalist world which dominates world-trade and which therefore determines the prices of the imports and the exports of the Second World and the volume of their foreign earnings. The anarchy of capitalism, which is beyond the control of the planners of the Second World, therefore affects the lives of consumers and enterprises in Kharkov and Havana as well as in Taipeh and Frankfurt. Food-queues in Warsaw are the consequence not only of an inadequate agriculture, but of the need to export food in order to pay that country's gigantic bill for goods imported from the West.

The social costs of the world arms-race are also visible in the First World. The co-existence of private affluence and public squalor has long attracted criticism and caused self-doubt even on the part of liberal US Ambassadors of good family. For wealth has been better distributed, and the quality of life has been superior to that of the USA in countries like Sweden, Switzerland, Norway and Denmark, not just for a rich minority, but for most people. Personal incomes may lag behind those in the USA (though they increased in France and Germany from a third of those in the USA in 1950 to three-quarters by 1976) but more of that wealth is used for public rather than purely individual ends. Whereas the USA had the lowest levels of infant and neo-natal mortality in the 1950s, by 1972 she had fallen behind France, Belgium, West Germany and England.[60]

The recession in the capitalist world has exacerbated these trends. Where people had come to expect a continuously rising standard of living, and a redistributive system of welfare, during the post-war decades, as of *right*, with recession they are now vulnerable to advocates of a scarcity psychology that sees Keynesian State intervention in both economy and society as not only impossible but unjustifiable in an era of decline, the remedies for which, they assert, must include the lowering of expectations. The social institutions built up by the working class in the past to protect their collective interests are less strongly defended in an era of demoralization and are more and more vigorously attacked.

None of this makes for radicalism, as theorists of the revolutionary consequences of immiseration have long preached. One reason is that the safety-net of the Welfare State now prevents total immiseration of the kind familiar in the 1930s in Britain and even in the USA. Another reason is that there is now a dual labour market. Those who have work feel that they own a valuable piece of property – a job. Where the rate of inflation is held down, too, they may even experience a rise in real earnings. Yet there are tens of millions who have only their labour-power to sell, but labour-power that nobody wishes to buy. Even for them, however, radical, let alone revolutionary responses still fail to materialize because no vision of an alternative society, no utopia in Mannheim's sense, has gripped the masses, and no revolutionary project, in Sartre's terms, therefore, exists. By revolutionary I do not mean the readiness to resort to violence or to meet force with force (though it includes those possibilities and could come to that in the future as it has done in the past) but that the idea of actually replacing the existing social system with a quite different *kind* of society only exists among a minority even of those who call themselves socialists and an even tinier proportion of the working class. Even when galvanized into a political confrontation with the State, as in France in 1968, the working classes of the Western world, and their organizations, have exhibited trade-union consciousness, taking their stand on enlarging their share of the national cake or defending that which they have. The idea of taking over the bakery has not occurred to them, or if it has, has frightened them.

One major reason, in the past, has been the deterioration of the major alternative vision that did exist, that of socialism, due to its being identified with the USSR. Stalin's terror ensured that. But a whole generation has grown up since then for whom Stalin is only a name in a history book. The international communist movement, moreover, led by the Italian Communist Party in the West and by Romania in the East has long accepted the principle that communism is now a polycentric, not a unitary phenomenon, despite Soviet opposition. That principle recognized the fact of differences in national forms of communism. But today, there are three major transnational forms of communism: the Soviet, the Chinese, and Euro-Communism, the last of which accepts the legitimacy of institutionalized opposition, plurality of political parties, the possibility of change of government, the protection and extension of civil rights, accountability, and other classic rights won during the bourgeois epoch.

But Soviet control of Eastern Europe has scarcely weakened, even if today the repression of working-class resistance is now carried out by the Polish rather than the Red Army. In Eastern Europe, paradoxically, the working class, which has never made a successful revolution in any capitalist country, advanced or underdeveloped, has consistently been the major force for social change and has borne the costs of resistance from the rising of the workers in East Germany in 1953, through the Hungarian Revolution centred on the factories of Csepel in 1956, to the 'Prague spring' of 1968 and the Solidarity movement in Poland.

Soviet-style socialism therefore remains a negative Utopia on other than economic grounds because it evokes a past of mass prison-camps and a present of much more selective psychiatric wards, gaols, and exile for those who dare to dissent.

To the working class in the West, then, the USSR – which they are constantly told is socialist – offers neither greater prosperity nor greater freedom. They are not prepared, therefore, to give up what they have, whatever its limits for millions of people, for less. Nor are they willing to trade freedom for material prosperity. To them, their bougeois liberties are rightly precious. Those on the Right who still expect to silence militant socialists by telling them to 'go back to Moscow' are therefore decades out of date, for Moscow has long been the symbol even to Marxists of what an earlier Trotskyist generation called a '*deformed* workers' state' of socialism gone wrong, which, though it provides some important lessons and models of how to plan and build a socialist economy, is also an anti-model of what to avoid.

The absence of revolutionism has not meant the absence of radicalism. The main organizational form of radicalism in the West since the Second World War, however, has not been the political party, but the *movement*. Once a more educated and affluent generation had developed an independent youth culture of its own, it was only a question of time before those social bonds would provide a ready-made basis for political community once the cause was present. In the USA, the cause arrived in the shape of the Vietnam war, in which, like all modern wars, young conscripts did the bulk of the fighting. The generation of women who had gone through the experience of mass higher education for the first time in human history only to find themselves back in that extra-mural world where their new skills and knowledge were still discounted, needed no other, specific cause, like Vietnam or the Bomb, to cause them to translate that common frustration into a movement for women's liberation.

Both these movements were able to follow styles of political organization pioneered outside the class-based parties which had hitherto been the main vehicles of radical protest. Black Power in the USA demonstrated how an *ethnic* group set about raising the consciousness that Black is beautiful so successfully that it could detonate nation-wide riots and bring about major political changes. Nuclear disarmers learned from those guided by what Max Weber called an 'ethic of absolute ends' – anarchists, pacifists and conscientious objectors, humanist, socialist and religious – that not only those who preached violence were unbending in their resistance and effective, and that revolutionaries had become conservative in their unwillingness to use direct action and in their acceptance of the unacceptable.

To label such primordial concerns as gender or ethnicity, or such ultimate matters as the very survival of humanity, single-issue campaigns is to demean them. Yet though these new movements are different in kind from class-based party politics, their elective affinity is with all those other groups which struggle against domination and exploitation. Hence though they have often conflicted with what C. Wright Mills called 'Victorian' Marxists and others for whom class was the only form of meaningful inequality and the politics of gender or race a 'deviation', in the end, most of the Left has come round to accepting that ethnic self-determination, women's liberation, nuclear disarmament, and even ecology, are issues it has to take up, even if they have still not developed the theoretical categories with which to express the overlaps and contradictions between class exploitation and exploitation based on gender or ethnicity.

Finding answers to those questions requires new convergences, moving 'beyond the fragments', and the modernization of traditional theories. The ideals that informed those theories remain valid, however, and need to be both reasserted and made relevant to modern problems. In the 1960s, it seemed to many that the ideals they believed in, sadly eroded during the Cold War, were being given new expression in the Third World in the positive neutralism that the Third World called 'non-alignment'. This has now been taken up in Europe in movements that seek to build bridges and to create or take advantage of whatever chinks in the wall between East and West there are and to remove nuclear weapons from countries on both sides of the divide, or that identification with the insulted and the injured, the wretched of the earth, which induces comfortable, non-political people to devote themselves to raise money, not just for the victims of the disasters that inevitably afflict whole peoples permanently on the edge of starvation, but in order to eliminate the structural causes of these famines.

It was these ideals that Mr Haig was trying to denigrate when he said that the Third World was a 'myth', and in particular the neutralist position that Third World countries had a perfect right to choose whether they would accept military, political and economic aid from the Second World or the First. Even reactionary Third World governments resented the limits placed on their autonomy by the leading Superpower.

The Second World originally attracted poor countries not just because its most powerful member was a potential source of material assistance, or because that country became the second greatest Power on earth within a generation, but because the smaller countries of the Eastern bloc, which were predominantly agrarian in 1945 (Czechoslovakia apart), all succeeded in industrializing themselves rapidly.

A country like the USA, during its development, was able to draw upon immense natural resources: it was a continent rather than a country. The two biggest communist countries likewise disposed of human as well as natural resources on an immense scale. Despite external pressures and war, the USSR between the World Wars and China up to the 1960s were able to build their economies autarkically, with a minimum of foreign trade or aid.

Yet the First World's efforts to discourage relations between the underdeveloped world and the Second World have been largely successful.

There has, too, been more than enough dismal evidence to support another aspect of what Mr Haig meant: that a situation of common poverty has not proved a viable basis for political co-operation. Inter-state organizations such as the Andean Pact have remained feeble, or, like the East African Community, have actually disintegrated. Since the Second World War, we are always being told, there has been no nuclear war. But the spread of nuclear weapons has not prevented the outbreak of wars waged with ever more sophisticated technological equipment, of increasing barbarity, nearly all of them in the Third World. They have cost the lives of 25 million people.

The ideals of the founding fathers of non-alignment have been sadly tarnished in the process. They have proved too much for poor countries to sustain. From Kampuchea to Uganda, Third World élites must bear their share of the responsibility for turning whole regions into slaughterhouses; it is not just the multinationals which bleed countries white and drive their leaders and their people to acts of chauvinist desperation. Nothing symbolizes that decay more than the occupation of the Presidency of the Organization of African Unity by Idi Amin.

In the face of these realities, Gramsci's famous assertion that he was an intellectual pessimist, but an optimist in spirit, is the only rational response. Optimism of the spirit has already seized the people of Greece, Spain and France. In the Third World, too, the non-aligned movement, despite its divisions, has grown, because the reality that sustains it – the facts of dependence and underdevelopment – have not gone away. The Third World, that is, is not a myth. The various meanings with which the term 'Third World' has been invested show family resemblances, even though they do not fully coincide. They have, that is, a common referent in the real world out there: the unequal, institutionalized distribution of wealth and illth on a world scale.

In a world capitalist recession, optimism about the possibility of growth has given way, over much of the Third World, to a new mood of pessimism, and in the West to new philosophies of 'limits to growth'. In Black Africa, the average annual growth of GNP *per capita* during the 1970s was a mere 0.8 per cent; by 1978, food production had declined to 80 per cent of what it had been in 1961; and by 1990, it is estimated the poorer African countries will have to import three times as much food simply in order to maintain already inadequate levels of nutrition. Uneven development is polarizing the Third World between the NICs at one extremity and the 'basket cases' at the other. More and more governments therefore see their main problem in the future no longer as one of how to industrialize themselves, but of how to feed their peoples. Any industrial development, they now believe, can only be based on the use of technologies appropriate to countries with plenty of labour but minimal capital.

Complementing this shift in Third World thinking is the growing belief that the drive towards infinity, both in production and consumption, which has powered modern capitalism has not only run down but is no longer a worthwhile focus for human energies anyhow; that US-style consumerism and the American way of life are not physically possible for the entire population of the globe, given that America presently consumes at least a third of many of the world's scarcest resources and that natural resources are a collective human heritage and not commodities to be sold on the market and consumed by the highest bidder. The drive to infinity has been equally characteristic of state socialisms, which in their formative years in particular have been so preoccupied with raising material living-standards in very poor countries that the maximization of production becomes an unquestioned primary goal to which everything else, including the toleration of alternative philosophies, is subordinated.

Optimists call this 'doom-watching' and point to the under-utilization of two-thirds of the world's cultivable land, and to the unknown and unused potential of the resources of the seabed and of outer space. Millions have died in famines in India and elsewhere, Sen has shown, not because there was not enough food, but because speculators hoarded it and poor people could not afford to buy it. 'The law', he concludes 'stands between food availability and food entitlement' – and laws can be changed.[61] There are even those who contemplate the unthinkable with confidence. Mao Tse-tung claimed that

> There is nothing in the world that does not arise, develop, and disappear. Monkeys turned into men, mankind arose; in the end, the whole human race will disappear, it may turn into something else [and] the earth itself will cease to exist. . . .
>
> When the theologians talk about doomsday they are pessimistic and terrify people. We say the end of mankind is something which will produce something far more advanced than mankind.[62]

Few share that sublime confidence. Today, capitalist and communist countries alike seek to yoke Third World countries to their chariot-wheels. Their rivalry divides the Third World and consumes resources which are more than ample to provide a life free from poverty for every one on earth and from the scandalous over-consumption of the First World.

But the greatest waste by far is the ever-escalating expenditure upon military weapons. World military expenditure is now roughly equal to the entire income in cash and in kind of the poorest half of the world's population. We have already noted the disastrous consequences of the world arms race and of the new Cold War for the economies of poor Third World countries and for a Second World which subordinates consumption to defence. Since the end of the Second World War, too, we have become more and more conscious that the two countries which were growing the fastest were those which lost the war, Germany and Japan, not just because they had re-equipped their industry with the latest in technology but because their research and investment was overwhelmingly devoted to civilian production. Britain took the opposite course, attempting to maintain her traditional status as a world Power, and now a nuclear one, with a declining economic base. Her rate of growth and her ability to compete on the international market steadily deteriorated. The two countries with the highest growth-rates today, Japan and West Germany, spend less than 7 per cent of their R&D budget on defence; Britain and the USA spend 30 per cent. In Britain, the Ministry of Defence is the largest employer of scientists and engineers. In the USA, after President Reagan took office, government defence R&D almost doubled to $31 billion, while civilian R&D fell from $17 to $14 billion a year.[63]

The costs of war have now begun to tell even on the economy of the world's No 1 capitalist country, for the USA is now able to balance its trade-account with Japan (aircraft sales apart) principally through the export of food, including, ironically, soya-beans, in order to pay for the Japanese electronics and cars which make steady inroads on the US domestic market. The machine-tools used in US industry are now twice as old as those used in Japan.

These economic consequences apart, the end-product of the arms race, if not halted, will be regression to a new epoch of hunting and collecting far more savage than the world before agriculture. Within the Third World, hitherto, the binary opposition between development and underdevelopment has been the overriding obsessional concern: in the First and Second Worlds, the Great Fear is, increasingly, the nuclear threat. There are different principal contradictions. This *was* understandable when underdeveloped countries did not possess nuclear weapons. But many soon will. Today, both these issues of underdevelopment and nuclear war are coming together. The last redoubts of colonialism, Israel and South Africa, probably already have the Bomb, and might well use it as a *Götterdämmerung* rather than recognize the rights of peoples they dominate. Authoritarian regimes from Brazil to Iraq are hell-bent on acquiring their own nuclear weapons, disguised, at first, as peaceful reactors. Their immediate cost will be not only the continuing poverty of their peoples, but their continuing repression. Their ultimate cost may well be a supporting role in a scenario of global destruction in which those who survive or who are merely spectators will be the most unfortunate.

Bourgeois democracy classically promised liberty in the form of political and civic rights for the individual. It still means these things, and has added to them a measure of redistribution of wealth which caters for the needs of the least privileged. That kind of democracy, painfully won over centuries, and then defended and extended by later generations, is embodied not just

in parliaments and courts, in questions in the House and Royal Commis-
sions, but in a whole political praxis of life in innumerable pressure-groups
and cause organizations, and in the possibility – almost the habit – of forming
new ones whenever they are needed, and in the expectation as of *right* that
those who rule them will be accountable to those they claim to represent.

These things are always under threat, however, and the liberal concept
still excludes both economic equality and fraternity, in the form of the
collective ownership and control of material resources, which lie at the heart
of socialism and which make equality more than a juridical or a minimalist
conception – the notion that 'the courts are open to rich and poor alike, just
like the Ritz Hotel'. To the poor of the Third World, the institutionalized
socialism of the communist countries is seen as a system which provides
bread, but not freedom. To even the least privileged in the First World, it
means the absence of both. Unless socialism promises more freedom and
greater prosperity, it will remain, in the West, a form of politics oriented to
humanizing capitalism rather than replacing it by another kind of society
altogether. Its project should be, therefore, not the abolition of the gains of
the bourgeois epoch, but their extension; of more democracy, not less; and
of a richer kind of co-operative life now, not in the future; and a promise,
too, not just of bread and TV sets, but of using the world's wealth so as to
meet the human needs of the majority of mankind rather than to make a very
few very rich indeed and to divide humankind into an aristocracy who live in
the First World and an underclass who live in the Third.

None of this is going to be achieved merely by increasing the flow of 'aid'.
Aid in its present form given to governments in their present form merely
increases a poor country's economic and political dependence. Its aim, Joan
Robinson has said, is 'to perpetuate the system that makes aid necessary'.
Conversely, it strengthens the export-industries of the rich countries and
provides profits for banks. The mere servicing of foreign debt (of which aid is
only one component) today absorbs more than half the export earnings of
many countries. Since 1972, the Third World has spent $268.5 million on
arms alone from the five biggest suppliers in the First World. Now, in an era
of recession, they are unable to cope even with interest payments, let alone
paying back the capital borrowed, causing countries to default and
threatening the stability of the entire world financial system.[64]

Nor does private aid make any significant difference. It is like trying to
sweep back the sea with a broom. Organizations like War on Want have
therefore shifted from a policy of simply giving to the world's poor to one of
enabling them to fend for themselves. Saving even the minority they can
assist from total starvation or slower death through diseases of poverty is
eminently worth-while and necessary. But for all its virtues, it does nothing
to change the structures which will continue to generate the disasters to
which people in the First World so compassionately respond.

We said at the outset that these countries are not naturally poor. They
have been made poor. Nor is their problem one of needing to be taught how
to produce. It is that the wealth they do produce ends up elsewhere. The
situation will continue as long as they receive low prices for their products
and pay high prices for what we sell them.

These poor countries are quite different from societies with 'Zen
economies' which the nineteenth century called 'primitive communism': the
'original affluent societies' in which people produce individually and
appropriate socially. Production is a necessary social activity and will remain
so. But those societies still provide us, as they provided Lewis Henry
Morgan, with evidence that there have been, and will be, societies in which
the economy is neither the primary preoccupation, nor an end in itself, but a
means of meeting human needs and satisfying social wants; evidence, in
Morgan's words, that 'a mere property career is not the final destiny of
mankind', and that 'the next higher plane of society' would be 'revival, in a
higher form, of the liberty, equality, and fraternity of the ancient gentes'. In
Marx's vision – so often reduced to a monochromatic economic determinism
– Economic Man, beloved of bourgeois political economy, would disappear
in the socialism of the future. We would enter the 'realm of freedom' only
when 'labour which is determined by necessity and mundane considerations'
ceased: 'in the nature of things . . . beyond the sphere of material
production'.

Socialism, Engels believed, would emancipate people from the domination by hierarchical structures which even the Labour movement had
produced. 'The German proletariat today', he wrote in 1885,

> . . . does not need any official organization any longer, either public or
> secret; the simply, self-evident interconnection of like-minded class
> suffices, without any statutes, committees, resolutions, or other tangible
> forms, to shake the whole German empire to its foundations. . . . The
> simple feeling of solidarity, based on the understanding of the identity of
> class position, suffices to create and hold together one and the same great
> party of the proletariat among the workers of all countries and tongues.[65]

Two decades later, Lenin repeated and extended that vision in *State and
Revolution*. Every cook would rule the State; all that was needed to run
society were the 'extraordinarily simple' skills of 'book-keeping and
control . . . , within the reach of anybody who can read and write and knows
the first four arithmetical rules'. Because he went on to create a centralized
society dominated by a centralized Party, we do not know, today, whether to
laugh or cry at these words.

Socialist societies, up to now, have been built by those for whom politics
was conviction politics. Their ideal of a co-operative and egalitarian society
drove them to organize parties powerful enough to overthrow the State, and

then to use the power of the new states they had created to pull and push, sometimes force, people along the path of their vision. It was also strong enough to induce millions of ordinary people to give their lives. But only a small proportion of the Chinese people, Mao once said, were socialists, and individual solutions to their problems still meet with a ready response today. Intransigent towards opposition and intolerant of diversity, iron resolution enabled the Bolsheviks to modernize the wretchedly backward Tsarist Empire despite famine, civil war and invasion; transformed a ruined China into a country where a billion people have enough to eat and whose health system commands the world's respect; and turned a sugar-plantation with a playground-cum-brothel enclave for the rich of Cuba and the USA into an inspiration for the poor of Latin America.

They are not the only kind of intransigent conviction politicians, but their goals are the opposite of those in the West who are using the power of the State to dismantle the machinery of social support for the disadvantaged built up over generations and to replace it by a society in which the race goes to the strong and the weak to to the wall. We know the consequences: the glitter and opulence of luxury hotels and condominiums, and the drug addiction centres in those devastated social battlefields called Harlem and the South Bronx.

It is possible to create an infinitely better society than that; possible, too, in countries where democracy has been developed over centuries, not driven underground, to create a much more participatory kind of society than that of the Second World. The problem, moreover, is not one of mobilizing people in order to create wealth, but the equitable distribution of the wealth that already exists. Marx, Warren has argued, was right after all: capitalism is developing in the Third World. He also believed that socialism would emerge first in the West. That belief was falsified by events. After the experience of Chile, that bourgeois, Europeanized and parliamentary society, it is hard to believe that ruling classes anywhere will give way to elected socialist governments with good grace. Class struggle might well give way to class war, in Miliband's words, even in the West.[66] In reaction, the organizations of those who seek change become themselves tougher and more rigid. But socialism in the West, if it ever comes, might well prove to be much closer to Engels' and Lenin's visions than the kinds of socialism that have emerged hitherto in poor countries with no heritage of democracy.

⌐ Democracy is necessary before soc⁼.

Appendix

The Urban Poor in the Workshop of the World

Henry Mayhew was an extraordinary man who lived in an extraordinary place at an extraordinary time. Apart from writing books and plays, promoting philanthropical reform, and even helping to edit *Punch* at one point, he devoted years of his life to the detailed ethnographic description of the life of the lower depths of London society.

London was not a centre of basic industry; as the capital, it had an unusually large tertiary sector which gave unstable employment to hundreds of thousands who ministered to the needs of the rich, from those in the garment-trades to servants.[1] But there were hundreds of thousands of others who led even more precarious lives.

Mayhew's study of them was by no means only a qualitative one, though it is so vivid that I cannot resist giving a sample of the richness of his descriptions below. In his personal lifestyle, he was an 'undisciplined . . . irreverent Bohemian'. But he was also an obsessional quantifier, who would spend hours calculating the weight of the excreta of the average horse (41lb, 9oz, 'in a fresh state') in order to arrive at an estimate of the total volume of horse-dung on the streets of London, or calculating that a ton of cigar-ends were thrown into the gutters every week (210,000 a week, equalling one ton).

His total dedication to discovering the truth disturbed others who preferred not to know about human misery or have it brought to public attention, and who therefore accused him of socialism, radicalism, and other bad things. But Mayhew was unstoppable.

He also rejected the categories used in official statistics, devising instead a classification of occupations of his own which, in true Victorian fashion, invoked moral and not only economic criteria. Workers were distinguished from non-workers; the former then divided into 'enrichers', 'auxiliaries', 'benefactors' and 'servitors'; the latter into 'those who cannot work' and 'those who will not'. He devoted only one page to 'those who *need* not work' because they draw their income from rent, dividends, yearly stipends, 'obsolete or nominal offices', 'trade in which they do not appear', etc., but the sarcasm is obvious. *Per contra*, there are many hundreds of compelling,

vivid pages about the poor, and very little moralizing even about prostitution. In discussing what others preferred to euphemize as the 'social evil' –
the lives of the various kinds of beggars, thieves and swindlers – he treats
them as a *subculture*, with values and an organized social life of their own.
Hence though he applied mathematical techniques to the study of the
economy, and of poverty, the poor, to him, were never 'economic man'.
Rather, as Yeo observes, he arrived at 'the crucial idea that economic
change was refracted through a cultural lens'.[2] He was, then, a pioneer of
urban ethnography. But he was also well aware of the findings of
comparative ethnology, drawing, in his study of prostitution, upon studies of
ancient societies and contemporary 'civilized', 'semi-civilized' and
'barbarous' peoples.

At the beginning of the nineteenth century, three windmills could still be
seen from the Strand and meadows and fields were to be found behind
Portland Place. But by 1830 the population had grown from 865,000 to one
and a half million, and in the next twenty years, another million poured in.[3]

The street-folk, he noted, 'differed as widely from each [other] in tastes,
habits, thoughts and creed, as one nation from another'. There were two
'distinct and broadly marked races': nomads and settlers; but all were
engaged in buying, selling or 'finding'. They ranged from the 'aristocracy' of
the costermongers (street-sellers), the 'patterers' (so-called because they
shouted their wares), down through the street entertainers and the street-
mechanics to the beggars 'driven to the streets by utter inability to labour',
unable to find regular employment. Ethnic varieties included Jewish
clothes-sellers, French singing women, German brass bands, Dutch 'buy-a-
broom' girls, and, above all, the colonial poor, the Irish, whose numbers
doubled during the Famine alone.

Mayhew also describes the *culture* of the street. They had their own
language, 'habits and amusements' (boxing, skittles, dancing, concerts,
card-playing, fighting, pigeon-shooting, and music-hall, especially the 'Vic'
gallery. Only about three in a hundred costermongers 'had ever been in the
interior of a church, or any place of worship, or knew what was meant by
Christianity'.[4] Their politics were 'detailed in a few words – they are nearly
all Chartists' who hated the police above all, and associated them with 'the
governing power'.[5] Only a tenth were married: 'there is no honour attached
to the married state, and no shame to concubinage'.[6] They had, however,
complex moral codes: the costers never stole from one another, even though
whole armies of thieves preyed on shop-keepers and the well-heeled. As for
the idea of 'penny capitalism':

> The costermongers, though living by buying and selling, are seldom or
> never capitalists . . . not more than one-fourth . . . trade upon their own
> property. Some borrow their stock money, others borrow the stock itself,

others . . . the donkey-carts, barrows or baskets, in which their stock is carried round . . . even the weights and measures by which it is meted out.[7]

If they did borrow, they had to pay an 'enormous' rate of interest (double the ordinary rate) which they had to pass on to their customers.

Apart from major markets such as Smithfield or Covent Garden, whole streets and zones were informal markets for nuts, oranges and lemons, greens, eatables and drinkables (pea soup, hot eels, pickled whelks, fried fish, sheep's trotters, baked potatoes, bread, hot green peas, ham sandwiches, meats, ginger-beer, coffee, cat and dog meat, elder wine, milk, curds and whey, rice-milk, water, pastries, boiled puddings, plum duff, pies, cakes, tarts, buns, crumpets, coughdrops, gingerbread nuts, and ice creams). They sold stationery, books and sensational literature, and popular songs, often on contemporary happenings like the burning of the House of Commons recited or sung by 'chaunters' and 'patterers', like the *repentistas* who improvise songs in markets of Brazil's north-east today. Letter-writers (including 'writers without hands'!) and petition-writers plied their trade together with sellers of cutlery, nutmeg-graters, tailor's needles, metal spoons, haberdashers and packmen selling clothing, new and second-hand corn-salve, crackers and detonating balls, cigar lights, toys, fly-papers, walking-sticks, whips, pipes, snuff and tobacco boxes, cigars, sponges, wash-leathers, spectacles and eye-glasses, dolls, rat-poison, tea, second-hand metal articles, musical instruments (including faked antiques); second-hand weapons and curiosities, telescopes and pocket glasses; animals, especially dogs and birds of all kinds, including birds' nests with eggs in them; goldfish, minerals, coal, coke, shells, rags, bottles, glass and bones, kitchen-stuff, grease and dripping, hare and rabbit skins.

At the bottom were the finders of rags and bones, the boy 'mud-larks' who felt with their feet for objects in the exposed banks of the Thames; the dredgers, the sewer-hunters who fought off packs of savage rats for the contents that sometimes went down five feet; the rat-killers, the nightsoil removers, sweepers and scavengers; the dustmen who, like Dickens traded in the 3½ million tons of coal-ashes *per annum*, and who, like Cali's 'vultures', were part of a complex chain.

Entertainment and the arts were sources of livelihood for Punch-and-Judy showmen (Mayhew even gives us the full text): the men who operated marionettes and mechanical figures, telescopes and peep-shows; the acrobats, strong men, street-jugglers, conjurers; the snake-, sword- and knife-swallowers; the reciters and musicians on every kind of instrument; the dancers and singers, the photographers, profile-cutters, pavement artists, exhibitors of trained animals, including dancing dogs; the cabinet-makers and doll's-eye makers; the coal-heavers and porters, ballast-gatherers, lightermen and heavers; 'lumpers' of timber, dock-labourers, watermen, steamboat men, omnibus workers and cab-drivers.

The poverty of the poorest was abysmal. In one lodging house, there were bunks

> . . . each about 7 feet long, and 1 foot 10 inches wide, and the grating on which the straw mattress is placed is about 12 inches from the ground. The wooden partitions between the 'bunks' are about 4 feet high . . . there are five rows of about 24 deep; two rows being placed head to head, with a gangway between each of such two rows, and the other row against the wall. The average number of persons sleeping in this house of a night is 60 . . . about 30 pick-pockets, 10 street-beggars, a few infirm old people who subsist occasionally upon parish relief and occasionally upon charity, 10 or 15 dock-labourers, about the same number of low and precarious callings. . . . At one time there were as many as 9 persons . . . who subsisted by picking up dog's dung out of the street, getting about 5s. for every basketful.[8]

Notes

Preface

1 Cajka (1978), p. 16.

1 Prolegomena

1 Harrison (1979), Chap. 1 and
   pp. 331–2.
2 Hill (1969), p. 82.
3 Rodney (1972).
4 Rowse (1950), p. 43.
5 Worsley (1964), Chap. 1.
6 Stavrianos (1981).
7 Preface to Fanon (1965), p. 7.
8 Bates (1979), p. 201.
9 Mason (1974), pp. 82–3.
10 Elliott (1970), p. 13.
11 Lockhart (1972).
12 Stone (1975), p. 51.
13 Elliott (1970), p. 170.
14 *Ibid.*, p. 177.
15 The complex system of
   corregidores and *oidores*, of
   lower-level *escribanos* and
   alguaciles, and of control through
   consultas, *visitas* and *residencias*, is
   described in Elliott, *op. cit.*,
   pp. 86–99 and 170–81, and in Ots
   y Capdequi (1957) and Phelan
   (1967).
16 Elliott, *op. cit.*, p. 117.
17 Stavrianos (1981), p. 83
18 Hemming (1970), p. 355.
19 Quoted in Stavrianos (1981),
   p. 93.
20 Buarque de Holanda (1969).
21 Lafaye (1974).
22 Mayer, J. (1973).
23 Porro (1977).
24 Wachtel (1971), Chap. 2.
25 Wachtel (1973), pp. 165–228.
26 Elliott, *op. cit.*, p. 147.

27 Hobsbawm (1968), p. 53.
28 Hobsbawm (1962), p. 72.
29 Hobsbawm (1968), p. 54.
30 Elliott, *op. cit.*, p. 367.
31 Alavi (1982), p. 50. Alavi calls the
   mercantilist phase of colonialism
   'pre-capitalist' and the industrial
   phase the 'colonial' mode of
   production.
32 Brockway (1979).
33 Stavrianos (1981), p. 48.
34 *Ibid.*, pp. 206 and 157.
35 *Ibid.*, p. 52.
36 *Ibid.*, p. 158.
37 van Leur (1955), p. 281.
38 Stavrianos, *op. cit.*, p. 230.
39 See the excerpt from Ch'ien
   Lung's speech in Worsley (1964),
   p. 1.
40 Hobsbawm (1962), p. 45.
41 Panikkar (1954), p. 88.
42 Stavrianos, *op. cit.*, pp. 117–18,
   206–29.
43 In Lerner (1968), p. 7.
44 Lipset (1960), p. 403.
45 Parsons (1951), pp. 46–51, 101–12.
46 Frank (1969), p. 34.
47 Shils (1972); Shils and Young
   (1953).
48 McClelland (1961).
49 Gouldner (1955).
50 Frank (1969), p. 24.
51 Bergesen (1980).
52 Warren (1980), pp. 67–8.
53 See the essays by Booth and
   O'Brien, respectively, in Oxaal *et
   al.* (1975).
54 Frank (1969 and 1971);
   Wallerstein (1974 and 1979);
   Amin (1974).

55 For Wallerstein's classification of
    countries as belonging either to
    the 'centre', the 'periphery', or the
    'semi-periphery' of the world
    system, and the difficulties this
    creates, see Worsley (1980).
56 Frank (1969), p. 45.
57 Booth (1975), p. 77.
58 Worsley (1981).
59 Gramsci (1957), p. 101; (1971),
    pp. 342–3.
60 Hodgson (1974).
61 Notes scribbled on an envelope
    found among his papers (Hughes
    (1959), pp. 71–2).
62 Hobsbawm (1972b), pp. 270–1.
63 Thompson (1978), p. 243.
64 Published in *Science at the
    Crossroads*, Kniga, Moscow, 1931.
65 Sahlins (1976), Chap. 3.
66 Gouldner (1970), pp. 215–16.
67 Nettl (1966).
68 Jay (1973).
69 Gouldner (1970), Chap. 12.
70 Though Gouldner addresses
    himself to some of the same issues
    in a later work, the categories he
    uses – 'Scientific' and 'Critical'
    Marxism – seem to me less
    illuminating (Gouldner (1980)).
71 Hall (1977), p. 59.
72 Beynon (1975), p. 319.
73 Harris (1968), p. 240.
74 Gamst (1980); Ross (1980).
75 Sahlins (1976), p. 156.
76 Foster-Carter (1978), p. 74.
77 Terray (1972).
78 Godelier (1978).
79 Krader (1968).
80 Though Anderson emphasizes the
    existence of Europe-wide
    institutions, and of symbiosis
    between East and West, both of
    which go back to the Roman
    Empire (and to a certain degree,
    even the boundaries), his basic
    unit of analysis, chapter
    by chapter, is the *country*.
    Curiously, though most backward

states, notably Russia, Austria and
Poland, are included, Portugal,
the first significant Power to
expand outside Europe (and which
plays a major part in Wallerstein's
study) receives no such attention
in Anderson's Eurocentric work
(Anderson (1974a and 1974b)).
81 See Worsley (1981), pp. 47–52.
82 For example, Harnecker (1974),
    Part 1.
83 See Parkin (1982), Chap. 4.
84 Weber, Max (1949), pp. 64–5.
85 Cabral (1971).
86 Anderson (1974a), pp. 131–7 and
    (1974b), pp. 24–9.
87 Alavi (1973).
88 Anderson (1976), p. 42.
89 Parsons (1951), Chaps 1 and 3.
90 The twenty volumes of Mariátegui
    published by Biblioteca Amauta in
    Lima remain mostly untranslated.
    Of those in English, *Seven Essays
    on Peruvian Reality* is the most
    important.
91 Mario Otero, though he retains
    the term 'ideology', has produced
    a very similar conceptualization of
    culture. 'Ideologies', he writes,
    'are of two kinds: religious and
    socio-political. . . . A socio-
    political ideology is a vision of the
    social world: it is a set of beliefs
    about the ordering and political
    control of community life. These
    beliefs can be grouped into four
    sets:
    (a) *ontological affirmations* about
        the nature of the person and
        the nature of society: what
        kinds of things persons are
        (material, spiritual, or a
        mixture of both), the way they
        combine to form communities
        and what these consist in
        (animal, cultural, or a mixture
        of both);
    (b) *affirmations about economic,
        cultural and political problems*

of these various kinds of communities: what the nature of these problems is and what priorities they indicate;

(c) *value judgements* about persons and their social activities as well as those about organizations and their ends; what is good and what is bad for society;

(d) a *programme of action* (or of *inaction*) for solving social problems (or simply maintaining the existing social order) and for bringing about the alignment of individual with social ends' (Otero (1980), p. 165).

Pierre Bourdieu likewise distinguishes between 'perceptions', 'appreciations', and 'actions' (Bourdieu (1972), pp. 174–8).

92 Worsley (1982).

93 Malinowski (1935), p. 132.

94 For one part of the rich and profound cosmology and philosophy of one Australian tribe, see Berndt and Berndt (1951 and 1952).

95 Etymology still preserves some traces of this ancient, unitary kind of culture:

Like 'ars' in Latin and 'art' in English, the German word 'Kunst' had originally two different meanings the second of which is now all but extinct. On the one hand, it denoted 'können', that is, man's ability purportly to produce things or effects, as nature produces such objects or creatures as stones, trees and butterflies, or such phenomena as rainbows, earthquakes and thunderstorms. On the other hand, it denoted 'kennen', that is, theoretical knowledge or insight as opposed to practice. In the first, or wider,

sense, the word 'Kunst' could be applied to the activities of any producer of things, as the architect, the carver, the embroiderer or the weaver; but also to the activities of any producer of effects, as the physician or the bee-keeper. In the second, or narrower, sense – which still survives in the expression 'Die freien Künste' or 'the Liberal Arts' – astronomy could still be called 'Kunst der Stern' ('art of the stars'). (Panofsky (1943), II, p. 242.)

96 See the fictitious 'miniature role system' on p. 73 of Nadel (1957).

97 Tylor (1871), p. 1.

98 Kroeber and Kluckhohn (1952).

99 Bauman (1973), Chap. 1.

100 Firth (1951), p. 27.

101 Shils (1968), p. 66.

102 White (1949), p. 365.

103 Sahlins and Service (1968).

104 White *op. cit.*, p. 39.

105 Eliot (1948), pp. 46, 101.

106 *Ibid.*, p. 36.

107 *Ibid.*, pp. 32–8.

108 *Ibid.*, p. 31.

109 Williams (1961), p. 230.

110 *Ibid.*

111 C. S. Ford, I. Rouse and Clark Wissler, cited in Kroeber and Kluckhohn, *op. cit.*, p. 128.

112 Williams (1977), p. 80.

113 Etzioni (1964).

114 Foster, J. (1974), pp. 223, 218.

115 Turner (1968).

116 de Heusch (1964).

117 Walter (1973).

118 The main attempt to theoretize the concept being Roszak's *The Making of a Counter-Culture* (1970). In academic circles, radical alternatives to orthodox theory proliferated in the form of journals and 'counter-courses' (Pateman (1972)).

119 Mao (1954), pp. 21–59.

120 Parkin (1954), Chap. 3.
121 The opening chapter of Hoggart's pioneering study of working-class culture captures both the persistence and variety of traditional forms and the constant emergence of new ones (Hoggart (1957)).
122 Moorhouse and Chamberlain (1974).
123 Moorhouse, H. F. (1976).
124 Runciman (1972).
125 Young and Willmott (1956).

2 The Undoing of the Peasantry

 1 Kumar (1978), pp. 132, 139.
 2 *Ibid.*, p. 164.
 3 Lévi-Strauss (1966), pp. 13–15.
 4 Peters (1960).
 5 Thompson, E. P. (1967).
 6 Holmberg (1950), pp. 30, 91.
 7 Sahlins, 'The Original Affluent Society', in Sahlins (1972), p. 36.
 8 *Ibid.*, p. 14.
 9 *Ibid.*, p. 9.
10 Lee (1979).
11 Malinowski (1922).
12 Salisbury (1962).
13 Malinowski, *op. cit.*, p. 515.
14 Lewis and Barnouw (1956).
15 Burgos (1977), Chap. 5.
16 Gluckman (1963).
17 J. Le Goff, quoted in Shanin (1982).
18 Weber, E. (1976), p. 115.
19 Dalton (1972), p. 399.
20 Ennew, Hirst and Tribe (1975), pp. 295–6.
21 Shanin (1971); Wolf (1966).
22 Chayanov (1967). The best summaries and appraisals of his work are Kerblay's Introduction to this work and Archetti's Introduction to the Spanish translation of Chayanov (1974).
23 Thus McGee (1973) uses the term 'urban peasantry' to describe the family household economy of 'marginal' subsistence entrepreneurs engaged in street trade (see below Chapter 3). Roberts' *Peasants in Cities* (1978), despite its title, is a 'macro' study of the political economy of migrants to the urban areas. The changes implicit in that title, involving the encounter between rural and urban values and behaviour patterns have been explored more explicitly, usually, by anthropologists such as Lloyd (1979).
24 Sahlins, *op. cit.*, p. 76.
25 This kind of analysis is, of course, equally applicable to industrial society. Thus, Rowntree found in his classic studies of York published in 1901 that poverty was in large measure a function of the phase reached in the family cycle. Its incidence was heaviest at two points: after the birth of the first child, when two incomes were suddenly reduced to one, and at the point when a man's physical powers began to decline (Rowntree (1901)). The difference from peasant society, however, is that the size of the enterprise (factory) is in no way conditioned by the size or composition of any particular family.
26 Wolf, *op. cit.*, pp. 3–10.
27 Redfield (1946); Lewis (1951).
28 Skinner (1964).
29 Chi (1936).
30 Skinner, *op. cit.*, p. 3.
31 *Ibid.*, p. 35.
32 *Ibid.*, p. 39.
33 Arensburg (1937), Chap. 5, 'Shops, Pubs and Fairs'.
34 Wolf (1957).
35 To be precise, the village community was called the *obshchina*; the *mir* was the council that ran the village. But the two terms have been used inter-

changeably and the latter has gained the wider currency.

36 Robinson (1932), pp. 71–5.
37 Sahlins (1972), p. 82.
38 Geertz (1963b).
39 Buchanan (1970), pp. 19-23; Ho (1959), Chap. 8.
40 Elvin (1973); Needham (1954–80).
41 Coulborn (1965), p. 4.
42 Anderson (1974b), Chap. 1.
43 Bloch (1961), p. 442.
44 Hill (1969), p. 29.
45 Ganshof (1952), p. 50.
46 Bloch (1961), p. 254.
47 Gouldner (1960).
48 Bloch (1961), p. 232.
49 Ganshof (1952), p. 130.
50 Wilhelm Abel, cited in Wolf (1966), pp. 5–6, 9.
51 Anderson (1974a), p. 151.
52 The primitiveness of the state machinery was mirrored in the primitiveness of the technological equipment used in administration. King Alfred, Bloch records, 'conceived the idea of carrying with him everywhere a supply of candles . . . to mark the passing of hours' (op. cit., p. 73). The administrative system of the Byzantine Empire, at the same time, was divided into many departments, each with a numerous staff trained in the keeping of elaborate records.
53 Macfarlane (1978), p. 163.
54 Ibid., pp. 83, 100.
55 Weber, Max (1961), Chap. 29.
56 Hill (1969), p. 98.
57 Ibid., p. 146.
58 Moore (1967).
59 Hilton (1973), p. 90.
60 Hill (1969), pp. 19, 56, 70.
61 Ibid., pp. 269–70.
62 Ibid., p. 267.
63 Hobsbawm and Rudé (1969).
64 Foster, J. (1974), Chap. 3.
65 Hill, op. cit., p. 261.

66 Hobsbawm (1962), p. 67.
67 Wittfogel's conception of 'Oriental Despotism' is not just one of a State 'stronger than society' but of one in which 'total terror', 'total submission', and 'government by flogging' are the routine bases of social order and the creation of 'total loneliness' a standard technique for preventing the consolidation of resistance (Wittfogel (1957)). For a study of an African state (the Zulu) in which terror was a normal instrument of rule, see Walter (1969).
68 Anderson (1974b), Chapter 1 in Parts 1 and 2 of that work.
69 Maynard (1962), p. 31.
70 Robinson (1949), p. 17.
71 Many into North America. Woodcock and Avakumovic (1968) relate how the Doukhobors were forced to leave their homeland for the Caucasus, then Cyprus, then for Canada, where they continued their resistance to military service and to secular education. Among their many metamorphoses and contradictions, these people, who believed that God was in every individual, produced the theocratic dynasty of the Verigins. For the Sons of Freedom, in Canada, during the Depression of the 1930s, their pacifism was perfectly compatible with the use of dynamite against an irreligious State power, and walking in processions, naked, to protest against military service and State education.
72 Macfarlane (1978), Chap. 7.
73 Cited in Gunawardana (1975).
74 Anderson (1974b), Note B, 'The Asiatic Mode of Production', pp. 462–549.

75 Elvin (1973), Chap. 10.
76 Essay on 'Sir James Mackintosh's History of the Revolution' in *Essays and Biographies* (1906), cited in Macfarlane (1978), p. 37.
77 Wilson (1970), p. iii.
78 Anderson (1974b), pp. 528–9.
79 Quoted in Gunawardana (1975).
80 Marx and Engels (1972), pp. 315, 84.
81 Leach (1959).
82 Anderson (1974b), pp. 491 ff.
83 Marx and Engels (1972), pp. 40, 86.
84 *Ibid.*, pp. 82–5.
85 *Ibid.*, p. 18.
86 Said (1978).
87 Marx and Engels (1972), pp. 41, 35–6.
88 Marx, cited in Halliday, F. (1974), p. 46.
89 Anderson (1974b), p. 488.
90 Srinivas (1952).
91 See the essays by Chattopadhyay and Kosambi, in Shah (1973).
92 Berreman (1979).
93 Mishra (1979), p. A-86-Z.
94 *Ibid.*, pp. A-89 and A-92.
95 Fairbank (1971), p. 20.
96 Wittfogel (1957).
97 Djilas (1957).
98 Amin (1974).
99 Wallace (1961), pp. 114–15. The social gulf between the aristocracy and the serfs is symbolized in the nineteenth-century Russian joke about how remarkably cultured the people of France were, since there even crossing-sweepers spoke French!
100 Wolf (1969), p. 77.
101 Robinson (1949), p. 61.
102 Shanin (1972), pp. 24, 19: Robinson similarly notes that they were a 'class [sic] marked off from the remainder of the population by special institutions and governed in part by laws quite

peculiar to itself' (*op. cit.*, p. 91).
103 Robinson (1949), pp. 131, 133, 255.
104 Nyerere (1967 and 1968); Kitching (1982).
105 Marx, letter to P. V. Annenkov, 28 December 1846, cited in Kitching, *op. cit.*, Chap. 2, which contains an analysis of populist thinking from its beginnings to the present day. See also Ionescu and Gellner (1969).
106 Wolf (1971), p. 64.
107 Thompson (1968), p. 11.
108 Shanin (1972), Chap. 3, traces the complex arguments.
109 *Ibid.*, p. 114.
110 Lewin, M. (1968), p. 28.
111 Alavi (1965).
112 Wolf (1971), p. 79.
113 Robinson (1949), p. 149.
114 *Ibid.*, pp. 191–2.
115 *Ibid.*, p. 194.
116 Shanin (1972), p. 38.
117 Berger (1980), pp. 195–213.
118 Wertheim (1974), pp. 105–10.
119 Berger, *op. cit.*, p. 199.
120 Scott (1976), p. 45.
121 Berger, *op. cit.*, p. 201.
122 Worsley (1968).
123 Cohn (1957).
124 Bancroft (1958).
125 Foster, G. M. (1967), Chap. 6. Those who think of peasants solely in terms of agriculture often fail to note that Foster defines as peasants all those who 'exchange a significant amount of their production for items they cannot themselves make, in a market setting that transcends local transactions stemming from village specialization' (p. 7). Only one in ten (15 per cent) of all Tzintzuntzeños do so via agriculture, the dominant occupation (55 per cent) being pottery-making. Potting, he notes, calls for close co-operation in the

family (p. 61); potters are also half as likely to innovate as non-potters (pp. 295–6). Conversely, for the minority which lives by agriculture, with little land to preserve and transmit, unlike many peasant societies, elopement is the dominant mode of initiating marriage rather than contractual alliances between families (p. 74); nearly half of all marriages are with persons from outside (p. 72); and girls are valued more highly than boys as domestic assets (p. 63). The image of the limited good, widely taken to be typical of *agricultural* peasants, thus seems to be based on the behaviour of *potters*.

126 Scott (1976), p. 54. Rulers tried to stop this by tattooing their subjects. Tattooing was also used, for very different purposes, by rebels: to provide magical immunity to bullets (*ibid*, pp. 149–50).

127 Marx (1938), pp. 791–2.

128 Selvaratnam (1976); Naidu (1980).

129 Tawney (1966), p. 62.

130 Redclift (1978), p. 68.

131 Mintz and Wolf (1950).

132 Geertz (1960), (1963a) and (1965).

133 Kahn (1978), p. 116.

134 Forman (1975), pp. 212–13.

135 *Ibid*., p. 217.

136 Turner (1968).

137 Turner (1974).

138 Hobsbawm (1959); (1969).

139 Lewin, B. (1957).

140 Gluckman (1963).

141 Forman (1975), pp. 76–8.

142 Trotsky (1959). For a similar analysis of Cuba on the eve of revolution, see Blackburn (1963).

143 In February 1917, Trotsky writes, when 2500 mill-workers were jamming the street in the Vyborg district of Petrograd, 'the officers first charged through the crowd.

Behind them . . . galloped the Cossacks. Decisive moment! But the horsemen, cautiously, in a long ribbon, rode through the corridor just made by the officers. "Some of them smiled", a participant recalls, "and one of them gave the workers a good wink". . . . In spite of renewed efforts from the officers, the Cossacks, without openly breaking discipline, failed to force the crowd to disperse. . . . Individual Cossacks began to reply to the workers' questions and even to enter into momentary conversation with them. Of discipline there remained but a thin transparent shell.' (Trotsky (1959), pp. 110–11).

144 Fainsod (1958), p. 35.

145 Eye-witness account from a village in Orel, quoted in Bauman (1979), p. 412.

146 Deutscher (1949), p. 140.

147 Trotsky (1957), p. 168.

148 Lane (1971).

149 Kautsky's *Die Agrarfrage* is still not translated into English largely because he fell from grace as the leading Marxist theoretician when he supported German involvement in the First World War and subsequently also denounced the fledgling Bolshevik state. He is therefore best known via Lenin's subsequent denunciation of him as a 'renegade', and his work, in consequence, has been largely ignored on the left.

150 Shanin (1972), p. 171.

151 It is rarely appreciated that Chayanov was by no means hostile to mechanized agriculture. The future of Russia was not to be a 'peasant Utopia': this he reserved for his satirical writings. From 1928 onwards, now responsible for planning the new State Farms, he

advocated the 'technical organization' of State Farms as veritable 'grain factories,' as well as expansion into new areas, thus anticipating Kruschev's 'virgin lands' policy by a quarter-century. His model, in *Life and Technology in the Future* (1928), was the mechanized dry farming of the American West on units of 8,000–12,000 hectares which would later be joined together to form farms of as much as 100,000 hectares in size. To make them viable, horses would have to be replaced by tractors, a transition 'comparable to the effect of the steam engine on industry. . . . Agricultural science would have to be thoroughly rethought [and] much of what we have hitherto considered as fundamental . . . relegated to the background.' Hence just as the artisanal workshop had had to give way to the modern factory, 'to defend peasant economy [was] to condemn several generations to slow death.'

Further into the future, his vision was even more apocalyptic: what we would now call hydroponics would render even the soil unnecessary: 'plants would be used purely for their decorative purposes and natural fruits for their inimitable perfumes'. Long before Stalin's visions of 'mastering Nature' via huge shelter-belts, Chayanov, the peasants' theorist, was looking forward to technical control of the climate which would make the precise forward planning of harvests possible.

152 Lewin, M. (1968), p. 150.
153 Bauman (1979), pp. 418–20.
154 Lewin, M. (1968), p. 260.
155 Deutscher (1949), pp. 324–5.
156 *Ibid.*, p. 325.
157 Conquest's estimate (1968). Lewin estimates that 10 million peasants were deported on 'death trains', of whom 'a great many' must have died (*op. cit.*, pp. 507–8).
158 Bauman (1979), p. 426.
159 Kerblay (1968).
160 Bauman (1979), p. 431.
161 Medvedev (1981). Sophisticated analysts in the West sometimes argue that the USSR deliberately chooses to sell oil abroad and import cheap food with the proceeds, rather than invest capital in improving their own agriculture – a view, however, which is not shared by the Soviet leadership who are constantly bemoaning the inadequacy of their agriculture. Much of the imported grain, it is believed, goes, however, to increase meat supplies, as animal-feed.
162 Tawney (1966), pp. 62, 66, 77.
163 Mao (1954), pp. 21–59.
164 *Ibid.*, p. 150.
165 Hinton (1966), p. 52.
166 *Ibid.*, pp. 7–8.
167 Shillinglaw (1971).
168 Mao (1974).
169 Skinner (1964), Part 2.
170 Kitching (1982). The classic source is Mitrany (1961). See also Narkiewicz (1976).
171 Lomnitz-Adler, C. (1979).
172 Guzmán (1965).
173 Manifesto to the Nation, 26 October 1915, published by Palafox and probably written by Soto y Gama (Womack (1969), pp. 246–7).
174 For the terms of the Agrarian Law of 1915, see Appendix A in Womack, *op. cit.*, pp. 405–91. Note the precision with which the peasants distinguished between types of land and distributed different amounts according to differences in climate, quality, and

whether it was rain-fed or irrigated.

175 See the description of the battle of the Cerro de la Pila, where the peons walked up the hill seven times in the face of artillery. Seven-eighths died in each attack, leaving behind seven distinct swathes of corpses (Reed (1969), pp. 247–53).

176 India: Agricultural Production Team (1959).

177 Moore (1967), pp. 392–410. See Tables 2 and 3 on output of rice, and yield per hectare compared to Japan, respectively.

178 See the survey of Latin America by Carroll in Worsley (1971).

179 See introduction to Worsley (1971).

180 For a typical African instance, see Saul, in Worsley (1971), for the history of the Victoria Native Cotton-Growers' Union in Tanzania.

181 *Ibid.*, p. 18.

182 Redclift (1978), p. 17, Table 3.

183 From the Manifesto of the European New Kenya Party, 1959, quoted in Leys (1975), on which the following account draws.

184 Lehmann (1976).

185 A further breakdown, in terms of the number of persons *supported* on a given unit (as distinct from *working* on it) would be needed to complement this analysis. The criterion of family/production unit is then used to construct a model of socio-economic stratification which distinguishes five types of enterprise: *latifundios*; producers on medium-sized multi-family farms; those on family farms; 'under-privileged farm people' on *minifundios*; and 'producers with administrator' (manager), each of these then being broken down further into owners, tenants, occupants, and 'mixed forms of tenure'. 'Administrators' are then analysed separately for all kinds of farming enterprise, and distinguished from 'technicians', as is the category 'workers', which includes share-croppers as well as permanent and temporary workers. A tabular summary, for one country, Brazil, is given in Forman (1975), Table 4, pp. 52–3.

186 Barnett (1975).

187 Byres (1972), where he surveys more than 100 studies of the Green Revolution in India.

188 Project planning in the FAO relies importantly on advice and assistance from transnational corporations, with advice and assistance of the Industry Co-operative Programme (which has a membership of some ninety transnational corporations). 'Inter-Agency Agreements' are drawn up with such agencies as the UN Development Programme, the ILO and UNICEF. (See Esteva and Feder in Oswald (1979), pp. 262 and 290. I also draw upon the contributions of Diaz Polanco, Oswald, Pessah, Cartas, and Echenique in the same volume.) This powerful pressure group thus shapes world food programmes much as the drug companies act as a pressure group in the field of world health programmes.

189 Feder (1977).

190 Oswald (1979), pp. 176–9.

191 Warman (1980).

192 Wolf (1966), pp. 23–9, and Geertz (1963b), pp. 13, 33.

193 Stavenhagen (1970), p. 256.

194 Omvedt (1975), pp. 118–19, and especially Table 1.

195 Brenner (1977), pp. 88–9.

196 The Great Plains, first thought of in quasi-mythological terms as

'Virgin Lands', a veritable 'garden of the world', struck many of those who first pioneered them as virtual deserts. If God had intended it to be productive, many argued, He would not have left it to the Indian and the buffalo (Smith, H. N. (1950); Shannon, (1968)). The inability of the Spaniards to colonize the Plains was due to their lack of three crucial technical devices which the Americans now possessed: the six-shooter (to deal with Indians and competitors); the wind-mill (to raise water); and barbed wire (to make private property in land a physical reality) (Webb (1961,) Chap. 4). Henceforth, the 'farmer and the cowboy could be friends' by keeping on their respective sides of the fence. By 1890, the Census Bureau declared, 'there can hardly be said to be a frontier line any more'.

197 The two largest concessions carved out of the Amazon (by Japanese and West German multinational corporations) were 2.2 million hectares in size and 1.7 million respectively. One Australian cattle-station is larger than Wales. For the wheat and cattle *estancias* of Argentina (where small-farming never developed), see Scobie (1964).

198 Massey (1982).

199 US Department of Agriculture (1976), Tables 30, 32, and 1. The high-point of population density was 1935, when 55 per cent of the land of the 48 states was divided between eight million farmers.

200 Nevins and Commager (1966), Chap. 17.

201 Hill (1969), p. 69.

202 Lipset (1950), p. 15. For Social Credit in Alberta, see Macpherson (1953).

203 Apart from religious and other utopian communities, the major North American exception has been the (not very numerous) co-operative farms formed by veterans of the Second World War in Saskatchewan, which owned or leased the land jointly, organized and divided up work at weekly meetings, for equal wages, and where even the houses were mostly owned by the co-operative. Within those houses, however, the normal individualistic patterns of behaviour and values of Canadian society obtained (Cooperstock (1964)).

204 Kline (1981), pp. 139–40. See also Crittenden (1981).

205 Franklin (1969); Galeski (1972).

206 This explains the apparent paradox that half a million of the 'affluent' and 'well-off' income categories reported no farm profits at all, whereas 87 per cent of the 'poor' operators did. The former are not really farmers at all, but set off their main income, which is non-farm, against their farm operations, as a tax loss. Less than 100,000 are classified as 'affluent' ($90,000 *p.a.*), 3 per cent of all farmers. Most (over a million) had average receipts of only $10,000. A half (52.5 per cent) of all cash receipts went to those running farms with sales of $40,000 and more (North Central Regional Publication (1972), pp. 6–11, 24–28).

207 1½ million had receipts of less than $5000 in 1967 and taxable income of less than $1000 while 3511 had receipts of over half a million dollars.

208 Kline (1981), p. 138.

209 *New York Times*, 1 September 1981.

210 Stavrianos (1981), p. 437.

211 *Ibid.*, p. 436.

212 Eckholm (1978).
213 Omvedt (1975), pp. 114–15.

3   The Making of the Working Class

1 Sahlins (1961).
2 Thompson, E. A. (1948).
3 Undoubtedly so for Spain, though Anderson expresses the usual view of Ottoman rule in Eastern Europe. 'For five hundred years', he writes, they 'camped in the continent without ever being naturalized into its society or political system'. They were an 'Islamic intrusion into Christendom'. The cultural barrier marked by religion is indisputable; but the research that would be needed to document the reality of the Turkish epoch has yet to be done (Anderson (1974b), p. 370).
4 See Castro (1975), Chap. 6, 'Al Andalus como una circunstancia en la vida española'.
5 Stambouli and Zghal (1976).
6 Wheatley (1971).
7 Elvin (1973), pp. 175, 85.
8 *Ibid.*, p. 177.
9 *Ibid.*, p. 250.
10 Aguirre Beltrán (1967).
11 Jara (1916).
12 Hopkins (1978), pp. 30, 38, 70, 104.
13 Nun (1969), pp. 178–237.
14 Tinker (1974). See also Naidu (1980) and Selvaratnam (1976).
15 First (1983).
16 Castles and Kosack (1973); Berger and Mohr (1975).
17 A UN survey found that a Kuwaiti civil servant works an average of seventeen minutes per day (Stavrianos (1981), p. 664).
18 Karpat (1976), pp. 10–11.
19 *New York Times*, 19 February 1982.
20 Berlinck (1975), Table 8, p. 50.
21 Aldunate *et al.*, Chap. 2, p. 10 and Table 10; and Chap. 3, p. 28 and Table 12.
22 See Mangin (1967); Morse (1965 and 1971); and Roberts (1978) for Latin America alone.
23 Moorhouse, G. (1971), pp. 95–101.
24 Cf. Lloyd's distinction between 'ego-oriented' views of society and those which concentrate on the analysis of 'externalized' structure (Lloyd (1979), Chap. 3). His own predilection is emphatically for the first.
25 Lomnitz (1975), unfortunately translated as *Networks and Marginality* in the English-language version.
26 Kapferer (1972), p. 206. The second sentence is somewhat confusing, but the first conveys the classical idealist interactionist message.
27 Lockwood therefore dismisses the antinomy between the problem of 'social integration' which focuses upon relationships between actors, and 'system integration', which focuses on relationships between the parts of a social system as 'wholly artificial', since the ends pursued by various kinds of groups, at different levels, and the interrelationships between them, have all to be taken into account in discussing the degree of coherence of a society, not just 'institutions' or 'classes', on the one hand, or 'primary groups' on the other (Lockwood (1964)).
28 Paine (1974), p. 159, Table 20.
29 See the photographs in Berger and Mohr (1975), pp. 46–51.
30 Paine, *op. cit.*, pp. 117–20.
31 Karpat (1976), p. 109.
32 Perlman (1975), p. 717.
33 Dahya (1974). Despite proclaiming a Weberian concern with 'the meaning of the action to the actor', the standard study by

British researchers (of the same community) is nevertheless largely a descriptive survey which admits to being 'only just able to scratch the surface' of Pakistani life, locally and nationally. These very entrepreneurial people are also treated as 'proletarians'. Though there is no doubt about the reality of discrimination on the part of Whites, the values and aims of the immigrants themselves are consistently underemphasized (Rex and Moore (1967), pp. 116–17).

34 Scobie (1964), pp. 60–1.
35 For Mozambique, First writes of 'incomplete and impermanent proletarianization' (First (1983), p. 185). For Peru, see Laite (1981).
36 Mayer, P. (1961).
37 van Onselen (1976).
38 Gluckman (1960), p. 57.
39 Epstein (1958).
40 Frank (1969).
41 Germani (1973). I draw heavily in this discussion of Latin American theorists on Berlinck (1975).
42 Ibid., p. 75.
43 Ibid., p. 88.
44 Ibid., pp. 87–8.
45 Marshall (1950); Bendix (1969).
46 Marx (1938), Chap. 25, Section 3.
47 Quijano (1966).
48 Quijano (1970).
49 For a representative English-language sample, see Quijano (1974).
50 Kumar (1978), Chap. 3; Nisbet (1967).
51 Simmel (1950).
52 Stonequist (1961), p. 10.
53 Merton (1963).
54 Movement from town to country, he wrote, 'has loosened local bonds, destroyed the cultures of tribe and folk, and substituted for the local loyalties, the freedom of the cities; for the sacred order of custom, the rational organization we call civilization'. In the process, individuals became 'not only emancipated, but enlightened' (Park (1928), pp. 889, 891). Hence, contact, though followed by competition and conflict, would eventually give way to accommodation and assimilation.
55 Wirth (1938).
56 Glass (1962).
57 Thompson's welcome Phillipic against the High Theory of Althusser unfortunately counter-poses 'experience' to 'theory' (Thompson, E. P. (1978)). But what people experience – what happens to them – is not perceived by all of them in the same way. It has to be interpreted. Experience, then, is not unproblematic or self-evident, since the interpretations people make of what happens to them depend upon the cultural assumptions (cognitive, normative and conative) they operate with, and which differ greatly, even for members of the same class. Consciousness, class or otherwise, cannot, therefore be 'read off' from economic situation; it is not a mere epiphenomenon. Being exposed to identical experiences, therefore, teaches people quite different things (Anderson (1980), pp. 25–9; Hall (1981), pp. 378–85).
58 Mills (1959).
59 The main critiques are Valentine (1968) and Leacock (1971), particularly Leeds' essay in the latter. I am indebted to Wendy Hoefler for her lucid summary of the debate.
60 Muñoz et al (1977), p. 90.
61 Karpat (1976), p. 39.
62 Ibid., p. 22.
63 Thus Nun (1969) observes that 26

per cent of non-agricultural labour was absorbed into employment between 1925 and 1960, but only 19 per cent between 1950 and 1960 (p. 215).

64 Muñoz et al., op. cit., Table 7–1, p. 92.

65 Kowarick, in Bromley and Gerry (1979).

66 UK Department of Industry (1977), Table 8, p. 118.

67 Association for Radical East Asian Studies (n.d.), pp. 70–1.

68 Fernández-Kelly (1982).

69 Kidron and Segal (1981), Map 37, 'The Islands of the Blessed'.

70 Middleton (1981), p. 173.

71 McGee (1973).

72 Tax (1953).

73 Bromley, R. (1978b).

74 Gloria Leff Zimmerman, quoted in Uno Más Uno, Mexico City, 30 January 1978.

75 Birkbeck (1979), p. 181, and (1978).

76 La Fontaine (1974).

77 Jocano (1975), pp. 25–27 ff. Many of these women (124 out of the 500 he studied) entered prostitution quite involuntarily, through 'trickery, coercion and subtle manipulation' (usually by their 'boy-friends'), including being raped, drugged and kidnapped, rather than taking it up in order to earn money, though the largest number (143) entered – from the age of fourteen upwards – via 'employment agencies'. Female 'friends', acting as 'bridges', recruited another 93. In Mexico City, where the number of prostitutes probably runs into hundreds of thousands rather than thousands, 90 per cent of the prostitutes who end up in one special prison (often because they failed to pay bribes to 'protectors', including the police) have venereal

disease; many are drug addicts or alcoholics (Uno Más Uno, 10 February 1978).

78 Ruiz-Pérez, in Bromley and Gerry (1979).

79 Jornal de Bahia, 13 May 1978.

80 Jocano (1975), p. 8.

81 In 'Left Wing' Communism, an Infantile Disorder', Lenin (1947).

82 Hart (1973).

83 'Uma nova classe operaria', Veja, 8 March 1978, pp. 85–7.

84 'Radiografia do Brasil', Veja, 18 July 1979, p. 89.

85 'Ameaça aos salarios', Isto É, 19 March 1980, pp. 64–72.

86 Townsend (1981).

87 Children of professional or clerical worker parents had sixty times more chance of entering secondary school in Ghana in 1961 as children whose parents were unskilled workers (Ibid., p. 67).

88 Lomnitz (1975), p. 96.

89 Rusque-Alcaino and Bromley, in Bromley and Gerry (1979) pp. 191–213.

90 Jones, G. S. (1971).

91 Lockwood similarly rejects the notion that clerical workers in Britain are victims of 'false consciousness', arguing that their job, market, and status situations have always been superior to those of manual workers, even if the gap has narrowed (Lockwood (1958)).

92 The average number of relatives supported per wage-earner in Dakar in 1965 was 9.6; cases of over 20 dependants were not unknown. The study, by Pfefferman, is cited in Rimmer (1970), pp. 56–7.

93 The variety of possible forms of the family, and of residence patterns, the types of networks developed, both of kin and non-kin; and of modes of mutual assistance, are indicated, for one

small shanty-town in Mexico City, by Lomnitz (1975). Sheth (1968) describes how workers in an Indian factory find jobs for their relatives and fellow caste-members.

94 Lomnitz (1975).

95 Jocano, *op. cit.*, pp. 7–8, 196–7.

96 Only two people were unemployed in 212 households in Chandigarh; less than 1 per cent in Delhi (1958), 38.5 per cent of them being skilled workers; while 86 per cent were employed in one Madras sample (1961), the rest being 'unemployed', 'unemploy-able', 'never employed' and 'students' (*sic*) Stokes (1962).

97 Germani (1973), pp. 103–11, including Tables 8, 9 and 10.

98 Muñoz *et al.* (1977), p. 94, including Table 7–2.

99 Cornelius (1975), p. 22. Most urban immigrants in Turkey got a job within a month and found it themselves (Karpat (1970), pp. 88–90).

100 Stokes (1962).

101 Perlman (1976), p. 149.

102 Cornelius (1975), p. 230.

103 Karpat (1976), p. 26.

104 Muñoz *et al.*, *op cit.*, p. 92, Table 7–1.

105 Godfrey (1970), pp. 237–8. *Laissez-faire* economists like Harry Johnson, Godfrey observes, defend this flow in the name of 'freedom of choice' and on the grounds that 'the international circulation of human capital is a beneficial process' (p. 239). In any case, they argue, there is no employment available for such people in backward economies, and the remittances sent back home benefit not only the immediate recipients, but the country as a whole. But only a tiny minority of the very privileged get into higher education and, over the generations, they become consolidated into a virtual caste. The freedom to earn at the price that their labour can command on the *international* market - the 'sacred principle of comparability' – means that even for those who return home, their salary-levels are related to high salaries overseas and helps sustain a high level of earnings for the educated as a whole. As a result, a tendency developed for domestic supply to exceed domestic demand for some categories (pp. 243–4). Needless to say, their services are hardly ever available to the poor. The way out of this vicious circle lies in expanding educational opportunities at home in fields indicated by national needs (manpower planning) rather than allowing the free play of the market to benefit a privileged minority at the cost of the unfortunate.

106 Sorokin (1956), Chap. 1.

107 Hart (1973).

108 Bromley, R. (1978a) and Moser (1978).

109 By one or two anthropologists; in Oliveira's 'Critica da razão dualista', in Brazil; and, in Africa, in Weeks' analysis of the 'unremunerated sector' in Bugisu and Wallace's study of Buganda (Bromley, R. (1978a), f.n.11).

110 Criticisms listed in Bromley, R. (1978a).

111 35 per cent of Cali's 9500 street-traders sell ice-cream, newspapers, soft drinks (as well as a variety of contraband, illegal, damaged, stolen, contaminated and sub-standard goods) or are dependent for supplies and credit on manufacturers, wholesalers and criminals to whom they pay high

prices and interest-rates (5–10 per cent a day). (Bromley, R. (1978b).)

112 MacEwen Scott (1979), p. 128.
113 Middleton (1981), Chaps 1 and 6.
114 Karpat, *op. cit.*, p. 38.
115 *Ibid.*, p. 106.
116 See the photo on p. 33 of Cornelius, *op. cit.*
117 Karpat, *op. cit.*, p. 58.
118 The theory that poor immigrants are great 'joiners', because they depend on others in cities where they are poor and do not know their way around, has been refuted, for Africa at least, where the majority do not join voluntary associations at all. It is people of higher socio-economic status who do the joining, just as it is with the middle class in Europe (Epstein (1967) and, for Europe, Bottomore (1954)).
119 Nash (1979), Chap. 5.
120 Mayer, P. (1980), pp. 69–70.
121 In an anomalous and atavistic regime like that of South Africa, it is the State which keeps the rural connection alive, via its *apartheid* policies: 'oscillatory' migration between the city and the rural areas of the Transkei – where 60 per cent of the households cannot produce enough to feed themselves – is so great that, today, it is no longer mainly the young who go to the mines and the factories, but most able-bodied males of all ages, and many of the younger women. In some villages, only the sick and unemployable remain. But though all want jobs, attitudes to the values of White-dominated society vary: migrants are therefore culturally heterogeneous not just in respect of their ethnic origins, but in their attitudes to life in the city and its values. Those who aspire to

Westernization (known as 'School' people), though as anti-White as the 'Reds' (so-called because they smear their bodies, in the traditional way, with ochre, not because they are leftists) – who reject the hegemonic subculture and defend their own cultural heritage – differ radically in their attitudes both to city life and Western values. Today, however, the younger generation increasingly rejects both and is turning to a variety of new modes of self-expression, from youth-gang rebellion to a more political Black Consciousness (Mayer (1980)).

122 See the chapters by Agassi and Goodstadt in Jarvie and Agassi (1969) and by Hopkins in Hopkins (1971).
123 The image of the housing, lives and social worth of immigrant workers as being similar to those enjoyed by inhabitants of chicken-runs has not escaped Olmi in his film *Bread and Chocolate*.
124 Similarly, Chandigarh, designed by Le Corbusier as the new capital of the Punjab, and a city of 'sun, space and greenery' in which, 'for the first time in Indian history, every household was going to have at least a two-roomed house with kitchen, bath and veranda, and . . . modern amenities like piped water, electricity, water-borne sewerage and drains', had degenerated, by 1971, into a place where 38 per cent of the households had one room each, with 3.4 persons on average, and another 35 per cent had two rooms with 2.3 persons per room; 15 per cent of the population were living in squatter settlements on the outskirts, and 54 per cent of the trading and service enterprises

were operating outside the planned structure (Sarin (1979)).

125 Cornelius, *op. cit.*, p. 80.

126 De Camargo *et al.* (1976), p. 28.

127 Karpat, *op cit.*, pp. 35 and 81. ninety-two per cent of married men and women interviewed in Turkey believed that their children would have a better life. In Rio, Caracas and Rabat, half to three-quarters expressed similar optimism: As a Rabat squatter put it, 'One doesn't have money but has hope.'

128 Mangin (1967), pp. 84–5.

129 Perlman (1976), p. 243.

130 Lomnitz (1975) found it necessary to distinguish four levels of poverty in Cerrada del Condor shanty-town.

131 Saldívar, 'Diferencias ideológicas entre obreros y empleados', in Muñoz *et al.*, *op. cit.*, Chap. 14.

132 Karpat, *op. cit.*, p. 44.

133 Fanon (1965), pp. 102–3.

134 Perlman, *op. cit.*, p. xvi.

135 Karpat, *op. cit.*, p. 234.

136 Cornelius, *op. cit.*, pp. 233, 80.

137 Perlman, *op. cit.*, p. 191.

138 Cornelius, *op. cit.*, p. 213.

139 Karpat, *op. cit.*, p. 233.

140 Cornelius, *op. cit.*, p. 106.

141 Kornhauser (1960).

142 Karpat, *op. cit.*, p. 65.

143 Vekemans (1967).

144 Oquist (1973).

145 Quoted in Davidson (1969), pp. 50–1. A markedly different translation of the whole text is given in Cabral (1971).

146 Fanon (1965).

147 See Hagopian (1974), pp. 171–7.

148 Warren (1980), pp. 128–40 'The General Effects of Colonialism', and 224–35.

149 Chile, Uruguay, Peru, Argentina and Mexico are studied in Mesa-Lago (1978).

150 Laite (1981).

151 'Social security has seldom been used as a social or economic indicator in Latin America or elsewhere. In a recent study by the Economic Commission for Latin America (ECLA) . . . [in which] forty-three socio-economic indicators were computed to measure and classify the level of development . . . none . . . [was] based on any aspect of social security' (Mesa-Lago, *op. cit.*, p. 3).

152 Two per cent of each firm's income-tax was paid into the fund instead of to the government. The firm added ½ per cent of their sales-turnover. Half was then divided between the firm's workers according to their annual wage; the other half according to seniority. The funds were invested on the stock exchange or to finance private enterprise. Each worker was issued with a pass-book, and withdrawals could be made for marriage, house-construction, retirement, invalidity, or death. Interest accumulated annually at 3 per cent (Bacha (1979), pp. 4.2–3, 4.30, 4.55, and 5.62–3).

153 Heath (1980), pp. 106–11.

154 Somarriba (1978); Junior (1976).

155 Gross and Underwood (1971).

156 Roxborough (1981).

157 Halliday, J., (1980), p. 7.

158 Quoted in Worsley (1975), p. 47.

159 Halliday, J. *op. cit.*

160 Dorfman and Mattelart (1972); a study whose publication in English was met with fierce counter-attacks from the Disney corporation's lawyers.

161 Lubeck (1980).

162 Thompson (1968), p. 9.

163 Cabral (1971), p. 48.

164 Nghe (1963).

165 Mayhew (1967); see Appendix below.

166 Harrington (1962).

4 Ethnicity and Nationalism

1 The fighting qualities of the Sikhs, Dogras, Rajputs or Gurkhas, were seen as rooted in a whole way of life, which could, however, become diluted. It was therefore important to distinguish the subcultural differences between 420 subdivisions of Dogras. Handbooks written for recruiting officers therefore were virtually anthropological monographs in which the British officer caste's 'obsession with precedence, breeding and heredity' was projected onto a society that was 'in movement, changing and melting', presenting, thereby, a spurious 'stationary picture of [the] social structure' (Mason (1974), pp. 35–6).

2 van Onselen (1976), pp. 153–4, the only pages, however, devoted to this crucial practice.

3 Barnett and Njama (1966).

4 Massey (1981).

5 Ahistoric analyses like Horkheimer's comparison of contemporary imigrants with Jews in Nazi Germany conflate the quite unlike situations of an 'internal' ethnic minority during an epoch of Depression and mass authoritarianism with an epoch of sustained economic growth and a democratic politics which rejected the Nazi past. For a brief critique of other aspects of Frankfurt School theories of authoritarianism, see Worsley (1976).

6 See the photo on p. 51 of the moving 'book of words and images' by Berger and Mohr, *A Seventh Man*.

7 Paine (1974), p. 116 (sample survey in 1971).

8 Massey (1981).

9 Analogies between free labour in Western Europe or South Africa and quite unfree labour during the Second World War – the 1.8 million prisoners of war and many millions more forced labourers – are not mere emotive rhetoric. 'Every fourth tank, lorry, field-gun, every fourth piece of ammunition was made by the hands of a foreigner in 1944' (quoted in Castles and Kosack (1973) p. 23). (This leaves aside the hundreds of thousands recruited into the Nazi armed forces and the hundreds of thousands more recruited through the labour market in the usual way.) At the beginning of the post-war immigration flow, a number of Italian, Spanish, and Greek workers in West Germany were actually housed in the huts of the former Dachau concentration camp. Many of the wardens of many German hostels, too, 'gained their "experience of dealing with foreign workers" during the War' (Castles and Kosack (1973), p. 262).

10 *Ibid.*, Chap. 4.

11 *Ibid.*, pp. 296–7.

12 Simons and Simons (1969), Chap. 13.

13 Two outstanding films capture their lot with singular poignancy: Fassbinder's *Fear Eats the Soul*, a study of a Moroccan immigrant whose marriage to a German cleaning-woman results in her being abandoned by her friends; and Brusati's *Bread and Chocolate*, about Italian workers in Switzerland. The ultimate irony is the stigma attached to being a Finnish immigrant worker in wealthy Sweden, where the Finns, despite their blond hair and blue

eyes, are still treated, as the Black South African sociologist, Mafeje, has observed, as 'Nordic Blacks'.

14 'The process by which social collectivities seek to maximize rewards by restricting access and opportunities to a limited circle of eligibles' (Parkin (1979) p. 44).

15 Gibb (1962), Chap. 5.

16 Halliday, F. (1974), p. 25. Thus the chapter on Iran, even the section on 'The New Opposition', discusses secular radicalism, but makes no reference to the religious movement that was to seize power five years later. A later study of Iran, written just before the collapse of the Shah's regime, does explore the mullahs and the bazaar merchants who were crucial in the formation of a Muslim opposition, but still concludes that 'religious leaders such as Ayatollah Khomeini . . . offer an ill-defined, ambiguous alternative', which is very rapidly passed over (Chap. 8.). Lest this be thought an uncharitable criticism with the benefit of hindsight, an Iranian specialist, writing a decade earlier, and focusing on the ulama and the merchants as the main enemies of the Shah, and concluded that 'Iranian national consciousness still remains wedded to Shi'i Islam, and when the integrity of the nation is held to be threatened by internal autocracy and foreign hegemony, protest in religious terms will continue to be voiced, and the appeals of men such as the Ayatullah Khumayni to be widely heeded' (Algar (1972), p. 255).

17 Mojahed (1980), p. 44.

18 Nairn (1975), p. 329.

19 Hobsbawm (1972a), p. 385.

20 Butterfield (1965), pp. 67–8.

21 Smith, A. (1971), pp. 194–9;

Breuilly (1982), pp. 15–18.

22 Smith, A. (*op. cit*), divides nationalisms into 'pre-Independence' and 'post-Independence'. Within the former category are three sub-categories, 'colonial', 'ethnic' and 'mixed', 'colonial' having two further sub-sub-categories ('heterogenous' and 'cross-cultural'), and 'ethnic' four ('secession', 'diaspora', 'irredentism' and 'Pan'). Post-independence movements are divided into 'recent' and 'sovereign' sub-categories, the former with three sub-sub-categories ('integration', 'protection' and 'expansion'), the latter with two ('renewal' and 'preservation'). These 'sub-stantive' nationalisms are then grouped into 'primitive', 'developed' and 'current', cross-classified into 'territorial', 'mixed' and 'ethnic', and finally graded according to 'formal (intensity and achievement) criteria' as either 'failed' or 'successful' (Tables 4 and 5, pp. 228–9). One is reminded of Lévi-Strauss' description of Elkin's taxonomy of totemism as one which, 'instead of helping to slay the hydra . . . has dismembered it and made peace with the bits' (Lévi-Strauss (1969) p. 66), or Sorokin's designation of Lloyd Warner's approach to the study of social class as 'meatball' sociology (Sorokin (1956), pp. 162–3).

23 Swartz, Turner and Tuden (1966), Introduction.

24 Kuper's phrase is therefore inappropriate (Kuper, 1947) to that extent, though it is presumably meant to emphasize that all Blacks are stigmatized in the same way.

25 Griffin (1961).

26 De Vos and Romanucci-Ross (1975), pp. 363–71. Or, as Gauguin put it, '*D'où venons-nous? Qui sommes-nous? Où allons-nous?*'

27 Kohn (1968), p. 63.

28 Benjamin Akzin's phrase, quoted in Bonfil (1981), p. 30.

29 Gulliver (1967), p. 260, p. 83 and p. 55 respectively.

30 Moerman (1968).

31 Leach (1954).

32 Colson (1968). Whilst accepting her view that the nation is equally a *construct*, one must dissent from her conclusion that 'tribalism . . . has the same qualities as nationalism and seems to arise under the same circumstances' (p. 201).

33 Evans-Pritchard (1937).

34 La Fontaine (1967), p. 189.

35 Despite taking formalist 'human ecology' and primary-group formation as his principal theoretical framework, Thrasher's classic 1927 study of *The Gang* does recognize that the gang was 'largely a phenomenon of the immigrant of the poorer type' (Thrasher (1963), Chap. 10, 'Race and Nationality in the Gang'). It was left to Wirth to develop the implications of this into a *theory* of the ghetto (Wirth (1956)).

36 Epstein (1958).

37 Mitchell (1956).

38 Grillo (1967).

39 Gellner (1964), p. 165. (I myself, with a Greek grandmother and two other grandparents from Northern and Southern Ireland respectively, am as English as they come in culture.)

40 Ware (1935), p. 152.

41 See Dahya (1974).

42 *Ibid.*, p. 163.

43 In Gulliver (1967), p. 340.

44 The inability of many to perceive this is reflected in the mistranslation of the title of Bendix's *Nation-Building and Citizenship* as *Estado y Nación* in the Spanish-language edition, thereby replacing the *relational* category 'citizenship' by the *collective* noun '*nación*', and substituting for the *processual* noun 'nation-*building*' the structural term '*estado*'. I draw heavily on Bendix's illuminating study in what follows.

45 The concept of the 'segmentary' state is taken from Southall's study of the Alur (Southall (1956)).

46 Srinivas (1952).

47 *Encyclopaedia of the Social Sciences* (1937), p. 322.

48 Abu-Lughod (1971), pp. 59, 24, 71.

49 Furnivall (1948), p. 34.

50 Hill (1969), p. 28.

51 *Ibid.*, pp. 36–8.

52 Hobsbawm (1972a), p. 388.

53 The most sycophantic worship of Gloriana occurs, fortunately, in an apocryphal play:
    This royal infant . . .
    Though in her cradle, yet now promises
    Upon this land a thousand thousand blessings . . .
    . . . She shall be . . .
    A pattern to all princes living with her,
    And all that shall succeed . . .
    (*Henry VIII*, v, iv) etc., etc.

54 Elliott (1970), p. 128.

55 Morris (1982), p. 144.

56 Macpherson (1962).

57 Gellner (1964), p. 156.

58 Bendix (1969), p. 84.

59 Carr (1968), p. 3.

60 Marx, 'The Chartists' (1852) in Bottomore and Rubel (1956), pp. 204–5 – a philosophy

symbolized in the person of the modernizing mill-owner, Robert Moore, in Charlotte Brontës *Shirley*, who loathes the reactionary Castlereagh and his Orders in Council, but fears his workers even more.

61 Hill (1968).

62 Briggs (1960).

63 German nationalism, seen often simply as Prussian militarism writ large, grew out of an equally Prussian tradition, that of a liberal bureaucracy that saw itself as applying Reason to the organization of the State. Pioneer German nationalism was 'against the jackboot'. Ironically, German unification came about in neither of these ways, but much more prosaically, through a customs union, the *Zollverein*, which achieved what Romantic nationalism could not, and was justly celebrated by the author of *Deutschland Über Alles*. It was

> Ham and scissors, boots and garters,
> Wool and soap and yarn and beer

which had unified the nation (Hobsbawm (1962), p. 165).

64 *Ibid.*, p. 169.

65 Gellner (1964), p. 150; Nairn (1975), p. 332.

66 Argyle (1967), pp. 41, 47.

67 *States'* rights were another matter. Interference with them was invoked to justify secession from the Union. In Lee's case, his belief in Virginia's political right to run its own affairs was strong enough to outweigh his objections to slavery and induce him to refuse the command of the Union forces.

68 Castro (1975), p. 269. This writer sees *hidalguismo* and the obsession with *limpieza de sangre* as the legacy of Arab (and even

Visigoth) conceptions of *their* social superiority *vis-à-vis* the Iberians they had conquered.

69 Ribeiro (1970).

70 Bonfil (1972).

71 Hemming (1970).

72 Anderson (1974a), pp. 24–5.

73 The same debates over slavery and Christianity took place in South Africa centuries later, with the same result: Christianized slaves remained slaves (Worsley (1964), p. 3).

74 Said (1978).

75 Also known as '*La Malinche*', her name has given rise to the term *malinchismo*: the excessive worship of things foreign as being intrinsically superior to things Mexican. It is a singularly, anachronistic notion, for since there was no 'Mexico' as we know it today, she could not be a traitor to it. She had, in fact, suffered greatly at the hands of the Aztecs, and was only too ready to ally with their powerful new enemies, the Spaniards. She can more aptly be regarded, therefore, as a patriot rather than a traitor.

76 Wagley (1959), pp. 534–5.

77 Torre Villar (1964), p. 110.

78 For the iconography of role-reversal during Carnaval (though not the nationalist dimension), see da Matta (1977 and 1979) and Leopoldi (1978).

79 González Navarro, in Caso, *et al.* (1954), pp. 115–19.

80 Cueva (1977), p. 7.

81 In a country that experienced no such revolutionary transformation, the lot of Indians in the Sierra of Ecuador was even worse. Any cash they earned through working on plantations or selling cash-crops went into the hands of the local *mestizo* shopkeepers. When they went to market, their

crops were literally wrested from them by the middlemen who gave them derisory payments. As late as the 1950s, when they bought cloth, a *vara de indios* measuring-stick was used, shorter than the *vara de blancos* used for Whites (see the picture in Burgos (1977), p. 227). They were even exploited in the public lavatories, by being charged for each piece of paper they used. When they spoke to Whites, they were expected to take off their hats and assume a respectful posture. When they died, they were charged for the number of times the church-bell was tolled.

82 Stalin, quoted in Deutscher (1949), p. 328.

83 Carr (1968), pp. 20–1.

84 Contemporary Soviet ethnography uses a definition of the 'ethnic community' which is practically identical with Stalin's (unacknowledged) definition of the nation. This wider conceptualization of ethnicity, however, involves a crucial loss: the connection between the emergence of the nation and the emergence of the modern State. We are left with a list of attributes (territory, language, common culture and values, etc.) which do not necessarily occur together. Where they do, the connections are not explained, nor those between cultural forms and political and economic institutions. Finally, the sociological significance of culture and of values is not theoretically conceptualized at all, but simply described in their empirical, institutional manifestations (differences of language, values, etc.) (Bromley, Y. (1974); Kozlov (1974)).

85 See the table on p. 512 of Stavrianos (1981), showing living-standards in Soviet Central Asia in 1926 and 1962, and comparing the latter with Turkey, Iran and India. In consequence, he observes, 'whereas the 1905 Russian Revolution contributed to the 1906 Constitutional Revolution [in Persia], the 1978–9 revolution against the Pahlavi dynasty incited no challenge to Soviet rule in the Azerbaijan Republic'.

86 A view most cogently argued by Kedourie (1960), and in the introduction to his later study (1970), the intellectual level and tone of which can be judged from his description of Lenin's *Imperialism* as a 'pamphlet' and 'the lucubrations of a revolutionary scribbler [who] made a modest but useful profit for Parus Publishers who brought it out' (p. 7).

87 'there was [no] natural racial or linguistic boundary . . . The exact line [of separation] in the end . . . was the result of political accident . . . Founded by foreigners, the Netherlands state continued to be ruled by foreigners' (Geyl (1932), pp. 29–30).

88 Weber, E. (1976), p. 66.

89 'Democracy in Brazil', Sergio Buarque de Holanda wrote in 1936, 'was always a lamentable misunderstanding' (cited in Forman (1975), p. 141).

90 Skidmore (1974), p. 101.

91 Pereira de Queiroz (1975).

92 Smith, A. (1971), p. 73.

93 Warren (1980), p. 93.

94 *Ibid.*, pp. 96–7. Chap. 4 of this work traces the evolution of Comintern policy *vis-à-vis* the struggle of colonial countries for self-determination.

95 *Ibid.*, p. 98.
96 Johnson (1970).
97 Hinton (1966), p. 54.
98 Chaliand (1969), pp. 132–4.
99 Davidson (1969), pp. 55, 83.
100 *Critique of the Gotha Programme*, cited in Bottomore and Rubel (1956), p. 263.
101 Worsley (1964), pp. 31–44.
102 See Stavrianos (1981), pp. 765–90; Robinson (1973).
103 Murra (1975).
104 Nairn (1975), p. 353.
105 Wolpe (1975), p. 215.
106 Parkin (1979), pp. 36–9.
107 Hechter (1975).
108 Lewis (1976), pp. 326–7.
109 Turnbull (1948), Chap. 10.
110 These and other modes of withdrawal into the 'little community' which provides the satisfactions of a dense, personal, shared, egalitarian and 'quotidian' life, are sensitively explored in Bonfil (1981).
111 Nairn (1975), p. 17.
112 *Ibid.*, p. 357.
113 Cueva (1977).
114 *Ibid.*, p. 49.
115 Cliffe (1971–2), pp. 95, 97 (1977).
116 Hobsbawm (1959), Chap. 7.
117 In the West, populism survives less as a kind of political movement than as a mood, in the form of critiques of society which blame the ills of this world on the rich or on governments but on 'bigness' – on Big Business, certainly, but also on too-big trade unions and on bureaucracies, including professions such as medicine or education which become self-producing organizations battening on the defenceless consumer. The problem, therefore, is how to humanize those structures by bringing them under popular control. Capitalist corporations ought therefore to be made more responsive to their 'customers, employees *and stock-holders*' (see Illich (1973), p. 88, my italics). As for socialism, it is merely the development of equally repulsive forms of bureaucracy. Such ideas are perennially popular among people rebelling against a world in which they are always under the authority of their elders at school, at work, and in the home. It surfaced powerfully during the epoch of student revolt, and was movingly captured in the film *One Flew Over the Cuckoo's Nest*.
118 For example Finer's discussion of *caudillismo* in countries of 'low' political culture (Finer (1962)).
119 Borón (1977), p. 493.

5 One World or Three?

1 Scott (1976), pp. 149 ff.
2 John Leonard, *New York Times*, 2 October 1981.
3 Worsley (1964), p. 93.
4 Jansen (1966).
5 *Ibid.*, pp. 240 ff.
6 Fanon (1965), p. 124.
7 Interview in the *Guardian* Third World Review, London, 8 January 1979.
8 Tordoff (1967), p. 152.
9 First (1970).
10 'Democracy' was similarly qualified. After listing the various forms of democracy in the new states: 'presidential democracy', 'basic democracy', 'guided democracy', 'organic democracy', 'selective democracy', 'neo-democracy', Finer wryly remarks that 'the one style missing here is "democracy", with qualification' (Finer (1962), p. 242).
11 Leys (1969), p. 247.
12 For Latin America, see Agee (1975); for Africa, Stockwell

(1978). Other studies of the CIA are cited in Stavrianos (1981), p. 464.

13 Stavrianos (1981), pp. 460 ff., 686–91.

14 The title of Pierre Moussa's book of 1959, mistranslated as *The Underprivileged Nations*.

15 Lacoste (1980), Vol. 1, p. 14.

16 *Measures for the Economic Development of Under-Developed Countries*, E/1986/ST/ECA/10 of 3 May 1951; cited in Wolf-Philips (1979), p. 106.

17 MacPherson (1962).

18 Horowitz (1966), p. 17.

19 Jen (1974). Recently, there has been a shift back to treating both Superpowers as equally deserving of condemnation.

20 Wallerstein (1974); Worsley (1980).

21 Wallerstein (1979), pp. 35, 68–9.

22 Halliday, F. (1982).

23 Thomas (1978); Kelemen (1982).

24 Djilas (1957).

25 Borón (1977), p. 528.

26 For Tanzania, see Shivjee (1976); for Kenya, see Leys (1975), Chap. 4. Technology royalties paid by Mexico have in recent years amounted to sixth of the value of her exports (Stavrianos (1981), p. 447).

27 Alan Cowell, 'The IMF's Imbroglio in Africa', *New York Times*, 14 March 1982.

28 Interview in the *Guardian*, Third World Review, London, 8 January 1979.

29 Address to the Convocation of the University of Ibadan, 17 November 1976, in Goulbourne (1979) Chap. 14.

30 *Ibid.*, p. 253.

31 Warren (1980), Chap. 8.

32 Ibarra *et al.* (1977), Vol. 1, pp. 108–9, Table 6; pp. 76–7,

Table 1 and p. 127, Table 14.

33 Goldthorpe (1975), Chap. 4.

34 For example, Wolf-Philips (1979). The term 'Fourth World' has also been applied to 'indigenous peoples who today are completely or partly deprived of the right to their own territory and its riches, and who have limited or no influence on their own destiny', in the words of the International Workshop for Indigenous Affairs (IWGIA) of Copenhagen, and, by extension, to 'describe the specially underprivileged in the "other America": not just the poor, but also the imprisoned, the sick, the elderly, and the underaged' (Hamalian and Karl (1976)).

35 World Bank 1982.

36 Debray (1974), pp. 35–8.

37 Jenkins (1970), p. 18.

38 Jalée (1968), pp. 5–6.

39 Buchanan (1963), p. 6.

40 Willets (1978), pp. 109, 145.

41 Salim (1981).

42 Interview in the *Guardian* Third World Review, London, 19 January 1981.

43 Interview in the *Guardian* Third World Review, London, 8 July 1981.

44 Ngugi wa Thiong'o, 'The Settlers under the Skin', the *Guardian* Third World Review, 19 November 1982.

45 Jonathan Steele, the *Guardian*, 7 September 1979.

46 For a survey of these meetings, see the section '*Economía*' in the *Guía del Tercer Mundo 1981*, pp. 480–540.

47 Taylor (1979), Chap. 2.

48 Quoted from *Fortune* magazine in Stavrianos (1981), p. 761.

49 *Guía del Tercer Mundo 1981*, pp. 7–8.

50 Halliday, F. (1982), pp. 78–80.
51 Worsley (1975), Chap. 4.
52 Dulles (1973).
53 Gott (1970), Part Five.
54 *Communist Manifesto*.
55 Dorfman and Mattelart (1972).
56 Vinnai (1974).
57 Quoted in Pollitt (1981), p. 260.
58 Jonathan Steele, the *Guardian*, 12 November 1982.
59 Nick Eberstadt, 'The Health Crisis in the USSR', *New York Review of Books*, 19 February 1981.
60 Edmund Stillman, *New York Times*, reprinted in the *Estado de São Paulo*, 25 April 1976.
61 Sen (1981).
62 Mao (1974), pp. 110, 127.
63 Martin Walker, 'Britain's self-inflicted wound', the *Guardian*, 25 August 1983. For the USA, see Melman (1974).
64 Payer (1974).
65 Conclusion to the *History of the Communist League*.
66 Miliband (1974).

Appendix   The Urban Poor in the Workshop of the World

1 Jones (1971).
2 Thompson and Yeo (1971), p. 84.
3 Quennel (1949), p. 15.
4 *Ibid.*, p. 54.
5 *Ibid.*, pp. 50–2.
6 *Ibid.*, p. 53.
7 *Ibid.*, p. 71.
8 Ibid., pp. 552–3.

Bibliography

Place of publication is London, unless otherwise stated.

Abu-Lughod, Janet L., 1971, *Cairo: 1001 years of the City Victorious,* Princeton University Press, New Jersey.

Agee, Philip, 1975, *Inside the Company: CIA Diary,* Penguin, Harmondsworth.

Aguirre Beltrán, Gonzalo, 1967, *Regiones de refugio,* Instituto Interamericano Indigenista, Mexico City.

Aguirre Beltrán, Gonzalo, 1972, *La población negra de México: estudio etno-histórico,* Fondo de Cultura Economica, Mexico City.

Alavi, Hamza, 1965, 'Peasants and revolution', in *Socialist Register 1965* (eds R. Miliband and J. Saville), pp. 291–335, Merlin Press.

Alavi, Hamza, 1973, 'Peasant classes and primordial loyalties', *Journal of Peasant Studies,* 1, no. 1, pp. 23–62.

Alavi, Hamza, 1982, 'India: transition to capitalism', in *Capitalism and Colonial Production* (eds H. Alavi, P. L. Burns, G. R. Knight, P. B. Mayer, and D. McEachern), pp. 23–75, Croom Helm.

Aldunate, Adolpho; Lamounier, Bolívar; Berquó, Elza; Cardoso, Fernando Henrique; José, Lenir; Loyola, M. Andrea; and Ruiz Matos, Marina, n.d., *Estudos de Populaçao 1: São José dos Campos: estudo de caso: dinâmica populacional, transformacões socio-econômicas, atuacão das institucões,* Centro Brasileiro de Análise e Planajemento, São Paulo.

Algar, Hamid, 1972, 'The oppositional role of the Ulama in twentieth-century Iran', in *Scholars, Saints and Sufis: Muslim religious institutions since 1500* (ed. Nikki R. Keddie), pp. 231–55, University of California Press, Berkeley.

Amin, Samir, 1974, *Accumulation on a World Scale: a critique of the theory of underdevelopment,* Monthly Review Press, New York.

Anderson, Benedict, 1983, *Imagined Communities: reflections on the origin and spread of nationalism,* New Left Books.

Anderson, Perry, 1962, 'Portugal and the end of ultra-colonialism', *New Left Review,* 15, pp. 83–102; 16, pp. 88–123; and 17, pp. 85–114.

Anderson, Perry, 1974a, *Passages from Antiquity to Feudalism,* New Left Books.

Anderson, Perry, 1974b, *Lineages of the Absolutist State,* New Left Books.

Anderson, Perry, 1976, *Considerations on Western Marxism,* New Left Books.

Anderson, Perry, 1980, *Arguments Within English Marxism,* New Left Books.

Arensburg, Conrad M., 1937, *The Irish Countryman: an anthropological study,* Macmillan.

Argyle, W. J., 1967, 'European nationalism and African tribalism', in Gulliver (1967), pp. 41–57.

Armstrong, W. R. and McGee, T. G., 1968, 'Revolutionary change and the Third World city: a theory of urban involution', *Civilisations*, 18, no. 3, pp. 353–77.

Bacha, Claire S., 1979, *The Emergence of Finance Capitalism in Brazil, 1930s to 1970s*, Ph.D. thesis, University of Manchester.

Banfield, Edward C., 1958, *The Moral Basis of a Backward Society*, Free Press, New York.

Barnett, Donald L., and Njama, Karari, 1966, *Mau Mau From Within: autobiography and analysis of Kenya's peasant revolt*, Monthly Review Press, New York.

Barnett, Tony, 1975, 'The Gezira Scheme: production of cotton and the reproduction of underdevelopment', in Oxaal *et al.* (eds), pp. 183–207.

Barraclough, Solon (ed.), 1973, *Agrarian Structure in Latin America*, D. C. Heath, Lexington, Mass.

Bates, Darrell, 1979, *The Abyssinian Difficulty: The Emperor Theodorus and the Magdala Campaign, 1867–68*, Oxford University Press.

Bauman, Zygmunt, 1973, *Culture as Praxis*, Routledge and Kegan Paul.

Bauman, Zygmunt, 1979, 'Stalin and the peasant revolution', pp. 403–33 (unpublished paper, University of Leeds).

Bendix, Reinhard, 1969, *Nation Building and Citizenship: studies of our changing social order*, Doubleday Anchor, New York.

Bennet, George, 1967, 'Tribalism in politics', in P. H. Gulliver (ed.), *Tradition and Transition in East Africa*, pp. 59–87.

Berger, John, 1980, *Pig Earth*, Knopf, New York.

Berger, John, and Mohr, Jean, 1975, *A Seventh Man: the story of a migrant worker in Europe*, Penguin, Harmondsworth.

Bergesen, Albert, 1980, 'From utilitarianism to globology: the shift from the individual to the world as a whole as the primordial unit of analysis', in *Studies of the Modern World-System* (ed. A. Bergesen), pp. 1–12, Academic Press, New York.

Berlinck, Manoel T., 1975, *Marginalidade Social e Relações de Classes em São Paulo*, Vozes, Petrópolis, Rio de Janeiro.

Berndt, R. M. and C. H., 1951, *Kunapipi: a study of an Australian religious cult*, Cheshire, Melbourne.

Berndt, R. M. and C. H., 1952, *Djanggawul: an aboriginal religious cult of northeastern Arnhem land*, Routledge.

Berreman, Gerald D., 1979, *Caste and other Inequalities: essays on inequality*, Folklore Institute, Meerut.

Beynon, Huw, 1975, *Working for Ford*, EP Publishing, Wakefield.

Birkbeck, Chris, 1978, 'Self-employed proletarians in an informal factory: the case of Cali's garbage dump', *World Development*, 6, no. 9/10, pp. 1173–85.

Birkbeck, Chris, 1979, 'Garbage, industry, and the "vultures" of Cali, Colombia', in Bromley and Gerry, Chap. 8.

Blackburn, Robin, 1963, 'Prologue to the Cuban Revolution', *New Left Review*, 21, pp. 52–91.

Bloch, Marc, 1961, *Feudal Society*, Routledge and Kegan Paul.

Bonfil Batalla, Guillermo, 1972, 'El concepto de indio en América: una categoría de la situación colonial', *Anales de Antropología*, 9, pp. 105–24, Mexico City.

Bonfil Batalla, Guillermo, 1981, *Utopía y revolución: el pensamiento político contemporáneo de los indios en América Latina*, pp. 11–53, Nueva Imagen, Mexico City.

Booth, David, 1975, 'André Gunder Frank: an introduction and appreciation', in Oxaal *et al.* (eds), pp. 50–85.

Borón, Atilio A., 1977, 'El fascismo como categoría histórica: en torno al problema de las dictaduras en América Latina', *Revista Mexicana de Sociología*, 39, no. 2, pp. 481–528.

Bottomore, T. B., 1954, 'Social stratification in voluntary associations', in D. V. Glass (ed.), *Social Mobility in Britain*, pp. 349–82, Routledge and Kegan Paul.

Bottomore, T. B., and Rubel, Maximilien, 1956, *Karl Marx: selected writings in sociology and social philosophy*, Penguin Books, Harmondsworth.

Bourdieu, Pierre, 1972, *Esquisse d'une Théorie de la Pratique, précédée de trois études d'ethnologie kabyle*, Droz, Geneva.

Brenner, Robert, 1977, 'The origins of capitalist development: a critique of neo-Smithian Marxism', *New Left Review*, 104, pp. 25–92.

Breuilly, John, 1982, *Nationalism and The State*, Manchester University Press.

Briggs, Asa, 1960, 'The language of "class" in early nineteenth-century England', in Asa Briggs and John Saville (eds), *Essays in Labour History presented to G. D. H. Cole*, pp. 43–73, Macmillan.

Brockway, Lucile H., 1979, *Science and Colonial Expansion: The role of the British Royal Botanic Gardens*, Academic Press, New York.

Bromley, Ray, 1978a, 'The urban informal sector: Why is it worth discussing?', *World Development*, 6, no. 9/10, pp. 1033–9.

Bromley, Ray, 1978b, 'Organisation, regulation and exploitation in the so-called "urban informal sector": the street-traders of Cali, Colombia', *World Development*, 6, no. 9/10, pp. 1161–71.

Bromley, Ray and Gerry, Chris (eds), 1979, *Casual Work and Poverty in Third World Cities*, Wiley, New York.

Bromley, Yuri, 1974, 'The term "ethnos" and its definition', in Yuri Bromley (ed.), *Soviet Ethnology and Anthropology Today*, pp. 55–72, Mouton, The Hague.

Buarque de Holanda, Sérgio, 1969, *Visão do Paraíso: os motivos no descubrimento e colonizacão do Brasil*, Companhia Editora Nacional, São Paulo.

Buchanan, Keith, 1963, 'The Third World: its emergence and contours', *New Left Review*, 18, pp. 5–23.

Buchanan, Keith, 1970, *The Transformation of the Chinese Earth*, Bell.

Burgos Guevara, Hugo, 1977, *Relaciones interetnicas en Riobamba: dominio y dependencia en una región indígena ecuatoriana*, Institute Indigenista Interamericano, Mexico City.

Butterfield, Herbert, 1965, *The Whig Interpretation of History*, Norton, New York.

Byres, T. J., 1972, 'The dialectic of India's Green Revolution', *South Asian Review*, 5, no. 2, pp. 99–116.

Cabral, Amilcar, 1971, *Revolution in Guinea: an African people's struggle*, Stage 1.

Cajka, Frank, 1978, *Peasant Commercialization in the Serranos of Cochabamba, Bolivia*, Ph.D. thesis, University of Michigan.

de Camargo, C. P. F. *et al.*, 1976, *São Paulo 1975*, Edicões Loyola, São Paulo.

Carr, Edward Hallett, 1968, *Nationalism and After*, Macmillan.

Carroll, Thomas F., 1971, 'Peasant co-operation in Latin America', in Worsley (1971), pp. 199–249.

Caso, Alfonso; Zavala, Silvio; Miranda, José; Gonzalez Navarro, Moises; Aguirre Beltrán, Gonzalo; Pozas, N. Ricardo, 1954, *Metodos y Resultados de la Política Indigenista en Mexico*, Memorias del Instituto Nacional Indigenista, vol. VI, Mexico.

Castles, Stephen and Kosack, Godula, 1973, *Immigrant Workers and Class Structure in Western Europe*, Oxford University Press.

Castro, Américo, 1975, *La realidad historica de España*. Porrua, Mexico City.

Chaliand, Gérard, 1969, *The Peasants of North Vietnam*. Penguin, Harmondsworth.

Chattopadhyay, D., 1973, 'Materialist and spiritualist traditions in India', in *Towards National Liberation: essays on the political economy of India* (ed. S. A. Shah), pp. 14–21, Montreal.

Chayanov, A. V., 1967, *The Theory of Peasant Economy* (eds D. B. Thorner, B. Kerblay, R. Smith), Irwin, Homewood, Illinois.

Chayanov, A. V., 1974, *La organización de la unidad economica campesina* (ed. E. Archetti), Ediciones Nueva Visión, Buenos Aires.

Chi Ch'ao-Ting, 1936, *Key Economic Areas in Chinese History as revealed in the development of public works for water-control*, Allen and Unwin.

Cohn, Norman, 1957, *The Pursuit of the Millennium: a history of popular religious and social movements in Europe from the eleventh to the sixteenth century*, Secker and Warburg.

Cliffe, Lionel, 1971–2, 'The political economy of planning in Tanzania', *Development and Change*, III, no. 3, pp. 77–98.

Cliffe, Lionel, 1977, 'Rural class formation in East Africa', *Journal of Peasant Studies*, 4, no. 2, pp. 195–224.

Colson, Elizabeth, 1968, 'Contemporary tribes and the development of nationalism', in Helm, June (ed.), *Essays on the Problem of Tribe*, pp. 201–6, University of Washington Press, Seattle.

Conquest, Robert, 1968, *The Great Terror: Stalin's purge of the thirties*, Macmillan.

Cook, Robert C., 1960, 'The world's great cities: evolution or devolution?', *Population Bulletin*, 16, pp. 109–30.

Cooperstock, Henry, 1964, 'Prior socialisation and co-operative farming', in *Canadian Society: sociological perspectives* (eds Bernard R. Blishen, Frank E. Jones, Kaspar D. Naegele and John Porter), pp. 227–42, Macmillan, Toronto.

Cornelius, Wayne A., 1975, *Politics and the Migrant Poor in Mexico City*, Stanford University Press, California.

Coulborn, Rushton (ed.), 1965, *Feudalism in History*, Archon Books, Hamden, Connecticut.

Crittenden, Ann, 1981, 'US farming: the changing landscape', *New York Times*, 1 February, p. E3.

Cueva, Agustín, 1977, *El Proceso de Dominación Política en Ecuador*, Solitierra, Quito.

Dahya, Badr, 1974, 'The nature of Pakistani ethnicity in industrial cities in Britain', in *Urban Ethnicity* (ed. A. Cohen), pp. 77–118, Tavistock Press.

Dalton, George, 1972, 'Peasantries in anthropology and history', *Current Anthropology*, 13, no. 3–4, pp. 385–414.

Davidson, Basil, 1969, *The Liberation of Guiné*, Penguin, Harmondsworth.

Debray, Régis, 1974, *A Critique of Arms*, vol. 1, Penguin, Harmondsworth.

Deutscher, I., 1949, *Stalin: a political biography*, Oxford University Press, London.

De Vos, George and Romanucci-Ross, Lola, 1975, *Ethnic Identity: cultural communities and change*, Mayfield Publishing Company, Palo Alto, California.

Djilas, Milovan, 1957, *The New Class*, Thames and Hudson.

Dorfman, Ariel and Mattelart, Armand, 1972, *Para leer al Pato Donald*, Siglo XXI, Mexico City (English translation, *How to Read Donald Duck*, I.G. Editions, New York).

Dulles, John W. F., 1973, *Anarchists and Communists in Brazil, 1900–1935*, University of Texas Press, Austin.

Eckholm, Erik P., 1978, *Losing ground: environmental stress and world food prospects*, Pergamon Press.

Eckstein, Susan, 1977, *The Poverty of Revolution*, Princeton University Press, Princeton, New Jersey.

Eliot, T. S., 1948, *Notes Towards the Definition of Culture*, Faber.

Elliott, J. H., 1970, *Imperial Spain 1469–1716*, Penguin, Harmondsworth.

Elvin, Mark, 1973, *The Pattern of the Chinese Past*, Eyre Methuen.

Ennew, J., Hirst, P., and Tribe, K., 1977, 'Peasants as an economic category', *Journal of Peasant Studies*, 4, no. 4, pp. 295–6.

Epstein, A. L., 1958, *Politics in an Urban African Community*, Manchester University Press.

Epstein, A. L., 1967, 'Urbanization and social change', *Current Anthropology*, 8, no. 4, pp. 280–2.

Etzioni, Amitai, 1964, *Modern Organizations*, Prentice-Hall, Englewood Cliffs, New Jersey.

Evans-Pritchard, E. E., 1937, *The Nuer: a description of the modes of livelihood and political institutions of a Nilotic people*, Clarendon Press, Oxford.

Fainsod, Merle, 1958, *Smolensk Under Soviet Rule*, Harvard University Press.

Fairbank, John King, 1971, *The United States and China*, Harvard University Press, Cambridge, Massachusetts.

Fanon, Frantz, 1965, *The Wretched of the Earth*, MacGibbon and Kee.

Feder, Ernest, 1977, *Strawberry imperialism: an inquiry into the mechanism of dependency in Mexican agriculture*, Institute of Social Studies. The Hague (Spanish-language edition *El imperialismo fresa*, Editorial Campesina, Mexico City).

Fernández Kelly, María Patricia, 1982, 'Mexican border industrialization, female labor force participation, and migration', in *Women, Men and the International Division of Labor* (eds Jane Nash and M. P. Fernández Kelly), State University of New York, Albany, New York.

Finer, S. E., 1962, *The Man on Horseback: the role of the military in politics*, Pall Mall Press.

First, Ruth, 1970, *The Barrel of a Gun: political power in Africa and the coup d'état*, Alan Lane/Penguin.

First, Ruth, 1983, *Black Gold: the Mozambican miner, proletarian and peasant*, Harvester Press, Brighton.

Firth, Raymond, 1951, *Elements of Social Organization*, Watts.

Forman, Shepard, 1975, *The Brazilian Peasantry*, Columbia University Press, New York.

Foster, George M., 1967, *Tzintzuntzan: Mexican peasants in a changing world*, Little, Brown, Boston.

Foster, John, 1974, *Class Struggle and the Industrial Revolution: early industrial capitalism in three English towns*, Methuen.

Foster-Carter, Aidan, 1978, 'The modes of production controversy', *New Left Review*, 107, pp. 47–77.

Frank, André Gunder, 1969, '*The Sociology of Development and the Underdevelopment of Sociology*', in *Latin America: Underdevelopment or Revolution? Essays on the development of underdevelopment and the immediate enemy*, pp. 21–94. Monthly Review Press.

Frank, André Gunder, 1971, *Capitalism and Underdevelopment in Latin America*, Penguin, Harmondsworth.

Franklin, S. H., 1969, *The European Peasantry: the final phase*, Methuen.

Furnivall, J. S., 1948, *Colonial Theory and Practice: a comparative study of Burma and Netherlands India*, Cambridge University Press.

Galeski, Boguslaw, 1972, *Basic Concepts of Rural Sociology*, Manchester University Press.

Gamst, Frederick C., 1980, 'Rethinking Leach's structural analysis of color and instructional categories in traffic control signals', in *Beyond the Myths of Culture: essays in cultural materialism* (ed. Eric B. Ross), pp. 359–90, Academic Press, New York.

Ganshof, F. L., 1952, *Feudalism*, Longman, Green.

Geertz, Clifford, 1960, *The Religion of Java*, Free Press, Glencoe, Illinois.

Geertz, Clifford, 1963a, *Peddlers and Princes: social change and modernization in two Indonesian towns*, University of Chicago Press, Chicago.

Geertz, Clifford, 1963b, *Agricultural Involution: the processes of ecological change in Indonesia*, University of California Press, Berkeley.

Geertz, Clifford, 1965, *Social History of an Indonesian Town*, MIT Press, Cambridge, Massachusetts.

Gellner, Ernest, 1964, *Thought and Change*, Weidenfeld and Nicolson.

Germani, Gino, 1973, *El concepto de marginalidad*, Fichas no. 29, Nueva Visión, Buenos Aires.

Geyl, Pieter, 1932, *The Revolt of the Netherlands (1555–1609)*, Benn.

Gibb, H. A. R., 1962, *Mohammedanism: an historical survey*, Oxford University Press.

Glass, Ruth, 1962, 'Insiders-outsiders: the position of minorities', *New Left Review*, 17, pp. 35–42.

Gluckman, Max, 1960, 'Tribalism in modern British Central Africa', *Cahiers d'Etudes Africaines*, 1, no. 1, pp. 55–70.

Gluckman, Max, 1963, 'Rituals of Rebellion in South-East Africa', in *Order and Rebellion in Tribal Africa*, pp. 110–36, Cohen and West.

Godelier, Maurice, 1978, 'Infrastructures, societies and history', *New Left Review*, 112, pp. 84–96.

Godfrey, E. M., 1970, 'The brain drain from the low-income countries', *Journal of Development Studies*, 6, no. 3, pp. 235–47.

von Goethe, J. W., 1963, *Elective Affinities*, Regnery, Chicago (first published 1809).

Goldthorpe, J. E., 1975, *The Sociology of the Third World*, Cambridge University Press.

Gott, Richard, 1970, *Guerrilla Movements in Latin America*, Nelson.

Goulbourne, Harry (ed.), 1979, *Politics and State in the Third World*, Macmillan.

Gouldner, Alvin W., 1955, 'Metaphysical pathos and the theory of bureaucracy', *American Political Science Review*, 49, no. 2, pp. 496–507.

Gouldner, Alvin, W., 1960, 'The norm of reciprocity: a preliminary statement', *American Sociological Review*, 25, no. 2, pp. 161–78.

Gouldner, Alvin W., 1970, *The Coming Crisis of Western Sociology*, Heinemann.

Gouldner, Alvin W., 1980, *The Two Marxisms: contradictions and anomalies in the development of theory*, Macmillan.

Gramsci, Antonio, 1957, *The Modern Prince*, Lawrence and Wishart.

Gramsci, Antonio, 1971, *Selections from the Prison Notebooks of Antonio Gramsci*, (eds Quintin Hoare and Geoffrey Nowell-Smith), Lawrence and Wishart.

Griffin, 1961, *Black Like Me*, Houghton Mifflin, New York.

Grillo, Ralph, 1967, 'The tribal factor in an East African trade union', in *Tradition and Transition in East Africa* (ed. Gulliver), pp. 297–321.

Gross, Daniel R. and Underwood, Barbara A., 1971, 'Technological change and caloric costs: social agriculture in North-eastern Brazil', *American Anthropologist*, 73, no. 2, pp. 725–40.

Gulliver, P. H. (ed.), 1967, *Tradition and Transition in East Africa: studies of the tribal element in the modern era*, Routledge and Kegan Paul.

Gunawardana, Leslie, 1975, 'The analysis of pre-colonial social formations in the writings of Karl Marx', *Sri Lanka Journal of the Humanities*, 1, no. 1, pp. 8–30, Peradeniya (reprinted in *The Indian Historical Review*, 2, no. 2, pp. 365–88, 1976).

Guzmán, Martin Luis, 1965, *Memories of Pancho Villa*, University of Texas Press, Austin.

Hagopian, Mark N., 1974, *The Phenomenon of Revolution*, Dodd, Mead, New York.

Hall, Stuart, 1977, 'The "economic" and the "political" in Marx's theory of classes', in *Class and Class Structure* (ed. A. Hunt), pp. 15–60, Lawrence and Wishart.

Hall, Stuart, 1981, 'In defence of theory', in *People's History and Socialist Theory* (ed. Raphael Samuel), Routledge and Kegan Paul.

Halliday, Fred, 1974, *Arabia Without Sultans*, Penguin, Harmondsworth.

Halliday, Fred, 1979, *Iran: Dictatorship and Development*, Penguin, Harmondsworth.

Halliday, Fred, 1982, *Threat from the East? Soviet policy from Afghanistan and Iran to the Horn of Africa*, Pelican, Harmondsworth.

Halliday, Jon, 1980, 'Capitalism and socialism in East Asia', *New Left Review*, 124, pp. 3–24.

Hamalian, Leo and Karl, Frederick R. (eds), 1976, *The Fourth World*, Dell, New York.

Harnecker, Marta, 1974, *El Capital: conceptos fundamentales*, Siglo XXI, Mexico City.

Harrington, Michael, 1962, *The Other America: poverty in the United States*, Macmillan, New York.

Harris, Marvin, 1969, *The Rise of Anthropological Theory: a history of theories of culture*, Routledge and Kegan Paul.

Harrison, Paul, 1979, *Inside the Third World: the anatomy of poverty*, Penguin, Harmondsworth.

Hart, Keith, 1973, 'Informal income and opportunities and the structure of employment in Ghana', *Journal of Modern African Studies*, 11, pp. 61–89.

Heath, John Richard, 1980, *The Formation of a Rural Proletariat: the case of Areia, North-east Brazil*, Ph.D. thesis, Faculty of Economics and Politics, University of Cambridge.

Hechter, Michael, 1975, *Internal Colonialism: the Celtic fringe in British national development, 1536–1966*, Routledge and Kegan Paul.

Helm, June (ed.), 1968, *Essays on the Problem of Tribe*, American Ethnological Society, University of Washington Press, Seattle.

Hemming, John, 1970, *The Conquest of the Incas*, Macmillan.

de Heusch, Luc, 1964, 'Mythe et société féodale: le culte du Kubandwa dans le Rwanda traditionnel', *Archives de Sociologie des Religions*, 18, pp. 133–46.

Hill, Christopher, 1968, 'The Norman Yoke' in *Puritanism and Revolution: studies and interpretations of the English Revolution of the 17th century*, pp. 58–125, Panther Books.

Hill, Christopher, 1969, *Reformation to Industrial Revolution*, The Pelican Economic History of Britain, vol 2, 1530–1780, Harmondsworth.

Hilton, Rodney, 1973, *Bond Men Made Free: medieval peasant movements and the English rising of 1381*, Temple Smith.

Hinton, William, 1966, *Fanshen: a documentary of revolution in a Chinese village*, Vintage Books, New York.

Ho, Ping-ti, 1959, *Studies on the Population of China 1368–1953*, Harvard University Press, Cambridge, Massachusetts.

Hobsbawm, E. J., 1959, *Primitive Rebels: studies in archaic forms of social movement in the 19th and 20th centuries*, Manchester University Press.

Hobsbawm, E. J., 1962, *The Age of Revolution 1789–1848*, Mentor Books, New York.

Hobsbawm, E. J., 1968, *Industry and Empire*, Weidenfeld and Nicolson.

Hobsbawm, E. J., 1969, *Bandits*, Weidenfeld and Nicolson.

Hobsbawm, E. J., 1972a, 'Some reflections on nationalism', in *Imagination and Precision in the Social Sciences* (eds T. J. Nossiter, A. H. Hanson and Stein Rokkan), pp. 385–406, Faber and Faber.

Hobsbawm, E. J., 1972b, 'Karl Marx's contribution to historiography', in *Ideology and Social Science: readings in critical social theory* (ed. R. Blackburn), pp. 265–83, Fontana/Collins.

Hobsbawm, E. J. and Rudé, George, 1969, *Captain Swing*, Lawrence and Wishart.

Hodgson, Geoff, 1974, 'The theory of the falling rate of profit', *New Left Review*, 84, pp. 55–82.

Hoggart, Richard, 1957, *The Uses of Literacy: aspects of working-class life with special reference to publications and entertainments*, Chatto and Windus.

Holmberg, Allan R., 1950, *Nomads of the Long Bow: the Siriono of Eastern Bolivia*,

Smithsonian Institution, Institute of Social Anthropology, Publication no. 10, Washington, DC.

Hopkins, Keith (ed.), 1971, *Hong Kong: the industrial colony*, Oxford University Press, Hong Kong.

Hopkins, Keith, 1978, *Conquerors and Slaves*, Cambridge University Press.

Horowitz, Irving, 1966, *Three Worlds of Development: the theory and practice of international stratification*, Oxford University Press.

Hughes, H. S., 1959, *Consciousness and Society: the re-orientation of European social thought 1890–1930*, MacGibbon and Kee.

Ibarra, David; de Navarrete, Ifigenia M.; Solís, Leopoldo, M.; Urquidi, Víctor L., 1977, *El perfil de México en 1980*, vol. I, Siglo XXI, Mexico City.

Illich, Ivan, 1974, *Deschooling Society*, Penguin, Harmondsworth.

Ionescu, Ghita and Gellner, Ernest (eds), 1969, *Populism: its meanings and national characteristics*, Weidenfeld and Nicolson.

Jaleé, Pierre, 1968, *The Pillage of the Third World*, tr. M. Klopper, Monthly Review Press, New York.

Jansen, G. H., 1966, *Afro-Asia and Non-alignment*, Faber and Faber.

Jara, Alvaro, 1916, *Guerre et Société au Chili: essai de sociologie coloniale*, Institut des Hautes Etudes de l'Amérique Latiné, Paris.

Jarvie, I. C., and Agassi, J. (eds), 1969, *Hong Kong: a society in transformation*, Routledge and Kegan Paul.

Jay, Martin, 1973, *The Dialectical Imagination: a history of the Frankfurt School and the Institute of Social Research 1923–1950*, Heinemann.

Jen, Ku-ping, 1974, 'Third World: great motive force in advancing world history', *Peking Review*, no. 44, pp. 6–8.

Jenkins, Robin, 1970, *Exploitation: the world power-structure and the inequality of nations*, MacGibbon and Kee.

Jocano, F. Landa, 1975, *Slum as a Way of Life: a study of coping behaviour in an urban environment*, University of the Philippines Press, Quezon City.

Johnson, Chalmers, 1970, *Peasant Nationalism and Communist Power: the emergence of revolutionary China, 1937–1945*, Stanford University Press.

Jones, Gareth Stedman, 1971, *Outcast London: a study in the relationship between classes in Victorian society*, Clarendon Press, Oxford.

Junior, Raimundo Arroio, 1976, 'La misería del milagro brasileño', *Cuadernos Políticos*, 9, pp. 31–48, Mexico City.

Kamenka, Eugene (ed.), 1973, *Nationalism: the nature and evolution of an idea*, Arnold.

Kahn, Joel, 1978, 'Ideology and social structure in Indonesia', *Comparative Studies in Society and History*, 20, pp. 103–22.

Kapferer, B., 1972, *Strategy and Transaction in an African Factory*, Manchester University Press.

Karpat, Kemal H., 1976, *The Gecekondu: rural migration and urbanisation*, Cambridge University Press.

Kedourie, Eli, 1960, *Nationalism*, Hutchinson.

Kedourie, Eli, 1970, *Nationalism in Asia and Africa*, Weidenfeld and Nicolson.

Kelemen, Paul, 1982, 'A critique of *The Ethiopian Revolution*', in *Socialist Register, 1982* (eds R. Miliband and J. Saville), pp. 239–58, Merlin Press.

Kerblay, Basile H., 1968, *Les Marchés Paysans en URSS*, Mouton, The Hague.

Kidron, Michael and Segal, Ronald, 1981, *The State of the World Atlas*, Pan Books.

Kitching, Gavin, 1982, *Development and Underdevelopment in Historical Perspective: populism, nationalism and industrialisation*, Methuen.

Kline, David, 1981, 'The embattled independent farmer', *New York Times Magazine*, 29 November, pp. 138–46.

Kohn, Hans, 1968, 'Nationalism', in *International Encyclopaedia of the Social Sciences* (ed. D. L. Sills), vol. 11, p. 63, Macmillan, New York.

Kornhauser, William, 1960, *The Politics of Mass Society*, Routledge and Kegan Paul.

Kosambi, D. D., 1973, 'Caste and class in India', and 'The past in India's present', in *Towards National Liberation: essays on the political economy of India* (ed. S. A. Shah), pp. 22–6 and 27–8, Montréal.

Kowarick, Lúcio, 1979, 'Capitalism and urban marginality in Brazil', in Bromley and Gerry (1979), pp. 69–85, Wiley.

Kozlov, V., 1974, 'On the Concept of Ethnic Community', in Yuri Bromley (ed.) (1974), pp. 73–87.

Krader, Lawrence, 1968, *Formation of the State*, Prentice-Hall, Englewood Cliffs, New Jersey.

Kroeber, A. L. and Kluckhohn, Clyde, 1952, *Culture: a critical review of concepts and definitions*, Papers of the Peabody Museum of American Archaeology and Ethnology, Harvard University, vol. LXVII, no. 1, Cambridge, Mass.

Kumar, Krishan, 1978, *Prophecy and Progress: the sociology of industrial and post-industrial society*, Penguin, Harmondsworth.

Kuper, Hilda, 1947, *The Uniform of Colour: a study of White-Black relationships in Swaziland*, Rand University Press, Johannesburg.

Laclau, Ernesto, 1971, 'Feudalism and capitalism in Latin America', *New Left Review*, 67, pp. 19–38.

Lacoste, Yves, 1980, *Unité et diversité du Tiers Monde*, 3 vols, Maspéro, Paris.

Lafaye, Jacques, 1974, *Quetzalcóatl and Guadalupe: the formation of Mexican national consciousness 1531–1813*, University of Chicago Press.

La Fontaine, J. A., 1967, 'Tribalism among the Gusii', in Gulliver (1967), pp. 177–92.

La Fontaine, Jean, 1974, 'The free women of Kinshasa: prostitution in a city in Zaïre', in *Choice and Change: essays in honour of Lucy Mair* (ed. John Davis), Athlone Press.

Laite, Julian, 1981, *Industrial Development and Migrant Labour*, Manchester University Press.

Lane, David, 1971, *The Socialist Industrial State: towards a political sociology of state socialism*, Allen and Unwin.

Leach, Edmund, 1954, *Political Systems of Highland Burma: a study of Kachin social structure*, Bell.

Leach, Edmund, 1959, 'Hydraulic society in Ceylon', *Past and Present*, 15, pp. 2–26.

Leacock, Eleanor Burke (ed.), 1971, *The Culture of Poverty: a critique*, Simon and Schuster, New York.

Lee, Richard Barshay, 1979, *The !Kung San: men, women and work in a foraging society*, Columbia University Press.

Leeds, Anthony, 1971, 'The concept of the "Culture of Poverty": conceptual, logical and empirical problems, with perspectives from Brazil and Peru', in Leacock (1971), pp. 226–84.

Lehmann, David, 1976, *A Theory of Agrarian Structure: typology and paths of transformation in Latin America*, Centre of Latin American Studies, University of Cambridge.

Lenin, V. I., 1947, ' "Left-wing" communisim, an infantile disorder', *Selected Works*, vol. 2, pp. 571–644, Foreign Languages Publishing House, Moscow (first published 1920).

Leopoldi, José Sávio, 1978, *Escola de Samba, Ritual e Sociedade*, Editorial Vozes, Petropolis.

Lerner, Daniel, 1958, *The Passing of Traditional Society: modernizing the Middle East*, Free Press, New York.

van Leur, J. C., 1955, *Indonesian Trade and Society: essays in Asian social and economic history*, van Hoeve, The Hague.

Lévi-Strauss, Claude, 1966, *The Savage Mind*, Weidenfeld and Nicolson.

Lévi-Strauss, Claude, 1969, *Totemism*, Penguin, Harmondsworth.

Lewin, Boleslao, 1957, *La Rébellion de Túpac Amaru y los orígines de la emancipación américana*, Hachette, Buenos Aires.

Lewin, M., 1968, *Russian Peasants and State Power*, Northwestern University Press, Evanston, Illinois.

Lewis, I. M., 1976, *Social Anthropology in Perspective: the relevance of social anthropology*, Penguin, Harmondsworth.

Lewis, Oscar, 1951, *Life in a Mexican Village: Tepotzlán restudied*, University of Illinois Press, Urbana, Illinois.

Lewis, Oscar, 1961, *The Children of Sánchez: autobiography of a Mexican family*, Random House.

Lewis, Oscar, 1962, *Five Families: Mexican case-studies in the culture of poverty*, Science Editions, New York.

Lewis, Oscar, 1964, *Pedro Martínez: a Mexican peasant and his family*, Secker and Warburg.

Lewis, Oscar, 1966, *La Vida: a Puerto Rican family in the culture of poverty*, Random House.

Lewis, Oscar and Barnouw, Victor, 1956, 'Caste and the jajmani system in a North Indian village', *The Scientific Monthly*, 83, no. 2, pp. 66–81.

Leys, Colin, 1969, 'The analysis of planning', in *Politics and Change in Developing Countries: studies in the theory and practice of development* (ed. C. Leys), pp. 247–75, Cambridge University Press.

Leys, Colin, 1975, *Underdevelopment in Kenya: the political economy of neo-colonialism, 1964–1971*, Heinemann.

Lipset, S. M., 1950, *Agrarian Socialism: the Co-operative Commonwealth Federation in Saskatchewan: a study in political sociology*, University of California Press, Berkeley.

Lipset, S. M., 1960, *Political Man*, Heinemann.

Lipset, S. M., 1964, *The First New Nation: the United States in comparative and historical perspective*, Heinemann.

Lloyd, Peter, 1979, *Slums of Hope? Shanty towns of the Third World*, Penguin,

Harmondsworth.

Lockhart, James, 1972, *The Men of Cajamarca: a social and biographical study of the first conquerors of Peru*, University of Texas Press.

Lockwood, David, 1958, *The Blackcoated Worker: a study in class consciousness*, Allen and Unwin.

Lockwood, David, 1964, 'Social integration and system integration', in *Explorations in Social Change* (eds G. K. Zollschan and Walter Hirsch), pp. 244–57, Routledge and Kegan Paul.

Lomnitz de Adler, Larissa 1975, *Como sobreviven los marginados?* Siglo xxi, Mexico City. (English translation: *Networks and Marginality: life in a Mexican shanty town*, Academic Press, New York, 1977.)

Lomnitz-Adler, Claudio, 1979, 'Clase y etnicidad en Morelos: una nueva interpretación', *América Indígena*, 39, no. 3, pp. 439–79.

Lubeck, Paul, 1980, 'Islamic networks and urban capitalism: an instance of articulation from Northern Nigeria', *Cahiers d'Etudes Africaines*, 21, 81–3, pp. 67–78.

MacEwan Scott, Alison, 1979, 'Who are the self-employed?' in Bromley and Gerry (1979), pp. 105–29.

McClelland, David, 1961, *The Achieving Society*, Princeton University Press.

MacFarlane, Alan, 1978, *The Origins of English Individualism: the family, property and social transition*, Cambridge University Press.

McGee, T., 1973, 'Peasants in the cities: a paradox, a paradox, a most ingenious paradox', *Human Organization*, 32, no. 2, pp. 135–42.

MacPherson, C. B., 1953, *Democracy in Alberta: the theory and practice of a quasi-party system*, University of Toronto Press.

MacPherson, C. B., 1962, *The Political Theory of Possessive Individualism: Hobbes to Locke*, Clarendon Press, Oxford.

Magdoff, Harry and Sweezy, Paul M., 1981, *The Deepening Crisis of US Capitalism*, Monthly Review Press, New York.

Malinowski, Bronislaw, 1922, *Argonauts of the Western Pacific: an account of native enterprise and adventure in the archipelagos of Melanesia and New Guinea*, Routledge and Kegan Paul.

Malinowski, Bronislaw, 1935, *Coral Gardens and their Magic*, vol. 1, *The language of magic and gardening*, Allen and Unwin.

Mangin, W., 1967, 'Latin American squatter settlements: a problem and a solution', *Latin American Research Review*, 2, no. 3, pp. 65–98.

Mangin, William (ed.), 1970, *Peasants in Cities: readings in the anthropology of urbanization*, Houghton Mifflin, Boston.

Mao Tse-tung, 1954, 'Report of an investigation into the peasant movement in Hunan', *Selected Works*, vol. 1, pp. 21–59, Lawrence and Wishart.

Mao Tse-tung, 1974, *Mao Tse-tung Unrehearsed: talks and letters 1956–71* (ed. Stuart Schram), Penguin, Harmondsworth.

Mariátegui, José Carlos, 1976, *Siete ensayos de interpretación de la realidad peruana*, Biblioteca Amauta, Lima (first published 1928), (English edition: *Seven Interpretative Essays on Peruvian Reality*, University of Texas Press, Austin (1971)).

Marshall, Tom, 1950, *Citizenship and Social Class*, Cambridge University Press.

Marx, Karl, 1938, *Capital: a critical analysis of capitalist production*, vol. 1. Allen and Unwin (first published 1867).

Marx, Karl and Engels, Frederick, 1972, *On Colonialism: articles from the New York Tribune and other writings*, International Publishers, New York.

Mason, Philip, 1974, *A Matter of Honour: an account of the Indian Army, its officers and men*, Cape.

Massey, Douglas S., 1981, 'Dimensions of the new immigration to the United States and the prospects for assimilation', *American Sociological Review*, 7, no. 1, pp. 57–85.

da Matta, Roberto, 1977, 'O carnaval como rito de passagem', in *Ensaios de Antropología Estructural*, pp. 19–66, Vozes, Petrópolis.

da Matta, Roberto, 1979, *Carnavais, Malandros e Heróis*, Zaher, Rio de Janeiro.

Mayer, Jean, 1973, *La Cristiada: la guerra de los cristeros* (3 vols), Siglo XXI, Mexico.

Mayer, Philip, 1961, *Tribesmen or Townsmen: conservatism and the process of urbanization in a South African city*, Oxford University Press.

Mayer, Philip (ed.), 1980, *Black Villagers in an Industrial Society: anthropological perspectives on labour migration in South Africa*, Oxford University Press.

Mayhew, Henry, 1967, *London Labour and the London Poor* (4 vols), Cass (first published 1851).

Maynard, Sir John, 1962, *The Russian Peasant and other studies*, Collier, New York.

Medvedev, Roy, 1981, 'Why the Russians can't grow grain', *New York Times*, 1 November, pp. 1, 17.

Melman, Seymour, 1974, *The Permanent War Economy: American capitalism in decline*, Simon and Schuster, New York.

Merton, Robert K., 1963, 'Social Structure and Anomie', in *Social Theory and Social Structure*, Chap. 4, Free Press, Glencoe, Illinois.

Mesa-Lago, Carmelo, 1978, *Social Security in Latin America: pressure groups, stratification and inequality*, University of Pittsburgh Press.

Middleton, Alan, 1981, *Poverty, Production and Power: capital accumulation and petty manufacturing in Ecuador* (unpublished MS, based on D.Phil. thesis, University of Sussex, 1979).

Miliband, Ralph, 1974, 'The *coup* in Chile', *Socialist Register 1973* (eds R. Miliband and J. Saville), Merlin Press.

Mills, C. Wright, 1959, *The Sociological Imagination*, Oxford University Press.

Mintz, Sidney W. and Wolf, Eric R., 1950, 'An analysis of ritual co-parenthood (*compadrazgo*)', *South-western Journal of Anthropology*, 6, no. 4, pp. 341–68.

Mishra, G. P., 1979, 'Distributional effects of rural development strategies: a case study', *Economic and Political Weekly*, Bombay, 14, no. 39, pp. A–86–92, 29 September.

Mitchell, J. Clyde, 1956, *The Kalela Dance: aspects of social relationships among urban Africans in Northern Rhodesia*, Rhodes-Livingstone, Paper no. 27, Living-stone.

Mitrany, David, 1961, *Marx against the Peasant: a study in social dogmatism*, Collier Books, New York.

Moerman, Michael, 1968, 'Being Lue: uses and abuses of ethnic distinctions', in *Essays on the Problem of Tribe* (ed. June Helm), pp. 201–6, University of Washington Press, Seattle.

Moore, jr., Barrington, 1967, *Social Origins of Dictatorship and Democracy: lord and peasant in the making of the modern world*, Beacon Press, Boston.

Moorhouse, Geoffrey, 1971, *Calcutta*, Weidenfeld and Nicolson.

Moorhouse, H. F., 1976, 'Attitudes to class and class relationships in Britain', *Sociology*, 10, no. 3, pp. 469–96.

Moorhouse, H. F. and Chamberlain, C. W., 1974, 'Lower class attitudes to property', *Sociology*, 8, no. 3, pp. 387–405.

Morris, John, 1982, *Londinium: London in the Roman Empire*, Weidenfeld and Nicolson.

Morse, Richard M., 1965, 'Recent research on Latin American urbanization: a selective survey with commentary', *Latin American Research Review*, 1, no. 1, pp. 35–74.

Morse, Richard M., 1971, 'Trends and issues in Latin American urban research, 1965–70', *Latin American Research Review*, Part 1, pp. 3–52, and Part 2, pp. 19–75.

Moser, Caroline O. N., 1978, 'Informal sector or petty commodity production: dualism or dependency in urban development?' *World Development*, 6, no. 9/10, pp. 1041–64.

Moussa, Pierre, 1963, *The Underprivileged Nations*, Beacon Press, Boston.

Muñoz, Humberto; de Oliveira, Orlandina; Stern, Claudio (eds), 1977, *Migración y desigualdad social en la ciudad de México*, El Colegio de México/UNAM, Mexico City.

Murra, John V., 1975, *Formaciones económicas y políticas del mundo andino*, Historia andina no. 3, Instituto de Estudios Peruanos, Lima.

Nadel, S. F., 1957, *The Theory of Social Structure*, Cohen and West.

Naidu, Vijay, 1980, *The Violence of Indenture in Fiji*, World University Service/ University of the South Pacific, Suva, Fiji.

Nairn, Tom, 1975, 'The modern Janus', *New Left Review*, 94, pp. 329–63.

Narkiewicz, Olga A., 1976, *The Green Flag: Polish populist politics 1867–1970*, Croom Helm.

Nash, June, 1979, *We Eat the Mines and the Mines Eat Us: dependency and exploitation in Bolivian tin-mines*, Columbia University Press, New York.

Needham, Joseph, 1954–80, *Science and Civilization in China* (5 vols), Cambridge University Press.

Nettl, Peter, 1966, *Rosa Luxemburg* (2 vols), Oxford University Press.

Nevins, Allan and Commager, Henry Steele, 1966, *America: the story of a free people*, Clarendon Press, Oxford.

Nghe, Nguyen, 1963, 'Franz Fanon et les problèmes de l'independence', *La Pensée*, no. 107, pp. 22–36.

Nisbet, Robert, 1967, *The Sociological Tradition*, Heinemann.

Nun, José, 1969, 'Superpoblación relativa, ejercito industrial de reserva y masa marginal', *Revista Latinoamericana de Sociologia*, 4, no. 2, pp.178–237.

Nyerere, Julius K., 1967, *Freedom and Unity: Uhuru na Umoja*, Oxford University Press.

Nyerere, Julius K., 1968, *Freedom and Socialism: Uhuru na Ujamaa*, Oxford University Press, Dar es Salaam.

Nyerere, Julius, 1979, 'The process of liberation' (address to the convocation of the University of Ibadan, 17 November 1976), in *Politics and State in the Third World* (ed. Harry Goulbourne), chap. 14, Macmillan.

O'Brien, Philip, J., 1975, 'A critique of Latin American theories of dependency', in Oxaal *et al.* (eds) (1975), pp. 7–27.

Omvedt, Gail, 1975, 'The political economy of starvation', *Race and Class*, 17, no. 2, pp. 111–30.

van Onselen, Charles, 1976, *Chibaro: African mine labour in Southern Rhodesia, 1900–1933*, Pluto Press.

Oquist, Paul, 1973, 'La participación en Chile', *Colombia: hacia una sociedad participante* (ed. Diego Uribe Vargas *et al.*), pp. 37–107, Fundación para la Nueva Democracia, Bogotá.

Oswald, Ursula (ed.), 1979, *Mercado y Dependencia*, Nueva Imagen, for CIS-INAH, Mexico City.

Otero, Mario, 1980, 'Examen filosófico del vocabulario sociológico', in *Epistemología: curso de actualización* (ed, Mario Bunge), Ariel, Barcelona.

Ots y Capdequi, J. M., 1957, *El estado español en las Indias*, Fondo de Cultura Economica, Buenos Aires.

Oxaal, Ivor; Barnett, Tony and Booth, David (eds), 1975, *Beyond the Sociology of Development: economy and society in Latin America and Africa*, Routledge and Kegan Paul.

Paine, Suzanne, 1974, *Exporting Workers: the Turkish case*, Cambridge University Press.

Panikkar, K. M., 1959, *Asia and Western Dominance: a survey of the Vasco da Gama epoch of Asian history*, Allen and Unwin.

Panofsky, Erwin, 1943, *The Life and Art of Albrecht Dürer*, (2 vols), Princeton University Press.

Park, Robert E., 1928, 'Human migration and the marginal man', *American Journal of Sociology*, 33, no. 6, pp. 881–93.

Parkin, Frank, 1972, *Class Inequality and Political Order: social stratification in capitalist and communist societies*, Paladin.

Parkin, Frank, 1979, *Marxism and Class Theory: a bourgeois critique*, Tavistock.

Parkin, Frank, 1982, *Max Weber*, Ellis Horwood, Chichester.

Parsons, Talcott, 1951, *The Social System*, Routledge and Kegan Paul.

Pateman, Trevor (ed.), 1972, *Counter-Course: handbook of course criticism*, Penguin, Harmondsworth.

Payer, Cheryl, 1974, *The Debt Trap: the IMF and the Third World*, Penguin, Harmondsworth.

Pereira de Queiroz, M. I., 1975, 'Les années brésiliennes de Roger Bastide', *Archives de Sciences Sociales des Réligions*, no. 40, pp. 79–87.

Perlman, Janice E., 1975, 'The slandered slum', *New Society*, 31, no. 650, pp. 717–9.

Perlman, Janice E., 1976, *The Myth of Marginality: urban poverty and politics in Rio de Janeiro*, University of California Press.

Peters, Emrys, 1960, 'The proliferation of segments in the lineage of the Bedouin of Cyrenaica', *Journal of the Royal Anthropological Institute*, 90, Part 1, pp. 29–53.

Phelan, John L., 1956, *The Millennial Kingdom of the Franciscans in the New World: a study of the writings of Gerómino de Mendieta, 1525–1604*, University of California.

Phelan, John L., 1967, *The Kingdom of Quito in the Seventeenth Century*, University of Wisconsin Press.

Pollitt, Penelope, 1981, *Religion and Politics in a Coal-Mining Community in Southern Chile*, Ph.D. thesis, University of Cambridge.

Porro, Antonio, 1977, *O Messianismo Maya no Periodo Colonial*, Ph.D. thesis, University of São Paulo.

Quennell, Peter (ed.), 1949, *Mayhew's London: being selections from 'London Labour and the London Poor'*, Pilot Press.

Quijano, Aníbal, 1966, 'Notas sobre el concepto de marginalidad social', CEPAL, Santiago.

Quijano, Aníbal, 1970, *Redefinición de la dependencia y marginalización en América Latina*, Faculdad de Ciencias Sociales, Universidad de Chile, Santiago.

Quijano, Aníbal, 1974, 'The marginal pole of the economy and the marginalized labour force', *Economy and Society*, 3, no. 4, pp. 393–428.

Redclift, M. R., 1978, *Agrarian Reform and Peasant Organization on the Ecuadorean Coast*, Athlone Press, London.

Redfield, Robert, 1946, *Tepotzlán, a Mexican village: a study of folk life*, Chicago University Press.

Reed, John, 1969, *Insurgent Mexico*, International Publishers, New York (first published 1914).

Rex, John and Moore, Robert, 1967, *Race, Community and Conflict: a study of Sparkbrook*, Oxford University Press.

Ribeiro, Darcy, 1970, 'The culture-historical configurations of the American peoples', *Current Anthropology*, 11, no. 4–5, pp. 403–34.

Rimmer, Douglas, 1970, *Wage Politics in West Africa*, Occasional Paper no. 12, Faculty of Commerce and Political Science, University of Birmingham.

Roberts, Bryan, 1978, *Cities of Peasants: the political economy of urbanization in the Third World*, Arnold.

Robinson, Geroid T., 1949, *Rural Russia under the Old Regime: a history of the landlord–peasant world and a prologue to the peasant revolution of 1917*, Macmillan, New York (first published 1932).

Robinson, Maxime, 1973, *Israel: a colonial-settler state?* Monad Press, New York.

Rodney, Walter, 1972, *How Europe Underdeveloped Africa*, Tanzania Publishing House, Dar es Salaam.

Ross, Eric B., 1980, 'Patterns of diet and forces of production: an economic and ecological history of the ascendancy of beef in the United States diet', in *Beyond the Myths of Culture: essays in cultural materialism* (ed. Eric B. Ross), pp. 181–225, Academic Press, New York.

Rostow, W. W., 1960, *The Stages of Economic Growth: a Non-Communist Manifesto*, Cambridge University Press.

Roszak, Theodore, 1970, *The Making of a Counter-Culture: reflections on the technocratic society and its youthful opposition*, Faber and Faber.

Rowntree, B. S., 1901, *Poverty: a study of town life*, Macmillan.

Rowse, A. L., 1950, *The England of Elizabeth*, Macmillan.

Roxborough, Ian [1981], *Unions and Politics in the Mexican Automobile Industry* (for publication.)

Ruiz-Pérez, Sonia, 1979, 'Begging as an occupation in San Cristóbal de las Casas, Mexico', in Bromley and Gerry (1979), pp. 251–66.

Runciman, W. G., 1972, *Relative Deprivation and Social Justice: a study of attitudes to social inequality in twentieth-century England*, Penguin, Harmondsworth.

Rusque-Alcaino, Juan and Bromley, Ray, 1979, 'The bottle-buyer: an occupational autobiography', in Bromley and Gerry (1979), pp. 185–215.

Sahlins, Marshall, 1961, 'The segmentary lineage: an organization of predatory expansion', *American Anthropologist*, 63, no. 2, pp. 332–45.

Sahlins, Marshall, 1972, *Stone Age Economics*, Aldine, Chicago.

Sahlins, Marshall, 1976, *Culture and Practical Reason*, Aldine, Chicago.

Sahlins, Marshall and Service, Elman R. (eds), 1960, *Evolution and Culture*, University of Michigan Press, Ann Arbor, Michigan.

Said, Edward W., 1978, *Orientalism*, Routledge and Kegan Paul.

Saldívar, Américo, 1977, 'Diferencias ideológicas, entre obreros y empleados', in H. Muñoz *et al.*, *Migración y desigualdad en la ciudad de México*, Chap. 14.

Salim, Ziad, 1981, 'ASEAN in the United Nations', *Indonesian Quarterly*, 9, no. 2, pp. 24–38.

Salisbury, R. F., 1962, *From Stone to Steel: economic consequences of a technological change in New Guinea*, Melbourne University Press.

Sarin, Madhu, 1979, 'Urban planning, pottery trading and squatter settlements in Chandigarh, India', in Bromley and Gerry (1979), pp. 133–60.

Scobie, James R., 1964, *Revolution on the Pampas: a social history of Argentine wheat, 1860–1910*, University of Texas Press, Austin.

Scott, James C., 1976, *The Moral Economy of the Peasant: rebellion and subsistence in South-east Asia*, Yale University Press, New Haven.

Selvaratnam, Viswanathan, 1976, *Metropolitan Control and South Indian Proletariat on the Malayan Plantation Frontier: the persistence and powerlessness of poverty*, Ph.D. thesis, University of Manchester.

Sen, Amartya, 1981, *Poverty and Famines: an essay on entitlement and deprivation*, Clarendon Press, Oxford.

Shah, S. A. (ed.), 1973, *Towards National Liberation: essays on the political economy of India*, Montréal.

Shanin, Teodor (ed.), 1971, *Peasants and Peasant Societies: related readings*, Penguin, Harmondsworth.

Shanin, Teodor, 1972, *The Awkward Class: political sociology of peasantry in a developing society: Russia, 1910–1925*, Clarendon Press, Oxford.

Shanin, Teodor, 1982, 'Defining peasants: conceptualizations and de-conceptualizations', *Sociological Review*, 30, no. 3, pp. 407–32.

Shannon, F. A. 1968, *The Farmer's Last Frontier*: agriculture, 1860–1897, The Economic History of the United States, Vol. V, Harper, New York.

Sheth, N. R., 1968, *The Social Framework of an Indian Factory*, Manchester University Press.

Shillinglaw, Geoffrey, 1971, 'Traditional rural co-operation and social structure: the communist Chinese collectivization of agriculture', in Worsley (1971), pp. 137–57.

Shils, Edward, 1968, 'The concept and function of ideology', *International Encyclopaedia of the Social Sciences*, vol. 7, pp. 66–75, Macmillan, New York.

Shils, Edward, 1972, *The Intellectuals and the Powers, and other essays*, vol. 1, *Selected papers*, University of Chicago Press.

Shils, Edward and Young, Michael, 1953, 'The meaning of the Coronation',

Sociological Review, 1, no. 2, pp. 68–81.

Shivjee, Issa, 1976, *Class Struggle in Tanzania*, Heinemann.

Simmel, Georg, 1950, 'The stranger', in *The Sociology of Georg Simmel* (ed. Kurt H. Wolff), pp. 402–8, Free Press, Glencoe, Illinois (first published 1908).

Simons, H. J. and Simons, R. E., 1969, *Class and Colour in South Africa, 1850–1950*, Penguin, Harmondsworth.

Skidmore, Thomas E., 1974, *Black Into White: race and nationality in Brazilian thought*, Oxford University Press, New York.

Skinner, G. W., 1964–5, 'Marketing and social structure in rural China', *Journal of Asian Studies*, 34, nos. 1–3, pp. 3–43, 195–227, 363–99.

Smith, Anthony D., 1971, *Theories of Nationalism*, Duckworth.

Smith, Henry Nash, 1950, *Virgin Land: the American West as symbol and myth*, Cambridge, Massachusetts.

Somarriba, Maria dos Mercês G., 1978, *Community Health and Class Society: the Health Programme of Norte das Minas, Brazil*, Ph.D. thesis, University of Sussex.

Sorokin, Pitirim, 1956, *Fads and Foibles in Modern Sociology and related sciences*, Regnery, Chicago.

Southall, Aidan, 1956, *Alur Society: a study in processes and types of domination*, Heffer, Cambridge.

Srinivas, M. N., 1952, *Religion and Society among the Coorgs of South India*, Clarendon Press, Oxford.

Stambouli, Fredj, and Zghal, Abdel-Kader, 1976, 'Urban life in pre-colonial North Africa', *British Journal of Sociology*, 27, no. 1, pp.1–20.

Stavenhagen, Rodolfo, 1970, 'Social aspects of agrarian structure', in *Agricultural Problems and Peasant Movements in Latin America*, Doubleday, Garden City, New York.

Stavrianos, L. S., 1981, *Global Rift. the Third World comes of age*, Morrow, New York.

Stockwell, John, 1978, *In Search of Enemies: a CIA story*, Norton, New York.

Stokes, Charles J., 1962, 'A theory of slums', *Land Economics*, 38, no. 3, pp. 187–97.

Stone, Samuel, 1975, *La dinastía de los conquistadores: la crisis del poder en la Costa Rica contemporánea*, Editorial Universitaria Centroamericana, San José, Costa Rica.

Stonequist, Everett V., 1961, *The Marginal Man: a study in personality and culture conflict*, Russell, New York (first published 1937).

Swartz, Marc J.; Turner, Victor W.; and Tuden, Arthur, 1966, *Political Anthropology*, Aldine, Chicago.

Tawney, R. H., 1966, *Land and Labour in China*, Beacon Press, Boston (first published 1932).

Tax, Sol, 1953, *Penny Capitalism: a Guatemalan Indian Economy*, Smithsonian Institution, Institute of social anthropology publication 16, Washington.

Taylor, John G., 1979, *From Modernization to Modes of Production: a critique of the sociologies of development and underdevelopment*, Macmillan.

Terray, Emmanuel, 1972, *Marxism and 'Primitive' Societies*, Monthly Review Press, New York.

Thomas, C. Y., 1978, 'The non-capitalist path', *Latin American Perspectives*, 17, vol. 5, no. 2, pp. 10–28.

Thompson, E. A., 1948, *A History of Attila and the Huns*, Clarendon Press, Oxford.

Thompson, E. P., 1967, 'Time, work-discipline and industrial capitalism', *Past and Present*, 38, pp. 56–97.

Thompson, E. P., 1968, *The Making of the English Working Class*, Penguin Books, Harmondsworth.

Thompson, E. P., 1978, *The Poverty of Theory, and other essays*, Merlin Press.

Thompson, E. P. and Yeo, Eileen (eds), 1971, *The Unknown Mayhew: selections from the* Morning Chronicle *1849–1850*, Merlin Press.

Thorner, David, 1966, 'Marx on India and the Asiatic mode of Production', *Contributions to Indian Sociology*, no. 9, December, pp. 3–66.

Thrasher, Frederic M., 1963, *The Gang: a study of 1,313 gangs in Chicago*, University of Chicago Press (first published 1927).

Tinker, Hugh, 1974, *A New System of Slavery: the export of Indian labour overseas, 1830–1920*, Oxford University Press.

Tordoff, William, 1957, *Government and Politics in Tanzania*, East Africa Publishing House, Nairobi.

de la Torre Villar, Ernesto; Navarro, Moisés; and Ross, Stanley, 1964, *Historia documental de México*, vol. 2. Instituto de Investigaciones Historicas, Universidad Nacional Autonoma de México, publicación número 71, serie documental número 4, Mexico City.

Townsend, Peter, 1981, 'An alternative concept of poverty: how it might be applied in national studies in developing countries', Study no. POV. 5, UNESCO, Paris.

Trotsky, Leon, 1959, *The History of the Russian Revolution: the overthrow of Tsarism and the triumph of the Soviets*, Doubleday, Garden City, New York.

Turnbull, Clive, 1948, *Black War: the extermination of the Tasmanian aborigines*, Cheshire, Melbourne.

Turner, V. W., 1968, *The Drums of Affliction: a study of religious processes among the Ndembu of Zambia*, Clarendon Press, Oxford.

Turner, V. W., 1974, 'Pilgrimages as a social process', in *Dramas, Fields and Metaphors: symbolic action in human society*, Cornell University Press, Ithaca, New York.

Tylor, Sir Edward Burnett, 1871, *Primitive Culture: researches into the development of mythology, philosophy, religion, language, art and customs* . . . , J. Murray.

Valentine, Charles, 1968, *Culture and Poverty: critique and counter-proposals*, University of Chicago Press.

Vekemans, Roger, 1967, *Algunos factores psico-sociales que condicionan el subdesarrollo latinoamericano*, DESAL, Santiago, Chile.

Vinnai, Gerhard, 1974, *El fútbol como ideología*, Siglo XXI, Buenos Aires.

Wachtel, Nathan, 1971, *La Vision des Vaincus: les indiens du Pérou devant la Conquête espagnole*, Gallimard, Paris.

Wachtel, Nathan, 1973, *Sociedad y ideología: ensayos de historia y antropología andinas*, Instituto de Estudios Peruanos, Lima.

Wagley, Charles, 1959, 'On the concept of social race in the Americas', *Actas del 33 Congreso Internacional de Americanistas*, 1, pp. 403–17, Lehmann, San José, Costa Rica.

Wallace, Sir Donald Mackenzie, 1961, *Russia on the Eve of War and Revolution*, Vintage Russian Library, vol. 724, New York (ed. Cyril E. Blade), (abridgement of 1912 edition; original 1877).

Wallerstein, Immanuel, 1974, *The Modern World-System: capitalist agriculture and the origins of the world-economy in the sixteenth century* (2 vols), Academic Press, New York.

Wallerstein, Immanuel, 1979, *The Capitalist World-Economy*, Cambridge University Press.

Walter, E. V., 1969, *Terror and Resistance: a study of political violence*, Oxford University Press, New York.

Walter, E. V., 1973, 'Pauperism and illth: an archaeology of social policy', *Sociological Analysis*, 34, pp. 239–54.

Ware, Caroline F., 1935, *Greenwich Village 1920–1930: a comment on American civilization in the post-war years*, Harper and Row, New York.

Warman, Arturo, 1980, *Ensayos sobre el campesinado en México*, Nueva Imagen, Mexico City.

Warren, Bill, 1980, *Imperialism: pioneer of capitalism*, New Left Books.

Webb, Walter Prescott, 1961, *The Great Plains*, Grosset and Dunlop, New York (first published 1931).

Weber, Eugen, 1976, *Peasants into Frenchmen: the modernization of rural France 1870–1914*, Stanford University Press, Stanford, California.

Weber, Max, 1949, ' "Objectivity" in social science', in *The Methodology of the Social Sciences*, Free Press, New York, pp. 49–112.

Weber, Max, 1961, *General Economic History*, Collier Books, New York (first published 1923).

Wertheim, W. F., 1974, *Evolution or Revolution? The rising waves of emancipation*, Penguin Books, Harmondsworth.

Wheatley, Paul, 1971, *The Pivot of the Four Quarters: a preliminary inquiry into the origins and character of the ancient Chinese city*, Edinburgh University Press.

White, Leslie A., 1949, *The Science of Culture: a study of man and civilization*, Grove Press, New York.

Willetts, Peter, 1978, *The Non-Aligned Movement: the origins of a Third World alliance*, Frances Pinter Ltd.

Williams, Raymond, 1961, *Culture and Society 1780–1950*, Penguin Books, Harmondsworth.

Williams, Raymond, 1977, *Marxism and Literature*, Oxford University Press.

Wilson, Bryan, 1970, *Rationality*, Blackwell, Oxford.

Wirth, Louis, 1938, 'Urbanism as a Way of Life', *American Journal of Sociology*, 44, no. 1, pp. 1–24.

Wirth, Louis, 1956, *The Ghetto*, University of Chicago Press (first published 1928).

Wittfogel, Karl A., 1957, *Oriental Despotism: a comparative study of total power*, Yale University Press.

Wolf, Eric R., 1957, 'Closed corporate peasant communities in Meso-America and Central Java', *South-western Journal of Anthropology*, 13, no. 1, pp. 7–12.

Wolf, Eric R., 1966, *Peasants*, Prentice-Hall, Englewood Cliffs, New Jersey.

Wolf, Eric R., 1969, *Peasant Wars of the Twentieth Century*, Faber and Faber.

Wolf, Eric R., 1972, 'Comment' on 'Peasantries in Anthropology and History' by George Dalton, *Current Anthropology*, 13, no. 3–4, pp. 410–11.

Wolf, Eric R., 1983, *Europe and the People without History*, University of California

Press, Berkeley.

Wolf-Philips, Leslie, 1979, 'Why Third World?', *Third World Quaterly*, 1, no. 1, pp. 105–14.

Wolpe, Harold, 1975, 'The theory of internal colonialism: the South African case', in Oxaal *et al.* (eds) (1975), pp. 229–52.

Womack, John, 1969, *Zapata and the Mexican Revolution*, Knopf, New York.

Woodcock, George and Avakumovic, Ivan, 1968, *The Doukhobors*, Faber and Faber.

Worsley, Peter, 1964, *The Third World: a vital new force in international affairs*, Weidenfeld and Nicolson.

Worsley, Peter, 1967, 'Groote Eylandt totemism and *Le Totémisme Aujourd'hui*', in *The Structural Study of Myth and Totemism* (ed. Edmund Leach), Association of Social Anthropologists, Monograph no. 5, pp. 141–59, Tavistock.

Worsley, Peter, 1968, *The Trumpet Shall Sound* (second edition), Shocken, New York.

Worsley, Peter (ed.), 1971, *Two Blades of Grass: rural co-operatives in agricultural modernization*, Manchester University Press.

Worsley, Peter, 1975, *Inside China*, Allen Lane/Penguin.

Worsley, Peter, 1976, 'Proletarians, sub-proletarians, lumpenproletarians . . .', *Sociology*, 10, no. 1, pp. 133–42.

Worsley, Peter, 1980, 'One world or three? A critique of the world-system theory of Immanuel Wallerstein', in *Socialist Register 1980* (eds Ralph Miliband and John Saville), pp. 298–338, Merlin Press.

Worsley, Peter, 1981, *Marx and Marxism*, Ellis Horwood, Chichester.

Worsley, Peter, 1982, 'Non-Western medical systems', *Annual Review of Anthropology*, 11, pp. 315–48.

Young, Michael and Willmott, Peter, 1956, 'Social grading by manual workers', *British Journal of Sociology*, 7, no. 4, pp. 337–45.

Young, Michael and Willmott, Peter, 1962, *Family and Kinship in East London*, Pelican, Harmondsworth.

Books and articles not by individually named authors

Association for Radical East Asian Studies, n.d., *Hong Kong: Britain's last colonial stronghold*, 2, no. 1.

Encyclopaedia of the Social Sciences, 1937, Macmillan, New York.

Guía del Tercer Mundo 1981, 1981, annual supplement to *Cuadernos del Tercer Mundo*, Mexico City.

Hong Kong Research Project, 1974, *Hong Kong: a case to answer*, Spokesman Books, Nottingham.

India: Agricultural Production Team, 1959, *Report of India's Food Crisis and Steps to Meet it*, sponsored by the Ford Foundation. Issued by the Ministry of Food and Agriculture and Ministry of Community Development and Co-operation.

Mojahed, 1980, 'How to study the Qoran', *Mojahed*, 1, no. 4, pp. 40–5.

North Central Public Policy Education Committee, 1972, *Who Will Control U.S. Agriculture?* North Central Regional Extension Publication 32 (Special Publication 27), College of Agriculture, Co-operative Extension Services, University of Illinois, Urbana, Illinois.

Times Atlas of the World, 1980, Bartholomew Times Books.

U.K. Department of Industry, 1977, *Report on the Census of Production 1972, Business Monitor*, PA 1000, Summary Tables, HMSO.

US Department of Agriculture, 1976, *Changes in Farm Production Efficiency*, Historical Series, Statistical Bulletin no. 61, Economic Research Series; US Department of Agriculture, Washington DC., September.

World Bank, 1982, *World Development Report, 1982*, Oxford University Press.

Index